AMERICAN WORKINGCLASS CULTURE

CONTRIBUTIONS IN LABOR HISTORY
SERIES EDITORS: MILTON CANTOR AND BRUCE LAURIE

AMERICAN WORKINGCLASS CULTURE

Explorations in American Labor and Social History

Edited by MILTON CANTOR

 Contributions in Labor History, Number 7

Greenwood Press
Westport, Connecticut • London, England

Library of Congress Cataloging in Publication Data

Main entry under title:

American workingclass culture.

(Contributions in labor history ; no. 7 ISSN
0146-3608)
Includes bibliographical references and index.
1. Labor and laboring classes--United States--
Addresses, essays, lectures. I. Cantor, Milton.
II. Series.
HD 8066.A73   301.44'42   78-59260
ISBN 0-313-20611-2

Library of Congress Catalog Card Number: 78-59260
ISBN: 0-313-20611-2
ISSN: 0146-3608

First published in 1979

Greenwood Press, Inc.
51 Riverside Avenue, Westport, Connecticut 06880

Printed in the United States of America

10 9 8 7 6 5 4 3 2 1

CONTENTS

ACKNOWLEDGMENTS

The essays by Michael Feldberg, Bruce Laurie, Paul Faler, John Cumbler, Thomas Dublin, Philip T. Silvia, Jr., Daniel J. Walkowitz, Michael A. Gordon, and Jean Ann Scarpaci originally appeared in *Labor History* over a number of issues. I am most grateful to Richard B. Morris, chairman of the editorial board, and to the board itself for permission to reprint them in this collection. A special debt of gratitude is also owed to Professor Bruce Laurie of the University of Massachusetts, who read a number of the essays in this collection and offered invaluable commentary on them.

AMERICAN WORKINGCLASS CULTURE

INTRODUCTION

Milton Cantor

There is no lack of literature dealing with industrialization, immigration, the labor movement, the changing nature of nineteenth-century private and institutional life, the ugly stereotypes of racism, the patently chauvinistic thought that drenched social and scientific journals, the popular attitudes toward unfamiliar dress, ideas, and language.[1] A very considerable body of historical scholarship focuses on what Ralf Dahrendorf once called "the virus of inhumanity" that afflicts a closed or threatened society.[2] Nonetheless it is useful to sketch the familiar—toward the end of adumbrating some neglected aspects of ethnic and workingclass history and culture.

It is a difficult assignment because we have only recently begun to learn of such matters, to become aware of the so-called inarticulate and their culture.[3] It is difficult, too, because of the variables in our cultural heritage and because these variables are often buried in the structure of prefactory work and life. The different strata and subcultures immensely complicate the task of detecting cultural factors and make it impossible to regard workingclass culture holistically. There are, for instance, local and industrial-growth variables, as well as the singular ethnic diversity of American society, and such factors have a centrifugal tendency that further discourages generalizations. This tendency toward differentiation is given added thrust, Stephenson observes, by the unwillingness of significant elements in the workforce to sink permanent roots and by the volatility of America's class structure.

Our focus is not on intellectual history—on the paranoid style of nativist organizations, the tangled skein of racism and xenophobia that colored the national mood, the late nineteenth-century invocation to Anglo-Saxon superiority. Nor is the concern with trade unionism, the lives of individual labor leaders, or workingclass strikes and economic demands at any given period. Rather the emphasis will be on cultural as well as economic forces, an approach set forth by Edward P. Thompson when considering that class is a historical relationship not exclusively defined by one's economic relations to the means of production, that it includes shared values and traditions that help shape, or fail to shape, class identity and which are necessary areas of discussion.

Such an approach raises a host of questions, the importance of which historians are only now beginning to recognize. What, for instance, is the relation of industrialization to community dislocation? What happens when a prefactory people is introduced into an expanding industrial order? What are the links between industrialization and nativism? How did ethnic antagonism affect workingclass consciousness and solidarity? Can we generalize in our answers? Or are these limited in time and space? These inquiries generate a gaggle of secondary questions. What were the national origins of workers who joined nativist societies, such as the American Republicans and the Order of United Americans? Why did they join? What ties exist between an evolving industrial morality, or reform crusades such as prohibition, and the transition from a preindustrial to an industrial society? Why was the diffusion of the dominant middle-class values more pervasive within one ethnic group than within another?

Some of the essays in this collection explore these problems; all recognize their importance. Hence a number are concerned with the use of leisure time, relations between the sexes, religious institutions and conflict, and familial traditions. When strikes are described, they are done in the context of the tensions of industrial society and the norms and expectations of the participants. A few essayists describe the disturbing phenomenon of change, the clash of irreconcilable ideas, the insufficiency of simple formulas, the complexity of men and society, the premonitory symptoms of the modern industrial community and workingclass. In seeking to enlarge upon these matters, to outline some of the causal relationships and to generalize, one is left with an overpowering sense of the need for an analytic framework —in which economic change is related to cultural, cultural to social, social to political, and so forth. These essays, taken together, are a starting point.

Industrialization has redirected the course of human history and is perhaps its most fundamental process. For us it begins in the 1820s, when the transition from a prefactory to a factory economy got underway. Until this time, America's economic landscape was dominated by the rural community, with its relatively low rates of geographical and social mobility, its high degree of residential stability, and its "peer group society," as Gans has called it.[4] Even the seacoast cities and commercial entrepôts of the interior comprised "loosely connected islands"—"the island community," in Wiebe's phrase.[5] They had a homogeneous occupational and/or ethnic character, face-to-face relations, and traditional social arrangements. These arrangements were personal and satisfying and people received respect, as Sennett and Cobb tell us, for who they are, not what they do.[6]

Schuylkill County was typical—with its cohesive little country towns mostly inhabited by Pennsylvania Germans—before Welsh and English immigrants, attracted to its mines, where they could exploit mining skills acquired at home, disrupted the region's ethno-religious homogeneity.[7] Fall

River underwent a similar process, being at first another small and sleepy community whose labor force was native born, drawn from surrounding farming areas; and then came the Lancashire Irish who helped transform it into a bustling factory city by 1850. Or in a later time and place, Ralph Mann carries us to the remote mining towns of California after the Civil War—and again the skilled, experienced, highly regarded English miners, especially Cornishmen, worked the diggings, and then the Irish and Chinese appeared, altering the towns' economic and social structures.

There was no overnight national transformation. For a century or more, the rural village and the old laboring districts of the larger town remained basic features of American life. While they did so, social patterns were not governed by the factory whistle and clock; and traditional institutions, such as family and churches, were dominant. Structure and consciousness interacted, a number of essays tell us, but this interaction was not unilinear and mechanical. Thus the perceptions and ideology spawned in a working-class community were not automatically those of class, and class consciousness was not the automatic and involuntary product of those having a strong sense of vocational cohesion.

The decades after 1820 brought mounting change: new roads, new commercial centers, railroads that transformed the physical environment, rising factories that altered a topography of small-scale producing units and low capital requirements. It was then that the old general merchant gave way to manufacturing specialties and to the wholesaler who served a regional market, that backcountry hamlets began to evolve into centers of capitalist agriculture and commercial enterprise, that the cohesive community first came under sustained attack. The shift from a mercantile to an industrialized, economically integrated regional society became apparent; low-status groups, like women, previously excluded from the skilled job market, came out of the home and the cottage industries and entered the factory; and the entrepreneur arose—who hired and fired, put out work and took control of a craft, introduced skill-destructive and wage-lowering technology.[8]

Such developments, as a number of essays indicate, have a spaciousness about them that transcend the pre-Civil War decades. Hannah Arendt has described what we refer to—the sense of a world that shifts, changes, transforms itself "with ever-increasing rapidity from one shape into another, as though we were living and struggling with a Protean universe where everything at any moment can become almost anything else."[9] Worldly permanence and reliability were gone, she asserted in *Between Past and Future*, and she might as well have been describing the full trajectory of nineteenth-century American society. Surely, then, Josiah Strong's forlorn inquiry of 1901 could have applied to some of the more developed urban centers of a half-century earlier: "When would these changes cease? How much of the old structure of society would they leave standing?"[10]

Industrialization would have a convulsive impact upon these old communities, urban as well as rural, and upon those who lived in them. It menaced social stability and community wholeness. It involved the painful process whereby an older way of life was discarded—the transition from eighteenth-century small-scale work to mid- and late-nineteenth-century large-scale specialized production. Industrialization signaled an entirely new reality for residents of the rural village, the small industrial towns, the prefactory communities—for those familiar with or those who recalled an older and more humane set of values and who resented the intrusion of the sharp change being thrust upon them from the outside. They were gradually losing social knowledge of one another and losing their sense of solidarity with the community itself.[11] Out of this dialectical tension produced by technological change, new urban workingclass communities evolved. Their inhabitants no longer mixed with formerly paternalistic employers or even with those in other occupations. They began to develop their own unique institutions.

By community, we mean the culture or the subculture of those who lived in a particular locality or region. This subculture nourished traditional customs and rituals, which were often brought over in the baggage of a new immigrant labor force—as Scarpaci, Bodnar, and Gordon observe. They included festivals and recreational activities that celebrated the Old World past and simultaneously affirmed the community in which its participants now lived.[12] The meaningful attachment to the past was largely ephemeral, to be sure, but for the time being—in these early days of the factory system and of the community that it engendered—traditional concerns and culture were important. They were played out, as a few of the essays note, in a way that did not clash with the somewhat different cultural values that governed society at large.

For the moment, however, it is enough to note the rise of a new working-class community, as well as the greater cohesiveness of the old craft community. And with these developments came the subculture that institutionalized customs and nostalgia—in the form of unions, taverns, fraternal orders, lodging homes. Thus Philadelphia's artisans, much like those of Boston and New York, sensing the loss of customary patterns of work, sociability, and informal community, joined new clubs and associations. They served in fire companies which, Laurie demonstrates, were a major local social-political institution, and they reinvested their loyalties in smaller, more manageable fraternal groups, usually formed along ethnic, religious, or craft lines.[13] Or turning to another kind of community, that comprising an entire town, its traditional values and unity would even take primacy over ethno-religious differences and all social classes might unite in hostility to disruptive elements. In western Pennsylvania—Gutman gives us the example of Buena Vista—those who lived and worked in small coal towns could join in response to the threat of outside strikebreakers; and when the local steel magnate attempted to import Italians—men strangers to the community in every sense—he was greeted by intense local antagonism.[14] Walkowitz and Cumbler show how two other industrial towns, Cohoes and Lynn, respectively, reacted to the introduction of nonlocal labor during strikes. Cohesiveness, of course, could also work against the best interests of a labor force: Scarpaci's Sicilians, with their tightly bound family and community ties, were insulated from the plight of other farm workers.

The community response that Walkowitz and Cumbler describe came easier when inhabitants were occupationally and geographically isolated or when, as in Lynn, the social structure and ideology of the town's workingclass was such that it sustained solidarity into the twentieth century.[15] Lynn in a way was typical. Its journeymen shoemakers lived in what was a struggling agricultural town until the 1820s. They shared a sense of community and ideology in common with the master cordwainers, as well as with other artisans. They kept it alive by virtue of a network of institutions that their fathers and fathers' fathers had evolved. They thought of their employers as virtuous men whose status and power testified to their industry, thrift, and skill. Unlike workers elsewhere in New England, they were not even ethnically segregated. Since immigrants did not come into town in overwhelming number, they were welcomed and eventually, after joining their own ethnic societies, were assimilated into Lynn's established and nonethnic associations. New and old workers would labor at the same workbench, lunch and play cards together, know and depend upon one another. Scranton's miners and machinists shared a similar pride in their work and their community, the same feeling of solidarity with fellow workers and, at least until the 1860s, with a paternalistic employer sector as well—which, of course, would dilute labor's awareness of a separate "them." They participated in local politics and community affairs, along with the town's elite, and, as Walker observes, both ends of the social spectrum shared feelings of mutual responsibilities. Unlike the absentee coal barons of western Pennsylvania mining towns, businesses in some of these bituminous mining towns of the Schuylkill region at this time were not the soulless and antisocial institutions described by the muckrakers twenty years later. Often the single most important source of employment in a town, the owner—and his achievement—could be readily identified with, and labor militancy might be diverted into a contest over job rights rather than direct confrontation with management. This is not to claim that class antagonisms were necessarily absent but simply that relations of both dependence and reciprocity evolving out of paternalism produced complex but usually inarticulated views, and a generally muted class consciousness mingled with a belief in the importance of loyalty to the legitimacy of managerial authority.

What is significant, however, is not the paternalism but the recognition that the residents of Lynn and Scranton often clung to their old ideas and identified with an idealized local community even after this phase in its history had passed. Such identification was as natural as breathing. The past was recent, though direct personal contacts and the resolution of conflict through mutual agreement were breaking down under the impact of industrialism. The skilled cordwainer and weaver had just graduated from the ranks of journeyman, and the small coal operator had been a miner himself. Understandably, then, the legacy of paternalism and the highly personal style of labor relations—the belief that industrial disputes were "essentially family matters"—eroded slowly.

Some communities, of course, experienced the social dislocations of industrialization later than others, paralleling the variables in technological advance and impact—some crafts entering a factory phase relatively early and others at a later date. Communities that were little more than farming and trading centers in the 1830s might become cities after the Civil War. Population centers certainly were less numerous and less well established in the late eighteenth century than they were in the nineteenth. Those that were not bustling colonial seaports, for instance, often concentrated on agriculture and household manufactures and recorded slower economic growth. At times they were composed of comparatively small-scale unincorporated enterprise. The Schuylkill Valley towns that Clifton Yearly describes were dominated by one or two industries, quite unlike the complex mercantile-manufacturing economy of older, frequently larger, urban centers.[16] Integrated into a national economic network at a later date, these towns preserved early patterns of community life, personal contact, and social organization well into the 1870s. Their residents, both employers and employees, felt related to each other by virtue of their common roots, their formalized interaction in such substructure institutions as lodges or unions, their notion of an autonomous and self-contained community in which personal association meant a great deal.[17] Sometimes this small-scale and highly informal community life would be transformed by the transportation revolution of midcentury, or by the needs of northern armies during the Civil War, as well as by the changing technology. Then, too, they might be affected by geographical considerations, such as proximity to the expanding coal industry, and by the new immigrants from Southern and Eastern Europe who were entering it.[18] Notwithstanding the relatively late maturation and uncomplicated economic structure of these towns, they were affected in much the same way and by much the same processes as those sprung from the colonial wilderness or from earlier nineteenth-century industrialization.

The immigrants, whether from Ireland, China, the Canadian maritime, or the European mainland, were strangers to these islanded communities. They existed on the periphery of organized culture, often shut out of established networks and clubs of old-stock Americans. Being excluded, they made a virtue of their exclusion and developed a pervasive informal structure of their own. Thus German and Irish immigrants in pre-Civil War Philadelphia and Newark knew the struggles and vicissitudes of an insecure life, and, deprived of the usual outlets for group loyalties, they turned to building their own lodges, associations, schools, newspapers. The Irish in Waltham and Newburyport, Steelton's Polish and Slavic steel workers, and Fall River's French Canadians held tenaciously to their own language, churches, and educational institutions.[19] Sicilians in Louisiana, Chinese in California's gold fields, Fall River's Portuguese did not experience even a modest acculturation, retaining instead the formal and informal ethnic institutions and practices that they brought with them.

A multitude of segregant organizations filled the leisure hours of those who lived in the emerging ethnic enclaves, and these compensated for the newcomers' anxieties, uprootedness, sense of loss and melancholia.[20] Much like rituals and festivals, these organizations served to duplicate the remembered past, though they also might be transformed into mechanisms for making the present more tolerable and the dominant cultural values more easily accepted. Writing of the early nineteenth-century English working-class, Asa Briggs has noted the "bond of attachment" to the world it had lost.[21] Unquestionably such a bond also existed among America's workers —whether native-born craftsmen wistful about the golden age of the past or newcomers recalling life in the Old World, its bitterly marginal conditions notwithstanding. But this bond did not have unequivocal dominance. It was in uneasy alliance with the Yankee emphases upon individual achievement—a hegemonic value if ever there were one—and pride in being "American." This clash of cultural values was never consciously articulated, and accommodation and reconciliation were usually effortless: witness, for instance, the three Fourth of July celebrations of 1854 observed separately by Newark's Irish, Germans, and "Americans."

Thus festivals as well as fraternal associations performed a useful assimilative function, bringing newcomers into the community's social life. Those of Newark's workers, like those of New York's or Philadelphia's— the fraternal benefit lodges, lyceums, mechanics' institutes, sports teams, volunteer fire brigades—suggest as much. But this socialization could also be highly selective, restricted to those of the same job sector or ethnic group. Hence the socializing function might perpetuate Old World ethnic, religious, or occupational feuds. Evidence abounds of how fragmentation sparked conflict among rival networks of associations, how it intensified mutual suspicions. The rivalry of Irish Catholic and Irish Protestant fire companies in Philadelphia is an example. And, to offer another instance, Newark workers created their own leisure forms, as Hirsh has shown us, and ethnic competition resulted.[22]

Subcultural institutions, then, could build and confirm a workingclass community, providing both continuity and a sense of solidarity. But if the immigrants were not integrated into the community, as in Lynn, then the reverse—a deepening antagonism borne of ethnic-religious hostility—might evolve. Whether institutions were able to maintain community and worker cohesiveness, whether they were able to enhance the workers' ability to see their cause as common, varied sharply from place to place, so much so that it is impossible to generalize.

Industrialization thus affected the workers as well as the community. Though only occasionally prompting Luddite protest—and Feldberg tells us of machine-breaking weavers in Philadelphia—it had a visceral impact on their lives. Technological change would render obsolete the preindustrial family as the basic unit of craft training and production. It would, almost immediately, produce a division of labor as production moved out of the home and the family lost its productive function.[23] It would make a mockery of the skills of the artisan—the yeoman mechanic who was part of a prefactory society. This craftsman, who worked with limited capital in his small shop, made the product entirely, bringing a piece of raw material to the final and completed stage; and he expected, with hard work, to become self-employed. He resented the loss of status and power in the local community, and he often found two outlets for his fears and frustrations: the trade union movement, which briefly flowered before the 1837 panic and then after the Civil War, and the links to tradition that allowed him to retain a set of standards with which to criticize the new industrial order. "The factory hand," Thompson has concluded, was "the inheritor . . . of *remembered* village rights, of notions of equality before the law, of craft traditions," and the recollected past enabled him to encounter the present and locate himself in history and society.[24] Consequently, as Frank Hearn shrewdly notes, one should not necessarily interpret workingclass discontent simply as a response to economic discontent. Rather, in J. L. Hammond's words, we must recognize that "the real passion of the working class revolt of this time was partly inspired by the envy of wealth, but ultimately in the main by a hostility to a view of life which outraged the poor man's self-respect and gave to his higher wants no place at all in its values."[25] Granted that Thompson, Hammond, and Hearn are writing about another country and time, there is no denying the fact that workingclass antagonisms were frequently directed against cultural as well as economic threats.

Understandably so. Artisans believed in work as a duty; they enjoyed it, and they were proud of their craft skills. Lynn's cordwainers were paradigmatic, as both Faler and Cumbler observe. Henry Clarke Wright, a hatter who became a prominent abolitionist, spoke to artisan pride: "Those who are ashamed to work with their hands ought to be ashamed to live." The family was perhaps the key institution that inculcated these virtues in children and, in home industries, in apprentices. Lowell mill girl Lucy Larcom explained: "We learned no theories about 'the dignity of labor,' but we were taught to work almost as if it were a religion; to keep at work, expecting nothing else." Labor was not an onerous burden; it was a source of pride and pleasure. "I felt real satisfaction in being able to make a hat," Wright testified, "because I loved to contemplate the work when finished, and because I felt a pleasure in carrying through the various stages."[26]

Naturally enough, these sentiments did not apply to the entire American workingclass, only to an upper stratum of skilled artisans who had a sense of their exclusiveness and superior social status—who usually considered themselves employers or prospective employers. This celebration of work appears to be a commitment to the values of the rising middle class but is not necessarily so; rather it provided artisans with a corporate identity that established their exclusiveness and stability in a society undergoing traumatic change.[27] Of course, craft institutions mediated the dominant industrial morality and ideology of work, which was partly reformulated to meet the requirements of all who labored, but that is another story. It is enough to observe now that the craft pride in work, much like their chanting of respectability—the values of family and home, of sobriety and propriety—marked off its champions from the disreputable Irish new-comers. Craft behavior, described by such epithets as "decent," "sober," "respectable," endowed artisans with a social status lacking in other segments of the labor force (much as it did for the late nineteenth-century Edinburgh aristocracy of labor according to R. S. Gray).[28]

Such distinctions as the artisans made reflected social tensions that existed within the workingclass and that spilled over into society itself. Another sort of distinction—the appeal of the success ethic—was strong enough to prevent the apprentice or journeyman from conceiving of himself as a member of the workingclass, and to have expectations of occupational mobility not held by many of the new ethnic groups. But this sense of expectancy did percolate down into society, taking on an axial role in middle-class cultural hegemony.

These very divisions within the labor force simply confirm our inability to advance any sweeping generalization for the American workingclass. On the one hand there was the artisan who defended the workplace against the inroads of monopolists; who celebrated the craftsman as "the life blood, bone, and sinew of the land," as a Newarker declared in 1829[29]; who transmitted the Protestant ethic of hard work and self-improvement, which some have interpreted as a triumph of middle-class values but can also be read as a fierce defense of the autonomy of craft and as resistance to the threat of subordination.[30] On the other hand, as Dawley, Faler, Kulik, and others have observed, artisan values and aspirations reached down into the ranks of the textile operatives of Pawtucket and the shoe workers of Lynn—to the "lower orders"—and thus the ordinary factory hand also absorbed a new industrial morality.

Industrialization changed the social existence of craftsmen in so many ways. However, as one scholar has commented, "Important developments in authority relationships and work roles occurred [even] prior to mechanization."[31] Whenever these changes occurred, they destroyed the craftsman's ideal of labor. The prefactory work and leisure lacked the regimented quality that the factory bell introduced. Artisans could no longer set their own pace of work or socialize with their fellows at any chosen time of the work day. The pace of machines prohibited socializing and drinking among fellow mechanics several times a day. Nor was there any leisure for impromptu festivities like sleigh rides and fishing trips, which, as both Hirsh and Thompson observe, were part of the prefactory routine.[32]

The craftsmen began to commute to the mills and to compete with untrained newcomers from Ireland and Germany. Small wonder that they—indeed most native-born workers—resented the constricted ways of factory life, the diminishing chances for success, the "brutalizing" system that made Lowell's textile operatives, for instance, "mere automaton appendages of machinery, and in the course of time lose almost all that is valuable in moral, intellectual and social character." The "force of habit"—factory discipline—was degrading, and factories were transforming "human beings into machines."[33] The reaction of craftsmen was predictable—an idealization of craft and of work-as-duty—and those who retained such values, who retained craft ways, retained a sense of status and exclusivity as well. The mechanics institutes of the early nineteenth century, which would further refine skills and education, were only the latest institutional symbols of such class identity and cohesiveness. They appeared at a time when industrialization was eroding the status and respect that society traditionally accorded artisans; and, like other residual associations, they tell us of the difficulty of understanding workingclass behavior and consciousness without an awareness of the divisions existing in the American working-class.

The German and Irish newcomers to Jacksonian America entered the urban workplace with their own values—as Gordon, Laurie, and Cumbler point out—and developed leisure forms and institutions that confirmed these values. The social life of the remembered past shaped these rituals and associations and at times served as a buffer to the harsh realities of life in an unfamiliar, sometimes hostile, present. On occasion, this bond of attachment was surrogate for retrogressive tendencies of protest. More often, it served as a stabilizing core of traditions, resistant to efforts by the elite to remake community values.

Industrialization severely tested and frequently overwhelmed such traditions and institutions, a number of authors make clear. The factory became the catalyst in transforming the human environment; and, as Thompson describes the maturing industrial society, it "entailed a severe restructuring of working habits—new discipline, new incentives, and a new human nature." Factory discipline, the division of labor, the demand for unskilled operatives produced new sensibilities and reordered class relations. Philadelphia's mills, which became the nation's largest, disturbed or obliterated existing class lines, ethnic patterns, political alignments. They produced a city pulsating with change.[34] In Lynn, new mills with power looms made cheaper cloth possible and made production by handicraft methods obsolete by the 1840s. The changes had not at first seemed wrenching because, as Dublin and Kulik describe it, the early labor force in Lowell and Pawtucket had been drawn from the surrounding rural communities. In Lowell, it was mostly the "attractive, well educated" New England farm girl whose stay was temporary and whose ties to the family homestead were deliberately maintained. Few adjustments were required, therefore, and the threat to existing craft practices seemed negligible.

But these changes, in textiles and other industries, were nonetheless profound—as Feldberg, Silvia, Faler, Cumbler, and Dawley all observe. Thus the literate and pious country girls, who had made up the bulk of textile operatives in Lowell, and their "sober, intelligent, and reliable" male counterparts departed from New England's mills, and from Fall River's shoe factories as well. They were displaced by Irish immigrants, along with some French Canadians. Lowell's earlier operatives had been familiar with long hours and hard chores on the farm, and Fall River's cordwainers were accustomed to the same. But they all had to adjust to changes taking place in leisure—to the factory clock and the machine pace in the new industrial environment. By the time that the immigrant workers arrived, the transition had been made, and they knew only the regularity and discipline of factory labor, something altogether alien from their own rural past—whether in rural Ireland, the Portuguese countryside, or Canada's maritime provinces. They could no longer labor at their own speed but worked to factory time and to machine pace. They had to accommodate to regular attendance and routinization of the workplace. Pollard, writing of English workers, phrased it aptly: "What was needed was regularity and steady intensity in place of irregular spurts of work."[35]

Workers could no longer regulate their activity in accordance with traditional holidays, festivals, fairs, religious celebrations. Irregular attendance, Thompson and Pollard found, was commonplace among prefactory people in the early factory system: "Spinners, even as late as

1800, would be missing from the factories on Mondays and Tuesdays, and 'when they did return, they would sometimes work desperately, night and day, to clear off their tavern score, and get more money to spend in dissipation.'"[36] These irregular labor rhythms had to be standardized to the rhythm of the machine. Factory bells in the Lowell mill cupolas reminded employees that time was money. Management campaigns equated leisure with idleness and idleness with sin, and urged that time away from the workbench be spent in self-improvement. Nor was idleness the only danger. The dissipation that Thompson attributed to English labor seemed a very real threat. Religious leaders joined entrepreneurs in warning against the deleterious effect of drinking, and employers pressed workers and their children to attend church services and school regularly.

The campaign to make operatives more amenable to factory discipline employed all the institutions and forms of social control: the school with its primers on thrift and industry, the lessons on sobriety taught at home, the sermons emphasizing a prudent morality, the popular didactic literature that rang the praises of hard work, thereby reinforcing the imperatives of a rising capitalism. The Lawrence Company rules, John Kasson states, stipulated that all employees "must devote themselves assiduously to their duty during working hours" and "on all occasions [demonstrate] a laudable love of temperance and virtue, and animated by a sense of their moral and social obligations."[37]

Much like Kulik writing about Pawtucket, Faler and Cumbler show how a new work ethic was formulated in Lynn's early nineteenth-century shoe industry, how it paralleled the shift from the artisan in his shack— the "ten footers"—and from the old premachine methods. As the factory took on recognizably modern lines, as specialization was increasingly practiced, the artisan's loss of control over the whole product became apparent. The very texture of the workingclass community—even the town's physical appearance—changed with the altered nature of work and the need for a full-time labor force.

Technological and community change, to repeat, was uneven. The hand-loom weavers continued to flourish in some branches of textile manufacture, while furniture and cigar manufacture was largely untouched by modernization in the pre-Civil War decades. But where industrialization occurred, it sharpened a consciousness of community—though it did not necessarily produce class consciousness, not even for those belonging to a single craft. Workers, after all, are governed more by relations with friends, neighbors, and relatives than by their economic category. Their ideological perceptions relate to the realities of their own lives, not social change remote from them. Hence they saw the class structure from the viewpoint of their own town or district, from their face-to-face encounters, and so, as Lockwood observes of English labor, they were likely to understand class relations in terms of income and material possession.[38] Usually, then, their discontent was generalized and the constraints of the social order accepted, however reluctantly. The discontented immigrant was naturally inclined toward an ethnic rather than an economic group.[39] Philadelphia and Newark mechanics, for instance, only rarely objected to industry and industrialization. They acquiesced in the rigidity of factory hours and machine-imposed time, their discontent being internalized—muted and mitigated in part by the informal social networks they created. Significantly, few urban craftsmen or workers expressed overt interest in the visionary schemes of Robert Owen or even George Henry Evans in the 1830s and 1840s.

This is not to conclude that the sense of class and class solidarity was entirely absent. It inevitably arose—as in Lynn and Philadelphia in the 1830s, Newburyport and the California gold towns in the 1870s—when, as Thompson concludes, "some men . . . feel and articulate the identity of their interests as between themselves, and as against other men whose interests are different from (and usually opposed to) theirs."[40] And it happens as a consequence of shifts from a prefactory setting—as the labor force responds to conditions of discontinuity in craft owing to modernization. Hence it can develop with the end of the putting-out system, the destruction of apprenticeship, the accelerating division of labor. Much of what we have already observed of nineteenth-century economic developments contributed: the separation of journeyman and master at the workplace, the cleavage between them that grew with market needs, the growing power of increasingly impersonal businesses and business relations, the development of viable workingclass institutions and networks within an area that had residential stability and a consciousness that gave labor identity and strength.

Nor did such developments alone contribute to class consciousness. Ethnic cohesion might be very influential. For example, there were the Slavic newcomers to Illinois' coalfields in the early 1890s, and their militancy swept everything before it.[41] More characteristic possibly was a mix of ethnic and class consciousness. In the California mining towns, Mann shows us, the Cornish maintained a fragile class solidarity with the Irish in the midst of a burgeoning nativism.[42] Despite intense anti-Catholic sentiment in Philadelphia, German shoemakers, Catholic weavers, and Presbyterian ship carpenters joined Irish textile hands and demonstrated substantial labor solidarity until the unions crumbled following the 1837 panic; only then did the competitive struggle for survival assume an ethnoreligious cast, with political alignments being based on it rather than on class interests.[43]

Depression, ethnic cohesion, confident radical thought—none of these automatically intensified class consciousness. Indeed hard times might have a crippling effect on union power. Nor did strikes guarantee a rising solidarity. But they could be a considerable factor at times. Witness, for instance, the Cohoes walkouts that Walkowitz comments upon and how Irish women worked and fought alongside English-speaking operatives, as well as the overwhelmingly unskilled French Canadians. Miners' strikes like those in California, Illinois, and Pennsylvania—the 1871 anthracite coal strike is typical—inevitably sharpened occupational, if not class, consciousness. It is understandable. Miners had a strong sense of occupational identity owing to the hazardous conditions of their work, which forced them to rely only on their fellow operatives. Their very social existence, in the isolated and homogeneous miner community—independent, self-contained, closed off from change—would breed occupational cohesiveness. Finally, though we will see contrary instances, even ethnic loyalties did not necessarily eliminate sharp economic struggle or class consciousness. When Irish master weavers sought to reduce piece rates, conflict between them and Irish workers continued through the depression years.[44] And if such conflicts existed within a single ethnic group, there certainly were occasions when single, multi-occupational ethnic groups could strike for higher wages and the ten-hour day. In 1835 when unskilled Irish coalheavers on the Schuylkill River docks walked out, they were followed by cordwainers, printers, bakers, and city employees, all with the same economic goals.[45]

The old immigrants, so-called by social historians, were crucial to industrial reorganization before 1860, much as the new immigrants were to postbellum factory growth. Both sets of newcomers had been recruited by factory managers and mine owners who were then modernizing their facilities. In each instance, the introduction of this new workforce created severe social dislocations, producing mounting tensions, and prompted intense racial animosities.[46] These tensions and the clashes that followed, it is not hard to establish, grew out of specific circumstances rather than inherent flaws in the American character or in human nature itself. They reflected the bewildering pace of economic growth, the disruptions to a once-stable community, the occupational derangement and worker discontent.

The Irish came first, debarking in flood proportions, having been driven out in a vast diaspora, bringing with them a Gaelic culture, rural folkways, the Catholic faith. They created a surplus labor pool, and they undertook the most arduous and menial jobs. They constructed Pennsylvania's canals and railways, as well as entered its iron foundries and textile mills. They enlisted in the building of Worcester's and Chicopee's canals in 1820 and 1829, respectively; invaded textile operations in Lynn and Lowell, comprising a third of mill workers by the mid-1840s; poured into Massachusetts factory towns into the 1870s; swelled New York City's longshore labor and boycotted antilabor employees; joined the German influx into Buffalo in the 1860s and again, as elsewhere, filled the bottom ranks of the workforce.[47] In Jersey City, for instance, they comprised 75 percent of the menial labor; in Lawrence and Cohoes, they were largely represented in unskilled catagories of work.

The results of the Irish entry into the labor force were nearly always the same, though there were a few significant exceptions. Fall River's Irish, John Cumbler notes, had first migrated to Lancashire and Blackburn, the English mill towns, and only then—after experiencing strikes and blacklists—had they arrived in Massachusetts. A skilled workforce with a record of workingclass militancy, they helped organize the town's first unions and associations. Jersey City's and New York City's Irish, as Shaw and Gordon, respectively, observe, transported Whiteboy violence and boycott practices along with their peasant folkways.[48] Surely more typical were the Irish of Newburyport. Their coming did not profoundly disturb things. True enough, it produced ethno-religious conflict, but such clashes posed no fundamental threat to the ruling circles—unlike Fall River's class conscious Irish and their antagonisms—and the town was remarkably stable between 1855 and 1880.[49]

More often than not, the Irish catalyzed the anxieties of both craftsmen and nativists, and each found a clear correlation between the newcomers and urban poverty, the decline in real wages, and the unraveling social fabric.[50] Predictably, laments were heard for the Yankee farm girls, then being displaced in the mills by Irish women—a "degraded" class that robbed the "employment of its former respectability."[51]

Equally unavoidable, Irish newcomers provoked a violent reaction at times. Jersey City, Newark, Boston, Worcester, Upper Michigan, Butte— the list is long—periodically erupted; and antiforeignism, antipapism, fear of the disorderly and dangerous poor was rampant among Protestants.[52] In Philadelphia, Feldberg and Laurie demonstrate, this menacing trinity of poverty, Catholicism, and unskilled labor prompted endemic violence— an epidemic of political factionalism, labor troubles, racial and religious riots—from the early 1830s to the late 1850s.[53] From the outset, it appears, unskilled and impoverished Irish immigrant weavers clashed with longtime residents, like the Protestant Scots-Irish, who were threatened by industrialization, occupational displacement, and erosion of community stability.[54] Nearly two decades later, antipapist Irish Protestants battled Irish Catholics in Kensington, a city suburb. These riots were sometimes fueled by such issues as the Protestant Bible in public schools and the liquor traffic and, channeled into political alliances, further heightened social tensions.[55]

Protestant nativists, it is significant, were not necessarily antilabor.[56] Indeed workers comprised the bulk of some nativist groups in Philadelphia, though its leaders were mostly professionals and small tradesmen.[57]

More to the point, these rank and file were drawn primarily from the crafts; they were still occupationally and psychologically committed to the old handicraft practices and to the traditional trades.[58] New England's nativists, those in Massachusetts' Know Nothing lodges, for instance, also included a disproportionate number of artisans—shoemakers, weavers, carpenters; the "vast majority" of Worcester's chief nativist organization came out of stores and artisans' shops, with 75 percent of the Know Nothings drawn from skilled manual trades.[59] In Jersey City, the story is the same: the town's skilled workers were largely native born, of which half voted Know Nothing in 1850.

Expressions of nativism are to be found everywhere and anywhere in nineteenth-century America; they were hardly limited to one ethnic group, one segment of the workforce, or a few well-known scenes of social turbulence. No one can fail to be impressed by the ethnic antagonism that divided and disorganized the labor movement in New York, Philadelphia, the Massachusetts mill towns, the Upper Michigan and California mining communities—and thereby weakened resistance to the worst abuses of early industrialism; no one can safely disregard the recurrent warfare among working peoples of different national origins, rather than between them and their employers.[60] Examples abound. There were the artisan-led assaults on Philadelphia's Irish workers in the 1830s and 1840s;[61] the deep hostility that cigarmaking craftsmen felt toward cheap Chinese labor;[62] the sharp divisions between Schuylkill County's ethnic labor force, such as between Irish Catholic and Welsh Protestant miners; the recurrent rioting and bloodshed between skilled Cornish miners and unskilled Irish mine laborers in the iron and gold fields, with the latter feared as Catholics and as cheap labor that would drive down wages;[63] the East European anthracite miners who disrupted stabilized patterns of ethnic group relations (the modus vivendi worked out by Irish, Welsh, and German miners) and thereby unleashed the familiar anti-immigrant sentiments.

At times an industrial dispute in the mine or mill prompted the local entrepreneur to seek new workers, often recruiting from outside. His action might trigger nativist reactions from virtually the entire community. There are many instances: Italians replacing striking Irish hod carriers in New York City, which galvanized the districts involved; North Adams shoe workers after Chinese shoe-and-boot workers were imported to break the 1870 strike; Swedish immigrants introduced into the Irish-dominated Cohoes textile mills with the same intent; English-speaking strikebreakers who went into the Ohio Valley iron foundries; blacks recruited for the Hocking Valley coal mines. When Italian laborers were conscripted for work in the homogeneous bituminous coal towns of western Pennsylvania, there was violent community reaction. So, too, when Slovak, Italian, and then Scandinavian workers arrived in central Illinois' coalfields;[64] or the

French Canadians in Chicopee and Fall River, during the bitter strikes of 1857 and 1873, respectively. Thus employer actions could ignite inter-ethnic strikes while simultaneously strengthening the class or occupational solidarity of the native-born or English miner, Irish weaver, or textile operative.

Sometimes a local industry producing at full capacity and having regional market expectations made a community attractive to foreign labor. Such was the case of Irish mill weavers in Chicopee and Holyoke. Slavic immigrants looking for any kind of work settled in the western Pennsylvania steel towns at a time when machines were being introduced to replace skilled labor. East Europeans also poured into Fall River to operate the newly installed automatic machinery and threatened to drive out the "better class" of workers—English, Irish, French Canadians—much as the last two nationalities had earlier evicted the Yankees from the mills.[65] Slavic and Italian workers entered the Illinois fields during a decade of modernization and depression.[66] And everywhere the newcomer would work longer hours for less pay, thereby permitting the introduction of labor-saving machinery that eliminated the need for traditional skills. And everywhere nativism erupted.

Occupational hierarchy also triggered ethnic conflict. Modernization always brought ethnic and occupational displacement in its wake, and this in turn disrupted hiring patterns.[67] The newcomers became easy targets. After all, they could readily be identified with technological change and a renovated factory hierarchy. The skilled had often been part of an aristocracy of labor earlier imported from countries then undergoing industrialization. They were now displaced by new technology that made their skills increasingly obsolescent. Pushed upward in the social and production hierarchy, they were replaced by the largely unskilled ethnic newcomers. Or else they were offered semiskilled work as machines took away their old craft jobs. Or they might be driven out of the mine and mill itself.[68] Industrial reorganization, consequently, whenever and wherever it occurred, displaced skilled labor in the occupation in question—as the specific craft was reshaped by modernization, labor-saving techniques, new social and market conditions.

The workplace hierarchy was sharpened by ethnic hierarchy, with predictable correlatives appearing. Catholic immigrants inevitably entered the urban labor force, usually the most menial, most unskilled, most lowly paid sector—whether because as newcomers it was their obvious place or whether, as Thernstrom has found in Newburyport, it was caused by a downward plunge from middle-class ranks.[69] So Irish peasants swarmed into jobs as Pennsylvania mine laborers, New York canal construction hands, Jersey City railway workers, or Massachusetts textile operatives and crowded into seemingly predetermined and lowly occupational strata in the workplace.[70] As early as the 1820s, Lowell had its "English Row" of supervisory personnel, and by 1840, English and Scottish workers had the better paying jobs; the Irish had the lesser, an occupational distribution common to thriving urban centers like Boston and New York and to smaller communities such as Warren in Pennsylvania, and Cohoes in New York State.[71] Welshmen monopolized the attractive surface work in the mining operations of eastern Pennsylvania, with German and Irish laborers seeking to supplant them.[72] Similar ethnic-hierarchical strata existed among Illinois' coal miners, with skilled and unskilled again following lines of national origins, and it accounts for feuding in workingclass ranks: English-speaking miners occupied the skilled jobs and Slavic newcomers worked as common laborers. In some regions of Pennsylvania, the miners paid the laborers directly—and inequitably—in the equivalent of a third of the coal mined; and they also sabotaged the surface laborers' right, after two years of apprenticeship, to become miners, a violation of state law.

Thus economic grievances attendant upon wage and job inequities confirmed and deepened ethnic antagonisms. Such ethnic-occupational tensions existed virtually everywhere—among Scranton's Irish coal miners who received a third less in wages than their Protestant enemies, the English and Welsh foremen, and who worked as mine laborers;[73] among Italians and other new immigrants who replaced the dominant Cornish, Irish, and North European workforce in Colorado mines by the mid-1850s; among Italian arrivals who swept Newark's streets in the 1880s, filled menial positions abandoned by upwardly mobile Germans and Irish, entered the construction industry;[74] among French Canadians who in the 1860s occupied the least skilled positions in the newly automatic mills of Holyoke, Chicopee, and Fall River, reducing wages and forcing some of the experienced, class-conscious Anglo-Irish upward in the job hierarchy.[75] Waltham's Irish, rather than being confined to one occupational category within an industry, were restricted to one industry—the dead-end jobs in textile mills where they performed simple, unskilled tasks—and the watch-making monopoly remained with the skilled and native-born, overwhelmingly Protestant, another form of ethno-religious segregation guaranteed to sharpen ethnic biases and antagonisms.[76]

Nor were matters helped when the newcomers established their own societies and, reinforcing the job hierarchy, did not mingle with Protestant workers or join Protestant societies.[77] Such parallel networks and associations simply made nativist stereotypes easier and more vivid. Not even religion was a solvent. Catholics did not automatically join together against the enemy—whether Protestant or employer.[78] But religion, as Jensen observes, was significant in an important way.[79] It invariably created subcultures and became a potent influence upon ethnic separateness and exclusivity. It became especially so when combined with ethnic sameness.

Such developments increasingly threatened community cohesiveness. Old-stock residents of such a community reinvested their loyalties in new clubs or refurbished their interest in traditional associations; and perhaps because these fraternal orders did not provide completely satisfying surrogates for the old community itself, they frequently displayed bitter hostility toward different and competing subcultural institutions.

Whenever the community was in the process of drastic change, this old and dominant socioethnic bloc was troubled by the diverse and frightening worlds below them; by what Antonio Gramsci, writing in another context and about a more homogeneous nation, has described as "the features of subordinate groups," which for the elite "always display something barbaric and pathological."[80] Not that the shock troops in this sustained, century-long assault against immigrant blocs were the elite; rather they were those most anxious about the transformation of their community's social and economic structure, those who felt deeply rooted ways of life and work were under attack, those who held onto the remembered past, what Gutman has called "particular visions of a just society."[81]

Conflict between seemingly incompatible cultures blurred class lines. The facts of job hierarchy within the mill or mine simply exacerbated matters. Scranton's Irish mine laborers at times displayed greater hostility toward the skilled miners directly above them in the job hierarchy than toward the mine owner; and the skilled in turn feuded with them both as Catholics and as cheap labor. Philadelphia's craftsmen, we have seen, deeply resented Irish immigrants for these same reasons, and the recurrent turbulence in this city often involved differing ethnic blocs of workers rather than anything resembling a class struggle. Witness, for instance, the 1844 Southwark riots, which were primarily an Irish-nativist clash in which laborer, clerk, artisan, and shopkeeper faced laborer, clerk, artisan, and shopkeeper.[82] The anthracite coal miners' strike of 1871 can also be cited, for it produced clashes between Welsh miners and the Irish-German labor force rather than between employees and employer. In the Illinois fields, the hostility was between first- and second-generation Americans and the "unassimilable classes." In the California gold fields, the Cornish-Irish antagonism produced bloody clashes—before they joined in a détente, along with other native-born and European immigrant labor, against the Chinese arrivals—that generated a crusade, which included lynchings, organized robbery, and traditional pogromist stereotypes; and the mine owners were lost sight of altogether.[83] Another racist clash occurred between skilled and unionized cigar workers, all of them Caucasian, and the Chinese who were displacing them in a rapidly modernizing industry that used an advanced division of labor and that drove out the small companies and their older craftsmen; and, once again, the manufacturer was largely forgotten in the ensuing nativist strife.[84]

Such ethno-religious divisions, then, often frustrated efforts at class solidarity. But a distrust of those who had risen economically, ad hoc workingclass militancy, and even class consciousness at times coexisted with these divisive factors. The amalgam might also include what Fried has called "the blandishments of potential success" and an unformed sense of class differences as well as community interests.[85] Often a mix of class and ethnic consciousness was apparent—as in Philadelphia in the 1830s; or in the California mining towns where the Cornish maintained a fragile class solidarity in the midst of a spreading nativism; or as native-born steel workers demonstrated in 1891 when they were in the militant vanguard of a mounting South European workforce; or as in the 1871 anthracite coal strike when Welsh foremen demonstrated loyalty to their fellow countrymen who were miners rather than to management, and when the Welsh miners continued the strike over the objections of their German-Irish miner allies who wished to return to work.[86]

Clearly, then, a broad spectrum of attitudes and factors must be considered in any exploration of workingclass culture in America: clashing sociohistorical experiences that produced differing values and traditions, the demands of a changing workplace, the community's geographical position, the manner in which new industrial recruits were integrated into the labor force, even the number and timing of their entry and their impact on community institutions. The effect of immigration and modernization upon communities or subcommunities with shared values is hardly predictable. Often it results in inhabitants' clinging ever more tenaciously to an older, psychologically more comfortable set of values, in contrast to the new industrial order and its ethical and work standards. Such a community might be quite united, with its local politicians, police, shopkeepers, striking workers, and nonstriking labor as well, in hostile confrontation against strangers who sought entry into the local workforce. That these strangers might thus blur existing class antagonisms is to be expected. But it is also problematic. In the context of an unfolding workingclass community, they might even interact with its historic culture. Certainly it is difficult to predict the community response because the process as well as the response is both uneven and complex.

Some patterns and results may be foreseen, however. We do know that industrialization created a central place of work and transformed the human environment as factory products began to fill the landscape. We also know that it produced changes in situation, sensibility, and consciousness, that it brought into shape a sense of the modern world. Industrialization also generated a new appreciation of social order and social control, a resurgent crusade for temperance or prohibition, a revived evangelicalism, and a virulent and widespread nativism. The last was one reaction toward newcomers, to the dependent relations introduced by the factory system, to

the erosion of insulated values of a preindustrial society. Those who resorted to it were in deadly combat with forces that they did not understand and that they felt did not understand them. This combat was largely defensive: restrictive ethnic membership practices, whether applied to unions, crafts, fraternal associations, the community itself. It spilled over into alignments of Protestant employer and employee against their opposite religious and/or ethnic number rather than into interethnic, interreligious class collaboration.[87] Hence it was a substitute at times for workingclass militancy and an oblique reflection on labor's powerlessness and misperceptions.

More than these tentatively advanced conclusions cannot be claimed; and what we need, as Hirsh suggests, are studies of specific industries and communities.[88] These would be case studies exploring the effect of industrialism on the community and on its workingclass culture. Such studies are the concern of all social, labor, and urban historians. The essays that follow, I believe, make a modest start in this direction.

NOTES

1. Typical of the books and articles dealing with such subjects, and among the very best, are John Higham, *Strangers in the Land* (New Brunswick, N.J., 1955); Barbara Solomon, *Ancestors and Immigrants* (Cambridge, Mass., 1963); Thomas Gossett, *Race: The History of an Idea in America* (New York, 1965); William Gribbin, "Antimasonry, Religious Radicalism and the Paranoid Style of the 1820s," *History Teacher* 7 (February 1974); David Brion Davis, "Some Themes of Counter-Subversion: An Analysis of Anti-Masonic, Anti-Catholic and Anti-Morman Literature," *Mississippi Valley Historical Review* 47 (September 1960): 205-224; Ray Billington, *The Protestant Crusade* (Chicago, 1964).

2. Ralf Dahrendorf, *Society and Democracy in Germany* (Garden City, N.Y., 1967), 331, 332.

3. Pathbreaking studies of the inarticulate are Jesse Lemisch, "Listening to the Inarticulate: William Widger's Dream and the Loyalties of American Revolutionary Seamen in British Prisons," *Journal of Social History* 3 (1969-1970): 1-29, and James Hutson, "An Investigation of the Inarticulate: Philadelphia's White Oaks," *William and Mary Quarterly* 28 (1970): 3-25.

4. Herbert Gans, *Urban Villagers* (New York, 1962), 36.

5. Robert H. Wiebe, *The Search for Order* (New York, 1967), 4, 44.

6. Richard Sennett and Jonathan Cobb, *The Hidden Injuries of Class* (New York, 1972), 28-29, 38, passim.

7. William Gudalunas, "Before the Molly Maguires: The Emergence of the Ethno-Religious Factor in the Politics of the Lower Anthracite Region" (Ph.D. diss., Lehigh University, 1973), 29-33. The best concise treatment of the social structure of the Pennsylvania anthracite region is Rowland Berthoff, "The Social Order of the Anthracite Region, 1825-1902," *Pennsylvania Magazine of History and Biography* 89 (July 1965): 261-291. On Welsh and English immigrants, see Wilbur Shepperson, *British Emigration to North America* (Minneapolis, 1957), Charlotte Erickson, *Invisible Immigrants: The Adaptation of English and Scottish Immigrants in Nineteenth Century America* (Coral Gables, Fla., 1972), and Rowland Berthoff, *British Immigrants in Industrial America* (New York, 1953).

8. On the wrenching structural changes in the economics of the communities, such as wrought by the railroads, see Michael F. Holt, "The Politics of Impatience: The Origins of

Know-Nothingism," *Journal of American History* 60 (September 1973): 309-331. When the railroads came to Jersey City, for instance, it resulted in a physical transformation in the old residential areas as well as a marked industrial growth. Douglas Shaw, "The Making of an Immigrant City: Ethnic and Cultural Conflict in Jersey City, New Jersey, 1850-1877" (Ph.D. diss., University of Rochester, 1973), chap. 1.

9. Hannah Arendt, *Between Past and Future* (Cleveland and New York, 1966), 95.

10. Josiah Strong, *The Times and Young Men* (New York, 1901), 14.

11. On community and the impact of its dislocation, see Richard Sennett, *Uses of Disorder* (New York, 1970), 38-44.

12. Richard Hoggert, *Uses of Literacy* (New York, 1957). On the "world of ceremony and seasonal celebrations" of the past, see also Alasdaire Clayre, *Work and Play* (London, 1974), 101.

13. Sam Bass Warner, *The Private City: Philadelphia in Three Centuries of Its Growth* (Philadelphia, 1968), 64, 65, 67. Dennis H. Clark, *The Irish in Philadelphia* (Philadelphia, 1973), is also useful. For a good discussion of the impact of the transportation revolution on Philadelphia's artisans and the growth of merchant capitalism in that city, see Stuart Blumin, "Mobility in a Nineteenth-Century City: Philadelphia, 1820-1860" (Ph.D. diss., University of Pennsylvania, 1968), chap. 1. There is a detailed account of the changes in the organization of the productive processes in shoemaking in John P. Hall, "The Gentle Craft: A Narrative of Yankee Shoemakers" (Ph.D. diss., Columbia University, 1953). For a study of fire companies, see Andrew Neilly, "The Violent Volunteers: A History of the Volunteer Fire Departments of Philadelphia, 1736-1831" (Ph.D. diss., University of Pennsylvania, 1959). See also Herbert Asbury, *Gangs of New York* (Garden City, N.Y., 1927), 1-45; Laurie, "Fire Companies and Gangs in Southwark: The 1840s," in Mark Haller and Allen Davis, eds., *The Peoples of Philadelphia* (Philadelphia, 1973). Also on New York City fire companies and their brawls, see Lowell M. Limpus, *History of the New York Fire Departments* (New York, 1940), 150-158.

14. Herbert G. Gutman, "The Buena Vista Affair, 1874-1875," in Peter Stearns and Daniel Walkowitz, eds., *Workers in the Industrial Revolution* (New Brunswick, N.J., 1974), 194-231.

15. On the socializing of Lynn's workers in ethnic clubs and societies, see Bessie Van Vorst and Marie Van Vorst, *The Woman Who Toils* (New York, 1903). Networks of associations as surrogates for trade unions are explored in H. A. Turner, *Trade Union Growth, Structure, and Policy* (Toronto, 1962), 85.

16. Clifton Yearly, *Enterprise and Anthracite: Economics and Democracy in Schuylkill County, 1820-1875* (Baltimore, 1961). On anthracite coal developments and their importance to the American economic scene, see also Alfred Chandler, "Anthracite Coal and the Beginnings of the Industrial Revolution in the United States," *Business History Review* 46 (Summer 1972): 141-181; see also Peter Roberts, *The Anthracite Coal Industry* (New York, 1901).

17. On the domination of community loyalties, rather than the emerging "society" interests of the Gilded Age, see Sam Hayes, "Political Parties and the Community-System Continuum," in William Chambers and Walter D. Burnham, eds., *American Party System* (New York, 1967), 52-58. On the community and idea of the walking city, see Sam Bass Warner, *Streetcar Suburbs: The Process of Growth in Boston, 1870-1900* (New York, 1971), 15-21. See his *Private City,* passim, as well. There is a useful discussion of subcommunal group solidarity, especially in the light of growing urban complexity, in Michael Feldberg, *The Philadelphia Riots of 1844: A Study of Ethnic Conflict* (Westport, Conn., 1975). And there are any number of studies of community. For a thoughtful and suggestive discussion of the city as a community, see Michael Frisch, *Town into City: Springfield, Massachusetts, and the Meaning of Community, 1840–1880* (Cambridge, Mass., 1972).

18. On Southern and East European immigrants and reactions to them, see Higham, *Strangers,* passim; Solomon, *Ancestors,* passim. See also Francis A. Walker, "Immigration and

Degradation," *Forum* 9 (1891): 644; "Which Shall Dominate, Saxon or Slav?" *North American Review* 166 (1898); on Polish immigration to western Pennsylvania steel towns, see David Brody, *Steelworkers in America* (New York, 1969).

19. Marcus Hansen and J. B. Brebner, *Mingling of Canadian and American People* (New York, 1970), 18, 124-125, 160-169. See also State of Massachusetts, *Report of the Bureau of Statistics of Labor* 11 (Boston, 1880): 59, and ibid. 13 (Boston, 1882), 64, on the French-Canadian practice of taking the place of striking English and Irish textile operatives. On Holyoke's French Canadians, see Kenneth Underwood, *Protestant and Catholic Century* (Boston, 1957), 211; Virginia B. Cunz, *The French in America* (Minneapolis, 1966), 81; Constance McLaughlin Green, *Holyoke, Massachusetts* (New Haven, 1968), 202, 369-370; U.S. Senate, *Labor and Capital* 1 (1885): 66-67. See also *John Swinton's Paper,* January 6, 1884. Newburyport's Irish Catholics, a fourth of the city's population in 1880, had their own churches, parochial school system, and social institutions. Stephan Thernstrom, "Laborer and Community in 1880," in Stearns and Walkowitz, *Workers in the Industrial Revolution*, 185.

20. Newark's benefit societies, which are multiclass and multicraft associations, were homogeneous ethnic organizations that cut across class lines and included employers and employees. Moreover, these "informal networks of friends," when in large factories, helped mitigate discontent. Susan Hirsh, "Industrialization and Skilled Workers, Newark, 1826 to 1860" (Ph.D. diss., University of Michigan, 1974).

21. Asa Briggs, "The Language of 'Class' in Early Nineteenth-Century England," in Asa Briggs and John Saville, eds., *Essays in Labor History* (London, 1960), 43-73.

22. Hirsh, "Industrialization and Skilled Workers," passim.

23. On the modernization of industry and its disruptions, see Cyril E. Black, *Dynamics of Modernization* (New York, 1966), 27-33; Ioan Davies, *Social Mobility and Political Change* (New York, 1970), 22; S. N. Eisenstadt, *Modernization: Protest and Change* (Englewood Cliffs, N.J., 1966), 5, 20; Neil J. Smelser, "The Modernization of Social Relations," in Myron Weiner, ed., *Modernization: The Dynamics of Growth* (New York, 1966), 119-121; Reinhard Bendix, *Nation-Building and Citizenship* (New York, 1964), 138-139; Irving Louis Horowitz, *Three Worlds of Development* (New York, 1966), 444; Lawrence Brown, *Immigration* (New York, 1969), 144; Higham, *Strangers*, 64, 86; Ronald Shanks, "Race and Ethnic Relations: A Modernization and Stratification Perspective, 1876-1896" (Ph.D. diss., University of California, Irvine, 1974), passim.

24. Edward Thompson, *Making of the English Working Class* (New York, 1963), 194 (emphasis added).

25. J. L. Hammond, "The Industrial Revolution and Discontent," *Economic History Review* 2 (1930): 227-228.

26. Quoted in Hirsh, "Industrialization and Skilled Workers," 11.

27. On the new work ethic, see Sidney Pollard, "Factory Discipline in the Industrial Revolution," *Economic History Review* 16 (1963): 260-269. See also Pollard, *The Genesis of Modern Management* (Baltimore, 1965), 213-214, for a discussion of the need for regularity and standardization.

28. R. Q. Gray, "Styles of Life, the 'Labour Aristocracy' and Class Relations in Later Nineteenth Century Edinburgh," *International Review of Social History* 18 (1973): 428-451.

29. Quoted in Hirsh, "Industrialization and Skilled Workers," p. 14.

30. Gray, "Styles of Life," 429.

31. Laurie et al., "Immigrants and Industry: The Philadelphia Experience, 1850-1880," *Journal of Social History* 9 (Winter 1975): 242.

32. For commentary on idleness, leisure, and factory discipline in Lowell, see John Kasson, *Civilizing the Machine: Technology and Republican Values in America, 1776–1900* (New York, 1976), 94-95. Clayre also discusses employer attempts to impose clock time and stamp out play and singing in *Work and Play*, 100. So, too, does Pollard, *Genesis*, 213; and Thompson

in a seminal article, "Time, Work-Discipline and Industrial Capitalism," *Past and Present* 38 (December 1967). See also Hirsh, "Industrialization and Skilled Workers."

33. B. Fosgate, "Social Influence of Manufacturing," *New World* 6 (June 3, 1843); John Greenleaf Whittier, *The Stranger in Lowell* (Boston, 1845), 84; *Voice of Industry* [Lowell], April 3, 1846; ibid., September 11, 1846; ibid., June 19, 1846; ibid., May 7, 1847.

34. Warner, *Private City*, 67.

35. Sidney Pollard, *The Genesis of Modern Management* (Baltimore, 1965), 22.

36. Pollard, *Genesis*, 213-214; Thompson, "Time, Work-Discipline and Industrial Capitalism," 76.

37. Kasson, *Civilizing the Machine*, 75.

38. David Lockwood, "Sources of Variation in Working-Class Images of Society," in Martin Bulmer, ed., *Working-Class Images of Society* (London, 1975), 21.

39. Seymour Lipset and Reinhard Bendix, *Social Mobility in Industrial Society* (Berkeley, 1959), 105.

40. Thompson, *Making of the English Working Class*, 9-10.

41. On the insistence of first- and second-generation Americans upon protection from the "demoralizing effects" of the new immigrants and on the pressure for immigration restriction, see Peter Roberts, *Anthracite Coal Communities* (Philadelphia, 1904), 22-38; Frank I. Warne, *The Slav Invasion and the Mine Workers* (Philadelphia, 1904); Victor Greene, *The Slavic Community on Strike* (Notre Dame, 1968), chaps. 2, 3, 6; Berthoff, *British Immigrants*, 54-58; Chris Evans, *History of the United Mine Workers of America* (Indianapolis, 1900), 2: 257, 269-270, 331, 348, 423.

42. On anti-Chinese sentiment with special reference to California and West Coast labor, see Alexander Saxton, *The Indispensable Enemy* (Berkeley, 1971). See also the special issue of the *California Historical Quarterly* (September 1951). Two additional references of value are Luther W. Spoehr, "Sambo and the Heathen Chinee: Californians' Racial Stereotypes in the late 1870s," *Pacific Historical Review* 42 (May 1973), and Roger Daniels and Harry Kilano, *American Racism* (Englewood Cliffs, N.J., 1970), 141-145.

43. David Montgomery, "The Shuttle and the Cross: Weavers and Artisans in the Kensington Riots of 1844," in Stearns and Walkowitz, *Workers in the Industrial Revolution*, 56-57. This essay makes a persuasive argument for cultural, ethnic, and religious divisions—usually in the form of nativist conflict—as reflecting a decline of class consciousness among Philadelphia's working people after the late 1830s.

44. Montgomery, *Shuttle and Cross*, 48-49. See also Leonard Bernstein, "The Working People of Philadelphia from Colonial Times to the General Strike of 1835," *Pennsylvania Magazine of History and Biography* 73 (1950).

45. Bernstein, "Working People of Philadelphia," 336-339.

46. On earlier instances of ethnic conflict and the rhetoric of violence, see Richard H. Brown, "Historical Patterns of Violence in America," in Hugh D. Graham and Ted R. Gurr, eds., *Violence in America* (New York, 1969), and also Warner, *Private City*, 125-157. See also David Craft, *History of Scranton* (Dayton, 1891), 220-226.

47. On Irish and Catholics in New York State, see Whitney Cross, *The Burned Over District* (Ithaca, 1950), esp. pp. 4-6, and John Horton et al., *A History of Northwestern New York* (New York, 1947). Irish canal labor is alluded to in a number of works, among them William D. Hurd, *The Catholic Church in New England* (Boston, 1899), 596, and Bernstein, "Working People of Philadelphia," 336-339. See also Laurence A. Glasco, "Ethnicity and Social Structure: Irish, Germans, and Native Born of Buffalo, New York, 1850-1860" (Ph.D. diss., State University of New York at Buffalo, 1973), 86, 93, 226. See also, on Irish canal labor, Vera Shlakman, *Economic History of a Factory Town* (Northampton, Mass., 1935), 49.

48. On rural Ireland, its society and violence, see Oliver MacDonagh, "Irish Famine Migration," in *Perspectives in American History* 10 (1976): 384-385. Jersey City's Irish are carefully discussed in Douglas Shaw, "Making of an Immigrant City."

49. Stephan Thernstrom, "Laborer and Community in 1880," in Stearns and Walkowitz, *Workers in the Industrial Revolution*, 188. In Jersey City, Shaw concludes, no cohesive community existed, but there was an Irish community, which included Irish shopkeepers, and it supported the Irish railway workers. These workers constituted only about 3.5 percent of the city's workforce—unlike Lynn, where the shoemakers comprised nearly 50 percent—but the Jersey City labor force was substantially Irish, with a tradition of nationalist agitation in the Sinn Fein movement, the Clan na Gael, and the anti-monopolist Land and Labor League, all post-Civil War associations.

50. "The Lower Classes," Order of United Americans (hereafter OUA), January 20, 1849; Samuel Busey, *Immigration: Its Evils and Consequences* (New York, 1869); Jesse Chickering, *Immigration into the United States* (Boston, 1848), 64; Robert Ernst, *Immigrant Life in New York City* (New York, 1949), 18-19.

51. Excerpts from unidentified Lowell newspapers, in *Boston Pilot*, August 16, 1851. See also OUA, January 13, 1849, and excerpt from *National Intelligencer,* in OUA, November 25, 1848; Oscar Handlin, *Boston's Immigrants* (Cambridge, Mass., 1941), 62-63; Max Berger, "Irish Immigrants and American Nativism as Seen by British Visitors, 1836-1860," *Pennsylvania Magazine of History and Biography* 70 (1946): 146-160; Carl Wittke, ed., *Irish in America* (Baton Rouge, 1956), 34; and Jean Hales, "Shaping of Nativist Sentiment, 1848-1860" (Ph.D. diss., Stanford University, 1973).

52. Clark, *Irish in Philadelphia*, chaps. 2, 4. Nativism as a reflection of change is discussed in Donald Kinzer, *Episode in Anti-Catholicism: The American Protective Association* (Seattle, 1964), 140. Racism and nativism as a reaction to the new social order is explored in Richard Weiss, "Racism in the Era of Industrialism," in Gary Nash and Richard Weiss, eds., *The Great Fear: Race in the Mind of America* (New York, 1970), 124-125. For a useful discussion of how and why immigrants were blamed for the disorganization of urban life, see Robert Wiebe, *Search for Order, 1877-1920* (New York, 1967), 54-56, and Bessie L. Pierce, *A History of Chicago*, vol. 3: *The Rise of the Modern City* (New York, 1957), 32-33. On early labor violence on docks and canals and railways, see Bernstein, "Working People of Philadelphia," 333-339. See also Warner, *Private City*, 61; John Schneider, "Community and Order in Philadelphia, 1834-1844," *Maryland Historian* 5 (Spring 1974). On New York City's riots, see Herbert Asbury, *Gangs of New York* (Garden City, N.Y., 1927), 1-45; Leon Richards, *Gentlemen of Property* (New York, 1970). See also Allan Grimshaw, "Lawlessness and Violence in America," *Journal of Negro History* 44 (January 1959): 52-55. On the urban poor, see Carol Groneman, "The 'Bloody Ould Sixth': A Social Analysis of a New York City Workingclass Community in the Mid-Nineteenth Century" (Ph.D. diss., University of Rochester, 1973), 179-180. For an illuminating discussion of the loss of community feeling in New York City and the corollary rise of new associations, see John Schneider, "Mob Violence and Public Order in the American City, 1830-1865" (Ph.D. diss., University of Minnesota, 1971). There is a very substantial literature on nativist riots. See, for example, on the St. Louis 1849 riot (of nativist fire companies versus Irish residents along the levee), Thomas Scharf, *History of Saint Louis City and County* (Philadelphia, 1883), 2: 836-837. On Know-Nothing violence, see W. Darrell Overdyke, *The Know Nothing Party in the South* (Baton Rouge, 1950). On the Boston (Charleston) riots of 1834, see Ray Billington, "The Burning of the Charleston Convent," *New England Quarterly* 10 (June 1937): 4-24; and on the Pennsylvania antiabolitionist riot of 1830, see Schneider, "Mob Violence," chap. 4. On a number of antiabolitionist mobs, see Richards, *Gentlemen of Property*, passim.

53. On the Manayunk workers, who were overwhelmingly Irish, and their sense of their plight and of the injustices done them, see John L. Commons et al., *A Documentary History of American Industrial Society* (Cleveland, 1910), 5: 331-334, 339.

54. Elizabeth M. Geffen, "Violence in Philadelphia," *Pennsylvania History* 36 (October 1969): 392. See also Billington, *Protestant Crusade*, and Thomas Scharf and Thompson Westcott, *History of Philadelphia* (Philadelphia, 1887), 1:663-668. On the 1844 riots, see

Feldberg, *Philadelphia Riots.* And see Schneider, "Community and Order in Philadelphia."

55. Philadelphia suffered from chronic nativist agitation, which mushroomed especially after the 1837 panic but had declined by 1844. See Montgomery, "Shuttle and Cross," in Stearns and Walkowitz, *Workers in the Industrial Revolution.* For comparable developments and issues in New York City, see Herbert I. London, "The Nativist Movement in the American Republican Party in New York City During the Period 1843-1847" (Ph.D. diss., New York University, 1966), 38, 56, 198-200. Lee Benson, *The Concept of Jacksonian Democracy* (Princeton, 1961), also emphasizes sociocultural developments and finds an economic explanation for developments too simplistic.

56. Order of United American Mechanics (hereafter OUAM) membership was almost exclusively drawn from mechanics' ranks, and it included, among others, cordwainers, tailors, and wheelwrights. OUAM Fredonia Lodge no. 52, West Philadelphia, "Records of the Society, 1850-1857." See also Hales, "Shaping of Nativist Sentiment," 137-143. Regarded as conservative and middle class, the Order of United Americans (OUA) also appealed to many workingmen. OUA members in New York City and Brooklyn, and United Sons of America members from Philadelphia and Camden, have been sampled by Hales: 40 percent of the OUA sample and a third of the USA sample were artisans and skilled labor. A similar organization is the Order of United Mechanics of America (OUMA), the third most important nativist society nationally, which drew almost exclusively upon mechanics. See also John Mulkern, "The Know Nothing Party in Massachusetts" (Ph.D. diss., Boston University, 1963), on the OUMA; Mary McConville, *Political Nativism in the State of Maryland, 1830–1860* (Washington, DC., 1928).

57. Thomas Whitney, *A Defense of the American Policy, as Opposed to the Encroachment of Foreign Influence* (New York, 1856), 261. See also Hales, "Shaping of Nativist Sentiment," on the conflict between Irish workers and organized nativism, which in Philadelphia, unlike other cities, was mostly (though even here, not wholly) middle class. Hence, as in the 1844 Southwark riots, it was primarily an Irish-nativist riot in which laborer and clerk faced laborer and clerk. Warner, *Private City*, 51.

58. On artisan and middle-class (working small-shop proprietors) adherents of Philadelphia's nativist movement, especially the American Republican Party, see Feldberg, *Philadelphia Riots*, 54. The prolabor bias that appears in much of nativist literature reflects the class origins and special interests of many nativists.

59. Charles Buell, "The Workers of Worcester" (Ph.D. diss., New York University, 1974). On Massachusetts Know Nothings, see Holt, "Politics of Impatience," 329.

60. Hales, "Shaping of Nativist Sentiment"; London, "Nativist Movement"; Benson, *Concept of Jacksonian Democracy.*

61. Montgomery, "Shuttle and Cross," 56-57.

62. Samuel Gompers, *Some Reasons for Chinese Exclusion* (Washington, D.C., 1902). Another pamphlet indicating Gompers' racism, coauthored with Herman Gutstadt, is *Meat vs. Rice: American Manhood Against Asiatic Collieism: Which Shall Survive?* (Washington, D.C., 1901). See also Saxon Mann, "Gompers and the Irony of Racism," *Antioch Review* 12 (June 1953): 205. Finally, there is Gompers, *Seventy Years of Life and Labor* (New York, 1925), 2: 152.

63. John Rowe, *Hard-Rock Men: Cornish Immigrants and the North American Mining Frontier* (New York, 1974), 118. On Irish-Cornish miner conflict in Upper Michigan iron mines, owing to "religious prejudices and fear of cheap Irish labor," see ibid., 269.

64. On the militancy of some new ethnic groups, particularly Slavic and Italian miners in Spring Valley, Illinois, in 1894 as well as in the Pennsylvania fields at this time, see Harry Barnard, *Eagle Forgotten* (New York, 1938), 276-279. These two groups of new immigrant miners and also those from Belgium spoke in terms of struggle and resorted to bloody actions in both Illinois and Pennsylvania in 1894, frequently clashing with the older miners. See also Richard Jensen, *The Winning of the Midwest* (Chicago, 1971), 254-255.

65. Hansen and Brebner, *Mingling of Canadian and American People*, 124-125, 160-169. Thirty percent of a sampling of French Canadian families had wives at work as late as 1909, compared to slightly over 10 percent for the Irish.

66. Herbert Gutman, "The Buena Vista Affair," in Stearns and Walkowitz, *Workers in the Industrial Revolution*, 194-231.

67. Handlin, *Boston's Immigrants*, 83; Richard Mayo Smith, *Emigration and Immigration* (New York, 1890), 126.

68. Thernstrom, "Working-Class Mobility in Industrial America," 287-288. Thernstrom describes the occupational mobility of the sons of unskilled and semiskilled workers and their movement into skilled or white-collar jobs in Boston. Eric Hobsbawm and Royden Harrison, writing of nineteenth-century English workers, have observed that only labor's aristocracy blended into lower middle-class ranks; but in the United States—or at least in Boston—the entire urban workingclass shared the possibility of upward mobility. Thernstrom is among many social historians who have noted the hierarchical arrangements at the workplace that found different ethnic groups having a near monopoly of different jobs in the process of production. See also, for instance, Donald Cole, *Immigrant City: Lawrence, Massachusetts, 1845-1921* (Chapel Hill, 1963), 116, and Robert Hunter, *Poverty* (New York, 1904), 294.

69. Thernstrom, "Working-Class Social Mobility," 292. On the self-advancement of Newburyport Irish, see Thernstrom, "Labor and Community in 1880: Toward Social Stability," in Stearns and Walkowitz, *Workers in the Industrial Revolution*, 186-189.

70. On the rise of urban poverty and slums, with the attendant destruction of residential areas, see Douglas Miller, *Jacksonian Aristocracy: Class and Democracy in New York, 1830-1860* (New York, 1967), 151; Handlin, *Boston's Immigrants,* 18-19, 88; *American Banner* (Philadelphia, February 28, 1852). On urban poverty and neighborhood blight, see *Philadelphia Public Ledger*, June 21, 1832; Norman Ware, *Industrial Worker* (Chicago, 1964), 12-16, 21, 27; Glasco, "Ethnicity and Social Structure," 43, 45.

71. Michael Weber, *Social Change in an American Industrial Town: Patterns of Progress in Warren, Pennsylvania from Civil War to World War I* (University Park, Penn., 1976), 74-75.

72. Alan Conway, ed., *The Welsh in America* (Minneapolis, 1961), 168. On Schuylkill miners and ethno-religious as well as political polarization in the 1840s, and its primacy for Welsh and English Protestant miners, see Gudalunas, "Before the Molly Maguires," 52, 63.

73. P. E. Gibbons, "The Miners of Scranton, Pennsylvania," *Harpers Magazine* 55 (November 1877): 923. On Welsh dominance of mining boss ranks, see H. M. Alden, "The Pennsylvania Coal Region," *Harpers Magazine* 27 (September 1963).

74. Churchill, *Italians of Newark*, 29.

75. On the importance of class solidarity to Fall River's English and Irish operatives, see "Testimony of Thomas O'Donnell," *Industrial Commission* 17, 56th Cong., 2d sess., House doc. 183, 1901, 567. On French Canadians as causing wage decreases, see Therese Bilodeau, "The French in Holyoke, 1850-1900," *Historical Journal of Western Massachusetts* 3 (Spring 1974): 6.

76. H. M. Gitelman, *Workmen of Waltham* (Baltimore, 1975), 2-3, 59.

77. Ibid., 152-155. Newburyport was similarly divided. Here too the "religious and ethnic differences had outweighed class considerations," and the simple class divisions were less important than those between Protestants and Irish Catholics. Thernstrom, "Labor and Community in 1880," 185.

78. On the identity of religious belief not necessarily creating a solidarity of attitude and response, see Underwood, *Protestant and Catholic Century*, 213-214. See also Bilodeau, "French in Holyoke," 6-7.

79. Jensen, *Winning of the Midwest*, 58. See also Frederick Luebke, *Immigrants and Politics* (Lincoln, Neb., 1969). On the social function of religion, see Henry Pelling, *Popular Politics and Society in Late Victorian Britain* (New York, 1968), 32-35. A useful discussion of the religion of Irish and German immigrants may be found in Gerhard Lenski, *The Religious*

Factor: A Sociological Study of Religion's Impact on Politics, Economics and Family Life (New York, 1961), 25.

80. Gramsci quote in Charles Tilly, "Collective Violence in European Perspective," in Hugh D. Graham and Ted R. Gurr, eds., *Violence in America* (New York, 1969), 12. For example, on anti-Irish and anti-Catholic views of Philadelphia's elite in the 1830s and 1840s, see P. Kenny, "The Anti-Catholic Riots in Philadelphia in 1844," *American Catholic Historical Researches* 13 (1896): 50-64, and also the testimony of Joseph Ripka in *Journal of the Senate of Pennsylvania* 2 (1838), 357-358.

81. Herbert G. Gutman, "Work, Culture and Society in Industrializing America, 1815-1919," *American Historical Review* 78 (June 1973): 531-587, contains important and instructive insights on this subject, and I have drawn upon this article at a number of points.

82. Warner, *Private City*, 51.

83. Saxton, *Indispensable Enemy*, 88. See also Robert McClellan, *The Heathen Chinese* (Columbus, Ohio, 1971), 61-63, on nativism in California mining communities; in Wyoming, specifically Rock Spring, where thirty Chinese were killed in 1855; and in other western communities, where Chinese quarters were burned down or the Chinese population deported (for example, Tacoma and Seattle incidents in 1886). See also Arthur C. Todd, *The Cornish Miner in America* (Glendale, Ill., 1967), 59, 61, 229, 256. See also Rowe, *Hard-Rock Men*, 118.

84. Gompers, *Seventy Years of Life and Labor*, 2: 152.

85. Marc Fried, *The World of the Urban Workingclass* (Cambridge, Mass., 1973), 94-95.

86. Lenski, *Religious Factor*, 25.

87. Nativism, as a movement that included skilled artisans—as distinct from unskilled foreign-born workers—is discussed in Hales, "Shaping of Nativist Sentiment," 136-147. See also Paul Kleppner, *The Cross of Culture: A Social Analysis of Mid-Western Politics* (New York, 1970), passim, and Jensen, *Winning of the Midwest*, passim, as well as a recent article by John Shover, "Ethnicity and Religion in Philadelphia Politics, 1924-1940," *American Quarterly* (December 1973), and Joseph Buenker, *Urban Liberalism and Progressive Reform* (New York, 1973), 167-181. These scholars, and Montgomery should be included, have examined political polarization along religious lines, with "pietistic" religions (such as Methodists and Baptists) aligned against those with a more "ritualistic" orientation (Catholics and Lutherans). Prohibition, they conclude, drained class militancy and was an issue upon which both immigrant and old-stock Americans divided, but these divisions were customarily along religious rather than class lines. Not that sociocultural issues were always clear-cut. Temperance, for instance, was not a Protestant or a middle-class monopoly in the 1880s. Pennsylvania's Catholics in the 1870s, Walker indicates, had an active Total Abstinence Union. Terence Powderly, an Irish Catholic and a machinist, was a temperance advocate. Unquestionably, for example, some mine foremen felt a greater sense of loyalty to their Welsh countrymen who were on strike than toward the companies for whom they worked. Indeed one Welsh foreman informed the Workingman's Benevolent Association of company plans to break the strike by using German workers. On the WBA, see Roberts, *Anthracite Coal Communities*, 69-70. Marvin Schlegel, "The Workingmen's Benevolent Association: First Union of Anthracite Miners," *Pennsylvania History* 10 (October 1943): 243-267; Harold Aurand, "The Workingmen's Benevolent Association," *Labor History* (Winter 1966): 19-34.

88. Hirsh, "Industrialization and Skilled Workers," 8.

A GATHERING OF STRANGERS? MOBILITY, SOCIAL STRUCTURE, AND POLITICAL PARTICIPATION IN THE FORMATION OF NINETEENTH-CENTURY AMERICAN WORKINGCLASS CULTURE

2

Charles Stephenson*

> Industrial giants impelling incessant speculation create a restlessness and haste among the skilled and unskilled masses of laborers that drive them in search of chances from town to town. Senseless competition keeps them in a state of constant migration from place to place, from street to street, from house to house. The sturdy artisans and poor day-laborers, the small tradesmen and mechanics, those having a little capital as well as those living on credit, all must follow the mysterious beck of the industrial magnates. The small householders fly hither and thither, where new hopes or better prospects brighten the horizon, or where there are grocers and butchers who do not know how much the newcomers owe in other quarters. Each business misfortune compels a change of residence, each promise of triflingly higher wages, as well as each reduction of income, creates a shiftiness and nervousness which cannot allow a thought of the common affairs to arise. There is either a general stagnation of business, which is to the industrial population like a whirlwind, scattering neighbors and separating too often fathers, mothers and children, while the cherished household goods go to the auction room or pawnbroker. Or there is a rush of business during which all make money and spend it foolishly. Why should the poor care?[1]

It has become commonplace to observe that population mobility in nineteenth-century America achieved stunning rates. We have sufficient evidence of the enormous and apparently constant turnover in population to cause us

*I would like to acknowledge the support of the Center for the Study of Metropolitan Problems, National Institute of Mental Health, for supporting this research under grant # MH 25860-02, and to thank Brian Greenberg, John Roberts, Walter Licht, and David Montgomery for reading earlier versions of this manuscript.

to wonder how stability was achieved at all. Study after study has shown that the larger part of a population found in a city in one year cannot be found in the same community several years later. In cities as diverse as Boston, Philadelphia, San Antonio, and San Francisco, in large urban complexes and small rural towns, the same general pattern has emerged. At the end of a period of analysis, generally a decade, from 30 to 70 percent of the original population were no longer resident.[2] The pattern is confirmed in Canadian studies as well, sometimes with even lower rates of persistence. David Gagan has found that over a period of twenty years, 95 percent of the population resident in rural Peel County, Ontario, in the first year had left. In his study of Hamilton, Michael Katz found that 25 percent of his population had left after only three months.[3] The pattern has appeared time after time, in study after study. Rates of persistence have proved to be particularly low among the workingclass. "In *no* American city," concluded one investigator, "has there been a large lower-class element with continuity of membership." In Boston, for example, "roughly a quarter of the population at any one date had not been living in the community *365 days* before."[4] Although we do not yet know precisely what the proportions of such a group were, we do know that working people constituted the majority of migrants and that the majority—the vast majority—of working people participated in this pattern of movement, many of them time after countless time.[5] Indeed Thernstrom and others have hypothesized the existence of a portion of the lower class characterized as a "permanent floating proletariat," "a class of permanent transients who continued to be buffeted about by the vicissitudes of the casual labor market."[6]

But although we have long been aware of the role of geographical movement in our society, American historians have developed little theory with which to deal with this omnipresent factor in our past. That which has addressed the question directly has stressed the social instability that it prompted and its debilitating effects upon the individuals and families involved. Eric McKitrick and Stanley Elkins spoke of "the lonely dwellers of the fast-growing cities." Rowland Berthoff, in urging adoption of "the central and continuous factor" of mobility as the unifying theme of social history, believed that the migration of nineteenth-century Americans "produced an American social disorder almost without parallel in the modern world" and posited a scheme in which "mobility and stability" were mutually exclusive phenomena—as Samuel Hays said, "Mobility and stability were incompatible."[7] The perception of the cost to the individual is exemplified by Thernstrom's characterization of repeating migrants as people who were "alienated but invisible and politically impotent."[8] It is as if workingclass communities were no more than a gathering of strangers and workingclass life an ordeal undergone in isolation.

It is becoming clear, however, that this entire approach is in great need of reevaluation and redefinition. We now have ample information concerning the nineteenth-century American workingclass to call into question these interpretations, indeed to contradict them, and to propose new hypotheses regarding the culture of the workingclass in industrial America. In considering our current state of knowledge, we should remember that much of the impetus behind the current emphasis on mobility studies has stemmed from two basic motivations. Well over a decade ago, many historians became aware that the history they were writing was one that focused upon a small minority of people while ignoring the remainder or making unfounded assumptions about them. In part the reaction to traditional historiography—its emphasis, its focus, its techniques—stemmed from ideological grounds. Historians who often were younger and politically active disdained the almost total concentration upon politicians, military leaders, kings and their courts, and other visible people.[9] They set out to write instead the history of the majority of people, who built the pyramids, fought the wars, tilled the fields.[10] As they did so, they found that more than ideology stood in their way. It was clear that traditional literary sources—diaries, newspapers, manuscripts, accounts of elections —had a class bias of significant proportions and seemed to offer little communication with the vast majority of Americans.[11] It was soon realized that the majority of people left few personal records that could be mined for new insights. They were not inarticulate while they had lived, but death seemed to have rendered them mute. In response to this challenge to avoid confusing "illustration with verification," some historians turned toward what they called a "social scientific" approach to the field (one that previously had been concentrated in economic history).[12] In dealing with questions of family structure, fertility, migration, and the like, these historians began to stress the importance of methodology, especially quantification and explicit model building. They began to deal, with an ever-increasing sophistication, with people in the aggregate in an attempt to fill in the void concerning the lives and behavior of the majority. Their sources were census manuscripts, city directories, birth, death, and marriage records, tax ledgers, immigration records, housing permits, and all manner of statistically manipulable materials that offered insight into the everyday lives of people.[13]

The achievements of this approach have been considerable, and social science history seems on the way to a well-deserved acceptance as a major field of endeavor in history.[14] Yet some questions have been raised regarding the basis of the approach, and we must look briefly at these. David Montgomery has criticized the approach, addressing especially the emphasis upon social mobility (from which he says it "may be said to have derived its basic concepts and methodology") as being fundamentally grounded in existing political assumptions. Montgomery believes that such an approach "contains an inherently self-confirming bias." "For the historian to concentrate his attention on the question deemed important" by advocates of an ideology of social mobility "is to rule out of consideration from the start any group cultures or values within the community other than those of the middle class, or to reduce the treatment of them to the level of social pathology." "As long as the historian's conceptual framework rests in the problem of social mobility," he warned, "endless investigation of 'mass behavior and social process' will reveal little about 'the ordinary people who make up the life of the city.'"[15] James Green has criticized the new historians on much the same basis. They refuse "to admit that methodology is related to ideology,"[16] and he urged others to adopt "behavioralism without fully explaining the ideological implications inherent in it."[17] He further chided those "consensus historians" who, seeing that quantification "would 'require no normative changes within the discipline,'" seek merely "to add scientific authority to their pluralist assumptions."[18] Allan Bogue, in another context, speculated that "the emphasis which behavioral historians are placing on the importance of ethno-cultural groups may in part reflect the fact that the ethno-cultural reference group is the easiest to identify in historical data."[19] Green noted further cases in which "the social analysis fails to integrate class and culture."[20] It is this attempt to bring a sophisticated view of culture to their analysis that has distinguished the proponents of the second approach, which has stemmed from the desire to "view history from the bottom up."

This approach, too, constituted a rebellion against institutional and elitist history, though in this case the institutions were labor unions and the elite were labor leaders. In attempting to follow Hyman Berman's dictum that "labor history is more than the rise and fall or the failures and successes of organizations . . . it also consists of elucidating the role of workers both organized and unorganized in the course of this country's historical development," these historians of the workingclass had come to realize that most working people never belonged to a union and that the vast majority of those who did never had been leaders in such an organization or indeed in any other organization.[21] Thus the history of the workingclass was enlarged to include the life of the average working person and not simply to detail the political involvement of visible members of leading organizations. The basis of the approach was the effort to detail the community culture of workers in all its manifestations and, especially in American terms, to analyze the wrenching transition from a traditional to an industrial-capitalist economy. The discovery of new sources was perhaps less sought after than was the imaginative use of old ones to answer new questions.[22] Historians in the United States, such as Herbert Gutman, Tamara Hareven, Paul Faler, Brian Greenberg, John Cumbler, Walter Licht, and Green, have attempted to follow the lead of the English historians who pioneered this approach, especially Edward Thompson and E. J. Hobsbawm.[23] While American historians—with the exception of Tryge

Tholfsen—have not yet achieved the methodological or ideological sophistication of Gareth Steadman Jones or John Foster, they are well on the way to doing so.[24] If the new social historians have attempted to enlarge the sociological aspect of history, the new workingclass historians —no less adaptors of social science history—have stressed what properly may be termed a variety of anthropological investigation, particularly in their emphasis upon further developing the central concept of culture. It is this concept that now offers the opportunity to develop a framework that can be used in answering the as-yet-unanswered questions regarding the crucial impact of geographical mobility upon the individual worker and the collective workingclass community in America.

"In England today," Gareth Steadman Jones tells us in his magnificent study of the workingclass in late nineteenth-century London, "the idea of a working-class culture, of a distinct working-class way of life, is practically a cliché."[25] "This working class culture," he continues, "was clearly distinguished from the culture of the middle class and had remained largely impervious to middle-class attempts to dictate its character or direction."[26] Such a proposition surely is not yet a cliché in terms of the American workingclass, but the distinctiveness of the life-styles and approaches of different groups is becoming more realized, especially due to recent work such as Gutman's. Yet Gutman's emphasis, in his article "Work, Culture, and Society in Industrializing America," is upon the diverse cultures found among different, ethnically defined, segments of the workingclass in America and less than upon the existence of working-class cultural patterns distinct from those of the (quite diverse) middle class. But it seems likely that the divide between behavior and the ideational patterns of the working and middle classes evinces cultures even more stark, and certainly more distinct, disparate, and separate, than those hypothesized by Gutman. Further, we must ask if the much-used distinction between nonindustrial "premodern" work habits and industrially adopted work habits is as useful as has been believed. Certainly the concept is a useful one in the analysis of social change and is necessary in the analysis of the nonindustrial or preindustrial peoples who came to the United States. If, on the other hand, the concept is used for its predictive value regarding opposition to an industrial-capitalist order, then its focus is misplaced. Indeed it may well prove that as great an opposition to industrialization stemmed from Americans born and bred into an industrial economy as came from those who had never known one. Familiarity sometimes breeds contempt, and familiarity did not necessarily soften the reaction to this form of oppression.[27] What we must investigate are the little-known contours of that workingclass culture as it operated on its own terms and in its conjunctures with the larger society, and the influence that constant and ever-present mobility had upon it.

For a key concept, my use of *culture* must seem notoriously amorphous. Of course I do not use it in the old sense of haute culture, though certainly differing social pursuits were characteristic of the differing life-styles I will address. This dilemma has a broader clientele than historians, however, for we have seen recently that even in cultural anthropology one "can search its records high and low for a satisfactory definition. For all the volumes written about it, the concept 'culture' has not become an incisive tool of thought. It remains a commodious cushion, a category in which anything can comfortably recline.'"[28] Yet, despite the fact that a commodious cushion could be quite useful at the present stage of our research, we can be a bit more precise regarding the elusive concept. When I speak of workingclass culture, I mean to designate a community characterized by "the special sets of behavior, norms, loyalties, beliefs, etc., manifested and internalized by its members.'"[29] Following Clifford Geertz's proposal that culture is a "system of ideas" animating social structure,[30] we can say that "culture is not behavior but the complex of rules and values which generate and guide behavior'"[31] and may be seen as "both a manner of ordering and structuring the individual's environment and a manner of correlating the arrangement of the individual's behavior with the arrangement of that environment.'"[32] In the terms in which culture will be used here, the definition centers about the reality of shared values, common patterns of thought, behavior, and association that cause members of a community or communities to coalesce at certain junctures rather than to repel. This definition is crucial to our study, for upon it is based the attraction of groups of many nationalities that shared the fact of being members of a workingclass. This is not to say that they always did coalesce —nothing so simplistic as that—but that the reasons for their failure to do so transcended their particular cultures and was centered in other phenomena.

Gutman has taken the initiative to propose a framework for what he has termed "a model subculture," which includes "friendly and benevolent societies, friendly local politicians, community-wide holiday celebrations, an occasional library, participant sports, churches, saloons, beer gardens, concert halls or music halls, [and maybe] trade unionists, labor reformers, and radicals.'"[33] To these designations we should add the particular patterns of family and kinship networks and customs and, sometimes, perceived hierarchies within the community. Such a set of associations offers the matrix within which community occurred and from which culture changed in America. This scheme offers historians a concrete beginning point for the study of the rich heritage of the diverse peoples who have populated the nation and puts the lie to schemes that prate of cultural anarchy and chaos. "It is time," says Gutman, "to discard the notion that the large-scale uprooting and exploitative processes that accompanied industrialization caused little more than cultural breakdown and social anomie." "Class and occupational distinctions within a particular ethnic group made for different patterns of cultural adaptation," he notes, "but powerful subcultures thrived among them all."[34] It was the strength of these powerful cultures, and the particular type and limits of assimilation and acculturation experienced in America, that furnished the peculiar adaptation of the workingclass to the constant mobility it experienced.

Certainly different ethnic and class groups were assimilated into the operational framework of the United States. Yet we now have accumulated sufficient evidence to discard the popular notion of the melting pot and to replace it with an understanding of the cultural diversity that has characterized our past. Milton Gordon has analyzed the way in which assimilation did take place and in so doing has pointed out the distinctions central to the process. Gordon has said that "the most salient fact" in the American experience "is the maintenance of the structurally separate subsocieties of the three major religions and the racial and quasi-racial groups, and even vestiges of the nationality groupings, along with a massive trend toward acculturation of all groups—particularly their native-born— to American culture patterns." Gordon prefers the term *structural pluralism* rather than *cultural pluralism*, believing it is "the major key to the understanding of the ethnic makeup of American society."[35] While the middle-class culture was attempting to shape the behavioral patterns of different ethnic groups, it resisted their integration into the social system. Colin Greer has noted that "behavioral conformity is achieved, but, in many cases, not structural integration. The great majority of newcomers and their offspring have held fast to a communal life made up of their fellow-immigrants."[36] S. N. Eisenstadt offered a more explicit model in *The Absorption of Immigrants.*[37] As Patrick J. Gallo explains,

> Eisenstadt makes a distinction between types of roles or values in a society. Three are noted: universal, specialities, and alternatives. A pluralist society demands complete fulfillment of the first only, allows the emergence of a particularist immigrant body within the general social structure with special roles allocated to it and a limitation on the scope of alternatives to it. The immigrants are acculturated to the degree that they internalize and express the major American patterns and values, and fulfill the universal roles of the society. They are permitted to retain certain particularistic traits from their native culture. Cultural assimilation does not demand complete uniformity.[38]

Thus the process of assimilation, or acculturation, is a dialectical one. As groups of immigrants bring with them to an American setting the values and patterns of behavior of their community, the new culture begins a process by which those values will be transformed; yet beyond the acceptance of modified behavior patterns, ethnic enclaves will be allowed, and in some cases encouraged, to exist. At the same time immigrants, often despite a desire to become "Americanized," will resist facets of the new values and attempt to maintain control over each aspect of their lives. The resultant cultural transformation will be a synthesis of the original values and the process of Americanization, with the characteristic expressions of communal life in many cases reserved for relations within the internal community and not in relations with the external society. It should not be supposed that this process is accomplished either rapidly or easily. Indeed the depth of resistance to it may perhaps best be seen in the primary forum where the two cultures meet—at the workplace. It was there that the resistance was centered and that it assumed its most violent and political forms, for that is where the applied pressure was greatest.

The end result of this process of acculturation, maintains Greer, was the allowed maintenance of certain ethnic characteristics but the removal of the active facets of class from ethnicity. Greer believes an emphasis upon pluralism is fallacious and that the fundamental factor in the process of acculturation is class. "The cues of felt ethnicity turn out to be the recognizable characteristics of class position in this society. . . . In reality most groups in American society have all been successfully integrated into a hierarchical class structure that expresses itself in ethnic categories."[39] Paul Buhle, in his analysis of the socialist movement in the early twentieth century, agrees: "For the foreign-born radical worker to become an American, in fact, was for him to join the consensual modes of the larger society (as most of the radicals' children did) and relinquish those very traits that had made him distinctively radical"—that is, the aspects of class that had informed his radicalism.[40]

The late nineteenth and early twentieth centuries, the period of greatest industrialization in the United States, was a time of great social conflict; the battle for hegemony was fought on the ground of culture. At first glance the battle might appear less than equal—after all, one of the combatants was continually being torn from his roots and his associations, while the other was distinctively stable. Yet we must constantly be aware of Amitai Etzioni's observation that "a group can maintain its cultural and social integration and integrity, without having an ecological basis." As Paul Gallo adds, "The subcommunity is not necessarily a geographical location but rather a social construct in the minds of its residents."[41] Human beings are raised into and assimilate a culture, and from that point on carry it with them whether it is changed or not. Clearly immigrants to the United States did not leave their values behind and did not exchange one set of cultural baggage for another upon stepping off the boat. Instead they carried the cultural baggage with them, whether they were immigrants who moved as communities from Europe or whether they were foreign- or native-born American workers who moved from city to city throughout this country. Culture was not ecological but social in nature, and it was transportable. For individuals, this form of movement occurred in two ways: movement among similar communities and among similar institutions.

Despite his assertion that mobility and stability do not mix, Samuel Hays has described the physical presence of the city as offering the illusion, and certainly to a degree the reality, of stability.[42] Buildings are always there, buildings for the maintenance of business to be sure, but also buildings of the people—workingclass housing, saloons, stores, churches. Institutions also persist: not only does business go on, but fraternal orders remain, and sports teams, mechanics' institutes, and many other institutions that serve both participatory and integrative functions. A city, or a neighborhood, thus can maintain itself regardless of the flow of population. By the same token, those who move from one place to another are greeted by the same institutions that they left. A south Italian coal miner from Allegheny who moves to a south Italian coalmining community in southern Illinois is an extreme example of the continuity that can be involved in migration, but he could as easily, and more often did, move from an Italian neighborhood in New York to live among "paisanos" in Buffalo, or Cleveland, or Chicago. Furthermore, in a large portion of moves, the family or kin network is involved in moving.[43] These networks of mobility existed not only among families, but among the institutions we have been discussing. Eric Hobsbawm has furnished us information on labor "tramping" in Britain, and Montgomery has offered us some insight into the process in the preindustrial American city.[44] We know that "urban tradesmen were both geographically mobile enough and sufficiently well informed about the state of the labor market elsewhere to maintain rather uniform standards throughout the northeastern cities." The circulation of information was well enough developed among working people that, for instance, "typographers who violated union rules and standards could not find refuge in other communities."[45] Labor unions, such as the Iron Molders, provided for the type of movement among members that Hobsbawm describes, as did voluntary associations. The Odd Fellows in America originated the use of a traveling card, which, as Brian Greenberg tells us, "allowed members to move about freely and still gain admission into proximate Odd Fellow lodges in the country." In 1870 the lodge in Albany established a relief agency "to assist distressed travelling members of the Order."[46] Many, and probably most, of those on the tramp, Greenberg says, were "unemployed and moved about looking for work, . . . a common practice in the nineteenth century.''[47] Writing of Lynn and Fall River, Massachusetts, John Cumbler describes the strength of workingclass institutions, which allowed them to ''[build] communities and [pass] on from generation to generation their culture and history.'' ''The viability of the working class institutions,'' he continues, ''affected the ability of the community to hold itself together over time, to maintain class solidarity, and to sustain collective action among its members.''[48] Examples of these practices are numerous, but the point should be clear: workers who moved to and in America in the nineteenth and early twentieth centuries did not leave their cultures behind each time they stopped. They moved between and among institutions, and they carried their values with them wherever they went. They built from the materials of their past the type of culture to which Montgomery referred, the ''elaborate pattern of economic and social differentiation'' evident in ethnic workingclass communities.[49]

Thus it becomes imperative to recast Thernstrom's dictum that ''the staggering turnover among those who did leave [the cities] prevented the formation of a fixed and stable working class which might have generated a revolutionary consciousness and institutions of its own.''[50] Clearly enough, migrants generated institutions of their own, but what of a ''revolutionary consciousness''? Of course we are coming dangerously close here to a basic problem in counterfactual history; we cannot assume that something like a revolutionary consciousness would have existed in any case, whether movement was present or not. We can, however, draw certain conclusions concerning the cultural orientation of some portions of the American workingclass during the period of industrialization. To do this we will look at workingclass behavior in two locations: the polls and the workplace.

Part of the reason for the retrospective despair of Thernstrom and others comes from the lack of workingclass participation in politics. Despite the examples that can be found to the contrary, the full range of workingclass activity was rarely expressed through electoral politics. This has led some scholars to attribute a lack of participation to the impact of alienation upon workers; on the other hand, others point to occasions when workers clearly did take part in elections as proof of their involvement in the electoral community. Both of these interpretations need to be revised.

Much more research needs to be done on nineteenth-century communities, but it is becoming unmistakably clear that the political and social structures were grievously fragmented. A brief look at recent studies shows that participation in the governing process was limited to specific groups. A study of a small midwestern town (Paris, Illinois) in the nineteenth century illustrates a pattern in which a small, elite group comprised the political and social leadership for the forty-year period studied.[51] This is not an unusual situation, for the stratified nature of the decision-making process in America is well documented,[52] even though the impact of movement upon it rarely has been considered.[53] In Paris population turnover was as extensive and as pervasive as it appears to have been elsewhere in the nation. "By 1860," Richard Alcorn tells us, "only 12 per cent of the household heads had lived in Paris for ten or more years."[54] With the impermanence of a population that never stayed longer than a few years, the question "Who ruled?" must be answered, "Those who stayed in the town." This group, Alcorn concludes, furnished the stability necessary to maintain the viability, and even the existence, of the community. Further, "in overall terms, the leadership of Paris from 1850 through 1855 was more persistent, wealthier, more likely to come from the ranks of the professions, commerce, or 'retired' farmers, and older than those they led."[55] "While the considerable outmigration during the period might seem to indicate that the community and its leaders failed to meet the needs of many people," Alcorn suggests, "even greater in-migration and the character of these shifting groups suggests that this population movement responded to the dynamic needs of the town's development. In any case, the continued acquiescence of the non-leaders and the evidence of a successful co-optation process indicate that the structural stability of the community was not challenged."[56]

The interpretation that emerged from this analysis is that, in a sea of change and flux, conceptually a combination of Wiebe's "island communities" and Thernstrom's "eternally sifting mass," responsible groups emerged to offer to the community a stability that it otherwise would not have had. "Chaos and order could exist," it is said, "with chaos actually enhancing order and stability."[57] Alcorn's study was greatly informed by Robert Wiebe's concept of a nineteenth-century America composed of isolated "island communities."[58] "The heart of American democracy," Wiebe states, "was local autonomy."[59] We were "a nation of loosely connected islands," with "limited communication and interaction among them."[60] The tension between these traditional patterns of life and the modernizing tendencies of a bureaucratic and centralizing entrepreneurial middle class defined the character of late nineteenth- and early twentieth-century America. Yet Wiebe's consideration offers an inadequately formed realization of the impact of population mobility upon the political and social structure of the nation. Alcorn's study of political leadership and decision makers is an attempt to reconcile that concept of island communities with the reality of continually high rates of movement. Clearly Wiebe's unstable American landscape dotted by island communities is incorrect in the sense intended. In another sense, however, an unintended one, it is a useful descriptive term. There were island communities in the United States, but the distinguishing characteristics of these communities were that they were not physically based but were instead functioning cultures, classes, separated by an apparently rarely violated chasm of residential stability. In the words of a Slavic immigrant, "My people do not live in America, they live underneath America."[61]

Other studies bear out Alcorn's conclusions regarding a ruling elite. Waltham, Massachusetts, exhibited the same "tendency to re-elect the same men" to office. Howard Gittleman found that "long-term persistence was virtually a prerequisite to office holding." "Those most often and repeatedly chosen for public office," he concluded, "were those who stayed in the community, who were known to it, and who had important stakes in it."[62] Countless others who have studied the period have come to the same conclusion. This much of the pattern is clear. What we must do now is address attention to the question of what happened in the cases where workers did participate in electoral politics. Gutman, Montgomery, and others tell of numerous such cases.

There are a number of questions involved in an examination of working-class political activity. The first deals with involvement. Who participated? If there was a portion who did not, were they alienated? Had they withdrawn from all activity from a feeling of powerlessness, and quietly accepted their "fate"? What effect did increasing legitimization on the part of workers of politics have? And finally, what is the relationship among politics, political or nonpolitical activity, and a workingclass culture?

Clearly workers participated in politics. "Because workers made up a large proportion of the electorate" of small industrial towns after the Civil War, Gutman tells us, "and often actively participated in local politics, they influenced local and regional affairs more than wage earners in the larger cities." He points out that not only were there workers who were postmasters but that, for example, "a labor party swept an election in Evansville, Indiana," workers sat on the city council in Joliet, Illinois, and Newport, Kentucky, others ran for seats in midwestern state legislatures, and the president of the Virginia City, Nevada, miners' union was elected to Congress.[63] David Montgomery offers more substantiation of labor's involvement in politics and adds to it the dimension Gutman had not dealt with: labor's political activity in the large cities.[64] Indeed the most prominent and notable political parties formed by workingmen were in metropolises. Beyond question workers were involved in the radical politics of the socialist movement during the period.[65] Yet there are two outstanding features of the type of political activity described here. First, those who participated seem to have been the more stable, skilled, and long-term resident workers. Second, political quarters rarely addressed questions of long-range importance to workingmen, nor were their leaders in most cases distinguished by being workers but by being members of a form of "labor aristocracy."[66]

The concept of the labor aristocracy is a much-used but little-defined area, the past use of which Gareth Steadman Jones labels "ambiguous and unsatisfactory," often "point[ing] toward a vacant area where an explanation should be."[67] Jones notes the uses to which the definition has been applied:

> For Engels, it meant the organized trade-union movement of the mid-Victorian period, by which he intended primarily those whose craft skill was not threatened by the machine. By Lenin it was variously applied to trade-union and social-democratic leadership, the upper strata of the working class and even, at some points during the First World War, the whole of the working class in imperialist countries. Since the Russian Revolution, in addition to its more traditional definitions, the term has also been used in conjunction with critiques of bureaucracy within the labour movement, or as a description of the relationship between an indigenous metropolitan working class and an immigrant, female or neo-colonial proletariat.

He notes that there is "as yet no definitive material theory of the labor aristocracy, and it is questionable whether there could ever be one."[68] I do not intend to develop one now. For the moment, I want to accept Engels's definition not only as a useful one to describe workingclass involvement in American politics but to point out that this is the definition implicit in most of the work that has been done on American workingclass politics. Gutman clearly has gone beyond this definition in more recent work, but his earlier studies, and those of Montgomery and others, despite their intentions to the contrary, have focused upon the analysis of upper strata and institutional factors.[69]

This is not surprising considering the pervasive lack of definition and conceptualization with which American labor historians have operated. It has been difficult enough to define "a workingclass" (an uncompleted task), and further refinement will require more mastery still. Yet we do have sufficient clues from which to gain considerable insight toward a definition. The distinction between skilled and unskilled workers is beginning to be addressed in terms of European history. Writing of England, Peter Stearns suggests that "the cleavage between skilled and unskilled workers constitutes the most obvious and durable division in the working class throughout the industrial revolution." The differences he details for industrializing Europe are stark: in employment rates, income, professional affiliation and assertion, hours, and other job-related fields, unskilled workers rated brutally low in relation to their skilled brethren.[70] There is reason to believe that the distinctions were not so sharp in the United States, but they clearly existed. The majority of those involved in the community activities discussed by these earlier historians were labor union or association related, as most American workers were not, and were skilled workers. Yet the majority of workers, especially foreign immigrants, were unskilled. Paul Buhle has discussed these questions at length in his consideration of the twentieth-century American workingclass and has found quite clear divisions among the skilled and unskilled workers, which in fact often were exploited by employers. Within the workingclass, Buhle says, lay "the reality of bitter division between native American, skilled workers and their foreign, unskilled counterparts (including women and children)."[71] "Would that all the proletariat of America were 'foreigners!'" cried Louis Fraina.[72] In fact many of them were. In Lawrence in 1912, "only 15 per cent of the eligible [voters] were citizens, and the majority in many American cities in 1880 were immigrants or their children.[73] The following proportions illustrate the situation: San Francisco, 78 percent; St. Louis, 78 percent; Cleveland, 80 percent; New York, 80 percent; Detroit, 84 percent; Milwaukee, 84 percent; and Chicago, 87 percent. "Not every foreigner is a workingman," Gutman quoted a clergyman as saying in 1887, "but in the cities, at least, it may almost be said that every workingman is a foreigner."[74] Most of them, he might have added, were unskilled and in a changing employment situation. The distinctiveness of the unskilled worker in America was compounded by the refusal of unions actively to organize them; even the Socialists "disdained [them] as a kind of 'lumpenproletariat' unworthy of their efforts."[75]

Yet we must not assume that the employment structure in the United States was stable even for skilled workers; clearly it was not. In the explosive industrial economy of the late nineteenth century, jobs were created and disappeared, sometimes quickly. But Thernstrom has pointed out that "since many of the craftsmen under pressure from technological change had rather generalized skills, they were able to move from a contracting to an expanding skill." He adds, "It is quite mistaken to assume that the sons of the threatened artisans were commonly driven down into the ranks of the factory operatives; they typically found a place either in the expanding skilled trades or in the even more rapidly expanding white-collar occupations."[76] Other studies have tended to bear out this pattern.[77] While unskilled workers sometimes rose into skilled categories, the changes undergone by the artisan and the skilled industrial worker, groups labeled "the American labor aristocracy," were much more diverse, and begin to provide part of an answer to the questions raised by Gutman's study of smaller communities.

Part of Gutman's purpose in many articles discussing the workingclass in smaller industrial towns was to challenge the notions "that the worker was isolated from the rest of society; that the employer had an easy time and a relatively free hand in imposing the new disciplines, [and] that the workers found little if any sympathy from non-workers."[78] These contentions he refutes directly and forcefully. In many cases, "town officials and other officeholders who were not wage earners sympathized with the problems and difficulties of local workers or displayed an unusual degree of objectivity during local industrial disputes."[79] In particular he relates cases in which strikes were prolonged by small merchants who defied large employers and extended credit to striking workers.[80] While Gutman attributes much of this to the "direct and everyday contact with the new industrialism and with the problems and outlook of workers and employers," more important, and something he also mentions, is that many of these small businessmen "had risen from a lower station in life and knew the meaning of hardship and toil."[81] What goes unsaid, but was more than likely, was that many of them would be workers again sometime soon.

The small shopkeeper to which Gutman refers was in one of the most unstable occupations. Conditions for the constantly struggling and frequently failing small businessman were sufficiently unstable most often to bar him from the ranks of the "stable elite." Many of these small entrepreneurs were workers who saved or borrowed enough money to start a small enterprise; they entered and exited the ranks of workers (here we are terming small businessmen of white-collar status) in large numbers. Clearly we need a new business history to investigate these questions and afford the small entrepreneur the same attention we are trying to give to workers. In a very real sense, many small businessmen were part of the workingclass. In addition, it is likely that such shopkeepers drew much of their trade from the people they had labored with. Not only was their sympathy with workers who may have struck, but it made good sense to extend credit, for their fortunes lay there too. We should remember that, as Michael Katz has written of Hamilton, Ontario, "What can be said about the life of entrepreneurial class in a general sense is that insecurity was the dominant tone."[82]

The experience of small entrepreneurs illustrates the volatility of the class structure in America. We would do well to keep in mind, however, the general position of the lower middle class. Arno Meyer recently has pointed out not only the amorphous nature but the importance of this group. He calls it "a complex and unstable social, political, and cultural compound" that "appears to be far more polymorphous and tangled than the landed aristocracy, the peasantry, the bourgeoisie, or the working class."[83] I would suggest that the ethos of the skilled worker and of the

small entrepreneur had commonalities, which should be explored in further research.

I began by talking about the relationship of the labor aristocracy to electoral politics. I do not wish to indicate that these groups—the petite bourgeoisie and the skilled strata of workers—were undifferentiated; rather first, that their inherent volatility, the continuing exchange among them, influenced their public nature, and second, that their political involvement does not characterize that of the entire workingclass. The thesis presented here is not that members of the remainder of the workingclass never participated in the electoral system. Rather it is that the electoral process was not the primary means of involvement, of expression, or of protest, and that ultimately electoral involvement, when it came, connoted a far different reality than might have been supposed. The assumption that all workers invariably participated in nineteenth-century politics is no better founded than that they invariably participated in labor unions in the nineteenth century. Studies of political structure seem virtually to accept on faith and to maintain the view that Americans of all strata have always participated in politics, and thus that a significant proportion of working-class Americans in the nineteenth and early twentieth centuries were concerned with and involved in political affairs on a continuing basis. These assumptions go beyond questions of whether physical participation necessarily connotes psychological enfranchisement and the subsequent legitimization of the system, and they deal only with the question of legal enfranchisement and participation. We must question how fully this latter could have been the case. Even the most sophisticated studies neglect to ask the basic question of who was present to participate and who did participate throughout the periods studied.[84] Those who claim that large numbers of American workers were involved in the affairs of a particular community over any length of time must explain how that community escaped, however briefly, the dramatic shifts in its composition that appear to have characterized the typical nineteenth-century American community.

If this thesis is correct, and many Americans had only a peripheral relationship to the electoral process in the nineteenth century, what were the reasons for political abstinence? In criticizing one of the standard works in the new ethnocultural history, James Green argues that a failure to vote could be as important a decision as voting and finds it "plausible to suggest that the voter opted out of the system when the political alternatives presented to him were meaningless." "If working-class voters felt that the alternatives which had been defined for them were irrelevant," Green says, "their failure to participate in elections would have been an important political phenomenon."[85] Yet although Green has pointed out one of the reasons for this phenomenon, his analysis continues to suffer from the specificity that has hindered an understanding of American politics. Green believes that voters made a decision in each election as to the relevance of the issues and that an election-by-election analysis will indicate the level of interest generated. While there is some truth to this, it is important to realize that a more general abstinence may have been the case.

We are told now by social scientists that the failure to vote reflects a general alienation, or anomie, on the part of industrial workers and others. Although it is a seminal concept that, like other central themes, has resisted precision in definition, alienation in contemporary sociological terms is applied to convey one or more of the following conditions: "power-lessness, meaninglessness, normlessness, isolation, and self-estrangement."[86] The term has powerful negative meanings and in most cases is intended to convey the growing inability of alienated individuals to cope with their surroundings. Yet except in Marx's use of the term to connote a worker separated from control over his own production, we should reject the negative meanings of the term when applied to the lower echelons of the nineteenth-century American workingclass. Instead their attitude toward politics was based on four things: first, the lack of centrality of politics to their culture; second, a realistic appraisal of the possibility of influencing the political structure as opposed to the structure of the workplace or the political economy; next, the centrality of that struggle to the culture; and finally, the perception of community as embracing their own family and kin networks, ethnic brethren, and class.

The expectation on the part of contemporary middle-class analysts that politics is central to daily life is mistaken both in its application to the nineteenth century and in its contemporary application. True, politics in America is a profound cultural expression (one writer recently called it "the binding secular religion"),[87] but participation in it does not connote psychological enfranchisement.[88] The abject lack of faith people perceive in their politicians today—and assuredly this is not a phenomenon of the Nixon years—has always been strong. Politics was perceived by many nineteenth-century workers as a forum with little power. When that situation, that perception, began to change, the nature of class relationships in America began to change. Instead the struggle lay in the workplace. It was here that the cultures clashed and that transformation would occur, and it was here that it was to be resisted. It is here, also, that we begin further to perceive the components of workingclass culture in America, for the resistance to the brutality of industrialization was more forthright, more steadfast, more violent in America than anywhere else in the world. Strikes and job actions were an ever-present phenomenon in this country, as was "violence" of every category. At times employers literally believed they were under siege, and this feeling gave rise to some of the bloodier responses of officials. These actions occurred throughout the nation in every industry and in every industrial town.[89]

Yet how could this have been the case? We seem entirely unprepared to explain this phenomenon in the light of new knowledge. If American workers moved as much as they appear to have moved, and stayed in places for short periods as they seem to have done, who provided the stability necessary for these strikes? Indeed who were the strikers? When David Montgomery analyzed the action of Philadelphia workers in the 1840s, or Herbert Gutman a strike in Paterson, Michael Frisch the social structure of Springfield, John Cumbler shoemakers in Lynn, or Brian Greenberg workers in Albany, how many people—how many workers—remained in the city throughout the period of analysis? Obviously this depends on how long the period of analysis is. If we study labor unrest in Newark during the course of a decade, we would assume that a smaller proportion of the population had persisted than had we discussed a three-month strike. On the other hand, we have no historical studies that correlate migratory behavior and labor unrest. Did social and economic conflict cause the timid to move away as soon as they were able? Or did the opportunity to strike a blow against the bosses hold workers, or perhaps even draw them in?

We need studies on these questions before we can deal with confidence with the issues raised, but we might make some general observations now about population change. In Philadelphia in the 1840s, for example, the persistence rate was 38 percent; 62 percent of the 1840 population was not in the city in 1850. Since persistence rates among lower and working classes certainly were lower, probably at least seven of ten workers exited during the decade. The actual rate of change was considerably higher. Thernstrom's figures confirm this for Boston, and the pattern would not have differed greatly for other American cities.[90] He tells us that "the number of newcomers entering the city" in the 1880s "was several times larger than the net migration calculations suggest" so that "the actual number of separate families who lived in Boston at *some* point in between 1880 and 1890 was a staggering 296,388, more than three times the total number residing there at any one time in this ten-year period!"[91] This is for a decade. If we apply Katz's figures from Hamilton, where over a three-month period 25 percent of his population apparently departed the city, we can begin to appreciate the difficulty of studying a three- or six-month strike in a major city. The theoretical problems are compounded when we begin to consider the sort of strike about which Gutman tells us: the 1910 action of Italian and Slavic workers in the western Pennsylvania coalfields when "eighteen [thousand] of twenty thousand miners quit work for *seventeen months*."[92]

It is not possible to hypothesize about the impact of such incidents until we have more information. We can, however, begin to answer the question of how such actions occurred over such a broad area of geography and time, and that is that organized and concerted action against employers had become as much a part of a mobile workingclass culture as the kin network itself. Yet this action showed limited political awareness—that is, awareness of its roles beyond the workplace. This was both its strength and its weakness.[93] We can gain perspective on this question if we remember the ever-present charges of "outside agitation" that wafted so freely among the middle class. At a meeting held in Saratoga Springs in the strike-torn depression year of 1877, for example, the president of a Connecticut charity organization observed that "the inner history of the recent disgraceful and disastrous riots" around the country "revealed how large detachments of 'our great standing army of professional tramps' rather than the 'so-called strikers' were mainly responsible for the destruction of valuable property."[94] Undoubtedly there were large numbers of transients during the economic miseries of that period who did participate in the extraordinary antiproperty actions that caused a widespread fear of "communism." But the workers who were termed "the 'very lowest layer' of the proletariat 'who would gladly participate in any mob actions'" were exemplary of a trend that apparently continued during the best of times. Depressions brought special hardships to the workingclass family, but the best of times did not alleviate it entirely. We have survey after survey that raises the question as to how they survived at all.[95] While studies indicate that migration was not correlated directly to unemployment, surely the shifting job market and the desire to better the family's position were influential in the decision to move.[96] What that continued migration did not do was emasculate the workingclass community. One of the most protest-filled years in our history, 1877, was a year among many years of phenomenal population turnover. Migrants were strikers too. They maintained their equilibrium because the ethnic and class neighborhoods of which they were a part furnished them with the social and psychological support and the self-actualizing reinforcement that is said to come from the modern day electoral participation of "political man."[97] The culture, community, and family patterns of the ethnic workingclass gave life to the worker, not a presumed participation in the futility of the electoral booth.[98] That, clearly, is a culture-bound, modern, and middle-class ideal.[99]

Yet the workingclass always was and remained at a disadvantage. The sum total of the courage, resourcefulness, and steadfastness in the struggle did not add up in its favor. By the 1920s the character of work, politics, and the workingclass itself had changed, and indeed the armed forces of the state had been replaced as the primary thrust of employer action by

Taylorism. We must always be aware of the complex matrix of relationships that existed during the period and of the pressures, both overt and subtle, that played upon the collective mind of a workingclass—which, though attempt after attempt was made, never coalesced into a class that could act in a concerted fashion against a common enemy. Perhaps the term *group* is best used to describe the "classes" of which we write: a group that existed and that had a consciousness of itself but that rarely exhibited the class consciousness necessary to join the issues of work.[100]

Much more needs to be done on the relationships between the working-class and politics in late nineteenth- and early twentieth- century America. Yet we may take clues from the British experience. Gareth Steadman Jones and Trygve Tholfsen, among others, have addressed this question and have found common answers to it. Both conclude that the acceptance of bourgeois political forms represented an acquiescence to the hegemony of bourgeois categories. Jones finds that at the same time as the Labour party was being founded, the workingclass was evincing an "estrangement from political activity as such."[101] Tholfsen also finds middle-class values slowly eroding the resistance of the workingclass—not by attacking them, but by reducing them, being reformist in nature. The end result of the creation and perseverance of a "cultural climate [which] tended to bring out the soft side of the working class social character"[102] was a political organization whose "mode of organization presumed mass passivity punctuated by occasional mobilization for the ballot box."[103] The institutionalization of an instrument for "working class political [electoral] expression," then, both represented and further engendered the retraction by workers of their own, self-legitimized authority. That is, the legendary structural process represented their withdrawal from psychological participation. "With the foundation of the Labour Party," Jones tells us, "the now enclosed and defensive world of working-class culture had in effect achieved its apotheosis." Paul Buhle indicates that much the same situation may have existed in the United States. Discussing the reforms enacted by the Progressive government in California, he argues that "these gains did not at all indicate the growing power of the working class. To the contrary," he observes in drawing closer to the British parallel, "they denoted the bourgeoisification of privileged sectors of the work force and, by and large, solidarity of these layers with the government and business against the interests of the unskilled workers."[104]

What we are dealing with is the adaptation of these cultures to the fact of mobility. Clearly mobility did not create new cultures from a void; instead it brought about new forms able to persevere. We can document this concept of "moving institutions" and understand the resolution it brings to the paradox of stability in the midst of vast movement. On the other hand, this does not bring the type of homogeneous resolution to the paradox put forward by Wiebe, Alcorn, and others. Instead it contradicts their approach and their conclusions. It is far too simplistic to accept the concept of basic institutions (politics and the like) as being the only ones, and indeed being even necessary ones, in which a workingclass separated and made distinct by the separateness of its culture would participate, or would be shaped by. Indeed the opposite would seem to be both the logical conclusion and the proper one. Politics in America has always been a cultural expression to a large degree, and its perceived omnipresence on the part of many factions of contemporary society has caused it to be evaluated as much more than it is. It is much more related, in a particular (and peripheral) form, to the cultural expressions of the nineteenth-century workingclass than to its self-perceived governance. Just as workers participated in many other activities when believed to be in their own best interests, they would participate in political life. That participation, when it happened, may have meant much less than it has been taken to mean. It may not have meant, for example, that blind and enthusiastic conferral of legitimacy that has been supposed, though eventually it came to mean that to the degree that the system was accepted, if cynically. There was, at the core of the industrial workingclass, in all its complexity, an identifiable culture that rejected certain bourgeois imperatives (such as politics). Industrial workers preferred to remain oriented inwardly, not, as Hareven has indicated—when discussing even the examples of "bourgeoisified resistance" and the adaptation of movement to the kin networks of immigrant labor in Manchester, New Hampshire—merely to their own family, but to their own devices and associations—to their own culture.[105] As David Gagan has said, we may have been studying local history, but we have not yet begun to study the history of the community.[106] What I hope I have made clear here is that the working-class community was no gathering of strangers but a culture that was vital, robust, complex, and capable of sustaining its self-esteem even in the face of the challenge, and subsequent victory, of American industrial capitalism.

As Jones has pointed out regarding England, the middle class was able to act as a catalyst upon the workforce. The latter began and ended with a distinct and a discrete culture. The middle class had imbued it with certain tendencies, however, and had brought it to accept and assimilate some manifestations of a middle-class orientation. The relationship was a dialectical one, and the transformation clearly was toward middle-class values, but this was achieved without vitiating and without exiling or destroying the separateness felt, and even cultivated, by the workingclass. The process was aided by the workingclass' efforts to work with and in the larger social order even while maintaining a desire and an impulse to remain distinct from it. Assimilation is far different from integration. Portions of the American workingclass still have not experienced the latter.

NOTES

1. The quotation is from Henry W. Cherauny, *The Burial of the Apprentice: A True Story from Life in a Union Workshop* (New York, 1900), p. 68, as reprinted in Irwin Yellowitz, *The Position of the Worker in American Society, 1865-1896* (Englewood Cliffs, N.J., 1969), p. 79.

2. For an overview, see Stephan Thernstrom and Peter R. Knights, "Men in Motion: Some Data and Speculations about Urban Population Mobility in Nineteenth Century America," *Journal of Interdisciplinary History* 1 (Summer 1970): 7-35. For a very cursory, obviously incomplete list of the mobility studies that have come about in the years since the publication of Thernstrom's seminal *Poverty and Progress: Social Mobility in a Nineteenth Century City* (Cambridge, Mass., 1964), see his *The Other Bostonians: Poverty and Progress in the American Metropolis, 1880-1970* (Cambridge, Mass., 1973), esp. pp. 222-223, and the concluding chapter ("The Boston Case and the American Pattern").

3. For information on the Canadian pattern, see David Gagan, "Geographical and Occupational Mobility in a Nineteenth Century Rural Canadian Community" (paper presented to the Great Lakes Regional History Conference, 1975); Gagan and Henry Mays, "Historical Demography and Canadian Social History: Families and Land in Peel County, Ontario," *Canadian Historical Review* 54 (March 1973): 37-47; interim reports from Gagan's Peel County history project; Michael Katz, "People of a Canadian City: 1851-2," *Canadian Historical Review* 53 (December 1972): 402-426; interim reports from the Canadian social history project; and Katz, *The People of Hamilton* (Cambridge, Mass., 1976).

4. Stephan Thernstrom, "Working Class Social Mobility in Industrial America," in Melvin Richter, ed., *Essays in Theory and History: An Approach to the Social Sciences* (Cambridge, Mass., 1970), pp. 227-228.

5. For a report on a project that attempts to trace migrants after they leave cities, see Charles Stephenson, "Tracing Those Who Left: Mobility Studies and the Soundex Indexes to the U.S. Census," *Journal of Urban History* 1 (November 1974): 73-84; "The Methodology of Census Record Linkage: A User's Guide to the Soundex," *Journal of Family History* (forthcoming); and "Determinants of American Migration: Methods and Models in Mobility Research," *Journal of American Studies* 9 (August 1975): 189-197.

6. See Thernstrom's work in general, but especially "Working Class Social Mobility," "Men in Motion," and "Urbanization, Migration, and Social Mobility in Late Nineteenth Century America," in Barton J. Bernstein, ed., *Towards A New Past: Dissenting Essays in American History* (New York, 1968).

7. Eric L. McKitrick and Stanley Elkins, "Institutions in Motion," *American Quarterly* 12 (Summer 1960): 188-197 (the quotation is from p. 191); Rowland Berthoff, "The American Social Order: A Conservative Hypothesis," *American Historical Review* 65 (April 1960): 495-514 (the quotations are from pp. 499, 507); Samuel P. Hays, "The Changing Political Structure of the City in Industrial America," *Journal of Urban History* 1 (November 1974): 6-38. See also Everett S. Lee, "The Turner Thesis Reexamined," *American Quarterly* 13 (Spring 1961): 77-83.

8. Thernstrom, "Urbanization," p. 173.

9. See Thernstrom's work for several statements and several articles by Jesse Lemish, who was one of the American historians who called for the history of the "common man,"

including his "The American Revolution Seen from the Bottom Up," in Bernstein, *Towards a New Past*, pp. 3-45; "Jack Tar in the Streets: Merchant Seamen in the Politics of Revolutionary America," *William and Mary Quarterly*, 3d series, 55 (July 1968): 371-407; and "Listening to the 'Inarticulate': William Widger's Dream and the Loyalties of American Revolutionary Seamen in British Prisons," *Journal of Social History* 3 (Fall 1969): 1-29.

10. For an eloquent statement of this approach, see, for example, Bertolt Brecht's "A Worker Reads History," in his *Selected Poems*, trans. H. R. Hayes (New York, 1947).

11. Michael Katz, in "People of a Canadian City," estimated that "at least ninety-five out of every hundred" people in Hamilton "remain invisible to the historian who consults only manuscript sources. While an imaginative use of nineteenth-century newspapers in Albany and Troy, New York, by Brian Greenberg indicates that this proportion will be somewhat different when other than news columns are consulted, the general point is quite surely accurate. See Greenberg's "Worker and Community: The Social Structure of a Nineteenth Century Commercial City—Albany, New York, 1850-1885" (in progress).

12. For an introduction to the approach, see especially Robert P. Swierenga, ed., *Quantification in American History: Theory and Research* (New York, 1970).

13. For an introduction to recent quantitative approaches to history, see Richard Jensen, "Quantitative American Studies: The State of the Art," *American Quarterly* 26 (August 1974): 225-240, and Robert P. Swierenga's excellent and informative survey articles, "Computers and Comparative History," *Journal of Interdisciplinary History* 5 (Autumn 1974): 267-286, and "Quantification in American History," *Journal of American History* (March 1974).

14. For example, the new Social Science History Association was formed in 1976, and it publishes a journal, *Social Science History*, which Swierenga edits.

15. David Montgomery, "The New Urban History," *Reviews in American History* (December 1974): 498-504 (quotations from pp. 502-503). See also Charles Stephenson, "The Cultural Context of Social Change: Social Mobility and the Contours of Community in America," *Societas* (forthcoming).

16. James R. Green, "Behavoralism and Class Analysis: A Review Essay on Methodology and Ideology," *Labor History* (1971): 89-106 (quotation from p. 92).

17. Ibid., p. 93.

18. Ibid.

19. Allan G. Bogue, "U.S.A.: The New Political History," *Journal of Contemporary History* 3 (January 1968): 24.

20. Green, "Behavioralism," p. 105.

21. Hyman Berman, review of Philip Taft, *Organized Labor in American History* (New York, 1964), in *Journal of American History* 51 (March 1965): 740-741.

22. The cultural approach to workingclass history received perhaps its greatest boost from the publication of E. P. Thompson's magnificent *The Making of the English Working Class* (New York, 1963), and the imaginative work of Eric J. Hobsbawm, especially *Labouring Men: Studies in the History of Labour* (London, 1964). An excellent introduction to the approach is found in the *Journal of Social History* 7 (Summer 1974), a special issue devoted to papers delivered to the Anglo-American Labor History Conference in 1973 at Rutgers University. For a further view of the American response, see Thomas A. Krueger, "American Labor Historiography, Old and New: A Review Essay," *Journal of Social History* 4 (Spring 1971): 277-285; Paul Faler, "Working Class Historiography," *Radical America* 3 (March-April 1969); and Will Brumbach, Jon Evanson, Laura Foner, Ruth Meyerowitz, and Mark Naison, "Literature on Working Class Culture," *Radical America* 3 (March-April 1969): 32-55.

23. See, for example, Gutman, "The Worker's Search for Power," in H. Wayne

Morgan, ed., *The Gilded Age: A Reappraisal* (Syracuse, 1963), 38-68; "Protestantism and the American Labor Movement: The Christian Spirit in the Gilded Age," *American Historical Review* 72 (1966-1967): 74-101; and "Work, Culture, and Society in Industrializing America, 1815-1919," *American Historical Review* 78 (June 1973): 531-588. Tamara Hareven, "Family Time and Industrial Time: The Interaction Between the Family and Work in a Planned Corporation Town: 1910-1924," *Journal of Urban History* 1 (May 1975): 365-389; "The Laborers of Manchester, New Hampshire, 1912-1922: The Role of Family and Ethnicity in Adjustment to Industrial Life," *Labor History* 18 (Fall 1975): 249-265; Paul Faler, "Cultural Aspects of the Industrial Revolution: Lynn, Massachusetts, Shoemakers and Industrial Morality, 1826-1860," *Labor History* 13 (Summer 1974): 367-394; Brian Greenberg, "Worker and Community: Fraternal Orders in Albany, New York, 1845-1885" *Maryland Historian* (Spring 1978):38-53; John Cumbler, "Continuity and Disruption: Working Class Community in Lynn and Fall River, Massachusetts, 1880-1950" (Ph.D. diss., University of Michigan, 1974), and "Culture and Community in Lynn and Fall River" in C. Stephenson, ed., *Life and Labor: Readings in the Social History of the American Worker* (Grand Rapids, Mich., forthcoming); Walter Licht, "The Nineteenth Century Railroad Worker" (Ph.D. diss., Princeton University, 1976), and "The Conditions of Labor," in Stephenson, *Life and Labor*; James Green, "The Brotherhood of Timber Workers, 1910-1913: A Radical Response to Industrial Capitalism in the Southern U.S.A.," *Past and Present* 60 (August 1973): 161-200.

24. See Gareth Steadman Jones, *Outcast London: A Study in the Relationship Between Classes in Victorian Society* (Oxford, 1971); "Working-Class Culture and Working-Class Politics in London, 1870-1900; Notes on the Remaking of a Working Class," *Journal of Social History* (Summer 1974): 460-508; and his review of the following book by Foster in *New Left Review* 90 (March-April 1975): 35-70. John Foster, *Class Struggle and the Industrial Revolution—Early Industrial Capitalism in Three English Towns* (London, 1974). Trygve R. Tholfsen, "The Intellectual Origins of Mid-Victorian Stability," *Political Science Quarterly* 86 (March 1971): 57-91.

25. Jones, "Working-Class Culture," p. 463.

26. Ibid., pp. 478-479.

27. Cumbler, "Culture and Community," makes the same point: "Not all workers in this country were newly arrived immigrant peasants, and those that were did not only enter the industrial factory, but also entered the urban world and the community of urban workers" (p. 3). He offers a number of examples of immigrants who were experienced industrial workers before they emigrated (p. 33). We know enough about the background of European and other immigrant groups to deny that all fell into any one category.

28. The question of culture in the anthropological literature is vast. Rather than listing a large number of books here, let me suggest some, beginning with Clifford Geertz, *The Interpretation of Culture: Selected Essays by Clifford Geertz* (New York, 1973); Geertz, ed., *Myth, Symbol, and Culture* (New York, 1971); and Alfred Krober, *Anthropology: Culture Patterns and Process* (New York, 1963), and suggest that useful, if necessarily limited, introductions for historians are Raymond Charles Miller, "The Dock-worker Sub-culture and Some Problems in Cross-Cultural and Cross-Time Generalizations," *Comparative Studies in Society and History* 11 (1969): 302-314; Robert P. Baker, "Labor History, Social Science and the Concept of the Working Class," *Labor History* 14 (Winter 1973): 98-105; and Zygmunt Bauman, "Marxism and the Contemporary Theory of Culture," *Co-existence* 5, pp. 161-171. The quotations are from Mary Douglas, "The Self-Completing Animal," *Times Literary Supplement* (August 8, 1975), a review of Geertz's *Interpretations*.

29. Miller, "Dock-worker Sub-culture."

30. Douglas, "Self-Completing Animal," and Geertz, *Interpretations*.

31. Baker, "Labor History."

32. Bauman, "Contemporary Theory."

33. Gutman, "Work, Culture, and Society," p. 564.

34. For purposes of clarity and simplicity, *culture* and *subculture* will be used essentially interchangeably in this essay.

35. Milton M. Gordon, *Assimilation in American Life: The Role of Race, Religion, and National Origins* (London, 1964). My discussion of Gordon is informed by and drawn from Colin Greer, ed., *Divided Society: The Ethnic Experience in America* (New York, 1974), especially Gordon, "Nature of Assimilation," pp. 39-51, and Greer, "Remembering Class," pp. 1-35.

36. Greer, "Remembering Class," p. 27.

37. S. N. Eisenstadt, *The Absorption of Immigrants* (London, 1954).

38. Patrick J. Gallo, *Ethnic Alienation: The Italian-Americans* (Rutherford, N.J., 1974), p. 89.

39. Greer, "Remembering Class," p. 34.

40. Paul Buhle, "Debsian Socialism and the 'New Immigrant' Worker," in William L. O'Neill, ed., *Insights and Parallels: Problems and Issues of American Social History* (Minneapolis, 1973), pp. 249-277.

41. Gallo, *Ethnic Alienation*, p. 117; the Etzioni quotation, first taken from Gallo (p. 117), is in "The Ghetto—A Re-Evaluation," *Social Forces* (March 1959): 255-262.

42. For reference to the Hays view, see Bruce Stave, "An Interview with Stephan Thernstrom," *Journal of Urban History* 1 (August 1975): 189-216. See also Hays's excellent, more recent, statement on the question of stability among migrants in his review of *The Other Bostonians* in *Journal of Social History* 10 (1976): 409-414.

43. See especially Hareven, "Laborers of Manchester," and Virginia Yans McLaughlin, "Like the Fingers of the Hand: The Family and Community Life of First-Generation Italian Americans in Buffalo, New York, 1890-1930" (Ph.D. diss., State University of New York at Buffalo, 1970); and "Patterns of Work and Family Organization: Buffalo's Italians," *Journal of Interdisciplinary History* 2 (Autumn, 1971): 299-314.

44. Hobsbawm, "The Tramping Artisan," in *Labouring Men*, pp. 34-63; David Montgomery, "The Working Classes of the Pre-Industrial American City, 1780-1830," *Labor History* 9 (Winter 1968): 3-22.

45. Montgomery, "Working Classes," p. 12.

46. Greenberg, "Fraternal Orders," pp. 12-13.

47. Ibid., p. 52, n.40.

48. Cumbler, "Culture and Community," p. 9.

49. Montgomery, "New Urban History," pp. 502-503.

50. See especially Thernstrom's "Men in Motion" and "Working Class Social Mobility."

51. Richard S. Alcorn, "Leadership and Stability in Mid-Nineteenth Century America: A Case Study of an Illinois Town," *Journal of American History* 61 (December 1974): 685-702.

52. The decision-making process is among the primary concerns of political scientists and sociologists, and the field is too large to allow any more than a cursory glance at the sources. For a general introduction to the field, see R. E. Agger, D. Goldrich, and B. E. Swanson, *The Rulers and the Ruled* (New York, 1964); Terry Clark, *Community Structure and Decision Making: Comparative Analysis* (San Francisco, 1968); Robert Dahl, *Who Governs?* (New Haven, 1961); Floyd Hunter, *Community Power Structure* (Chapel Hill, 1953); Robert V. Prethus, *Men at the Top: A Study in Community Power* (New York, 1964); Nelson W. Polsby, *Community Power and Political Theory* (New Haven, 1963); and C. Wright Mills, *The Power Elite* (New York, 1956). A useful starting place for the sociological literature is T. R. Bottomore, *Elites and Society* (Baltimore, 1967).

53. John M. Orbell and Toro Uno, "A Theory of Neighborhood Problem Solving: Political Action *vs.* Residential Mobility," *American Political Science Review* 66 (June 1972): 471-489, and a book that informed the article, Albert Hirschman, *Exit, Voice, and*

Loyalty: Responses to Decline in Firms, Organizations, and States (Cambridge, Mass., 1970). Orbell and Uno is one of the first solid pieces to deal with the question of migration and politics in an analytical fashion, although literature on migration and mental health is large, as are studies of neighborhood formation and change. See Howard Chudacoff, *Mobile Americans: Residential and Social Mobility in Omaha, 1880–1920* (New York, 1972), esp. chap. 8, "Voting and Mobility," pp. 130-148, for an attempt to deal with the question in historical terms. Also see Michael Parenti, "Immigration and Political Life," in Frederick C. Jaher, ed., *The Age of Industrialism in America: Essays in Social Structure and Cultural Values* (New York, 1968), pp. 79-99.

54. Alcorn, "Leadership and Stability," p. 691.

55. Ibid., p. 699.

56. Ibid., p. 701.

57. Ibid., p. 702.

58. Robert H. Wiebe, *The Search for Order, 1877–1920* (New York, 1967).

59. Ibid., p. 4.

60. Ibid., p. xiii.

61. The quotation is from ibid., p. 9. Wiebe at one point seems to perceive the outlines of such a situation but does not carry it further. "Apart from the rest," he says (pp. 3-4), "urban elites of wealth and family . . . also qualified as small self-contained communities." These so-called island communities—different cultures—were separated not only by great wealth but also by their relationship to the governance of the community.

62. Howard M. Gittleman, *Workingmen of Waltham: Mobility in American Urban Industrial Development 1850–1890* (Baltimore, 1974), p. 115.

63. Gutman, "Workers' Search for Power," pp. 37-38.

64. David Montgomery, *Beyond Equality: Labor and the Radical Republicans, 1862–1872* (New York, 1967).

65. Buhle, "Debsian Socialism."

66. Questions that interested workingpeople were discussed and were fought over, but they were issues such as the eight-hour day and a Greenback policy. There is evidence that many workers did not consider them crucial, looking at them as issues shaped by the bourgeoisie and the labor aristocracy.

67. Jones, "Class Struggle," p. 61.

68. Ibid.

69. For example, in his "Statistical Outline of American Social Stratification, 1870," appendix A of *Beyond Equality* (pp. 448-452), Montgomery divides the workforce into several large categories but does not distinguish between or attempt to identify skilled and unskilled workers.

70. Peter N. Stearns, "The Unskilled and Industrialization: A Transformation of Consciousness," *Archiv für Sozialgeschichte* 16 (1976): 249-82. (The quote is from p. 249). See also Joan Wallach Scott, *The Glassworkers of Carmaux: French Craftsmen and Political Action in a Nineteenth Century City* (Cambridge, Mass., 1974); Bernard Moss, "Origins of the French Labor Movement: The Socialism of Skilled Workers" (Ph.D. diss., Columbia University, 1971).

71. Buhle, "Debsian Socialism," pp. 260-261. See also Leon Fink, "Class Conflict in the Gilded Age: The Figure and the Phantom," *Radical History Review* 3 (Fall-Winter 1975): 56-73.

72. Buhle, "Debsian Socialism," p. 262.

73. Ibid., p. 263.

74. The percentages and the quotation are found in Gutman, "Work, Culture, and Society," p. 561.

75. Buhle, "Debsian Socialism," p. 269. Edward Bemis' "Restriction of Immigration,"

Andover Review 9 (March 1880): pp. 256-257, in Yellowitz's *Position of the Worker*, pp. 64-65, estimates the proportion of skilled and unskilled among the male immigrants over fourteen who arrived between 1880 and 1886. He categorized some 53 percent as unskilled. Considering that his figures were drawn largely from Western European countries and included only males, it is easy to see that the proportion of unskilled workers during this period was not only a significant majority but was growing.

76. Thernstrom, "Urbanization," p. 171.

77. In "Culture and Community," John Cumbler offers a fascinating account of the skilled-unskilled question. As late as the 1920s, skilled shoe workers in Lynn voted to forego membership in a stronger union that would bring them more benefits because the group would not protect the unskilled workers adequately. But in Fall River in 1919, ethnic divisions had so split the workers that during a strike of unskilled mill hands, skilled workers scabbed against them in order to break the strike (pp. 17, 37-38).

78. Gutman, "Workers' Search for Power," p. 33.

79. Ibid., p. 38.

80. Ibid., pp. 38-39.

81. Ibid., p. 38.

82. Michael B. Katz, "The Entrepreneurial Class in a Canadian City: The Mid-Nineteenth Century," *Journal of Social History* (Fall, 1975).

83. Arno J. Mayer, "The Lower Middle Class as Historical Problem," *Journal of Modern History* 47 (September 1975): 409-436. Mayer posits that "in the United States, the presumed differences between large sectors of the lower middle class and large sectors of manual labor are being eroded" (p. 423). I suggest that this in fact happened much earlier in this country.

84. See, for example, W. Dean Burnham, "The Changing Shape of the American Political Universe," *American Political Science Review* 59 (March 1965): 7-28. Gittleman says that in Waltham, many of those who paid a poll tax "were disqualified from voting because they had not registered." One-third were unregistered in 1890. In addition he estimates that over half of the foreign-born males were not citizens. *Workingmen of Waltham*, pp. 119-120. A number of the contributions in Yellowitz's *Position of the Worker* call attention to the fact that many immigrants, both alien and nationalized, were not literate.

85. Green, "Behavioralism and Class Analysis," pp. 104-105.

86. Alienation is another seminal but vaguely defined social science concept. See Simon Marcson, ed., *Automation, Alienation, and Anomie* (New York, 1970) (quotation from p. 377); Ephraim H. Mizruchi, "Alienation and Anomie: Theoretical and Empirical Perspectives," in Irving Louis Horowitz, ed., *The New Sociology: Essays in Honor of C. Wright Mills* (New York, 1964), pp. 253-267, and a shorter version, "Alienation, Anomie, and the American Dream," in Mizruchi, ed., *The Substance of Sociology* (New York, 1967), pp. 550-560; Gallo, *Ethnic Alienation*; and William A. Rushing, *Class, Culture, and Alienation: A Study of Farmers and Farm Workers* (New York, 1972).

87. Steven R. Weisman, *New York Times Book Review*, May 11, 1975, p. 1, quoting Theodore H. White, *Breach of Faith* (New York, 1975).

88. David Montgomery has suggested that "the two party system was splendidly adapted at the local level to serving the needs of the upwardly mobile of each ethnic group . . . and thus preserving a vertical, rather than class division of partisan loyalties, which attached the electorate of each ethnic bloc to its own middle class leaders through cultural issues of intense and intimate importance to daily life." *European Labor and Working Class History Newsletter* 8 (November 1975):47. Beyond his error in equating a horizontal division with a class loyalty, Montgomery fails to consider the impact of the non-upwardly mobile—the role of the unskilled or semiskilled portion of the workingclass.

89. Historians of the workingclass finally have begun to treat the "crowd" as more than a "mob" and to realize the disciplined form that labor violence took. For the European view,

see especially E. P. Thompson, "The Moral Economy of the English Crowd in the Eighteenth Century," *Past and Present* 50 (February 1971): 76-136; several works by George Rudé, for example, *The Crowd in the French Revolution* (New York, 1959); and Charles Tilly, Louise Tilly, and Richard Tilly, *The Rebellious Century, 1830-1930* (Cambridge, Mass., 1975). For several views of American violence, see Hugh Davis Graham and Ted Robert Gun, *The History of Violence in America* (New York, 1969). For an account of a particularly violence-prone era, see Robert Bruce, *1877: Year of Violence* (New York, 1961).

90. Stanley Engerman, "Up or Out: Social and Geographic Mobility in the United States," *Journal of Interdisciplinary History* 5 (Winter 1975): 469-489, properly points out that rates may have been higher in Boston because it was a port city through which many immigrants moved. A comparison of rates for other cities, however, reveals a general pattern in large measure apparently unaffected by such considerations. Year-by-year figures on migration in a number of towns would be useful here.

91. In *Workingmen of Waltham*, Gittelman finds an even higher rate of turnover (see esp. pp. 23-49). At one point, for example, he believes that inmigration exceeded that recorded by 55 percent, while outmigration exceeded that recorded by 119 percent (p. 30).

92. Gutman, "Work, Culture, and Society," p. 580.

93. Buhle, "Debsian Socialism," p. 251, observes the following: "The hostility of workers toward the new modern wage slavery was expressed in a characteristic American fashion with sporadic militance involving considerable violence while lacking any but the most limited political implications." Indeed this does seem to have been characteristic of the resistance of the period—by and large, a lack of sustained action directed toward alternative conceptions of industrial organization.

94. Paul T. Ringenbach, *Tramps and Reformers: The Discovery of Unemployment in New York* (Westport, Conn., 1973), p. 14.

95. See, for example, the discussion of workingclass family income in Henry F. May, *The Protestant Response to Industrial America* (New York, 1966); and by Montgomery, "Working Classes;" and the discussion of the employment cycle in Thernstrom, *Poverty and Progress*. When asked by a congressional investigating committee if married bronze workers were able to save from their wages, brass workers' union member Joseph Finnerty answered, "No sir; they do not. If they happen to be able to make both ends meet at the end of the year they are doing wonders." Yellowitz (pp. 84-86) citing U.S. Senate, Education and Labor Committee, *Report Upon the Relations between Labor and Capital* (Washington, D.C., 1885), 1: 744-45. See also the workingclass family budgets that Yellowitz (pp. 74-76) draws from the Illinois Bureau of Labor Statistics, *Biennial Report*, no. 3 (1884). One family of five (no. 39, Scandinavian), for example, earned $605 yearly from the father and an eleven-year-old son, while living expenses were $632.

96. Statistical studies indicate that labor migration was not correlated most highly to employment patterns. For analyses of the relationship between migration and economic factors, see Jeffrey Williamson, *Late Nineteenth Century American Economic Development: A General Equilibrium Model* (Cambridge, England, 1974); Richard A. Esterlin, *Population, Labor Force, and Long Swings in Economic Growth: The American Experience* (New York, 1968); Brinley Thomas, *Migration and Economic Growth* (Cambridge, England, 1954); Simon Kuznets, *Toward a Theory of Economic Growth* (Baltimore, 1956); Everett S. Lee et al., *Population Redistribution and Economic Growth: United States, 1870-1950*, vol. 1: *Methodological Considerations and Reference Tables* (Philadelphia, 1957); various articles in Philip M. Hauser and Otis Dudley Duncan, eds., *The Study of Population: An Inventory and Appraisal* (Chicago, 1959); and various articles in the journal *Explorations in Economic History*.

97. The issue is a central one, but despite its importance, it is far too complex to deal with in any depth here. Literature in political science and political psychology is vast. For

an introduction, see, for example, Robert E. Lane, *Political Life: Why People Get Involved in Politics* (Glencoe, Ill., 1959), *Political Thinking and Consciousness* (Chicago, 1969), and *Political Man* (New York, 1972).

98. See especially Cumbler, "Culture and Community;" Conzen, "Ethnic Community;" and Hareven, "Laborers of Manchester."

99. The scheme of social organization hypothesized by William Appleman Williams might, in conjunction with Orbell and Uno, offer significant insight into the cultural distinctions that we have observed. In *The Contours of American History* (Chicago, 1966), Williams suggests the existence of several types of political arrangements within societies, in particular those in which an elite, minority group "accept[s] the responsibility for meeting the fundamental economic and political requirements of living together as an organized society. And they also grant the many a rudimentary respect: within specified areas, and within certain limits, the few leave the many alone to their own devices. For their "passivity about power," on the other hand, "the many are rewarded with an opportunity, restricted though it is, to create a limited community of their own." "It is crucial to realize," Williams continues, "that the resulting culture of the many under [this type of arrangement] has often been vital and warm, if also crude and circumscribed" (see esp. pp. 6-9, 17-23, 479-488). Orbell and Uno (in an application of the type of themes suggested by Hirschman, *Exit, Voice*) suggest that individuals who live in a community and who are not satisfied with it or with their lives in it in general have three primary alternatives. The first is essentially to do nothing about the situation, to settle in and try to adjust to it. The second alternative, and the one for which most Americans have opted in the past, is to leave the community, to extricate themselves from disagreeable surroundings, and to go elsewhere. The third alternative is to stay and try to change the situation. It would be easy to oversimplify these suggestions, but we must remember the intricate and complex issues that they address. The position of the workingclass in late nineteenth- and early twentieth-century America was one in which a rich cultural community furnished spiritual sustenance to its members yet was divorced from the larger realms of politics or of governance. Beset by economic hardship, yet unable for many reasons to coalesce into a sustained class, workingclass families moved from place to place in search of economic stability. They did not abrogate their perceived responsibilities to the self-governance of the community; quite the contrary, they mounted continual, though ordinarily undirected, action at the place of work, the place where their cultures clashed most immediately with the demands of industrial capitalism. Nonetheless the realm of politics reasonably seemed closed to them, had they been interested in approaching it, and thus they were rendered "impotent" and "inarticulate" in the councils of state. It is in this sense that Williams' hypothesis has much to offer in the analysis of the American workingclass community. Indeed we should be aware of a recent study (the only type that deals with these questions) which indicates that individuals with higher self-esteem might be more likely to be residentially mobile than those with greater self-derogation, although it was posited also that residential mobility increased "the probability of subsequent self-derogation." See Howard B. Kaplan, "Black Self-Derogation and Residential Mobility," *Journal of Health and Social Behavior* 16 (September 1975): 283-290.

100. I have deliberately avoided dealing with the larger questions of class in this essay, although I plan to do so elsewhere, because of the amorphousness of the use of the term. If we accept, as we should, Thompson's description of class as a process, as a historical relationship, then we must understand the basis from which that process begins. While American workers have seldom had a sustained consciousness of class, they often have had and have proceeded upon a recognition and consciousness of group. It is most often in the soil of these groups that the seeds of class are planted. American historians, however, have dealt very little with the conceptual demands of definition, usually approaching class in a forthrightly tautological fashion: "These workers all were members of what I call the working class, there-

fore they were a class.'' Definition must be brought to the concept; meanwhile the term *group* is considerably more accurately employed.

101. Jones, "Working-Class Culture," p. 462.

102. Tholfsen, "Intellectual Origins," p. 89.

103. Jones, "Working-Class Culture," p. 500.

104. Buhle, "Debsian Socialism," p. 270.

105. I use the phrase "bourgeoisified resistance" because of the insular non-work-oriented consciousness of the workers she described. While, on the other hand, it is likely that workers who emigrate only to accumulate capital and to return to their home base do not fit into this category, the French Canadians in Manchester seem to have adapted to middle-class styles.

106. Gagan, "Mobility in a Canadian Community," p. 14. Gagan believes that "for those people who dwelt only fleetingly in Peel County, as they must have done in other communities, 'community' could have no more meaning than simply next place they came to as replacements for those who had just left." "At the very least," he continues, "there were two 'communities' in nineteenth century Peel County, a small community of itinerants, who, in any case, were merely a fragment of an even larger totality for whom all of Ontario was their 'community.'"

WORKINGCLASS CULTURE AND POLITICS IN THE INDUSTRIAL REVOLUTION: SOURCES OF LOYALISM AND REBELLION

3

Alan Dawley and Paul Faler

I

It is the goal of revolution to change human nature. All the major political revolutions of modern times have tried to create a new kind of person liberated from the corruption of the old order: the Citizen of the French Revolution, the Proletarian Hero of the Bolsheviks, the New Man and New Woman of Cuba and China. The same is true of the Industrial Revolution. It gave birth to a new person among the laboring classes of Europe and America, one who put his/her own needs ahead of the demands of kin and community, who acknowledged no master but the self, and who located the virtues of self-control, self-denial, and self-improvement at the center of the moral universe. To working people, long accustomed to servitude and other forms of personal subordination, this new individualism fomented a fundamental challenge to customary ways of living. It divided people along cultural lines between the traditionally minded, who clung to old values and beliefs, and the modern-minded, who adopted the new personality. Further, the modern-minded worker, coming of age in the industrial era and faced with brutal attacks on his/her new-found sense of personal dignity, wrestled with the question of whether to be loyal to the system of industrial capitalism or to rebel against it. The central task of this essay is to sort out the origins of loyalism from the origins of rebellion, and to assess the relative historical impact of both.

We will proceed to that task in a moment, after setting out the boundaries of the subject. Although the ideas herein have a broad relevance to industrialization wherever it has occurred, we focus on the political and cultural experience of workers in the United States. We worked out the basic analysis in exhaustive studies of the shoe industry and the shoemaking community of Lynn, Massachusetts.[2] The shoe industry was of considerable importance to the American economy in the nineteenth century, second only to textiles at mid-century in numbers employed and product value. Its capital, its technology, and the bulk of its labor were all home-grown, and so its roots reach deep into the American economic subsoil. Lynn, for its part, was the largest center in the industry and was more fully dominated by shoe manufacturing than its close rival, Philadelphia. Together, then, Lynn and the shoe industry were a microcosm of the Industrial Revolution.

We have attempted to bridge the microcosm of Lynn and the macrocosm of the Industrial Revolution. Recognizing that the Lynn experience was not the

only route to industrialization, we have attempted to take from Lynn only those
ideas about the whole process that have some verification in the specific
circumstances of other communities. Thus it may be that Lynn had more than
its share of rebel workers while Boston abounded in bread-and-butter loyalists
and Pittsburgh was filled with traditionally minded peasants, but this tripartite
division between rebels, loyalists, and traditionalists appeared everywhere as the
basic cultural cleavage among American working people through most of the
nineteenth century. The time boundaries of the essay run from the rise of
industrial capitalism in the Era of Good Feeling to its supremacy in the Gilded
Age.

Lynn embarked on the path of industrialism in the 1820s and 1830s when a
reorganization in the production of shoes underminded the old artisan/mercan-
tile way of life and created a new social structure based on capitalist manufacturers and wage earners, the two core groups of the industrial class system. In
the same two decades, the community saw the beginnings of industrial class
conflict (strike organizations), the formation of working-class institutions (journeymen's societies and workingmen's parties), and the emergence of a new
industrial culture — all before the advent of the factory system. The importance
of this period is underlined by the fact that the main ideas, forms of organization, and social cleavages that developed before the factories would persist for a
full generation under the factory system.[3]

None of these early innovations was more far-reaching than a new industrial
morality. This moral code was characterized by a panoply of individualist values:
self-discipline, self-control, and self-reliance. "Trust thyself," Emerson intoned,
"every heart vibrates to that iron string." The code promised self-fulfillment
through the faithful devotion to regular habits of toil. It stressed the virtue of
work for its own sake, not as an expression of some higher calling. It demanded
industry (labor aimed at self-improvement), frugality (economic self-sacrifice),
and temperance (sensual self-denial). In the new code of morality, the self was at
once supreme and suppressed, deified and denied, liberated and enchained.

Industrial morality bore a certain resemblance to an earlier set of virtues. It is
clear that industry, frugality, and temperance had preindustrial (though not
precapitalist) origins, and that an ethic of competitive individualism had put in
an appearance among eighteenth-century laboring classes (among mechanics, at
any rate, if not slaves, servants, or common laborers). But it is equally clear that
the moral universe in which these values appeared remained bounded by traditional forms, and that those forms were broken only by the rise of industrial
capitalism in the nineteenth century. In preindustrial times, individualism had
been incorporated into a pattern of deference to social superiors, but in the new
setting individualism was alloyed with a belief in equality of opportunity.[4] At
one time industry had meant hard work; now it was redefined as devotion to a
methodical work routine. Frugality was once consistent with charity; now it
became associated with a definition of poverty as crime and a new stringency in
poor relief. Temperance once meant moderation in drinking habits and prudent
sexuality; now it was redefined as total abstinence and prudish sexuality. Thus,
the new values were the result of the reassertion of traditional attitudes in new
surroundings and represent both the effort of preindustrial America to keep
itself going along traditional lines and the failure of that effort. This paradox of
change emerging from an effort to conserve the past pervades American history

in the 1820s and 1830s. To take another example, the Jacksonian movement sought to restore the foundations of the old Republic, but instead fostered the new democratic styles in politics and the very expansion in industry that undermined it.[5] The dialectical process of breakdown and repair thus resulted in the creation of something quite different than was intended.

We emphasize that industrial morality was a general feature of the industrial class system as a whole, not the particular values of one class within the system. It was neither bourgeois nor proletarian. It caused businessmen to organize the Society for the Promotion of Industry, Frugality, and Temperance, and prompted wage earners to join the Washingtonian Total Abstinence Society. It inspired businessmen to promote their new Institution for Savings with appeals to popular thriftiness, and it encouraged many working families to practice thrift at the expense of current living standards.[6]

Because industrial morality defined what industrial workers and industrial capitalists had in common with one another, it also defined how their values differed from the libertine culture of preindustrial class systems. The contrast is most striking when we compare industrial morality with the culture of slavery: individualism versus paternalism; the work ethic versus an ethic of leisure; free labor versus bond labor. Just as the industrial classes drew upon a common cultural reservoir, so, too, the classes of slavery drew their values from common preindustrial sources. Despite vast inequalities between slaves and masters, they shared certain cultural outlooks that set them farther apart from the industrial classes than from each other.[7] (This point will take on added importance later when we consider the political impact of the Civil War.)

Industrial morality was a source of cleavage within the working class between "traditional" and "modern" values. As each generation of preindustrial laborers came into contact with industrialism, some adopted the new code, while others rejected it and clung to preindustrial values. We term the latter "traditionalists" because they refused to give up their casual attitudes toward work, their pursuit of happiness in gaming and drinking, and the raucous revelry that accompanied fire and militia musters. Traditionalists still deferred to the silk vest, the gold watch, and the ivory-handled cane, still expected a rum ration from their employers, and still claimed Saturday afternoon and Monday morning as their own time. In 1820 virtually all the shoemakers in Lynn were traditionalists, and continual infusions of people with preindustrial backgrounds from the hills of New Hampshire and the rills of County Cork insured that a variety of traditional customs would persist well into the industrial period.

A second group adopted the new morality, and we term them "modernists." In terms of moral character, modernist workers resembled their employers (most of whom were also modernists) more than they did their traditionalist co-workers. They joined their employers in shunning the very things traditionalists cherished — the warm sociability of the drinking club, the "wasteful" amusement of the circus and the Jim Crow show, the easygoing work rhythm.[8]

If morality were the only determinant of behavior, then neither group of workers would have mounted an organized challenge to their employers — the traditionalists because they believed their employers were their betters and the modernists because they believed their employers were no different than themselves. But other factors threw wage earners into conflict with their employers and tapped industrial morality as both a motivation for struggle and as a means

to wage that struggle. The economic changes of the industrial revolution intensified competition among wage earners, cheapened their skills, undercut their
security, attacked their standard of living, increased their dependency, and
lowered their social position. In each case these changes conflicted head-on with
the values of industrial morality: self-reliance, self-discipline, and self-improvement. Given the situation in which scores of people were dependent upon a
single individual for their livelihood, what other recourse was there for those
who believed in equal rights and self-improvement but to take collective action?
Social and economic changes impelled the individualism of the modernists in
collective directions toward the mutualism of the benefit society, the fraternity
of the lodge, the common front of collective bargaining, and the solidarity of the
strike.

All the modernists were caught up in this process, but not all in the same
way. Some hastened its work; they devoted all their spare time to the moral
elevation of the laboring classes, sold subscriptions to labor newspapers, canvassed the town to promote support for a strike, and, after attending a temperance rally on Friday, spoke at a meeting of the journeymen's society on
Saturday. Others, however, slowed the process; they subscribed to a community
newspaper but not a labor journal, told the canvasser a strike was ill-advised, and
spoke at the temperance rally, but probably did not attend the journeymen's
meeting. In other words, the modernists subdivided into two different groups;
the first we term "rebels," the second, "loyalists." The rebels laid the foundations of the labor movement, saw sobriety and literacy as matters of self-pride
and as means to proclaim their independence from the external commands of
employer and liquor, and did not shrink from the prospect of a strike. On the
other hand, loyalists held aloof from the labor movement (or joined only in a
crisis), wore their sobriety and literacy as badges of middle-class respectability,
and tried to evade the issue of class conflict altogether. It is this division between
rebels and loyalists that commands our attention for the remainder of the essay.

Since rebels and loyalists shared the same underlying moral character, they
did not part company with each other (or with their bosses) over this cultural
issue. Rather, they divided over the question of political economy. Where the
loyalists saw an overriding mutuality of interests between labor and capital,
offset only by minor differences, the rebels saw an overriding antagonism, offset
only by minor points of agreement. To the loyalist, capital and labor were
mutually dependent, and each was entitled to a just reward — the entrepreneur a
fair profit, the laborer a fair wage. To the rebel, however, capital and labor stood
in direct opposition, since the interest of the former was to get as much work
from the latter for the lowest possible wage.

The explanation for this difference in outlook — a difference with vital
bearing on the question of class consciousness — lies in part outside the realm of
culture. A long period of economic prosperity reinforced the loyalist position,
while depression reinforced the rebels; by the same token, the loyalist argument
made more sense to well-paid, secure, skilled workers than to people who were
poorly paid and insecure (indeed, the true labor aristocrats in the shoe industry
— the cutters — were unquestionably the most loyal). But below the level of the
cutters, alignments were only tendencies, not hard and fast lines of demarcation.
In fact, the two outlooks cut across skill and wage differentials and must be
understood first on their own ground as cultural phenomena.

The breach in outlook was caused by the rebels' application of artisan radicalism to their own situation. They updated the egalitarian ideas of the American Revolution, the French Revolution, and English Jacobinism,[9] and combined them with the labor theory of value to produce an incisive critique of industrial capitalism. Believing that only labor could create value, they concluded that capital was nothing but the congealed labor of the producing classes. By itself, capital was inert and lifeless, not the living "head" of production, as the loyalists believed. Rebels argued that the large manufacturer who no longer performed labor in the shop and whose control over production rested exclusively on his ownership of capital was both a parasite and a thief. A Lynn cordwainer explained the labor theory of value to the readers of *The Awl* in 1844: "Is it not clear that the businessman stands debtor to the world for all which he receives over and above the amount of labor given? And is it not equally clear that the mechanic, I mean particularly the mechanics of Lynn, receives *less* than a compensation for the amount of labor given? It appears, therefore, that the world stands debtor to the mechanic for this surplus labor."[10] Pursuing this logic, rebels further contended that because the rise of capitalist manufacturing had divided labor from capital, and because labor suffered the consequences, the only road to reunion of labor and capital and the only ultimate remedy for the plight of the laborer was cooperative ownership.

This is as far as the early rebels took the labor theory. They were not Marxian socialists. While their views showed an affinity for socialism, largely because socialism rested on the same theory, they did not propose to seize existing private property rights. Nor were they middle-class reformers. While they often stood shoulder to shoulder with petty bourgeois democrats listening to some agrarian or currency reformer hawk his particular panacea, they maintained a distinct identity of their own. Some historians with ideological commitments to pure and simple trade unionism have mistaken the rebels as utopian middle-class meddlers, but these writers have missed their mark. The rebels were bona fide wage earners, not some offshoot of middle-class reformers.[11] Nor were they muddle-headed reactionaries who opposed the whole advance of industrialism; unlike the traditionalists, they did not seek cures for present ills in a return to the world of the past.

The accomplishments of the rebels were considerable and were far out of proportion to their numbers. A distinct minority, the rebels were, nonetheless, the catalytic element in Lynn and in the American working class as a whole. Their penchant for autodidacticism, their self-discipline, and their high level of literacy gave them the personal skills necessary to be effective organizers, and they took the lead in establishing unions, cooperatives, newspapers, workingmen's parties, and central labor councils. They authored the most incisive criticisms of industrial capitalism one can find in the annals of nineteenth-century social protest, and their ideas dominated the mainstream of the labor movement from the journeymen's societies and workingmen's parties of the 1830s through the National Labor Union, the Eight-Hour Movement, and the Knight of Labor after the Civil War. Thus the most vigorous opponents and the most trenchant critics of industrial capitalism were those workers who had accepted cultural values which they shared with their employers but used in their own class interest.

The foregoing discussion has shown that industrial morality was both a source of accord and a source of discord between labor and capital. Neither the stability of the industrial class system nor a revolutionary threat from below could be predicted on the basis of cultural influences alone. Thus before we make any final judgments on the fundamental cleavages of nineteenth-century American history, we must assess the weight of other factors. We will look further at the impact of economic changes before turning later to a consideration of political influences.

II

Surely the record of American industrial relations between the Civil War and World War II was a story of constant turbulence interrupted only intermittently by periods of relative peace. In this respect Lynn in 1860 represented what the United States would become, because in that year its shoemakers staged a massive walkout that soon became the largest strike the country had ever seen.[12]

In the five years before the strike, the chronic deterioration of the old artisan/mercantile order entered an acute phase in which the breakdown was especially severe. First, machine methods replaced hand methods in binding, the branch of the trade that had historically belonged to women. For more than a generation women had constituted about half the total workforce, but the establishment of several sewing-machine shops run as proto-factories compelled many married women with children to leave the trade completely. These changes also undermined the wages and security of women who could afford to buy a sewing machine and work at home, because household producers could only compete by accepting less pay for more work. Second, factory methods were introduced into certain branches of the trade, notably heeling, where machines had not yet been invented. Third, shoe bosses were sending an increasing part of their orders to domestic workers in the countryside, giving preference to outsiders at the expense of Lynn citizens. Lastly, the panic of 1857 lengthened into three years of hard times with resultant wage reductions and layoffs.

Virtually everyone was affected by the crisis at hand, but only the rebels had developed the methods to meet it. Only their analysis of the division between capital and labor made sense out of the recent economic changes and justified a strike as the means to combat them. Only their recognition of the need for the organization of labor and their organizing talents were adequate to the situation. In 1859 they formed the Lynn Mechanics Association and began publishing the *New England Mechanic*. In the winter of 1859-60 they called mass meetings and canvassed the city for strike support. They took the lead in a movement that gathered widespread support from loyalists and traditionalists alike, and on Washington's birthday in 1860 they led virtually the entire city out on strike.

The strike was a lesson in class conflict that strengthened the rebel outlook within the working class, even as it left the shoemakers in a weaker position vis-a-vis the manufacturers. Indeed, the very fact that the bosses had resolutely defeated the strike by sending work outside of town and importing out-of-town police to keep order verified the rebel analysis. Taken by surprise, many loyalists grew bitter over the manufacturers' resolve to defeat and disgrace them and swung over to the rebel position.

Economic changes over the next several years powerfully reinforced this trend. Although the economic squeeze was eased a bit by the return of prosperity during the war, the breakdown of the old order and the construction of the new was completed when the shoe industry converted to a full-fledged factory system by 1868, with all the accompaniments of a widening gap between capital and labor, a greater subordination of the wage earner to the owner's will, and an increasing share of wealth going to the owners. Traditionalists found it harder to hold on to the preindustrial ways, and loyalists found it harder to evade the issue of inequality. Consequently, the rebels were able to organize shoeworkers of all three types into the Knights of St. Crispin, a militant union of modern industrial workers that began its meteoric rise in Lynn in 1868.

Within two years the Knights of St. Crispin signed up more than half the male shoeworkers in the city as dues-paying members, mobilized hundreds more in a city-wide strike in 1870 that rivaled the magnitude of the Great Strike of 1860, and joined forces with the Daughters of St. Crispin, a sister organization that represented several hundred women shoeworkers. On a national scale the union's growth was equally impressive, making it the country's largest trade union. Labor historians have long recognized the importance of this remarkable group of unionists, but until very recently they have been just as mistaken in assessing who the Crispins were as they were correct in assessing their importance. Following John Commons, the original student of the order, they identified Crispins as old-time, skilled craftsmen fending off the influx of green hands.[13] Based on new evidence obtained from census information on 1000 names in the dues book of a Lynn Lodge, it is now possible to show conclusively that Commons was wrong. Crispins were not the most stable or the most highly skilled artisans, the groups who were assigned first rank in the order by the Commons interpretation. Instead, most Crispins were modern industrial workers: in terms of skill, income, property ownership, birthplace, and geographical mobility they represented a cross-section of the work force.[14]

Further insight into Crispin strength and militancy is provided by looking at three groups in the union whose background suggests traditionalism but whose behavior implies rebellion. First, Irish immigrants, who were less than a fifth of the work force, filled nearly a quarter of the Crispin membership rolls. The special Irish affinity for the union, a pattern repeated in the Knights of Labor a decade later, indicates that the factory system was fast undermining the peasant's traditional deference toward his employer and devotion to casual work rhythms. However, the size of the Irish contingent indicates the union contained men from both sides of the cultural divide — modernists who denounced the evils of demon rum for the Father Matthew Total Abstinence Society and traditionalists who found the convivial atmosphere of the drinking circle more to their liking. The union's adaptation to this hold-over from traditionalism broadened its base and put a larger army in the field under rebel leaders at strike time.

Second, Yankees from rural areas filled another quarter or more of the rolls. The small-town cobblers and farmer shoemakers who migrated to Lynn had been schooled in the values of rugged individualism, a fact which hastened their conversion to industrial morality and sharpened their reaction to the factory system. They were not used to being bossed, and their fierce independence clashed with the authoritarian rule of the factory, which not only drove them into the union but made many of them union militants.

Third, the prominence of women in Lynn's labor movement reveals the decline of patriarchy, a fundamental pillar of the traditional order. Women had benefited least from the great popular emancipations of the nineteenth-century laboring classes — the disappearance of servitude, the abolition of slavery, the opening of career opportunities, the granting of suffrage and other rights of citizenship — so that in the 1870s women retained their status as personal subordinates of their fathers and husbands. Yet the Daughters of St. Crispin, like the women strikers of 1860, held mass meetings, conducted work stoppages, and talked the rebel language of "equal rights." Clearly, the modern temper had invaded the "women's sphere" and weakened traditional beliefs. Once again, the base of the union was broadened, its position strengthened, and its militancy intensified.

As traditionalism waned, loyalism shifted ground. The inescapable inequality between employer and worker in the factory system caused the loyalists to reassess their position further, and they finally conceded the necessity for organization among the toilers. They no longer held aloof from the labor movement and even the most loyal of the loyalists, the cutters, eventually joined the Knights of Labor.

The rebels reassessed their outlook, too. In the 1870s and 1880s they showed an increasing affinity for a class analysis of the conflict between labor and capital. Crispin conventions discussed the concept of wage slavery and emphasized the abolition of the wage system through cooperation as the only true solution to the labor problem. Some of the letters in local newspapers and some of the testimony reported by the Massachusetts Bureau of the Statistics of Labor protested that the country was ruled by the industrial and financial monopolists. Some adherents of the Eight-Hour Movement located the source of social and political inequality in the exploitative process by which the worker was compelled to work a portion of each day solely for the profit of the owner. The Lynn Labor Reform party called for the nationalization of the means of communication and transportation.[15]

The overall impact of the economic changes in the shoe industry after 1860 was to reduce the cultural divisions within the working class. The factory system inducted traditionalists into the modernist viewpoint faster than any pre-factory experience. It persuaded loyalists to join the labor movement. And it produced tons of grist for the rebels' mill.

III

Taking stock of the argument so far, we have seen the development of a new type of person — one who believed that he could improve his lot in life by following a strict regimen of regular labor and by avoiding the pitfalls of excessive drink and excessive spending. In contrast to the traditionalist, who clung to the libertine morality and customs of an earlier era, the modernist lived by a tighter code of personal and social conduct that he shared with his employer. This cultural bond became the basis for political loyalty for some workers, but we have also seen an opposing development: the emergence of a rebel outlook from the clash between the worker's individualist beliefs and his actual economic situation, in which he was dependent on a money wage and subordinated to his employer's command. Further, we have seen the growing strength of the rebel outlook within the working class, the intensification of class conflict, rising organization and militancy, and the increasing affinity of the rebel outlook for a class explanation of labor's predicament.

Surely this is sufficient to demonstrate the potential for the development of a pervasive, class-conscious, radical outlook among American workers. By the 1870s workers in Lynn, as in other sections of the country, appeared ready to believe that the unequal distribution of wealth and power was caused by an interlocking economic, social, political, and cultural mechanism that brought about the oppression of all who labored with their hands.

But this potential was never fully realized. By the end of the century most workers probably linked their desire for collective self-help to a conception of labor as an interest group rather than a class. What, then, had contained the spread of radicalism? What historical alchemy had transformed rebellion into reconciliation?

The question is no less interesting for not being new. In one variation or another, it has been posed in a dozen ways ranging from the ridiculous (Daniel Bell) to the sublime (Selig Perlman).[16] The most recent answers have frequently taken one of two forms: (a) the diverse ethnic and religious origins of the American working class have divided it internally against itself, thus blocking the development of a common group identity; or (b) the high incidence of social mobility – in particular, movement up the ladder – gave workers a satisfying taste of success within the existing system and thwarted class identity.[17] While both perspectives shed considerable light on the question, and the second has opened a treasure chest of new evidence, neither constitutes a decisive solution to the problem. Diversity did not prevent the formation of the collectivist notion of labor as an interest group, and the incidence of rapid social mobility was consistent with a high level of class consciousness in several European countries.

Our own answer focuses on the intersection of working-class culture and American politics and is divided into three parts: (a) the ritual of democracy, (b) the impact of the Civil War, and (c) the interclass character of the party system.

During the 1820s and 1830s American politics became a mass ritual for the expression of popular culture. For the first time anywhere in the world, ordinary folk (at least the white males among them) regularly expressed their values and beliefs in the ongoing political process through the hoopla of conventions, the pageantry of parades, the camp-meeting style of rallies, the frenetic electioneering of voting day, and the final victory celebrations. All the bunting, brass bands, banners, and flags that festooned election campaigns merely demonstrated that politics had become a popular form of mass entertainment.

Industrial morality had a key role to play in the new ritual of democracy. Working people who believed in their own self-worth, and no longer deferred to the silk vest, the gold watch, or the ivory-handled cane, insisted that their own voices be heard and their own votes counted. Sooner or later most politicians learned to court them with phrases about the bone and sinew of society that flattered even their own high self-esteem. Democrats were the first to adopt the new style, but Whigs were not far behind, as they proved in the Log Cabin and Hard Cider campaign of 1840. The new style, with its banners, floats, and parades, thus incorporated into the election campaign itself many of the tamer features of old 'Lection day, a preindustrial festival of popular culture abolished by the Massachusetts General Court in 1831.[18] In other words, the ritual of democracy reinforced the individualist code of ethics adopted by modernist workingmen, but also provided popular entertainment for the traditionalists.

Further, the ritual emphasized the common political culture workers and employers shared. In contrast to several European countries, political democracy did not arise in the United States from the class demands of dispossessed workers against the propertied interests that controlled the state. Instead, it arose from an interclass movement that included both propertyless workers and small entrepreneurs, and was dominated by property-owning artisans and farmers. Thus the first generation of industrial workers often cooperated with industrial employers in joint political ventures. Lynn shoemakers who saw the wealth and power of some manufacturers increasing daily at their expense could turn to politics and make common cause with other manufacturers against an enemy — real or imagined — of the democratic political culture. In this fashion, antimasonry swept Lynn with a call to alarm against a secret, conspiratorial aristocracy. Nativism arose out of the fear of an internal threat to American republicanism posed by an authoritarian foreign power that used ignorant Irish Catholics as its pawns for gaining control. The powerful Free Soil movement attacked the Southern slaveocracy on the grounds that it was the epitome of aristocratic power, a death threat leveled at the producing classes, and the antithesis of industrial morality. Finally, the conflict between workers and employers was frequently softened by their joint cooperation as producers against the parasitic money power.[19] Just as inequality waxed in economics, it seemed to wane in politics.

Thus for the first generations of industrial workers, politics was a continual re-enactment of a ritual embodying the social relations of an earlier era of unity among the "producing classes." Industrial culture interacted with the political system in just the opposite way that it interacted with the economic system. The consequence was to retard the spread of rebellion and to advance the politics of loyalism.

The Civil War gave an enormous impetus to the politics of loyalism. At the outset of the War, Lynn was bitterly divided along class lines drawn during the strike of 1860. Strike passions boiled over into electoral politics as strike leaders organized a Workingmen's party to vent their outrage against the use of out-of-town police and their frustration over losing on all their formal strike demands. As the economic struggle resolved into a political struggle, economic defeat was offset by an overwhelming political victory. The Workingmen's party captured nearly every position in the Lynn city government. But then, just at this decisive moment, Fort Sumter fell. Rebel workingmen got back in step with their employers, strikers and bosses submerged their differences in the Yankee cause, and together they marched off to fight confederate traitors. The effect of the War on class consciousness was written in the next election returns: the Republican party, dominated by local shoe manufacturers, won its first city election, and soon worker opposition withered away to nothing. Literally *nothing*. Not a single vote was cast against the incumbent Republican mayor in 1863.[20]

The suffocating embrace of wartime unity persisted through the next decade as the issues created by the War continued to dominate the nation's political affairs, again despite massive economic dispute and division. Questions of reconstructing the Union overshadowed the social and economic issues of industrialization, so that when labor discontent re-emerged after the War, it did not define the main lines of political debate. Thus during the most critical years of industrialization, the United States was more keenly divided politically between industrialism and slavery than between industrial workers·and industrial capitalists.

The War gave workers and manufacturers a common historical legacy. Both groups agreed that the history of their country after 1850 was, in effect, the history of class struggle. They regarded bleeding Kansas, the John Brown raid, the Civil War itself, and the military occupation of the South afterwards as incidents in a mortal battle for state power waged by antagonistic social and economic interests. Workers and manufacturers regarded their joint victory as a judgment on the superiority of the northern, industrial way of life. Both groups rejoiced in the defeat of the common enemy, the vindication of industrial morality, and the preservation of democratic values against their subversion by a would-be aristocracy. Both believed that the Federal government and the Union armies had served their basic interests well.

Class consciousness, like all forms of collective thought, is based on actual historical experience transformed into myth. The mythology that arose from the Civil War tended to persuade workers that their power and destiny were inextricably linked to the military heroes, civilian leaders, and the existing frame of government that had won the war. It was not necessary for bourgeois ideologists to go about preaching a "false" consciousness to working people who had risked their lives to bring down the slave power; workers needed only to compare their death toll at the hands of the slaveocracy with their death toll at the hands of company guards, police, and militia. Although the violent suppression of the Mollie Maguires and railroad workers in 1877 began to add up, the result was still dozens against thousands.[21] Had the war ended differently, with the Union in disgrace, or had slavery not been rooted so deeply in American history that it required the greatest military effort of the nineteenth century to extirpate it, the experience and the myths would have been different. Perhaps the conflict between the industrial and preindustrial systems would have been less severe and the conflict between the industrial classes more severe, but as it turned out, things ran the other way. The War took grist from the rebels' mill and gave it to the loyalists.

Working-class political culture emerged from conflicting cross-pressures, some encouraging and others discouraging a class view. As the effect of the Civil War waned, perhaps the most crucial pressure against class consciousness and the major outlet for working-class discontent was electoral politics. Its effect derived from the interclass character of the political parties, and it was crucial because it bore directly on the rebel worker, without whom no widespread radical movement was possible. Whether a rebel became a Democrat, Republican, Labor Reformer, or Greenbacker, he invariably came into close contact with middle-class politicians (a point David Montgomery has emphasized in his perceptive analysis of postwar politics), and this itself demonstrated the openness of the political process. No one has captured the essential relation between social discontent and electoral politics better than Wendell Phillips, firebrand of social reform, Labor Reform candidate for governor of Massachusetts, and hero to rebel workers. "We rush into politics," Phillips explained, "because politics is the safety-valve."[22]

The most powerful political organization in Lynn between 1878 and 1890 was a Workingmen's party that emerged under exactly the same circumstances as its predecessor in 1860: outrage and frustration in a strike launched a political movement for revenge against city officials that carried a Workingmen's candidate to overwhelming victory. The candidate, George P. Sanderson, was a man of clear rebel credentials. The son of a small-town, New Hampshire preacher, he had been a partner in a shoemakers' cooperative. His campaign was infused with rebel rhetoric about the conflict between labor and capital, a conflict personified by Sanderson himself, who had been a shoeworker most of his life, and his opponent, who was the owner of the largest shoe factory and the largest fortune in the city.

But soon after taking office, the rebellion petered out. Although Sanderson acted on his promise to fire the hated police chief, he brought forth nothing else in the way of a distinctive labor program. Having turned the rascals out of office and satisfied the popular taste for revenge, he had nothing further to do except reward the party faithful. Once in office, he became a loyalist by default.

The pattern set by Sanderson persisted throughout the Workingmen's reign. The party was effective in winning elections, manipulating city contracts and patronage jobs, and in controlling the local police force. Each of these accomplishments was important to the city's labor movement, and it is not necessary to belittle the bread-and-butter benefits provided by the Workingmen's party to make the point that it did nothing to pursue the broader interests of the class or to take the rebel outlook into such areas as municipal ownership, health and safety regulations in the factories, or expanded assistance to the poor. The Workingmen's party avoided areas of potential friction between wage earners and middle-class supporters and, instead, sought out the areas of agreement between them.[23] The Workingmen's party was not a party of the proletariat.

IV

We have seen that the Industrial Revolution twice divided American society: first, along industrial and preindustrial lines, and second, along class lines within the industrial order itself. The first division pitted a modern code of morality against a traditional code, industrialism against slavery, the Union against the Confederacy, and it proved to be the deeper division. The second pitted labor against capital, strikers against employers, rebels against owners, and in the time span we are considering from 1820-1890, this division was not as deep. Indeed, industrial class conflicts were often resoived in common struggles against preindustrial influences: the movements for moral reform, the ritual of democracy, and the war against the slave power united wage earners with their employers in battles against common preindustrial enemies.

Recognition of this double division — one between classes, the other between class systems as a whole — clarifies the conflicting cross-pressures that bore down on the nineteenth-century industrial worker. The pressures generated in class conflict tended to make the worker rebellious in his attitudes toward capital and conscious of his own class interests, whereas those generated by conflicts between the preindustrial and the industrial systems tended to make him loyal to the existing order, despite its gross inequalities. American historians, who have ignored such complexities too often, would do well to pose questions that recognize these divergent potentials. Historians who ask only, "Why isn't the

American worker class conscious?" get flat, one-dimensional answers. Better to ask "What conditions promoted class consciousness and what promoted the interest group mentality?" Why, for example, did vigorous strike activity, on any comparative basis, arise amid relatively docile politics? Likewise, historians who wonder, "Why is there no socialism in the United States?" get caught flat-footed when confronted with actual workers who had socialist ideas. Better to ask "Why is socialism weak among certain groups of workers, but strong among others?"

The experience of the first generations of industrial workers influenced the cultural and political development of later generations as America's industrial society matured in the twentieth century. First, the "traditionalist" was reborn whenever a displaced ex-peasant immigrated to America and set about to find work. While some of the children of the immigrants found steady employment and adopted modern ways, others became trapped in an economic maelstrom of low wages and high unemployment that made a mockery of the modern virtues of thrift, temperance, and self-improvement. Before the mid-twentieth century, the descendants of European immigrants would be joined by southern Blacks, Appalachian whites, and Puerto Ricans in this economic underworld. The tragedy of these hard-living, street-corner, marginal workers was that, having lost the anchor of traditional values, they became demoralized when they were unable to find a replacement. Neither traditional nor modern, their aimless, hopeless, disorganized life style was as much the cause as the consequence of their entrapment in a vicious cycle of poverty.

Second, the loyalists not only made peace with the labor movement, but took over large segments of it. Ironically, they often operated under the leadership of conservative ex-rebels like Samuel Gompers in the AFL and James Tobin in the Boot and Shoe Workers' Union. They came to see the trade union as a vital ally in their drive for economic security within the system, and, concurrently, they became bulwarks of the two-party system as an expression of their overall loyalty to the existing order. Their loyalty was severely tested by the Great Depression, but they jumped at the chance to reaffirm it by voting in droves for Franklin Roosevelt and enlisting to fight the fascist armies of Hitler and Tojo. Much like the Civil War, the Second World War strengthened loyalism in the American working class; so much, in fact, that it could be perverted to support the totalitarian, antiradical impulse in the country after the War.

Finally, the rebels cut a channel in American soil that enabled the egalitarianism of the late eighteenth-century revolutions to flow into the twentieth-century labor movement and join up with the streams of immigrant socialism. Rebels established a pattern of labor support for third parties that influenced the formation of socialist and labor parties in the first half of the twentieth century. Although frequent setbacks to industrial unionism and the post-World War II purges of radicals weakened the rebels' influence in the labor movement, the contemporary relevance of their ideas becomes apparent whenever hardship and frustration expose the cruelties of modern industrial capitalism and drive its victims to revolt.

FOOTNOTES

1. An earlier version of this article was presented at the 1974 meeting of the American Historical Association.

2. The ideas herein are a synthesis of the views of both authors; however, we have approached the subject from different perspectives. Paul Faler has specialized on the cultural life of pre-factory artisans, and he originated the cultural typology and terminology used here ("traditionalists," "rebels," "loyalists," industrial v. libertine morality). He introduced this material in "Cultural Aspects of the Industrial Revolution, Lynn, Massachusetts, Shoemakers and Industrial Morality, 1826-1860," *Labor History,* vol. 15, no. 3 (1974): 367-94. Alan Dawley has specialized on the economic and political life of factory workers and has written on these subjects in *Class and Community: The Industrial Revolution in Lynn* (forthcoming, Harvard University Press). In addition, see the following works: Dawley, "The Artisan Response to the Factory System: Lynn, Massachusetts, in the Nineteenth Century" (Ph.D. diss., Harvard University, 1971); Faler, "Workingmen, Mechanics, and Social Change: Lynn, Massachusetts, 1800-1860" (Ph.D. diss., University of Wisconsin, 1971); and Faler, "Working Class Historiography," *Radical America,* vol. 3, no. 2 (1969): 56-68. These studies revise an earlier body of literature on the shoe industry, of which the leading work is John Commons, "American Shoemakers 1648-1895: A Sketch of Industrial Evolution," *Quarterly Journal of Economics* 74 (1909): 39-84. Two other important works are Blanche Hazard, *The Organization of the Boot and Shoe Industry in Massachusetts Before 1875* (Cambridge, Mass., 1921), and Don Lescohier, "The Knights of St. Crispin," *Bulletin of the U. of Wisconsin,* no. 355 (Madison, 1910): 19-24.

3. Between 1830 and 1837 the first strike meeting occurred, the first journeymen cordwainers' society was formed, and the first workingmen's party appeared.

4. The co-existence of individualism and deference in preindustrial New England is described by Charles Grant, *Democracy in the Connecticut Frontier Town of Kent* (New York, 1961); an interesting recent perspective on the decline of deference can be found in James S. Young, *The Washington Community, 1800-1828* (New York, 1966).

5. The paradox has been explored by Richard Hofstadter, *The American Political Tradition* (New York, 1948); Marvin Meyers, *The Jacksonian Persuasion* (New York, 1957); and Oscar Handlin, *Commonwealth* (New York, 1947).

6. There was an "interlocking directorate" between the Society for the Promotion of Industry, Frugality, and Temperance and the Lynn Institution for Savings, both founded in the late 1820s; the full impact of the temperance movement on working people came in the early 1840s with the rise of the Washingtonian Total Abstinence Society.

7. Eugene Genovese has explored the culture of the slave system in *Roll, Jordan, Roll: The World the Slaves Made* (New York, 1974).

8. See Faler, "Cultural Aspects."

9. For a good introduction to eighteenth-century artisan radicalism, see the handy summary of E.P. Thompson's work on England and Albert Soboul's on France by Gwynn Williams, *Artisans and Sans-culottes: Popular Movements in France and Britain during the French Revolution* (New York, 1969).

10. *The Awl,* Aug. 7, 1844.

11. For a case of mistaking the origin and identity of the rebels see Norman Ware, *The Industrial Worker, 1840-1860* (Chicago, 1964).

12. Amazingly, Commons and his followers ignored the strike. The best treatment is in Philip Foner, *History of the Labor Movement in the United States* (New York, 1947), 1: 240.

13. The "green hands" theory can be found in Commons et al., *History of Labour* (New York, 1966), 2: 78; Lescohier, "Knights of St. Crispin," pp. 19-24; and Norman Ware, *The Labor Movement in the United States, 1860-1895* (New York, 1929), p. 20.

14. David Montgomery was the first to see through the "green hands" theory in *Beyond Equality* (New York, 1967), p. 154; full documentation for the Lynn Crispins is in Dawley, "Artisan Response," pp. 212-20.

15. Cooperation was endorsed in the *Proceedings* of the Third Annual Crispin convention, pp. 23-24; consecutive issues of the *Lynn Transcript* in January 1880, contained letters from "Scrib," who demanded an end to the political stranglehold of the rich; a Lynn respondent in the *Fourth Annual Report* of the Massachusetts Bureau of the Statistics of Labor (1873, p. 306), warned that the results of the factory system "have been altogether in favor of capital and against labor"; a letter (July 25, 1885), in the *Knight of Labor* said failure to enact an eight-hour law was like taxing labor for the benefit of capital, and the result would be the same as the outcome of unjust taxation in 1776.

16. For an example of the former see Daniel Bell's brilliantly written but foolishly conceived *Marxian Socialism in the United States* (Princeton, 1952); for an example of the latter see the best single work of the Wisconsin school, Selig Perlman, *Theory of the Labor Movement* (New York, 1928).

17. The first argument can be found in David Brody, *Steelworkers: the Non-Union Era* (Cambridge, Mass., 1960), and Marc Karson, *American Labor Unions and Politics* (Carbondale, Ill., 1958). The second argument has been set forth in recent quantitative studies; the study of working-class social mobility is virtually synonymous with Stephan Thernstrom's pathbreaking *Poverty and Progress* (Cambridge, Mass., 1964), and his more recent *The Other Bostonians* (Cambridge, Mass., 1973).

18. The abolition of 'Lection Day is discussed in Faler, "Cultural Aspects," pp. 381-82.

19. The political movements are treated in Dawley, *Class and Community*, chs. 2, 8.

20. Dawley, "Artisan Response," pp. 252-56.

21. Other relevant body counts include the death toll in the June Days of 1848, and the slaughter of the Paris communards.

22. Montgomery, *Beyond Equality*, passim; Wendell Phillips, quoted in Richard Hofstadter, *The American Political Tradition* (New York, 1948), p. 160.

23. The city government elected at the height of the Workingmen's strength was composed of almost equal numbers of working-class and middle-class council members.

THE CROWD IN PHILADELPHIA HISTORY: A COMPARATIVE PERSPECTIVE*

4

Michael Feldberg

In recent years, a growing number of scholars have become interested in American "pre-industrial" collective behavior.[1] Most acknowledge, to varying degrees, a debt to the European historians who first blazed a path in this area: notably George Rudé, Eric Hobsbawn, E. P. Thompson, and Charles Tilly.[2] Rudé, especially, has provided a model of European pre-industrial violence against which those who have studied violence on both sides of the Atlantic have measured the motives, beliefs, and behaviour of crowds in history. In his careful studies of French and English uprisings in the period 1740-1848, Rudé had undermined the stereotyped image of the bloodthirsty and irrational "mob" created by such nineteenth-century critics as Hyppolite Taine and Gustave LeBon. Rudé has concluded that collective violence was a reaction by the disfranchised and

---

* An earlier version of this paper was delivered at the American Historical Association Convention, New Orleans, Louisiana, December 29, 1971.

[1] Among the most important contributions in this area are Leonard Richards, *Gentlemen of Property and Standing* (New York, 1970); Pauline Maier, "Popular Uprisings and Civil Authority in Eighteenth-Century America," *William and Mary Quarterly*, XXVII, 1 (1970), 3-35; Jesse Lemisch, "Jack Tar in the Street: Merchant Seamen in the Politics of Revolutionary America," *ibid.*, XXVV, 3 (1968), 371-401; Gordon S. Wood, "A Note on Mobs in the American Revolution," *ibid.*, XXIII, 4 (1966); John Runcie, " 'Hunting the Nigs' in Philadelphia: The Race Riot of August 1834," *Pennsylvania History*, XXXIX, 2 (1972), 187-218.

[2] Among the best-known works of these authors are numbered Rudé *The Crowd in History: A Study of Popular Disturbances in France and England, 1730-1848* (New York, 1964); Rudé and Hobsbawm, *Captain Swing* (London, 1969); Hobsbawm, *Primitive Rebels: Studies in Archaic Forms of Social Movement in the 19th and 20th Centuries* (New York, 1959); Thompson, *The Making of the English Working Class* (New York, 1963); and Tilly, "Collective Violence in European Perspective," in Hugh Davis Graham and Ted Robert Gurr, eds., *Violence in America: Historical and Comparative Perspectives* (New York, 1970), 4-45.

Source: From *Labor History* 15, no. 3 (Summer 1974): 323-336.

relatively powerless "lower orders" against innovative technologies, government policies, and capitalist market relationships that threatened their security or stability. His insight has been refined and elaborated on by Tilly in particular, who has expanded it into the basis for a theory of modern European history that will be discussed below. Rudé's observations have also proven helpful in understanding the peculiar nature of American resistance to British authority before the War of Independence.[3] But can his findings be applied to later periods of American history? In many ways, Jacksonian Philadelphia provides an even better test than Colonial America of the validity — and problems — of transferring the European model of pre-industrial collective violence to America.

Rudé focuses primarily on events in post-1770 England and Revolutionary France because it was during those periods in those two countries that pre-industrial, localized economies were becoming industrialized, and politically-centralized national units. Rudé argues, and Thompson, Hobsbawm, and Tilly generally agree, that as France and England switched from one productive mode to another, their social and political structures were transformed. These changes, in turn, elicited violent responses from the "lower orders." Through their uprisings, urban and rural rioters struggled to preserve the traditional social and economic systems within which they had always lived. Professor Tilly has labelled these crowds "reactive," or backward-looking.[4] They were groups of wage-earning peasant or artisan protestors seeking to prevent a new capitalist commercial order from replacing their own vestigial medieval economic value systems. Their pre-industrial values, Thompson points out, provided the rioters with "legitimising notions,"[5] such as "natural justice" and "just price," in whose name they carried out so many bread riots and rick burnings. Theirs was violence to protect the old order, not to abolish it.

This backward-looking orientation among European pre-industrial crowds was fated to disappear. With the imposition from above of an industrial, capitalist, politically centralized social order, rioters ceased hoping to preserve a golden age.[6] All four historians argue — and it is a

---

[3] The best application of Rudé's ideas to the coming of the American Revolution is Wood, "Note on Mobs," cited in note 1. For a different view of "mobs" in the Revolution, see Lloyd Rudolph, "The Eighteenth-Century Mob in America and Europe, *America Quarterly,* XI (1959), 447-59.

[4] Tilly, "Collective Violence in European Perspective," 16.

[5] Thompson, *Making of the English Working Class,* 68.

[6] In reality, this break was not so abrupt as this sketch implies. See, for example, Hobsbawm, *Primitive Rebels,* for the survival of archaic forms of backward-looking social protest.

crucial hypothesis for us in our comparison between Europe and America — that after the triumph of liberal capitalism, the French and English lower orders became a working class. Their organization, goals, and violent tactics changed along with their status. Instead of rioting to regain such vanished ends as the assize of bread, or to prevent such innovations as power looms, the newly-unified masses began to organize politically and industrially to demand their fair share in — or, in some cases, control of — the new economic order. They continued to oppose unpopular policies with violence, but now with a new kind of mass violence, involving much larger crowds who were brought together not on the basis of neighborhood residence or craft but simply by their respective memberships in the new urban working class. Thus the crowd at the Champs de Mars sought not the restoration of fair prices but guarantees of political rights for artisans and shopkeepers; the Chartists defended neither "Church and King" nor outmoded handlooms, but rather sought to enfranchise millions of English workers. Violence by both working people and the state went hand in hand with union organization, strikes, and mass political agitation. And indeed, the more the dominant capitalist state used force against working-class organization, the more it encouraged working-class unity. For the English historians, then, resistance to authority was an indicator not only of changes in the economic and social structure, but of the emergence of working-class consciousness as well.[7]

Does this European schema apply to Jacksonian Philadelphia? Chronologically, in the two decades between 1830 and 1850, the city passed from its pre-industrial to an early industrial stage.[8] Factories and machines invaded such Philadelphia industries as textiles, clothing, and shoemaking, while they created others like machine tool and locomotive manufacture. These innovations led to dislocations and unemployment, especially among portions of the city's skilled artisan community. Philadelphia craftsmen had a reputation for turbulence, and when the factory system and machine production directly threatened their livelihoods such men did not passively accept these industrial innovations. Several times in this period violent strikes disturbed the city's peace. At the same time, Philadelphia's commerce was drawn by the new canal and railroad network into the emerging national market for food and manufactures. In this competition for outlets, New York took a predominant commercial posi-

---

[7] This point is made explicit by Rudé, *Crowd in History*, 234.

[8] For a description of Philadelphia's industrial transformation, see Sam Bass Warner, Jr., *Private City: Philadelphia in Three Periods of Its Growth* (Philadelphia, 1968), ch. iv.

tion, while inland centers such as Buffalo and Cincinnati grew up at Philadelphia's expense. By the Jacksonian era, Philadelphia's trade was losing ground to other ports while cheap manufactures from New England flooded her shops.[9]

Between 1830 and 1850, Philadelphia's economy was generally in poor shape, a condition that only exacerbated the social tensions growing out of non-economic conflicts among various groups in the city. To name just one problem, there was the race issue. Since Philadelphia bordered on the Upper South, it attracted significant numbers of free blacks and runaway slaves, much to the dismay of many white Philadelphians. Similarly, as a port-of-call for Atlantic traders, Philadelphia also received a steady flow of South Irish peasants, many before 1846, but a veritable flood after the potato famine struck in full force. Blacks and Irishmen in particular did not mix well with each other or with the native white population.

The period's economic and demographic strains were reflected in episodes of collective violence — the Jacksonian decades were the most turbulent in Philadelphia's history. To mention only the city's dozen or so largest riots in chronological order, natives fought Irish weavers in 1828, blacks fought whites in August 1834, and again in July 1835, and a turbulent dockworkers' strike took place that same year. Eighteen thirty-five was also notable for an incident in which a "respectable" crowd dumped abolitionist literature into the Delaware River. This action foreshadowed the burning of abolitionist-built Pennsylvania Hall in May 1838. On the same night the hall was destroyed, a crowd also attacked the Friends' Shelter for Colored Orphans. Two years later, in June 1840, residents of Front Street, Kensington (in what is now North Philadelphia), rioted to prevent the construction of a railroad on their neighborhood streets, and continued to riot off and on for two years until the project was finally abandoned. The summer and fall of 1842 witnessed an Irish attack on black temperance marchers, followed by a protracted and often violent Irish handloom-weavers' strike. The strikers were bold enough to attack a *posse* and severely manhandle the sheriff. This flood of violence peaked in the great riots of 1844 that pitted Irish Catholics against native Protestants, most of them skilled artisans. The fighting occurred in two stages, the first in May, the second in July 1844. At least thirty were killed, an equal number seriously wounded, and scores more

---

[9] For the impact of "internal improvements" and their relationship to industrialization, see George Rogers Taylor, *The Transportation Revolution* (New York, 1951) chs. ii, x-xiii.

hurt. In the July episode, the nativists even fought a pitched cannon battle with a State militia company. In 1849, an election riot turned into a full-scale race war known as the "California House" riot. In addition to all this major bloodletting, Jacksonian Philadelphia was also plagued by a near-constant scourge of increasingly brutal firemen's fights and gang wars. The gangs and fire boys had become so regularly disruptive by the mid-1840's that the Philadelphia *Public Ledger* took special pains to announce one Monday, with both irony and relief, that the previous day had actually been a *"Quiet Sunday."* A Sabbath had finally passed without the fireboys running to false alarms that they had set themselves in hopes of clashing with a rival company.[10]

Much of this disorder follows closely the standard European pre-industrial behavior patterns described by Rudé, Tilly, Hobsbawm, *el al.* According to Rudé, the hallmark of a European pre-industrial "mob," contrary to the very connotations of that term, was its restraint. Crowds proceeded with "remarkable single-mindedness and discriminating purposefulness." They rioted for "precise objects and rarely engaged in indiscriminate attacks on either property or persons." Most attacks were in fact limited to property, and when directed at persons rarely produced fatalities. While there was sometimes bloodshed, Rudé notes, "it was authority, rather than the crowd that was conspicuous for its violence to life and limb."[11] Collective violence for Rudé, as well as for Tilly, Hobsbawm, Thompson, and many others, was less an irrational outburst of emotion than a consciously chosen form of protest against governmental policies or social conditions. Riots were intended as a means for the politically powerless to express limited and well-defined protest, and were not intended to injure persons gratuitously.

This pattern of goal-oriented violence marked by restraint clearly characterized the Philadelphia handloom weavers' strike of 1842. It presented a classic example of what Eric Hobsbawm has called "collective bargaining by riot."[12] The striking weavers used machine breaking, intimidation, destruction of unwoven wool and finished cloth, house wrecking, and the threat of even worse destruction for two connected reasons: first, to force their employers to accede to their demands, and second to keep strike breakers from accepting work. Problems in the Philadelphia

---

[10] For the interconnectedness of these riots, see Warner, *Private City*, ch. vii; and Elizabeth M. Geffen, "Violence in Philadelphia in the 1840s and 1850s," *Pennsylvania History*, XXXVI (1969), 381-410.
[11] Rudé, *Crowd in History*, 253-57, 60, 224.
[12] Hobsbawm, *Labouring Men*, 9.

weaving community actually began with the economic depression of 1837, when local employers felt compelled to lower wages. The industry never fully recovered from the slump, or from the competition of New England's more efficient textile mills. When, in 1842, employers lowered piece rates yet again, this time below what the organized handloom weavers considered a subsistence level, they struck. Unfortunately, their solidarity was undermined by the severe hard times in the weaving trade, which meant that many men and their families needed desperately to work at almost any wage, and the influx of semi-skilled Irish immigrants into the industry willing to accept employment at a time when the journeymen weavers' association was trying to maintain solidarity and stop production.[13]

Thus the need to force production to shut down. Breaking into several factories and workshops in the fall of 1842, strikers tried to drive out "scabbing" workers and to punish employers for not restoring the higher piece rates that had previously prevailed. Since much of the handloom weaving in Philadelphia was done by outworkers, periodically the strikers would march with fife and drum to the homes of families taking work from recalcitrant employers, break into the house, wreck the worker's loom and ruin his wool skein, destroy some furniture, apologize to his neighbors for the disturbance, and march peacefully away. In late September 1842, a band of Kensington strikers concocted a scheme to destroy Kempton's water-powered weaving mill in suburban Manayunk which "manufactured, by a much cheaper process, an article of cotton goods . . . hitherto . . . made by the handloom weavers." While the attack was driven off, two constables were wounded when they intercepted the weavers on their way to burn the mill.[14]

Although the strike was to last until winter 1843, these wounded constables were the only seriously injured individuals in over a half-year of strikers' protest marches and demonstrations, loom smashings and factory attacks. The more normal pattern of confrontation between the weavers and either their employers, or scabs, or the authorities was the one illustrated by the humiliating defeat inflicted by strikers on the Philadelphia county sheriff that climaxed their walkout. On January 9, 1843, approximately 300 weavers turned out for a solidarity march in suburban Moyamensing, which along with Kensington was a center of the handloom-

[13] For conditions among the handloom weavers, see David Montgomery, "The Shuttle and the Cross: Weavers and Artisans in the Kensington Riots of 1844," *Journal of Social History*, V, 4 (1972), 412-416.
[14] Philadelphia *Public Ledger*, August 29; September 3, 8, 24, 26; October 27, 1842. For the attack on Kempton's mill, see *ibid.*, September 26, 1842.

weaving industry in the city. As always, they broke into scab weavers' homes and destroyed their looms and goods. When they reached the southern boundary of the city proper (Philadelphia County was divided into over thirty different jurisdictions in this period), the mayor and his police turned them back. Determined to march in Kensington, the weavers gathered there two days later. Once again parading and entering homes, the weavers were challenged by two aldermen who tried to arrest a striker for rioting. The officers were beaten for their efforts. At a rally that afternoon, the weavers vowed to punish any other authorities who interfered with internal affairs in the weaving community. The sheriff arrived soon afterwards, hoping to address the meeting. When his pleas for peaceable behavior were hooted down, he resolved to raise a *posse* and put an end to the strikers' freedom of action.

Returning with his friends in late afternoon, the sheriff met with a rousing reception by several hundred well-prepared strikers carrying bricks, clubs, and guns. A volley of stones dispersed the unarmed volunteers, who fled forthwith. Only the sheriff and three valiant friends remained to face the great mass of aroused weavers, and they were quickly overwhelmed. Knocked down and badly bruised by stones, the sheriff was allowed to escape before he sustained serious injury, save that to his pride. He then called on the State militia, who entered Kensington in large numbers and pacified the area. The soldiers then kept guard in the district while their commanding general oversaw deliberations between the weavers and their employers that ended the strike in favor of the latter.[15]

The Kensington anti-railroad riots, which began in 1840 and recurred sporadically until 1842, also reflected tensions between the new industrial order and older community values. The trouble began when the Philadelphia and Trenton railroad corporation persuaded the Pennsylvania legislature to grant it the right to lay tracks on the streets of Kensington. The legislature aspired to make Philadelphia an important entrepôt for the rail traffic between New York and the Deep South. Kensington's weaving and truckmen's community, as well as their landlords, would have nothing to do with the scheme. The early "iron horse" spewed hot coals directly from its smokestack and would have posed a fire hazard to surrounding wooden houses. Property values in general were likely to drop sharply if trains passed through the neighborhood. Furthermore, tracks on the street threatened to disrupt local wagon traffic, an important ele-

---

[15] *Public Ledger,* January 12, 13, 1843.

ment in the district economy. Finally, there was the very real danger that pedestrians, and especially children, would be killed by passing trains. Despite the danger to life, property and commerce, opponents of the railroad, joined by several Democratic politicians seeking to profit from this David and Goliath confrontation between big business and a defenseless neighborhood, ultimately chose to make their strongest objections on ideological grounds: the notion of political rights and constitutional liberties. "A PUBLIC HIGHWAY CAN NOT BE LEGALLY OR PROPERLY CHARTERED OUT TO A PRIVATE CORPORATION!" they proclaimed. "NO MONOPOLY! FREE PASSAGE TO ALL! . . . THE CONSTITUTION PROTECTS THE PEOPLE IN THE USE OF THEIR HIGHWAYS." In this way the anti-railroad coalition translated Jacksonian anti-monopoly rhetoric into a set of "legitimising notions" that justified their violence.[16]

Behaviorally, the anti-railroad resistance was even more limited — and, as it turned out, effective — than the striking weavers' violence. No member of the railroad work crews was hurt, probably because they ran as soon as the first paving stones were thrown, Once a *posse* unsuccessfully tried to guard a construction crew but it, too, was dispersed with a minimal show of force on the protestors' part. That night, demonstrators burned a local tavern that had been used as the *posse's* headquarters. The crowd may have known that the tavern's landlord was also the railroad's president. After four or five false starts, all of which provoked riots, the railroad abandoned its efforts and the state legislature finally repealed its grant. When the revocation was announced in June 1842, the neighborhood celebrated with two days of fireworks and block parties.[17]

Jacksonian Philadelphia also produced an example of yet another classic type of pre-industrial violence, the "Church and King Mob." This was a crowd that used violence to defend established values from unpopular minority groups whose beliefs seemingly challenged prevailing orthodoxies. Just as in 1780 the Gordon rioters turned on London's Catholics when Parliament lifted the traditional civil disabilities from that group, Jacksonian era Philadelphians almost unanimously turned on abolitionists whose doctrines and actions threatened the city's own prevailing mores. In 1838, a crowd composed of both well-dressed

---

16 Reports of the anti-railroad riots appeared in the *Public Ledger* on March 3, 13, 14 and August 4, 1840, as well as June 22, 1842. The quotation is from the latter date. The resistors included several prosperous landlords and even a district constable who lived in the neighborhood. For the identity of landlords, see the tax assessors' ledgers for Kensington, 1844, preserved in the Philadelphia City Archives, City Hall, Philadelphia.
17 *Public Ledger,* June 22, 1842.

gentlemen and turbulent native and Irish workingmen moved to defend the city from the opening of Pennsylvania Hall, a convention center for the national abolition movement. The anti-abolition crowd that ultimately burned the hall was opposing the dual blight of radical political doctrines and racial "amalgamation" (the contemporary term for miscegenation). A flyer announcing an opposition rally just before the hall's burning warned that "a convention to effect the immediate emancipation of the slaves throughout the country is in session in this city, and it is the *duty* of citizens who entertain a proper respect for the Constitution of the Union and the right of property *to interfere, by force if necessary* [emphasis added]." Even those without concern for constitutional niceties could find ample grounds for outrage upon learning that the abolition convention meeting at Pennsylvania Hall "presented, for the first time since the days of William Penn, the unusual union of black and white walking arm in arm in social intercourse." Since the law could do nothing to interfere with the abolitionists' rights of free speech and assembly, white citizens were "forced" — in their own minds — to defend society by direct, if extra-legal, action. This was quintessential "Church and King" behavior. Yet even righteous anger did not lead the Pennsylvania Hall crowd to lose its collective head: when firemen arrived to fight the blaze, they were compelled to play their hoses not on the hall but on adjoining buildings so that none but the abolitionists would suffer loss. No individual was attacked, not even the abolitionists. The crowd moved with a deliberateness and calm that was striking to all observers. Of course, since they were unopposed by either the hall's owners or legal authorities, there was really no need for the rioters to take hasty or ill-conceived actions.[18]

While the anti-abolition crowd's behavior kept within conventional bounds common to both European and American pre-industrial crowds, the nature of its hostility was characteristically American. The popular objections to abolitionism might have been constitutional and political, but the hostility to "amalgamation" was purely racist. And racism was not an important part of the European pre-industrial tradition. While the histories show that European pre-industrial crowds intensified their efforts as they developed class consciousness, the increase in racial and ethnic violence in Jacksonian Philadelphia occurred outside the consciousness of class. This is not to say that economic factors played no

---

[18] For the characteristics of "Church and King Mobs," see Rudé, *Crowd in History*, ch. ix; for the burning of Pennsylvania Hall, see Warner, *Private City*, 123-37.

role in exacerbating racial or ethnic animosities, for indeed they did, but in America violent ethnic and racial conflict has, for the most part, cut across class lines.[19]

Race wars and ethnic clashes in America have never been limited to a particular economic or technological setting; they appear to be endemic. While they have done their greatest damage within lower- and working-class communities, they have never, unlike pre-industrial European conflicts, shown consistent respect for class distinctions, social distance, or "better" neighborhoods. Philadelphia's native artisans battled Irish immigrant laborers and weavers from the 1830s to the Civil War, at first partly for economic reasons; the semi-skilled Irish replaced skilled native workmen in some of the city's industries. Even after the pre-industrial distinctions between craftsmen and laborers disappeared, however, and both Irish and native-born Americans were merged into a single "wage earning class," the two groups never did manage to suppress their feud. Similarly, poor whites have fought poor blacks at all stages of our history, pre-industrial and industrial, in prosperous times as well as bad, in rural and urban settings, in the North as well as the South. And, again, ethnic and racial violence has known no class distinctions. The American Republican party, for example, whose political rallies led directly to the great Philadelphia Native American Riots of 1844, had a substantial middle-class leadership and rank-and-file. The crowd that burned Pennsylvania Hall was led by "gentlemen of property and standing."[20]

Even though ethnic and racial violence in Jacksonian Philadelphia cannot be fully explained by the European pre-industrial model, it does help illuminate certain aspects of some violent episodes in the period. A surprising degree of restraint characterized Philadelphia's ethnic conflicts. At the outset of the bloody Native American Riots, the nativists on first entering the Irish ward in Kensington to do battle came unarmed. Only when it became clear that they were caught in a planned crossfire did they go home to get their guns. Even when their counter-attack was successful, and they were in a position to retaliate against the entire neighborhood, they only destroyed those houses from which gunfire had emanated, deliberately passing by dwellings of the old, in-

---

[19] David Montgomery, in his "The Shuttle and the Cross," argues that ethnic conflict between native-born Protestant artisans and Irish weavers destroyed the class-conscious labor movement that had been developed by Jacksonian Philadelphia's working population.

[20] The last phrase is taken from Leonard Richards' excellent book, see *supra,* fn. 1.

firm, or neutral. It was the Irish who first broke the city's tradition of not using firearms in collective disorders. Fighting between the Irish and the nativists seems to have escalated to the use of weaponry on a permanent basis thereafter. Bloodshed and loss of life became a much more common feature of Philadelphia rioting after the 1840s.[21]

The pre-industrial model offers yet another insight into Philadelphia violence in the Jacksonian era. The preoccupation of Rudé, Tilly, and others with working-class rioters reminds us that even though there were middle- and upper-class faces in Jacksonian crowds, for the most part these crowds were drawn from the ranks of the city's artisans, sailors, and laborers. Indeed, just as ethnicity and race seem to have become Philadelphia's chief sources of violence, so they became the chief sources of self and group identity for members of the working class. Thus ethnic and race wars satisfied individual competitive instincts and the need to "belong." But psychic rewards were not the only benefit that Philadelphia's workingmen gained from ethnic conflict. The many gang wars and fire fights, for example, also provided an opportunity for physical recreation. Fire fights most frequently occurred on Sundays or in the evenings, when young apprentices and journeymen had time off from their labors.[22] These battles took a form not so different from Eskimo football; each side brawled to attach its hose to a fire plug before the other, or to tip over the other's hose carriage. After all, what other outlets were there for hard-working youths in a city without public recreational facilities?

There were also good "hard" returns to the winners in ethnic and racial confrontations. Control of jobs, housing, and neighborhoods was often on the line. For example, the whites who invaded the black ghetto in 1842 were not drawn randomly from the white population; the crowd was spearheaded by Irish coalheavers who lived next door to the black ghetto. There is evidence that black and Irish coalheavers were competing directly for control of the city's docks.[23] Indeed, in several occupations Irish immigrants replaced long-established free Negroes, driving down the latter's standard of living.[24] Similarly, middle-class

---

[21] For the sequence of gunfighting in Kensington, see Michael Feldberg, "The Philadelphia Riots of 1844: A Social History," unpublished doctoral dissertation (University of Rochester, 1970), ch. v.

[22] Bruce Gordon Laurie, "Firemen and Gangs in Southwark, 1843-1853," *The Peoples of Philadelphia,* Mark H. Haller and Allen Davis, eds. (Philadelphia, 1973).

[23] Laurie, "The Working People of Philadelphia, 1827-1853," unpublished doctoral dissertation (University of Pittsburgh, 1971), 113.

[24] For a discussion of downward social mobility among Philadelphia's blacks in the Jacksonian period, see Theodore Hershberg "Slavery and the Northern City: The Case of Ante-Bellum Black Philadelphia," Haller and Davis, eds. *Peoples of Philadelphia.*

Irish politicians clashed with their native American counterparts in the Democratic Party over the division of political patronage. Around half of the Philadelphia American Republican Party was composed of native-born ex-Democrats who had left their old Party when, among other things, it began rewarding its Irish supporters with places on the night watch and the staff of the public markets in Democratic districts. The native Jacksonians also resented the Party's willingness to support the immigrants on such questions as temperance and Sunday licensing laws, just as they disliked the favorable response that Democrats offered to the plea by the Catholic Church to permit Catholic children to read their version of the Bible in the public schools.[25]

If, then, violence flowed out of ethnic, racial, cultural, and religious conflicts as well as the dislocations of modernization and industrialization, can we find among the works of scholars of European collective violence a theory more wide ranging than the technologically-bound notion that changes in the nature of collective violence in the nineteenth century reflected the transition from pre-industrial to industrial society? In this regard, Charles Tilly has moved beyond the influence of Rudé and Hobsbawm into the realm of political sociology. He has argued that, irrespective of the technological environment, violence will occur when competitive social groups are gaining or losing influence in the political structure. By politics here, Professor Tilly means the bargaining process by which groups divide and distribute the various economic and prestige rewards that a society has to offer. As he puts it, "Far from being mere side effects of urbanization, industrialization, and other large structural changes, violent protests seem to grow most directly from the struggle for established places in the structure of power."[26]

Applying this theory is most helpful in our own case: Philadelphia's working- and middle-class nativists were losing control of the Democratic Party to Irish Catholic immigrants; American-born craftsmen, and even laborers, were losing certain jobs to these same semi-skilled Irish hands or to machines manned by Irish men, women, and children. In the eyes of native-born Americans, control of the Democratic Party, their schools, or their jobs were prerogatives worth fighting for. The Irish, on the other hand, were agitating to remove the Protestant bias in the public schools while struggling to maintain their religious and cultural autonomy. At the same time, despite hostility from the native-born, the

---

[25] Laurie, "Working Peoples of Philadelphia," ch. vii.
[26] Tilly, "Collective Violence in European Perspective," 10.

Irish *were* making substantial gains in the Jackson Party and capturing a lowly but acknowledged place in the city's economy. Seeing themselves as upwardly mobile, if only in a limited way, the Irish identified with, and even went beyond, Philadelphia's accepted hostility toward blacks. For lower-class Irishmen, physical attacks on their black rivals helped them feel equal to other white groups in the city and superior to the numerically smaller black community. This violence also had the added benefit of driving blacks out of certain Irish-dominated occupations. At the same time, Philadelphia's blacks did not passively accept their own downward mobility. When they fired guns at the Irish coalheavers invading their neighborhood in 1842, they were fighting for their jobs, fighting to keep the ghetto boundaries from being blocked by surrounding Irish expansion, and fighting for their dignity.[27]

And what were the respectable middle and upper classes doing to protect their standing in the community during this time of upheaval and disorder? In the 1840s, the merchant, manufacturer, and Quaker elite busily lobbied for a modern professional police force and a city-paid, locally-stationed militia company. In 1844, the two city councils voted funds for the militia company, and after the California House riot of 1849, the State authorized Philadelphia County to create a full-time, uniformed police department. Thus those at the top increased *their* ability to use violence in defense of their property and authority. One of the major themes in American urban history since the 1850s has been the struggle of municipal authorities and their business-class allies to gain a monopoly on the use of violence. The problem was not that elected officials lacked a monopoly on the use of legally authorized violence; rather, they struggled to convince turbulent portions of the populace that all other violence was illegitimate.[28]

In the Jacksonian era, Philadelphia's municipal officials had neither the physical capacity nor the recognized legitimacy to control fully public disorder. Before the 1850s, government machinery was weak, police forces almost non-existent, legal powers severely curbed. When public officials intervened in riots, it was usually (and reluctantly) to part the two fighting sides long after hostilities had gotten out of hand. On the contrary, in the many riots studied by Hobsbawm, Rudé, and Thompson,

---

[27] For black self-defense, see Warner, *Private City*, 140.

[28] For the creation of the policy, see *ibid.*, 155-57; Montgomery, "Shuttle and Cross," 437-39. On government's struggle for legitimacy, see Alan Silver, "The Quest for Order in Civil Society," *The Police: Six Sociological Essays*, David J. Bordua, ed. (New York, 1967), 1-24.

the crowd almost always fought on one side and representatives of the state on the other. Not so in the American case, or at least not in the case of ethnic or racial violence. Often, when private groups fought each other, government would stand aside. In this era, law-enforcement officials served through popular election. Only exceptional politicians protect unpopular minorities from aroused majorities. In Jacksonian Philadelphia, public officials were at all times slow to separate fighting elements among the lower classes, but they were especially slow in responding to attacks on the black ghetto. If they moved at all, it was because the fighting or burning threatened respectable neighborhoods. When abolitionist Pennsylvania Hall was burned, the sheriff failed to rouse his *posse,* and told the crowd that he would not call out the militia. And when the army defended a Catholic church in Southwark from a nativist crowd in July 1844, it did so only because two months earlier, during the Kensington riots, upper-class critics were roused to a frenzy when a Catholic church in a respectable downtown neighborhood was burned. Although a church in the Irish ward of Kensington had also been put to the torch, much less was said about that.[29]

Jacksonian Philadelphia lacked strong or purposeful authority to mediate between groups or keep them from each other's throats; riot thus was easily employed as a direct-action method by which groups regulated their relations. Violence did not replace politics, but rather was a part of politics. Violent conflict was used by ethnic groups to win and distribute jobs or political power; laboring groups like the weavers used it to raise their wages; Irish coalheavers used it to drive black rivals from the docks; Kensington's anti-railroad rioters used it to control their streets and counteract the legislative influence belonging to a railroad corporation; and the anti-abolitionists used their force to purge the city of unwanted radicals. The use of violence was inseparable from the process of social bargaining by which groups measured each other's strength and distributed power and influence accordingly.[30]

---

[29] For the sheriff's behavior at Pennsylvania Hall, see Warner, *Private City,* 134. For the upper-class reaction to the church burnings, see Feldberg, "Philadelphia Riots," ch. vi, *passim.*

[30] For violence as a method of community control and regulation in an earlier period of American history, see Maier, "Popular Uprisings and Civil Authority." Cf. H. L. Neiburg, *Political Violence* (New York, 1969), 5.

"NOTHING ON COMPULSION": LIFE STYLES OF PHILADELPHIA ARTISANS, 1820-1850

5

Bruce Laurie*

Labor historians are only beginning to appreciate the cultural dimensions of working-class life. Progress has been slow principally because students of working people find it difficult to transcend the legacy left by John R. Commons and his associates. Commons and company were institutional economists who focused on the position of wage earners in the marketplace and the adjustments they made to new modes of distribution and production. Workers, to them, were members of trade unions who did little else than defend their immediate and long-range interests by striking or by voting for third parties when the opportunity presented itself. They ignored working-class attitudes towards the market itself, or towards work for that matter, and consequently left the impression that workers are mono-dimensional men obsessed with economic matters of one sort or another and condemned to a life of incessant toil. This paper attempts to go beyond the narrow constraints of institutional history in order to explore preindustrial working-class culture and to examine how and why that culture changed between 1820 and 1850 in the city of Philadelphia.

Philadelphians saw their world dramatically altered by wholesale changes in transportation between 1820 and 1850. Private promoters and the state legislature invested heavily in transportation, developing in the process a network of canals and railroads which linked Philadelphia with New York and Baltimore, the coal region of northeastern Pennsylvania, and interior towns and cities in the west. Seagoing trans-

*I wish to thank the National Endowment for the Humanities for its support of a portion of the research that went into this article.

Source: From *Labor History* 15, no. 3 (Summer 1974): 337-366.

portation developed and boomed as Philadelphians, following their more innovative rivals in New York, introduced packets in the coastal and transatlantic trade in the 1820s. More reliable than regular traders or transients, packets made scheduled runs and merchants quickly took advantage of them. By 1827 they carried more than half the city's coastal trade, delivering agricultural products and manufactured goods to southern and Caribbean ports in return for cotton, hides, and other vital raw materials.[1]

Improvements in transportation paved the way for mass production by reducing shipping costs and penetrating new markets. Manufacturers of textiles, shoes, clothing, and other commodities gained access to the rich markets in Pennsylvania's back country as well as in the Ohio Valley and also strengthened traditional ties with the South.[2] The textile industry, in turn, spurred the city's small but innovative machine tool industry, which was the envy of many foreign observers. By the Civil War, Philadelphia was surpassed only by New York as a manufacturing center.

Rapid population increases and ethnic diversification went hand in hand with economic change. The population of Philadelphia County tripled between 1820 and 1850, increasing from about 136,000 to just over 408,000. The factors which contributed to such impressive growth are not yet known, but it is probable that natural increase and in-migration from nearby farm areas gave way to immigration from western Europe. Ireland and Germany sent the bulk of the immigrants, and the greatest inflows probably occurred in the late 1820s-early 1830s and the mid 1840s. By 1850, the first year for which we have accurate data on nationality, the Irish comprised 27 percent of the population and the Germans accounted for 11.4 percent.[3]

Immigrants and native-born Americans clustered in select tiers of Philadelphia's highly diversified occupational hierarchy by 1850 but also overlapped at certain points. The Irish, who arrived in America

---

[1] On the development of railroads and canals, see George R. Taylor, *The Transportation Revolution, 1815-1860* (New York, 1951), 45-8, 78; Albert Fishlow, *Railroads and the Tranformation of the Ante-Bellum Economy* (Cambridge, 1965), 242-43; and Carter Goodrich, ed., *Canals and American Economic Development* (New York, 1961), 62-72. On the rise of packet lines, see Robert G. Albion, *The Rise of New York Port, 1815-1860* (New York, 1939) and *Square Riggers on Schedule* (Princeton, 1938).

[2] The classic statement on this process is John R. Commons, "American Shoemakers, 1648-1895," in Commons, *Labor and Administration* (New York, 1913), 219-77.

[3] Compiled from United States Census Office, *Census of the United States Population Schedule, County of Philadelphia, 1850* (microfilm, National Archives) by the Philadelphia Social History Project, Univ. of Pennsylvania, Theodore Hershberg, Dir. Hereafter cited as *7th Census*, MSS.

without benefit of skills, concentrated at the bottom, performing the most menial tasks. Over 42 percent of them toiled as day laborers, carters, teamsters, and the like. An equal proportion reported skilled occupations at mid-century, but they were chiefly confined to the most "dishonorable" trades. Many of them had manned hand looms in Ireland and England and dominated this easily learned trade in Philadelphia. Others moved into trades undergoing the division of labor and dilution of skill, such as tailoring and shoemaking, and by 1850 the Irish comprised nearly 25 percent of the city's tailors and shoemakers. Germans practiced skilled trades in the Old World and readily assumed the role of craftsmen in American. Slightly more than two-thirds of them plied skilled trades in Philadelphia by 1850. They had a special affinity for woodworking, tailoring, and shoemaking, which together accounted for nearly 20 percent of their number. Native-born Americans could be found in the most prestigious occupations. About a third of them worked at non-manual jobs, while only 10 percent, the smallest proportion of all groups, were unskilled laborers. They supplied a smaller proportion of their number to the crafts (57 percent) than did the Germans, but dominated the most honorable trades, such as printing, the building trades, and the metal trades.[4]

Most working people resided in the county's industrial suburbs, which formed a semi-circular ring around the old port city. They clustered according to occupation, ethnicity, or both, and lived in close proximity to their place of employment.[5] Indeed, dwelling and shop were one for hand loom weavers as well as for many tailors and shoemakers who worked at home under the putting-out system. For the great majority of the labor force, the shop was not the mill or factory which we commonly associate with the "take-off stage" of economic growth. The average shop size in 1850 hovered around ten workers; the median was slightly less than four. Most of these workers, moreover, did not operate power-driven machinery. Three-quarters of them were handicraftsmen employed by bosses whose sole source of power was the journeyman himself.[6]

---

[4] *Ibid.*

[5] Sam Bass Warner, Jr., *The Private City* (Philadelphia, 1968). Warner unfortunately underestimates the extent of ethnic clustering by using ward boundaries as geographic divisions, despite the fact that ethnic neighborhoods overlapped ward boundaries. See pp. 49-78.

[6] Compiled from United States Census Office, *United States Census, Manufacturing Schedule, County of Philadelphia, 1850* (microfilm, National Archives). Hereafter cited as *Manufacturing Census*, MSS.

Even without the aid of mechanization this emerging capitalist order bore down heavily on the wage earner. Merchant capitalists captured mass markets by contracting with buyers in distant markets and with producers in Philadelphia. Most of these producers were small employers who increased productivity by closely supervising teams of highly specialized workers and by slashing piece rates at every opportunity. Master shoemakers cut the rates on first-rate boots from $2.75 to $1.12 a pair, and reduced the scale on "cheap work" 30 percent in the late 1820s and early 1830s, which compelled journeymen to turn out "triple the quantity . . . to obtain a living. . . ."[7] Some employers compounded this insult by demanding better craftsmanship without additional compensation, which moved one journeyman to protest that the "improvement in the finish of every article produced by the Mechanic, requiring thereby more time in its production, and the improvement bringing with it no extra remuneration, was in fact a reduction of . . . wages. . . ."[8] Carpet weavers lodged a similar protest in 1836, staging a strike when offered an advance in rates to weave a new design. The new pattern required "extra work," and the "extra labor required reduced the quantity each could turn out," which cancelled the advance.[9]

The response of these wage earners to such exploitation in the 1830s has been well charted. It is now common knowledge that between 1834 and 1839 all manner of wage earner — skilled and unskilled, native-born and foreign-born — formed trade unions and joined together under the aegis of the General Trades' Union of the City and County of Philadelphia in protest against low wages and excessive toil. The Trades' Union reached its membership peak in 1836 when it represented over fifty unions and 10,000 workers, but it is best remembered for the general strike of the previous summer. In early June carpenters and shoemakers affiliated with the Trades' Union dropped their tools and joined day laborers on strike for a ten-hour day. Bearing signs with the slogan "6 to 6," they paraded through Philadelphia, attracting supporters along the way. Within a week the cause spread to every conceivable trade, including factory hands, and thereby produced the first general strike in our history. Such unprecedented solidarity convinced most employers and the city council to grant a ten-hour day.[10]

---

[7] *Pennsylvanian*, April 4, 1834. All newspapers cited were published in Philadelphia.

[8] Letter signed "SHERMAN," *United States Gazette*, Apr. 2, 1836. Hereafter cited as *U.S.G.*

[9] *Public Ledger*, December 1, 1836. Hereafter cited as *P.L.*

[10] Leonard Bernstein, "The Working People of Philadelphia from Colonial Times to the General Strike of 1835," *Pennsylvania Magazine of History and Biography*, LXXIV

For most workers, however, the general strike proved to be a pyrrhic victory. The devastating depression of 1837 depleted the ranks of many trade unions and destroyed others, leaving workers defenseless against employers determined to restore the long work day. Millowners imposed longer hours when prosperity resumed,[11] and those who did not do so accomplished the same result by cutting piece rates. One of their victims complained in 1849 that "almost every pursuit of labor, has within ten or fifteen years . . . been shorn of from one-third to one-half of its former gains; or where the rates remain nominally the same, instability of employment . . . has produced the same effect; though in a majority of cases, an actual reduction of rates is the active cause."[12] Numerous artisans pointed out the obvious consequence of plummeting piece rates, namely a longer workday to compensate for their loss and more intensive pace of work.[13]

Yet these same wage earners complained about unemployment as bitterly as they complained about overwork. They repeatedly lamented the days, weeks, and even months spent jobless or in search of work, though historians have been more attentive when they protested against excessive toil, perhaps because such protests normally precede or accompany dramatic events which make for exciting reading.[14] This oversight is unfortunate, since it has encouraged a narrow view of working-class experience.

A number of factors contributed to sporadic employment, one of which was the nature of the transportation system. The very system which made mass production and its consequences possible also contributed to slack times. The "Transportation Revolution" may have penetrated new markets, but it did not reduce irregularities and discontinuities in supply and demand. Delays, spoilage, and loss of goods plagued Penn-

(July 1950), 322-39 and William A. Sullivan, *The Industrial Worker in Pennsylvania, 1800-1840* (Harrisburg, 1955), esp. 133-36.

[11] *Pennsylvanian,* July 17, 20, 1848.

[12] Letter signed "A REFLECTING OPERATIVE," *Spirit of the Times,* October 9, 1849. Hereafter cited as *S.T.*

[13] On tailors, see *P.L.* Mar. 15, 1844; on shoemakers, see letter signed, "ONE OF THE CRAFT," *ibid.,* March 25, 1850; and on construction workers, see *ibid.,* July 31, 1850.

[14] See, for example, letter of saddlers, *Pennsylvanian* July 30, 1835; letter marble cutters, *ibid.,* November 3, 1835; letter of house carpenters, *ibid.,* March 21, 1836; letter of plasterers, *P.L.* July 31, 1850; and letter of G. W. Heilig, *American Banner,* September 21, 1850. Hereafter cited as *A.B.* Even millhands, who experienced more regimentation than any group of workers, complained about slack times. See letter signed, "A Jeffersonian American Working-Man," *Germantown Telegraph,* September 18, 1833. English labor historians have been more attentive to this issue. See E.J. Hobsbawm, "The British Standard of Living, 1790-1850," in *Labouring Men* (Garden City, 1964) 75-121 and E.P. Thompson, *The Making of the English Working Class* (New York, 1964), 234-68.

sylvania's canals. The Main Line, which connected Philadelphia with Pittsburgh by a series of canals, railroads, and a motorized inclined plane, angered merchants and manufacturers because of high costs and delays caused by bottlenecks at transshipment points as well as by excessive lockage on waterways. Some of them grew so frustrated that they preferred to use the Erie Canal, despite the inconvenience of shipping through New York City. Others gave up on the Main Line and moved to New York to take even greater advantage of the Erie.[15]

Railroads conquered the weather but little else. Lines that employed steam engines were so beset by breakdowns that they kept teams of horses in reserve. Service improved with advances in steam engines, but many problems remained. Faulty track, poor scheduling, and plain carelessness caused repeated wrecks and derailments, giving antebellum railroads a "nightmarish quality." Connections between different lines were lacking because competitors refused to adopt a standard gauge. The Pennsylvania and Ohio lines had seven distinct gauges, which inspired contemporaries to dub their rivalry the "war of gauges."[16]

Coastal packets offered the most dependable mode of shipment, but they had their own drawbacks. They made scheduled sailings only during the "season," which stretched from early fall to late spring. Shippers cut back in summer, transferring some craft to the transatlantic run and sending others northward or southward only when guaranteed adequate cargo. Coastal packets therefore resembled ordinary traders in the warm months when they were governed by profits rather than schedules. Merchants and manufacturers sometimes waited months for an arrival.[17]

The capriciousness of these transportation facilities may well have aggravated the nagging problem of erratic deliveries of goods.[18] Such unpredictable deliveries inevitably made work itself unpredictable and helped shape the work habits of artisans. Wage earners could expect fairly steady employment when markets were good and raw materials available, but faced frequent lay offs when raw materials failed to arrive on time, if at all. This was the assessment of an Englishman who spent part of a tour of America toiling in a hatter's shop. He reported that journeymen anticipated being laid off when they exhausted the supply of fur and leather. Rather than spread the work by slowing down, how-

---

15 Goodrich, *Canals,* 228, 240. See also, Ralph D. Gray, *The National Waterway* (Carbondale, Ill., 1967), 134.
16 Thomas C. Cochran, "Business Organization and the Development of an Industrial Discipline," in Harold F. Williamson, *The Growth of the American Economy* (New York, 1944), 312. Fishlow, *Railroads,* 8.
17 Albion, *Riggers,* 65-7, 69.
18 Stanley Lebergott, *Manpower in Economic Growth* (New York, 1965), 143, 241-53.

ever, the more experienced hands made hats as quickly as possible in order to garner enough money to tide them through the impending lay off.[19] In slack times hatters and other journeymen either left the city to search for work elsewhere or took whatever employment they could find. Many shoemakers and tailors found temporary employment in repair work or day labor; some hand-loom weavers were so accustomed to shifting into casual labor during periodic downturns that they considered themselves weavers/laborers.[20]

Winter months were unusually trying. Frozen waterways curtailed trade and brought on the slack season, throwing journeymen out of work for long periods and forcing them to seek relief from Philadelphia philanthropists who distributed soup, bread, and fuel. Seasonal fluctuations in trade also determined wage rates. Journeymen, aware that the warm months normally ushered in brisk business, negotiated differential wage scales, demanding higher rates in spring and summer. Carpenters, for example, earned about 10 percent more per day in spring and summer than in fall and winter.[21] Hand-loom weavers negotiated contracts twice yearly — in early spring and late fall — and exacted higher rates in the warm season.[22]

The shape of Philadelphia's industrial plant also determined the quantity and quality of employment. The dominant form of business organization, the small shop, was extremely fragile. Owners operated on hopelessly thin profit margins and were so anxious to reduce costs that they slashed employment rolls at the "slightest hint" of a downturn in trade.[23] They kept the best workers, leaving slower, less experienced hands to forage for work or wait until business improved.[24]

Incessant toil, in a word, was not the bane of Philadelpia's antebellum artisan. What really gnawed at him was the combination of plummeting wage rates and the fitful pace of work, the syncopated rhythm of the economy with its alternating periods of feverish activity broken by slack spells. In slow months, the dull season, or periods with

[19] James D. Burn, *Three Years among the Working Classes in the United States during the War* (London, 1865), 185-86.

[20] On repair work, see *Manufacturing Census*, MSS, *passim*. On weavers, see *7th Census, Moyamensing*, MSS.

[21] *P.L.*, December 14, 1843.

[22] David Montgomery, "The Shuttle and the Cross: Weavers and Artisans in the Kensington Riots of 1844," *Journal of Social History*, 6 (Summer 1972), 417.

[23] Burn, *Three Years*, 189. On the fragility of small business, see Stuart M. Blumin, "Mobility and Change in Ante-Bellum Philadelphia," in Stephen Thernstrom and Richard Sennett, eds., *Nineteenth Century Cities* (New Haven, 1969), 165-208.

[24] Letter signed "A Journeyman Printer," *Daily Sun*, August 27, 1850. Hereafter cited as *D.S.*

"broken days," he was on his own, without work or the ability to meet day-to-day costs of running the household. Such times could be extremely demoralizing and may be a factor in the frequency of working-class suicides reported in local newspapers. In the case of shoemaker William Reed there is no question about the cause. January 2, 1845, marked his sixth week without work: "The prospective appeared gloomy, and starvation apparently surrounding him, caused him to seek repose in death" by slitting his throat with his shoemaker's knife.[25]

Fluctuations in trade were not the only determinants of employment. Popular attitudes towards work also figured prominently in the equation, for many artisans who lived in the transitional period between the pre-industrial and industrial age adhered to values, customs, and traditions that went against the grain of early industrial discipline. Prizing leisure as well as work, they engaged in a wide spectrum of leisure-time activities, ranging from competitive sport to lounging on street corners. Many of them also belonged to volunteer organizations, which successfully competed with their places of employment for their attention and devotion.

Traditions die hard, and perhaps none died harder than preindustrial drinking habits. Advances in science and medicine, early industrial change and, as we shall see, the advent of revivalism, eroded customary drinking habits among some sectors of the medical profession, the clergy, and the emerging industrial elite. But the old commercial classes and most artisans still clung tenaciously to older ways. They valued alcohol for its own sake and used it as a stimulant or as medicine to combat fatigue, to cool the body in summer or warm it in winter, and to treat common illness.

Numerous contemporaries report that artisans were not particular about where they imbibed. Presbyterian minister Sylvester Graham found them drinking in workshops as well as at home in the early 1830s and, he lamented, they especially enjoyed a drink in the late afternoon when "treating" time arrived and journeymen took turns sipping from a jug.[26] Graham's observations are supported by Benjamin T. Sewell, a tanner and vice president of the Trades' Union in 1834 and 1836 who became a Methodist minister in the 1850s. Looking back on his days as a journeyman, Sewell recalled that young apprentices learned

---

[25] *D.S.*, January 3, 1845. See also, *ibid.*, June 3, 15, 1845 and March 29, 1848.
[26] Pennsylvania Society for Discouraging the Use of Ardent Spirits, *Anniversary Report of the Board of Managers* (Phila., 1831), 22-3.

to drink while they learned a trade. Journeymen arrived at work with flasks and appointed an apprentice to make periodic trips to the local pub in order to have them filled, "for which service" he "robs the mail . . . takes a drink before he gets back. . . ."[27] This training ground turned many young wage earners into hardened drinkers, inclined to go on an occasional binge. Such workers, said another observer, toil "soberly and industriously for a season, and then, by way of relaxation, indulge in a carouse, often of some day's continuance. The saturnalia, and its effects being terminated, they again return to their former occupations and habits of very moderate drinking."[28]

Employers winced at such behavior, but one ought not assume that all of them were martinets who enforced regulations against drink. Owners of textile mills could afford to do so because they relied upon a semiskilled labor force which could be replaced with relative ease. The concentration required by operators of power-driven machinery, moreover, caused some workers to relinquish drink without much prompting from employers. The millhands of Manayunk, for example, boasted in 1835 that they formed a temperance society "without the aid or countenance of the influential or talented members of the community," for experience taught them that drinking was a liability which tended to "confuse the brain, cloud the mind, and warp the judgment, thereby rendering the person who indulges in them [textile mills] totally unfit to superintend the movements of complicated machinery."[29] Smaller employers, on the other hand, were more tolerant of workers who drank. Reverend Thomas P. Hunt went so far as to claim that masters also enjoyed an occasional dram or two. He knew a young man who was fired on account of "idleness and neglect of business but not for drinking; for they all [including the employer] drank themselves."[30] We should allow for some exaggeration on Hunt's part, but there is truth in his assessment. Many, if not most, small employers were former journeymen themselves steeped in preindustrial culture, and those who did custom work anticipated fluctuations in trade and therefore tolerated irregular work habits. These employers "expected" journeymen to shun the shop on holidays — official as well as self-proclaimed — and they endured drinking, as long as their journeymen worked "tolerably regularly" and managed to avoid getting

[27] Benjamin T. Sewell, *Sorrow's Circuit, or Five Years' Experience in the Bedford Street Mission, Philadelphia* (Phila. 1860), 273.
[28] *Fountain,* February 20, 1838.
[29] *Germantown Telegraph,* May 20, 1835.
[30] Rev. Thomas P. Hunt, *Jesse Johnson and his Times* (Phila., 1845), 11.

"absolutely drunk."[31]

Most artisans did their drinking in pubs, and pubs probably assumed greater importance in their life after some employers began to prohibit drinking in the shop. Working-class pubs had a style all their own. Signs with piquant inscriptions hung above entranceways and stood in bold contrast to the sedate placards which graced the vestibules of middle-class establishments. "The Four Alls," a public house in Moyamensing, owed its namesake to the following apothegm:[32]

1. *King* — I govern all.
2. *General* — I fight for all.
3. *Minister* — I pray for all.
4. *Laborer* — And I pay for all.

Immigrant taverns sometimes advertised popular political causes. An Irish tavern in Kensington, for example, sported a placard with a bust of Daniel O'Connell and the slogan:[33]

'Hereditary bondsmen! who would be free,
Themselves must strike the blow.'

These taverns offered a wide variety of entertainment, illicit and otherwise. Cockfighting, a popular spectator sport in colonial times but eschewed by people of social standing thereafter, prospered in the working-class pubs of antebellum Philadelphia. Cockfights drew either handfuls of fans or large crowds, depending upon the size of the facility. One of the larger and more popular cockpits could be found in William Cook's pub in Moyamensing. Cook constructed an amphitheater around the pit, which comfortably seated seventy-five enthusiasts. He also concealed it in the tavern loft, since cockfighting invited betting, which was illegal.[34]

Working-class gamblers not excited by cockfights could try their hand at games in the gambling halls or the taverns. Policy houses, which operated lotteries, dotted Philadelphia and concentrated in the suburbs. Furtively located on side streets and in back alleys, they lured workers who wagered from "3¢ to 50¢ with the sanguine hope of having this money returned fourfold. . . ."[35] Taverns sponsored games that probably

31 *Fountain*, February 24, 1838.
32 J. Thomas Scharf and Thompson Wescott, *History of Philadelphia,* 3 vols.· (Philadelphia, 1884), II, 987.
33 *Ibid.*, 986.
34 *P.L.* November 24, 1851. See also Scharf and Wescott, *Philadelphia*, II, 941 and *D.S.*, March 5, 1846.
35 Society of Friends, *Statistical Inquiry into the Condition of the People of Color of the City and Districts of Philadelphia* (mss, 1847, American Philisophical Society, Phila.), 124.

resembled "menagerie," in which participants sat around a circular board divided into pie-shaped units, each of which bore the picture of an animal. Each player placed a coin on his choice and waited breathlessly while a pinwheel whirled and designated the winner upon coming to a stop.[36]

Despite these attractions most workers, we may believe, visited pubs for the sake of camaraderie. At the end of the workday homebound artisans made detours to their favorite taverns, where they exchanged stories or discussed politics over drams or mugs of a variety of malt liquor. Outworkers broke the boredom of toiling alone by visiting the local pub during the day, and shopworkers probably went there to celebrate the completion of a task or an order. Most observers agree that tavern traffic increased dramatically on Sunday night and in winter when trade slowed.[37]

Circuses and road shows also captured the fancy of workingmen. Heavily publicized in newspapers and in broadsides posted on fences, such entertainments rarely respected the industrial time clock. Occurring on weekdays as well as on weekends, they dazzled throngs of onlookers with bizarre acts and feats. One of the most prestigious companies that thrilled Philadelphians was the internationally acclaimed team of Messrs. LaConta and Gonzalo and Master Minich of exotic Spain. LaConta captured the limelight in the Pennsylvania Museum when he danced the popular "fisherman's hornpipie on the tight-rope, and performed the much more difficult exercise of saltation on the same rope with a living boy tied to each foot."[38] Less elaborate but equally exciting fare took place in the streets when daredevils or athletes visited Philadelphia. Sizable crowds gathered to watch balloonists ascend or to witness competition staged by tramping athletes. Long-distance runner William Jackson, affectionately known as the "American Deer," attracted a crowd upon challenging all bettors that he could run eleven miles in less than an hour. The outcome of this race against time is unknown, but those who gathered at the finish line had quite a time "gambling, fighting, drinking, etc."[39]

Though fascinated by these events, artisans especially enjoyed pastimes in which they could participate. They simply loved shooting matches and hunting small game, according to an observer who bemoaned that

---

[36] Scharf and Wescott, *Philadelphia*, II, 941-42. See also, *P.L.* May 4, 1836, March 29, 1838, June 25, 1847.
[37] Charles Quill [pseud. James W. Alexander], *The American Mechanic* (Philadelphia, 1838), 12-15, 21-22, and 61-62. See also, *P.L.*, April 17, 1839, September 21, 1849.
[38] Scharf and Wescott, *Philadelphia*, II, 957.
[39] *D.S.* June 16, 1846. See also, *P.L.*, August 14, 1837.

"every fair day" yielded a "temptation to forsake the shop for the field." The most avid hunters, he contended, were artisans who toiled indoors, for they found a jaunt in the fields especially relaxing.[40] Artisans who resided in the same neighborhood sometimes set aside time for exercise by declaring holidays and staging competitive games; hand-loom weavers, for instance, often did so. In August 1828, those living near Third and Beaver streets laid down their shuttles and passed the day — a classic "Blue Monday" — footracing and merrymaking.[41]

Sport, merrymaking, and drinking were also staples at ethnic gatherings. English, German, and Irish immigrants honored Old World customs and traditions, celebrated weddings and holidays, or gathered simply in order to socialize regardless of the time of day or day of the week. Germans, for instance, set aside Monday as their "principal day for pleasure," and festivities could spill into the middle of the week.[42] Würtemburgers once journeyed to Philadelphia's rural suburbs for a *Volksfest* which stretched from Sunday to Tuesday, ample time for them to consume untold kegs of beer, participate in games, and dance in honor of newlyweds.[43] The Irish were also known to set aside Monday for outings in the suburbs.[44] Their national games, the Donneybrook Fair, traditionally attracted hundreds of enthusiasts and no self-respecting Irish Protestant missed the annual July 12 parade commemorating the glorious victory on the banks of the Boyne in 1690. On July 12, 1831, Orangemen marched through Philadelphia and taunted angry Catholic bystanders with offensive songs such as "Kick the Pope" and "Croppies Go Home." Tensions built steadily until the Catholics, unable to restrain themselves any longer, attacked the paraders, touching off a melee which led to many arrests. Witnesses from both sides appeared in court, including journeyman James Mitchell, a perky young artisan who, speaking in behalf of his class, testified that he joined the procession because "all work and no play makes Jack a dull boy, . . ."[45]

An elderly tailor elaborated upon this point. Reclining in a field with

---

[40] Alexander, *Mechanic,* 87. William Cobbett, *A Year's Residence in the United States of America* (Carbondale, Ill., 1965), 205-06.

[41] *U.S.G.,* August 14, 1828. See also, *P.L.,* June 6, 1843.

[42] *Manayunk Sentinel,* June 5, 1874. Although the references to these events are from the 1870s, they clearly took place before the Civil War but received scant attention from the English-language press. See, for example, *P.L.,* August 8, 1854.

[43] *Ibid.,* September 17, 1875.

[44] Irish weddings also had a tendency to keep workers from their shops, see *Evening Bulletin,* June 11, 1855.

[45] *A Full and Accurate Report of the Trial for Riot before the Mayor's Court of Philadelphia . . . Arising out of a Protestant Procession.* (Philadelphia, 1831), 44.

a companion, he met James W. Alexander, a Presbyterian minister from nearby Princeton, who sought their reaction to the 1837 depression. Alexander assumed that hard times kept both men from their workplace. "Not at all," snapped the quick-witted old man, "we are only enjoying the *Tailor's Vacation. Pressure* is well enough, to be sure," he went on, "as I can testify when the last dollar is about to be pressed out of me; but *Vacation* is capital. It tickles one's fancy with the notion of choice. 'Nothing on compulsion' is my motto."[46]

Membership in voluntary fire companies also interrupted the daily work routines of Philadelphia artisans. Indeed, the city fire department enjoyed its greatest growth between 1826 and 1852, when sixty-eight new companies appeared. The department was nearly equally divided between hose companies, which connected lengths of hose to fire plugs and to pumps, and engine companies, which transported mobile pumps. City law limited engine companies to fifty members and hose companies to 25, but the ordinance was a dead letter. Memberships swelled and sometimes reached two or three hundred to the company.

Firemen were fierce competitors. Hose companies fought for the fire plugs nearest a blaze, and engine companies did battle for rights to the prime hose locations. Firemen loved racing their gaudy tenders and hose carriages through the city streets and went to extraordinary lengths to preserve their pride, shoving wrenches into the spokes of a rival rig, cutting its tow ropes, or assaulting its towers. Races usually ended in brief scuffles, but competition reached fever pitch in the 1840s when ethnic tensions polarized Philadelphians and artisans formed fire companies along ethnic lines. Irish Catholic, Irish Protestant, and nativist companies emerged and allured gangs of intensely loyal young toughs, so that when rivals crossed paths riots ensued which caused enormous property damage and some loss of life.[47]

As competition increased, so did the devotion of firemen. An observer knew a volunteer who "work[ed] better after a long sun and race with the P___ and had beaten her, but if his company was waxed, he could'[nt] (sic) work at all and had to lose a day." The most devoted firemen earned the title of "bunkers." Spending the night in the firehouse, they took turns watching for fires from the house tower in the hope of getting the jump on rivals and arriving first at the scene of a blaze. Some of them even

[46] Alexander, *Mechanic,* 66-67.
[47] Bruce Laurie, "Fire Companies and Gangs in Southwark: The 1840s," in Allen F. Davis and Mark H. Haller, eds., *The Peoples of Philadelphia* (Phila., 1973), 71-88.

"delighted in a day watch."[48]

These pursuits and activities—drinking and gaming, participating in popular sports and in fire companies—characterized a vibrant pre-industrial style of life. A number of factors underpinned this style, the most significant of which were demographic and material. First, as Herbert Gutman notes, it was repeatedly replenished by waves of immigrants and rural-urban migrants, who came from widely divergent sub-cultures but whose values and behavior collided with the imperatives of early industrial discipline.[49] Second, and perhaps more important, at mid-century many wage earners worked in traditional (as against modern) settings which, together with the boom-bust quality of the economy, supported sporadic work habits. Those who knew this environment best were outworkers — especially hand-loom weavers, shoemakers, and tailors — who toiled at home without direct supervision of employers and custom workers, who fashioned consumer goods to the taste of individuals and who thereby evaded the more vigorous regimen of workers producing for the mass market.

Outworkers and custom workers displayed traditional forms of behavior in that they made no sharp distinction between work and leisure. Blending leisure with work, they punctuated workdays with the activities sketched above. Nor did they respect the specialization of role and function which normally accompanies modernization. Instead they persisted in assuming the dual role of artisans and firemen in the face of strong opposition from urban reformers who wished to relegate firefighting to paid professionals. It is probable, moreover, that the values, activities, and organizations of this style of life filled the basic needs of its adherents by sanctioning and supplying vehicles for recreation, neighborhood cohesion, ethnic identity, and camaraderie.

At the same time, however, there emerged a competing culture with its own organizations and institutions. Unlike preindustrial culture, it made a sharp distinction between work and leisure and regarded pre-industrial culture as wasteful, frivolous and, above all, sinful. Sanctioning

---

[48] Frank H. Schell, "Old Volunteer Fire Laddies, the Famous, Fast, Faithful, Fistic, Fire Fighters of Bygone Days," unpublished mss. (Frank H. Schell Papers, Historical Soc. of Pennsylvania), Ch. 11, 2.

[49] Othneil A. Pendelton, Jr., "The Influence of the Evangelical Churches upon Humanitarian Reform: A Case Study Giving Particular Attention to Philadelphia, 1790-1840," *Journal of the Presbyterian Historical Society*, XXV, No. 1 (1947), 14-45. Hereafter cited as Pendleton, "Evangelical Churches." George M. Marsden, *The Evangelical Mind and the New School Experience* (New Haven, 1970) and Robert W. Doherty, "Social Basis for the Presbyterian Schism of 1837-1838: The Philadelphia Case," *Journal of Social History*, 2 (Fall 1968), 69-79.

a more modern style of life, it originated not among the working class but with the emerging industrial elite and the Presbyterian clergy. This elite was in the process of displacing the old Quaker oligarchy and included manufacturers who represented the most advanced industries, such as locomotive builder Matthias W. Baldwin, as well as merchants and professionals with investments in industry and transportation, such as Matthew Newkirk, a dry goods merchant, banker and railroad promoter, and the merchant-investor Alexander Henry. Nearly all of them shifted their political loyalty from the Federalists to the Whigs. They filled the first pews of the fashionable Presbyterian churches of the center city, and some were attentive to evangelical ministers like Albert Barnes. Adapting Protestantism to industrial capitalism, Barnes assaulted the embattled ramparts of orthodoxy (paving the way for the 1837 schism), and preached a brand of Protestantism that bordered on arminianism. Such ministers did not proselytize for the vindictive, arbitrary God of John Calvin, but a benevolent deity who promised salvation to all who willed it, rewarded wordly success with grace, and exhorted His people to do good in the world. God thus freed men to accumulate wealth without the pangs of guilt that had tortured the orthodox conscience and He inspired them to launch a moral crusade against sin.[50]

These ministers and their lay advocates did not regard sin as doctrinal error but as moral laxity of the sort displayed by Philadelphia's working class. Such behavior threatened the material progress sanctioned by God himself, and those who crusaded against preindustrial behavior did God's work and their own at the same time. The elite pursued its God-given commission with staggering energy, forming and funding a spate of moral reform organizations, beneficial societies, and lobbies designed to proscribe working-class pastimes and to teach working-class children the value of deference and self-discipline.[51]

It is difficult to assess the extent to which reformers succeeded in some of these efforts, but it is doubtful that they enjoyed much success prior to the Civil War. While they convinced the State to establish a system of free public schools in 1834, working-class parents did not immediately take advantage of it. Parents appear to have more interest in teaching a trade to their children than in schooling them, which may account for low

---

[50] Herbert G. Gutman, "Work, Culture, and Society in Industrializing America, 1815-1919," *American Historical Review,* 78 (June 1973), 531-88.

[51] Montgomery, "Shuttle and the Cross," 423-25. See also, Pendleton, "The Influence of the Evangelical Churches upon Humanitarian Reform: A Case Study Giving Particular Attention to Philadelphia, 1790-1840," unpublished doctoral diss. (Univ. of Pennsylvania, 1945).

and erratic attendance in antebellum classrooms.[52] The elite found it difficult to regulate working-class pastimes because it did not have authority over the police, the principal agent of social control. Each suburban district raised its own police force prior to 1854 from the very population the elite wished to control, and voluntary policemen were notoriously lax in their day-to-day duties. They exerted authority only in cases of emergency.[53]

Temperance may have been another matter entirely. The elite, and large factory owners in particular, found working-class drinkers quite troublesome and equated them with gremlins whose behavior interrupted operations in mills and factories. The "steady arm of industry," went one bizarre metaphor, "withers" from drink.[54] And so the elite channeled its energies into changing the drinking habits of wage earners.

Philadelphia's temperance movement formally began in 1827 when parishioners in the stylish Second Presbyterian Church joined like-minded ministers, physicians, and industrialists and formed the Pennsylvania Society for Discouraging the Use of Ardent Spirits. The Society's name belied its intentions, however, since it soon advocated the extreme position of total abstinence from all intoxicants, as did the Pennsylvania Temperance Society which succeeded it in 1834. These organizations supported lectures and distributed polemics which linked intemperance to poverty and economic ruin and marshalled the latest medical opinion about drinking on their side. They relied heavily on Presbyterian ministers, some of whom, like evangelists Thomas P. Hunt and C. C. Cuyler, rejected arminianism but endorsed revivalism and preached temperance in the late 1820s and early 1830s. Their efforts swelled the rolls of Presbyterian churches, filling the pews with thousands of converts, who formed local temperance societies and affiliated with the Pennsylvania Society. By 1834 the Pennsylvania Society boasted a following of 4,300.[55]

Membership lists of these affiliates do not survive, which makes it difficult to assess their class composition. But it appears that the movement did not reach very deeply into the social structure, except perhaps in Southwark and Northern Liberties where aggressive ministers con-

---

52 See, for example, Michael B. Katz, "Four Propositions about Social and Family Structures in Pre-Industrial Society" (paper prepared for Comparative Social Mobility Conference, Institute for Advanced Study, Princeton, June 15-17, 1972), esp. 7-8.

53 David R. Johnson, "Crime Patterns in Philadelphia, 1840-70," in Davis and Haller, eds., Peoples, 89-110.

54 Journal of the American Temperance Union (January, 1837), 11-13. Hereafter cited as A.T.U.

55 Pendleton, "Evangelical Churches," 29-37.

verted some artisans.[56] The typical temperance advocate of the 1830s is best described, however, as a church-going member of the middle and upper-middle classes.[57]

The temperance crusade of the late 1820s and 1830s aroused the suspicion of most wage earners because it was so closely identified with the Presbyterians and advocated total abstinence. Presbyterian domination of the temperance movement did not sit well with most workers whose religious interests ranged from the popular sects to Free Thought and skepticism and who looked upon the crusade as a subterfuge for Presbyterian influence or for creeping priestcraft.[58] Some workers were offended by the Presbyterian's upper-class pretentiousness; so was Thomas P. Hunt, a Presbyterian minister himself, who accused his colleagues of being "too conservative" and prone to "cast a look of suspicion upon all workingmen."[59] Wage earners, moreover, endorsed temperance, if anything, in the 1830s and equated partisans of total abstinence with "fanatics." Holding this opinion, Benjamin Sewell recalls having had "no objection" to moderate drinking in that decade. "My company all drank, a little," he remembered, "'but nothing to hurt' we used to say."[60] Men like Sewell and his friends were so accustomed to drinking, so convinced of its value, that they could not break the habit — even if so inclined — simply by signing their names to a total abstinence pledge, which the Pennsylvania Temperance Society naively considered "essential to the support and prosperity" of the cause.[61] They needed the encouragement and understanding of peers, but most workers were not yet prepared to lend such support. Sewell, for example, recounts the tragedy of a young friend who signed a total abstinence pledge against the advice of his comrades, who suggested that he simply "cut down." Stigmatized as a teetotaler and chided by his friends, he relapsed into heavy drinking and

---

[56] This matter is too complex to treat in this paper, but it should be noted in passing that Presbyterian ministers in the working-class suburbs considered themselves a group apart from the Presbytery. They received very little support from the Presbytery. See, for example, Rev. William Ramsey, *Diaries, 1822-49*, mss. 23 vols. (Presbyterian Historical Society).

[57] One of the largest societies that claimed to speak for workingmen was actually led by some of the wealthiest master mechanics and industrialists and probably attracted the middle class more readily than the working class. See Albert Barnes. *The Connexion of Temperance with Republican Freedom: An Oration Delivered on the Fourth of July before the Mechanics and Workingmens Temperance Society of the City and County of Philadelphia* (Phila., 1835).

[58] See, for example, letter signed "Obadiah, *"Mechanic's Free Press,* October 31, 1829 and editorials in *ibid.,* July 10, 24, 1830.

[59] Rev. Thomas P. Hunt, *Life and Thoughts* (Wilkes-Barre, Pa., 1901), 300.

[60] Sewell, *Sorrow's Circuit,* 274.

[61] American Temperance Union, *Report of the Executive Committee* (Philadelphia, 1838), 5.

lost his job. So he left for a suburb in west Philadelphia in order to "hunt work and reform," but was told by an employer acquainted with his drinking problem "we have no work for *you.*" Distraught and demoralized, he wandered aimlessly for a few days and then hanged himself.[62]

Between 1837 and 1843, however, a new temperance crusade suddenly developed, which bore little resemblance to the older movement in terms of organizations, constituency, and tactics. It appeared in the form of temperance-beneficial societies which were located in the industrial suburbs. The membership lists of these organizations indicate they were dominated by skilled journeymen and master craftsmen with small numbers of small shopkeepers, clerks, and unskilled workers as well.[63] Their supporters were critical of the older societies, which had "no provision by which all members may be brought together at short intervals" so as to exert their "united influence."[64] Temperance-beneficial societies remedied this glaring shortcoming by holding frequent meetings, sometimes nightly gatherings, not just in churches but in the streets and public squares — or anywhere they could attract a crowd. In anticipation of the Washingtonians, they appealed to hardened drinkers and drunkards, whom the older societies had studiously ignored and who would become featured speakers at temperance rallies, visible examples of the possibility of self-reform.[65] Such tactics yielded striking results. Temperance-beneficial societies mushroomed between 1837 and 1841, when the *Public Ledger* counted 17,000 teetotalers in the country and exulted that, in two months of 1841 alone, 4,300 formerly wayward souls enlisted in the crusade.[66] These organizations did not necessarily turn drinkers into teetotalers overnight. Apostasy continued to plague them, but they did establish a significant foothold among the lower middle class and working class by employing peer-group pressure, eternal vigilance, and the power of example.

To what can we attribute the sudden emergence of this temperance movement? We ought to extend credit to those who pioneered the

---

[62] Sewell, *Sorrow's Circuit,* 275-76.
[63] For example, the occupations of the members of the Temperance Beneficial Association, Southwark Branch, No. 1, were: Artisans (92), unskilled workers (13), low white collar (9), small shopkeepers (8), professionals and clergy (7), public officials (5), and manufacturers (3). The occupations of the members of Western Branch, No. 2 were: artisans (19), small shopkeepers (2). See, *Charter and By-Laws of the Temperance Beneficial Association, Western Branch, No. 2.* (Philadelphia, 1837). This pamphlet contains membership lists of both organizations. Hereafter cited as *Charter.*
[64] *Fountain,* December, 1837.
[65] *Ibid.* See also, *D.S.* January 28, 1845.
[66] *P.L.,* March 20, 1841.

crusade, since some of their converts emerged in the temperance-beneficial societies.[67] But the movement would not have enjoyed such a mass
following without the economic turmoil of the late 1830s and early
1840s. The new movement flourished in the wake of the 1837 panic, the
most devastating and prolonged economic downturn in Philadelphia's
experience. Press and pulpit concurred in attributing hard times to God's
wrath visited upon people fallen from grace and, it is hardly surprising,
the depression triggered a new wave of revivals.[68] Revivalists were especially active in the industrial suburbs, where their protracted meetings
made thousands of conversions and brought hundreds into the churches.[69]
There was unprecedented growth for Methodists, though it is difficult
to determine the precise rate because they suffered defections in 1828
and 1843 which tend to skew the figures before and during the depression. Even with these losses, however, they made impressive gains. Between 1815 and 1836, for example, Methodists enjoyed fairly steady
growth, attracting about 240 members per year, while they lost about
140 members yearly between 1844 and 1850. But during the depression
years (1837-1843), they more than doubled the previous rate of growth,
taking in slightly less than 540 new members a year. This accretion is
probably several times greater than it appears because hundreds who
experienced conversion attended church but did not become members.[70]

The depression not only swelled the membership of the Methodist
Church (and other denominations as well), it also altered the message
its ministers conveyed to communicants. Methodists lagged behind the
Presbyterian vanguard in adjusting their discipline to the exigencies of
industrial capitalism. The General Conference, for instance, did not restore Wesley's ban on buying and selling liquor, repealed in 1791, until
1848. The reasons for this lag are not entirely clear, though we might
consider the fact that the Methodist ministry was recruited from the
lower classes and less influenced by the industrial elite than were Pres-

---

[67] A number of artisans who belonged to the First Presbyterian Church of Southwark and
who endorsed total abstinence in the middle of the 1830s became members of the
Temperance Beneficial Association, Southwark Branch, No. 1. See, *Minutes of the First
Presbyterian Church in Southwark, 1830-1840*, mss. (Presbyterian Historical Society)
and *Charter.*

[68] John Allen Krout, *The Origins of Prohibition* (New York, 1925), 239; Doherty, "Presbyterian Schism," 79; and *P.L.*, May 8, 1843.

[69] *P.L.*, May 11, 1843. See also, Centennial Publishing Committee, *History of Ebenezer
Methodist Church of Southwark, Philadelphia* (Philadelphia, 1890), 112-16; John C.
Hunterson, *Echoes of Fifty Years: Memorial Record of the Wharton St. M.E. Church*
(Philadelphia, 1892), 42; and Ramsey, *Diaries*, XXII.

[70] Compiled from *Minutes of the Annual Conferences of the Methodist Episcopal Church*
(1815-1850).

byterian clergymen. Whatever the reason, the Methodists did not wax enthusiastic over the prospect of a prosperous, industrial America until the 1830s. Some of them then hailed the rise of railroads and steam power as evidence of God's blessing and "man's elevation" and began to attack behavioral patterns that impeded such progress, emphasizing instead "habits of industry."[71] Most Philadelphia ministers, however, showed precious little enthusiasm for temperance or total abstinence until the depression, which they interpreted as God's punishment for man's depravity. Hard times strengthened the resolve of some clergyman to tighten morality and converted others to the cause, for when the Philadelphia Conference met in 1841, it suspended a rule permitting the use of alcohol for medicinal purposes, resolved to recommend "total abstinence from all intoxicating liquors as a beverage" to "all our people," and applauded the "triumphs" in the crusade against liquor "during the past year."[72]

These ministers had every reason to be pleased. They played a key role in delivering messages of total abstinence to the working class by joining together with other revivalists as well as laymen to form the temperance-beneficial societies. Working people who flocked to these societies in the late 1830s formed their own temperance societies, often along craft lines, in the early 1840s.[73]

The revived temperance crusade turned into the first of a series of events which pitted middle-class and working-class Protestants against the city's growing Catholic minority. Catholics perceived a threat to their culture in the evangelical zeal of the movement and began to disrupt temperance rallies.[74] Their activity aroused the anger of Protestant workingmen chastened by hard times and disposed to look for scapegoats. Catholics were the most convenient targets, and they became even more vulnerable when their leaders protested against Protestant domination of the public schools. They objected to the use of anti-Catholic texts and to the reading of the King James Bible during opening exercises

[71] Rev. Fitch Reed, "The Influence of Moral Principle, Secured by Early Culture, Essential to National Prosperity," in Shipley W. Willson and Ebenezer Ireson, eds., *The Methodist Preacher: or Monthly Sermons from Living Ministers* (Boston, 1832), 355-73 and Rev. J. Kennady, *Sermon, Delivered before the Sunday School Teachers' Union of the M. E. Church of Philadelphia* (Philadelphia, 1840).

[72] *Minutes of the Philadelphia Conference of the Methodist Episcopal Church 1833-1846,* esp. (1841), 11-12.

[73] A number of trade-union leaders who were charter members of the Temperance Beneficial Society, Southwark Branch, No. 1 founded temperance societies among fellow tradesmen. Compare the names found in *Charter* with the leaders of temperance organizations of shoemakers, printers, and tailors, *P.L.* Feb. 21, 1842, Jan. 25, 1839, and Aug. 14, 1841.

[74] *Temperance Advocate and Literary Repository,* Apr. 28, 1841 and June 18, 1842. Hereafter cited as *T.A.*

and requested that the school board permit their children to hold separate religious exercises. This emotionally charged issue incited revivalist ministers (who were also involved in the temperance crusade) to form the American Protestant Association in the winter of 1842-43, which interpreted the Catholic request as a veiled threat to "kick" the King James Bible out of the public schools and to undermine American institutions. The convergence of the school controversy and the temperance crusade breathed life into nativist American Republican Associations which had been operating without much success since 1837. Middle-class temperance advocates led by Lewis Levin, editor of the *Temperance Advocate and Literary Repository,* fused their cause with the nativists, drawing thousands of working-class teetotalers with them. American Republicans scored a landslide victory in the 1844 municipal election which proved to be ephemeral in the center city as voters returned to the Whig fold the following year. But in most formerly Democratic suburbs the American Republicans showed more staying power and tallied solid majorities at the polls in the 1840s.[75]

American Republicans did not enlist all working-class temperance advocates. Some of them remained loyal Democrats, but the temperance movement of the depression and American Republicanism shared much the same constituency. American Republicanism, repellent to the Presbyterian and Quaker elite, drew its strength from the native-born Protestant middle class and working class. Such people fancied themselves the solid "middle" of society, bone and sinew of Protestant Republicanism. Their leaders continually stressed the connection between temperance and prosperity. Total abstinence, one of them was convinced, "restores the drunkard to his prosperity, and makes him secure. . . ."[76] Another gave assurance that the cause inspired people to "maintain their *glorious independence,* which has contributed so essentially to their health, happiness, respectability and worldly prosperity."[77] Such claims were clearly those of ambitious people, but American Republicanism was not simply the mother's milk of *parvenus* or of paranoids suffering from fear of domination by immigrants. It was more complex and more subtle than that. It conveyed a strong sense of class identity and what might be called a modern work ethic.

American Republicans cut their teeth on the labor theory of value.

---

[75] Montgomery, "Shuttle and the Cross," 423-37.
[76] *T.A.*, May 6, 1843.
[77] *Ibid.,* letter signed, OLD JEFFERSONIAN, June 17, 1843.

This doctrine, which had informed the General Trades' Union and which existed in the popular mind well into the 1890s, held that labor is the source of all wealth. People created wealth by blending their labor with the soil or with raw materials, and those who did so were considered to be "producers," chiefly mechanics, farmers, or anyone who produced commodities by working with his hands. Those who did not work with their hands—doctors, lawyers, merchants, bankers, landlords, and the like—but who amassed wealth by selling commodities made by producers, by performing services, or by investing capital, were stigmatized as "accumulators." They were drones and parasites, but nonetheless powerful people who exacted special privileges from legislators in the form of bank and corporate charters, land grants, and the like. They were responsible for the enormous maldistribution of wealth and for the misery of the majority.[78]

This analysis of American Republicans allowed for only two classes, and middle-class nativists differed over where employers fit in. A minority, comprised of former journeymen, considered small, traditional masters to be "producers" and, defending them, contrasted these small masters with the ambitious, innovative bosses who squeezed workingmen. One of them contended that a "conscientious man in these times, can scarcely expect to earn more than a *competency*. If more than this is aimed at, man is apt to become the oppressor of his fellows — taking advantage of their necessities and obtaining the fruits of their labor without rendering them a just recompense."[79] On another occasion he admonished, "National prosperity, as it is generally described, (that is, the prosperity of the wealthy classes, or capitalists,) is perfectly reconcilable with a prostrate and miserable condition of the laboring people."[80] Oliver P. Cornman, who rose from journeyman house painter to editor of the principal organ of the American Republican Party, the *Daily Sun,* aped the leaders of the General Trades' Union when, in the late 1840s, he drew a distinction between masters and employers.[81] As a former workingman he was well acquainted with the "soulless men who would grind down the journeyman to the point of starvation and

[78] The most definitive expression of this can be found in the addresses of William Heighton, *An Address, Delivered before the Mechanics and Working Classes Generally* . . . (Phila., 1827) and *The Principles of Aristocratic Legislation* . . . (Phila., 1828). The Maldistribution of wealth was indeed staggering, Blumin, "Mobility and Change." 204-05 estimates that by 1860, 10 percent of the population owned 89 percent of the wealth.
[79] *American Banner,* August 24, 1850. Hereafter cited as *A.B.*
[80] *Ibid.,* March 15, 1851.
[81] Letter signed "SHERMAN," *U.S.G.* April 6, 1836.

drive his family to the point of desperation." Such men were " 'masters' in name [only]. . . ." Honorable masters respected the maxim that the journeyman was worthy of his hire and of being paid a just wage.[82]

Most middle-class nativists, however, found fault only with the crudest, most grasping employers such as those who exploited women and children. They normally praised entrepreneurs and endorsed those who accumulated wealth. Commending employers, master printer H. H. K. Elliott exhorted an audience of mechanics to "Look around . . . and . . . discover in your own city, among those who now have high places, great wealth and much respect, very many who started in life as, and who continue to be mechanics."[83] Master craftsmen, after all, were producers whose honest labor had created capital and "capital acquired by labor," claimed a nativist editor, "is a friend of labor. . . ."[84]

Middle-class American Republicans in fact had nothing but disdain for detractors of employers. They looked upon the class warfare of the previous decade with some regret and imagined their cause as a bridge between employer and employee. Levin, for example, considered temperance the "most effectual means of closing this fatal chasm in our social system, of knitting up those sympathies again. . . ."[85] And while Levin and his middle-class colleagues recognized working-class poverty, they sought to convince workers that their immiseration had less to do with the advance of industrial capitalism than with the crimes perpetrated by accumulators and immigrants.

These American Republicans pronounced accumulators guilty of cultural and economic crimes, each of which caused poverty in its own way. These accumulators had a style of life which bred intemperance and disrespect for hard work and honest toil. Levin thus traced the "rise and prevalence of intemperance" to the "mushroom aristocracy" who "rioted on the wealth bequeathed to them by their fathers, affected to despise the honest industry by which it had been acquired, and by their upstart and debauched habits set a pernicious example. . . ."[86] Levin's colleagues further charged that the same people who led others to ruin by spreading depravity also controlled the vital purse strings of the economy and exploited masters and journeymen alike. Employers were simply the *"agent[s] of capital,"* beholden to the iron laws of supply and demand.

---

[82] *D.S.,* August 3, 1850.
[83] *Ibid.,* March 27, 1847.
[84] *Ibid.,* March 8, 1847. See also, *ibid.,* February 26, 1847.
[85] *T.A.,* September 25, 1841.
[86] *P.L.,* January 24, 1842.

When capital was plentiful, wages were high and everyone benefited. But when the money market contracted, masters had to slash wages or lay off workers.[87] The real culprits were monied aristocrats, bankers, and speculators who had the "leisure to combine . . . scheme and make enormous profits, sometimes without investing a cent. . . ." They also had the "power to elevate or depress the market . . . make money plenty [sic] or scarce . . . gamble with impunity, and even control, by combination and monopoly, the very circulating medium. While they lounge at ease in their palatial mansions, or roll about in their carriages, in elegant indolence and luxury. . . ."[88]

Catholics, on the other hand, threatened native-born workers from the bottom of society. They depressed the wages of honest workers because they flooded the labor market and because they were accustomed to "liv[ing] on less than the Native" and more than willing to work for pittance. Unchecked immigration promised to "reduce" American workers to the level of Irish peasants.[89] American Republican politicians rarely missed an opportunity to raise this specter, but did not object to the Irish simply because they competed with native-born workers in the labor market.

Middle-class American Republicans harbored an image of a Catholic lifestyle at variance with the new virtues of sobriety, respectability, and self-control. And since they measured Catholics by the same standard they applied to accumulators, they employed common metaphors to describe both groups and held strikingly similar images of them. Both groups loved to drink, and "riotous," wreckless accumulators had counterparts among Catholics who engaged in "disgusting debauchery" and "rioted" in the city streets as every observer of the 1844 riots was aware.[90] At least one nativist conceded that all Catholics were not necessarily lower class. Some were aristocrats, others mobocrats. "If the former class, they are generally the profligate gambler, spendthrift or worse. If the latter, they are either lazy, drunken paupers, or transported felons. . . ." The aristocrats, like their American counterparts, spent their life in "riotous living"; the others were a "riotous, drunken set. . . ."[91]

---

87 *D.S.*, March 16, 1847.
88 *Ibid.*, April 15, 1848.
89 *Ibid.*, March 16, 1847. See also, *ibid*, February 26, March 19, 1847.
90 See, for example, *ibid.*, February 8, 1848. See also, *A.B.*, October 12, 1850 and August 30, 1851.
91 Letter signed, "AMERICUS," *A.B.*, September 20, 1851.

Nor did the Irish qualify as producers in the opinion of nativists. "Three-fourths of the grocery stores, and nine-tenths of the liquor stores, in this country," one of them declared, "seem to be kept by Irishmen." These stores, he emphasized, "are not *productive* occupations. . . ." Irishmen who did find honorable employment did not linger there very long, because "as soon as they get five or ten dollars 'ahead,' we find them opening grog shops, peddling lemons, or . . . in some other occupation which is little better than idleness, or perhaps a little *worse*."[92] That some Irish did accumulate property did not surprise another nativist. They saved enough money to purchase property by "living in mean, squalid, filth and degradation . . . and harder landlords than these are seldom to be found."[93]

American Republicanism, then, can be viewed as the amalgam of the labor theory of value and the revivalism of the depression years. This merger provided native-born, middle-class Protestants with their own sense of identity, a means of distinguishing themselves from the mercantile and financial upper class and the foreign-born lower class. And while it is difficult to distinguish the contributions each of these forces made to the American Republican synthesis, it may be said that revivalism imbued Party members with faith in industrial capitalism, intolerance of immigrants, and a moral code which deprecated moral laxity and stressed sobriety, diligence, and respectability. The labor theory of value imparted a peculiar class analysis of society which located exploitation not in the relationship between employer and employee but in the relationship between producers and accumulators. The synthesis of these forces, in turn, offered a multi-causal analysis of the plight of producers. That is, workers were impoverished because they did not work hard enough and because immigrants depressed wages. And all producers — journeymen and masters — were not justly rewarded because of the machinations of accumulators.

At first glance it appears that native-born wage earners accepted this analysis. In 1845, for example, a handful of skilled workers and master mechanics met at the Jefferson Temperance Hall and formed the Order of United American Mechanics (U.A.M.), which quickly established branches throughout the county. Membership was limited to native-born producers — masters and journeymen — who upheld the new respecta-

[92] *Ibid.,* August 30, 1851.
[93] Letter signed "B.B.," *D.S.,* February 4, 1848.
[94] Order of United American Mechanics, *Journal of the State Council* (Philadelphia, 1845-53), 3, 254-55. Hereafter cited as *Journal.*

bility by pledging to honor "Honesty, Industry, and Sobriety," and by listening attentively to lectures on how to save money and to accumulate property. Ostensibly a fraternal-beneficial organization, the U.A.M. sponsored a funeral fund and paid benefits to members too ill to work.[94] It also vowed to employ "every honorable means to obtain a 'fair day's wage for a fair day's work' " so that workers could "support themselves and their families in comfort and respectability . . ." and "accumulate a sufficient sum, during many months of toil, to support and sustain them through the mischances and mishaps of a 'rainy day'. . . ."[95] The U.A.M. thus put pressure on employers to hire native-born Americans only and encouraged consumers to patronize American craftsmen and to boycott business owned by foreigners in the hope that American employers would increase their businesses and then pay better wages.[96] But higher wages alone did not guarantee that journeymen would live a respectable life. So members policed one another's morality to guarantee that they did not engage in dissipation, reporting cases of intemperance and frivolity and visiting those who claimed eligibility for welfare payments — in order to make sure that they did not feign illness. Members found guilty of immoral conduct were either reprimanded or expelled.[97]

Like most other nativist organizations, the U.A.M. assumed that employers and employees had common interests, that journeymen did not have interests peculiar to them as a class. But the model nativist worker who joined a temperance society, belonged to the U.A.M., and voted for or held membership in the American Republican party was also likely to be a militant working-class spokesman. Leaders of unions of house carpenters, printers, shoemakers, saddlers, and other trades belonged to both organizations.[98] They firmly believed the labor theory, but unlike their middle-class coreligionists, they endorsed the corollary that the wage earner was entitled to the full product of his labor. Precisely what they meant by this remains somewhat of a mystery. But it clearly implied that wage earners had rights to what *they* produced and were entitled to wages sufficient to support themselves and their families in dignity and respectability. This theory, moreover, armed workers with a principle that distinguished their interests from those of employers.

American Republican wage earners, consequently, found themselves

95 *A.B.*, June 1, 1850.
96 *Ibid.*, and *Journal*, 254-55.
97 *Journal, passim.*
98 Bruce Laurie, "The Working People of Philadelphia, 1827-1853," unpublished doctoral diss. (Univ. of Pittsburgh, 1971), Appendix C.

pursuing the illusory goal of aspiring to a respectable life style on sub-sistence wages. One such American Republican was George F. Turner, a founding member of the United American Mechanics and President of the Association of Journeymen House Carpenters in 1850-51. Like most oth-er unions led by nativists, the carpenters refused to organize the foreign-born members of their trade until they learned that this strategy was counter-productive: It invited immigrants to undermine the bill of prices which the union had sacrificed so much to establish, and by the late 1840s and early 1850s the carpenters dispatched organizers to Irish districts dur-ing "standouts," as their walkouts were called.[99] One of these strikes was particularly bitter and protracted. It began in the fall 1850, collapsed, and then recommenced the following spring. It elicited numerous letters from strikers to local newspapers, one of which was by Turner. Describing the dilemma of the respectable artisan, he asserted that the "worthy me-chanic" was entitled to "a house . . . on a front street, three stories high, bath room, hydrant, good yard, cellar . . . house furniture, bedding, cloth-ing, amusements. . . ." But the cost of these "necessities" left him without sufficient income to feed his family adequately. The only course of action bringing respectability to the journeymen was pursuit of their class in-terests: "Unite to work fewer hours, and organize and inquire into that system of acquisition and distribution of the products of their own in-dustry. . . ."[100] Carpenters who had failed to obtain the rate advance followed Turner's advice and formed their own producers' cooperative.[101]

Printers behaved in much the same manner. American Republicans who belonged to temperance societies or the U.A.M. occupied nearly every elective office in the printers' union, the Franklin Typographical Associa-tion.[102] They steadfastly declined to cooperate with a union of German printers until 1850, when they launched a work stoppage for a series of non-wage demands and a rate advance.[103] Those who failed to convince employers of the justice of their cause also formed a cooperative. Their leader, George W. Heilig, revealed the mentality of the newly-evan-gelized workingman when he explained that man was no longer content simply to "eat and clothe himself," because science and art "have at this day disclosed an *artificial, intellectual, moral, and social life,* which . . . is as essential to maintain as the merely natural; and, as it is more refined

---

[99] *Ibid.,* 193-98.
[100] *D.S.,* April 25, 1851.
[101] *P.L.,* March 4, 6, and April 16, 17, 1851.
[102] Laurie, "Working People," Appendix C.
[103] *Ibid.,* 198-201.

and exalted, so also does it require a freer and more liberal nourishment."
Printers who worked for Philadelphia's large book houses did not earn
enough money "to meet the demands of this more elevated life, which
. . . is the religious as well as the political duty of every American to seek
and maintain. The *true light* now lighteth every man that cometh into
the world, and *it will be received*. We must, therefore, also be in a condition that will enable us to contribute to the support of churches and other
associations that will afford us the opportunity of engaging in such religious exercises and social duties as may tend to bring into genial activity
our religious feelings and moral affections."[104]

Not all native-born Protestant workers who enrolled in the American
Republican Party and its auxiliary organizations necessarily subscribed
to these values. A sizable sector of the Party, which appears to have been
comprised of young, unmarried men, embraced nativism simply because
they hated Catholics. They adhered to older values and forms of behavior,
shunning the church, frequenting pubs, taverns, and gaming houses, joining fire companies, and engaging in the rough-and-tumble life of the
streets. On the other hand, some nativist workers endorsed the middle-
class version of American Republicanism and became obsequious employees, repelled by trade unionism and radicalism alike. There is no way of
knowing the origins of these people, though it is probable that they were the
most upwardly mobile artisans and recent rural-urban migrants who lacked
the laboring traditions of the city's more experienced workers.

The more vocal working-class partisans of American Republicanism,
however, did not fulfill the expectations of their middle-class exponents
by acting the part of submissive workers wedded to employers by common
economic and cultural interests. Day-to-day experience with entrepreneurs
who refused to recognize their rights to what they produced made a compelling case that "wage slavery" was more responsible for poverty than
intemperance, a glutted labor market, or the exploitation of accumulators. But while they rejected the American Republican analysis of immiseration, they did not cast off the new morality imparted by it. The
irony is that this morality of sobriety, self-control, and respectability emphasized the grim reality; namely, that workers could not support a respectable style of life on wage labor alone. It is also ironic, as Paul Faler
suggests, that this morality fortified workers in their struggle against
competitive capitalism by arming them with a sense of self-discipline and

---

[104] *A.B.*, September 21, 1850.

commitment to purpose. The final irony may be that in employing the new morality in their own interests, they followed the advice of a middle-class nativist who described the ideal society as one which recognized the maxim: *"Act well thy part—there all the honor lies."*[105]

One can safely equate nativist morality with the "cult of respectability," which British labor historians associate with the Victorian middle class and the "aristocracy of labor." The nature of this morality is not in dispute. Most writers agree that it rejected the spontaneity and moral laxity of preindustrial culture for a morality that valued sobriety, hard work, and respectability. Instead, what appears to be at issue is the means by which wage earners became exponents of it.

Implicitly or explicitly, most American writers argue that the new morality was foisted upon workers by Whig industrialists and Presbyterian clergymen who operated through the government and private organizations. While it is clear that these reformers erected the organizational apparatus with which they could manipulate or control their social inferiors, it is improbable that they experienced much success in the period under discussion. The evidence presented here suggests an alternative explanation.

There is little doubt that early industrialization gave rise to a new form of evangelical Protestantism which emphasized the morality of self control. Nor is there much doubt that workers engaged in those modern industries which required the most discipline — textile mills for example — endorsed evangelical Protestantism and the new morality in the late 1820s and early 1830s. But these workers were a decided minority both in terms of their work environment and religious convictions. Most artisans worked either in traditional or transitional settings at mid-century, laboring at home or in small shops without power-driven machinery. Those who produced for mass markets were forced to toil more intensively as time wore on, and some of them may have been inspired to adopt the new morality. But trade was also rather erratic. Consequently, the work environment of most artisans encouraged sporadic work habits, not steady application to work. And precious few artisans, or Methodist clergymen, found the new morality appealing prior to the depression of 1837.

The chilling effect of hard times appears to have changed their attitudes dramatically. The depression expedited the conversion of Methodist divines to the new morality and made the lower middle class as well

---

[105] *Ibid.*, April 19, 1851.

as the upper echelon of the working class receptive to it. Methodists and New School Presbyterians in the industrial suburbs struck a resonant chord among these elements in the social strata when they claimed that the depression was inflicted by a God of wrath, angered over the moral depravity of man. They converted thousands of Philadelphians to the new morality, which gained political salience in the American Republican party and its auxiliary organizations. Nativism, then, was the means by which many artisans registered their commitment to a more modern work ethic, and those who converted them were not the elite and its clergy but their own clergy and that of the lower middle class.

Just as preindustrial culture filled the needs of its adherents, so nativism catered to the needs of its followers. It offered both the lower middle class and the upper level of the working class a coherent and seemingly credible explanation for their plight, which the rigors of hard times and the strain of industrial change had brought. It enabled them to assert their dignity and sense of self-worth. It held out prospect of prosperity and worldly success to those who would shun drink, the gaming room, and moral laxity in favor of sobriety and self-discipline. It promised to eliminate class conflict by uniting employers and employees on cultural issues.

Yet nativism fell short of being this cement for masters and journeymen. Those who were native born were, to be sure, united at the polls and in various nativist organizations, but parted ways over divisive class issues in the work shop. Journeymen mediated nativism through values which proclaimed their right to the full product of their labor.[106] Grafting nativist morality onto this formula they emerged as militant spokesmen for their class.

[106] See, for example, R. Q. Gray, "Styles of Life, the 'Labour Aristocracy,' and Class Relations in Later Nineteenth Century Edinburgh," *International Review of Social History* 18, pt. 3 (1973), 428-52.

CULTURAL ASPECTS OF THE INDUSTRIAL REVOLUTION: LYNN, MASSACHUSETTS, SHOEMAKERS AND INDUSTRIAL MORALITY, 1826-1860*

6

Paul Faler

Industrialization is usually described in connection with machinery, factories and workers; or, when considered as a part of labor history, changes in wages, hours, and working conditions. Undeniably, all are crucial aspects. But what of the social and cultural side? The industrial revolution, after all, was more than a series of economic changes in the means of production. It was revolutionary as well in its transformation of traditional society; scarcely any part of the old order escaped its impact. Its cultural dimension is more easily grasped if one keeps in mind an earlier but now seldom used definition of industry—the earnest and constant attention to work. This ethic spills over into the social life of those who took it up.

The cultural aspects of life in Lynn, Massachusetts, is the subject of this study. For Lynn's inhabitants, most of them shoemakers and their families, industrialization meant inner discipline and a tightening up of the moral code through either the abolition or drastic alteration of those customs, traditions, and practices that interfered with productive labor. More than ever before, life became oriented toward work. The objective was an orderly society, a "minature likeness of a well-regulated republic," as one Lynn reformer described it. Citizens would be self-reliant, hard-working, and sober; obedient to their superiors; attentive to their labors; and self-disciplined in all their pursuits. A new morality based on the para-

---

* An earlier version of this paper was prepared for the meeting of the Organization of American Historians in Chicago on April 11-14, 1973.

Source: From *Labor History* 15, no. 3 (Summer 1974): 367-394.

mount importance of work was taking shape, an industrial morality that was the cultural expression of the industrial revolution.

Industrial morality was not, as some have suggested, a product of the factory alone. The application of the work ethic in Lynn began long before the 1860s, when machinery and factories first appeared. The shoemakers were handworkers then, not factory operatives. The workplace was the shop or manufactory, not the factory. A cultural apparatus of ideas and institutions outside the work place was chiefly responsible for inculcating the new values.

Industrial morality profoundly affected the lives of Lynn's shoemakers, both within and outside the workplace. This paper will examine several areas of change: poverty and dependency, temperance, recreation, and education. It will also attempt to explain why the new code of morality became a source of discord among the shoemakers and shaped their response to the Industrial Revolution,

Efforts to strengthen the new morality formally began in 1826 with the founding of the Society for the Promotion of Industry, Frugality and Temperance. The Society's founders and officers were prominent townfolk, mostly shoe manufacturers and leather dealers, but with a handful of clergymen and lawyers among them as well. Of the ward officials of the Society, the shoe bosses easily made up the largest element. Leading members included Thomas Bowler, Republican town clerk; Micajah Pratt, Lynn's largest shoe manufacturer; Jonathan Buffum, shoe manufacturer, hardware and paint dealer, and publisher of the *Lynn Record,* the community's largest paper from 1830 to 1840; Jonathan Bacheller, owner of a prosperous dry goods store and Lynn postmaster from 1808 to 1829; and two other leading shoe manufacturers, Isaiah Breed and Ebenezer Brown.[1] Among the ward representatives were several of Lynn's 700 shoemakers, 60 percent of the town's adult population, whose support would be crucial to the Society's success.

As the Society's name indicated, members sought to promote values that would foster industry and help Lynn prosper as a manufacturing center. Industry required self-discipline, emphasis upon productive labor, and condemnation of wasteful habits. Industry, frugality, and temperance, if conscientiously followed, would result in savings that would bring material reward to the wage earner and well being to the community.

---

[1] *Lynn Mirror,* December 30, 1826; *Weekly Messenger,* December 15, 1832. For statement of purpose and constitution of the Society, see *Lynn Mirror,* December 23, 1826. A Lynn citizen later estimated that 143 people joined the new society. "Lynn Scrapbooks," XXIV, II. Scrapbooks in Lynn Public Library.

Several officers of the Society, not unexpectedly, were also founders and directors of the Lynn Institution for Savings which opened its doors in 1826, the year that the Society itself was founded. Isaac Story, a native of Marblehead and brother of Supreme Court Justice Joseph Story, was cashier. The directors included Josiah Newhall, a shoe manufacturer; Isaac Bassett, a leather dealer and shoe boss; and Robert Trevett, Lynn's first lawyer.[2]

One group of prominent citizens was absent — the merchants of West Lynn, men engaged in mercantile activities rather than in manufacturing. Theirs was the section of Lynn that most nearly resembled the mercantile centers of the North Shore in which the libertine morality of the eighteenth century was most deeply entrenched. Differing social and political forms emanated from distinctive economies. Lynn was Republican, Methodist, anti-Masonic, Democratic, and Free Soil; Salem was Federalist, orthodox or Unitarian, and Whig. The temperance movement in particular was strongest in rising manufacturing and farming towns; weakest in port cities, such as Salem and Boston. After 1826, rum sellers in West Lynn would be an annoying impediment to that sobriety manufacturing interests desired.[3]

The Society for Industry, Frugality, and Temperance — having 143 members in 1826 and increasing to 450 in 1830 — had close ties to Lynn's religious bodies. Its meetings were alternately held at the Methodist and Congregational churches. Each of the town's remaining half dozen or so denominations—Quakers, Baptists, Unitarians, chief among them — sent delegations, suggesting that industrial morality had taken hold among the Congregationalists and Quakers as well as among the evangelical Methodists and Baptists who are usually identified as the authors of the new morality. The churches became vehicles for inculcating the values of this new morality. Preachers pledged themselves to temperance or abstinence and expected their parishioners to do the same. Beginning in the 1840s, thousands of students from the newly-formed Sunday Schools marched under the banner of the cold-water army in monster temperance parades. Some churches established special courts that tried cases of infidelity, drunkenness, or immoral conduct. Morality and religion have obvious, intimate, and familiar ties, but the link between industrial morality and religion on the one hand and the industrial revo-

---

[2] *Lynn Mirror,* January 20, 1827.
[3] For resistance from West Lynn, see *The Star,* August 20, 1836, October 1, 1836; *Lynn Bay State,* November 22, 1849.

lution on the other has never been fully explored. A brief sketch of the religious revival in Lynn from 1790 to about 1840 suggests the nature of the connection.

Before 1790, organized religion exerted little influence over Lynn's shoemakers. The town had only two religious bodies — the orthodox Congregationalists and the Society of Friends. The former, by 1790, had dwindled to a dozen or so male members, though the congregation had many times that number. The Friends numbered perhaps thirty families. The rejuvenation of piety began in 1790 with the appearance in Lynn of Jesse Lee, an itinerant Methodist preacher whom Methodist Bishop Francis Asbury dispatched from New York City to New England. Making his way across Connecticut to Boston, Lee everywhere met with failure. After nearly three months of preaching in Boston, he claimed only a dozen converts. But the same length of time in Lynn produced scores of believers. Some 108 converts organized the First Methodist Church, the first of its kind in New England,[4] and Lynn would be the Methodist stronghold in New England for a century. By 1850, for example, there were 2,000 members in eight churches served by eight pastors and six lay preachers. The revival broadened in the three decades after 1790. A Baptist church was founded in 1816, an Episcopal chapel in 1819, a Unitarian Congregation in 1826. Congregationalism's decrepit First Church, cleansed of dissenters by the withdrawal first of Methodists, then of Unitarians, suddenly expanded with dozens of new members.

This broadly-based religious revival in Lynn seems to support Donald Mathews' observation that the formation of churches during the Second Great Awakening was "an organizing process that helped give meaning and direction to people suffering in various degrees from the social strains of a nation on the move into new political, economic and geographical areas."[5] Churches lent a sense of purpose and community to a people whose ties to established institutions had been loosened by a quickening of economic activity. But if this is true of the founding of religious institutions, what of their adoption of a stern code of morality that became a hallmark of Protestantism?

---

[4] George Henry Martin, "The Unfolding of Religious Faith in Lynn," *The Register of the Lynn Historical Society*, XVI 16 (1912), 60-65. A hostile critic of Methodism, Parsons Cooke of the Calvinist First Congregational Church, asserted that Methodism succeeded because "it took hold of the doctrines which lay in the minds of almost all men here, and wrought them with the steam, levers, and pulleys of a new engine." Parsons Cooke, *A Century of Puritanism and a Century of Its Opposites* (Boston, 1855), 258.

[5] Donald G. Mathews, "The Second Great Awakening as an Organizing Process, 1780-1830: An Hypothesis," *American Quarterly*, XXI (Spring 1969), 25-43.

First, although suspicion about sins of the flesh has been characteristic of Christianity, its intensity has varied considerably from generation to generation. A rigid moral code, in other words, is not inherent in Protestantism. Methodism is a case in point. Although its founder, John Wesley, had frowned on liquor, America's Methodists did little in the eighteenth, and early nineteenth centuries to reinforce his strictures. As late as 1812, the General Conference refused to censure those Methodist preachers who sold "spirituous or malt liquors." It permitted preachers to sell and consume alcohol, and allowed church members to distill, retail, and drink liquor.[6] But the church moved steadily toward temperance and then abstinence over the next two decades until, by the 1820s, Methodists were in the vanguard of the prohibition movement. Had a rigid morality inhered in Methodism, it seems obvious, there would not have been such early laxity.

Secondly, nearly all Protestant demoninations took an increasingly hard line against alcohol after 1820. The Congregational church in eighteenth-century Massachusetts had amply demonstrated that heavy drinking and a degree of sexual profligacy could coexist with religion. Ordination ceremonies invariably included liquor for the celebrants, and anywhere from a third to a half of refreshment expenses went for alcoholic beverages.[7] When a congregational minister called on a parishioner, he was usually offered a glass of brandy. Congregationalists also seemed indifferent to the fornication that frequently accompanied the custom of bundling. Such practices would be unthinkable by the 1840s. Lynn's moral reformation, however, had secular, not religious, origins. They derived from the pressure for greater discipline and control demanded by a competitive market economy.

To locate the social conditions that spawned the movement for industrial morality, it is necessary to trace briefly the changes in Lynn's social economy.

Shoemaking is essentially a series of cutting and stitching operations. The eighteenth-century shoemaker or cordwainer fashioned shoes from

---

[6] *The History of American Methodism,* I (New York, 1964), 257-258; Charles W. Ferguson, *Organizing to Beat the Devil: Methodism and the Making of America* (New York, 1971), 359.

[7] Robert Rantoul of Salem attended an ordination in 1785 at the First Parish of Beverly. One-third of the total expenses went for strong drink, "which I suppose was not an unusual proportion of the expenses on such occasions. Ordinations were scenes of conviviality to the people generally, who assembled from all the towns in the neighborhood. Fiddling, dancing and various other sports were common." "Mr. Rantoul's Establishment in Business — Intemperance and Pauperism," Essex Institute *Historical Collections,* V no. 6 (December, 1863), 241-247.

leather and fabric, performing each operation with his own hands. America's colonial status along with the lower price of British shoes limited the market for those women's shoes made in Lynn. In 1750, only three shoemakers sold enough of their wares to warrant the assistance of journeymen. Most of the town's shoemakers were self-employed farmer-craftsmen. A limited domestic market thus limited production. But expulsion of the English from this market, recognition of a national economy with ratification of the Constitution, a tariff on shoes imported from abroad, and improvements in transportation combined to expand greatly the potential market for Lynn shoes. Several changes followed to expand production. First, Lynn's residents gradually abandoned farming and devoted their full attention to shoemaking. The worked at their craft under the roofs of specialized structures which started to appear in the 1780s. Consequently, while the population remained constant at 2,000, production nonetheless increased from 60,000 pairs in 1770 to 175,000 in 1785. And although the population doubled from 2,000 to 4,000 by 1810, shoe output increased five fold.[8] Second, women began to be employed. To speed production, cordwainers began to call upon their wives and children for assistance in stitching together the upper portion of the shoe in preparation for bottoming or making—that is, attaching the upper to the soles. Women were soon employed on a massive scale, filling jobs that ordinarily might have given work to the men of Lynn. But trade and shipbuilding in the ports of Essex County had attracted male wage earners to seafaring occupations, leaving openings for women whose traditional skills in sewing garments could be applied to shoes. In the post-Revolutionary decades, then, increased production came about through a shift in the work force from agriculture to manufacturing, the employment of women, and an enlarged labor supply.

During this phase in the evolution of shoe making, the merchant was the dominant entrepreneurial figure. Access to a vast market and command of capital were the twin sources of his power. He supplied Lynn's shoemakers with materials, then sold the finished product to shoe dealers and shopkeepers. The Lynn shoemakers, who formerly worked their own stock and sold directly to the customer, became subcontractors to the merchant, taking their pay in the commodities he provided. If the shoe-

8 Alonzo Lewis and James R. Newhall, *History of Lynn, Essex County Massachusetts . . .* (Boston, 1865), 335, 371; James R. Newhall, *Centennial Memorial of Lynn, Essex County, Massachusetts* (Lynn, 1876), 75, 63; United States Census Reports for 1810, 1830, 1850 and 1860; Commonwealth of Massachusetts, Secretary of the Commonwealth, *Statistics of the Condition and Products of Certain Branches of Industry in Massachusetts,* 1837, 1845, 1855.

maker employed journeymen, the master paid them in kind. This system of production contained a serious defect that led to its collapse. Although the merchant had access to the market and owned the raw materials, he had no control over the productive process. Wasteful and inefficient use of materials and shoddy goods were the results. Lynn's largest shoe merchant in the 1780s and 90s, Ebenezer Breed, complained furiously about the shoes he received from inept craftsmen; "confounded fools," he called them.[9] As the merchant suffered severe reverses, there appeared another class of entrepreneur who would eventually become the "shoe manufacturers." Tough, austere, methodical, and ambitious, they would transform the shoe industry and, simultaneously, usher in a set of personal and social values that eventually became industrial morality.

Like the merchant, the manufacturer possessed property — land, a retail store — which he translated into capital in the form of raw materials. Sometimes he obtained credit from a larger capitalist. Unlike the merchant, however, the manufacturer took command of the productive process by establishing a central shop that housed the sophisticated putting-out system prevailing in Lynn from about 1820 to the introduction of machinery and factories in the 1860s. Depending on the size of his business, the manufacturer's central shop was a one- or two-story wooden frame building. Several vital functions took place here, each performed by the boss or under his close scrutiny. First, the cutting of stock with a minimum of waste. No longer would the shoemaker be allowed to misuse the employer's stock and keep for himself enough material ("cabbage") to make and sell a few shoes on the side. The boss himself or an expert cutter would wield the knife. Secondly, the boss would personally inspect the finished product brought in by the binders and shoemakers. If dissatisfied, he would reprimand or fire the mechanic on the spot. Finally, the central shop was partly a commissary from which the boss dispensed commodities to workers in payment for their labor.[10]

The shoe manufacturers were numerically a large group. In 1832 there were about forty — with the largest bloc, nearly all Quakers, each employing several or more cutters and hundreds of binders and shoemakers. Each sold tens of thousands of pairs of shoes, mainly through their own outlets in the South and West. Smaller bosses did their own

---

[9] For an account of Breed's career, see Newhall, *Centennial Memorial,* 59-61.
[10] Blanche E. Hazard, *The Organization of the Boot and Shoe Industry in Massachusetts Before 1875* (Cambridge, 1921); *"Lynn Scrapbooks,"* II, 15, 50-53; vol. 11, 23. John Philip Hall, "The Gentle Craft: A Narrative of Yankee Shoemakers" (Unpublished Ph.D. Thesis: Columbia University, 1953).

cutting, employed as few as two to four binders and jours (who attached the uppers to the soles, doing whatever fitting, stitching and trimming was needed to finish the product); and then they peddled a few hundred pairs directly to customers or merchants in Boston.

The bulk of Lynn's population was made up of shoemakers and binders. The binders, or stitchers, were mostly women, either the daughters and wives of the shoemakers, or unattached women in surrounding towns. Working in the home, they stitched together the pieces that formed the upper part of the sole and then returned the uppers either directly to the shoemakers or to the boss in the central shop. The shoemakers (cordwainers, jours, mechanics) were white males. They worked by the piece in the home or, more often, in a small shop (commonly called a ten-footer) together with several other shoemakers who made up the shop's crew. They owned their own kit of tools but depended on the boss for lasts and leather. Most of the shoemakers were native born, having grown up in Lynn or migrated to the town from the hard-pressed farming areas of eastern Massachusetts, southern Maine, or New Hampshire. The heavy influx of Irish immigrants tended to bypass Lynn in favor of the port cities and textile factory towns. They made up only 9 percent of the town's population in 1850 and 15 percent in 1860. By 1860, approximately 10 percent of Lynn's shoemakers were Irish. Of the 840 shoemakers in Lynn in 1832, 56 percent were born in town. By 1860, however, the natives accounted for only 25 percent, the majority now being immigrants from elsewhere in New England.[11]

Lynn's putting-out system lacked machinery and factories, but the town itself resembled an immense manufactory, a coordinated mechanism of interrelated parts — morocco leather dressers and dealers, manufacturers and cutters, binders and shoemakers — each performing a specialized task necessary for completion of the finished product.

The architects and directors of the putting-out system were the manufacturers. They were, to repeat, the first to adopt the values that made up the new industrial morality. Hardworking, self-reliant, resourceful and shrewd, they were a tough and hardy breed. Their qualities of character had been forged and tempered in the market place. The formula for business success and personal fulfillment was simple: it combined prudence,

---

[11] Barbara M. Solomon, "The Growth of the Population in Essex County, 1850-1860," Essex Institute *Historical Collections*, LIXV (1959), 82-103. Samples of 100 shoemakers from *Lynn Directories* of 1832, 1851, and 1860. Place of birth from *Vital Records of Lynn, Massachusetts to the End of the Year 1849*, 2 vols (Salem, 1905, 1906).

economy, and the self-disciplined renunciation of the pleasures of the flesh. Benjamin Franklin Newhall, for one, recalled that he kept close check of his accounts, met all obligations promptly, and as a result reaped both a material and spiritual reward. Success prompted in him a feeling of great elation, pride in achievement, and an inner tranquility that suggested divine approbation.[12] The Lynn entrepreneurs were not unique. A similar process was unfolding elsewhere as shrewd and ambitious young men responded to the opportunities provided by an expanding market place.

About this time, a few miles away, in Groton, young Amos Lawrence began his apprenticeship as a shopkeeper-merchant. He was determined to avoid the "miserable bog or slough" of failure that swallowed up the improvident and careless who had not learned to put "restraint upon their appetite." The pitfalls he identified were the habit and customs of a libertine morality that prevailed in much of eighteenth-century America. Drinking was one of the most insidious and deadly, and the first that Lawrence overcame:

> We five boys were in the habit, every forenoon, of making a drink compounded of rum, raisens, sugar, nutmeg, &, with biscuit, — all palatable to eat and drink. After being in the store four weeks, I found myslf admonished by my appetite of the approach of the hour for indulgence. Thinking the habit might make trouble if allowed to grow stronger, without further apology to my seniors I declined partaking with them. . . . During that whole period [five years] I never drank a spoonful though I mixed gallons daily for my old master and his customers. I decided not to be a slave to tobacco in any form, though I loved the odor of it then, and even now have in my drawer a superior Havana cigar . . . but only to smell of.

From then on Lawrence lived by a stringent code of conduct, his life governed by habits of "industry, economy and sobriety." He learned the wisdom of placing "business before friends," of judging all things by their utility, of "putting down every cent you receive and every cent you spend," of being "accurate," of having "system" in one's affairs at all times, and of eating "the bread of industry and quietness." He learned, above all, that "patience and perseverance will overcome all obstacles." Here in the making was a wealthy and powerful capitalist and the embodiment of a new morality. A merchant indeed, but cut from a different fabric than that of an eighteenth-century predecessor

---

[12] Benjamin F. Newhall, "Sketches of Lynn," numbers 33 and 34, in scrapbook, Lynn Historical Society. For biographical sketch of Newhall, Lewis and Newhall, *History of Lynn,* 570-571.

such as John Hancock: if Hancock can be likened to fine silk, Lawrence was like wire mesh.[13]

John C. Warren, a Boston physician whose life spanned the period from 1778 to 1856, discerned the shift in values that began around 1800. In his early life, he said, "the general and pernicious habit of a morning draught of flip or other stimulant" prevailed. Men of all classes spent the morning drinking hot punch, porter, brandy and water, and eating bread and cheese while arguing and chatting about topics of the day. "It may readily be imagined," Warren recalled, "that a conversation under such circumstances was not likely to be brief, and that no small part of the morning was wasted in this relaxation." The reason for such indulgent customs was that "time was not very important to most men at that period." Consequently, he stated, "from the peace of '83 until near the beginning of the present century very little business was done in Boston. About half a dozen merchants were sufficient to carry on the greater part of the foreign trade; and the rest were condemned to small business, which did not fill up their vacant hours."[14] Quickening economic activity led some Americans to view old ways differently. Entrepreneurs like Amos Lawrence and the Lynn shoe manufacturers were among the first to recognize that the slack and leisurely practices of the old culture were incompatible with the opportunities, and dangers, presented by the new order. Worse, in business self-indulgence would mean certain failure.

Entering a competitive market place that was a continual trial of their shrewdness and steadfastness, the rising entrepreneurs carried with them a conviction of their own personal righteousness. They confidently attributed their success to strength of character, self-discipline and the correctness of the moral code by which they lived. They also recognized an obligation to others: "to whom much is given, of him will much be required." Here was a prescription for social leadership that they exercised with zeal and skill. And in the case of Lynn, they also recognized that success depended not only on their own industry, frugality and temperance but upon like values from those they employed. All were parts of a single social entity. The idle, drunk, and dissolute were a burden upon the industrious wage earners and, unless reformed, would drag all into a "miserable bog or slough." The manufacturers exhibited a

---

[13] William R. Lawrence, ed., *Extracts from the Diary and Correspondence of the Late Amos Lawrence* (Boston, 1855), 24ff.
[14] Edward Warren, ed., *The Life of John Collins Warren*, I (Boston, 1860), 15-19.

mature class consciousness that equated society's interests with their own. Those who gathered in December 1826 to form Lynn's Society for the Promotion of Industry, Frugality, and Temperance intended nothing less than a moral reformation in the culture of an entire city.

Lynn's poor were among the first to attract the Society's attention. That indifference which characterized the eighteenth century view of paupers and poor relief quickly came to an end in the 1820s. No longer would reformers fatalistically accept the view that "the poor ye always have with you." They attacked the causes of poverty which they identified as idleness, intemperance, and lax self-discipline. In the case of idleness, they would "banish it from the world" with a mandatory work regiment. For inmates of the poor house, confinement would become "a punishment and a terror to the intemperate and idle," and would instill a "strong sense of fear accompanied by absolute humility and contrition."[15] Although reformers sometimes made a distinction between the worthy and unworthy poor, the distinction rapidly crumbled in their eagerness to deal with "willful" offenders.

Lynn's poor fell roughly into two groups: those who were completely dependent upon the town for food and shelter, and who resided at the Alms House which the community had built in 1819; and those who were partly dependent and who lived at home but received some support from the town. Aid to the first group was in-the-house relief; aid to the second was out-of-the-house relief. The reformers proposed measures that significantly affected each group.

The slack discipline that permitted Alms House residents to wander the streets and converse with ordinary townsfolk ended in 1828. The town meeting, at the Society's urging, established regular visiting hours; at all other times the inmates would be isolated from the outside world. To enforce its order, the town appropriated $100 to construct a ten foot wooden fence topped with iron spikes. "This is the beginning of our economy in the poor house establishment," the *Lynn Mirror* proclaimed.[16] Overseers of the Poor transferred male inmates from farm work to shoe-making with materials furnished by Isaiah Breed, himself an Overseer, shoe manufacturer, and owner of the store that supplied

---

[15] *Lynn Mirror,* May 5, May 19, 1827, February 9, 1828. The Movement in Lynn was similar to efforts elsewhere to understand the causes of deviancy and dependency. See David Rothman, *Discovery of the Asylum: Social Order and Disorder in the New Republic* (New York, 1971). It is not unfair to assert that the reformers who Rothman studies would have preferred the entire society to run according to the principles and regimen of the asylum.

[16] *Lynn Mirror,* May 10, 1828.

commodities to the indigent shoemakers.[17] In 1828, the town deprived the poor of liquor; $120 had been spent on alcoholic beverages for the poor in the previous year. Although rejecting the recommendation of one reformer who proposed a diet of bread and water for able-bodied males on relief, the Overseers did apply sound business principles, and effectively reduced Poor House maintenance costs to a minimum. All three Overseers responsible for implementing the new policy were Quakers, and two were officers in the Society for the Promotion of Industry, Frugality, and Temperance. Their control over poor relief gave them a splendid opportunity to put their reforms into practice. But without approval of the town meetings that elected them, the changes could not have been made.

Reformers also changed the method of dispensing goods to the poor living outside the Alms House, many of them unemployed shoemakers whom depression periodically reduced to want. Overseers in the past gave needy citizens orders or credits drawn on local stores, allowing the recipient free choice in selecting those items he most needed. But a special committee reported that the poor did not choose wisely. They might buy meat instead of fish, flour instead of Indian meal, coffee instead of potatoes. The town therefore abolished the order system and directed the Overseers to stock staple commodities at the Alms House, doling these out in the amount they deemed sufficient.[18] One reformer also wished to humiliate the poor by publicly posting their names. Lynn's physicians aided the movement to banish idleness by agreeing in 1828 not to attend any family whose head was poor and a drunkard.

Massachusetts also lent support to local proponents of industrial morality. In 1831 it repealed an 1815 law prohibiting the use of cadavers for medical purposes. Many people thought it horrifying and disgusting to have one's body or that of a loved one desecrated by dissection. But the new measure did grant medical schools the right to practice anatomy on deceased paupers whose bodies were not claimed within twenty-four hours. Consequently, this law met research needs and also, in light of widespread opposition, calmed the fears of respectable and self-reliant citizens.[19]

Action to bring about temperance was another outgrowth of the movement for industrial morality and was, in the eyes of its advocates,

---

17 *Weekly Messenger,* March 9, 1833.
18 *Lynn Mirror,* March 15, 1828.
19 *Essex Democrat* (Salem), March 18, 1831. Letter from a "Poor Man" protesting the law, *Lynn Mirror,* February 5, 1831.

the most effective way of insuring diligence and frugality. Before temperance reform began in Lynn, shoemakers and other citizens drank heavily and often. There were grog shops in every part of town, and "it was not a rare sight to witness the apprentice, and even the school boy, laying his change on the counter, and receiving his evening dram." Every visitor was offered the decanter, the tumbler, and sugar bowl as a gesture of welcome. No storekeeper could survive if he did not sell liquor by the glass or mug, and occasionally treat his customers to a drink. No workingman would labor unless his employer provided a half pint of liquor per day as part of his wages.[20]

In the shoe shops of Lynn, many cordwainers drank their daily pint of "white eye" and there were some "who went the whole quart." At eleven and four each day, a boy went to the rum shop with a two-quart bottle for a supply of "black strap," a popular drink of rum sweetened with molasses. The shoemaker who made the best shoe treated his fellows to drinks; so did the one who made the worst. "Every birthday of each operative was a 'treat', every holiday was a regular 'blowout' — and every 'raising,' training, election of civil or military officers, and even the ordination was an occasion for the circulation of the pail of punch." The man who reached his "majority" laid in a supply of the choicest liquors for visiting well wishers. Shoemakers who went to the shore for an outing "would as soon think of sailing on dry land as of having a 'good time' without plenty of punch." Drinking was indulged in by all — ministers, doctors, and teachers as well as by clerks, artisans, and workingmen, by young and old, by male and female.[21] These drinking patterns were part of a preindustrial culture that did not stress self-denial, self-discipline, or the subordination of pleasure to productive labor.

The emerging code of industrial morality gave work paramount place in life. Whatever distracted from this duty of work became objectionable. Lebbeus Armstrong, an early temperance advocate in New York, reported that "the effect of intoxicants on labour efficiency was the strongest argument that could be presented in support of temperance."[22] Temperance must be viewed as an integral part of the larger process of

---

[20] "Lynn Scrapbooks," XXIII, 6. Nathan Chase, a Lynn shoe manufacturer, recalled that he hired carpenters in 1823 to construct his first central shop. They threatened to quit unless he provided a liquor ration. "Lynn Scrapbooks," XXIII, 7.

[21] For descriptions of drinking customs in Lynn, see "Lynn Scrapbooks, XXIII, 6, 7, 27; XXIV 6, 11; *Lynn Mirror,* August 12, 1837; *Lynn News,* September 3, 1847; *Lynn Record,* July 24, 1839.

[22] Quoted in John Krout, *Origins of Prohibition* (New York, 1925), 79.

social disciplining and not merely as a "symbolic crusade."[23] Its connection with other reforms is especially close in the early years, for drinking seemed conducive to every vice — poverty, debauchery, crime, idleness, brawling, civil disturbances — that frustrated the new order. As the Lynn town meeting expressed it in 1835, "the use of intoxicating liquors is the source of more disturbance, crime and misery than all other causes together."[24] Lynn's inhabitants apparently agreed with the Society for the Promotion of Industry, Frugality, and Temperance which had earlier, in 1832, deleted "industry" and "frugality" from its name on the grounds that temperance would insure these virtues.

In the vanguard of the temperance movement, Lynn was one of the first towns in Massachusetts to request a prohibition on the sale of spirituous liquors.[25] An elderly minister from Brookline who had attended ninety-four ordinations reported that one such ceremony in Lynn in 1843 was the first at which liquor was absent and ladies were present.[26] To encourage temperance, reformers used both moral suasion and legal coercion, as well as methods that fell somewhere in between. Some shoe manufacturers employed no worker who drank. "You alone," one temperance advocate announced to bosses, "must take the bold, manly and decisive measure to make all your workmen temperate, industrious, punctual and faithful in their business."[27] Nathan and Isaiah Breed, two of the town's largest employers, also invested heavily in real estate. Owning much of central Lynn, they leased no land to anyone who permitted liquor on the premises. In their own businesses, they hired only teetotalers.[28] Militia captains, agreeing to dispense with ardent spirits, limited their men to cider and beer.[29] Some fire companies, made up primarily of shoemakers, inserted temperance clauses in their by-laws to ban spirits from their meeting houses. Some doctors renounced the use of liquor for medicinal purposes and adopted the cold-water theories of Vincenz Preisnitz (1790-1851), the German doctor who, for good health, prescribed cold baths and a diet that included copious amounts of cold water (20-25 glasses per day) and cold, unseasoned

23 Joseph Gusfield makes this argument in *Symbolic Crusade* (Urbana, 1963), especially 5-6.
24 *Lynn Record*, May 28, 1835.
25 *Lynn Record*, March 27, 1833, for report of town meeting.
26 David N. Johnson. *Sketches of Lynn: The Changes of Fifty Years* (Lynn, 1880), 412-413. Robert Rantoul, "Mr. Rantoul's Establishment in Business — Intemperance and Pauperism," Essex Institute *Historical Collections*, V, no. 6 (December 1863), 246.
27 *Lynn Mirror*, November 24, 1827.
28 "Life and Times of Nathan Breed," *Daily Evening Item*, April 10, 1908.
29 *Lynn Mirror*, May 17, 1838, *The Locomotive*, June 8, July 27, 1842.

food. Young ladies were urged to rebuff courting young men who drank.[30]

The principal coercive agents here were the law and the police. Temperance reformers succeeded in converting the new moral values into a binding legal code enforced by Lynn's constables.[31] In the past, the main task of the police had been to canvass Lynn before the town meeting and read the warrant explaining the business agenda to each citizen. Chosen annually by the selectmen, the constables were not professionals. They received no regular pay, wore no uniforms, and carried no weapons. Their badge of office was a long staff ringed at the top with alternating bands of colored stripes. But their function and composition changed as they were called upon to enforce the new code of industrial morality. In the late 1840s, the traditional staff was cut into pieces to make billy clubs. At about the same time, some constables became permanent members of the force.[32] A survey of arrests in Lynn during the late 1850s shows that the majority were for the illegal sale of liquor, drunkenness, and disorderly conduct, and not for serious crimes against persons or property.[33]

Many shoemakers, adopting the new moral code, altered their forms of recreation and leisure. Perhaps the most popular holiday for the pre-industrial mechanic was 'Lection Day, celebrated in Massachusetts for nearly two centuries before its abolition in 1831. The last Wednesday in May marked the election of representatives to the General Court. Festivities began on this day and continued until the following Monday, though "the entire week partook of the flavor of a holiday." Tame activities included visiting friends, gathering spring flowers, and eating 'Lection Cake, a special pastry made with molasses, wine, fruits and spices and covered with a sugar glaze. There were also athletic contests like jumping and wrestling, and games of chance — pitching coppers, throwing props, and card playing. But these were not the diversions that alarmed the partisans of industrial morality. 'Lection Day was also a time of heavy drinking, gambling, and wild and bawdy dancing at roadhouse taverns. Young men from the Lynn-Salem area journeyed to public houses on the Danvers Road or to Putnam's Tavern on the Dan-

---

[30] *Lynn Mirror*, July 26, 1828.

[31] There were periodic demands by groups of "citizens" for constables to crack down on liquor sellers. See *Lynn News*, December 16, 1853, March 3, 1857, for items on petition campaigns headed by Nathan and Isaiah Breed, two of Lynn's manufacturers.

[32] Henry Fenno, ed., *Our Police: The Official History of the Police Department of the City of Lynn* (Lynn, 1895). The police received pistols in 1878 during a strike of shoe workers. Also see *Lynn Scrapbooks*, XXXVI, 14-15.

[33] For police report on illegal drinking and gambling, see *Lynn Pioneer*, April 15, 1847. Arrest statistics for 1850s are in annual reports of the city marshal.

vers Plain to consume an assortment of drinks — egg pop, beer punch, flip and toddy. Adults paused between drinks long enough to watch horse races on Danvers Plain.[34] In 1831, the year 'Lection Day was abolished, Alonzo Lewis, Lynn historian and poet, commemorated the holiday with a poem describing the manner in which it had been celebrated by towns-folk:

> And is Election Day no more?
> Good old 'Lection . . .
> No more shall we go up
> To see "Old Willis!"
> He has hung up his fiddle
> On the last peg.
> The days of old 'Lection are over.
> The glorious days of "Landee John!"
> When "Gid" used to hustle coppers,
> And the niggers play "paw-paw"
> On Boston Common.
> No more shall we eat 'Lection Cake,
> Or drink muddy beer,
> Misnomered "ale,"
> At "Old Bly's."
> The days of dancing "Suke" are done,
> And fat "Bet" shall shake her jolly sides no more
> To the merry winding about
> Of linked sweetness, long drawn out,
> From old "Pompey's fiddle!"
> No more shall "the Governor"
> Sit in his great arm-chair,
> To encounter the stare
> Of the idle mixed multitude,
> "Black spirits and white,
> Blue spirits and gray,"
> Barefoot and booted,
> Maudlin and merry.
> Yes, 'Lection is done
> With all its paraphernalia
> Of cocked-up hats and fun. . . .[35]

Although it is doubtful that a holiday celebrated for two centuries sud-denly disappeared, traditionalists would hereafter make merry only under the ban of respectable opinion.

---

[34] Robert Rantoul, "Mr. Rantoul's Connexion with Town and Parochial Affairs — His Views of Religion," Essex Institute *Historical Collections,* VI, no. 2 (April 1864), 84. "Lynn Scrapbooks," 1, p. 7.
[35] *Lynn Mirror,* May 28, 1831.

Lynn shoemakers, like New Englanders generally, were also citizen soldiers. In the years following the war of 1812, they converted militia training days into occasions for boisterous fun. They ordinarily assembled once or twice a year, presumably for marching, shooting, and mock warfare. The purpose of training day, then, was to prepare for fighting, but it became a rolicking fall festival, one additional manifestation of eighteenth-century libertine morality. Proponents of industrial morality were understandably hostile. "Scenes of riot and drunkenness" were "disgusting and harmful." "Men and boys in a brutal state of intoxication, and even large numbers of females were to be observed mixing with the motley crowd." Militiamen attracted a large crowd of camp followers who gathered around "the numerous shanties located about the muster field." The enterprising proprietors of these "shanties" dispensed "ardent spirits" which encouraged "tumults and riots." Training day also attracted "pickpockets, gamblers, drunkards, profane swearers, with many others of a similar stamp." Worst of all, the excitement of parades, cannon fire, and soldiers in uniform enticed "innocent children and youths" to the field. They were youngsters "whom curiosity brought together, but whom nothing but night send home more corrupted than they went." "More mischief is here done in one day, more vicious inclinations here take root, than home, or the pulpit, can eradicate in a year." Military commanders contributed to the disorder by treating their men to rum dispensed from large barrels hauled on wagons.[36]

The abolition of compulsory militia training aided the cause of morality, but the volunteer fire companies that replaced the militia also offended reformers. Each unit, which numbered sixty men, was made up primarily of the neighborhood's shoemakers who supplied the muscle to operate the hand-pumped apparatus.[37] The companies frequently engaged in competitive musters that tested their speed, strength, and accuracy. But the fire houses also became important social and political centers in which the enginemen met for discussions generally well-lubricated by liquor. Fire company musters in the 1840s attracted several thousand onlookers who, at the conclusion, joined the festivities that accompanied the collation, or banquet, and the firemen's ball. The muster was the nineteenth-century equivalent of modern spectator sport. An 1846 contest, for example, drew 2,000 spectators; another in 1848 at-

---

[36] *Lynn Mirror,* July 1, 1826, October 6, October 27, 1827.
[37] Membership lists often included with constitutions and by-laws of the units. All are in the manuscript collections of the Lynn Historical Society. Also see *Lynn Tattler,* February 19, 1849.

tracted 2,500.[38] The temperance movement made inroads among the shoemaker-enginemen. Some units became temperate; others remained drinkers. Those converted provide another indication of success of industrial morality among shoemakers, altering their lives outside the shop.

Informal and spontaneous expressions of a loose morality on the part of the shoemakers also changed. In 1828, Lynn adopted a series of by-laws to prohibit objectionable forms of social behavior. Placed under the ban was the use of profane, obscene, or insulting language; shooting dice in any street, land, or alley; making tumultuous noises, and being rude in either speech or gesture toward females.[39] Furthermore, no person would be permitted any longer to bathe or swim in the nude within 200 feet of a dwelling.

Beginning in the 1830s and 1840s, the shoemakers lost access to the common lands to which they had gone for picnics and outings. Nahant Peninsula, for generations a favorite of shoemakers who wished to fish, drink, and relax, became a resort for the wealthy, most of them from Boston. By the 1840s, one could find on this rugged and scenic site "the Boston Butterflies who fly up and down between Boston and Nahant during the summer, luxuriating on the money which they have cajoled out of the people." It became the place "where the Boston aristocracy airs itself every summer and braces up for the dissipation of the coming winter." Another portion of Lynn's open land fell into the hands of Richard S. Fay, a wealthy Boston capitalist who guarded "his grounds from the profane step of Lynn shoemakers by a pack of savage dogs."[40] Although traditional forms of leisure and recreation did not suddenly cease, the changes that accompanied the industrial revolution were altering the shoemaker's life both in and outside the workplace.

Lynn's schools, as might be expected, helped to inculcate the new values, becoming an important instrument in shaping good character. Indeed, the annual reports of its school officials often read like the proceedings of the Society for the Promotion of Industry, Frugality, and Temperance. No longer could children be ignored or allowed to be initiated into society through the public house or neighborhood gang. Bad habits or dangerous opinions, once formed, would be difficult to change.

---

[38] Lynn Forum, September 15, 1846; *Lynn Tattler,* April 1848; *Lynn Pioneer,* March 2, April 12, 1848.

[39] *Lynn Directory,* 1832, 29-31, lists by-laws adopted in 1828.

[40] *Essex County Washingtonian,* September 12, 1844; *Lynn News,* December 17, 1847. For Nahant's conversion to a wealthy resort, see Alonzo Lewis and James R. Newhall, *History of Lynn,* 62-63. *Lynn Pioneer,* May 24, 1848.

Schools were a strong antidote. They were "the very places for cultivating self-restraint, order, decency and a regard for all the proprieties of life." In addition to useful knowledge, educators would teach "morals and manners," particularly "sobriety, industry and frugality, chastity, moderation and temperance." They also had to foster "habits of application, respect to superiors, and obedience to law."[41] One such habit was punctuality, "a habit invaluable to individual credit, successful business, and general tranquility." The importance of "having a place, time and order for everything, and everything in its order, time and place" was the all-encompassing maxim to be taught.[42]

Control over education shifted from the neighborhood prudential committee to the town school committee with enlargement of the administrative unit from the neighborhood to the town.[43] This administrative change led to the accession to office of Lynn's prominent and wealthy rather than the obscure and middling townsfolk. The school committee stripped the prudential committees of the power to hire and fire teachers, to set the curriculum, and to prescribe a code of student conduct. Consonant with an 1826 State law, the school committee required of teaching candidates "evidence of good moral character." Reformers at the State level supplied such candidates by opening several normal schools for the purpose of properly training teachers. Emphasis upon "moral character" occurred simultaneously with the assignment to women of the primary responsibility for child rearing and for the defense of a stern moral code. Partly for this reason perhaps, a shift from male to female teachers took place in the elementary schools.

Reformers often encountered indifference to their efforts to tighten school discipline. Truancy was a major problem. In 1838, one third of those enrolled in Massachusetts' public schools were absent during the winter months. In the summer, this figure increased to 40 percent. The situation was worse in Lynn. Of the 1,430 town children in 1830 between four and fourteen years of age, 1,130 were enrolled in the common

---

[41] Commonwealth of Massachusetts, State Board of Education, "Report from Lynn," in *Eighteenth Annual Report of the Board of Education* (Boston, 1855), 128. For a broader view of changes in the schools, see Michael B. Katz, *The Irony of Early School Reform: Educational Innovation in Mid-Nineteenth Century Massachusetts* (Cambridge, 1968).

[42] Town of Lynn. School Committee, *Annual Report for 1847-1848* (Lynn, 1848), 7. Also see statement by City Solicitor and former school committee member, J. C. Stickney, *Lynn News*, December 20, 1853.

[43] For transfer of power see Commonwealth of Massachusetts, State Board of Education, *First Annual Report of the Board of Education* (Boston, 1838), 28-37; *Tenth Annual Report*, 148-152.

schools. Average attendance was about 650.[44] If the minds of the young were to be shaped properly, a way was needed to compel enrollment and attendance. Beginning in 1851, Massachusetts passed the first compulsory attendance laws. In subsequent years truant officers tracked down the runaways.

Reformers also encountered the obstinate cultural legacy of the eighteenth century, an age that had been indifferent to self-discipline, obedience to authority, and self-imposed restraints on natural impulses, or that had encouraged their opposites. The clash between the new nineteenth-century morality and the earlier immorality produced conflict in the schools. In 1838, the State Board of Education reported that 150 or more schools were "broken up by the insubordination of the scholars."[45]

Compliance to rules of behavior that students had not acquired in the home was the goal of Lynn's reformers and the teachers they hired. Because the great majority of students under twelve were the sons and daughters of shoemakers, their behavior provides a glimpse of their families and of their rearing. Many families apparently did not stress the dictum of "everything in its time, order, and place." The eighteenth century tended to ignore truancy and tardiness. Students who went off to the beach at Nahant or berrying in the woods were simply imitating their parents' behavior. The school committee recognized the source of such disobedience: "Right control at home will generally secure obedience at school. Its want is often the true cause of the child's ill conduct and punishment."[46] To gain student compliance to the new rigorous code, teachers and school officials employed both persuasion and coercion. They preferred a "kind and paternal discipline," but used the whip and stick when paternalism failed.

The beating of "refractory" students caused heated controversy in Lynn. Josiah Hand, for one, was flogged with a wooden stick two-feet long and half-an-inch thick for refusing to sweep the classroom. City and school officials at first defended such practices. They argued that the teacher was an agent of the parent and thus entitled to treat the child as the parent would. But some parents did not share the values advanced by the teacher or the school board. On several occasions angry parents

---

[44] State Board of Education, *First Annual Report*, 37. "Lynn Town Records, 1822-1835," 373. MS in Lynn City Hall.
[45] State Board of Education, *Seventh Annual Report of the Board of Education* (Boston, 1844), 66-67. The secretary happily reported in 1844 that "at the present time, the breaking up of schools, through a successful insurrection of the scholars, is an exceedingly rare event. This is most gratifying."
[46] Town of Lynn, School Committee, *Annual Report for 1847-1848*, 7.

whose children had been physically chastised invaded the classroom and either berated or beat the teacher.[47] School officials therefore altered their position. Once the child entered the classroom, they claimed, the authority of the parent ended. Too many parents, one critic charged, "were total strangers to all discipline, whether mental or moral."

Massachusetts school reformers also began to segregate the sexes in the public schools. Floor plans for "model" schools provided for separate playgrounds, entrances, stairways, and halls. Boys and girls would be together in the classroom, to be sure, but always under the watchful eye of an instructor of sound moral character.[48]

The clash within the schools between the loose morality of the past and the more rigorous industrial morality was part of a broader struggle, one which encompassed such issues as poor relief, drinking habits, forms of recreation, leisure activities, sexual practices, and work habits. Advocates of industrial morality made significant gains over two decades, but complete success eluded them, Many townsfolk, though vulnerable to hardship and poverty, struggled mightily to avoid becoming public charges. Yet the number of inmates in the Alms House increased and relief rolls grew — not proportionate to population growth, to be sure, but upward nonetheless. Some of Lynn's inhabitants renounced drink in favor of cold water, but others persisted in heavy and frequent tippling. The boisterous brawling and earthiness of the eighteenth century disappeared from many public places but continued in a moral underground, away from the scrutiny and censure of respectable opinion.

What of the overall affect of industrial morality on Lynn shoemakers and, if Lynn is at all representative of other manufacturing towns, of workingmen elsewhere?

Certainly, the impact of poor relief reform was especially profound. Long before the appearance of factories, the shoemaker was dependent on wages for his livelihood. Norman Ware is misleading (in his *American Industrial Worker, 1840-1860*) when he asserts that "in 1830 nearly all the shoemakers of Lynn had owned their homes with some land about them." "Almost every family kept a pig and many had their own cow." Tax records do not support this view. Scarcely 10 percent of Lynn's adult males owned a pig, fewer still owned a cow. Less than 50 percent of the

---

[47] For flogging cases in schools, see *Lynn Bay State*, June 13, 1850, January 23, 1857; *Lynn News*, July 26, 1850, February 20, 27, 1852, December 20, 1853, February 3, May 5, 1857. Town of Lynn. School Committee, *Annual Report for 1847-48*, 5.
[48] State Board of Education, *Fifth Annual Report of the Board of Education* (Boston, 1842), 126; *Tenth Annual Report* (Boston, 1847), 253

entire adult male population owned any real property whatever. Most shoemakers owned nothing. Ware's description may have been accurate for the cordwainers of 1800, but it was not true of the shoemaker from 1830 to 1860.[49] As early as 1830 the shoemaker was vulnerable to the vicissitudes and insecurity of a competitive capitalist market economy.

Changes in poor relief produced a dread of dependency in the shoemakers, and a compulsive drive to do all that was humanly possible to avoid pauperism — precisely the objective sought by the Society for the Promotion of Industry, Frugality, and Temperance. The depression of 1837-44 severely tested the resourcefulness of Lynn's shoemakers. Many foraged the woods for fuel, dug dandelions and clams for food, bartered with neighboring farmers or fishermen — anything to avoid going to the Overseers of the Poor.

A dread of pauperism is expressed in a letter to the *Lynn Pioneer* in 1848: "No person can contemplate the idea of becoming a pauper, without a feeling of horror. It seems like becoming a criminal. Many would as soon go to prison, as to a poor-house, and others would sooner go to their graves than to either."[50] That death would be preferable to dependency is evident in the suicide note left by an aging shoe cutter, Joseph Dwyer:

> As I grow old, and my health fails, and I find myself less able to provide for myself and live as I want to, and not to be dependent on others, who have as much as they can do to provide for themselves (no doubt they would do what they could for me in an emergency, but I prefer to help myself, one way or another), I take the method you will find when it happens. I have enjoyed life as well as the most of men, but cannot bear the idea of being a helpless, dependent old man. I paid my way so far, and owe nothing. Goodbye to all.[51]

The State's new poor houses were more feared than the local almshouses. When inmates of the Lynn Alms House were transferred to the new institution in Tewksbury, many were "dragged out screaming."

Equating dependency with shame deepened the shoemakers' determination to fight for their rights. Upon being told by one manufacturer that poor workmen should not have children, a mechanic angrily asked: "What impudence! Who made them rulers over us." The specter of poverty and the horror of dying among paupers and criminals was great-

---

49 Norman Ware, *The Industrial Worker, 1840-1860* (Chicago, 1964), 39-40. Town of Lynn, "Assessments and Taxes," 1832, MS, Lynn City Hall.
50 *Lynn Pioneer*, March 15, 1848.
51 "Lynn Scrapbooks," XVII, 45.

est for mechanics, who could no longer be assured of acquiring a "competency" under the rigorous competitive system. The word itself has disappeared from our vocabulary, but the pre-industrial mechanic looked upon a "competency" as a reward to which every able-bodied, diligent mechanic was entitled. He believed that during his working life as a mechanic — the years from 16 to 50 or 55 — he would be able to set aside enough money to support himself after retirement. The period from retirement to death was "a portion of time which was never intended for a season of labor."[52] But under the new system, the shoemaker would have to labor until the moment "the green sod is closed over him." Those shoemakers who were determined to acquire "an honest maintenance" and escape pauperism succeeded only by "unparalleled exertions," often laboring twelve to sixteen hours a day in the crowded, poorly ventilated little shop of seven by nine feet. Such exertions might produce an unintended result. Lynn health officials reported that the life expectancy of Massachusetts shoemakers was twenty years less than for farmers.[53] The work day for shoemakers became longer, the labor more arduous. By the 1840s, shoemakers commonly worked beyond dark, taxing their eyes by the dim light of candle or lamp, and earning an average of $5 per week.

To avoid the shame of becoming a public charge some shoemakers turned to collective self-help, often in an informal way. They frequently aided one another by giving sustenance to a jobless shoemaker or loaning out a small boat for fishing. In the small shop where each crew of journeymen worked, a jour possessing a special skill might perform that skill for his fellow wage earner so that the employer would not "cut him down" (reduce his wages) or give him "the sack." Shoemakers also formed six cooperative stores and affiliated with the New England Protective Union, a federation of several hundred cooperatives that covered much of the New England region. Manned by volunteer help and operating on a strictly cash basis, these stores enabled the shoemaker to obtain more goods for less money. New England workingmen and mechanics established the most extensive network of cooperative stores in the region's history.

The shame and odium attached to poverty also caused shoemakers to reject charity from manufacturer-philanthropists whom they viewed as

---

[52] *The Awl*, August 21, 1844.

[53] Lynn. *Annual Report of the Board of Health of Lynn*, 1850, City Document #7, p. 14. Average age at death for Massachusetts farmers was sixty-five; for shoemakers forty-three.

"plundering drones" responsible for their plight. When Isaiah Breed, one of Lynn's largest manufacturers and most prominent apostles of reform, proposed a soup kitchen to provide some relief during the 1837-44 depression, the mechanics responded with angry ridicule. They wanted work at good wages, not charity from the hands of a "grinder" from "extortion hollow" who lived off them.[54] They reacted in a similar manner a decade later when depressions struck the shoe trade with ominous regularity.[55] Their reluctance to accept poor relief stemmed from a public policy and pervasive ethos that made self-reliance a virtue and dependency a humiliation.

In considering other aspects of industrial morality — temperance, forms of recreation, codes of personal behavior — three groups of shoemakers are discernible by their differing responses. That the mechanics, like Americans generally, divided along cultural lines is familiar enough. Less well known or understood is the relationship between industrial morality and class consciousness.

One group of shoemakers were traditionalists, the bane of the reform forces. They stubbornly clung to customs and habits inherited from the loose eighteenth-century morality. They patronized rum dealers, beer and cider shops, attended Jim Crow shows and circuses, and frequented the town's saloons. Within their fire companies they carried on the raucous activities that had been such an important part of 'Lection Day and militia training. Despite condemnation by the reformers, they still played props and cards, hustled coppers, and danced to the fiddle. Many traditionalists lived in Lynn's western portion, once the site of modest mercantile activity and of the loose morality which that form of economy had produced. In West Lynn stood Caleb Wiley's grog shop. Frequently charged with selling liquor, Wiley was often acquitted of such violations because of the helpful testimony of his shoemaker customers. These traditionalists were mostly Democrats, usually of the Hunker or orthodox variety rather than anti-Masonic or, later, Free Soil wing. Ideologically and socially they remained aloof from the efforts of other shoemakers to form producer cooperatives and thus create, in embryonic shape, an alternative to capitalism. A desire for higher wages united them with other shoemakers, but the traditionalist was unlikely to respond to radical plans for social reconstruction. And if one is to accept the innuendoes of their critics, the traditionalists were men of inferior skill in shoemaking. They

---

[54] *The Awl,* March 1, 1845.
[55] *Lynn News,* November 24, 1857.

made "cacks" and "slaps" exclusively rather than the finer welted walking shoe. Their lack of skill may in fact have produced a diminished self-esteem that made them more accepting of their lot, more limited in their demands, and less eager for social reconstruction than the skilled shoemaker. In any case, those who clung to a traditional code and resisted the new industrial morality did not mount an articulate, organized challenge to the economic power of the shoe manufacturers.

A second group of shoemakers were the loyalists, who combined the new morality with deference toward their employers. They were model workers: self-reliant, self-disciplined, sober — and unprotesting, They were among the rank and file of the moral reform movement. Some joined the Society for the Promotion of Industry, Frugality, and Temperance and in town meetings voted for statutes that would chastise the poor, reshape the schools, deny licenses to liquor dealers, punish drunkards, and ban circuses and Jim Crow shows. Their signatures were probably among the 2,000 affixed to the petitions circulated by manufacturers Isaiah and Nathan Breed calling upon Lynn officials rigorously to enforce temperance laws. They often provided the convicting testimony in court cases against liquor dealers. Many loyalists were bound by ties of kinship, religion, or neighborhood to those shoe employers prominent in the moral reform movement. One can identify dozens of journeymen who were the brothers, sons, or fathers of manufacturers; often they worked for their relatives as wage earners. If one were to assess the numerical strength of the loyalists solely on the basis of elections, they and their employers made up a bare majority of Lynn's population. Like the traditionalists, they remained aloof from the efforts of other shoemakers to build class institutions as alternatives to those dominated by entrepreneurs. And like the entrepreneurs, they attributed poverty to idleness and self-indulgence rather than to exploitation.

Rebel mechanics were the third group. Culturally, they were nearly indistinguishable from the loyalists: each practiced temperance and frugality, and respected the canons of propriety in dress, speech, and demeanor. But the rebel mechanic was a vigorous critic of both capitalist exploitation *and* drink, economic injustice *and* moral degradation. Where the loyalist shoemakers attributed the employers' wealth to hard work, self-reliance, and shrewdness, the rebel claimed it was a product of petty fraud and heartless exortion. And where the loyalist attributed poverty to drink, the rebel mechanic reversed the causal connection and attributed drink to poverty and despair. His role in Lynn prompts the suggestion that the connection between working-class radicalism and a code of morality that was later termed "middle class" is the reverse of what some interpreters have argued. The most vigorous opponents of capitalist exploitation were those wage earners who had accepted a code of morality which they shared with their employers but used in their own class interest.

The rebel mechanics were the catalytic force among the shoemakers. They organized the Journeymen Cordwainers Society, drafted the circulars and constitution, edited the newspapers, founded the producers and consumers cooperatives. Yet at the same time their social gatherings, the cordwainers' tea parties, were models of teetotal decorum. They valued learning and education as a means of protecting themselves from the gullibility and ignorance that aided their oppressors, but insisted that shoeworkers and not employers control the schools. They also founded a workingmen's library as an auxiliary to their trade society. The rebel shoeworker might speak at the Washingtonian Total Abstinence Society on Friday night and the cordwainers' society on Saturday. From their work in the temperance movement, they learned how to use outdoor public meetings to solicit support from other shoemakers. In sum, the rebel mechanic combined the currents of moral reform and an emerging working-class consciousness.

The rebel mechanic exhibited a strong sense of self-dignity, pride, and self-esteem which served to stiffen his resistance to conditions he viewed as degrading. His heightened sense of worth derived from an ideology formed from three sources — the labor theory of value, republicanism, and, to a lesser extent, Christianity. This ideology enabled the rebel mechanic both to interpret what was happening to him and to fashion a cooperative network of social relations, as an alternative to competitive capitalism. From 1830 to 1860, the skilled shoemaker was in social decline, largely owing to the intense competition among wage earners for the right to work and, it follows, the right to live. The rebel mechanic identified the source of his trouble as the exploitation of employers whose control of raw materials enabled them to take from the mechanic a portion of everything he produced, leaving a wage that barely supported him and his family. Here was the root cause of both economic and moral degradation and here, too, was the point at which the rebel mechanic parted company with the loyalist.

Resolving to resist his degradation, the rebel mechanic sought to embrace industrial morality and unite with others like himself in a joint effort of collective self-help. Self-imposition of a rigorous code of moral conduct was not a way to respectability but rather a means of preserving personal pride and obtaining a sense of power and self-confidence at a time when the worker always seemed subject to outside control. He was proclaiming his independence from those external forces that governed him — whether employer or liquor. Obedience to the commands of another was slavery in his eyes; so, too, was his surrender to temptations that came from within. Addiction to alcohol was one form of bondage. Sam Hayward of Boston, a mechanic and a temperance lecturer who was a favorite among Lynn's artisans, explained his own conversion: "I was a football when a drunkard, kicked around by everybody." Hayward became temperate during the 1837-44 depression when a Washingtonian approached him and asked, "Sam, don't you want to be a *man* again?"

The drunkard, furthermore, was useless to everyone—family, friends, and, most important, to himself. The mechanic interpreted drunkenness as an admission of despair and surrender, a sign that the victim had succumbed, leaving him without will or direction. But the rebel shoeworkers who organized the Cordwainers Society and the Good Samaritan Temperance Society neither condemned the drunkard nor withheld their support from him. "Never forsake a brother — if he fail once, twice, or even the third time, receive him again."[56] Renouncing coercion, they chose moral suasion and mutual support, and thereby were distinguished from their temperate employers who readily employed coercion against the traditionalists among the shoeworkers.

Cultural differences impeded but did not prevent concerted action by shoemakers for limited ends. The traditionalists were neither inert nor hidebound. And even the loyalists' patience had its limits. A series of severe depressions in the 1850s brought about an economic crisis that united shoemakers in a common effort to protect their economic interests. The result was the great shoemakers' strike of 1860, perhaps the largest strike in New England's history, involving nearly 20,000 binders and shoemakers in the region's most important industry.

But despite the impressive solidarity of the moment, cultural tensions would remain. The cultural side of the industrial revolution — the new attitudes toward dependency, sexuality, drink and self-discipline, and

---

[56]*Essex County Washingtonian*, March 30, 1843. For a brief account of the mechanics' presence in the Washingtonian movement, see John Krout, *Origins of Prohibition*, 182-202.

the new forms of education, pleasure, and recreation — became a source of discord among shoemakers, dividing them along cultural lines, restricting social contact, and circumscribing the formation of class consciousness.

LABOR, CAPITAL, AND COMMUNITY: THE STRUGGLE FOR POWER

7

John T. Cumbler

In an article published in 1954, Clark Kerr and Abraham Siegel argued the importance of local conditions in determining the propensity to strike.[1] Picking up on that theme, especially in the last ten years, labor historians have further emphasized the impact of local conditions on labor consciousness and struggles. Unfortunately in many cases when historians have tried to put the worker in his own context, rather than in a national political or labor organization, their emphasis has been upon the dramatic strikes, usually located in large urban areas, involving radical or revolutionary groups. In recent years, however, scholars have begun to investigate the workers, rather than their formal national organizations, in smaller industrial cities. They have looked to the daily struggles to maintain what the workers considered living wages, "short enough hours," and the dignity and community of wage earners of which they believed themselves a part.[2]

In New England's industrial towns, separated from such national commercial and intellectual centers as Boston and New York by the activities and tedium of their own industry, wage earners were integrated in their communities.[3] Not all of these workers had been torn from peasant backgrounds and thrown into the army of industrial workers to suffer trauma and anxiety owing to the loss of their traditional ways of life. Many had inherited a long history of industrial work and felt proud of their role as producers of the wealth of their communities. They reacted to their social and economic environment as industrial workers, not as urbanized peasants, and their reactions tell us something about the patterns of industrial workers not peasants, in transition. In Lynn, Massachusetts, workmen, whether or not they were recent immigrants, considered themselves part of a tradition of shoe manufacturing that went back to the early part of the nineteenth century. These workers felt a deep tie to their town and to their trade.[4]

Labor organizations in these industrial centers were apt to be localized. Even locals of national organizations had little connection with the national unions.[5] Local conditions, along with local consciousness, determined the direction that labor organizations took, and when local rank-and-file interests conflicted with national directives, local secessions often resulted.[6]

Source: An earlier version of this article was published in *Labor History* 15 (Summer 1974): 395-415.

Consequently when they did affiliate with national organizations, local concerns and group loyalty transcended national policies. The important ties with other outside unions were informal. Ties to nonlocal workers and unions were usually confined to feelings of brotherhood and solidarity, which manifested themselves in aid for union struggles.

In examining a strike of little national significance, that of leather workers in the city of Lynn, Massachusetts, this paper will look at how the workers viewed their environment and attempted to deal with the tactics of the manufacturers within the context of an industrial community. It will show how the workers rallied their community of fellow workers to fight against the companies. Since Lynn's wage earners viewed their city as a community of workers, the strike provides a picture of a community in struggle. The community gave the workers strength and support to resist the employers; their friends and relatives were workers and union members, and their unions controlled most of the shops in Lynn. The same community, however, also gave them a false sense of their power to effect their demands against organized capital.

In the late nineteenth century, Lynn claimed to be the largest shoe manufacturing center in America. Its shoe industry supported a community of workers who traced their heritage back to the earliest shoe factories in the country. Its "ten-footers," as the early shoe shops were known, nurtured craft pride and dignity. These ten-footers were forums for social and political discussions, as well as workplaces, and even into the twentieth century shoe workers talked nostalgically about the lost days when workers made shoes by hand and felt themselves the social equal to any citizen.[7] From the mid-nineteenth century, Lynn had been the nation's largest shoe center, surpassing Philadelphia and Newark, because machines and the factory system had been introduced first in Lynn. Like all other industrial centers at the turn of the century, Lynn had a mixed ethnic community; but unlike the textile towns of New England, Lynn's workers did not segregate ethnically, and no single ethnic group dominated the city. Shoe and leather workers in the late nineteenth century lived in the Brickyard, a large workingclass residential area located southeast of the downtown shoe and leather shops. The Brickyard had a mixed population of natives: Irish, English, Canadian, German, Scandinavian, and, at the turn of the century, Southern and Eastern Europeans.[8] Although Lynn had a more mixed community than the textile towns did, the owners still lived in the "diamond district" around Ocean Street, and the workers lived in crowded triple-decker tenements in the densely populated third, fourth, and sixth wards.[9]

Native-born workers continued to be employed in large numbers throughout the nineteenth and early twentieth centuries, usually at the more skilled jobs of cutting or lasting. In 1895, 75 percent of Massachusetts shoe workers were native born; the number decreased to 46 percent by

1903. Of those workers of foreign descent, the Irish, with over 28 percent, were the largest group; and the French Canadians, with over 9 percent, the Canadian English, with over 6 percent, and the English, with almost 5 percent, followed.[10] With its proximity to Boston and its expansion during the late nineteenth and early twentieth centuries, Lynn probably accounted for a larger percentage of the foreign shoe workers than the state figures would indicate.[11]

Despite the fact that male leather workers averaged slightly higher yearly wages than male shoe workers, there were far more foreign born in the former category than in the latter. In 1895, 61 percent of the state's leather workers were foreign born, and this figure increased to more than 78 percent by 1903. Those of Irish descent accounted for almost 53 percent of the state's leather workers. The French Canadians with more than 6 percent, English with more than 3 percent, and Germans with just under 3 percent again followed the Irish.[12]

Native wage earners avoided leather work because of the poor working conditions and the unpleasant labor. Although leather processing involved more skilled positions and a higher degree of skill than shoemaking, the work was heavy, wet, and distasteful. The leather worker was often splashed with odious chemicals, and had to breathe noxious fumes as well. The largest majority of foreign workers worked in the early processing stages, which, though requiring skill and judgment, were the most offensive. Few of the positions in the leather factories were unskilled, and most of these were filled by young or transient laborers or unemployed native shoe workers, especially during the slack season in the shoe trade.[13]

Leather, or morocco leather (an important leather for shoemaking), manufacturing had always been an important shoe-related industry in Lynn. As early as 1800 there were firms manufacturing leather used by the Lynn shoe workers. Following the Civil War, the leather industry mechanized along with the shoe industry to meet growing demands, and by 1880 it accounted for roughly $2 million of business. The three largest Lynn firms accounted for almost half the trade. The few families who began the morocco trade in the early nineteenth century continued to dominate the industry into the early twentieth century. One of Lynn's largest firms and a central employer in the 1890 strike was the Joseph Moulton Company, begun in 1835.[14]

A strike of leather workers in Newark, New Jersey, in the 1880s, and the advantage of being in the heart of the shoe manufacturing district brought even more leather manufacturing firms to Lynn, so that by 1890 Lynn closely rivaled Philadelphia, which was then the largest morocco leather manufacturing city in the United States. Although leather manufacturing (its rise depended upon the demand of Lynn shoe workers) was originally connected with the town's shoe industry, by 1892 only a small portion of the morocco leather was sold to Lynn shoe manufacturers.[15]

Lynn's leather workers took pride in their work, despite its unpleasant aspects. That they did feel strongly about it was due to the continuing importance of each worker's judgment and experience in the production process. Although the industry mechanized to some extent in the early 1880s, the workers still had to be able to judge for themselves the hides and the chemical fluids they worked with, so that the hides would not be destroyed by too little or too much time in the processing fluids. The beamster, who cleaned and trimmed the hides, had to be a skilled workman in order not to damage the hides through cutting or to waste the leather. Miscalculation or carelessness on the part of the leather worker could destroy a hide and cut considerably into company profits.[16] The workers believed their skill was indispensable to the manufacturers, and they used that position to build their union and bargain for higher wages.

Leather workers were skilled operatives. They worked in small shops that employed between thirty and fifty workers; usually only a couple of workers were involved in each stage of the operation. They knew each other and depended upon union solidarity. They felt that Lynn's skilled labor had created the value of the product.[17] Despite the large number of foreign leather workers, many had relatives in the shoe trade. The leather factories were located next to the shoe shops in the city's downtown area. Leather and shoe workers took their lunch breaks together in the downtown cafés and lunchrooms.

Lynn morocco leather workers, like Lynn shoe workers, had a durable tradition of militancy and unionism behind them. When Lynn shoe workers began building strong Knights of Labor lodges in the shoe factories, the leather workers organized as well. By 1890 almost all of Lynn's leather factories were union shops. Concentration of the shoe and leather factories in the downtown area facilitated workingclass cohesion. Workers would gather and talk together at the doors of the factories before and after work, as well as over their lunch. The factories were so close that in 1896, when the secretary of the Lasters Union was denied entrance to a fifth-floor factory, he went next door and called out instructions to the lasters from the fifth-floor window of the neighboring factory.[18]

Lynn operatives felt close ties with their unions and with their trade. The union hall was more than a meeting place for business; it was the center for social activity for shoe and leather workers. After work and on Saturday afternoons and evenings, card tables would be set up in the main meeting rooms. Workers would come into the union hall and play cards throughout the night, with as many as fifty games going on at once. There was always plenty of talk and comradeship at the union hall.[19] The Lynn Lasters Union had a pool and billiard room, which was crowded with union members and netted the union between ten and twenty dollars a week.[20]

In good weather, shoe and leather workers would gather in Central Square, where Simon's poolroom and the various bowling alleys and lunchrooms provided activity as well as information for friends and fellow workmen. Shoeworkers who were laid off would spend their days at Hunt's Cafe, known as "Crispin's Congress," because of all the shoe workers who frequented it. Here they would meet with friends and ask about job openings. Hunt's had difficulty staying in business because of the shoe workers' habit of coming in, ordering one cup of coffee, and staying all day to socialize. Like other cafés and lunchrooms in downtown Lynn, it functioned much like French bistros for the Lynn shoe workers.[21]

Through such formal and informal institutions, Lynn workers integrated the new workers into the community, teaching them the history and lessons of past struggles and the meaning of community and union solidarity.[22] In addition to the unions, workers in Lynn had numerous clubs, benefit societies, and lodges, which tied them to the community. A turn-of-the century observer noted that "the social side of [Lynn] wage-earner's life seem[ed] to be developed through lodges and benefit organizations."[23]

Lynn's tradition as a strong union town went back to the pre-Civil War period. In the 1840s the city's workers published the *Awl*, a workingman's paper that advocated the dignity of labor, freedom for the workingman, and the social equality of all producers. The antebellum workers formed cooperatives, debating societies, and clubs for journeymen cordwainers to further their education and improve their economic condition. When the wages of these early nineteenth-century workers were cut, they fought back. In 1843 Lynn morocco and kid finishers struck, successfully, for a wage increase. In 1860 the militant independence born of the early days, when journeymen and masters were considered social equals, collided with the developing factory system in Lynn, and the town became the focal point of the nation's largest strike up to that time. Thousands of workers paraded through the city's streets. The strike was set off by wage reductions and layoffs in the 1850s, but behind the strike lay the bitterness of proud artisans and journeymen who felt their labor and position in society were being undermined by the factory system.[24]

In the 1870s Lynn's workers published the *Little Giant*, dedicated to workingclass solidarity and unity. They supported one of the nation's strongest and most militant branches of the Knights of St. Crispin. The Crispins not only negotiated for higher wages and acted as a vigilant spokesman for the interests of Lynn's workers but functioned as a social center for the workers as well. The Crispins provided community and fellowship for their members through an intricate pattern of social functions, picnics, dances, benefits, and lodge meetings. The Lasters continued the tradition of informal activities after the Crispins collapsed following the loss of the 1878 strike. The Lasters held dances and benefits and maintained a mutual aid association, a pool and billiard room, and a reading and social room, which included a piano for informal singing.[25]

In the 1880s the Knights of Labor filled the gap left by the end of the

Crispins for those shoe and leather workers who were not Lasters. The Lynn Knights were neither utopian nor backward looking. They were a strong class-conscious industrial union, dedicated to wresting from capital the laborer's full share, which in the long run they felt was the full worth of his product.[26] By 1886 they were so powerful that the *Boston Evening Transcript* accused them of having "almost absolute control in the workrooms of every important factory."[27]

The Knights were not the only militant unionists in Lynn. In the late 1890s the city's carpenters left the Brotherhood of Carpenters and Joiners of America because of its conservatism. Believing that the Brotherhood was spending too much time and money on benefits and too little for organizing, they attempted to build a New England organization dedicated to militant unionism and to the leadership of the region's eight-hour-day movement.[28] The Machinists Lodge 471, with many members in the city's growing electrical industry, was also composed of strong, independent unionists. In 1898 they set up meetings to discuss means of broadening their activity beyond "simple trade unionism." They held a special convention to discuss the merits of joining the Socialist Trade and Labor Alliance.[29] The building trades were also well organized and contributed much support to the local labor movement, both independently and through Lynn's Central Labor Union. The city's union movement, then, was one of the strongest in Massachusetts throughout the late nineteenth and first part of the twentieth centuries.[30]

Although leather workers had been averaging slightly higher yearly wages than shoe workers in the late 1880s, their wages declined in the latter part of the decade. In 1890 the leather business improved, and leather workers believed the time had come for a major confrontation with the manufacturers.[31]

On July 25, 1890, more than six hundred workmen from the various branches of the morocco leather trade crowded into the union hall for a mass meeting to discuss the situation of Lynn leather workers. To prevent compromising any of the participants, they voted to exclude the nonlabor press. The workers demanded that leather work should be done no more than nine hours a day. They considered this an issue of health as well as a labor right, for they had to work amid foul toxic fumes given off in leather processing. The leaders of the Knights of Labor, Leather Workers Assembly, under the direction of Master Workman John McCarthy, felt that because of the general prosperity of the industry, a strike would be successful.[32] The men decided to walk out on August 12, 1890.

A month later, on August 22, the leather manufacturers, representing Lynn's twenty-eight leather shops, gathered in closed meeting to decide what tactics they should adopt to deal with the strike and with what they considered to be an infringement on their priorities by the local Knights of Labor. The manufacturers agreed to fight the union and bring the open shop into all the Lynn leather factories. One manufacturer declared that "if the shops [have] to remain closed for ten years [we will not let] the men [come] back as Knights of Labor."[33] Being members of the National Association of Leather Manufacturers, centered in the Middle Atlantic states, the manufacturers decided that the NALM, which was originally organized to protect the manufacturers from the control of labor by unions and the monopoly of supply by the packers, would be the means used to break the union.[34]

These leather manufacturers confronted two major problems in their attempt to break the power of the local Knights in their leather factories. First, they needed some guarantee that the lockout would not threaten their position with buyers. Leather manufacturers sold in a highly competitive market. In order to survive, they depended upon cultivating regular buyers. The loss of these customers could cripple the industry in Lynn. Second, they also needed some assurance that skilled leather workers from outside the city were available so that they could continue operating while locking out the local Knights. The NALM offered a solution to both problems for the Lynn employers. It pledged that during the strike, competitive members of the NALM would not steal the regular buyers of the Lynn companies. It further assured the Lynn companies that skilled workers from Newark were available for use in the effort to break the power of the local Knights.[35]

At the start of the strike, the workmen were convinced that they would be successful. Their meetings and rallies were jubilant. On Labor Day the morocco leather workers turned out in strength with banners proclaiming their demand for a nine-hour day.[36] The striking workers spent their days at the union headquarters on Monroe Street. They felt that this walkout would be as successful as past struggles. At union headquarters they waited for strike news. The strike provided an excuse for coming to the union hall, playing cards, and renewing old friendships. Many drifted to Central Square in hopes of hearing about jobs elsewhere. The social aspect of unionism was heightened during the strike as the union hall became an all-day social center.[37]

On September 11, 1890, after four weeks, the strike changed complexion. John T. Moulton, son of Joseph Moulton, the founder of one of the early leather factories, with the backing of the NALM, opened his factories to nonunion workers. Lynn's NALM members agreed to have "no Knight of Labor work for [them]." Moulton sent his foreman to Montreal to enlist French Canadian workers who were not affiliated with the Knights.[38] The leading Lynn paper, on September 16, 1890, observed that the companies were bringing in "foreign labor" to break the union; it also reported that the companies were advertising in foreign papers for workers. A German worker claimed to have seen the notice in a German paper.[39] Eventually it became evident that most of the strikebreakers were no more "foreign" than the Lynn workers, but these early tactics on the part of the manufacturers raised the fear of foreign strikebreakers, which continued throughout the strike.

The union began to rally the community around the striking workmen and against the outsiders. Strikers tried to enlist financial support from various tradesmen and merchants in Lynn, who realized that in order to maintain their good standing among the city's workmen, they had to support the strike. To do otherwise would have appeared antiunion and antiworkingclass. Even reluctant merchants went along "in the interests of the city" and hoped for an early settlement.[40] "Refusals from those thus approached were rare."[41] The striking leather workers called a mass meeting on September 16 to keep the spirit of the strike alive and to explain the new threat to the workingpeople in Lynn.[42]

The author of a letter to the *Lynn Daily Bee* expressed the feelings of many workmen in Lynn when he wrote as "a citizen of Lynn": "I feel deeply interested in the contest which is going on between capital and labor in this city. As a wage earner . . . I offer my protest to the methods adopted by certain manufacturers to crush out the manly hopes and inborn liberty of American citizens. As all wealth is the product of labor, labor should receive its just reward."[43] The wage earners of Lynn felt that theirs was a city of wage earners and that an attack against organized labor was an attack against the whole community.

The appearance of growing numbers of outside strikebreakers visibly strengthened the community's support of the strike. Local hotels refused to board strikebreakers. H. Hitcock, proprietor of the Ideal Dining Room, stated to the local newspaper that he refused to have anything to do with them; he "did not want such boarders."[44] On October 5, 1890, the Central Labor Union of Lynn, which represented all of Lynn's organized workers— American Federation of Labor, Knights of Labor, and independent unions—held a mass meeting in support of the strikers. The Central Labor Union sent out a telegram to labor organizations across the nation: "Fellow workers: again has a fierce attack of organized capital compelled an appeal from organized labor of this city to its friends throughout the country."[45] A committee was formed to go to the different city agencies to help strikers and keep the scabs out. It informed the city hospital that if it continued to admit scabs suffering from noxious fumes while boarding within the factories, the unions would "withhold their patronage of that institution amounting to one thousand dollars yearly."[46]

Strikers went to the stores in Federal Square and "ordered [the proprietors] to refuse to supply the special officer employed at the Moulton Factory with any goods under fear of losing the trade of the workmen."[47] Only one merchant refused this demand, and his store was successfully boycotted by Lynn's workingclass.[48] Retailers began to insert notices on the front page of the city's leading paper denying selling to or having any connection with the scabs or struck companies. T. J. Ready repudiated a "report" that he had sold beds or bedding to any manufacturers.[49] Strikers' successes in rallying Lynn's merchants and tradesmen forced manufacturers to import food and goods for the strikebreakers from Boston.[50]

Even Lynn's Republican Mayor Newhall, concerned about the upcoming election, and the citizens' fear of the specter of strikebreakers being brought in, promised that he would try "to bring about the adoption of some measure which should tend to check the bringing of any further numbers of men into Lynn."[51] The mayor, having failed in his attempt to stop the importation of outside labor, blamed the situation on the NALM, "who had taken the situation out of the control of the Lynn manufacturers."[52]

As the strike progressed, the local unions took an increasingly active role in supporting the strikers against what they came to believe was the beginning of an all-out struggle of labor against capital. On October 18, 1890, they decided to boycott leather from the manufacturers who participated in the lockout. The shoe cutters promised to aid the leather workers by refusing to work on boycotted leather.[53] On November 14, 1890, the boot and shoe unions held a mass meeting in support of the morocco leather workers. The unions decided to "canvass the various branches of industry in the city for aid for the morocco workers."[54] The Lynn Lasters Protective Union gave strike leader John McCarthy two hundred dollars a month until late December when a shrunken treasury forced it to reduce this amount.[55] The Plumbers Protective Union, AFL of Lynn, sponsored a band concert and dance for support of the strikers who were Knights of Labor, despite the fact that nationally the two organizations were competing for the control of organized labor in America.[56] Lynn's workers, then, responded to local workingclass needs rather than to the national directions of organized labor. Even the *Lynn Daily Item*, the town's conservative paper, stated in a front-page story that "for maintaining a determined and well fought battle against the opposing forces of capital, the men are to be complimented."[57]

Meanwhile schoolchildren also responded, gathering around the struck factories after class ended and throwing rocks at the windows and doors, requiring police to protect the property.[58] Then, on September 18, 1890, John T. Moulton began operating his factory with scabs. The strikers assembled outside the factory to greet those among their former co-workers who had rejected the unions. When the whistles of the surrounding shoe factories blew at quitting time, men emptied into the streets and marched down to join the strikers. The local paper described the situation where well over a thousand men had gathered: "It seemed that everyone who had finished their day's work stopped at the factory on their way home."[59] At quitting time the crowd began throwing bricks at the building. The few scabs who finally appeared were met with a barrage of insults and threats. One strikebreaker from Lynn was followed home by a small committee of strikers who tried to persuade him to join the strike. According to accounts in the paper, he was neither threatened nor intimidated. He agreed, after listening to their arguments, not to return to work.[60]

The scabs who were not from Lynn received different treatment. They were followed by the crowd with taunts and threats, punctuated by occasional bricks, from the factory door to the train depot. At the train depot the threats became explicit. "Do you want to get out of this town alive? . . . Well you won't if you come here again!"[61] When the train pulled into the station the crowd pushed in closer, and, to convince the strikebreaker of the error of his ways, he was kicked and shoved as he tried to board it. Someone tried to pull him off the train for further convincing. When he finally managed to struggle aboard, a stone crashed through the window. As the train departed, a union representative hopped aboard. He tried to explain to the "outsider" that Lynn was a union town and that the scab should not return to work for a company being struck. The strikebreaker on at least this occasion reportedly agreed to remain home.[62]

During such confrontations, the police, realizing there was little they could do, stood by without interfering. They were hesitant to act against the strikers. Moreover, they were far outnumbered, and so were the scabs. Furthermore the strikers were also citizens, and their organization was one of the strongest and most powerful in Lynn. The outsiders were not citizens, and at this point did not seem to be represented by any powerful local organization. Ever since the 1878 strike, when they came under attack by the newly elected workingman's mayor, George Sanderson, the police had tried to remain neutral in labor conflicts, and without direct orders the officers on duty decided to avoid provoking the strikers by protecting the scabs.

At a mass meeting following the confrontation with the scabs as well as later, at the factory door, the strikers were warned of "a hundred and twenty-five Armenians" who were in Boston, hired by Moulton, and waiting to be brought in as strikebreakers.[63] Rumors of "Armenians" continued throughout the walkout, despite the fact that relatively few of the strikebreakers were in fact Armenian; most came from Newark and were approximately the same ethnic mix as the strikers themselves.[64] The threat of Armenians was a symbol that reflected the Lynn strikers' fear of the outside. They felt that they could control the situation in Lynn since they had the community support. But they could not depend on the outside, the unknown community. They had no sense of how outsiders would react to pleas of solidarity and workingclass traditions.

At the strikers' mass meeting, the union called for peaceful picketing of Moulton's and asked union men to stay away unless they were there to picket. This appeal kept strikers from the factory door, but not from the railroad depot, and scabs, waiting for the train back to Boston, continued to be abused. One striker told a strikebreaker: "If you choose to remain a scab, you must accept the consequences and I think your days in that line are numbered."[65]

On September 20, 1890, a crowd of women and children, plus the "hoodlum element," gathered around one of the struck factories and attacked a fireman as he left. But he identified himself as a Lynn man not involved in the strike and was escorted to his home by a group of strikers.[66]

By September 22, the police had received clear orders from Lynn's Republican administration, which had a strong local tradition of law and order, that they would be used to protect strikebreakers. They escorted the scabs from the train depot to the factory and back again at the end of the day.[67] Tensions catalyzed by the use of scabs finally brought the community into a confrontation with the police. A large crowd, including many women and children, gathered by five o'clock Monday on Marion and Center streets. It swelled rapidly, and the strikers were soon in the minority as other workers joined them at quitting time. Over two thousand wage earners pushed into the square. By six o'clock the Thompson-Huston Electrical Works (later to become the Lynn General Electric Company) sounded its whistle, and the crowd was further augmented by the electrical workers, many of whom had relatives among those already present. Believing that they could not control this crowd, the police read the "riot act" to those present and drove them back with clubs, in the process arresting John W. Twombly, a shoe worker who had refused to move on and kept returning to the scene.[68]

John Moulton, in the vanguard of the NALM's attack on the Knights, responded to these threats to scab labor, and the general community resistance to it, by housing the strikebreakers inside his factory. The Knights of Labor shavers, who had not been on strike, now went out in support of the strike and to protest the housing of scabs in the factories. The strikers set up twenty-four pickets, twenty-four hours a day, at all the struck factories. The companies sent employment notices all over New England and, according to a local paper, "employment seekers [came to Lynn] . . . unaware of any existing trouble and not knowing that they [were] to take the places left vacant by men who [were] fighting for their bread."[69] When the new workers arrived, they were "met and the state of affairs explained to them." In most cases, according to the Democratic paper, the strikebreakers refused to work and, in the case of thirty New Hampshire men, returned to discourage others from coming to Lynn.[70]

By September 26, coordinated by the NALM, factories began operating "free shops" with workers imported from out of town, many of whom it brought from Newark.[71] The manufacturers placed cots inside the factories for their new workers and petitioned the police for special protection against community anger over scab labor. John Moulton, leading the attack on the Knights, began to build a boardinghouse adjacent to his factory, anticipating a protracted conflict with local organized labor. His willingness to invest in the construction reflected both his commitment to defeating the union and his understanding of the extent of community hostility toward his new workers. He knew that the anger directed against the scabs would not recede in a few days or even a few weeks. His investment suggested his awareness of the inadequacy of a temporary solution and of the need to provide protection over a long period of time.[72] The manufacturers claimed that the strike would end only with the complete destruction of the Knights of Labor in the morocco leather trade, no matter how long it took. "I don't believe in crowding a man simply because you have the best of him," one stated, "but when you have a fight I believe in thoroughly whipping the adversary."[73]

The strikers, however, were confident that they would win despite the imported scabs. Their strong community identification convinced them that only Lynn workers were skilled enough to handle the hides correctly and that production costs, driven up by the waste and inefficiency of the new workers, would soon cause the manufacturers to turn back to the men of Lynn and accept them and their organization. Their ranks held steady, and after six weeks of striking, more than half of the original eight hundred strikers had found jobs elsewhere to tide them over during the strike. Those who were unable to find work received aid from brother Knights.[74]

On October 13, 1890, Grand Master Terence Powderly of the Knights of Labor came to Lynn. Several thousand crowded into the hall to hear him denounce the un-American act of importing scabs to break the movement of working people. Much was made at this rally of the righteousness of the cause of labor. One speaker, for example, claimed that he was a "Knight of Labor because [he] believed it to be [his] duty."[75]

On December 23, 1890, after more than four months on strike, the strikers held a mass parade through the streets of Lynn to emulate the massive marches of the famous 1860 walkout. More than a thousand marched through the city in preparation for a gigantic rally at the Odd Fellows Hall. The marchers, led by labor leaders from all the trades of Lynn, held banners proclaiming opposition to the organization of employers and supporting the dignity of labor: "Employers organise but deny us the same right"; "Labor produces all wealth, all wealth should belong to those who produced it"; "To labor, to learn, to love is the destiny of mankind"; "Our cause is just, public sympathy is with us." Speakers at the rally ranged from the head of the Carpenters Union to the leader of the local Knights.[76]

With the new year, a new mayor took over the Lynn city hall. Mayor E. Knowlton Fogg was a Knight of Labor himself and had campaigned for neutral police protection. Lynn's workmen had a long tradition of "throw-the-bum-out" politics. Following the 1860 strike, when police and military units had been called up against the strikers, the shoe workers elected one of their own number as mayor and completely reorganized the police department. During the Civil War, the manufacturers were able to regain control of the city government through the Republican party, and they governed for the next seventeen years. In the 1878 strike, police were again employed as an antilabor weapon. Following the loss of the strike, the workers mobilized and elected as mayor George Sanderson, an ex-shoe worker and strike leader.[77] Workers continued to dominate city government until the late 1880s. Newhall's use of police to protect scabs and against the strikers, and his inability to block the importation of strikebreakers, gave Fogg an issue that turned out the labor vote.

Fogg tried to bring the manufacturers to the conference table to negotiate a peace, but the companies refused. They were particularly emphatic because of Fogg's union membership and sympathies. They were convinced that their former employees were beaten and that the strikers would renounce their organization in a matter of weeks and return to work as nonunion men. Lynn's manufacturers had initiated the NALM attack to destroy the power of the Knights of Labor in the leather industry. The issue could no longer be compromised.[78] Most of the companies had opened up again with imported nonunion help and, with the support of the national organization, felt that they could last longer than the union.

By February, six months after the strike had begun, local Lynn men were deserting the union and asking for work in the open shops. On February 20, 1891, five hundred workmen gathered outside one of the factories being struck and attacked a former union man who had gone back to work. The crowd grew to more than a thousand as it followed him home, jeering and heckling the man for turning against his comrades. Meanwhile the companies had been able to operate despite the strike in a union town. The men realized that though they had the public sympathy, the support of the labor community, and the backing of the labor movement, they were not as powerful as the factory owners, especially if the latter had the well-coordinated support of the NALM. The union town could not protect union men against the combined and determined efforts of the national organization of manufacturers. To even the most loyal union supporter, it had become obvious that the companies could hold out and that the longer the union fought, the more new people would come into Lynn looking for work in the open shops.

On February 28, 1891, the head of the leather workers, Master Workman McCarthy, was arrested for conspiracy. His trial drew huge crowds. It ended with both sides declaring a victory, McCarthy being found guilty but given a minor sentence, but the trial represented only a last gasp of activity in a dying cause. The crowds that came to support McCarthy could do no more to protect him than they could do to prevent the companies from running their shops.

On April 8, 1891, after eight long months of struggle, the men gave up and returned to work in nonunion shops. Their battle was lost. The support of the community, although a key factor in helping to keep the ranks solid for so many months, had not been enough to defeat the determined efforts of the nationally oriented manufacturers, who viewed the struggle in Lynn as part of a national plan to break the strength of the Knights of Labor in the leather manufacturing industry.[79]

Ironically what gave Lynn's workers the strength to hold out for so long also contributed to their weakness. Their perception of themselves as powerful members of a workingclass community endowed them with an unreal sense of their own power. In Lynn they were powerful. They could elect one of their own if the city government interfered with what they considered their rights. They were surrounded by union members or supporters.[80] Believing that all the world was Lynn and all men were union men with the exception of the "bosses" and the outside "Armenians," they thought themselves unbeatable. But the world of the manufacturers was larger than Lynn. It had the aid of a national organization. Manufacturers knew that the NALM would not let them flounder while other companies picked up their orders. Although the workmen also considered themselves part of a national body, they were basically a community movement with a local strategy.[81] As long as the companies were locally oriented and owned and in competition with others locally and nationally, a local union movement could effectively unite its community against the company and last out the strike. When the companies became part of a national organization, they overcame the community efforts of the union men.

The conviction that only Lynn workers could process the leather correctly because of their superior skill also reflects the workers' local orientation. The Lynn workingclass community gave the workers the strength to fight but narrowed their vision with its parochialism. Their defeat did not destroy unionism or even the Knights of Labor in Lynn. The community strength kept the Knights active even into the twentieth century.[82] The morocco workers, though they lost the 1890 strike, built a new union, which led to another lockout nine years later. In 1899 it was Thomas Kelley and Company that boarded and lodged new workers in its factory in order to break the strike of the morocco leather workers of the Socialist Trade and Labor Alliance. Lynn's wage earners maintained their militant independence after the Knights faded but tempered it with a realization of the importance of strong national trade-union organizations. The conflict between local militance and the desire for national coordination and organization led them in and out of the Boot and Shoe Workers Union, the ST and LA, and other national union movements.[83] Although the strike of 1890 was not Lynn's largest or even its most dramatic, it does indicate the relationship between class solidarity and community support and the insufficiency of that relationship in the struggle between labor and capital.

NOTES

1. Clark Kerr and Abraham Siegel, "The International Propensity to Strike—An International Comparison," in Arthur Kornhauser, Robert Dubin, and Arthur Ross, eds., *Industrial Conflict* (New York, 1954), 189-212. Kerr and Siegel put forward the hypothesis that isolation of groups of workers doing the same type of work and the absence of a mediating middle class most fully explains the propensity of some industrial workers to strike.

2. Much of this work was pioneered by Herbert Gutman in his work on the industrial worker in the Gilded Age, which emphasized the conflict between the local workers and their community and the developing capitalist system. Gutman points to the importance of the workers' preindustrial cultural and social traditions in their resistance to capital. Herbert Gutman, "Protestantism and the American Labor Movement: The Christian Spirit in the Gilded Age," in Alfred Young, ed., *Dissent* (DeKalb, 1968), 139-174; see also Gutman, "The Worker's Search for Power; Labor in the Gilded Age," in H. Wayne Morgan, ed., *The Gilded Age* (New York, 1963), pp. 38-68. For other innovative studies, see David Brody, *Steelworkers in America: The Non-Union Era* (Cambridge, Mass., 1960); Stephan Thernstrom, *Poverty and Progress: Social Mobility in a Nineteenth Century City* (Cambridge, Mass., 1964), and David Montgomery, *Beyond Equality: Labor and the Radical Republicans, 1862–1872* (New York, 1967).

3. Jonathan Lincoln in a speech commemorating the opening of a new mill in Fall River, Massachusetts, commented that in Boston and New York, Fall River was considered a culturally backward and unsophisticated place because all its energy was put to the single task of industry and prosperity. J. Gilmer Speed, *Fall River Incident* (Fall River, 1895), 18.

4. In a taped interview I made with retired shoe workers who entered the shoe trade in the early twentieth century, Frank Cacicio remarked: "I was a shoe worker all my life and I am not sorry; I'm proud of the shoe workers."

These tapes were made in group sessions in order to gain a broader sample of experience. Many of the shoe workers did not want to give their names but were willing to talk in the broad forum of the group. Because much of the information cited here was the product of the group rather than single individuals, they will be referred to hereafter as "tapes." The tapes are also available at the Lynn Historical Society.

The workers who came to this country to work in the shoe and leather industries were not all unskilled workers. U.S. Congress, Senate, Immigration Commission, *Immigrants in Industry*, vol. 74, 61st Cong., 2d sess., S. Doc. 633, 1909-1910, 225, 377.

5. Local studies of the Knights of Labor show that despite the national's position against strikes, local assemblies used them continually in order to gain wage and job condition improvements.

6. Lynn's labor history was full of secession movements and the formation of local independent unions.

7. David Johnson, *Sketches of Lynn* (Lynn, 1880), ii, 21-52; Paul Faler, "Workingmen, Mechanics and Social Change: Lynn, Massachusetts, 1800-1860" (Ph.D. diss., University of Wisconsin, 1970).

8. William Betts, "Lynn, a City by the Sea," *Outlook* 68 (May 1901): 209; see also the papers of the Lynn Associated Charities, Family Service of Greater Lynn; Papers of the Gregg

House, Swedenborg School of Religion, Newton, Mass., for descriptions of the mixed ethnic community in the Brickyard; tapes, Lynn Historical Society.

9. See Betts, "Lynn," 201, for a description of the Lynn tenements at the turn of the century.

10. Immigration Commission, *Immigrants in Industry*, 225; *Massachusetts State Census, 1895* (Boston, 1896), 4:392; *Thirty-fourth Annual Report of Massachusetts Bureau of Statistics of Labor, 1903* (Boston, 1904), 181.

11. The names in the dues books of the Lynn Lasters Union, vols. 14-19, 1870-1900, indicate more foreign shoe workers in Lynn than the state statistics would suggest. Lynn Lasters Union Papers, Baker Library, Harvard University.

12. *Massachusetts State Census*, 390; *Thirty-fourth Annual Report*, 119.

13. U.S. Department of Labor, Bureau of Statistics of Labor, *Description of Occupations, Boot, and Shoe, and Tanning* (Washington, D.C., 1918), 63-70; Leo C. Brown, *Union Policies in the Leather Industry* (Cambridge, Mass., 1947), 180-181; tapes.

14. Johnson, *Sketches*, 320-31.

15. "Shoe Manufacturing in Lynn," *Boot and Shoe Recorder* (Lynn, 1892), 14.

16. Department of Labor, *Description of Occupations*, 63-70; Leo C. Brown, "Collective Bargaining in the Leather Industry" (Ph.D. diss., Harvard University, 1940), 14.

17. See Robert Blauner, *Alienation and Freedom* (Chicago, 1964), for a discussion of skill and the worker's consciousness of the total production process in contributing to solidarity.

18. "Minutes of Lynn Lasters Union," vol. 1, June 23, 1896, Lynn Lasters Union Papers.

19. Taped interviews with retired shoe workers of Lynn reflecting back on when they first entered the trade before World War I and what their parents, who were also shoe workers, told them. See also Allen Dawley, "The Artisan Response to the Factory System: Lynn, Massachusetts" (Ph.D. diss., Harvard University, 1971); "Testimony of Horace Eaton, Sec'y. of Lynn Lasters," *Report* of the U.S. Industrial Commission, vol. 7, 56th Cong., 2d. sess., H. Doc. 495 (Washington, D.C., 1900-1901), 364.

20. Lynn Lasters Union, receipt book, vol. 10, Lynn Lasters Union Papers.

21. Tapes. Advertisements were placed in the local union reports by local lunchrooms and cafés that emphasized the social and political aspect of the eating places. Mackenzie's Lunch claimed to be a "strictly union house," and Wyman's Lunch on Monroe Street, where there were a large number of shoe and leather factories, noted that they were open all night for socializing and gathering.

22. Tapes.

23. Betts, "Lynn," 210; Nathan Hawkes, "An Historical Address Delivered before Bay State Lodge, #40, I.O.O.F., 1894," unfiled ms., Lynn Historical Society.

24. See Faler, "Workingmen," chap. 11.

25. Minutes of Lynn Lasters Union, vol. 1, Nov. 9, 1898; dues book, vol. 10, 1894-1896; Minutes of Benefit Assoc., vol. 24, Sept. 10, 1894; record book, Lasters Aid Assoc., vol. 26, June 1890, Nov. 1890, Lynn Lasters Union Papers.

26. The banners at the 1890 Labor Day parade reflected this aspect of strong class-conscious unionism, with such slogans as: "To Labor Belongs All the Value!" "Together We Stand!" "Labor Pays Taxes Without Representation." *Lynn Daily Bee*, Sept. 2, 1890.

27. *Boston Evening Transcript*, Nov. 13, 1886. Although the number of local assemblies of the Knights of Labor had decreased in the second half of the 1880s, Lynn still had between four and fourteen strong local assemblies, mostly of shoe and leather workers. Jonathan Garlock and N. C. Builder, *Knights of Labor Data Bank* (Ann Arbor, Mich., 1973). I would like to thank Eric Austin of ICPR for his help in procuring the listing of the Knights of Labor Assemblies data.

28. *Thirtieth Annual Report of Massachusetts Bureau of Labor Statistics, 1889* (Boston, 1900), 197.

29. Ibid.

30. In the late nineteenth and early twentieth centuries, Lynn had the third largest number of trade unions of any city in the state. Massachusetts Bureau of Statistics of Labor, *Massachusetts Labor Bulletin*, nos. 1-38 (Boston, 1897-1905).

31. *Lynn Transcript*, Aug. 1, 1890; *Massachusetts State Annual Report of Manufacturers, 1891* (Boston, 1892), 255.

32. *Lynn Transcript*, Aug. 1, 1890.

33. *Lynn Daily Item*, Oct. 2, 1890.

34. *Annual Report, Shoe and Leather Reporter, 1886* (Boston, 1886).

35. Brown, *Union Policies*, 24-25, 31; *Lynn Transcript,* Aug. 29, Sept. 5, 1890; *Lynn Daily Item*, Oct. 4, 1890.

36. *Lynn Transcript*, Sept. 5, 1890.

37. *Lynn Daily Bee*, Sept. 4, 1890.

38. *Lynn Daily Item*, Sept. 11, 1890.

39. Ibid., Sept. 16, 1890.

40. Ibid., Sept. 14, 1890.

41. Herbert Gutman has called attention to the support of strikers by merchants and small businessmen in his work. See, for example, Gutman, "Workers Struggle for Power," 20. The difference between the support Gutman saw in the small industrial towns that he studied and the support by Lynn's merchants was one of motivation. Gutman attributed the merchants' support to personal ties between workers and small businessmen, which went back to earlier stages of development. In Lynn, although personal ties were clearly a factor in much of the support, many of the merchants acted because of the economic power of the organized workers in the city. The workers in Lynn were accustomed to using their buying power as a means of punishing local merchants and tradesmen for not supporting strikes. In 1894, for instance, the Lynn Lasters Union refused to buy coal from the Lynn dealers because the local dealers were "not progressive," and had failed to support the city's workers. Minutes book, Lynn Lasters Benefit Association, vol. 24, Sept. 10, 1894, Lynn Lasters Union Papers.

42. *Lynn Daily Item*, Sept. 16, 1890.

43. *Lynn Daily Bee*, Sept. 24, 1890.

44. Ibid., Sept. 20, 1890.

45. *Lynn Daily Item*, Oct. 6, 1890.

46. Ibid.

47. Ibid.

48. Ibid.

49. Ibid., Oct. 9, 1890.

50. Ibid.

51. Ibid., Oct. 4, 1890.

52. Ibid.

53. Ibid.

54. Ibid., Nov. 15, 1890.

55. Lynn Lasters Union Treasurer's cash book, vols. 3, 4, Sept. 5, 29, Oct. 13, 28, Nov. 25, Dec. 23, 1890, Jan. 20, Feb. 21, June 1, 1891, Lasters Union Papers.

56. *Lynn Daily Item*, Jan. 1, 1891.

57. Ibid., Oct. 6, 1890.

58. Workingclass children of the Brickyard from an early age identified with local workingclass peer groups, which were centers for their activity and were in constant conflict with the police. Much of their activity was directed against the symbols of the controlling elites of the city, such as factories and abandoned tenement buildings. Papers of the Gregg House (nineteenth-century settlement house), *Scrapbook* 1, 1907.

59. *Lynn Daily Bee*, Sept. 19, 1890.

60. *Lynn Daily Item*, Sept. 19, 1890.

61. Ibid.

62. *Lynn Daily Bee*, Sept. 19, 1890.

63. Ibid., Sept. 23, 1890.

64. *Lynn Transcript*, Oct. 3, 1890. On Sept. 22 strikers remained on vigil all night "waiting in expectation of the Armenians." *Lynn Daily Bee*, Sept. 23, 1890.

65. *Lynn Daily Item*, Sept. 20, 1890.

66. Ibid., Sept. 22, 1890.

67. Ibid.; Dawley, "Artisan Response," 308.

68. *Lynn Daily Item*, Sept. 23, 1890.

69. *Lynn Daily Bee*, Sept. 24, 1890.

70. Ibid.

71. *Lynn Transcript*, Sept. 19, Oct. 3, 1890; *Lynn Daily Item*, Oct. 2, 1890; *Lynn Daily Bee*, Sept. 27, 1890.

72. *Lynn Daily Item*, Sept. 26, 1890.

73. Ibid., Oct. 2, 1890.

74. *Lynn Daily Bee*, Sept. 27, 1890.

75. *Lynn Daily Item*, Oct. 13, 1890.

76. Ibid., Dec. 24, 1890.

77. Dawley, "Artisan Response," 307-309.

78. *Lynn Daily Item*, Oct. 4, 1890.

79. During the strike in Lynn, leather manufacturers began locking out Knights of Labor workers in New York City.

80. In an interview with Thomas Coleman, an eighty-year-old retired shoe worker, at the Lynn union hall, United Shoe Workers, I asked Mr. Coleman what nonshoe workers such as salesmen or real estate agents did in their spare time. Mr. Coleman responded that "in the old days there were only shoe workers in Lynn." Interview, Dec. 13, 1972.

81. Although the men were part of the Knights of Labor with its national organization, the Knights were unable to coordinate an effective national boycott against scab leather. The power of the Knights in Lynn was in the local support they enjoyed. The manufacturers dealt mostly with nonlocal markets. Shoe towns like Brockton and Haverhill were not as organized as Lynn in the 1880s, and coordination and communication were not sufficiently developed to organize an effective statewide boycott.

82. In 1903 the cutters' local of the Knights of Labor successfully struck against the United Boot and Shoe Workers Union, AFL, to maintain control over the Lynn cutters and stitchers. Ellen Wetherell, *After the Battle* (Lynn, 1903), 1-6.

83. Minutes of Lynn Lasters Union, vol. 1, Aug. 23, 1899; *Thirtieth Annual Report,* 197; A. E. Galster, *Labor Movement in the Shoe Industry* (New York, 1924), 145-155; Edward Bert, *The Shoe Craft* (Boston, 1917), 69; John Laslett, *Labor and the Left* (New York, 1970), 70, 72, 75, 83-88. The Lynn Lasters Protective Union, which helped form the Boot and Shoe Workers Union in Lynn late in the 1890s, split off from the BSWU and joined the ST and LA. The Lasters soon afterward left the ST and LA. In the early twentieth century many other Lynn shoe workers broke off from the BSWU to form the United Shoe Workers, as well as several independent unions.

WOMEN, WORK, AND PROTEST IN THE EARLY LOWELL MILLS: "THE OPPRESSING HAND OF AVARICE WOULD ENSLAVE US"

8

Thomas Dublin

In the years before 1850 the textile mills of Lowell, Massachusetts, were a celebrated economic and cultural attraction. Foreign visitors invariably included them on their American tours. Interest was prompted by the massive scale of these mills, the astonishing productivity of the power-driven machinery, and the fact that women comprised most of the work force. Visitors were struck by the newness of both mills and city as well as by the culture of the female operatives. The scene stood in sharp contrast to the gloomy mill towns of the English industrial revolution.

Lowell, was, in fact, an impressive accomplishment. In 1820, there had been no city at all — only a dozen family farms along the Merrimack River in East Chelmsford. In 1821, however, a group of Boston capitalists purchased land and water rights along the river and a nearby canal, and began to build a major textile manufacturing center. Opening two years later, the first factory employed Yankee women recruited from the nearby countryside. Additional mills were constructed until, by 1840, ten textile corporations with thirty-two mills valued at more than ten million dollars lined the banks of the river and nearby canals.[1] Adjacent to the mills were rows of company boardinghouses and tenements which accommodated most of the eight thousand factory operatives.

As Lowell expanded and became the nation's largest textile manufacturing center, the experiences of women operatives changed as well. The increasing number of firms in Lowell and in the other mill towns brought the pressure of competition. Overproduction became a problem and the prices of finished cloth decreased. The high profits of the early years declined and so, too, did conditions

Source: From *Labor History* 16, no. 1 (Winter 1975).

for the mill operatives. Wages were reduced and the pace of work within the mills was stepped up. Women operatives did not accept these changes without protest. In 1834 and 1836 they went on strike to protest wage cuts, and between 1843 and 1848 they mounted petition campaigns aimed at reducing the hours of labor in the mills.

These labor protests in early Lowell contribute to our understanding of the response of workers to the growth of industrial capitalism in the first half of the nineteenth century. They indicate the importance of values and attitudes dating back to an earlier period and also the transformation of these values in a new setting.

The major factor in the rise of a new consciousness among operatives in Lowell was the development of a close-knit community among women working in the mills. The structure of work and the nature of housing contributed to the growth of this community. The existence of community among women, in turn, was an important element in the repeated labor protests of the period.

The organization of this paper derives from the logic of the above argument. It will examine the basis of community in the experiences of women operatives and then the contribution that the community of women made to the labor protests in these years as well as the nature of the new consciousness expressed by these protests.

The preconditions for the labor unrest in Lowell before 1850 may be found in the study of the daily worklife of its operatives. In their everyday, relatively conflict-free lives, mill women created the mutual bonds which made possible united action in times of crisis. The existence of a tight-knit community among them was the most important element in determining the collective, as opposed to individual, nature of this response.

Before examining the basis of community among women operatives in early Lowell, it may be helpful to indicate in what sense "community" is being used. The women are considered a "community" because of the development of bonds of mutual dependence among them. In this period they came to depend upon one another and upon the larger group of operatives in very important ways. Their experiences were not simply similar or parallel to one another, but were inextricably intertwined. Furthermore, they were conscious of the existence of community, expressing it very clearly in their writings and in labor protests. "Community" for them had objective and subjective dimensions, and both were important in the experience of women in the mills.

The mutual dependence among women in early Lowell was rooted in the structure of mill work itself. Newcomers to the mills were particularly dependent on their fellow operatives, but even experienced hands relied on one another for considerable support.

New operatives generally found their first experiences difficult, even harrowing, though they may have already done much hand-spinning and weaving in their own homes. The initiation of one of them is described in fiction in the *Lowell Offering:*

> The next morning she went into the Mill; and at first the sight of so many bands, and wheels, and springs in constant motion, was very frightful. She felt afraid to touch the loom, and she was almost sure she could never learn to weave . . . the shuttle flew out, and made a new bump on her head; and the first time she tried to spring the lathe, she broke out a quarter of the treads.[2]

While other accounts present a somewhat less difficult picture, most indicate that women only became proficient and felt satisfaction in their work after several months in the mills. [3]

The textile corporations made provisions to ease the adjustment of new operatives. Newcomers were not immediately expected to fit into the mill's regular work routine. They were at first assigned work as sparehands and were paid a daily wage independent of the quantity of work they turned out. As a sparehand, the newcomer worked with an experienced hand who instructed her in the intricacies of the job. The sparehand spelled her partner for short stretches of time and occasionally took the place of an absentee. One woman described the learning process in a letter reprinted in the *Offering*:

> Well, I went into the mill, and was put to learn with a very patient girl . . . . You cannot think

> how odd everything seemed . . . . They set me to
> threading shuttles, and tying weaver's knots, and
> such things, and now I have improved so that I can
> take care of one loom. I could take care of two if
> only I had eyes in the back part of my head.[4]

After the passage of some weeks or months, when she could handle
the normal complement of machinery — two looms for weavers
during the 1830s — and when a regular operative departed, leaving
an opening, the sparehand moved into a regular job.

Through this system of job training, the textile corporations contributed to the development of community among female operatives. During the most difficult period in an operative's career, the
first months in the mill, she relied upon other women workers for
training and support. And for every sparehand whose adjustment
to mill work was aided in this process, there was an experienced
operative whose work was also affected. Women were relating to
one another during the work process and not simply tending their
machinery. Given the high rate of turnover in the mill workforce, a
large proportion of women operatives worked in pairs. At the
Hamilton Company in July 1836, for example, more than a fifth of
all females on the Company payroll were sparehands.[5] Consequently, over 40 percent of the females employed there in this
month worked with one another. Nor was this interaction sur-
reptitious, carried out only when the overseer looked elsewhere;
rather, it was formally organized and sanctioned by the textile
corporations themselves.

In addition to the integration of sparehands, informal sharing of
work often went on among regular operatives. A woman would occasionally take off a half or full day from work either to enjoy a
brief vacation or to recover from illness, and fellow operatives
would each take an extra loom or side of spindles so that she might
continue to earn wages during her absence.[6] Women were generally
paid on a piece rate basis, their wages being determined by the total
output of the machinery they tended during the payroll period.
With friends helping out during her absence, making sure that her
looms kept running, an operative could earn almost a full wage
even though she was not physically present. Such informal work-

sharing was another way in which mutual dependence developed among women operatives during their working hours.

Living conditions also contributed to the development of community among female operatives. Most women working in the Lowell mills of these years were housed in company boarding houses. In July 1836, for example, more than 73 percent of females employed by the Hamilton Company resided in company housing adjacent to the mills.[7] Almost three-fourths of them, therefore, lived and worked with each other. Furthermore, the work schedule was such that women had little opportunity to interact with those not living in company dwellings. They worked, in these years, an average of 73 hours a week. Their work day ended at 7:00 or 7:30 P.M., and in the hours between supper and the 10:00 curfew imposed by management on residents of company boarding houses there was little time to spend with friends living "off the corporation."

Women in the boarding houses lived in close quarters, a factor that also played a role in the growth of community. A typical boarding house accommodated twenty-five young women, generally crowded four to eight in a bedroom.[8] There was little possibility of privacy within the dwelling, and pressure to conform to group standards was very strong (as will be discussed below). The community of operatives which developed in the mills carried over into life at home as well.

The boarding house became a central institution in the lives of Lowell's female operatives in those years, but it was particularly important in the initial integration of newcomers into urban industrial life. Upon first leaving her rural home for work in Lowell, a women entered a setting very different from anything she had previously known. One operative, writing in the *Offering*, described the feelings of a fictional character: ". . . the first entrance into a factory boarding house seemed something dreadful. The room looked strange and comfortless, and the women cold and heartless; and when she sat down to the supper table, where among more than twenty girls, all but one were strangers, she could not eat a mouthful." [9]

In the boarding house, the newcomer took the first steps in the process which transformed her from an "outsider" into an accepted member of the community of women operatives.

Recruitment of newcomers into the mills and their initial hiring was mediated through the boarding house system. Women generally did not travel to Lowell for the first time entirely on their own. They usually came because they knew someone — an older sister, cousin, or friend — who had already worked in Lowell.[10] The scene described above was a lonely one — but the newcomer did know at least one boarder among the twenty seated around the supper table. The Hamilton Company Register Books indicate that numerous pairs of operatives, having the same surnames and coming from the same town in northern New England, lived in the same boarding houses.[11] If the newcomer was not accompanied by a friend or relative, she was usually directed to "Number 20, Hamilton Company," or to a similar address of one of the other corporations where her acquaintance lived. Her first contact with fellow operatives generally came in the boarding houses and not in the mills. Given the personal nature of recruitment in this period, therefore, newcomers usually had the company and support of a friend or relative in their first adjustment to Lowell.

Like recruitment, the initial hiring was a personal process. Once settled in the boarding house, a newcomer had to find a job. She would generally go to the mills with her friend or with the boarding house keeper who would introduce her to an overseer in one of the rooms. If he had an opening, she might start work immediately. More likely, the overseer would know of an opening elsewhere in the mill, or would suggest that something would probably develop within a few days. In one story in the *Offering*, a newcomer worked on some quilts for her house keeper, thereby earning her board while she waited for a job opening.[12]

Upon entering the boarding house, the newcomer came under pressure to conform with the standards of the community of operatives. Stories in the *Offering* indicate that newcomers at first stood out from the group in terms of their speech and dress. Over time they dropped the peculiar "twang" in their speech which so amused experienced hands. Similarly, they purchased clothing more in keeping with urban than rural styles. It was an unusual and strongwilled individual who could work and live among her fellow operatives and not conform, at least outwardly, to the customs and values of this larger community.[13]

The boarding houses were the centers of social life for women operatives after their long days in the mills. There they ate their meals, rested, talked, sewed, wrote letters, read books and magazines. From among fellow workers and boarders they found friends who accompanied them to shops, to Lyceum lectures, to church and church-sponsored events. On Sundays or holidays, they often took walks along the canals or out into the nearby countryside. The community of women operatives, in sum, developed in a setting where women worked and lived together, twenty-four hours a day.

Given the all-pervasiveness of this community, one would expect it to exert strong pressures on those who did not conform to group standards. Such appears to have been the case. The community influenced newcomers to adopt its patterns of speech and dress. In addition, it enforced an unwritten code of moral conduct. Henry Miles, a minister in Lowell, described the way in which the community pressured those who deviated from accepted moral conduct:

> A girl, suspected of immoralities, or serious improprieties, at once loses caste. Her fellow boarders will at once leave the house, if the keeper does not dismiss the offender. In self-protection, therefore, the patron is obliged to put the offender away. Nor will her former companions walk with her, or work with her; till at length, finding herself everywhere talked about, and pointed at, and shunned, she is obliged to relieve her fellow-operatives of a presence which they feel brings disgrace. [14]

The power of the peer group described by Miles may seem extreme, but there is evidence in the writing of women operatives to corroborate his account. Such group pressure is illustrated by a story (in the *Offering*) in which operatives in a company boarding house begin to harbor suspicions about a fellow boarder, Hannah, who has received repeated evening visits from a man whom she does not introduce to the other residents. Two boarders declare that they will leave if she is allowed to remain in the household. The housekeeper finally informs Hannah that she must either depart or not see the man again. She does not accept the ultimatum, but is promptly discharged after the overseer is informed, by one of the boarders, about her conduct. And only one of Hannah's former friends continues to remain on cordial terms.[15]

One should not conclude, however, that women always enforced a moral code agreeable to Lowell's clergy, or to the mill agents and overseers for that matter. After all, the kind of peer pressure imposed on Hannah could be brought to bear on women in 1834 and 1836 who, on their own, would not have protested wage cuts. It was much harder to go to work when one's roommates were marching about town, attending rallies, or circulating strike petitions. Similarly, the ten-hour petitions of the 1840s were certainly aided by the fact of a tight-knit community of operatives living in a dense neighborhood of boarding houses. To the extent that women could not have completely private lives in the boarding houses, they probably had to conform to group norms, whether these involved speech, clothing, relations with men, or attitudes toward the ten-hour day. Group pressure to conform, so important to the community of women in early Lowell, played a significant role in the collective response of women to changing conditions in the mills.

In addition to the structure of work and housing in Lowell, a third factor, the homogeneity of the mill workforce, contributed to the development of community among female operatives. In this period, the mill workforce was homogeneous in terms of sex, nativity, and age. Payroll and other records of the Hamilton Company reveal that more than 85 per cent of those employed in July, 1836, were women and that over 96 per cent were native-born.[16] Furthermore, over 80 per cent of the female workforce were between the ages of 15 and 30; and only 10 per cent were under 14 or over 40.[17]

Workforce homogeneity takes on particular significance in the context of work structure and the nature of worker housing. These three factors combined meant that women operatives had little interaction with men during their daily lives. Men and women did not perform the same work in the mills, and generally did not even labor in the same rooms. Men worked in the initial picking and carding processes, in the repair shop, and on the watchforce and filled all supervisory positions in the mills. Women held all spare-hand and regular operative jobs in drawing, speeding, spinning, weaving and dressing. A typical room in the mill employed eighty women tending machinery, with two men overseeing the work and two boys assisting them. Women had little contact with men other than their supervisors in the course of the working day. After work, women returned to their boarding houses, where once again there were few men. Women, then, worked and lived in a predominantly female setting.

Ethnically the workforce was also homogeneous. Immigrants formed only 3.4 per cent of those employed at Hamilton in July, 1836. In addition, they comprised only 3 per cent of residents in Hamilton Company housing.[18] The community of women operatives was composed of women of New England stock drawn from the hill-country farms surrounding Lowell. Consequently, when experienced hands made fun of the speech and dress of newcomers, it was understood that they, too, had been "rusty" or "rustic" upon first coming to Lowell. This common background was another element shared by women workers in early Lowell.

The work structure, the workers' housing, and workforce homogeneity were the major elements which contributed to the growth of community among Lowell's women operatives. To best understand the larger implications of community, it is necessary to examine the labor protests of this period. For in these struggles, the new values and attitudes which developed in the community of women operatives are most visible.

II

In February, 1834, 800 of Lowell's women operatives "turned-out" — went on strike — to protest a proposed reduction in their wages. They marched to numerous mills in an effort to induce others to join them, and, at an outdoor rally, they petitioned others to "discontinue their labors until terms of reconciliation are made." Their petition concluded:

> Resolved, That we will not go back into the mills to work unless our wages are continued . . . as they have been.

> Resolved, That none of us will go back, unless they receive us all as one.

> Resolved, That if any have not money enough to carry them home, they shall be supplied.[19]

The strike proved to be brief and failed to reverse the proposed wage reductions. Turning-out on a Friday, the striking women were paid their back wages on Saturday, and by the middle of the next week had returned to work or left town. Within a week of the turn-out, the mills were running near capacity.[20]

This first strike in Lowell is important not because it failed or succeeded, but simply because it took place. In an era in which women had to overcome opposition simply to work in the mills, it is remarkable that they would further overstep the accepted middle-class bounds of female propriety by participating in a public protest. The agents of the textile mills certainly considered the turn-out unfeminine. William Austin, agent of the Lawrence Company, described the operatives' procession as an "amizonian [sic] display." He wrote further, in a letter to his company treasurer in Boston: "This afternoon we have paid off several of these Amazons & presume that they will leave town on Monday."[21] The turn-out was particularly offensive to the agents because of the relationship they thought they had with their operatives. William Austin probably expressed the feelings of other agents when he wrote: " . . . notwithstanding the friendly and disinterested advice which has been on all proper occassions [sic] communicated to the girls of the Lawrence mills a spirit of evil omen . . . has prevailed, and overcome the judgement and discretion of too many, and this morning a general turn-out from most of the rooms has been the consequence."[22]

Mill agents assumed an attitude of benevolent paternalism toward their female operatives, and found it particularly disturbing that the women paid such little heed to their advice. The strikers were not merely unfeminine, they were ungrateful as well.

Such attitudes notwithstanding, women chose to turn-out. They did so for two principal reasons. First, the wage cuts undermined the sense of dignity and social equality, which was an important element in their Yankee heritage. Second, these wage cuts were seen as an attack on their economic independence.

Certainly a prime motive for the strike was outrage at the social implications of the wage cuts. In a statement of principles accompanying the petition which was circulated among operatives, women expressed well the sense of themselves which prompted their protests of these wage cuts:

UNION IS POWER

Our present object is to have union and exertion, and we remain in possession of our unquestionable rights. We circulate this paper wishing to obtain the names of all who imbibe the spirit of our Patriotic Ancestors, who preferred privation to bondage, and parted with all that renders life desirable — and even life itself — to procure independence for their children. The oppressing hand of avarice would enslave us, and to gain their object, they gravely tell us of the pressure of the time, this we are already sensible of, and deplore it. If any are in want of assistance, the Ladies will be compassionate and assist them; but we prefer to have the disposing of our charities in our own hands; and as we are free, we would remain in possession of what kind Providence has bestowed upon us; and remain daughters of freeman still. [23]

At several points in the proclamation the women drew on their Yankee heritage. Connecting their turn-out with the efforts of their

"Patriotic Ancestors" to secure independence from England, they interpreted the wage cuts as an effort to "enslave" them — to deprive them of their independent status as "daughters of freeman."

Though very general and rhetorical, the statement of these women does suggest their sense of self, of their own worth and dignity. Elsewhere, they expressed the conviction that they were the social equals of the overseers, indeed of the mill owners themselves.[24] The wage cuts, however, struck at this assertion of social equality. These reductions made it clear that the operatives were subordinate to their employers, rather than equal partners in a contract binding on both parties. By turning-out the women emphatically denied that they were subordinates; but by returning to work the next week, they demonstrated that in economic terms they were no match for their corporate superiors.

In point of fact, these Yankee operatives were subordinate in early Lowell's social and economic order, but they never consciously accepted this status. Their refusal to do so became evident whenever the mill owners attempted to exercise the power they possessed. This fundamental contradiction between the objective status of operatives and their consciousness of it was at the root of the 1834 turn-out and of subsequent labor protests in Lowell before 1850. The corporations could build mills, create thousands of jobs, and recruit women to fill them. Nevertheless, they bought only the workers' labor power, and then only for as long as these workers chose to stay. Women could always return to their rural homes, and they had a sense of their own worth and dignity, factors limiting the actions of management.

Women operatives viewed the wage cuts as a threat to their economic independence. This independence had two related dimensions. First, the women were self-supporting while they worked in the mills and, consequently, were independent of their families back home. Second, they were able to save out of their monthly earnings and could then leave the mills for the old homestead whenever they so desired. In effect, they were not totally dependent upon mill work. Their independence was based largely on the high level of wages in the mills. They could support themselves and still save enough to return home periodically. The wage cuts threatened to deny them this outlet, substituting instead the prospect of total dependence on mill work. Small wonder, then, there was alarm that "the oppressing hand of avarice would enslave us." To be forced, out of economic necessity, to lifelong labor in the mills would have indeed seemed like slavery.[25] The Yankee operatives spoke directly to the fear of a dependency based on impoverishment when offering to assist any women workers who "have not money enough to carry them home." Wage reductions, however, offered only the *prospect* of a future dependence on mill employment. By striking, the women asserted their actual economic independence of the mills and their determination to remain "daughters of freemen still."

While the women's traditional conception of themselves as independent daughters of freemen played a major role in the turn-out, this factor acting alone would not necessarily have triggered the 1834 strike. It would have led women as individuals to quit work and return to their rural homes. But the turn-out was a collective protest. When it was announced that wage reductions were being considered, women began to hold meetings in the mills during meal breaks in order to assess tactical possibilities. Their turn-out began at one mill when the agent discharged a woman who had presided at such a meeting. Their procession through the streets passed by other mills, expressing a conscious effort to enlist as much support as possible for their cause. At a mass meeting, the women drew up a resolution which insisted that none be discharged for their participation in the turn-out. This strike, then, was a collective response to the proposed wage cuts — made possible because women had come to form a "community" of operatives in the mill, rather than simply a group of individual workers. The existence of such a tight-knit community turned individual opposition to the wage cuts into a collective protest.

In October, 1836, women again went on strike. This second turn-out was similar to the first in several respects. Its immediate cause was also a wage reduction; marches and a large outdoor rally were organized; again, like the earlier protest, the basic goal was not achieved: the corporations refused to restore wages and operatives either left Lowell or returned to work at the new rates.

Despite these surface similarities between the turn-outs, there were some real differences. One involved scale: over 1500 operatives turned out in 1836, compared to only 800 earlier.[26] Moreover, the second strike lasted much longer than the first. In 1834 operatives stayed out for only a few days; in 1836, the mills ran far below capacity for several months. Two weeks after the second turn-out began, a mill agent reported that only a fifth of the strikers had returned to work: "The rest manifest *good 'spunk'* as they call it."[27] Several days later he described the impact of the continuing strike on operations in his mills: "We must be feeble for months to come as probably not less than 250 of our former scanty supply of help have left town."[28] These lines read in sharp contrast to the optimistic reports of agents following the turn-out in February, 1834.

Differences between the two turn-outs were not limited to the increased scale and duration of the later one. Women displayed a much higher degree of organization in 1836 than earlier. To coordinate strike activities, they formed a Factory Girls' Association. According to one historian, membership in the short-lived association reached 2500 at its height.[29] The larger organization among women was reflected in the tactics employed. Strikers, according to one mill agent, were able to halt production to a greater extent than numbers alone could explain; and, he complained, although some operatives were willing to work, "it has been impossible to give employment to many who remained." He attributed this difficulty to the strikers' tactics: "This was in many instances no doubt the result of calculation and contrivance. After the original turn-out they [the operatives] would assail a particular room—as for instance, all the warpers, or all the warp spinners, or all the speeder and stretcher girls, and this would close the mill as effectually as if all the girls in the mill had left."[30]

Now giving more thought than they had in 1834 to the specific tactics of the turn-out, the women made a deliberate effort to shut down the mills in order to win their demands. They attempted to persuade less committed operatives, concentrating on those in crucial departments within the mill. Such tactics anticipated those of skilled mulespinners and loomfixers who went out on strike in the 1880s and 1890s.

In their organization of a Factory Girl's Association and in their efforts to shut down the mills, the female operatives revealed that they had been changed by their industrial experience. Increasingly, they acted not simply as "daughters of freemen" offended by the impositions of the textile corporations, but also as industrial workers intent on improving their position within the mills.

There was a decline in protest among women in the Lowell mills following these early strike defeats. During the 1837-1843 depression, textile corporations twice reduced wages without evoking a collective response from operatives.[31] Because of the frequency of production cutbacks and lay-offs in these years, workers probably accepted the mill agents' contention that they had to reduce wages or close entirely. But with the return of prosperity and the expansion of production in the mid-1840s, there were renewed labor protests among women. Their actions paralleled those of working men and reflected fluctuations in the business cycle. Prosperity itself did not prompt turn-outs, but it evidently facilitated collective actions by women operatives.

In contrast to the protests of the previous decade, the struggles now were primarily political. Women did not turn-out in the 1840s; rather, they mounted annual petition campaigns calling on the state legislature to limit the hours of labor within the mills. These campaigns reached their height in 1845 and 1846, when 2,000 and 5,000 operatives respectively signed petitions. Unable to curb the wage cuts or the speed-up and stretch-out imposed by mill owners, operatives sought to mitigate the consequences of these changes by reducing the length of the working day. Having been defeated earlier in economic struggles, they now sought to achieve their new goal through political action. The Ten Hour Movement, seen in these terms, was a logical outgrowth of the unsuccessful turn-outs of the previous decade. Like the earlier struggles, the Ten Hour Movement was an assertion of the dignity of operatives and an attempt to maintain that dignity under the changing conditions of industrial capitalism.

The growth of relatively permanent labor organizations and institutions among women was a distinguishing feature of the Ten Hour Movement of the 1840s. The Lowell Female Labor Reform Association was organized in 1845 by women operatives. It became Lowell's leading labor organization over the next three years, organizing the city's female operatives and helping to set up branches in other mill towns. The Association was affiliated with the New

England Workingmen's Association and sent delegates to its meetings. It acted in concert with similar male groups and yet maintained its own autonomy. Women elected their own officers, held their own meetings, testified before a state legislative committee, and published a series of "Factory Tracts" which exposed conditions within the mills and argued for the ten-hour day. [32]

An important educational and organizing tool of the Lowell Female Labor Reform Association was the *Voice of Industry*, a labor weekly published in Lowell between 1845 and 1848 by the New England Workingmen's Association. Female operatives were involved in every aspect of its publication and used the *Voice* to further the Ten Hour Movement among women. Their Association owned the press on which the *Voice* was printed. Sarah Bagley, the Association president, was a member of the three-person publishing committee of the *Voice* and for a time served as editor. Other women were employed by the paper as travelling editors. They wrote articles about the Ten Hour Movement in other mill towns, in an effort to give ten-hour supporters a sense of the larger cause of which they were a part. Furthermore, they raised money for the *Voice* and increased its circulation by selling subscriptions to the paper in their travels about New England. Finally, women used the *Voice* to appeal directly to their fellow operatives. They edited a separate "Female Department," which published letters and articles by and about women in the mills.

Another aspect of the Ten Hour Movement which distinguished it from the earlier labor struggles in Lowell was that it involved both men and women. At the same time that women in Lowell formed the Female Labor Reform Association, a male mechanics' and laborers' association was also organized. Both groups worked to secure the passage of legislation setting ten hours as the length of the working day. Both groups circulated petitions to this end, and when the legislative committee came to Lowell to hear testimony, both men and women testified in favor of the ten-hour day.

The two groups, then, worked together, and each made an important contribution to the movement in Lowell. Women had the numbers, comprising as they did over 80 per cent of the mill workforce. Men, on the other hand, had the votes, and since the Ten Hour Movement was a political struggle, they played a crucial part. After the State committee reported unfavorably on the ten-hour petitions, the Female Labor Reform Association denounced the committee chairman, a state representative from Lowell, as a corporation "tool." Working for his defeat at the polls, they did so successfully and then passed the following post-election resolution: "*Resolved*, That the members of this Association tender their grateful acknowledgements to the voters of Lowell, for consigning William Schouler to the obscurity he so justly deserves . . . ."[33] Women took a more prominent part in the Ten Hour Movement in Lowell than did men, but they obviously remained dependent on male voters and legislators for the ultimate success of their movement.

Although co-ordinating their efforts with those of working men, women operatives organized independently within the Ten Hour Movement. For instance, in 1845 two important petitions were sent from Lowell to the state legislature. Almost 90 per cent of the signers of one petition were females, and more than two-thirds of the signers of the second were males.[34] Clearly the separation of men and women in their daily lives was reflected in the Ten Hour petitions of these years.

The way in which the Ten Hour Movement was carried from Lowell to other mill towns also illustrated the independent organizing of women within the larger movement. For example, at a spirited meeting in Manchester, New Hampshire, in December, 1845 — one presided over by Lowell operatives — more than a thousand workers, two-thirds of them women, passed resolutions calling for the ten-hour day. Later, those in attendance divided along male-female lines, each group meeting separately to set up parallel organizations. Sixty women joined the Manchester Female Labor Reform Association that evening, and by the following summer it claimed over three hundred members. Female operatives met in company boarding houses to involve new women in the movement. In their first year of organizing, Manchester workers obtained more than 4,000 signatures on ten-hour petitions.[35] While men and women were both active in the movement, they worked through separate institutional structures from the outset.

The division of men and women within the Ten Hour Movement also reflected their separate daily lives in Lowell and in other mill towns. To repeat, they held different jobs in the mills and had little contact apart from the formal, structured overseer-operative relation. Outside the mill, we have noted, women tended to live in female boarding houses provided by the corporations and were isolated from men. Consequently, the experiences of women in these early mill towns were different from those of men, and in the course of their daily lives they came to form a close-knit community. It was logical that women's participation in the Ten Hour Movement mirrored this basic fact.

The women's Ten Hour Movement, like the earlier turn-outs, was based in part on the participants' sense of their own worth and dignity as daughters of freemen. At the same time, however, it indicated the growth of a new consciousness. It reflected a mounting feeling of community among women operatives and a realization that their interests and those of their employers were not identical, that they had to rely on themselves and not on corporate benevolence to achieve a reduction in the hours of labor. One woman, in a open letter to a state legislator, expressed this rejection of middle-class patenalism: "Bad as is the condition of so many women, it would be much worse if they had nothing but your boasted protection to rely upon; but they have at last learnt the lesson which a bitter experience teaches, that not to those who style themselves their 'natural protectors' are they to look for the needful help, but to the strong and resolute of their own sex."[36] Such an attitude, underlying the self-organizing of women in the ten-hour petition campaigns, was clearly the product of the industrial experience in Lowell.

Both the early turn-outs and the Ten Hour Movement were, as noted above, in large measure dependent upon the existence of a close-knit community of women operatives. Such a community was based on the work structure, the nature of worker housing, and workforce homogeneity. Women were drawn together by the initial job training of newcomers, by the informal work sharing among experienced hands, by living in company boarding houses, and by sharing religious, educational, and social activities in their leisure hours. Working and living in a new and alien setting, they came to rely upon one another for friendship and support. Understandably, a community feeling developed among them.

This evolving community as well as the common cultural traditions which Yankee women carried into Lowell were major elements that governed their response to changing mill conditions. The pre-industrial tradition of independence and self-respect made them particularly sensitive to management labor policies. The sense of community enabled them to transform their individual opposition to wage cuts and to the increasing pace of work into public protest. In these labor struggles women operatives expressed a new consciousness of their rights both as workers and as women. Such a consciousness, like the community of women itself, was one product of Lowell's industrial revolution.

The experiences of Lowell women before 1850 present a fascinating picture of the contradictory impact of industrial capitalism. Repeated labor protests reveal that female operatives felt the demands of mill employment to be oppressive. At the same time, however, the mills provided women with work outside the home and family, thereby offering them an unprecedented independence. That they came to challenge employer paternalism was a direct consequence of the increasing opportunities offered them in these years. The Lowell mills both exploited and liberated women in ways unknown to the pre-industrial political economy.

NOTES

1. *Statistics of Lowell Manufacturers,* January 1, 1840. Broadside available in the Manuscripts Division, Baker Library, Harvard Business School.

2. *Lowell Offering* I, p. 169.

3. *Ibid.* IV, p. 145-148, 169-172, 237-240, 257-259.

4. *Ibid.* IV, p. 170.

5. These statistics are drawn from the author's dissertation, "Women at Work: The Transformation of Work and Community in Lowell, Mass., 1826-1860" (Columbia Univ., 1975).

6. Harriet Hanson Robinson, *Loom and Spindle, Or Life Among the Early Mill Girls* (New York, 1898), p. 91.

7. Dublin, "Women at Work," Chapter 4. Statistics are based on linkage between company payrolls and register books of the Hamilton Manufacturing Company. The register books were alphabetically organized volumes in which operatives were signed into and out of the mills. They gave the nativity and local residence of operatives as well as additional data. For a detailed discussion of the linkage methods used see the appendices of "Women at Work."

8. Dublin, "Women at Work," Chapter 5. Statistics based on analysis of federal manuscript census listings of Hamilton boarding houses in 1830 and 1840.

9. *Lowell Offering* I, p. 169.

10. *Ibid.* II, pp. 145-155; I, pp. 2-7, 74-78.

11. *Hamilton Manufacturing Company Records,* vol. 283, *passim.* This volume, along with all the other company records cited in this article, is located in the Manuscript Division of Baker Library, Harvard Business School.

12. *Lowell Offering* IV, pp. 145-148.

13. *Ibid.* I, p. 5; IV, p. 148.

14. Henry A. Miles, *Lowell As It Was and As It Is* (Lowell, 1845), pp. 144-145.

15. *Lowell Offering* IV, pp. 14-23. Like so many of the stories in the *Offering*, this one has a dramatic reversal at its conclusion. We learn at the end that Hannah's visitor is her brother, whose identity could not be revealed because he was afraid that the woman he was courting might learn that his sister was an operative.

16. These statistics are based on the linkage of payroll and register books of the Hamilton Company as were the data on residence presented above. See Chapter 4 and Appendices of Dublin, "Women at Work."

17. These data are based on an analysis of the age distribution of females residing in Hamilton Company boarding houses as recorded in the federal manuscript censuses of 1830 and 1840. See Dublin, "Women at Work," Chapter 4.

18. Federal Manuscript Census of Lowell, 1830.

19. Boston *Evening Transcript*, February 18, 1834.

20. *Lawrence Manufacturing Company Records*, Correspondence, Vol. MAB-1, March 4 and March 9, 1834.

21. *Ibid.,* February 15, 1834.

22. *Ibid.,* February 14, 1834.

23. Boston *Evening Transcript,* February 18, 1834.

24. Robinson, *Loom and Spindle.* p. 72; *Lowell Offering*, February 1841, p. 45. For an interesting account of conflict between an operative and an overseer, see Robinson, p. 57.

25. The wage cuts, in still another way, might have been seen as threatening to "enslave." Such decreases would be enacted by reductions in the piece rates paid women. If women were to maintain their overall earnings, given the wage cuts, they would have to speed up their work or accept additional machinery, both of which would result in making them work harder for the same pay. Opposition to the speed-up and the stretch-out were strong during the Ten Hour Movement in the 1840s, and although I have found no direct evidence, such feeling may have played a part in the turn-outs of the 1830s as well.

26. Robinson, *Loom and Spindle,* p. 83; Boston *Evening Transcript*, October 4 and 6, 1836.

27. *Tremont-Suffolk Mills Records*, unbound letters, Vol. FN-1, October 14, 1836.

28. *Ibid.,* October 17, 1836.

29. Hannah Josephson, *The Golden Threads: New England's Mill Girls and Magnates* (New York, 1949), p. 238.

30. *Tremont-Suffolk Mills Records,* Unbound Letters, Vol. FN-1, October 10, 1836.

31. *Hamilton Manufacturing Company Records,* Vol. 670, Correspondence of Treasurer, March 14, 1840; Lowell *Advertiser,* June 6, 1845, gives data on 1842 wage cuts.

32. Massachusetts *House Document* No. 50, 1845. Quoted in full in John R. Commons et al., *A Documentary History of American Industrial Society* (Cleveland, 1910), Vol. 3, pp. 133-151.

33. *Voice of Industry,* November 28, 1845.

34. Based on author's examination of Ten Hour Petitions at Massachusetts State Archives, 1845, 1587/8 and 1587/9.

35. *Voice of Industry,* December 5 and 19, 1845, July 24, 1846, October 30, 1846, December 4, 1846, January 8, 1847.

36. *Voice of Industry,* March 13, 1846.

THE POSITION OF WORKERS IN A TEXTILE COMMUNITY: FALL RIVER IN THE EARLY 1880s

9

Philip T. Silvia, Jr.

The growth of Fall River, Massachusetts, in population, mills, capitalization, machinery, and total production was phenomenal during the fifteen years following the Civil War. Among the various reasons for this leap forward, none was more important than the adaptation of the effective use of steam power which conveniently coincided with the attainment of maximum potential water usage of the Quequechan River. New sites, less dependent upon a water source, could now be constructed by enterprising capitalists who also recognized certain advantages afforded by the Fall River location, particularly in the more economical transporting costs of cotton and coal as compared to competitive areas elsewhere in New England. Other attractions, such as direct steamship connection with New York City—the great center of textile marketing—lower taxes than assessed by a rival city such as Lowell, and even a probable climatic advantage due to a more humid atmosphere than competitors, all combined to induce local entrepreneurs to build Fall River into the greatest textile center in America.[1]

Figures best reveal their achievement. Fall River manufacturers of print cloth fared unexpectedly well during the Civil War for, despite the difficulty in securing cotton, there was an increase of nearly $1 million in capitalization between 1860 and 1865. Then came a period of exciting business expansion down to 1880, a period of peaks and valleys which ended with a sevenfold capital investment increment totaling nearly $15 million. This period included the fan-

Source: From *Labor History* 16, no. 2 (Spring 1975):230-248.

tastic years of "Great Expansion" from 1870 to 1872, when most of the 1,390,830 spindles operating in Fall River a decade later were first put in place. By 1880 there were five spindles for every one that had existed at the close of the war and, except for Massachusetts itself and neighboring Rhode Island, Fall River's total spindleage as a city could not be matched by that of any other state in the Union. From 1865 to 1878 production in yards of cloth multiplied thirteenfold, reaching an awesome annual yield of 391,725,000 yards. Fall River specialized in print cloth production, and by 1875 it was manufacturing nearly 57 percent of the national output. This enormous capacity for producing print cloth and other goods was due to the founding of new mill complexes. The five corporations existing in 1860 had increased to twenty-two within fifteen years, and by 1881 the city could proudly display its fifty-two cotton mills, plus a print works, and a bleachery, all of which were owned by thirty-six corporations. This magnificent array of mills enabled the Spindle City, as Fall River came to be called, to far outstrip its chief competitors, Lowell and Lawrence, whose total number of corporations combined only equaled 80 percent of Fall River's. Its predominance would continue unabated throughout the 1880s, for in 1883 more than one-seventh of all spindles and three-fifths of all print cloth production in the entire nation were centered in Fall River. By 1889 approximately 2,100,000 spindles were operational, or three for every two that were in place in the entire South, despite a surging textile growth below the Potomac in the 1880s.[2]

Fall River soon evolved into a one-industry city. By 1875 more than 80 percent of its invested capital, and more than 85 percent of the value of manufactured products, were in the textile industry. Huge numbers of operatives, attracted by the opportunities afforded in these new cotton mill complexes, soon ended the immediate post-war labor shortage. The 2,654 textile workers of 1865 blossomed to nearly 7,000 by 1868 and then to 15,000 by 1872, before leveling off during the middle and late 1870s. Fall River's population growth earned the city last place

2 *Ibid.*, 53-71; *Fall River Daily Globe*, October 6, 1890; *Fall River Daily Herald*, October 8, 1890; Sylvia C. Lintner, "A Social History of Fall River, 1859-1879" (unpublished Ph.D. diss., Radcliffe College, 1945), 564; Henry H. Earl, *Fall River and Its Manufactories, 1803-1884* (Fall River, 1885), 27, *Fall River and Its Manufactories, 1803-1875* (1876), 41 (editions one-four, carrying through 1876, were entitled *Fall River: Its Rise and Progress*); Mass. Bureau of Statistics of Labor, *Thirteenth Annual Report* (1882), 228-229; Victor S. Clark, *History of Manufactures in the United States* (New York, 1929), II, 394.

in a listing — the 1870 federal census report — of the fifty principal cities of the United States. The population nearly tripled in the decade after 1865, jumping from 17,481 to 45,340; then the pace slackened, reaching 48,961 by 1880. This influx included a steady stream of foreign-born, many of whom were attracted to the unskilled job opportunities in the mills. By 1878 approximately 75 percent of the city's factory workers were foreign-born, having come almost exclusively from England, Ireland, and Canada. Fall River was well on its way to becoming the nation's leading immigrant city. In 1870 newcomers comprised 42.9 percent of its 26,766 inhabitants, while five years later, numbering 23,866, they represented 52.6 percent.[3]

Among Fall River's foreign-born population, immigrants from England, especially skilled mule spinners, had organized worker resistance to wage reductions of approximately forty percent during the 1870s. While the workers lacked the economic stamina to defeat a Manufacturers Board of Trade, they had rocked Fall River with protest demonstrations, sporadic violence, calls to revolution by radical labor leaders, and large-scale strikes during 1870, 1875, and 1879. An exhausted populace welcomed the uneasy industrial peace that prevailed between 1880 and 1883.

Even with the absence of strikes, mill workers often dwelled upon the shortcomings of their vocation. Besides low wages, they emphasized poor working conditions within the mills and poor living conditions outside them. Problems about working conditions can be subdivided into those affecting all workers, and those troubling one group of textile workers, the spinners. The universal complaint most closely associated with wages was the policy of piecework payment, whereby quantity of output determined income. Fortunately, direct testimony about this and other points of contention has been preserved in two invaluable printed sources. Under the auspices of Carroll Wright, the Massachusetts Bureau of Statistics of Labor's *Thirteenth Annual Report* included a 220-page section capsulizing an investigation undertaken from June to November 1881 by Bureau agents seeking answers to the following question which had been addressed to Wright: "Why is it that the working

---

[3] Mass. Bureau of Statistics of Labor, *Thirteenth Annual Report* (1882), 200, 204; William W. Armstrong, *Industry and Statistics of Cotton Manufactories of Fall River* (Fall River, 1868); Lintner, 564; U.S. Bureau of the Census, *Ninth Census of the United States: 1870. Population*, 380-391; Commonwealth of Mass., Bureau of Statistics of Labor, *Census of Massachusetts: 1885. Population and Social Statistics*, I, pt. 1, 66-67.

people of Fall River are in constant turmoil, when at Lowell and Lawrence they are quiet?" Two years later a United States Senate committee met with several prominent citizens of Fall River in an attempt to better understand the relationship between capital and labor.[4]

Both these studies contain recurrent complaints about the evils attendant upon the "drive" to increase the productive capacity of Fall River's mills. Several manufacturing establishments were violating the ten-hour law, workers testified, while at the same time all mills resorted to an excessive speed-up of machinery. By being on the job at an illegally early hour many mill workers took advantage of capital's "beneficence," which allowed them extra time to produce more piece work. The speed-up practice hardly declined between 1881 and 1883, causing experienced British workers to lament their decision to settle in Fall River. In England they were not worked "like horses or slaves." Efforts to maximize profits led to another exploitative practice, that of "cheating" weavers and spinners. There were numerous complaints about false measurements of a weaver's normal "cut" of forty-five yards of cloth, the standard length upon which wages were based and in itself longer than the thirty-six yards which had been the standard a quarter century earlier. Weavers swore that they were only credited with a cut after an output of as much as fifty yards, thus giving the mill a freely woven five extra yards. Such malpractice directed against the eight-loom weaver could mean nearly one free cut per week for a mill corporation. Many spinners also grumbled about mills that paid the coarse filling price to those deserving a higher price for working finer filling. The overseers, who were identified principally as Englishmen in this testimony, were most directly blamed for these practices, but they also were perceived to be only the lowliest cog in an unjust system. Such practices were ultimately attributed to the competitive drive of mill susperintendents and treasurers who wished to manufacture the greatest amount of cotton textile products at the least possible cost. Following in the wake of this capitalistic rivalry came a descending chain of command within the factories that produced its own special tensions. Treasurers drove superintendents, who pushed overseers, who pressured workers who were themselves subjected to added anxiety by their co-workers. And even this pressure to produce was heightened by the mill practice of chalking individual cut production yield on slates. Such publicity served the speed-up, as neighboring mill hands raced to ex-

---

[4] Mass. Bureau of Statistics of Labor, *Thirteenth Annual Report* (1882), 195.

ceed listed outputs.[5]

Before returning to a discussion of these general problems, it would be useful to turn to the organized spinners who, predictably, most lamented factory life. Their leader, Robert Howard, stated that no son of his would enter the mills; if his offspring became a chimney sweep, Howard claimed, it would be a preferable vocation. Such a reaction was understandable. Mule spinners had exhausting physical labors. Howard, an astute observer, reckoned that because of increased machinery speed, they walked more than the eighteen to twenty-five miles per day that a commission appointed by the English government had discovered was the average for mule spinners in their tasks. When Howard called for special spinner union meetings in 1881 to discuss vocational complaints, these were succinctly characterized as "high speed, low wages, and insufficient gas lights." Many an older spinner went into involuntary retirement because poor lighting caused his eyesight to fail, which diminished his ability to detect any breaks in the 1,600 threads that would have to be retied. A spinner noted that one mule alley in a mill where he had worked in New Bedford was as well lit as were entire sections of mules in Fall River mills. Besides these physical hardships, every spinner who spoke to Wright's agents in 1881 mentioned the tendency of mill treasurers to purchase poor cotton, and this meant more frequent breakage, with consequent time-consuming repairs that lowered wages because of decreased filling production.[6]

[5] *Ibid.*, 301, 306-307, 354, 359, 405; U.S. Congress, Senate, *Report of the Committee of the Senate Upon the Relations between Labor and Capital*, 4 vols., S. Rept. 1262, 48th Cong., 2d Sess., Vol. I, 1885, 631 (hereinafter referred to as U.S. Senate, *Labor and Capital*); David S. Lawlor, *The Life and Struggles of an Irish Boy in America* (Newton, Massachusetts, 1936), 26; Rowland Berthoff, *British Immigrants in Industrial America* (Cambridge, 1953), 26. Manufacturers explained that their chalking individual production cut on slates was solely for the benefit of weavers, so they would know they were receiving proper credit for the amount of cloth woven.

[6] U.S. Senate, *Labor and Capital*, I, 1885, 633, 647. Howard (1845-1902) had been born in England of Irish parents and came to Fall River in April, 1873. He began working as a piecer in a silk mill when eight years of age, and at fifteen was a journeyman spinner working at Stockport. Before leaving England he had been selected as president of the Stockport Spinners' Union. He earned a reputation for extraordinary skill in operating mule frames at several Fall River mills before the organized spinners voted a salary grant permitting him to devote full time as secretary of their union from 1878 to 1897. Howard, a conservative, believed in dealing on a friendly basis with management, although he could be fiercely belligerent when spinner demands were flagrantly ignored. His influence in transforming the hot-headed labor movement of the 1870s into a more cautious approach to labor disputes affected his own craft union. Other organizations of mill job specialists emulated his policy when they achieved respectability in the mid-1890s. A contributor to the *Atlantic Monthly* noted as early as 1879 that secretary Howard was "a very good natured fellow" who "appeared to regard the owners and agents as reasonable men, who were disposed to deal justly with the laborers. . . ."Mill capitalists first came to appreciate Howard when he headed off strike sentiment in 1880. Declaring him to be "level-headed" and the "only man fit" to be a labor leader,

These annoyances were endured by spinners enjoying steady employment. Many were not so fortunate, for Fall River had a back-up force of sick-duty spinners who secured employment only when they could replace regulars requiring a few days off every month to recuperate from their physically taxing work. The inundation of skilled mule spinners may be partially explained by the practice, begun in 1879, of replacing mules with ring spinning frames. This innovation left a thousand spinners competing for 800 jobs. Thomas O'Donnell, an English-born spinner who was adversely affected by this surplus, has described the brutal story of his struggle for existence. O'Donnell was able to work for $1.50 per day so infrequently that his annual earnings for 1882 only amounted to $133; but this income, he testified, was as great as that brought in by more than one thousand other Spindle City families. These funds, along with wood, coal, and clams scavenged in and around Fall River's vicinity, were the entire resources upon which O'Donnell, his wife, and two children subsisted during that year. The family dressed pitifully, and the youngsters could not attend school during the winter months because they did not have adequate shoes. Upon relating this tale of misery, O'Donnell was asked why he did not, following Horace Greeley's advice, begin life anew by moving westward and establishing a homestead, all of which could be done at a cost of $1,500. His reply to the Senator's inquiry was convincing: "Well, I never saw over a $20 bill, and that is when I have been getting a month's pay at once. If someone would give me $1,500 I will go. . . ."[7]

---

they supported Howard's successful campaign to become a state representative. By 1881 Howard's fame had spread to labor circles outside Fall River. For further details on Howard's life, see *Fall River Daily Herald*, November 7, 1881, December 2, 1882, August 27, 1883; *Fall River Daily Globe*, April 28, 1902; Clifton K. Yearley, Jr., *Britons in American Labor; A History of the Influence of the United Kingdom Immigrants on American Labor, 1820-1914* (Baltimore, 1957), 148-149; "Study of a New England Factory Town," *Atlantic Monthly*, XLIII (June 1879), 695; Robert Howard "Progress in the Textile Trades", in *The Labor Movement: The Problems of Today*, ed. George E. McNeill (Boston, 1887), 228; John R. Commons, *et al.*, *History of Labour in the United States* (2 vols.; New York, 1918), II, 22, 321; Federation of Organized Trades and Labor Unions of the United States of America and Canada, *Report of the First Annual Session, 1881* (1882), 8, 11; *Second Annual Session, 1882* (1883), 7; American Federation of Labor, *Proceedings of the Fourth Annual Convention* (1889), 12, 43. *Fall River Daily Herald*, October 10, 1881. At this time employees of the Shove mill praised management for its introduction of electric lighting (*ibid.*, October 21, 1881). Mass. Bureau of Statistics of Labor, *Thirteenth Annual Report* (1882), 310. One ex-back boy, who was an assistant to a spinner, recalled a time when one spinner who was working on poor grade cotton shouted to another: " 'Hey, Jack, a nigger's pair of boots just came through; I expect very soon the nigger himself will come along.' " (Lawlor, 29). *The New York Times*, April 3, May 7, 1882; *Fall River Daily Evening News*, July, 1882. "Filling" refers to the material that comes off the mule and goes to the spinner.
7 *Fall River Daily Herald*, February 26, 1884; *Fall River versus the Mass. Bureau of Sta-*

O'Donnell also mentioned the manufacturers' inclination to substitute ring for mule spinning frames. Apparently, there were two reasons for this innovation: a technological advantage which meant less expensive ring-frame costs, and the undermining of the one strong trade union that had withstood all other adversity. In the early 1880s, the latter consideration dominated. Available testimony demonstrates entrepreneurial exasperation with spinner unionism. Anger mounted as organized labor employed such tactics as having a leader buy a few shares of stock in one mill, thereby permitting attendance at stockholder meetings where ammunition for future complaint was unobtrusively gathered. Manufacturer displeasure was directed against Howard and other officials of the spinners' union, who were denounced as selfish "agitators" and as "men on the 'make,' " seeking to use workers' prejudices to better themselves. Howard's business, one manufacturer testified in 1881, was to "find fault and make trouble all the time," an effort facilitated by the one or two committee men from each mill who, besides collecting monthly dues, also reported to Howard "how their mill *is* run and how it *should* be run." For such reasons, this manufacturer stated, conveniently forgetting the pre-Howard days when the Board of Trade had been molded as an anti-union weapon, capital had recently deemed it necessary to adopt protective measures.[8]

The ring spinning substitution was ultimately the greatest protection for entrepreneurs. Wholesale conversion to it did not take place, however, for financial reasons. As early as 1866 manufacturers were weighing the costs of a cheaper, readily obtainable pool of labor against that required by ring-frames, which needed greater amounts of horsepower per thousand spindles. By 1871 certain technical problems associated

---

tistics (Fall River, 1882), 8, 10; Mass. Bureau of Statistics of Labor, *Thirteenth Annual Report* (1882), 207-308; U.S. Senate, *Labor and Capital,* III, 1885, 452, 453, 455; *Fall River Daily Herald,* October 19, 1883; O'Donnell's testimony reproduced in *Labor and Capital in the Gilded Age* ed. John A. Garraty, (Boston, 1968), 33-36, provided an interesting comparison with the similar situation that befell John Jones in 1879, a mule spinner whose family was reduced to poverty by cutdowns and the strikes of the 1870s (*Fall River Daily Herald,* September 2, 1879). The *Fall River News* was happy to report O'Donnell was arrested for drunkenness shortly after testifying—the true reason for his poverty (*Fall River Daily Evening News,* October 20, 26, 1883.) Another factor contributing to the immobility of textile workers was noted by Rowland Berthoff, who quoted from an 1875 writer: the dissatisfied Fall River cotton weaver from Lancashire " 'remains in Fall River; he does not attempt any other work; he is simply a Fall River weaver, and at the bottom of his heart he stoutly believes that the world owes him such a living as he fancies by weaving, and that if he does not get it somebody is wronging him.' " (Berthoff, 88-89; see also *Fall River Daily Herald,* October 2, 1880).

8 "New England Factory Town," 696; U.S. Senate, *Labor and Capital,* III, 1885, 413; Mass. Bureau of Statistics of Labor, *Thirteenth Annual Report* (1882), 397.

with ring-frame spinning had been overcome, and by 1881 several Fall River manufacturers acknowledged that they were adopting these machines, which could be operated by females and young boys, as speedily as possible. It was believed correctly, that the days of the mule spinner were numbered. But this development did not, as many expected, occur overnight, for mule spinners remained the vital element in Fall River's unionized labor force until at least 1895, and possibly even into the twentieth century. The primary reason for such stability was the cost of technological change. Many of the mills constructed since 1870 were originally equipped with mules and, understandably, there was hesitation about disposing of this expensive machinery before it became worn out. One superintendent disclosed that mule obsolescence was a twenty-five year process. Even in 1881, therefore, when there was considerable friction between mule spinners and manufacturers, statistics compiled from twenty-nine Fall River cotton textile corporations reveal that almost 73 percent of their spindles were still in the mule category.[9]

Management's other effective "protective" device was the blacklist. When the field team of the Massachusetts Bureau of Statistics of Labor was undertaking its investigation in the latter part of 1881, it often extracted information from workers only after promises of anonymity because, as one spinner said, "my bread is at stake." He and others had, fresh in their minds, the memory of spinners who had been dismissed during the spring, after testifying about work conditions in Fall River mills before a state House legislative committee. The city's Board of Trade began a "secret service" in the fall 1880 and, with inside information provided by a union member named Wilkinson, blacklisted twenty-six to thirty men who were then compelled to work at distant mills if they wished to continue at mule spinning.[10]

Despite these attacks, Howard's 1883 testimony confirms that he was then attempting to placate the manufacturers, and was optimistically inclined to believe that a period of better relations had arrived. He

9 New England Cotton Manufacturers' Association, *Proceedings*, XV (1873), 6-37; Herbert Lahne, *The Cotton Mill Worker* (New York, 1944), 178; Mass. Bureau of Statistics of Labor, *Thirteenth Annual Report* (1882), 313-31, 315; U.S. Senate, *Labor and Capital*, III, 1885, 451; *Fall River Daily Herald*, February 7, 1884.

10 *Labor Standard* (Fall River), April 2, 1881; Mass. Bureau of Statistics of Labor, *Thirteenth Annual Report* (1882), 347. A native of Oldham, England, Wilkinson received money for turning over the names of the union's executive committee and other prominent union members, particularly dues collectors. When the union became suspicious, the manufacturers paid to remove him and his family to parts unknown (Howard, 235). *Ibid.*, 236; Mass. Bureau of Statistics of Labor, *Thirteenth Annual Report* (1882), 345-347. See also Lillie B. Chace Wyman, "Studies of Factory Life: Black-Listing at Fall River," *Atlantic Monthly* LXII (Nov., 1888), 605-612.

thought that Fall River was unfairly maligned because of the excessive zeal of newspaper reporters, for "if a man only makes a change in his breakfast table" it appeared in print. Of course, so did minor labor disputes; and with local reporters being paid by New York City and Boston newspapers for contributions, such accounts were widespread, causing Fall River to acquire notoriety as the most turbulent cotton textile center in the United States. Howard carefully emphasized that distinctions had to be made, that there were manufacturers who were fair and willing to treat him with respect. Entrepreneurs were often oblivious to friction within the mills. Overseers were the troublemakers, as they sought to ingratiate themselves with the manufacturers, even if it meant driving and cheating the help. Giving "due credit" to management, Howard stated that, except on the question of wages, he could generally expect satisfaction when seeking to eliminate inequities.[11]

Howard thought that the key to industrial peace rested with the workers themselves. Labor warfare, which was "becoming a rare thing" in Fall River, would cease as soon as a more thorough organization of workers arose. Then a new, more sophisticated era in labor-capital relations would be ushered in, and the strike would be dimly recalled as a relic of barbarous days. The spinners' union was paving the way and proving that organization brought strength, which in turn brought recognition. One method of flexing union muscles was the practice of depositing spinner funds, which were accumulated at the rate of one dollar per month from each of 700 members, into one of the manufacturer-controlled banks, to show capital that resistance against injustice could assume formidable proportions.[12]

Finally, after finding that the possibility of industrial peace revolved around labor conferences among equals, Howard appraised his own role as a labor mediator:

> Our work there [Fall River] is very hard, and there are many things that need to be remedied, but I think if we could get the same spirit shown by the manufacturers generally that is shown now by a few of them who are willing to meet . . . and talk affairs over—I think if we could have that

---

[11] U.S. Senate, *Labor and Capital*, I, 1885, 632, 636-637.

[12] *Ibid.*, 632. The mule spinners were worthy adversaries. Wilted by three strike defeats in the 1870s, their union had not withered away. Adding to the stability and attractiveness of the union were new association rules, as announced by Secretary Howard in February 1881, which provided generously for members in good standing. These craftsmen were thenceforth cushioned against the hazards of mill fires, failures, and breakdowns, as well as against blacklisting. Benefits for sickness, old age, physical impediment, death, and burial were also provided (*Fall River Daily Evening News*, February 7, 1881).

spirit made general among them, strikes would come to an end in that city. I have been congratulated a good deal within the last three years for keeping the men quiet and getting little grievances rectified without trouble, which it would be impossible for the men to get rectified by treating directly with the bosses. . . .[13]

Protests against various aspects of mill life, by all categories of Fall River workers, occurred in these years. A major grievance was embodied in Howard's observations that the "bosses, some of them, don't like to stoop down and talk with the men." For workers threatened by technology with anonymity and displacement, the absence of familiarity with a friendly feeling of management was keenly felt. This feeling of anxiety was compounded by arbitrary entrepreneurial attitudes. Nearly every worker testified that workers brazen enough to request redress of a grievance were almost invariably met with the rejoinder that, if dissatisfied, they were free to leave. Furthermore, "obnoxious" individuals were dismissed without warning, despite a state statute intended to protect workers from this practice. While manufacturers ignored this law, workers could not afford to violate another statute requiring them to render a ten-day notice before leaving, since they would not be paid for their final week's work by the company.[14]

Another familiar problem related to the wage-scale — namely, that only a family with several working members could expect to accumulate any savings. In order to do so, or merely to maintain a subsistence level, parents frequently had to neglect young children. Offspring might be locked inside the home or left free to wander without supervision, often with only a piece of bread for food, as they awaited the return of adults who were at work for more than ten hours. Moreover, the health of both adults and adolescents, even those under age whose birth dates were forged by working parents, was endangered by excessive heat in

[13] U.S. Senate, *Labor and Capital*, I, 1885, 632. Howard had been most optimistic in 1883, seeing himself as the indispensable intermediary link between trade unionism and capitalism. But his mood darkened with one of the "old kind" of Fall River strikes. After spinners refused to report to work in February 1884 because of another wage-cut announcement, management warned Howard and his spinner unionists of their intention to "starve us into submission." They held out for eighteen weeks. Capitulation became inevitable when the union treasury had been so depleted that strikers were barely given enough to purchase the "coarsest kinds of necessaries." One consequence of defeat was the blacklisting of fifty to sixty spinners. Howard, still hopeful, predicted correctly that "like Banquo's ghost" the union would rise again, overcoming the adversity being inflicted upon it (*Fall River Daily Herald*, May 12, June 9, 11, 1884; *John Swinton's Paper* (New York), June 1, 8, 22, 1884).
[14] Mass. Bureau of Statistics of Labor, *Thirteenth Annual Report* (1882), 358, 338, 328-329.

the mills. This was particularly the case in the weave departments, which were almost unbearable in the summer when windows remained closed and atomizers were utilized to fill the rooms with hot steam in order to keep warp filling damp. Colds and pneumonia were common, especially when workers left the job and went out into icy winter winds. Workers' lungs also were affected by flying cotton fibers that sometimes filled rooms and settled on machinery to the extent that it seemed like a "heavy frost." The weavers also had the unsanitary duty, gone uncorrected since exposed a decade before by Dr. John Whitaker, of placing one's mouth against, and sucking thread through, shuttles. Physical weariness, especially among women, was an inevitable feature of mill work and it resulted from long hours of standing and the necessity of concentrating on the task at hand, not so much from strenuous activities.[15]

Social Ills: Two Viewpoints

Having read the 1882 report of the Massachusetts Bureau of Statistics of Labor and been disturbed by the adverse criticism contained in it, the Fall River Board of Trade members prepared and published a rebuttal to what they termed this "worthless rubbish." The essentially negative bureau study was not effectively repudiated, although Wright was justifiably reproached for including statements from individuals obviously biased against life in Fall River as compared with that in Lowell and Lawrence. The only point on which the state report and manufacturer response agreed was the cause of Fall River's labor disputes. Both felt that the city's "sudden and abnormal growth" in one type of manu-

---

[15] *Ibid.*, 114, 300; George E. McNeill, *Factory Children: Report upon the Schooling and Hours of Labor of Children* (Boston, 1875), 28; Mass. Bureau of Statistics of Labor, *Thirteenth Annual Report* (1882), 282, 222. By 1881 the harmful practice of steaming the rooms was beginning to be alleviated, at least in one mill, the Granite, where an effective humidifier piped "jets of cold vapor" into the weaver quarters (Smith, 58). "New England Factory Town," 691; *Fall River Daily Herald*, October 20, 1883, December 13, 1892. More than a decade earlier, Dr. Whitaker, a working-class sympathizer, professed to recognize eighteen dangers to body and soul related to labor in Fall River cotton mills. These ranged from intemperance and depression to physical deterioration and the "predisposition to sexual abuse. There is no doubt that this is very much increased, the passions being excited by contact and loose conversation; there cannot fail to be among so many brought together many evil disposed and immoral persons." While concerned about possible evil consequences resulting from such transgressions, he observed, as a good friend of the common people, that in his opinion there was not so much sexual abuse as "among the opulent who have nothing to do. . . ." He vividly described the sucking procedure and its results: "The weavers suffer most from sucking the threads through the shuttles, particles of cotton getting into their mouths, which they keep chewing and often swallow. I have been called to cases where I suspected this to be the cause of trouble in the stomach. After getting an emetic, they have in some cases vomited little balls of cotton." Mass. Bureau of Statistics of Labor, *Second Annual Report* (1870-1871), 504-508.

factured product had created a strong spirit of trade unionism.[16]

Apparently, given their reply, Fall River entrepreneurs were disturbed less by the exposé of conditions facing mill workers than by the suggestion that excess profits were being made. Expressing their firm belief in government noninterference, they asked:

> What business has he [Wright] to be meddling with the manufacturer's profits at all? The State has not yet the authority to determine what share of the profits made by a manufacturing company shall be given to the stockholders, and what share to the operatives. No doubt the labor reformers would like this to be so, but up to the present time they have not gained their object. Until they have, the Bureau of Statistics will do better to let the question of profits alone.[17]

In their report, the manufacturers displayed a booster consciousness, which reflected that of Fall River newspapers and of all segments of the community. Boosterism, for instance, may be seen in their denial of malicious reports about drinking in the Spindle City. Statistics, they claimed, demonstrated that total arrests and arrests for drunkenness were lower in Fall River than in either Lowell or Lawrence, though these two communities had a larger population. There is a certain inconsistency on the part of Fall River's entrepreneurs. Preserving their city's reputation against untrue detractors, they nonetheless considered the misery of workers to be primarily self-inflicted, owing to excessive consumption of liquor. Their only solution was city-enforced temperance. Indeed, the only positive testimony by non-workers, contained in the Bureau of Statistics and the Senate committee's reports, came from two clergymen. One of them proposed the establishment of coffee shops and reading rooms for workers' relaxation as alternatives to the saloon, and the other touched upon what would soon become the great political issue of the day, when he suggested selective enforcement of the liquor license law, which would have the additional value of saving Fall River from labor malcontents, most of whom he equated with wastrels who spent their wages on rum.[18]

---

16 *Fall River versus the Mass. Bureau of Statistics,* 20, 6-8, 21-23, 31.
17 *Ibid.,* 23.
18 *Ibid.,* 20. Fall River's Irish were arrested in excess of any other ethnic group from 1874 to 1881; they made up 5227 of 13,743 arrests (Mass. Bureau of Statistics of Labor, *Thirteenth Annual Report* (1882), 257). A limited self-help ethos among mill operatives was evident during the latter half of the 1870s when a flourishing Workingmen's Co-operative Association, officered almost exclusively by male mill hands, attempted to serve as a buffer against extraordinary wage cuts. By 1882, with the return of prosperity and a lessening of labor-capital friction, this Association ended its existence. A Free Discussion Association, headed by a reporter for the local *Labor Journal* newspaper, as well as an Overseers

Working-class representatives held a different outlook. While not denying the problem of intemperance, they chose to focus on its cause rather than its effect. Robert Howard recalled how workers, including women weavers "stripped almost to the skin, wearing only a kind of loose wrapper" during the summer months, self-consciously slunk into the nearest liquor store after an exhausting day's work. Drink, an unnamed worker stated, was often the only way to stimulate an appetite. Then there was the heat, especially in the summer, produced by cooking an evening meal in a kitchen which doubled as the sitting room for most workers, and it might drive to the saloon even those who made it directly home from work. Querying workingmen about the influence of liquor, one physician learned that it served as a relaxant. It helped them to forget fatigue, and to mix socially during the evening. Futhermore, it lightened spirits by serving temporarily as surcease from painful reality or, in the doctor's words, paraphrasing those of the workers, " 'it covers that all up; we lose all thought of that, and for the time being we feel well.' "[19]

Obviously, then, as with other aspects of Fall River life, the perspectives of employee and employer widely varied on this issue. Commenting upon these differing perceptions of the problem, Robert Howard testified: "I have often argued myself that if our manufacturers would give over preaching so much about temperance and other things and try to bring about a reform in the condition of their operatives, it would be better than all the many thousand temperance lectures and temperance

---

Reading Room Association, also functioned briefly during 1876. Thoughts about a worker-capitalized mill which could serve as a yardstick measuring the profit margin were aborted during 1875 because of a general lack of enthusiasm and the realization that the cost was prohibitive. In the early 1880s self-improvement organizations affected only a nominal number of workers. There was one reading room organized by twenty-five "foreigners," that is, English-born mill workers, who used small initiation fees and weekly dues to purchase a small shop which served as a "library." It consisted of forty-three books along with magazines and newspapers. The newspapers were auctioned at the close of each week to the highest-bidding member, who would frequently forward them to acquaintances in his native land. There were some books in the mule spinners' hall as well as a large blackboard used by one untalented spinner who had artistic pretensions. There were several fraternal lodges and church-affiliated or nationality-based organizations usually dedicated to temperance enforcement and occasionally to cooperative purchasing and insurance protection. But there were no temperance-crusading worker organizations. In fact, spinner Secretary Howard was called an irresponsible inebriate by his critics, and on one occasion was arrested and forced to pay a token fine for what seems to have been a trumped-up arrest charge for drunkenness. He admitted to a couple of beers while attending a party but denied staggering along the streets after the festivities had ended. (Fall River, *City Directory*, 1870-1885; *Fall River Daily Herald*, November 29, 1882, January 9, 11, 1884; *Fall River Daily Evening News*, November 12, 1883; Wyman, 605-608).

[19] Mass. Bureau of Statistics of Labor, *Thirteenth Annual Report* (1882), 256; U.S. Senate, *Labor and Capital*, I, 1885, 647. III, 1885, 409-10.

tales."[20]

Such reforms were not forthcoming; no provisions were made during the 1880s for either coffee shops or reading rooms. Spindle City workers were left to fend for themselves in leisure hours outside the mill. Much of this time was spent in the tenements built specifically for them. Such housing did not compare with that of the uniquely designed granite mill buildings themselves. In 1874 an investigatory report on conditions within these mills was, on the whole, quite complimentary, especially in describing the clean, well-ventilated rooms which housed machinery with safety innovations. Sanitary conditions also received generally favorable mention eight years later when the Massachusetts Labor Bureau published its rather critical thirteenth annual report.[21]

The mills might provide a bearable working environment but housing, to repeat, was another matter. Owing to Fall River's rapid population influx, the village became a tenement-clotted city with clusters of multi-family dwellings surrounding the mills. Moreover, Fall River had a greater number of people per dwelling than either Lawrence or Lowell by 1880. The mill-working populace had no choice other than these rented tenements. Unable to acquire any substantial savings, they rarely purchased their own home.[22]

Two motives, Sylvia C. Lintner has shown, governed the interest groups that invested in tenement construction — and neither concerned the welfare of the prospective tenants. Primarily, company tenements were for management a necessary adjunct to the mills then also being built, especially to those mills constructed in such uninhabited, open-field areas as the Flint and in what became known as Mechanicsville. By 1876 Henry Earl, a historian, had compiled a somewhat incomplete listing which revealed that twenty-one of thirty-three mill corporations owned and operated over 1400 mostly wooden-framed multi-tenement dwellings which provided living quarters for more than 14,000 people.

---

20 *Ibid.*, I, 646; *Fall River Daily Herald*, April 2, 1884. Mass. Bureau of Statistics of Labor, *Fifth Annual Report* (1874), 117-154. Two of the older mills provided glaring exceptions. The Pocasset mill was reported as "old, and has old machinery. Rooms low-studded, badly ventilated, and carding and weaving room very dark. Was lighted with gas at two o'clock in the afternoon when visited. In the Quequechan mill the picker-room is clean and well-guarded; carding-room very dark. Gears overhead low and unprotected. Some of the main belts come through the floor, entirely unprotected, and are dangerous. Privies in spinning-room in a filthy condition; floor wet and soaking with filth; can smell it all through the mill." (*Ibid.*, 144).

21 *Fall River versus the Mass. Bureau of Statistics*, 9.

22 Lintner, 83; *Fall River versus the Mass. Bureau of Statistics*, 11; Mass. Bureau of Statistics of Labor, *Thirteenth Annual Report* (1882), 215, 296-297.

When the decade closed three years later, the mills owned nearly 2,000 of these structures.[23]

Although such company construction did much to alleviate the housing problem, there was still opportunity for a second interest group, the private speculators, who built for profit alone and without concern for the comfort of tenants. The 1874 state report, underscoring the inferiority of their dwellings, pronounced hundreds of them "unfit to live in."

The twin abuses of interior crowding and lack of proper sanitation remained uncorrected into the 1880s. In 1883 trade unionist Frank K. Foster devoted considerable testimony, before the United States Senate Committee on Education and Labor, to reading verbatim from a section of the Massachusetts Bureau of Statistics of Labor's thirteenth report which focused on the generally deplorable housing conditions of Fall River workers. Later in the year a subcommittee of United States senators saw these conditions for themselves and filed a report — after visiting several other mill towns and cities — which concluded that Fall River living accommodations for workers were " 'worse than that of any other place visited.' " Senators Nelson W. Aldrich of Rhode Island and James Z. George of Mississippi were directed on a tour through several company-owned tenements by Robert Howard and Henry Fenner, agent of the Slade mill. Fenner had an uncomfortable time, for the senators judged the Slade tenements the worst of several corporation-owned tenements that they investigated. Their estimate was not surprising. The Slade tenements had acquired a notorious reputation for being poorly constructed and ill situated near a swampy area of stagnant pools, which created an unbearable stench and a mosquito menace in the summertime. These Slade dwellings, futhermore, were in serious disrepair, and, overall, were "a noisome, disgusting place" where all families had only one outside faucet to supply them with water.[24]

---

[23] Lintner, 88; Robeson mill treasurer, *Second Annual Report* (in the files of the Fall River Historical Society, Box B-1878). Fall River's unique geographical complexion took shape in the 1870s when tenement villages evolved in sprawling fashion throughout the city, centering around the mills that were built wherever flat land was available. Urban development was costly. This lack of a central and cohesive town meant abnormal expenditure for interconnecting road systems, sewers, water pipes, and schools for each separately built-up area. The three major areas were to the south of the Quequechan River around Cook Pond, sometimes called Laurel Lake, where Globe village grew; above the falls of the Quequechan near South Watuppa Pond, where the Flint village mills were constructed; and well north of the Quequechan, along the Taunton River, where Mechanicsville sprang up. (See Smith, 71-76, especially for his map marking the evolution of Fall River's mill pattern, 1850-1920.) Henry H. Earl, *A Centennial History of Fall River, Mass.* (New York, 1877), 118-146; Lintner, 84.

[24] Mass. Bureau of Statistics of Labor, *Fifth Annual Report* (1874), 94. The Mass. Labor Bureau's material had more than a contemporary fascination; both Lintner and Lamb,

Howard proposed that the Senate subcommittee visit Fall River's worst section which suggestion Fenner, saving himself from further embarrassment, managed to deflect by claiming that the area was unrepresentative. But its representative character is best captured by an in-depth analysis of the tenements of nine corporations which labor bureau investigators undertook in 1881. Conditions in four of them were wretched in almost all respects, a fifth had good and bad features, while the remaining were considered quite satisfactory. As to the quartet that had been condemned, their faults were enumerated by exterior and interior, with the former thus described: buildings stood on swampy land; refuse littered the yards, and decaying vegetable matter and other rubbish and even, according to one source, dead chickens as well as rats, were scattered about; and, among other complaints, lack of private sewerage, dirty and odorous outdoor privies, and infrequent painting. Complaints about the interiors centered around poor ventilation, flooded cellars, and an inadequate indoor water supply.[25]

This investigation, nevertheless, did indicate that there were corporations which owned neat dwellings and that a few did employ maintenance men. Corporate managers defended the quality of their tenements, pointing out that none were as bad as "Little Canada" in Lowell where tenements were built on marsh land filled in by garbage, including readily distinguishable "tin cans, bottles, swill, ash-barrels, general household refuse and a quantity of wool and cotton waste." Furthermore, the crowded tenement construction of New York, Boston, or even Lowell had been and was being avoided. Adequate sunlight, proper ventilation, and an absence of claustrophobic, dark living quarters were features associated with nearly all Fall River tenements. Despite worker complaints, mill tenements usually provided accommodations superior to those that were privately owned.[26]

in their Ph.D. dissertations, also quoted from the Massachusetts report, even though it went chronologically beyond the self-imposed limitations of their respective studies (Robert K. Lamb, "The Development of Entrepreneurship in Fall River, 1813-1859" [unpublished Ph.D. diss., Harvard University, 1935], chap. 14, 3-11; Lintner, 87). *Fall River Daily Herald*, September 5, December 11, 1883. Fenner would become, in the early twentieth century, the successor to Earl as Fall River's historian. He would write a flattering official account, one devoted especially to recording the exploits of outstanding capitalists who were responsible for phenomenal industrial growth of the Spindle City. U.S. Senate, *Labor and Capital*, III, 1885, 669-670; *Fall River Daily Herald*, September 2, 1879; U.S. Senate, *Labor and Capital*, III, 1885, 411.

25 Mass. Bureau of Statistics of Labor, *Thirteenth Annual Report* (1882), 272-80; Lintner, 102. *Fall River Daily Herald*, September 5, 1883; "New England Factory Town," 690-692.

26 Mass. Bureau of Statistics of Labor, *Thirteenth Annual Report* (1882), 263-64, 272-83; *Fall River Daily Evening News*, September 9, 1876.

The manufacturers' position was that faulty tenement conditions should not be attributed to them, but to the workers themselves. The foreign workers flocking to the city, declared the *Fall River News* in the early 1870s, were personally unclean. They refused to acknowledge that throwing garbage into streets and yards was a potential health hazard; they were indifferent to the care of privy vaults; and they tested the efficiency of the board of health by their efforts to turn tenement quarters into "pig styes." City authorities and critics outside of Fall River believed that primary responsibility for the upkeep of their property rested with mill officials. But the manufacturers thought otherwise. Those interviewed by Wright's Bureau agents for the most part defended the quality of their tenements, and accused the tenants of improper care. Drunkenness, it was asserted, was a major factor in their neglect. Inebriates misused tenements as if they were barrooms, testified one entrepreneur, while a few, more realistic, admitted that the tenements "are not as good as we would like to have them, but good enough for the operatives" who preferred to make places dirtier rather than keep them clean.[27]

Apologists for the workers countered that money was lacking for improvements, and that, moreover, the typical working wife had no time for more than a minimal amount of cleaning. Preparing the main meal and dinner-pail mill lunches occupied the work week, they said, while Saturday afternoon was devoted to the basic necessities of washing, shopping for food, ironing, and baking.[28]

Fall River manufacturers, it is apparent, proved to be a socially conservative lot. Their philosophical approach to the treatment of mill workers remained basically unchanged over the course of a generation. They were firm believers in—and, more importantly, practitioners of — the ideal of laissez-faire. Consequently, just as they expected to acquire profits unhindered by state action, so they also defended the right of workers to choose to work whenever employment opportunities were available—even if this meant serving as strike breakers.[29]

Carried one step further, as applied to mill workers' living quarters, entrepreneurs usually respected the independence of their workers. Nor-

[27] *Ibid.*, July 18, 1872; "New England Factory Town," 692; letter of city marshall to Thomas J. Borden, 1866 (in the files of the Fall River Historical Society, Box B-1866); Mass. Bureau of Statistics of Labor, *Thirteenth Annual Report* (1882), 275-276.
[28] *Ibid.*, 288.
[29] *Fall River Daily Herald*, February 23, 1884. *Fall River Weekly News*, August 29, 1894. This attitude was most clearly stated, at a later date, by an editorial written in the manufacturers' newspaper, which was headlined "The Right to Work."

man Ware has contrasted this attitude with that held by Lowell capitalists during pre-Civil War days. By the 1850s, Spindle City entrepreneurs had adopted a policy of noninterference, following a precedent that had been established by cotton mill pioneer Samuel Slater in Rhode Island. This meant that the watchful oversight governing the paternalistic Lowell system was avoided in Fall River. For better or for worse, the activities of Spindle City workers were regulated only when they were inside the mill. Their life outside the factory gates was their own affair. This viewpoint remained unaltered into the early 1880s. By then, Fall River's early years of mill growth were gone; so, too, were the company-owned boarding houses that might regulate the personal lives of inhabitants. The resulting freedom, however, had its drawback; left to fend for themselves, workers could not expect help in the form of manufacturer-sponsored reading rooms or coffee taverns that might improve their lot. As Ware observed of the 1850s, the cage was "gilded" in Lowell but "dirty and unkempt" in Fall River. Nevertheless, the private lives of Spindle City workers were usually unobstructed by shackling rules.[30]

To be sure, the realities of a situation did not always correspond with this ideal. Workers, as observed, were sometimes compelled to live in mill-owned tenements, which was a means to curtail union activities. In the 1870s it was also a common practice for the leases of company tenements to stipulate that, in return for the privilege of living there, the family would supply a certain number of employees for the mill. But even this constraint, except in time of labor crisis, was lessening in the 1880s, as many corporations began selling their property and concentrating solely upon cotton production. Generally, the Fall River worker was "left perfectly free."[31]

The Fall River entrepreneurs took pride in this laissez-faire attitude, and defended it in their 1882 reply to Carroll Wright. As one manufacturer summed it up: "what they do outside of the mill we don't care anything about, so long as they come to the mill sober and able to do their work." Wright had criticized this approach, contrasting it unfavorably with the continued enforcement of regulations in the cor-

---

30 Norman Ware, *The Industrial Worker, 1840-1860*, (Chicago, 1964), 74-78; *Fall River Daily Herald*, May 8, 1882; *Fall River versus the Mass. Bureau of Statistics*, 10.

31 *Weekly Visitor* (Providence, R. I.), March 26, 1881; *Labor Standard*, March 26, 1881; *Fall River Daily Herald*, April 23, 1884, September 13, 1889, April 14, 1895; Lintner, 85, 92; Mass. Bureau of Statistics of Labor, *Thirteenth Annual Report* (1882), 220. Disposal by the corporations accelerated during the 1890s (Richard Borden Manufacturing Company, *Record Book*, 1880-1890, Fall River Historical Society Collection).

porate-controlled dwellings of Lowell and Lawrence. Fall River manufacturers wanted it understood that strictures should instead have been directed at a policy that did not leave "every man to himself, and to the dictates of his own manhood." Their only concern would be violations of this ideal. They were troubled when the unfettered Spindle City mill worker failed to grasp this precious gift of individual freedom and renounced it in favor of trade unionism, thereby becoming a slave to majority sentiment. This hostility toward organized labor, though modified in later years, contributed to Fall River's unenviable and long-lasting reputation as a center of industrial discord.[32]

PATTERNS OF RESISTANCE TO INDUSTRIAL CAPITALISM, PAWTUCKET VILLAGE AND THE STRIKE OF 1824

10

Gary B. Kulik

In the late spring of 1824, a textile workers' strike closed the spinning and weaving mills of Pawtucket, an industrial village on the Rhode Island-Massachusetts border. In the same village a generation earlier, Samuel Slater had introduced water-powered machine spinning into the United States, signaling the beginnings of mass manufacture and the factory system. This strike added to Pawtucket's fame. It was both the nation's first textile strike and the first of any kind in which American women participated. The strike deserves attention not simply because of its historic priority, but because it laid bare stark social cleavages between millowners and the general community. During the week-long strike, the owners faced determined and well-organized workers, the hostility of angry village crowds, and the threat of arson. Community outrage was sufficient to compel a compromise settlement. Such a settlement in a period when workers generally lost strikes is noteworthy and indicates both a measure of worker power and the community's ability to impose effective sanctions on the behavior of mill owners.[1]

The strike dramatically underlined the attitude of Pawtucket's workers, artisans, and farmers to textile industrialism. It was neither the first act of community resistance nor the last. Resistance to the textile industry was visible in Pawtucket from 1790 through the 1830s and was punctuated by conflict over water power, taxes, wages, work routine, and the recording of factory time. This was conflict engendered by the rapid expansion of the textile industry in the years prior to 1830 and the substantial social changes it brought in its wake. The most important of those changes was the formation of a distinct social class of millowners and their merchant supporters who attempted to impose their will on the village's farmers, artisans, and mill workers. While farmers and artisans joined forces against the millowners only on occasion, conflict over work, time, and leisure sharply and continuously divided workers and owners.

This study focuses on the strike of 1824 but is centrally concerned with the continuity of local resistance to textile mills and millowners. Its primary assumption is that capitalist industrialism did not sink its roots into American soil quickly or without opposition. It draws support from the work of Herbert Gutman who, in his study of the industrial towns of the Ohio River Valley in the 1870s, has found extensive evidence of community support for striking workers. Gutman has interpreted the evidence to suggest that in a time of rapid social change, an "ideology alien to industrialism retained a powerful hold on many who lived outside large cities."[2] Gutman did not specify the contents of that ideology, but in a later, influential article, drawing on the work of English historians E. P. Thompson and E. J. Hobsbawm, he argued that first-generation migrants to American industrialism—from Yankee farm girls to Slavic day laborers—brought with them preindustrial work and leisure habits.[3] These habits persisted and formed the core of private and, at times, collective resistance to the values of industrial capitalism. Such habits, expressed through seasonal definitions of time and task-specific work behavior, formed one part of an ideology, or culture, resistant to industrial capitalism. Another part of that culture was formed in industrializing communities among residents recently subject to the changes brought by large-scale industry. This study draws evidence from both the workplace and the community, from both individual and collective action, to demonstrate the resistance offered by one village to the values of industrial capitalism.

Pawtucket is situated four miles northeast of Providence at the last fall before tidewater on the Blackstone River. Built on both sides of the river, the village spanned two states until 1862: Massachusetts on the east bank and Rhode Island on the west. According to an 1819 gazetteer, the part of the village in Rhode Island contained eighty-three houses, twelve stores, two churches, a bank, and two or three schools in addition to its industry. On the Massachusetts side, there was an industrial village of about the same size. Both industrial areas were part of larger rural townships—North Providence, Rhode Island, and Seekonk, Massachusetts—and consequently no clear population figures are available. The 1820 population of the industrial community surrounding Pawtucket Falls can, however, be estimated at approximately three thousand.[4]

From 1790 to 1820, Pawtucket was the most important industrial village in the United States. The textile industry began there in 1790 with Samuel Slater's introduction of the Arkwright system of carding and spinning. By the early 1820s, there were eight textile mills on both sides of the river, six of them likely involved in both spinning and weaving. The largest and most active of the mills were the two-story, wood-frame Slater Mill, built in 1793 and owned by Slater and by two Providence merchants, William Almy and Smith Brown, kinsmen of the wealthy Quaker merchant Moses Brown; the "White Mill," built in wood around 1800, expanded in stone in 1813, and owned by the skilled and socially mobile artisan Oziel Wilkinson and three of his sons-in-law; the four-story "Yellow Mill," built in 1805, expanded in 1813, and owned by a group of prominent local merchants, including Major Ebenezer Tyler, Nathaniel Croade, Oliver Starkweather, and Eliphalet Slack; and the four-story, stone Wilkinson Mill, built in 1810-1811 by Oziel Wilkinson and operated by his son, David. By the early 1830s, the village's textile industry ran approximately fourteen thousand spindles and over three hundred and fifty looms, and it employed about five hundred workers.[5]

Textile mills did not wholly dominate the local economy. Pawtucket had been an ironworking center from the mid-seventeenth century. By the early nineteenth century, the village produced anchors, nails, screws for oil and paper pressing machinery (some cast, the others turned on David Wilkinson's screw cutting machine, the American forerunner of the sliderest, industrial lathe), cannons, hollow ware, and assorted castings. The work was done in numerous small forges located along the river and in a rolling and slitting mill operated by the Wilkinsons. In addition to the ironworking shops, Pawtucket's artisans ran a grist mill, a tannery and bark mill, three snuff mills, one linseed oil mill, three fulling mills, and a clothier's works. The village also had a sizable shipbuilding industry. Between 1794 and 1805, one builder, George Robinson, employed nineteen to twenty ship carpenters and built seventeen vessels ranging in size from eighty to two hundred and eighty tons. This local industry provided a market for the village's ironworkers, but when shipbuilding collapsed during the embargo years, most of the ship-related iron business collapsed with it. The growth of the textile industry, however, provided a new market for the village's ironwork. A few artisans, including the Wilkinsons, had previous experience in building textile machinery, but significant expansion did not occur until 1812-1813. By 1819, on the Rhode Island side alone, there were six shops that manufactured machinery. One year later, the census taker remarked that the machine shops employed "a great number of hands" and built "all kinds of mill machinery." This was a sophisticated and nationally important industry, nurturing such prominent inventors and machine builders as David Wilkinson, Asa Arnold, John Thorp, Larned Pitcher, and James Brown.[6]

Pawtucket, like many English towns, was an industrial village prior to the introduction of textile mills. Unlike the large urban complexes on the Merrimack River or the smaller villages on the Blackstone and Pawtuxet rivers, Pawtucket experienced capitalist industrialization in a context of both rural experience and artisan tradition. This was not a village like Slatersville, Rhode Island, for example, where the entire physical plant— mills, canals, and class-structured housing—was implanted in an isolated rural community, crystallizing at one moment in time a set of hierarchical relationships that would seem to later generations to be both permanent and inevitable. Pawtucket in 1800 was a community of artisans and farmers with distinct industrial and preindustrial traditions, a community in which wealth, status, and power had not coalesced into a consistent pattern.[7]

Class, and class consciousness, emerged in Pawtucket as the textile industry developed. A distinct economic elite, consisting of textile mill-owners and wealthy merchants with textile investments, formed prior to 1820. The common needs of textile capitalists—to recruit and discipline labor, to secure uncontested rights to water power, and to exercise political and social control in the village—drew Pawtucket's millowners together in fundamental ways. Despite early conflict between Moses Brown and Samuel Slater over the building of the White Mill, Brown wrote in 1802 that "in order to save the business from immediate ruin We thought best to so far unite so as not to interfere with each other in workmen nor wages."[8] This early agreement set the tone for future cooperation. By the 1820s, Pawtucket's millowners were accustomed to meeting together to regulate hours and wages and to discuss other matters of common interest.[9]

Economic interest was reinforced by kinship and religion. Three of Oziel Wilkinson's sons—Abraham, Isaac, and David—and four sons-in-law—Samuel Slater, Timothy Greene, Hezikiah Howe, and William Wilkinson—worked with him in textile mill ownership. A few of the owners, like the Wilkinsons and the Browns, were Quakers, and a distinct network of Quaker businessmen developed along the East Coast, a network important in the sale and distribution of yarn. Other owners were Baptist or Episcopalian, but sectarian ties were never strong enough to limit cooperation. Millowners of different religions dominated the founding of Pawtucket's Sunday school and, along with their wives, played a critical role in the formation and administration of the Baptist and Episcopal churches, the Pawtucket Moral Society, and the Female Beneficent Society. Such activity expressed more than a simple, shared piety. In forming these institutions, millowners were attempting to convey their own standards of industry, propriety, and religion to a community of laborers and artisans only partly receptive to them.[10]

The millowners were most conspicuously different from their poorer neighbors in their patterns of consumption and display. They were, for example, Pawtucket's primary users of carriages. Though the carriages were said to be simple and utilitarian (Samuel Slater rode in a "shabby old one horse wagon" even after acquiring wealth, and Oliver Starkweather's chaise had a "pink stern, flat top, and was very ugly looking"), they clearly marked the millowners as different from more humble folk. The millowners' houses were the most visible manifestation of their wealth. Early in the century, Abraham Wilkinson, who had textile mill interests in Pawtucket, Valley Falls, and Albion, Rhode Island, erected his "mansion house" on two lots at 23 and 27 East Avenue. Major Ebenezer Tyler, a man of "substance and prominence," part owner of the "Yellow Mill," built on the corner of Main Street and East Avenue about 1800. His house was "then the only three story dwelling in the place." Samuel Slater and his second wife finished a brick structure, begun by Hezikiah Howe, on three lots at 67, 69, and 71 East Avenue. The property was bought from Howe on February 22, 1819, for $6,500. The "Slater Mansion" was richly decorated. Wallpaper depicting Oriental scenes embellished one parlor, and the walls of another featured scenes from Scott's *Lady of the Lake.* Barney Merry, the village's first dyer and bleacher, built on three East Avenue lots just south of Slater. In the late nineteenth century, his large house still presented a "fine appearance." On the east side of the river, Oliver Starkweather, a merchant and cotton manufacturer, built his "mansion house" about 1800. Sited on a bluff overlooking the river, the Starkweather house was a two-story wooden structure built in the federal style. Its elaborate detail, quioned corners, ornate entrance, and gabled dormers rivaled the finest houses of the period. In 1815, Colonel Eliphalet Slack, involved with Starkweather and Tyler in mill ownership, built a substantial brick house for himself. "For a long period these two were the finest dwellings in Pawtucket on either side of the river. The Walcotts and the Pitchers, who were interested in the cotton manufacture and other industries, erected mansion houses about this time."[11] Here was starkly visible evidence of the changes brought by the advance of the textile industry. The stately houses of Pawtucket's newly rich were not isolated in rural retreats or even in separate neighborhoods, as they would be later, but were built in more than one neighborhood and in the midst of ruder housing. For some they were affronts to the traditional order; and for the striking workers of 1824, they served to focus community animosity.[12]

Pawtucket's textile workers were generally recruited in family units from nearby farms. Large families were prized by the early spinning mills because of the industry's need for child labor. The Slater Mill in 1820 employed fifteen men, five women, and fifty-two children. In the same year, children constituted more than two-thirds of Pawtucket's textile workforce. A sizable number of adults, and some children, were employed outside the factories, however, for this was an industry only partly mechanized. In its first twenty to thirty years, the spinning mills of Pawtucket depended on hand-loom weavers and handpickers. The latter, who worked in their own homes, opened the raw cotton by hand, separated the fibers, and removed the excess dirt and seeds. The weavers, often part-time farmers, produced finished cloth from yarn furnished by the mills at a rate fixed by the millowners.[13]

The need to rely on outworkers limited production and increased the millowners' uncertainty about the quality, amount, and promptness of the work. Handpickers and weavers worked at their own rhythms isolated from the direct commands of an overseer. One Rhode Island manufacturer, Zachariah Allen, complained that "webbs were sometimes out a year, before being returned . . . , and the cloth was sometimes appropriated by the weavers to their own use."[14] Despite the problems it created for mill-owners, this form of cottage industry survived in Rhode Island for approximately thirty years, until new technology made change possible.

The mechanization of picking and weaving in cotton textiles took place between 1814 and 1825 and was largely complete in Pawtucket by the early 1820s.[15] Machine pickers and power looms increased production and altered the composition of the workforce. More young women entered the factories to tend the new power looms. Labor was sufficiently scarce throughout this period to require millowners to lure their new labor with cash wages. One Pawtucket company advertised in 1821 for "twenty-four good Water Loom Weavers, to whom good wages will be given, part cash, or all, if particularly required."[16] The increased rate of work made it difficult for small children to keep pace, and by the 1820s they were rarely used as production workers. They remained in the mills in a variety of auxiliary jobs, most of which involved moving stock from one point in the production process to the next. The percentage of children in Pawtucket's cotton mills declined from almost 70 percent of the total workforce in 1820 to approximately 40 percent in 1831. Over the same period, the percentage of women increased from about 16 percent to over 30 percent, while males increased from about 15 percent to about 25 percent. Males dominated the skilled jobs, working as mule spinners (the mule was a machine for fine spinning partially powered by hand) and as overseers. They also worked as dresser tenders, sizing the warp yarns with a starch solution, as carding room hands, and as unskilled watchmen, draymen, and yardmen. Women, earning one-half to one-third less than most men, tended looms, throstle spinning frames, drawing frames, winding machines, and warpers and also drew in the individual warp yarns by hand in preparation for weaving.[17]

Pawtucket's mill workers did not adjust easily to the demands of industrial capitalism. Freshly drawn from the tasks of farm labor, they were not yet accustomed to the methodical, attention-demanding, and repetitive nature of factory work or to the new strictures of a day's work defined solely by the factory bell. They expressed their independence from the millowners in a number of critical ways. During various times in the industry's first decade, parents disrupted production by removing their children from Slater Mill at random moments in the day, handpickers refused to work with dirty cotton, children refused to clean ice from the water wheel, five to six male workers left Slater's employ in a dispute over wages to begin a mill of their own, and during berry picking season in July 1796, most of Slater's outworkers chose to pick whortleberries rather than clean cotton.[18]

The village's textile workers expressed their independence outside the factory as well, to the discomfort of middle-class observers like the Baptist minister, David Benedict:

> The cotton mill business had brought in a large influx of people who came in the *second-class* cars. Such was the prejudice against the business that few others could be had, and the highways and hedges had to be searched even for them. . . . There was a set of old and staid inhabitants of a very respectable class, who had made up their minds to live here the best way they could. But when strangers came here who had been accustomed to a good state of society, they made loud complaints, and their censures were frequent and free. *Bang-all, Hard-scrabble, Bung-town, Pilfershire,* etc., were with them appropriate epithets for the place.[19]

Elsewhere, Benedict referred to Pawtucket as a "nest of corruption and disorder,"[20] and one of the village's nineteenth-century historians argued that the first generation of local mill workers had a reputation for "rough, rude, and boisterous behavior, for drunkenness and debauchery."[21]

These are, of course, the comments of biased observers, but they indicate the extent to which Pawtucket's workers lived beyond the comfortable propriety of the church-going middle class. By all accounts, local mill workers drank heavily. The village's dozen taverns were not closely licensed, and local production of liquor was extensive. In 1820, there were sixteen cider mills in North Providence producing nine hundred barrels a year. In the same year, a single local resident, Oliver Holmes, brewed eight hundred barrels of beer, and a local cooper, Edmund Shelton, worked full time in the production of rum barrels. The minister and deacons of Pawtucket's First Baptist Church continually expressed concern over the drinking habits of church members. They were equally pre-occupied with sexual misdeeds. Even among church members, a decided minority of the population, the incidence of premarital and extramarital sex was marked, though only women seem to have been singled out for the ritualized investigations, most often followed by confession, ex-communication, and on occasion readmission to the church fellowship. In their drinking habits and their sexual behavior, the village's workers conformed to the more openly secular standards of the late eighteenth century, a period noted for its alcoholic consumption and for its high rate of premarital pregnancy, the highest of any period in American history prior to the 1960s.[22]

The mill workers also distinguished themselves from the millowners and their supporters by their recreation. The primary summer sport, both for children and adults, was swimming in the Blackstone. The nude swimming of adolescent boys elicited middle-class outrage, but not as much as the practice of high diving. It became customary for boys, swimming both at noon and after work, to challenge each other to jump from large rocks at the river's edge and from the Main Street bridge into the eddy below the falls. The boldest of the jumpers was the mule spinner, Sam Patch, who began his short but brilliant career as a nationally prominent daredevil by jumping off the four-story Yellow Mill into the river. Patch, the best-known Pawtucket resident of his time, attracted large local crowds and, according to one account, left the village after "people began to object" to his performances. He became a traveling "professional," immortalized in nineteenth-century folklore.[23]

The millowners made concerted efforts to control the behavior of the village's workers. They established churches, moral reform societies, and temperance organizations, institutions designed to buttress the values and ideology of industrial capitalism. Their efforts, reflecting a desire to achieve cultural hegemony in the village, were similar to those of American industrialists elsewhere in this period. Paul Faler, in his study of Lynn, Massachusetts, in the early nineteenth century, has described the attempt of local manufacturers to create an "industrial morality," emphasizing order, inner discipline, propriety, and the work ethic.[24] Pawtucket's millowners adhered to the same morality and attempted to extend its reach to the entire village. In 1815, two years after a significant expansion in textile mill capacity, the owners formed the Pawtucket Moral Society to "combat the irreligion and licentiousness" said to be connected with the rapid population increase. Millowner Timothy Greene was its first president, Oliver Starkweather and Samuel Slater, its first vice-presidents. Its objects were to "suppress intemperance," "profane swearing," and "breaches of the Sabbath."[25] The last problem was particularly vexing. It became customary for the Baptist church to appoint a committee each year "to preserve order in and about the meeting house in time of service."[26] Like the children of Slatersville, Rhode Island, who in this period played ball "before the doors" of the meeting house "all the time of service," most of Pawtucket's workers viewed Sunday not as a day of religious observance but as one for rest and recreation.[27] Recognizing the difficulty of changing the behavior of workers through voluntary organizations, local millowners also attempted to increase police power. In June 1814, millowners and their supporters petitioned the Rhode Island General Assembly for authorization to form a local police force "for the punishing of such persons who may be disturbers of the peace." The twenty-five signers admitted that "it has often been found difficult to preserve order and due subordination."[28]

Throughout this period, few mill workers joined churches. The First Baptist, formed in 1805 and strongly influenced by millowners Starkweather, Tyler, Croade, and Slack, had fewer than two hundred members in 1820. Some mill workers clearly joined the church, particularly in periods of economic depression, but they did not do so in great number.[29] St. Paul's, an Episcopal church formed in 1815 and dominated by Slater, David Wilkinson, Barney Merry, and the Greenes, had 309 members in 1824, many of whom were children. For a time, it faced the village's "bitter hostility," perhaps because of its associations with British aristocracy and high-church ritual. It is likely that the only workers who joined were recent British immigrants like Edward Jones, who in 1820 lived in a mill worker tenement.[30] The one church free of millowner influence at its inception was Free-Will Baptist, formed by Ray Potter in 1820 with a membership of only sixty or seventy. In 1821, Daniel Greene, a millowner and church member who was hostile to Potter's encouragement of revivalism and religious "enthusiasm," set a portion of the congregation against Potter and gained control of the church. Potter's published defense was cast in the form of a sermon on a biblical text: "Do not rich men oppress you? lo to ye rich men, weep and howl for the miseries that shall come upon you."[31] Greene's successful bid to control Free-Will Baptist established the authority of millowners over the village's only evangelical sect, one whose beliefs were implicitly democratic and whose practice was, on occasion, disruptive of public order.[32] No more than 15 percent of the area's population belonged to Pawtucket's churches.[33]

The independence of Pawtucket's mill laborers was nurtured on the rocky soil of New England's farms and derived in part from preindustrial standards of work and leisure. It was reinforced and strengthened by the democratic ideology of the American Revolution. The village and its neighboring townships had provided active support for the Revolution and maintained strong democratic traditions. A majority of the east side's farmers, for example, supported Shays's Rebellion, and the freemen of North Providence took an active part in efforts to expand the restrictive Rhode Island suffrage.[34] As a consequence of these traditions, many of the village's residents opposed the textile industry as a British importation. It was, of course, not uncommon in this period for many Americans to view British manufacturing as a threat to democratic liberties and as an assault upon equality. According to Benedict, there was prejudice against Slater because he was an Englishman, prejudice that "lasted some time, and attached to everything pertaining to cotton manufacturing."[35] Pawtucket's workers thus inherited a culture both democratic and egalitarian, a culture suspicious of millowners and resistant to industrial values. This culture was stronger than it otherwise might have been because millowners had to build their institutions, and impress their values, within a preexisting community. As a consequence, the hegemony of millowners in this period was never secure. Indeed, the buttressing institutions of industrial capitalism were weaker in Pawtucket than elsewhere in New

England. The village had no rows of company housing, no church until 1805, no temperance movement until 1826. There was one company-run store, but it had no monopoly of local business since it sold its wares alongside numerous other stores. Mill worker independence was also reinforced by local artisans, some of whom shared similar work and leisure values.[36]

In 1820, 65 percent of the village's manufacturing labor did not work in the textile mills. The majority of these workers were artisans, but that single term encompassed a variety of trades—ironworker, machinist, miller, carpenter, tinsmith, shuttle-maker, cabinetmaker, mason, housewright, millwright, patternmaker, and so on—and masked subtle differences in status, work routine, wealth, and power. Most artisans worked in small shops, sometimes as proprietors but more often as apprentices or journeymen. Their working conditions were markedly better than those of the textile workers. They generally had greater control over their workday and performed at a variety of separate tasks, working as long on a specific job as their skill demanded. They were rarely required to simply tend machinery, though a few, like the operators of nail-making machines, worked at tasks as monotonous as any in the textile mills. Unlike textile workers, most artisans worked under recognized apprenticeships. In general, artisans received higher pay than textile workers did, usually in the form of a price for goods finished rather than as a wage for time spent.[37]

Pawtucket's artisans were men poised in the middle, the lure of independent proprietorship on the one side, the disgrace of downward mobility into the ranks of factory labor on the other. Historians know more about the successful, those like Oziel Wilkinson who rose to industrial prominence and took a leading part in town politics. But for every Wilkinson there were many more like the Smithfield shoemaker, Stafford Benchley, forced to give up his trade and to enter a local textile mill with his family in order to meet mounting debts.[38]

The chance for upward mobility was one factor affecting whether artisans adhered to traditional or industrial forms of morality. Some artisans, particularly master machinists who saw their fate directly linked to the textile industry, accepted the values and ideology of millowners. They were among the village's "respectables." Others, like the ship carpenters whom Benedict described as "wanting in stability," adhered to a looser, more traditional morality. They were the natural allies of the "disorderly" textile workers. But independent proprietorship and "respectable" behavior did not necessarily imply deference to millowners. There was a small third group of artisan radicals, similar to those in Lynn and Philadelphia described by Paul Faler, David Montgomery, and Bruce Laurie, who combined opposition to industrial capitalism with an acceptace of a type of "industrial morality." For example, the Pawtucket radical Henry

Earl (or Earle) served as a member of the editorial committee of the labor paper, the *New England Artisan*, in 1832 while earlier supporting the local temperance movement as a way of increasing the self-respect and political effectiveness of the laboring classes.[39]

Even among those respectable artisans who seemed to subscribe to the values of millowners, there was considerable ambivalence. In the early 1820s, local artisans formed the Pawtucket Mechanics Society apart from the earlier organization of the millowners and their agents. None of the society's numerous officers were millowners. At a dinner meeting of the society held in the Smithfield Hotel on March 20, 1828, the artisans offered toasts to the "American System," to Henry Clay, the "Champion of Freedom," and to General Jackson, "in the hands of a mad opposition he would cut the throat of his country." Each of these toasts reflects a political culture shared by millowners and artisans. However, the meeting was held in celebration of the traditional ending of evening labor in the textile mills. This was a genuine element of workingclass culture in New England mill towns. In Lowell, gala balls marked March 20, when the approach of the summer solstice made artificial light in the mills unnecessary, and similar celebrations continued in Rhode Island at least into the 1850s.[40]

It is not surprising that Pawtucket artisans did identify with those below them in the new industrial hierarchy. Many had experienced the social changes brought by industrial capitalism. They observed for themselves the increased use of unskilled women and children, the new discipline of the factory, and the emergence of a wealthy elite. Some may have had children of their own working in the mills. By the late 1820s, local artisans were declining in status and, if they did not oppose industrialism itself, few deferred to the encroaching power of textile millowners. In the early 1830s, Pawtucket artisans played a critical role in the formation of the area's first labor paper, the *New England Artisan,* and in the establishment of the first regional labor organization, the New England Association of Farmers, Mechanics, and Other Workingmen.[41]

Local farmers constituted a fourth group, one whose boundaries in this period were quite flexible. Some area farmers worked at seasonal trades, such as shipbuilding and grist milling, and went home when their work ended. Ironworkers left their forges in the slack periods to return to the family farms. Some farmers and many of their kin alternated between farm and factory labor, and many farm families had previous experience as textile mill outworkers. The overlapping boundaries among farm, artisan, and factory labor ensured that numerous farmers and their families in the outlying areas of North Providence and Seekonk had direct ties to industrial work in Pawtucket village. In addition, local farmers were indirectly linked to the village in two ways. First, the largest farmers, those who did a cash crop business, were dependent for their sales on the mill villages of Pawtucket, Rehoboth, North Providence, and Smithfield. Second, freehold farmers who lived within the corporate limits of North Providence and Seekonk shared in political decisions affecting Pawtucket village. Whether their ties were direct or indirect, area farmers could not escape the influence of a changing industrial landscape, nor could they fail to develop attitudes about the growing power of textile millowners.[42]

The response of New England farmers to the coming of the spinning mills was complex and has been poorly studied. In some communities, settled farmers were the first to express opposition to the mills. In Waterford, Rhode Island, for example, farmers opposed the building of a woolen mill and "placed all the obstacles which they could in its way."[43] Conflicts over water rights, tax policy, the location of town meetings, and the building of roads divided southern New England farmers from textile millowners throughout the early nineteenth century and, on specific occasions, drew farmers and laborers together in explicit alliance. In Pawtucket, local farmers initially opposed the encroachments of millowners and thereby established a pattern of community resistance. By the 1820s, the dense and interlocking connections among farmers, artisans, and mill laborers helped to solidify community support for militant action against the mill-owners.[44]

The textile strike of 1824 was the clearest and most intense act of resistance to industrial capitalism in Pawtucket, but it was not the first such expression of community resistance. Opposition to the textile industry occurred early. The damming of the Blackstone River in 1792-1793 caused serious division in the village. The new dam was built just upstream of the lower one (first built in 1718) and in conjunction with a power canal for the Slater Mill. Its construction resulted in at least one act of sabotage. The owners of the new dam—Almy, Brown, and Slater—charged the occupants of the lower privilege, the ironworkers, John, Stephan, and Eleazer Jenks, with "illegally and violently" pulling down the upper dam. The building of the upper dam posed complicated problems for a fair apportioning of water among competing industrial users. Much of the early nineteenth-century conflict aroused by the building of the dam pitted artisans against textile capitalists. The issue prompted rancorous litigation and divided the village for years.[45]

For residents upstream, the dam accentuated two problems. First, the building of a new dam increased the risk of flooding. In some cases, such as in Valley Falls, Scituate, and Manville, all Rhode Island towns, arable farmland was flooded. In Valley Falls and Scituate, the aggrieved farmers won court cases against the millowners. The fines imposed, however, were not high, and the upstream lands remained under water.[46] The flooding of good farmland caused bitterness. One resident of Valley Falls, a mill town just upstream of Pawtucket, pointedly complained that "one or two of the best farms in the region [were] forever submerged under the water of the created [mill] pond."[47] Second, the building of dams the width of the river forced curtailing the seasonal fish runs. Reducing the number of fish in the river had serious consequences for farmers and fishermen accustomed to the traditional spawning of shad, alewives, and salmon at Woonsocket Falls. Before the extensive damming of the Blackstone, according to one report, "salmon were very plentiful, so much so that they formed the chief article in the farmer's bill of fare."[48] Conflict over fishing rights had divided the village previously. In 1714, local residents cut a fishway, known as Sargeant's trench, around the Pawtucket Falls on the west bank. When the fishway failed in its purpose, anti-industrial interests were strong enough to have the Rhode Island General Assembly declare the Blackstone a public river and to make it lawful to break down or blow up the rocks at the Falls to "let fish pass up."[49] The controversy festered until the damming of the river in 1792-1793, and the refusal of both the court of common pleas in Taunton, Massachusetts, and the Rhode Island General Assembly to act against the millowners effectively ended any hope of redress for the farmers and fishermen.[50]

Conflict over taxes also divided the village. When Oziel Wilkinson, Samuel Slater, and others built the White Mill in what was then Rehoboth, Massachusetts, they petitioned the Massachusetts legislature for a tax exemption. The town opposed the exemption, but without success. The millowners were able to appeal over the heads of local interests to the state, an authority more amenable to their influence. Such conflict was not rare or confined solely to Pawtucket. In 1823, the town of Smithfield, Rhode Island, voted a tax to be levied on the Blackstone Manufacturing Company. In the same year, the town instructed its representative to vote against the company's petition to the general assembly in opposition to that tax. The effort to tax the company apparently failed. Four years later, the town tried a new approach, instructing its representative to propose a tax on cotton and woolen machinery. There is no indication that the town was any more successful, and the efforts appear to have been dropped.[51]

Throughout this period, millowners attempted to increase their power and influence in Pawtucket village. They ran for local office, established churches, moral reform societies, and other institutions of social control, and tightened discipline on the factory floor. The majority of the villagers remained hostile to their efforts. Despite their wealth and despite the restrictive suffrage, millowners rarely controlled town politics. This was clearly demonstrated in 1823 when a local justice of the peace convicted a mill overseer for assault and battery on a female child despite the overseer's argument that the child's parent had properly delegated his authority to punish. When the case was heard in an appellate court in

Taunton, Massachusetts, however, the decision of the Pawtucket justice of the peace was reversed.[52]

By the early 1820s, there was the outline of an oppositional tradition in Pawtucket, hostile to millowners and supported, at various times and for partly different reasons, by farmers, artisans, and mill laborers. This was not a tradition punctuated by daily conflict, but it did provide a cultural resource, in times of periodic crisis, for those opposed to textile mills and millowners. It was a tradition partly rooted in eighteenth-century standards of work and leisure, in the democratic heritage of the Revolution, and in the experience of adjusting to the changes introduced by textile industrialism. In their first thirty years in Pawtucket, textile millowners altered the physical landscape with their large mills and stately houses, greatly increased the numbers of unskilled laborers with their employment of women and children, introduced new definitions of time, work, and leisure, and attempted to secure political and cultural hegemony in the village. They met opposition at every turn, and in the late spring of 1824, that opposition crystallized in the first strike of textile workers in North America.

The strike was precipitated by the decisions of local millowners on Monday, May 24, to run their mills one hour longer and to reduce by approximately 25 percent the wages of "those who weave by the yard."[53] The owners, acting in concert, intended the changes to take effect on June 1. Increasing the workday was to be accomplished by reducing the "time allowed at the several meals."[54] This would bear equally on all workers. Reducing weaving piece rates, however, would affect only the young female weavers.

The owners' rationale was explicit. They referred to conditions of "general depression" in a report justifying their actions, which was published after the strike.[55] They believed they were paying 10 to 20 percent more for the same work than "any manufacturing district in the union."[56] Their factories, to their knowledge, were running fewer hours than those elsewhere. One newspaper report mentioned the recent tariff as the cause of the millowners' action, but the owners themselves did not discuss it.[57] They displayed a remarkable willingness to reveal their competitive disadvantages. But if the economic arguments were not sufficient to convince a hostile community that their actions were responsible, the owners summoned one further argument. Female weavers, they claimed, were making two dollars a week "above their board," and this was "generally considered to be extravagant wages for young women." It was, the owners continued, much more than the women could earn elsewhere and was a sum "out of proportion to the wages of other help." This latter statement can be interpreted to mean that some weavers, at least, were making more money than unskilled men.[58]

There is no evidence that there was a general depression in 1824. It is clear, however, that by the early 1820s the cotton textile industry was first feeling the effects of the capitalist trade cycle. Earlier periods of economic crisis could be traced partly to political causes. The stronger producers had weathered the overexpansion of the embargo years and the subsequent dumping of British goods at the close of the War of 1812. Beginning in 1819-1820, however, the entire industry began to experience periodic bursts of overproduction and declining cloth prices in the context of a volatile and largely uncontrolled market—conditions that haunted the industry throughout the nineteenth century. In the early nineteenth century, markets could not be created fast enough, or be sufficiently stabilized, to keep pace with the thrusts of technological innovation.[59]

Productivity, measured by annual cloth output, rose between 1820 and 1824 by a factor of four: from 13,844,000 yards to 55,777,000 yards. This was primarily the result of the introduction of the power loom. Over the same period, and following the same logic, the average annual price of brown sheeting on the New York market dropped precipitously, from 24.4 cents per yard to 14.6 cents per yard, the sharpest drop coming between 1823 and 1824 (20.7 cents per yard to 14.6 cents per yard). Combined with a steep rise in the average annual price of middling cotton (11.4 cents per pound in 1823 and 14.8 cents per pound in 1824), these figures suggest that New England textile millowners found themselves in the spring of 1824 in deteriorating economic circumstances.[60]

These trends are generally reflected in Pawtucket. The Pawtucket Cotton Manufacturing Company (the name of the Yellow Mill company by 1832) experienced a decline in the price of brown shirting from 30 cents per yard in 1816 to 12.5 cents per yard in 1824. Profits for 1824 were 8 percent, compared to 15 percent the year earlier and to 10 percent in each of the two subsequent years. The early 1820s were also years of serious drought in Pawtucket. Lack of water forced mills to lie idle in the late summer, further contributing to the economic difficulties of local millowners.[61]

It is not surprising then that Pawtucket millowners sought to cut labor costs, for these were the only major expenses over which they had control. Their decision to reduce the rates of female weavers may be seen as shrewd calculation. The weavers were the newest entrants to the factory system. Since no real labor market existed for women prior to textile mill development, it can be assumed that young female weavers had no highly developed sense of a customary wage. The millowners evidently believed that the weavers would not respond to a wage cut as forcefully as male laborers would. And since piece rates for power weaving were a new and still experimental form of payment, it is likely that female weavers of sufficient skill and dexterity were able to make more money than unskilled males, as the owners seemed to charge. The owners were willing to exploit the issue, perhaps assuming that it would divide the workforce. They badly miscalculated.[62]

Though the increase in hours and reduction in rates were not to go into effect for a week, the workers responded immediately. The local manufacturers' press provided a detailed, if biased, account of the beginning of the turnout:

> When the laboring part of the community learned the result of the meeting [the meeting of owners on May 24], they very generally determined to work only the usual hours; and when the bell rang to call them to their employment, they assembled in great numbers, accompanied by many who were not interested in the affair, round the doors of the mill, apparently for the purpose of hindering or preventing the entrance of those [willing to work], no force, however, was used.[63]

The turnout closed all the textile mills in the village and was supported by many who did not work in the mills. Moreover it elicited the spontaneous and militant action of the young female weavers. The *Manufacturers' and Farmers' Journal* continued its account with patriarchal disdain.

> The female weavers assembled in parliament to the number, it is stated of *one hundred and two*—one of the most active, and most talkative, was placed in the chair, and the meeting, it is understood, was conducted, however strange it may appear, without noise, or scarcely a single speech. The result of the meeting was a resolution to abandon their looms, unless allowed the old prices.[64]

It is unfortunate that virtually nothing is known about these women or any of the other striking workers. No labor records for Pawtucket's mills in the 1820s have survived, no millowners' letters refer to the strike, and newspaper accounts provide no clue to the workers' identities. It can be assumed that most of the weavers were the daughters of local artisans, farmers, and factory workers. Some, no doubt, lived with their families. The millowners' reference that the weavers were making two dollars a week above their board is a clear indication that most were living either in boardinghouses specially adapted for the purpose or were boarding with families in the village. This contradicts the conventional assumptions about the dominance of a family labor system in Rhode Island and has consequences for understanding the strength of popular protest in Pawtucket. If many of the weavers lived together in a single boardinghouse, as they did in Lowell and later communities organized by Boston capitalists, they would have experienced that same sense of cohesiveness reflected in the strike behavior of Lowell mill women in the 1830s. However, the women of Lowell had few ties to the local community, and both of their major strikes were failures. The weavers of Pawtucket not only drew strength from each other but, since they did have local ties, from the community as well.[65]

On the evening of May 26, mill workers and artisans engaged in crowd behavior threatening to the millowners. According to the *Journal*:

> On Wednesday evening a tumultuous crowd filled the streets, led by the most unprincipled and disorderly part of the village, and made an excessive noise—they visited successively the houses of the manufacturers, shouting, exclaiming and using every imaginable term of abuse and insult. The window in the yellow mill was broken in—but the riot, considering the character of those who led, and the apparent want of all reflection in those that followed, was not so injurious to property and personal security, as might have been reasonably apprehended. The next day the manufacturers shut their gates and the mills have not run since.[66]

The *Journal's* tone is deceptive and its use of the term *riot* misleading. Read closely, the passage indicates that Pawtucket's workers behaved in a restrained, organized, and purposeful manner. With some measure of informal leadership, they visited "successively" the homes of millowners, subjected the owners to extensive verbal abuse, but engaged in no real violence. Though there is no line of direct continuity, precedents for this kind of organized crowd behavior can be found thirty years earlier in the actions of the Revolutionary crowd. Like the eighteenth-century mobs analyzed by recent historians, the crowd in Pawtucket acted in defense of accepted community standards and of a broadly defined notion of the public good. The owners' intention to cut wages and increase hours, though justified by the new standards of capitalist entrepreneurship, threatened to degrade the village's mill laborers and to intensify their exploitation. The community's immediate and unambiguous response served notice of a different set of standards, those rooted in an artisan culture with its profound sense of the dignity of labor. It is significant that the community chose the millowners' houses as objects of its anger, for they were the village's chief symbols of aristocratic pretense, the physical embodiments of the antidemocratic thrust of textile industrialism.[67]

The strike continued through the remainder of the week and into the next. The *Journal's* account, published on Saturday, May 29, indicates continued unrest: "The citizens of Pawtucket have, for a few days past, been in a state of excitement and disorder, which reminds us of the accounts we frequently read of the tumults of manufacturing places in England, though unattended with the destruction and damage usually accompanying those riots."[68] There is no record of further organized and public activity by the strikers. However, on early Tuesday morning, June 1, an attempt was made to set fire to a section of the Yellow Mill then owned by Edward Walcott. The *Journal* remarked that it was "evidently the work of an incendiary." Fire enveloped seven bales of cotton near a window, but it was apparently discovered quickly enough to prevent major damage.[69]

This is a difficult act to interpret. It could simply have been the work of rebellious children and only indirectly related to the strike. But it did occur during the strike, in fact on the morning the proposed changes in hours and rates were to have gone into effect. And significantly, the fire was set in the mill of Edward Walcott, a manufacturer who took a leading part in the millowners' deliberations. It is reasonable to assume that the attempted arson was directly related to the strike, either as an act of anger and retribution or as a calculated and measured warning. The mill, after all, did not burn and perhaps was not intended to, the warning being deemed sufficient.[70]

The deliberate burning of textile mills was not uncommon in early nineteenth-century New England. One historian of industrial Rhode Island asserted that "many of the early mill fires were reported to be of incendiary origin."[71] In Pawtucket alone more than five attempts were made to burn cotton mills or related structures between 1811 and 1820. On October 5, 1811, at 1:30 A.M., the slitting mill of Oziel Wilkinson was burned, and the fire spread to a workshop owned by Almy, Brown, & Slater, causing considerable damage.[72] Three nights later, fire was discovered in the Slater Mill, but it was put out before serious damage was done. Samuel Slater, in a letter to Almy & Brown, stated that "many are of opinion it was set on fire wilfully," though Slater himself did not wish to believe it.[73] On February 1, 1814, the *Rhode Island American* reported that "several attempts have been made to set fire to the cotton mills in Pawtucket." The newspaper interpreted the attempts as political attacks against the Federalist millowners.[74] Then in early May 1820, three fires were set in a five-day period, two of which involved cotton mills.[75]

There is no evidence that these fires were set by workers, but given the nature of the act, evidence should not be expected. There is sufficient circumstantial proof to see the burning of textile mills as acts of anonymous protest and as part of a larger underground tradition employing arson for the redress of grievances, both public and private. And if we wish to glimpse something of the attitude of millworkers to the burning of their mills, there is the remarkable statement of a nineteenth-century Rhode

Island historian who, in commenting on the changing relations of workers and owners since the depression of 1837, asserted that "no body of men would now stand by and cheer at the destruction of their employers's mill, as they did when that of William Harris, at Valley Falls, was being devoured by the flames."[76]

Millowners in this period were well aware of the possibility of arson. The attempt to burn Walcott's Mill may have encouraged them to settle quickly, for the strike came to an end almost immediately after. Only two pieces of evidence relate to the strike's conclusion. On Thursday, June 3, the *Journal* reported that the "ferment" in Pawtucket had "subsided," and the mills were "generally in operation."[77] On Saturday, the *Providence Patriot* stated that "the Pawtucket mills are again in operation, under a compromise between the employers and the employed."[78] This is nothing like unqualified victory, but the compromise settlement underscores both the inability of Pawtucket's millowners to dominate the village and the strength of the oppositional tradition shared by farmers, artisans, and mill laborers.

The day after the fire at Walcott's Mill, Wednesday, June 2, the owners met at Blake's Hotel and appointed a committee of five to draft a statement for the local newspapers. Among other things, the statement was designed to refute "a report . . . industriously circulated" that the recent changes were "for the purpose of tyrannizing over, and oppressing the people employed in [the owners'] factories."[79] The committee consisted of William Harris, whose mill later burned at Valley Falls, John Gardner, Holder Burden, J. C. Starkweather, and Henry Marchant. The committee secretary was Edward Walcott, and the chairman was Ebenezer Tyler.[80] Two days later, after the strike had been settled, the owners met to issue their report. This is the same report that freely and candidly revealed the wage scale, the hours of operation, and the comparative disadvantages of Pawtucket's millowners. The tone is defensive and the act of writing clearly deliberate. This was no hasty or poorly conceived response but the act of a committee proceeding with due consideration and attentive to public opinion. The strike was clearly perceived as a matter of consequence. The owners took seriously the threat to their reputation and went to unusual lengths to "remove all impressions . . . prejudicial to the manufacturers" of their village.[81] On one level, this response reflected their fear that if such impressions gained currency, they would have a harder time recruiting workers. On another, more fundamental level, it indicated the incomplete and still fragile hegemony of industrial capitalism. Despite the workers' recourse to the strike, a weapon both new and of doubtful legality, it was the owners who felt called upon to defend themselves.

The text of the owners' report is significant—both for what it says and for what it does not say. With the exception of their aggressive stance on the wages of female weavers, they made no direct attack on the workers.

They did not mention the organized crowd, the insults and epithets, the damage to property, or the attempted arson. Within the developing ideology of industrial capitalism, the owners could have used any or all of these incidents to mount a damning attack on Pawtucket's workers. But they did not. Given the history of Pawtucket, the millowners' defensiveness is understandable. They knew that a direct attack on the workers would not have been supported by the community. This is not the sort of defensiveness one expects to find among nineteenth-century capitalists, but in 1824 the future success of industrial capitalism was far from assured. If the millowners of Pawtucket did not act like men confident of their own values, there were reasons for it deeply rooted in the village's past.

In the immediate aftermath of the strike, a special meeting of the North Providence Town Council was called. With authorization provided by the annual town meeting two days earlier, Abraham Wilkinson, Timothy Greene, and Caleb Drown petitioned the council to appoint a night watch in the fire district of Pawtucket. The town granted the petition, and the three were authorized to select a watch and "provide a suitable building as a Watch house and Bridewell to confine any person or persons . . . disturbing the peace and quiet."[82] The watch, established because of the owners' fear of continued arson, was organized to guard the town and the owners' property from 9 P.M. to sunrise. The cost would be borne by the petitioners, not the town; the townsfolk were sympathetic to the owners' fear, but only to a point.[83]

While the millowners and freemen of North Providence considered the role of local government in protecting private property, local mule spinners were busy organizing. For approximately three weeks, both the *Journal* and the *Patriot* carried notices announcing a meeting of "Mule-Spinners in the State of Rhode Island and vicinity" to be held Monday, July 5, at 11 A.M. at Joseph Randell's Inn in Smithfield, just one mile from Pawtucket. The purpose of the meeting was to organize a society of mule spinners and "to establish rules and regulations for the government thereof." In many ways it was a remarkable notice, indicative of the spinners' newly felt power. The spinners could have met on the previous day, the Fourth of July. They chose instead to meet in the middle of a working day, curtailing production for the time they were out. Unfortunately we know nothing more. The press carried no account of the meeting, and organizational records have not survived.[84]

Confronted by efforts to organize workers, the millowners continued their attempts to control the culture. In the fall of 1826, two hundred residents met in the Pawtucket Hotel in support of the newly organized temperance movement. A petition, signed by the village's leading figures, was addressed to the Rhode Island General Assembly asking for authorization to pass more stringent licensing laws. It was granted immediately but, because

of local opposition, could not be effectively implemented in the village.[85]
On July 4, 1827, the owners sponsored their most impressive act of public
theater. Three hundred to four hundred young boys from the village's
Sunday schools, wearing "the look of health, cheerfulness and prosperity,"
paraded alongside a gala float drawn by six white horses. The float contained a loom and spinning frame operated by a crank leading from one of
the axles.

> On a flag floating over the machinery, were the names,
> H. Clay, H. Niles, and M. Carey [three of the manufac-
> turers' most effective propagandists], and attached to the
> flag-staff was a placard *"Encourage National Industry,
> under this we prosper."*[86]

The loom wove either eight or fifteen yards of cloth, depending on
accounts, in the course of the parade.[87]

The effectiveness of these developments was limited. Most of Pawtucket's
workers remained unruly and resistant to the values of middle-class
propriety. In March 1828, the millowners on the Massachusetts side offered
one answer. After a petition to the Massachusetts legislature, the town of
Pawtucket, Massachusetts, was constituted as a distinct entity. Its first
town clerk was J. C. Starkweather, and its three selectmen were millowners,
as were five of its seven tax assessors. For the first time, millowners controlled at least part of the village. Rhode Island millowners made similar
efforts. At the August town meeting, they proposed to split Pawtucket
from North Providence. The proposal was first postponed and later
dropped. Pawtucket was not separated from North Providence until
1874.[88]

The millowners' efforts at political control aroused new opposition. In
the fall of 1828, the editorial column of the *Pawtucket Chronicle* gave
notice of a significant, and perhaps unique, effort at community alliance
against the millowners. The villagers had "promptly and liberally" raised
five hundred dollars at public subscription for a town clock to be placed in
the new Congregational church then being built on the Massachusetts side.
The *Chronicle* expressed the need for such a clock with clarity.

> A time-piece which can be depended upon as a regulator,
> located in so central and public a situation as the new
> Congregational Church, will be of great utility in this vil-
> lage—All are aware of the vexatious confusion occasioned
> by the ringing of the factory bells at this time, and which
> can only be remedied by erecting a clock that will always
> give *"the time of day."*[89]

The clock was erected to counter the millowners' monopoly of public time. In the absence of such a public clock, the village and its workers were at the mercy of the factory bells and the owners' definition of time. We have this complaint from Thomas LeFavour who, prior to becoming a millowner himself, worked from dawn to 7:30 P.M., "or what they called half-past seven, for the clock used to be figured to suit the owners."[90] Even advertisements for workers carried references to a workday defined not by the number of hours but by the factory bell. J. Underwood and Company advertised in the fall of 1821 for twenty to thirty weavers "willing to work six whole days in each week, and attend their Looms all bell hours."[91] The clock, as the *Chronicle* indicated, would reduce confusion, but more importantly, it would directly challenge the millowners' power to define public time.[92]

Less than one year later, in the midst of a serious textile depression, the *Chronicle* turned its fire directly on the millowners.

> Every village, as well as every monarchy, has its tyrant. Wealth or talents constitutes someone to domineer over the multitude, and to keep down the poor and the indigent. We have seen more of this in manufacturing communities than any other—we have seen it in our own village. . . .
>
> There are individuals, in manufacturing communities, who from the habit of ruling the children in their mills with a rod of iron; and from dealing out to them . . . barely enough to cover their nakedness . . . , have acquired the belief that they may step out into the community with the same air, and brow beat all who came in their way, as if they too were dependent on them for a subsistence. . . . What is this but tyranny . . . ? Nothing to which the human mind is subjected is so degrading as this—it converts man, free, independent man, into a tool, to be used for the very worst of purposes.[93]

The editorial went on to praise men (perhaps like the writer himself) "who will not bow and fawn" to the millowners. The tone of the editorial was republican, and the contempt ran deep. The writer scarcely concealed his feeling that the recent failures—of the Wilkinsons, the Greenes, William Harris, and John Gardner, among others—were retributive and just: "Need we look twice, in the circle around us, for distress and poverty among those who have lorded it, with a high hand over their poorer neighbors?"[94]

Two conflicting trends are visible in the 1830s. The early years of the decade saw the first flowering of national labor unrest with the formation of trade societies, labor newspapers, regional labor associations, and the workingmen's parties. But the militance of labor radicals, like the Rhode Island carpenter, Seth Luther, was at times tinged with despair. Luther saw the power and influence of labor slipping away. He believed that the press was not open to the laboring class, that the control of millowners over their workers was becoming more overt, and that the possibility for education was increasingly beyond the grasp of working people. In this period, millowners were consolidating their power, tightening discipline in the factory, and increasing the pace of production. Potential labor alliances were weakened because of the small number of mill workers who participated in sustained organization.[95] The New Haven delegates to the third convention of the New England Association of Farmers, Mechanics, and Other Workingmen complained in October 1833 that

> the absence of delegates from the factory villages gives reason to fear that the operatives in the factories are already subdued to the bidding of their employers—that they have felt the chains riveted upon themselves and their children and despair of redemption. The Farmers and Mechanics, then, are the last hope of the American people.[96]

Despite the absence of mill workers in the counsels of the New England Association, Pawtucket's tradition of opposition to textile industrialism did not die entirely. Its outlines are visible throughout the early 1830s in continued conflict over the millowners' definition of time, in the organization of a cooperative store, and in the formation of the *New England Artisan*. With the depression of 1837, the base for continued opposition was weakened. The depression took its toll, closing mills and scattering workers. Pawtucket did not recover until the coming of the railroad, and the Irish, in the late 1840s. Even in the 1840s, however, there is evidence of a continuation of Pawtucket's antiauthoritarianism. Like other mill villages, it provided critical support for the prosuffrage party of Thomas Dorr. Efforts to revise the colonial charter and to expand the suffrage beyond its restrictive property qualifications were first led by laborers and artisans. Though the movement was later dominated by middle-class elements, and its goals watered down, its primary popular support was found in the mill villages of the Blackstone and Pawtuxet River valleys. But the prosuffrage forces lost the Dorr war, and the Irish quickly replaced the Yankees in Rhode Island's mills in the late 1840s and early 1850s. The possibilities for sustained class-consciousness had been weakened by depression, the loss of the free suffrage fight, and the encroaching power of the millowners. Now with wholesale demographic change, the owners would be faced with new problems in trying to discipline a second group of preindustrial migrants to the work habits of industrial capitalism, but they would not have to face a culturally unified workingclass with a forty-year tradition of opposition to textile industrialism.[97]

Opposition to textile mills and millowners marked Pawtucket's history from 1790 to 1830. Millowners disrupted traditional uses of water power, rearranged the class structure and status order of the village, and imposed new standards of time and work on the factory floor and a more rigid and sober definition of leisure in the community. Few in the village accepted the changes easily. Opposition ranged from political pressure to strikes, from sabotage to arson, from workplace resistance to the erection of a town clock to counter the owners' monopoly of public time. The strength of that opposition derived from a preindustrial culture, democratic traditions, and the villagers' stark awareness of the changes brought by textile industrialism. The history of that opposition, lost for so long, undercuts the Tocquevillian assumption, underlying most of American historiography, that industrial capitalism sanks its roots into American soil quickly and without opposition.

NOTES

1. On Slater, see George S. White, *Memoir of Samuel Slater* (Philadelphia, 1836). On the strike, see John Commons et al., *History of Labour in the United States* (New York, 1918), 1:156. Commons refers to it as the "first instance of women participating in the activities of labour organization." He does not argue that it is the first textile strike in North America, but I have found no reference to an earlier one.

2. Herbert G. Gutman, "The Worker's Search for Power: Labor in the Gilded Age," in H. Wayne Morgan, ed., *The Gilded Age: A Reappraisal* (Syracuse, 1963).

3. Gutman, "Work, Culture, and Society in Industrializing America, 1815-1919," *American Historical Review* 78 (June 1973); E. P. Thompson, *The Making of the English Working Class* (London, 1963); Thompson, "Time, Work Discipline, and Industrial Capitalism," *Past and Present* 38 (1967); Thompson, "The Moral Economy of the English Crowd in the Eighteenth Century," *Past and Present* 50 (1971); E.J. Hobsbawm, *Laboring Men* (London, 1964).

4. For the boundary settlement, see Massena Goodrich, *Historical Sketch of the Town of Pawtucket* (Pawtucket, 1876), p. 15. The 1819 gazetteer is quoted in Leonard Bliss, Jr., *The History of Rehoboth, Bristol County, Massachusetts* (Boston, 1836), p. 235. In 1820, because of a diligent census taker, the village of Pawtucket was listed separately from North Providence. Its population was 1,287. Seekonk, Massachusetts, had a population in the same year of 2,775. About half that number lived in the four square miles of industrial village on the east side of the river. We can estimate this because that area contained 1,458 people in 1828 when Pawtucket, Massachusetts, was constituted. This gives us an estimate for both villages of approximately 3,000. *1820 U.S. Census* (Washington, D.C., 1821); Goodrich, *Historical Sketch*, p. 5.

5. "Financial Statements, 1800-1830," Almy, Brown, & Slater Papers, Rhode Island Historical Society; William Bagnall, *The Textile Industries of the United States, 1639-1810* (Cambridge, 1893), 1:253-256, 379-382; Robert Grieve, *An Illustrated History of Pawtucket, Central Falls, and Vicinity* (Pawtucket, 1897), pp. 136ff; Richard Bayles, *History of Providence County, Rhode Island* (New York, 1891), 2:42; *Transactions of the Rhode Island Society for the Encouragement of Domestic Industry in the Year 1861* (Providence, 1862), pp. 76-118.

Estimates of spindlage compiled from Louis McLane, *Report of Secretary of the Treasury, 1832, Documents Relative to the Manufactures in the United States,* House Documents, 22d Cong., 1st Sess., 1833, doc. 308.

6. Grieve, *Ilustrated History,* pp. 32-44; David Wilkinson, "Reminiscences," in *Transactions,* pp. 76-99, 101-118; Timothy Dwight, *Travels in New England and New York* (New Haven, 1821), 2:27; *Pawtucket Past and Present* (Pawtucket, 1917), p. 36; Bliss, *History of Rehoboth,* p. 235; *1820 Census of Manufacturers, Schedule for Massachusetts and Rhode Island;* Joseph W. Roe, *English and American Tool Builders* (New Haven, 1916); Robert S. Woodbury, *Studies in the History of Machine Tools* (Cambridge, Mass., 1972); David J. Jeremy, "Innovation in American Textile Technology during the Early Nineteenth Century," *Technology and Culture* 14 (January 1973); Brenden Gilbane, "Pawtucket Village Mechanics, Iron, Ingenuity, and the Cotton Revolution," *Rhode Island History* (February 1975).

7. On Slatersville, see Bayles, *History,* pp. 485-500. The final sentence is not a claim that inequality did not exist but that wealth did not necessarily buy political power, nor did its absence necessarily reduce status. On wealth and occupation, see the raw data compiled by Lisa Krop from probate records, North Providence, on file in the Slater Mill Historic Site. On wealth and political power, see note 50. For mill village development in this period, see Caroline Ware, *The Early New England Cotton Manufacture* (Boston, 1931), Vera Shlakman, "Economic History of a Factory Town: A Study of Chicopee, Massachusetts," *Smith College Studies in History* 20, nos. 1-4 (October 1934-July 1935); Constance Green, *Holyoke, Massachusetts: A Case Study of the Industrial Revolution in America* (New Haven, 1939). There is still no adequate study of Rhode Island mill villages. See Bayles, *History,* J. R. Cole, *History of Washington and Kent Counties, Rhode Island* (New York, 1889). See also the photos in H. R. Hitchcock, *Rhode Island Architecture* (Providence, 1939), and Joseph McCarthy and Samuel Greene, "Rhode Island Mills and Mill Villages," WPA, 1940, Nickerson Collection, Providence Public Library. My ideas on wealth, status, and power in New England villages prior to textile industrialism have benefited by conversations with Jonathan Prude. Cf. Jonathan Prude, "The Coming of Industrial Order: A Study of Town and Factory Life in Rural Massachusetts, 1813-1860" (Ph.D. diss., Harvard University, 1976).

8. Moses Brown to Elisha Waterman, February 23, 1802, Almy, Brown, & Slater Papers, Rhode Island Historical Society, quoted in James L. Conrad, Jr., "The Evolution of Industrial Capitalism in Rhode Island, 1790-1830: Almy, the Browns, and the Slaters" (Ph.D. diss., University of Connecticut, 1973).

9. See the charter of the millowners' organization, the Pawtucket Association of Mechanics and Manufacturers, Rhode Island Charters, June 1810, Rhode Island State Archives; "Petition of Cotton Manufacturers of Providence and vicinity to the Senate and House of Representatives, U.S. Congress, October, 1815," Timothy Pickering Papers, Massachusetts Historical Society; Brenden F. Gilbane, "A Social History of Samuel Slater's Pawtucket" (Ph.D. diss., Boston University, 1969), pp. 376-377.

10. Grieve, *Illustrated History,* pp. 80, 84-87; Conrad, "Evolution"; records of the Catholic Baptist Society, Dec. 1792-March 1838, bound, and records of the First Baptist Church, August 1805-November 1837, bound, First Baptist Church, Pawtucket; Rhode Island petitions, 1811-1812, p. 60, Rhode Island State Archives; Rev. Edward H. Randall, *A Discourse Commemorative of the 50th Anniversary of the Consecration of St. Paul's Church, Pawtucket, R.I.* (Pawtucket, 1868); Goodrich, *Historical Sketch,* pp. 152-153, *Rhode Island American,* September 8, 1815; David Benedict's speech, *Report of the Centennial Celebration of the 24th of June, 1865, at Pawtucket, of the Incorporation of the Town of North Providence* (1865).

11. Grieve, *Illustrated History,* p. 137.

12. The quotes in this paragraph are from Grieve, *Illustrated History,* pp. 54-56, 100, 136-137, 140; Bliss, *History of Rehoboth,* p. 233; David Benedict, "Reminiscences No. 2," and

"No. 26," *Pawtucket Gazette and Chronicle*, February 4, 1853, and December 16, 1853; Gilbane, "A Social History," p. 210. He interprets this well: "From about 1800, when the Starkweather mansion went up on the Massachusetts side to the development of the larger houses on Quaker Lane and on the Jenks plat at the extension of that lane in the 1820's, the social gap was there for anyone to see."

13. Ware, *Early New England*, pp. 198-235; Susan Basham, "The Greene Manufacturing Company" (ms., 1973, Old Sturbridge Village); H. N. Slater, Sr., "Reminiscences of Father," April 26, 1884, Slater Mill Historic Site; *1820 U.S. Census.*

14. Allen, "Diary, 1853," pp. 67-68, Rhode Island Historical Society.

15. Samuel Batchelder, *Introduction and Early Progress of the Cotton Manufacture in the United States* (Boston, 1863); *Transactions*, pp. 101-118.

16. *Manufacturers' and Farmers' Journal*, June 18, 1821.

17. *1820 U.S. Census; McLane Report;* Batchelder, *Introduction;* James Montgomery, *A Practical Detail of the Cotton Manufacture of the United States* (Glasgow, 1840); Robert Baird, *The American Cotton Spinner* (Boston, 1854).

18. Slater to Almy & Brown, September 25, 1795, box 2, no. 256; Slater to Almy & Brown, July 19, 1796, box 3, no. 352, Almy, Brown, & Slater Papers, Rhode Island Historical Society; White, *Memoir of Slater*, pp. 98, 106.

19. Benedict, "Reminiscences No. 23," *Pawtucket Gazette and Chronicle*, October 28, 1853.

20. *Report of the Centennial Celebration*, p. 88.

21. Grieve, *Illustrated History*, p. 94.

22. *1820 Census of Manufacturers;* Grieve, *Illustrated History*, pp. 54, 67, 118, 127; letter on the history of Seekonk, Massachusetts, no author, to Wm. Jennison, November 20, 1823, ms. bound, 1820-1837, Massachusetts Historical Society; records of the First Baptist Church, 1805-1837, bound, First Baptist Church, Pawtucket. See the meetings of December 5, 1818, January 7, July 28, 1819, February 5, March 1, August 7, September 28, 1820, June 28, 1821; Bruce Laurie, " 'Nothing on Compulsion': Life Styles of Philadelphia Artisans, 1820-1850," *Labor History* (Summer 1974); Paul Faler, "Cultural Aspects of the Industrial Revolution: Lynn, Massachusetts, Shoemakers and Industrial Morality, 1826-1860," *Labor History* (Summer 1974); Daniel Scott Smith and Michael Hindus, "Pre-marital Pregnancy in America, 1640-1971," *Journal of Interdisciplinary History* (Winter 1976).

23. Grieve, *Illustrated History*, pp. 100-101; Richard M. Dorson, "The Wonderful Leaps of Sam Patch," *American Heritage* 18 (December 1966).

24. Faler, "Cultural Aspects." For similar efforts by upper-middle-class interests elsewhere, see Raymond A. Mohl, *Poverty in New York, 1783-1825* (New York, 1971); Michael B. Katz, *The Irony of Early School Reform: Educational Innovation in Mid-Nineteenth Century Massachusetts* (Cambridge, Mass., 1968); Carroll Smith-Rosenberg, *Religion and the Rise of the City: The New York City Mission Movement, 1812-1870* (Ithaca, N.Y., 1971); Stanley K. Schultz, *The Culture Factory: The Boston Public Schools, 1789-1860* (New York, 1973).

25. *Rhode Island American*, September 8, 1815.

26. Records of the First Baptist Church, 1805-1837. See the annual meetings usually held in June of each year.

27. Rev. E. A. Buck, *An Historical Discourse Delivered at the . . . Anniversary of the Slatersville Congregational Church, 9 September 1866* (Woonsocket, R.I., 1867), p. 14.

28. Rhode Island petitions, 1815, p. 43, Rhode Island State Archives. See also North Providence Town Meeting records, 1808-1855, meeting of November 18, 1812, Pawtucket City Hall, Clerk's Office.

29. Membership computed from *Manual of the First Baptist Church, Pawtucket Rhode Island* (Providence, 1884). Fifty-three people joined the church prior to 1813. In the years of textile mill expansion, 1813-1815, 70 new members joined. Membership rates dropped after 1816 (only 18 new members joined from 1817 to 1820, and slightly increased from 1820 to

1824, the years when the power loom was being introduced; 60 new members joined in that five-year period). By 1820, there were 186 members of First Baptist, but there is reason to believe this is an overestimate. A total of 203 joined the church prior to August 1820 (the month the federal census was completed), and 17 were recorded as having died, moved, or been excommunicated. For many members, however, there was no date given for termination of membership. It is likely that more than 17 left the church from 1805 to 1820. Membership increased sharply in years of depression: 45 joined in 1816, 75 in 1829. For evidence of millowner influence, see the records of the First Baptist Church, 1805-1837, and Grieve, *Illustrated History*, pp. 176-178, and the records of the Catholic Baptist Society, 1792-1838.

30. Vital records, bound, St. Paul's Church, Pawtucket, membership list of October 13, 1824, St. Paul's; Frederick Houk Law, *The History of Old St. Paul's of Pawtucket* (Providence, [c. 1900]); Randall, *Discourse*, p. 6; *1820 U.S. Census*.

31. Ray Potter, *A Poor Man's Defense* (Providence, 1823), p. 10; Potter, *Memoirs of the Life and Religious Experience of Ray Potter* (Providence, 1829); Grieve, *Illustrated History*, pp. 179-180.

32. For the democratic thrust of evangelical religion, see William G. McLoughlin, *New England Dissent, 1630-1833: The Baptists and the Separation of Church and State* (Cambridge, Mass., 1971); McLoughlin, "Charles Grandison Finney," in David Brion Davis, *Ante-Bellum Reform* (New York, 1967). For local examples, see Bliss, *History of Rehobeth*, pp. 214-228. For revivalism and public order, see Jacob Frieze, *Two Discourses . . . on Religious Excitements Delivered at the Universalist Church, Pawtucket* (1829). For the example of a Free-Will Baptist minister who supported a Fall River strike, see A. D. Williams, *The Rhode Island Free-Will Baptist Pulpit* (Boston, 1852), pp. 248-249.

33. This estimate is derived from the two church lists, for First Baptist and St. Paul's, and from Potter's membership claim for Free-Will Baptist. These were the only churches in the village in 1820. The number of adults was computed from the 1820 census. The total population serviced by the village's churches was estimated to be all of North Providence and Pawtucket village, Massachusetts. Comparison between church lists and the 1820 census clearly indicates that the village's churches drew from both rural North Providence and from Massachusetts. The claim of 15 percent church membership may seem surprisingly low, but there is reason to believe that it is actually too high. First, the formation of both St. Paul's and First Baptist was assisted by Providence residents, members of Episcopal and Baptist congregations in Providence, who remained as Pawtucket church members. If it were possible to identify them precisely and exclude them from the estimate, the number of Pawtucket church members would, of course, decline. Second, I did not include the populations of Seekonk or Rehoboth, Massachusetts, in the estimate, though it is possible that the village's churches drew some members from these areas. There is also written evidence of the weakness of organized religion in Pawtucket. See Benedict, "Reminiscences No. 23," *Pawtucket Gazette & Chronicle*, October 28, 1853, and Law, *History of Old St. Paul's*. It should not be concluded that the unchurched population was necessarily irreligious. In this period, itinerant revivalists did visit the village. See Williams, *Free-Will Baptist Pulpit*, pp. 76-77, 108.

34. Bliss, *History of Rehoboth*, p. 158; North Providence town meeting records, 1808-1855, meeting of January 20, 1797; Gilbane, "A Social History," pp. 364-367; Peter J. Coleman, *The Transformation of Rhode Island, 1790-1860* (Providence, 1969), p. 268.

35. *Report of the Centennial Celebration*, pp. 87-88.

36. On housing, see Conrad, "Evolution," pp. 112-113; Gilbane, "A Social History," pp. 282-283. On stores, see Grieve, *Illustrated History*, p. 93; Bliss, *History of Rehoboth*, p. 235. On temperance, see Rhode Island petitions, 1826-1827, p. 47, Rhode Island State Archives; North Providence town meeting records, 1808-1855, meeting of April 15, 1829.

37. *1820 Census of Manufactures*; McLane Report; *Transactions*, pp. 101-118; Slater, Sr., "Reminiscenses." Rich sources for artisan life in this period are the depositions in the Sargeant's trench case, *Ebenezer Tyler et al.* v. *Abraham Wilkinson et al.* (1826), Federal Case

No. 14,312, Federal Records Center, Waltham, Massachusetts.

38. Rhode Island petitions, 1815, p. 11, Rhode Island State Archives.

39. *Report of the Centennial Celebration*, p. 87; Grieve, *Illustrated History*, pp. 98-99; *New England Artisan*, May 24, 1832; Rhode Island petitions, 1826-1827; Faler, "Cultural Aspects"; Laurie, " 'Nothing of Compulsion' "; Montgomory, "The Shuttle and the Cross: Weavers and Artisans in the Kensington Riots of 1844," *Journal of Social History* 5 (Summer 1972).

40. *Manufacturers' and Farmers' Journal*, August 23, 1824; *Pawtucket Chronicle*, March 22, 1828, August 29, 1829. See also the membership list of the artisans' militia unit, the Fayette Rifle Corps in Grieve, *Illustrated History*, p. 218. It included no millowners. On the celebrations each March 20, see *Pawtucket Gazette & Chronicle*, March 18, 1853, and Hannah Josephson, *The Golden Threads: New England's Mill Girls and Magnates* (New York, 1949).

41. *Pawtucket Chronicle*, April 25, 1829; Grieve, *Illustrated History*, pp. 98-99. The *New England Artisan* was published in Pawtucket from January 1832, when it was founded, until October 1832, when it was moved to Boston. The best history of the New England Association is still that written by Helen Sumner for Commons et al. *History of Labour*, vol. 1.

42. *1820 U.S. Census; 1820 Census of Manufactures*; Ware, *Early New England*; Basham, "Greene Manufacturing." See also John Borden Armstrong, *Factory Under the Elms: A History of Harrisville, New Hampshire, 1774-1969* (Cambridge, Mass., 1969). For the shifting boundaries between farmers and laborers, see the depositions in the Sargeant's trench case.

43. William Bagnall, "Contributions to American Economic History," typescript, ed. V. S. Clark (1908), 2:999, Baker Library, Harvard University.

44. See John G. Metcalf, *Annals of the Town of Mendon, Massachusetts, 1659-1880* (Providence, 1880), pp. 489, 506, 517, 524, 528ff, 537, all on conflicts over roads or bridges. On the formation of the Farmers and Workingmen of Mendon, see the *Woonsocket Patriot*, January 18, February 5, March 22, 1834. For conflict between millowners and farmers, see the efforts at town division in Jonathan Russell et al., "To the Honorable Senate and the Honorable House of Representatives . . . ," Mendon, Mass., c. 1820s, Massachusetts Historical Society; Metcalf, *Annals*, pp. 586ff; Bliss, *History of Rehoboth*, pp. 161ff, 237ff; Grieve, *Illustrated History*, p. 125; William T. Davis, "Webster," in D. Hamilton Hurd, ed., *History of Worcester County, Massachusetts* (1889), 1:362ff. Jonathan Prude first alerted me to the importance of town division conflict.

45. Moses Brown, "Deposition," August 31, 1792, cited in the *Flyer*, January 1972, publication of the Slater Mill Historic Site; Grieve, *Illustrated History*, pp. 104ff; David Green, "Battle for Water Power: The Sargeant's Trench Case, Pawtucket, 1826" (ms., 1976, Slater Mill Historic Site).

46. For Valley Falls, see the Samoset Dam file, state of Rhode Island, Department of Natural Resources, Division of Planning and Development. For Scituate, see the agreement between Paris Hopkins and Peleg Walker, agent to the Foster Woolen Manufacturing Company, September 10, 1819, in the possession of Elinor Larson, North Scituate, who graciously allowed me to cite it. For Manville, see Thomas Steere, *History of the Town of Smithfield* (Providence, 1881), pp. 101ff.

47. Lillie B. C. Wyman, *Elizabeth Buffam Chace, 1806-1899* (Boston, 1914), 1:73.

48. Bayles, *History*, p. 235.

49. Rhode Island collection of records, vol. 7, pp. 222, 248, cited by Grieve, *Illustrated History*, p. 105. See also the conflict over fishing rights on the Palmer River, Rehoboth, in Bliss, *History of Rehoboth*; p. 91; Rehoboth town records, vol. IV, 1780-1792, meeting of May 14, 1792.

50. Conrad, "Evolution," p. 91.

51. Rehoboth town records, vol. V, 1793-1808, meeting of April 13, 1799; Bagnall, *The Textile Industries*, p. 252; Steere, *History*, pp. 65-66.

52. Millowners did hold town office in both Seekonk and North Providence, but they never dominated those offices. In North Providence in 1800, only one millowner served in one of the sixteen major offices: moderator, clerk, treasurer, town sergant and tax collector, town council (seven), overseer of the poor and assessor of rates (three), and representative to the state house (two). There was no sharp increase in millowner participation until 1815, when four of the top sixteen officeholders were millowners. By 1820, however, millowners held only two offices. The failure of millowners to control town politics is all the more surprising given the restrictive suffrage. Most mill workers and some artisans did not possess enough real property to qualify. The conclusion is clear that propertied farmers and artisans did not choose to be dominated by millowners. See Bliss, *History of Rehoboth*, pp. 170-172, 191-198, 201-202; North Providence town meeting records, June 2, 1800, June 4, 1810, June 15, 1815, June 5, 1820. On the number of people voting, see the meetings of April 15, 1818, August 29, 1820, April 18, 1821, June 3, 1822, and Gilbane, "A Social History," pp. 354-355. For the assault and battery case, see the *Manufacturers' and Farmers' Journal,* September 22, 1823.

53. *Manufacturers' and Farmers' Journal,* June 7, May 31, 1824. The *Journal* reported on May 31 that the reduction was 20 percent and that it affected all piece workers. The letter written by the millowners and published in the *Journal* on June 7 referred only to weavers. The owners' own figures constituted a wage cut of 25 percent.

54. *Providence Patriot*, May 29, 1824.

55. *Journal*, June 7, 1824.

56. Ibid.

57. *Providence Patriot*, May 29, 1824.

58. *Journal*, June 7, 1824. If the weavers were being paid two dollars per week above their board, it was slightly more than was being paid to Harvey Scranton, a watchman hired by the Greene Mfg. Co., Warwick, R.I., February 2, 1824. Scranton's contract called for eight dollars per month. See the volume of Labor Contracts, 1814-1832, Greene Manufacturing Company Papers, Rhode Island Historical Society.

59. Ware, *Early New England*, pp. 39-59; Melvin T. Copeland, *The Cotton Manufacturing Industry of the United States* (Cambridge, Mass., 1917).

60. Figures from Robert Brooke Zevin, *The Growth of Manufacturing in Early Nineteenth Century New England* (New York, 1975), tables 1, 3; *U.S. Historical Statistics*, Series E104; Evelyn Knowlton, *Pepperell's Progress: The History of a Cotton Textile Company, 1844-1915* (Cambridge, Mass., 1948), app. 12, 15, tabulated by John M. Cudd, *The Chicopee Manufacturing Company, 1823-1915* (New York, 1974), app. 16.

61. *McLane Report*, Massachusetts, document 3, no. 51.

62. When the power loom was first introduced into Fall River in 1819, it was so imperfect that piece rates could not be maintained, and weavers were allowed to work by the day. See the recollections of Hannah Borden, a weaver, in Bagnall, "Contributions," 3:1918.

63. *Journal*, May 31, 1824. The account was reprinted in the *Rhode Island American*, June 1, 1824, and in the *Rhode Island Republican*, June 3, 1824.

64. *Journal*, May 31, 1824.

65. Records consulted include the Lonsdale Collection, the Almy, Brown, & Slater Papers, the records of the Greene Mfg. Co., the papers of Zachariah Allen and Asa Arnold, all in the Rhode Island Historical Society; the Brown & Ives Papers, John Carter Brown Library, Brown University; the Slater Papers, Baker Library, Harvard University; plus the town records of North Providence and Seekonk. On strikes in Lowell, see Thomas Dublin, "Women at Work: The Transformation of Work and Community in Lowell, Massachusetts, 1826-1860" (Ph.D. diss., Columbia University, 1975).

66. *Journal*, May 31, 1824.

67. Gordon S. Wood, "A Note on Mobs in the American Revolution," *William and Mary Quarterly* (October 1966); Pauline Maier, "Popular Uprisings and Civil Authority in Eighteenth Century America," *William and Mary Quarterly* (1970); Dirk Hoerder, "Boston Leaders

and Boston Crowds: 1765-1776," in Alfred F. Young, ed., *The American Revolution, Explorations in the History of American Radicalism* (DeKalb, Ill., 1976).

68. *Journal*, May 31, 1824.

69. Ibid., June 3, 1824; *Patriot*, June 5, 1824.

70. *Journal*, June 7, 1824.

71. Joseph Brennen, *Social Conditions in Industrial Rhode Island, 1820-1860* (Washington, 1940), p. 33.

72. Slater to Almy & Brown, October 9, 1811, Almy, Brown, & Slater Papers, box 7, no. 944.

73. Ibid.

74. *Rhode Island American*, February 1, 1814.

75. The *Pawtucket Gazette and Chronicle* ran a series on the history of firefighting in Pawtucket. See the issues of August 2, 9, 16, 1861.

76. Brastus Richardson, *History of Woonsocket* (Woonsocket, 1876), p. 173.

77. *Journal*, June 3, 1824.

78. *Patriot*, June 5, 1824.

79. *Journal*, June 7, 1824. The reference seems to indicate that this was a printed report. There is no other reference to a report and, if it was printed, it has yet to turn up in local or regional collections. There is a reference to a letter written by "Hector" from Pawtucket on the strike and submitted to the *Beacon*. The paper refused to publish it. See the *Beacon*, June 26, 1824. Earlier, the same paper refused to carry any notice of the strike. They did not wish to advertise the "private feuds of individuals" (May 29, 1824).

80. For biographical information on the millowners, see Grieve, *Illustrated History*, pp. 138, 54, 100, 200, 90, 143, 161, 170; Bayles, *History*, 2:240, 440-441, 236-237, 239; White, *Memoir*, pp. 106-107; Bliss, *History of Rehobeth*, 228, 233.

81. *Journal*, June 7, 1824.

82. North Providence town meeting records, 1808-1855, meetings of June 7, 9, 1824.

83. Ibid.

84. *Providence Patriot*, June 16, 19, 1824; *Journal*, June 14, July 1, 1824.

85. Rhode Island petitions, 1826-1827, p. 47; North Providence town meeting records, 1808-1855, meetings of April 15, 1829, September 17, 1831.

86. *Journal*, July 5, 1827; *Pawtucket Chronicle*, July 7, 1827. A more spontaneous children's parade, and one closer to the sources of workingclass culture, occurred on the last night of lighting-up when Pawtucket's children "paraded the streets, bearing torchlights, and shouting at the top of their voices . . . and the little devils would give three cheers for 'Liberation' [this was a political slogan for the release of the imprisoned Thomas Dorr, the leader of the prosuffrage forces in the Dorr war, but the children may have had their own "liberation" in mind] themselves just liberated for a brief season from within the walls of a factory. Who can blame them." *Providence Daily Gazette*, 24 March 1845, cited in Brennen, *Social Conditions*, p. 48.

87. Ibid.

88. Town meeting records, Pawtucket, Massachusetts, 1828-1854, meeting of March 4, 1828, records in Pawtucket City Hall, Clerk's Office; North Providence town meeting records, meetings of August 26, 1828, April 15, 1829; Grieve, *Illustrated History*, p. 126.

89. *Pawtucket Chronicle*, October 18, 1828.

90. Benedict, "Reminiscences," *Pawtucket Gazette and Chronicle*, June 10, 1853.

91. *Journal*, September 27, 1821.

92. For an earlier effort to erect a bell and clock in the steeple of First Baptist, see the records of the Catholic Baptist Society, meeting of June 28, 1815. Millowners were the primary contributors. A bell was put in place but no clock was ever obtained. The bell was to be rung on Sunday and on all "public occasions and especially in case of fire." The church

would allow it to be rung on weekdays only if a "majority of freeholders living in the compact part of the village" had a special meeting, "convened for the purpose," and brought to the church a petition signed by seven of their number ten days previous to the date requested. The expense was to be borne by the town. Clearly the bell was not to compete with the factory bells.

93. *Pawtucket Chronicle*, August 29, 1829.
94. Ibid.
95. Seth Luther, *An Address to the Working-Men of New England* (Boston, 1832).
96. Quoted in Commons, *History of Labour*, p. 306.
97. Grieve, *Illustrated History*, p. 102; Dan King, *The Life and Times of Thomas Wilson Dorr*, 1859 (reprint, New York, 1969), pp. 147-148; Marvin Gettleman, *The Dorr Rebellion: A Study in American Radicalism* (New York, 1973), pp. 18ff, 130-134. *The New England Artisan*, January 26, February 16, November 29, 1832. See also John Commons et al., *A Documentary History of American Industrial Society* (Cleveland, 1910), 5:196-197.

STATISTICS AND THE WRITING OF WORKINGCLASS CULTURE: A STATISTICAL PORTRAIT OF THE IRON WORKERS IN TROY, NEW YORK, 1860-1880

11

Daniel J. Walkowitz

During the 1960s American historians began the wholesale adoption of statistical methods in social history. At the time this innovation seemed to many a progressive turn in the profession — part of an attempt to introduce new source materials on lower-class life. Census tracts, tax and church records, and labor and population data were enlisted in the struggle against an elitist history and a sentimental, antiquarian treatment of the poor. Elitist history has focused almost exclusively on individual achievements of "great" men who had held the reins of economic and political power. For labor history this usually has meant writing either entrepreneurial history or institutional union history. By this criterion, the vast majority of working-class people — the unorganized, the unemployed, or the invisible (blacks, chicanos, women and children, for example) — have not been deemed historically significant.[1]

Several social historians writing in the 1960s began to rescue the American working class from the historical graveyard. Such American historians as Stephan Thernstrom, David Montgomery, Herbert G. Gutman, and their students have pioneered a new social history strongly

---

[1] Two recent review essays nicely summarize labor historiography and convey something of this development. *See,* Robert Zieger, "Workers and Scholars: Recent Trends in American Labor Historiography," *Labor History,* 13, No. 2 (Spring, 1972), 245-66, and Thomas A. Krueger, "American Labor Historiography, Old and New: A Review Essay," *Journal of Social History,* 4, No. 3 (Spring, 1971), 277-85.

Source: From *Labor History* 15, no. 3 (Summer 1974):416-460.

influenced by British models — most notably by the works of Eric J. Hobsbawm and Edward P. Thompson.[2] This history has been successful in important ways: for example, it has begun to document substantial conflict and violence earlier ignored by consensus historians. The task now at hand is to explain such disorder. This essay will try to suggest ways in which historians can begin to understand the organization and protest that marked so many mid-nineteenth-century working-class communities, and the way statistics can be effectively used toward that beginning.

Such radical historians as Jesse Lemisch and Staunton Lynd deserve much of the credit for the new interest and concern for the history of the lower-class.[3] Thernstrom's 1964 study of laborers in Newburyport, Massachusetts, *Poverty and Progress,* demonstrated a method by which census data in particular could be utilized.[4] Social historians "discovered" the local manuscript population census: Clyde Griffin for Poughkeepsie, Peter R. Knights for Boston, Theodore Hershberg for Philadelphia, Michael Katz for Hamilton, Ontario, to name but a few.[5] Interesting

[2] See, Edward P. Thompson, *The Making of the English Working Class* (New York, 1963); Eric J. Hobsawm, *Primitive Rebels* (New York, 1959), and *Laboring Men* (New York, 1964); Stephan Thernstrom, *Poverty and Progress; Social Mobility in a Nineteenth Century City* (Cambridge, Mass., 1964), and *Nineteenth-Century Cities: Essays in the New Urban History,* edited with Richard Sennett (New Haven, 1969); and David Montgomery, *Beyond Equality: Labor and Radical Republicans, 1862-1872* (New York, 1967). The latest of Herbert G. Gutman's many articles, "Work, Culture, and Society in Industrializing America, 1815-1919," appeared in the *American Historical Review,* 78, No. 3 (June 1973), 531-88.

[3] See, Jesse Lemisch, "Jack Tar in the Streets: Merchant Seamen in the Politics of Revolutionary America," *William and Mary Quarterly,* 3rd Ser,, XXV (July 1968), 371-407, and "The American Revolution Seen From the Bottom Up," in *Towards a New Past: Dissenting Essays in American History,* Barton J. Bernstein, ed. (New York, 1968), 3-45; and Staughton Lynd, *Anti-Federalism in Dutchess County, New York; A Study of Democracy and Class Conflict in the Revolutionary Era* (Chicago, 1962).

[4] Thernstrom, *Poverty and Progress.* In fact, historians responding to Frederick Jackson Turner's frontier hypothesis had made extensive use of census tracts earlier in attempts to reconstruct community life in midwest frontier towns. See, for example, Merle Curti, et al., *The Making of an American Community: A Case Study of Democracy in a Frontier County* (Stanford, 1959).

[5] Many of the essays in *Nineteenth-Century Cities,* Thernstrom and Sennett (eds.) offer examples. Thus, see Clyde Griffen, "Workers Divided: The Effect of Craft and Ethnic Differences in Poughkeepsie, New York, 1850-1880," in *Nineteenth-Century Cities,* 49-97; Michael B. Katz, "Social Structure in Hamilton, Ontario," in *Nineteenth-Century Cities,* 209-244; and, Peter R. Knights, "Population Turnover, Persistence, and Residential Mobility in Boston, 1830-1860," in *Nineteenth-Century Cities,* 258-274. Peter R. Knights, *The Plain People of Boston,* 1830-1860 (New York, 1971) is perhaps the most flagrant example of the singular dependence on statistical data. Many others, for example such students of Herbert Gutman as Lawrence Glasco, Virginia McLaughlin, Carol Groneman, and the author, have also worked in some depth with local census tracts. Not all have limited themselves to such data, but a significant part of this group has focused on occupational classification. See, Michael B. Katz, "Occupational Classification in History," *The Journal of Interdisciplinary History,* III, No. 1 (Summer 1972), 63-88; and, Clyde Griffin, "Occupational Mobility in Nineteenth-Century

data have been collected, ordered and published. But the method has become reified. In a characteristic American way, facts have too often simply been accumulated, as if their sheer weight could argue historical truth.

The abuse, rather than the use, of statistics has compartmentalized and broken down the historical experience in two troublesome ways. First, recent histories of the American working-class have not been sufficiently rooted in the context of behavior, or in the context of working-class culture. Second, while statistical details have correctly made us sensitive to cleavages and distinctions, ambiguities and conflicts, within the working-class community, minute attention to detail has led to historical paralysis — an unwillingness or inability to synthesize tremendous quantities of information. In sum, too much recent work has suffered serious failings: it has been ahistorically rooted in one or two static instants in time; it has failed to place descriptive data in a broader analytic historical context where it could be balanced, amplified, and substantiated by narrative sources; and it has tended to obscure class concerns in a welter of data.[6]

Statistics can organize much raw data into useful information, but this data must be placed within the context of behavior, difficult cultural traditions, and the impact of different institutions. Historians of the lower-class need to examine many other cultural aspects of social existence and especially the varying ways in which the industrial experience, ethnicity, and diverse social and ethical structures shape social history. Without this expansive vision, the historian runs the risk of grossly misjudging the social consciousness, including attitudes, values, motives, perceptions, awareness. For instance, the mobility of Irish workers who rose from unskilled to semi-skilled and skilled status must be evaluated in terms of the goals and value-system of Irish culture. Moreover, care

---

America: Problems and Possibilities," *Journal of Social History*, 5, No. 3 (Spring 1972), 310-30. There are on-going research projects that symbolize this phenomena: the Canadian Social History Project directed by Michael B. Katz, and the Philadelphia computer project directed by Theodore Hershberg are examples.

[6] The concluding meeting of the conference on "Immigrants in Industrial America," sponsored by The Balch Institute and the Eleutherian Mills Historical Library in Wilmington, Del., (November 103, 1973) dealt with occupational classification and provoked these observations. For two recent examples of the ways in which census data can be integrated with the social and cultural experiences of a lower-class community, see, Judith R. Walkowitz and Daniel J. Walkowitz, " 'We Are Not Beasts of the Field': Prostitution and the Poor in Plymouth and Southampton Under the Contagious Diseases Acts," *Feminist Studies*, I No. 3 (Winter/Spring 1974), 73-106; and, William H. Sewell, "The Working Class of Marseille Under the Second Republic: Social Structure and Political Behavior," in *Workers in the Industrial Revolution*, P. Stearns and D. Walkowitz, eds. (New Brunswick, N.J., 1974).

must be taken not to impose an historical prejudice against manual labor on mobility. Our biases notwithstanding, in order to write the history of the working class, the distinct character of each person's life needs to be drawn sympathetically along both horizontal and vertical lines: *across* the spectrum of social institutions (such as religious, factory, and community) and *within* each institution (such as trades, skills, ethnicity, and marital status).

Edward Thompson has well articulated this expansive treatment of culture. Class, for Thompson, is defined not as simply an economic relationship, but as an historical one: people behaving together in historical events. Thompson acknowledges that class relationships are "largely determined by productive relations into which men are born." However, in Thompson's understanding, class extends beyond economics: as a result of common experience men "feel and articulate the identity of their interests between them." And, however much the class defines itself within its laboring context, common experiences are expressed in cultural terms: traditions, ideas, value-systems and institutional forms.[7] The relationship between cultural pre-conditions and economic conditions, basically the extent to which class and culture reinforce, inhibit, or condition different responses and attitudes, is a little understood and very much open question.

Class and culture are intrinsically related. The precise ways they relate defines the consciousness of the workers under study. Social behavior — manifestations of shared experiences — provides a critical dimension in which to frame the history of the working-class and its culture. Certain interesting historical events in the life of a people may be uncovered, but they remain fragments until the social historian identifies the actors and explains their cultural and social context. Here statistics can help.

Stephan Thernstrom's pioneer study of social mobility in nineteenth-century Newburyport demonstrated innovative ways to use census and tax records to explore dimensions of working-class life. In subsequent work, Thernstrom and others have elaborated and refined much of what we know about mobility in America. But there is an important need to re-evaluate the parameters of mobility. For the behavior of these workers involves more than a question of mobility; central to understanding their actions is the social and cultural context in which they found themselves. These issues involve the inner dynamics of American society and

---

[7] E. P. Thompson, op. cit., 9-10.

suggest the pressures and contradictions that direct and riddle the consciousness of workers living the American experience.

This essay draws a statistical profile of one group of factory workers — the iron workers in Troy, New York, between 1860 and 1880 — in order to examine the relationship between class and culture in industrializing America. A few pages give a brief background about that city's major industry, the iron manufacture, and its founders and workers. Hints follow about the particular quality of social and cultural conflict in Troy. These summaries — each deserving of extended analysis — are only meant to set the stage for the larger theme of this essay: the ways in which census data and quite simple descriptive statistics permit the reconstruction of cultural and class configurations that shape working-class behavior and make it possible to explore the origins and nature of organization and protest in one nineteenth-century American industrial city. Furthermore, this essay reports on work in progress. Statistical data alone can not begin to encompass all the dimensions of culture. A model for understanding working-class culture will have to integrate and balance such statistical information with more traditional literary sources (in historiographical terms, Thernstrom with Thompson), but the focus here will be on statistics. Information drawn from manuscript censuses — data about working-class skills and age levels, property ownership, ethnicity, and marital status — describes more than just social mobility: it allows us to study community structure and ethnic subculture and their relations to family life and occupational structure. In sum, it makes it possible to re-examine the working-class social structure at a given time and the cultural dimensions of particular ethnic workingclass life-styles. Only then can historians begin to understand "random" behavior and consciousness in order to raise questions about social patterns of continuity and change within the working-class world.

Troy is a good place to study. Although it does not tell the "whole story," it has certain ideal qualities. It was a major American manufacturing city, and one to which the large, modern factory came quickly. Moreover, immigrants dominated the city's working-class during its early period of major growth and transformation. It allows us to examine carefully the ways in which radical technological and social change, a fluid but discernable class structure, and immigrant culture affected working-class life. In addition, it is possible to study the reverse process: the extent to which the conditions of working-class life and culture influenced particular technological changes and social behavior.

Located on a narrow plateau along the east bank of the Hudson River
at the confluence of the Mohawk River, the town of Troy was formed in
1789, more than a century after the old Dutch city of Albany some five
miles to the south. Troy was well situated geographically for rapid
growth. It serviced the north country of New England and, after 1825,
served as the terminal port westward and northward for the Erie and
Champlain Canals. It had a ready labor force: between 1820 and 1840
the town's population increased fourfold to nearly 20,000 as settlers from
Massachusetts, the Connecticut Valley, and Vermont migrated westward
to the new urban marketplace where they could work in the fledgling nail,
iron, and textile factories. Between 1840 and 1860 Troy's population
doubled again to nearly 40,000. Increasingly, French Canadians and
British Canadians (especially Irish immigrants) migrated from Canada,
while German, Irish, English and Scottish immigrants arrived yearly by
boat from New York ports. Finally, mountain streams spilling out of the
ranges to the east provided Troy with power for its mills.

Troy developed rapidly during the second quarter of the nineteenth
century, but in a special way. Unlike many other American cities, not one
but two industries shaped its growth: the shirt and collar industry and
the iron industry. Still called the "Collar City," Troy remains today a
mere shadow of its former self with only one shirt factory left and with
a defunct iron industry. But by the mid-nineteenth century, these two industries dominated a bustling urban economy in which men labored in
the iron mills and foundries and women stitched, ironed, and finished
shirts and collars in large factories.[8]

The iron and the shirt and collar industries not only paced Troy's
growth but shaped it in particular ways, so that the city's social structure
and much else continually reflected the presence of these twin giants of
enterprise, Although we concentrate here only upon the iron industry, it
is important to note that employment opportunities for women in Troy's
specialized collar and shirt factories made for a more balanced sex ratio
than in nearby Cohoes, where the single cotton mill dominated that town
which depended so heavily on female labor as to upset the sex balance.[9]

[8] Arthur J. Weise, *Troy's One Hundred Years, 1789-1889* (Troy, 1891), 407-415, counts
twenty-two shirt and collar factories in Troy in 1890. He states these factories employed
over seven thousand Trojan girls and women and an additional seven thousand from
neighboring towns.
[9] *See,* Daniel J. Walkowitz, "Working-class Women in the Gilded Age: Factory, Family
and Community Life Among Cohoes, New York, Cotton Workers," *Journal of Social
History* (Summer 1972), 464-90. Troy's sex distribution reflected the slightly larger
percentage of women nationally. Females comprised 53.9 percent of the population in

TABLE I

Troy Population Statistics, 1860 and 1880

	1860	1880
Total population	39,237	56,747
Non-white	611	577
Foreign born	13,461	16,938
Native born	25,774	39,809
Foreign extraction[a]	23,000 (est.)	36,000 (est.)
percent of total pop.	59% (est.)	64% (est.)
Males 15 and over[b]	12,018 (est.)	18,884 (est.)

[a] "Foreign extraction" refers to immigrants and those with a foreign-born father.
[b] Estimate based on Rensselaer County figures for 1860, New York State figures for 1880.

Troy counted 39,325 residents in 1860, and 56,747 twenty years later (table 1).[10] Immigrants and their children were in a clear majority. In 1860 three of every five Troy inhabitants was foreign-born or the son or daughter of an immigrant. Between 1860 and 1880 a steady stream of immigrants arrived in the city. While the population increased slightly less than 45 percent over the twenty-year span, the number of immigrants and of those Americans with a foreign-born father rose more than 56 percent. By 1880 immigrants and their children were nearly two of every three (64 percent) residents. The iron industry absorbed more than its share of these new workers. About 2,000 men labored in the city's iron works in 1860. Put another way, almost one of every six Troy males over the age of fourteen worked in an iron mill or in an iron foundry. In 1880 roughly 4,500 men worked in this industry, and the ratio had climbed to one in four. Thus the iron industry's share of Troy's work force had outpaced that of the city's population growth. Within particular immigrant

Cohoes in 1860. In contrast, Troy's two industries nicely balanced one another: women comprised 51.8 percent and 50.7 percent of the Troy population in 1860 and 1880 respectively.

[10] Unless otherwise noted, data for this essay has been compiled from Federal manuscript census schedules for 1860 and 1880. See, U.S. Census Office, 8th Census, 1860, *Population of the United States in 1860;* U.S. Census Office, 8th Census, 1860, *Manufactures in the United States in 1860;* U.S. Census Office, 10th Census, 1880, *Population of the United States in 1880;* U.S. Census Office, 10th Census, 1880, *Manufacturers in the United States in 1880;* U.S. Census Office, 10th Census, 1880, Census Reports, *Tenth Census, June 1, 1880,* I, pt. 2, "Statistics of the Population."

groups this ratio climbed even higher. Among the Irish, for example, who made up the largest number of the workers, about three of every eight adult males over fourteen worked in the iron industry in 1880. The ratio of Scot and English iron workers was slightly higher, and that of the Canadians, Germans and native Americans lower.[11]

What, then, of the iron industry which dominated the lives of so many Troy male workers and their families? Its development can be reconstructed from local town histories and from the federal manufacturing censuses of 1860, 1870, and 1880. Not surprisingly, the city's iron industry had modest beginnings, but expanding markets and the direction given these firms by several wealthy capitalists and creative inventors caused the industry to grow steadily. The Civil War brought large orders for horseshoes and iron plate to Troy, greatly stimulating iron manufacture. Finally, the city's iron industry had developed from a series of small mills in the first half of the nineteenth century. In contrast, after the war, the mills began to amalgamate and work concentrated increasingly in a small number of large mills and foundries.

Arthur James Weise, the nineteenth-century Troy local historian, described how the Albany Rolling and Slitting Mill opened on the north side of the lower falls of Wynants Kill in 1807. Two years later a similar mill, built by "other capitalists," started on the upper falls of the Kill.[12] These were small mills and nothing much is known of them. Yet within fifteen years, two men moved to the Troy area and developed their respective enterprises into multi-million dollar businesses by 1880: Erastus Corning, an Albany entrepreneur, and Henry Burden, a Scottish immigrant inventor. In 1826 Corning purchased the lower mill, which was renamed the Albany Iron Works in 1838. By the outbreak of the Civil War this Works, run by Corning and a Vermont-born iron manufacturer named John F. Winslow, had become a major Troy industry that employed 500 men and boys in the manufacture of bar and sheet iron. Under

---

11 These are not precise estimates. The Irish estimate is based on the percentage of iron workers of Irish extraction (estimated at 59.5 percent) compared to the percentage of Troy's population that is of Irish extraction (estimated at 40.4 percent) for the year 1880. I have estimated the number of Irish iron workers because the totals in the manufacturing census conflict with figures compiled from the manuscript population census. The discrepancy is much larger in 1860 and is due to several factors. Some trades are "mixed": engineers and machinists, for instance, worked both in and outside of the iron mills. Many workers were listed by the 1860 census takers simply as laborer." Some workers probably lived outside the city limits. These and other problems involved with using these statistical materials are detailed in a series of essays edited by Seymour Martin Lipset and Richard Hofstadter, *Sociology and History: Methods* (New York, 1968). A comparison of the percentages in columns 1 and 10 in Table 5 gives approximate ratios for the other ethnic groups in Troy in 1880.

12 Weise, *op. cit.,* 264.

the direction of Corning and Winslow, the iron plates for the *Monitor* were made in Troy during the Civil War. Renamed Erastus Corning Company in 1867, it merged with John A. Griswold & Co.'s (Griswold was the other prominent Troy iron master) Rensselaer Iron Company and Bessemer Steel Works to form the gigantic Albany and Rensselaer Iron and Steel Company. The Rensselaer Iron Works had emerged in 1854 from the Troy Vulcan Company (1846) rolling mill in south Troy. By 1860 the mill (controlled in a partnership by Griswold and Corning and their sons) employed 350 men and boys in the manufacture of bar and sheet iron. Lastly, the Bessemer Steel Works started in Troy in 1863 when three of the city's capitalists, Winslow, Griswold, and Alexander L. Holley, bought the American patent for the Bessemer Process. On February 16, 1865, iron was converted to steel for the first time in a new mill south of the mouth of Wyants Kill. After an extensive fire nearly destroyed the works in 1868, John A. Griswold & Co. became owners. With the merger of all three operations — the Troy Iron Works, the Rensselaer Iron Works, and the Bessemer Steel Works — by 1880, the new Albany and Rensselaer Iron and Steel Company probably employed at least 1,500 men. This amalgam was incorporated as the Troy Steel and Iron Company in 1885 and capitalized at $2,500,000.[13]

Henry Burden's achievement was no less remarkable. The small mill begun in 1809 had become the Troy Iron and Nail Factory Company by 1813. Henry Burden, an engineer and inventor, arrived in America in 1819 from Scotland. In 1822 he was appointed superintendent at the Nail Factory. During the next twenty-five years, Burden held patents on a wrought iron nail and spike machine, as well as many refinements on this and other machines. Finally, in 1848, he assumed control of the Troy Iron and Nail Factory. During the Civil War, his 370 employees produced horseshoes in great number for the Union Army. The mill expanded rapidly and added forty-five acres along the Hudson, north of the Wynants Kill. When Henry Burden's two surviving sons, James A. Burden and I. Townsend Burden, incorporated the Burden Iron Company in 1881, the plant employed over a thousand men and boys in the production of wrought iron bars ("Burden's Best"), as well as bolts, rivets, and spikes.[14]

---

[13] The employment figures are estimated from Weise, and U.S. Census Office, 9th Census, 1870, *Manufactures in the United States in 1870*. The manufacturing census available for 1880 was incomplete for Rensselaer County.
[14] See Burden, *Iron*, advertising pamphlet published by the Burden Iron Company (Troy, 1920); Weise, *op. cit.*; 8th Census, 1860, *Manufactures*; 9th Census, 1870, *Manufactures*; and, 10th Census, 1880, *Manufactures*.

by Fuller and Warren & Co., for example, had grown from modest beginnings as the Troy Air Furnace in 1818 to become the city's largest foundry. In 1860 it employed 200 men and boys, or more than 25 percent of the city's foundry workers, and by 1880 the number had risen to 550 men or 29.6 percent of all foundry hands. In fact, while the Clinton Works clearly dominated the Troy foundry industry, the large foundries, those employing one hundred or more men, all cast stoves and ranges during both census years. Thus, Troy's average foundry hand worked in a large stove foundry, and more likely than not he worked in the Clinton Works.

The average iron mill hand also labored in a large factory. In 1860 the iron mills already employed, on the average, 307 hands; by 1880 this figure more than doubled to 882. In contrast, the Fledgling Malleable iron mill was small. In 1860 it employed eight men. By 1880, however, it had also grown quite large and employed 140 men and boys. Specialty iron mills complicated the scene. Several hundred additional workers in Troy labored in industries that either made iron products or used iron in the productive process, turning out such items as boilers, chains, files, scales, car wheels, springs, edge tools, shovels forks, brackets, railings, wire cloth, and tin, copper, and sheet iron ware. These establishments ranged in size from L. Lillie's Safe Factory employing one hundred men to Andrew Stearn, a self-employed bracket maker.

In summary, Troy's iron industry had expanded greatly from 1860 to 1880. Several of the iron mills merged, and all became vast enterprises involving, by contemporary measures, large-scale operations. New businesses started, but the trend toward larger operations, especially in the manufacture of stoves and ranges, continued. Taken together, 82.8 percent of the iron workers in 1860 labored in mills and foundries that employed at least one hundred men. By 1880 the percentage had risen to 84.4 percent. Moreover, several hundred men worked in iron-related industries. The entire city depended on the iron industry and especially on a few large mills. When the iron industry suffered through a depression or a strike, the entire community was immediately and intensely affected.

Troy's iron worker community did not develop in a social vacuum. During the years after the Civil War, industrialization and the demands of the highly competitive profit system forced extensive and rapid changes in the conditions of labor and the social order. Workers resisted these changes, and the era between 1860 and 1880 was not merely the age of enterprise. It was also the age of resistance: American entrepreneurs struggled among themselves to gain control of burgeoning markets, while working men fought an internal struggle against management for control over conditions central to working-class life. Violence and disorder characterized this period and surrounded the lives of the iron workers. Skilled workers, molders and puddlers in particular, led the resistance. While studying the whole iron worker community, we will pay special attention to these skilled workers.

To start with the iron molders, their union lasted through the period. Born in the wake of the widespread wage reductions and hardships that attended the 1857 depression, the Troy iron molders' union rapidly gained first local, then national, prominence. After Philadelphia's iron molders organized in the mid-1850s, they issued a call for national unionization, and the Troy molders were to respond first. On April 28, 1858, the latter held their first meeting at Druids Hall "for the purpose if possible to enhance the position of the Molders and likewise to maintain and if necessary to raise the prices and for other purposes deemed expedient by them."[15] Within a year, the union claimed nearly 300 members from Troy and nearby areas, developed a disciplined and intricate body of customs, rules and regulations, sustained strikes in several local foundries, and stimulated the formation of a molders' union in Albany. The union began mainly among the Clinton Stove Foundry workers, the largest foundry, but by 1860 included dues-paying representatives in thirteen stove foundries in the Troy vicinity.

Throughout the next twenty-odd years, the molders' union — primarily stove and range molders during much of the early period — remained one of the strongest and most militant unions in Troy and in the United States.[16] It provided political and financial aid to the Iron Molders' International Union in the 1860s, when the Union led the struggle for national organization. Similarly, in Troy itself, the molders' union remained in the forefront of the developing local labor movement. Strikes occurred regularly, and new unions formed in trades both related to and outside the iron industry. Molders sparked and supported such movements. On April 30, 1864, for instance, when several thousand workingmen held a mass protest meeting to demonstrate against re-

---

[15] Troy Molders Union, No. 2, *Minutes,* April 28, 1858.
[16] This is frequently reiterated by the editors of the major labor magazines. See *Fincher's Trade Review* (Philadelphia), 1863-1866; and *The Workingman's Advocate* (Chicago), 1866-1872. William H. Sylvis, president of the Iron Moulders International Union in the early '60s supports this view in *Fincher's.*

pressive State labor legislation, Henry Rockefeller, president of Iron Molders' Union, No. 2, of Troy, was the main local speaker. *Fincher's Trade Weekly* reported this event and emphasized, "[the workingmen of Troy] partake of the same spirit of determination which marked the other great demonstrations in the state, only a little more so."[17] In the next month Rockefeller made a similar address at a rally in support of the massive cotton spinners' strike in neighboring Cohoes' Harmony Mill. Hundreds of Troy workingmen accompanied Rockefeller, watching him donate $200 from the city's molders to their sisters in Cohoes. That same month a Stove Mounters' Association, the first in the nation, was formed in Troy, with sixty-two members. Nor was this all. By August 1864 a Trades Assembly had been formed with seventeen participating local unions. Troy's trades unions, now united, displayed their solidarity and strength in a picnic run by the molders that same month. A parade also marked the picnic, as an estimated 2,000 workmen met and marched through the city streets "to show the capitalists . . . the strength of the working class when combined."[18] Later that day, almost 4,000 persons (roughly 10 percent of Troy's total population) frolicked and listened to speeches by Rockefeller, by William Sylvis, President of the Iron Molders' International Union, and by a State Assemblyman. The proceeds went towards the establishment of a free reading room.[19] By the end of 1864, Troy workers boasted of some twenty trades unions; a year earlier, only two had existed. Of these twenty at least three were in the iron trades: the Molders' Union claimed 700 members, the Stove Mounters' Union 170, and the Iron Rollers' Association (drawn from the Troy Nail Works) 150.[20] By the end of the following year, a new Puddlers' Union had organized as well with ninety members. In addition a Heaters' Union had formed. Under the chairmanship of a leading molder, the Trades Assembly had just enrolled an entirely different group of workers — in a Laborers' Union, which was a development of awesome potential.[21] Finally, the flourishing Troy Trades Assembly helped the underpaid tailoresses organize, had begun construction of a free reading room and library, and had started a co-operative store for the union members.

---

17 *Fincher's*, April 30, 1864.
18 *Ibid.*, August 20, 1864.
19 *Ibid.*, as reported from the *Troy Press*.
20 *Ibid.*, December 24, 31, 1864; and *Troy Daily Times*, June 22, Sept. 27, 1864.
21 *Troy Daily Times*, November 27, December 11, 1865. Scattered reports in the local papers suggested the Laborers' Union grew rapidly at first. Little, however, is heard of it in subsequent labor conflicts. In 1866 it had five hundred members.

Such developments meant that a large number of Troy iron workers labored in mills of considerable size dominated by local capitalists. In addition to these iron mills, the Troy iron industry included many foundries that molded finished iron products, especially stoves and ranges, stove patterns, wheels, and bells. Foundry workers, however, worked in mills that varied in size, so their work experience differed within the industry and from that of the iron mill workers. Iron foundries provided employment for hundreds of skilled and unskilled iron workers. Though half of Troy's fourteen foundries in 1880 employed less than fifty men, the typical foundry worker actually found himself in a considerably larger factory (table 2). Between 1860 and 1880, he most likely worked in a large stove foundry. While 86.1 percent and 96.9 percent of the foundry workers labored in plants of at least moderate size in 1860 and 1880 respectively, all eight stove and range foundries in 1860 employed at least fifty hands. Large stove foundries predominated in Troy, although small specialized foundries supplemented them. For example, in 1880 eight of the ten small foundries cast patterns, wheels, or belts. In other words, the largest foundries, led by the large Clinton Stove Works, were almost without exception stove foundries. The Clinton Works, operated

TABLE 2

Foundry and Mill Size in Troy, 1860 and 1880

Number of Employees	Foundries		Mills	
	1860	1880	1860	1880
Under 10	3	7	1	
11-19	2	0		
20-49	2	3		
50-99 (moderate)	4	8		
100+ (large)	3	4	3	3
Total factories	14	22	4	3
Total employees	796	1860	1228	2646 (est.)
Average size (mean)	56.9	84.5	407	882 (est.)
% employees in factory with 50+ men	86.1%	96.9%	99.3%	100%
% employees in factory with 100+ men	57.2%	62.7%	99.3%	100%

"Lazy Ned," the colorful and enthusiastic Troy correspondent to *Fincher's Trade Review,* observed these accomplishments and noted with pride that the molders had begun work at 7 A.M. now in order to help at home and see their children by daylight. In the context of the Civil War labor struggle, these seemingly modest gains promised great victories for Troy's workmen, so that "Lazy Ned" could exclaim, " 'God bless the movement.' "[22]

Despite organized opposition, the Troy molders sustained their union after the Civil War and won important victories. In 1866, iron foundries owners in Troy and other cities met in Albany to consider ways to destroy the fledgling union. They formed a national trade association, but drew support mostly from Troy's manufacturers. One Troy entrepreneur, Charles Eddy, headed the association, and fourteen of its thirty-three manufacturers were also from that city, while nine came from Albany. The owners resolved to post notice in the foundries that in the future they and not the Moulders' Union would regulate the number of apprentices. Furthermore, they would "outlaw shop committees," and "control . . . [their] own workshops."[23] Central to this lockout was not only the continued existence of the union, but the regulation of the work force, and the source of power and authority within the industry. In asserting their right to control the number of new workers, the manufacturers struck at the heart of the union's power — its ability to regulate the supply of new workers. In a letter to the *Workingman's Advocate* written several years later, Troy's Dugald Campbell, a Scottish immigrant tavern owner, sometimes iron worker, and outspoken labor organizer, understood this when he complained that "overproduction in the foundry line is the curse of Troy." He argued that the men undercut their own demands by giving the employers more service than their salaries merited, simultaneously providing surplus goods to glut the market.[24] New workers meant higher production and lower salaries. If conditions did not improve, the workers would start their own cooperative foundries in which they could control and regulate production and wages. So, on March 17, 1866, immediately after the notices of the manufacturers' association appeared, the Troy molders, 745 in number, quit work. They were promptly joined by the stove mounters and pattern makers.

---

22 *Fincher's,* October 15, 1864.
23 The American National Stove Manufacturers' and Iron Founders' Association resolutions, quoted in the *Troy Daily Times,* March 17, 1866.
24 Dugald Campbell to the editor, *The Workingman's Advocate,* May 1, 1869.

One month after the lockout began, with the molders ready to break ground for a cooperative foundry, the entrepreneurial group gave in. The molders gained much from this victory. Not only did they defeat an association of Troy's most powerful and wealthy men, but they also established the city's first cooperative foundry;[25] and two more followed before 1870. These same years saw other workers assert their interests through collective action. The Sons of Vulcan, a union of boilers and puddlers, sustained strikes for higher wages in the large iron mills. In 1869, the Collar Laundresses' Union, known as one of the few *"bona fide* female unions in the country,"* struck Troy's other important industry and won support from the city organized male workers.[26] Although the iron workers were on reduced schedules, following the depression and price decline of 1868, they and other male operatives supported the women. Upwards of 7,000 workingmen, many of them related to the striking women, assembled to demonstrate their solidarity with the laundresses, and later they helped them organize a cooperative laundry. Such successes, however, were not the full story of the immediate post-war years. Troy workers could not, for example, sustain a local labor newspaper, the *Troy Herald.* Dugald Campbell argued in vain against their support of a local press owned by "Mr. Shoddy." He urged the workers to act in ways that would put "Mr. Shoddy and his paper . . . [in] a bed in the deepest part of the Hudson,"[27] but the *Herald* folded in the spring of 1869, a few months after its first issue.

The collective strength of each side continued to be tested into the 1870s, but the temper and tone of such encounters changed sharply, especially after the 1873 depression began. Lengthy strikes and recurrent violence marked the depression years from 1873 to 1878. The bitterness and much of the violence continued through 1885. At issue were more than purely economic questions; the struggles were fought over the introduction of work discipline into the mills, the regulation of apprentices, and the power of the union or management to enforce control over the work place.

The period of turmoil began in spring 1873, when Troy's manufacturers, faced with competition from manufacturers west of the Appalachian mountains, united to control prices, effect wage reductions, and impose a more regimented work discipline in the iron mills. In the early

---

25 *Troy Daily Times,* April 16-May 12, 1866; *Troy Daily Whig,* April 17-May 12, 1866; and *The Workingman's Advocate,* April 21, 1866.
26 Dugald Campbell to the editor, *The Workingman's Advocate,* May 1, 1869.
27 *Ibid.* Campbell was made superintendent of the laundry co-operative.

spring, Chester Griswold, proprietor at the Bessemer Steel Works, failed in his efforts to convert wages to piece-rates — from the "day system" to the "ton system"[28] — and then also retreated from an attempt to impose a "ticket system" — time cards — when the workers threatened to strike.[29] The major conflicts during the decade, however, involved the puddlers and the molders. On June 10, the puddlers at Burden's Nail Factory, who were members of the Empire Forge of the Sons of Vulcan, struck against an arbitrary foreman and a *de facto* company blacklist. Briefly, a foreman had refused to assign a puddler to a furnace he had been working at and insisted he could move or discharge any worker at his pleasure. The company fueled resentment by refusing to issue discharge papers without which no other employer would hire a worker. Despite the depression, the strike continued six months. When it ended in mid-December, the Vulcans had won an agreement from the Burdens that they would oversee the forge department personally and end the "discharge system."[30]

Strikes occurring over the next three years were settled less peaceably. From October 1874 to April 1875, 258 members in five forges of the Sons of Vulcan fought a lockout by the manufacturers rather than accept a 22 percent wage reduction on top of a 20 percent reduction imposed in November-December 1873. Despite attempted police intimidations, the puddlers' union emerged victorious from the thirty-one week strike. Violence in Troy, however, continued. But its origins are not as clear as the term "labor violence" suggests. As a testimony to the aggressive role of management, non-union men were brought into Troy's Bessemer Steel Works on January 17, 1876, and war broke out. Gun fire could be heard that very day, and men were injured. Two days later, a non-union molder was assaulted, and the following night the workers held a mass meeting to consider developments. By April the molders of Troy had struck against the use of scabs. From then until end-of-year elections attracted the workingmen's interest, there were at least five different incidents in which non-union molders were violently attacked or assaulted: non-union molders were stoned and there was one attempt to burn the barn of a manufacturer who employed scabs. Three of the at-

---

[28] *Troy Daily Press,* January 23, 1873; and *Troy Daily Times;* January 15-30, 1873.

[29] *Troy Daily Press,* May 6, 1873; and, *Troy Daily Times,* May 5, 1873.

[30] For a more detailed discussion of these strikes and lockouts and their relationship to the political and social history of the Troy working-class, see Daniel J. Walkowitz, "Working-Class Culture in the Gilded Age: The Troy New York Iron Worker Community and the Cohoes, New York, Cotton Worker Community, 1855-1884," unpublished doctoral dissertation (Rochester, 1972).

tacks involved, according to the Republican *Troy Times*, from thirty-to-forty armed molders.[31] Violence escalated in the spring of 1877. Incendiary fires and stonings now occurred at regular intervals, and the violence began to resemble the Sheffield "outrages" of the mid-1860s in England,[32] or the terrorist tactics of the Molly Maguires: systematically, almost every second or third day, a non-union molder was shot or attacked. When the manufacturers attempted to employ convict labor to augment the non-union molders, they only provoked further mass meetings and attempted murders. According to the *Times*, "A Reign of Terror" existed. When several molders were finally apprehended, tried, and convicted, the union suffered a temporary setback.

During the 1880s, a resurgent unionism in the iron industry returned to do battle for the rights of the workingmen. Again the patterns of violence resumed. And again the violence escalated: after the manufacturers armed and protected their mills with special police, for example, a union molder was killed in 1883.[33] By mid-December molders and mounters, organized in both the Knights of Labor and the Federation of Organized Trades, remained locked in a complex struggle with stove manufacturers for recognition.[34]

These long strikes and violent events cannot be dismissed merely as economic struggles for higher wages and shorter hours. As mentioned earlier, the manufacturers' attempt to regulate apprentices threatened the unions' security and power; and the strikes after 1873 reflected similar concerns. Issues of work discipline and power within the industry again were central. After 1873, the dominant factor was aggressive employer behavior: for instance, when manufacturers introduced time cards into the mills and foundries, they thereby threatened to impose a rigid discipline on the workers, who saw their independence and integrity as workmen sacrificed to the demands of efficiency and control. In the industrializing world, craftsmen missed the personal satisfaction, the dignity, and the sense of achievement formerly felt by the independent artisan. Industrialization reduced these skills to technical functions, to nuts-and-bolts operations, with the result that workers felt

[31] Troy *Times*, April 27, 1876; October 2, 1876.
[32] Sidney Pollard, *A History of Labor in Sheffield* (Liverpool, 1959), 152-8.
[33] *Progress* (New York), June 23, 1883.
[34] The beginning of this period in Troy's history is discussed more fully in my dissertation and still deserves careful attention. Something of the complexity can be garnered from the discussion of national labor developments in Norman J. Ware, *The Labor Movement in the United States, 1860-1895* (New York, 1929), and Gerald N. Grob, *Workers and Utopia: A Study of Ideological Conflict in the American Labor Movement, 1865-1900* (Evanston, 1961).

themselves becoming industrial functionaries. Time cards were viewed as an attempt to regiment the workers, and their response against them was part of their response against the modern industrial process itself. Similarly, management tried to use scab workers and convict labor to destroy the union movement and to assume what regulatory power the unions possessed. The duration of the strikes and the extent of the violence at this time suggests the intensity of employee resistance. In order to overcome such obstacles, employers were forced to appeal to the political authorities — the police, the mayor, the national guard, and the courts — to discipline the workers. Consequently, events of these years must be discussed, not only in economic but in political terms as well. Finally, those committed to resistance were not just iron workers, or just "immigrants," but (as mentioned earlier) were largely Irish iron workers. So, to the economic dimension and the political dimension must be added the ethnic dimension.

In all of the events after 1873, Irish political culture played a conspicuous role. For instance, the 1873 strike was complicated by a police imbroglio. The manufacturers, and Republicans in general, had applied pressure to have the Rensselaer County police replace the Troy police, a largely Irish police force with family and community ties to the Irish laborers. The County police force replaced the city's on August 7, 1873, in the midst of the protracted Sons of Vulcan strike. When the Troy police returned to power in mid-November, 5,000 workingmen filled the streets and rejoiced.[35] This cordial relationship between Irish police and Irish iron workers, especially reinforced by the Irish community's refusal to aid the authorities, made the apprehension of "criminals" difficult for employers. During the 1877 "reign of terror," for instance, the *Troy Times* complained that the "outrages" continued while "inefficient" police "ignored" the attacks. Furthermore, the newspaper suggested, the molders' behavior and the response of the community were intricately connected: prosecution was made most difficult because community opinion sided with the molders. During one exchange of shots, for instance, in which a non-union molder was wounded, some of the residents of south Troy, where the iron workers lived and worked, were unable to recall witnessing the incident.[36] Small wonder that employers had to turn to the courts and the national guard. Court actions did finally blunt

---

[35] A similar contest, with results less satisfactory to the iron worker community, took place in 1882-83 during a bitter molder strike. See, Daniel J. Walkowitz, "Working-Class Culture" (Ph.D. thesis).

[36] *Troy Times*, April 30, 1877.

the union attack temporarily. Nonetheless, during the great railroad strike of late July 1877, New York national guard troops had to be called into Troy to avert trouble. Yet the two companies of the 10th Regiment, known to be composed almost entirely of molders, were deliberately not activated.[37]

Troy iron workingmen, most particularly the Irish, had political, social, and cultural lives that extended outside their purely labor activities, yet remained related to those activities. The 1863 Troy draft riot underscores the political and religious connections of these Irish workmen. During the riot, several thousand workmen marched from the Nail Factory to the *Troy Times* building and attacked it while the Catholic priest pleaded that they stop.[38] In addition, Mayor Edward Murphy, Jr., perhaps the first Irish mayor of Troy, was re-elected for the second year in the midst of the explosive events of the 1877 "terror," after winning the endorsement of the Workingmen's Convention.[39] Finally, Irish nationalist movements were very strong in Troy. The Fenian national convention met in Troy in 1866, and several hundred of the city's stalwart Irishmen attacked Canada during the 1866 raids, while thousands rallied daily in Troy to cheer their advance.[40] And even more significant, the highly secretive, militant, and revolutionary Irish brotherhood, the Clan na Gael, supposedly claimed Mayor Murphy as well as Troy's police chief and comptroller as members. According to Thomas N. Brown, "Troy, New York, had the distinction of being the home of the largest and perhaps the most influential city organization" of the Clan.[41]

In summary, during the post-bellum years, a fluctuating economic market and the demands of increased competition compelled the iron manufacturers to cut costs — to make their operation more efficient, and to introduce new methods and procedures into the mills. The unions stood in their way. In the face of the new regimented work discipline and employer encroachment on union power, the workers resisted. They applied all the pressure they could bring to bear in an attempt to preserve some control over their work and, in many ways, over their lives. Violence often resulted. Manufacturers, on the other hand, confronted strong and united workingmen organizations; more precisely, Irish work-

---

37 *Troy Times,* July 25, 1877.
38 Weise, *op. cit.,* 198-200.
39 The preceding mayor, Thomas B. Carroll, was probably the city's first Irish mayor; he contributed heavily to the Fenian expedition from Troy he had helped organize.
40 Troy Times, April-June, 1866; William D'Arcy, *The Fenian Movement in the United States* 1858-1886 (Washington, D.C.), 1947.
41 Thomas N. Brown, *Irish-American Nationalism* (Philadelphia, 1966), 66.

ingmen, who were knit together on social, political, and economic levels. A strong union movement, an effective Irish-dominated political machine, a cohesive Irish working-class community, and militant and well-organized Irish nationalist organizations all resisted the manufacturers and presented serious obstacles to the control that the latter so desired. Before the manufacturers could gain complete control over their workers in their industry, they had to restore order to Troy. This required social and political domination. Consequently, at various times they legislated against the City police force, complained about police "inefficiency," or argued that police collusion permitted the fraudulent election of Mayor Murphy. Thus we see that formal working-class protest in Troy between 1855 and 1885 extended to social and political institutions as well as questions of immigrant or ethnic culture. In order to examine and assess these patterns, we need a closer picture of the iron workers, especially the dominant Irish.

Considerable violence, we have observed, marked Troy's history during the post-bellum decades. Fuller explanation of such violence lies beyond the scope of this essay, and is to be found in the closer study, for example, of individual molders and puddlers. But the data does reflect something of the collective organization, achievement, and anger of the working-class community. Despite continual problems of underemployment and unemployment, lengthy strikes, and unhealthy living and working conditions, Troy's workers developed closely-knit industrial, political and ethnic organizations during this period. It remains to be seen how the persistence of strong cultural bonds might be reflected in coherent ethnic residency patterns and in distinct ethnic family statistics. Similarly, data confirming property attainment, occupational mobility, and strong two-parent families might suggest the sense of achievement or deprivation felt by the iron worker community from the expectations of their pre-immigration existence. If the city's iron workers can be identified and their social mobility and family patterns traced, it might then be possible to begin to estimate the relative impact of different social and cultural institutions on behavior.

Who were the Troy iron workers in these central decades? Data compiled from the 1860 Federal population census calls attention to the central role played by immigrant Irishmen (table 3). Such was the case even *before* the outbreak of the Civil War. Oscar Handlin's classic study of Boston's Irish reinforced the traditional image of "Paddy" working as a day laborer in the streets and ditches of urban cities or as domestic

TABLE 3

Selected Iron Workers and Ethnicity, 1860[a]
(Raw totals, and percentage of the total in the trade)

Iron Workers' Birthplace	Population [1]b	Managerial [2]	Laborer [3]c	Molder [4]	Puddler [5]	Heater/ Roller [6]	Stove Mounter [7]	Pattern Maker [8]	Machinist [9]	TOTALS (Columns 3-9) [10]
Native U.S.A.	25,774	85	77	209	31	60	44	53	188	622
Father's Birthplace										
U.S.A.	37.8%	82 (78.8)	47 (18.0)	152 (31.2)	19 (11.5)	43 (25.9)	42 (58.3)	53 (71.6)	169 (57.0)	525 (33.9%)
Ireland	46.0%	8 (7.6)	174 (66.6)	266 (54.7)	66 (40.0)	92 (55.4)	18 (25.0)	10 (13.5)	55 (18.5)	747 (46.9%)
England	5.4%	5 (4.8)	16 (6.1)	19 (3.9)	62 (37.5)	22 (13.2)	7 (8.7)	4 (5.4)	32 (11.8)	162 (10.2%)
Canada	4.1%	2 (1.9)	16 (6.1)	21 (4.3)	12 (7.2)	4 (2.4)	5 (6.9)	4 (5.4)	12 (4.4)	74 (4.6%)
Scotland	2.6%	4 (3.8)	5 (1.9)	18 (3.7)	3 (1.8)	3 (1.8)	0 (0)	1 (1.3)	17 (6.3)	47 (4.6%)
Germany	4.1%	3 (2.9)	3 (1.1)	10 (2.0)	0 (0)	4 (2.4)	4 (5.5)	2 (2.7)	9 (3.3)	32 (3.0%)
Other	0.2%	0 (0)	0 (0)	0 (0)	3 (1.8)	0 (0)	1 (1.4)	0	2 (.8)	6 (2.0%)
Total	39,235	104	261	486	165	166	72	74	296	1593

a For a more complete breakdown of all the iron workers, see, Daniel J. Walkowitz, "Working-Class Culture," (Ph.D. thesis).
b The ethnic breakdown is based upon a 5 percent sample population of every twentieth person listed on the 1860 manuscript census tract.
c This total is low: it does not include men listed as "laborer" unless "in iron mill" was specified.

help. Other historians have subsequently tended to adopt this view un-critically.[42] However, Boston, a port city, does not tell the full story. Handlin wrote that the Irish, unlike the city's other new immigrant groups, "remained unneeded and unabsorbed . . . [and] had the service occupations almost entirely to themselves. . . . Even the Negroes, who stood closest to the Irish in occupational experience, fared better than they."[43] Troy suggests otherwise. Thomas N. Brown noted that in Troy's factories, as everywhere in urban America, the Irish were a pool of "cheap, unskilled labor."[44] But while the Irish made up the bulk of unskilled Troy day laborers and service workers, they were much more than ditch diggers and coachmen.

The Troy Irish filled vital roles, both skilled and unskilled, in the city's expanding iron industry; moreover, they had secured that foothold by 1860. Not all Irishmen worked in factories, but in 1860 the typical iron factory worker, skilled or unskilled, was Irish. What was more, in each of the three largest skilled trades — molders, puddlers, and heaters and rollers — the Irish constituted the largest number of workers. Among unskilled workers, the Irish constituted 66.6 percent; among the skilled trades the Irish constituted 54.7 percent of the molders, 40 percent of the puddlers, and 55.4 percent of the heaters and rollers. Considering that most had lived in Troy, and perhaps even in the country, little more than a decade, such figures show considerable upward mobility for these newcomers.[45]

Except for the boiler makers, a trade closely related to the puddlers, native Americans filled most of the other skilled iron trades. Native-born workers held a particularly high percentage of positions as pattern makers in the foundries and as nailers and spikers (39 of 61 places) in Burden's Nail Factory. In the latter trade, those of Canadian origin — some 454 workers — also had relatively high concentration. Though the sample is small (there were 13 Canadian nailers in 1860), this evidence suggests

---

42 *See,* Oscar Handlin, *Boston's Immigrants, 1790-1865: A Study in Acculturation* (Cambridge, Mass., 1941), 61-75; Brown, *op. cit.,* 18-19; William V. Shannon, *The American Irish* (New York, 1963), 28, 95; Carl Wittke, *Irish in America* (Baton Rouge, 1956).

43 Handlin, *op. cit.,* 61-75.

44 Brown, *op. cit.,* 18.

45 In comparison, few if any blacks gained entrance into the iron industry even as unskilled workers and, almost to a man, they worked as day laborers or in service positions. Troy's population increased 45 percent between 1860 and 1880, while the number of blacks and mulattoes in Troy declined almost 9 percent during these years (table 1). Since Troy witnessed dramatic industrial growth, this decline suggests that racial prejudice worked against the blacks. In an industrial city with opportunities in expanding iron and shirt factories, these jobs went almost exclusively to whites; blacks filled service positions or migrated elsewhere.

that ethnocentricity, a concern with both status and security, as well as bias may each have motivated such an ethnic group to enter a given trade at a given time. In any case, once a trade opened to an ethnic group, workers tended to congregate in ethnic circles.

Table 4 suggests the degree to which the various trades were "open" to ethnic groups in 1860. If an ethnic group has a proportion of workers in a trade equal to the proportion of that group in the population, it will have a base figure of 100 in the table. Thus, in 1860, while native Americans and Scotsmen held 78.8 and 3.8 percent of all the managerial positions (manufacturers, stove dealers, and superintendents), the relative concentration of both groups was disproportionately high, being 206 and 146 respectively.[46] Among the unskilled workers, the Irish, who constituted the largest number, also had the highest relative concentration. The figures for all the immigrant groups, however, with the exception of the small German population, were above average.

In the skilled trades the pattern of mobility reflects the large blocks of immigrants that had already populated the industry: the Irish had relative concentrations close to or above the base figure in each of the three larger trades; the native-born figure exceeded 100 in all the other major trades. The English and Scottish immigrants, and even the Canadians, although small in number, had a relatively easier time than the Irish in gaining entrance to all the skilled trades. Finally, two figures are of special note: while the English puddlers were fewer in number than the Irish, the relative concentration of English puddlers was an extraordinarily high 694; and, though the samples are somewhat scanty, relative to the other immigrant groups, the Irish had a low relative concentration in the two skilled foundry trades — stove mounters and pattern makers.

Thus, by 1860, immigrants, and especially the Irish, had gained ready access into the iron industry; and those who worked in it had clear-cut ties to ethnic culture. The well-organized and more militant molders', puddlers', and rollers' unions were probably dominated by Irish workers. And, finally, first generation immigrants constituted the bulk of these ethnic groups, further suggesting that newcomers entered the iron mills and foundries with ease. As column 10, table 3 shows, only 97 of the "native U.S.A." iron workers, slightly more than 6 percent of all iron workers, had immigrant fathers.[47] Of that group more than three-quarters

---

[46] The Scottish were the Burden's, in this case a highly successful and powerful foursome in Troy.

[47] The difference between the "native U.S.A." and "U.S.A." figures in table 3 represents

(76) ,were of Irish origin, and two-thirds of those (49) were molders. In other words, soon after arriving in this country, immigrant Irishmen were able to find employment in the Troy iron industry. But what had been the Irishman's pre-Troy factory experience? Some had worked in the English factories before coming to America. Some were pre-famine immigrants. Increasingly, they were rural peasants, fleeing famine, and for these the rapid adjustment must have been tremendous. But they quickly made up the backbone of the skilled as well as unskilled workers that built the industry and constituted a powerful bloc in the labor force. Like their Scottish neighbors, the Irish were even able to secure jobs for their sons, friends, and neighbors as skilled molders. It was the Yankee and his son who soon felt compelled to look for employment elsewhere.

What happened between 1860 and 1880? In 1880, English, Canadian, and German workers constituted a relatively larger share of the population than they had in 1860, while the percentage of native Americans and Irish declined almost five and one points respectively. The figures in 1880 reinforce the picture in 1860 and demonstrate the continued Irish domination of the burgeoning iron industry (tables 4 and 5). Whereas 6.1 percent of the iron workers in 1860 had been sons of immigrants, 34.6 percent of all iron workers in 1880 were second-generation immigrants. Just as in 1860, more than three-quarters of these (77.3 percent) were of Irish parentage. In total, six out of every ten iron workers were of Irish extraction by 1880.

By their sheer numbers the Irish now overwhelmed the other ethnic groups among the unskilled and skilled workers in the major iron trades. By 1880 the percentage of skilled Irish workers had risen in every iron trade, and especially among the molders, the puddlers, and the rollers, roughers, and heaters. The number of native-American molders remained constant, while the number and percentage of Irish molders doubled. The number of English puddlers dropped to one-third of its 1860 total, while the Irish total increased two-and-a-half fold to a point where the Irish totally dominated the trade. The number of heaters, rollers, and roughers of American extraction declined to less than one-third its 1860 total, while the Irish total almost doubled. Even the stove mounters, an occupation predominantly filled with native-born workers in 1860, was now dominated by the Irish. Of the skilled trades in and related to the iron industry, only the pattern makers, engineers, and machinists were

---

the small number of second generation immigrants, American-born children of an immigrant father, working in the iron factories in 1860.

TABLE 4

Relative Concentration of Selected Iron Workers, 1860 and 1880
(Proportion among gainful workers in all occupations = 100)

Birthplace of Iron Workers' Fathers	Managerial	Laborers	Molder	Puddler	Heater/Roller	Stove Mounter	Pattern Maker	Machinist
1860								
U.S.A.	208	48	83	30	69	154	189	151
Ireland	17	145	119	87	120	54	29	40
England	89	113	72	694	244	161	100	219
Canada	46	149	105	176	59	168	132	107
Scotland	146	73	142	69	69	0	50	242
Germany	71	27	49	0	59	134	66	80
1880								
U.S.A.	140	35	58	7	18	91	133	120
Ireland	34	134	133	170	158	101	41	49
England	297	175	125	170	205	90	215	295
Canada	66	94	52	84	31	185	140	68
Scotland	380	333	233	60	60	0	140	607
Germany	38	56	64	6	20	86	216	105

TABLE 5

Selected Iron Workers and Ethnicity, 1880
(Raw totals, and percentage of the total in the trade)

Iron-Workers Birthplace	Population (1)[a]	Managerial (2)	Laborer (3)	Molder (4)	Puddler (5)	Heater Roller Rougher (6)	Stove Mounter (7)	Pattern Maker (8)	Machinist (9)	TOTALS (Columns 3-9) (10)
Native U.S.A.	39,809	87	730	497	12	82	148	86	182	1837
Father's Birthplace										
U.S.A.	34.8%	54	169	153	5	13	58	58	108	564
		44.6	11.2	18.5	2.3	5.8	29.0	42.3	38.1	16.7%
Ireland	46.4%	19	936	511	166	171	94	26	65	1969
		15.7	62.4	61.9	79.0	73.3	47.0	18.9	22.9	58.2%
England	6.1%	22	161	63	22	28	11	18	51	354
		18.1	10.7	7.6	10.4	12.5	5.5	13.1	18.0	10.5%
Canada	6.2%	5	88	27	11	4	23	12	12	177
		4.1	5.8	3.2	5.2	1.9	11.5	8.7	4.2	5.3%
Scotland	1.5%	7	75	29	2	2	0	3	26	137
		5.7	5.0	3.5	.9	.9	0	2.1	9.1	4.0%
Germany	6.4%	3	55	34	1	3	11	19	19	142
		2.4	3.6	4.1	.4	1.3	5.5	13.8	6.7	4.2%
Other	1.6%	1	23	8	3	3	3	1	2	43
		.8	1.5	.9	1.4	2.3	1.5	.7	.7	1.3%
Total	56,747	111	1507	825	210	224	200	137	283	3386

[a] The ethnic breakdown is based upon a 4 percent sample population of every twenty-fifth person listed on the 1880 manuscript census tract.

TABLE 6

Relative Concentrations of Selected Workers in Troy and the United States, 1880

(Proportion among gainful workers in all occupations = 100)

Birthplace	A Troy Unskilled Iron Workers	B Nat'l Iron & Steel Oper. (a)	C Troy Laborers (b)	D Troy Cotton & Wool Oper. (b)	E Troy Police (c)	F Troy Carpen- ters (b)	G Troy Cigar makers (b)
U.S.A.	69		46	117	47	82	93
Ireland	179	278	294	42	215	98	31
Great Britain	265 (Eng.) 419 (Scot.)	315	96	186	64	243	167
Canada	136	99	175	72	52	396	50
Germany	73	126	93	42	30	94	658

Source: (a) A. E. Hutchinson, *Immigrants and Their Children, 1850-1950* (New York, 1956), 103-4.
　　　(b) Based upon Troy figures in Census, 1880, *Reports*, 1, pt. 2, Statistics of the Population," 905.
　　　(c) Compiled from manuscript population census, 10th census, 1880, *Population*.

dominated by ethnic groups other than the Irish.[48]

Although the Irish comprised the largest and most powerful bloc among Troy's iron workers in 1880, those of Scottish and English extraction had the highest relative concentrations within any ethnic group (table 4). Both groups had doubled their size in Troy in the twenty-year period, and the new immigrants evidently found easy access into the iron industry at all levels. On the other hand, those of German, Canadian, or American origins fared worse in the iron mills.[49] Between 1860 and

---

[48] The Irish constituted 33.7 percent of the engineers, but eleven of the thirteen men listed as firemen in the ironworks were Irish. These firemen are usually combined with the engineers but they clearly had different ethnic patterns.

[49] Immigrants from Great Britain assumed managerial posts and became skilled machinists, engineers, molders, boiler makers, and pattern makers. But, interestingly, the English had one of the highest proportional rises in relative concentration in the unskilled positions. Though those of German, Canadian, or American origins fared worse, all three groups did have near or above-average relative concentrations in two stove-related trades: stove mounters and pattern makers. The Germans had a particularly high concentration of pattern makers, a skill that may have involved the sort of woodwork training many had received in their native Germany. In fact, the Irish were the only major immigrant group to have a relative concentration of pattern makers that was

1880 it was the Irish who became established and secure in the iron mills and foundries. Why, then, did violence and disorder occur? Just what did the high proportion of Irish workers signify?[50] And how did employment patterns in the iron industry compare with figures for other Troy trades (table 6)? These questions and others require a careful study of Irish workers and their culture.

Social status and occupational mobility are related but distinct measures of social position. Although historians have surmised that the high proportion of Irish iron workers by 1880 coincided with a decline in the status of iron workers, such may not have been the case in Troy.[51] For the Irish, Troy's largest ethnic group (46.4 percent), jobs in the iron industry may well have afforded some measure of both status and achievement.

The relative concentration figures for other Troy occupations suggest that being a skilled iron worker may have held less status for the English immigrant or native American, but might well have been the mark of a successful Irishman. In general, the high concentration of workers of the different ethnic groups in different trades may not have reflected merely the decline of a trade's status, nor a technologically-related decline in the skill involved in a trade, nor the lack of mobility into a trade for an ethnic group, though each of these may be the case. For beyond these factors lies the distinct possibility that the cultural pattern and communitarian cohesiveness of an ethnic group attracted these men into certain trades. Certain high relative concentration figures demonstrate how different ethnic groups entered different trades at different rates: in Troy there were German cigarmakers (658), Canadian carpenters (396), English carpenters (243), and Irish policeman (215). Each group took pride in "their" men's ability and in the place their jobs occupied in the Troy economy. Since many Irishmen came to America without factory skills, they did much of the unsatisfying manual labor in America. Yet, the fact remains, they quickly filled most of the skilled iron trades. Certain jobs in the iron industry, to be sure, were dirty, hot,

---

below average. Lastly, men of American extraction had slightly above normal concentrations in managerial positions and as engineers and machinists; and engineers of Canadian extraction and machinists of German extraction were slightly above average in their relative concentrations of workers.

50 A. E. Hutchinson, *Immigrants and Their Children,* 1850-1950 (New York, 1956), 103-4, lists the relative concentration nationally of immigrant iron and steel operators in 1880: for men born in Ireland the figure is 278, and for men born in Great Britain the figure is 315. These figures compare well with Troy's foreign-born Irish (179), English (265), and Scottish (419).

51 For example, see Handlin, *op. cit.,* 78.

and unpleasant, but the increasing number of Irish workers may still have found stature and a steady income in this industry and thus willingly stayed. The native American worker might not have wished to associate with a particular trade any longer, especially if it were dominated by a particular ethnic group with which he did not wish to be identified.

However, there is no reason to assume that skilled iron workers did not find skilled manual labor satisfying. Work conditions, work relations, and social pressure and attitudes that belittled a man's work encourage alienation. But skilled labor in and of itself is not a destructive or alienating experience. Conditions that fostered alienation deserved attention, but the Irish-American might still have found molding a stove a rewarding experience. It is striking that union militancy, strikes, protests, and even violence emerged after 1870, at the same time that manufacturers tried to impress such controls as the time-cards on skilled workers. A closer look at certain skilled and unskilled Troy workers during this period discloses cohesive family and cultural patterns that helped to knit the iron worker community together. These patterns may provide clues to the attitudes, values, and life style that influenced the social behavior of these workers.

Troy runs north and south on the plain along the Hudson River and extends up the side of a mountain ridge that traces the path of the river. The iron workers lived in both ethnic and occupational neighborhoods. Between 1860 and 1880 virtually every known unskilled worker in the Troy iron and steel mills lived in the two or three southernmost wards of Troy, usually on the streets and alleys nearest the river and the mills. North of those workers, yet below the central business district, lived many of the skilled iron workers in the Clinton foundry and the skilled iron mill hands — the puddlers, the rollers, roughers, and heaters, and the molders of iron bars. The northern wards contained only the skilled foundry workers — pattern makers, stove mounters, and stove molders — who were employed in the several foundries in that part of the city.

Those skilled iron workers who were more "independent," such as the engineers and machinists, tended to locate in the same northern and southern wards as the molders. Few workers lived in either the exclusive

Troy center wards or in the baronial estates that overlooked the city. Otherwise, while unskilled workers appeared least mobile and concentrated in the southern wards, evidence indicates that among skilled workers the ethnic makeup of a local area and the location of one's employment had greater influence on where one lived than the nature of one's skill. The Irish "community" gathered around the iron mills located in the south wards although, as could be expected of such a large group, they were well represented throughout all but the city's center wards. The Scottish iron workers had a small but concentrated "community" in the midst of these southern "Irish" wards called Scotch Hill. And similar patterns existed throughout Troy for the various ethnic and/or religious groups. Only the small number of blacks were excepted. They worked as coachmen or maids for families scattered throughout the city, or they gathered in shanty enclaves in the alley dwellings in the center wards or near the river. Thus, with the important exception of the blacks, Troy's workers had congregated in well-defined, cohesive residential communities.

The manufacturers, on the other hand, lived in one of two almost classic settings: in an aristocratic, Henry James-like setting of a brownstone mansion near the business district on Washington Square; or in the semifeudal ambience of a brick mansion with abundant servants atop the hillside dominating their industrial serfs. In order to see Henry Burden and his family, for example, an iron worker had to look up the hill toward heaven.

By 1860 Henry Burden's wife had died, and he lived alone with his sons James and I. Townsend and his daughter Jessie. The eldest son, William, dwelt in another house on the estate with his wife and two children. In the census, the two households together claimed to have $85,500 in the bank, and Henry listed his real estate holdings as worth $96,000. The eight Burdens, then, were very comfortable. They had eleven servants to tend to their needs: one housekeeper, one chambermaid, one cook, two waitresses, two coachmen, and four other servants. In 1880 the surviving Burden sons, I. Townsend and James, had married and had three and four children respectively. The eleven Burdens now had between them seventeen servants, two of whom were married with two small children of their own. The Burden family, in sum, had weathered the social crises of the two decades very well.

Iron workers, one need scarcely add, were less affluent. Some sense of their lives can be constructed from census data and information can be found there that raises numerous important questions. Did marital status, age, property holdings, or family structure encourage or inhibit working-class activism, especially during the turbulent years after 1870? What effect did urbanization and industrialization have on the iron worker and his family? This data can only partially answer such questions, but when the iron workers and their family structure are broken down according to trade and ethnic origins and then analyzed, certain characteristics and

TABLE 7

Marital Status and Age of Unskilled Iron Workers and Molders, 1860 and 1880

UNSKILLED

AGE	1860			1880		
	single	mar.	Per cent of total	single	mar.	Per cent of total
0-19	68	1	27.7%	386	1	25.7%
20-29	52	35	34.9%	352	135	32.3%
30-39	9	39	19.3%	79	218	19.7%
40-49	1	26	10.8%	17	184	13.3%
50-59	1	8	3.6%	6	75	5.4%
60+	0	9	3.6%	3	52	3.6%
TOTALS	63	117		457	664	
AGE 20+						
(%)	35.0	65.0		40.8	59.2	

MOLDERS

AGE	1860			1880		
	single	mar.	Per cent of total	single	mar.	Per cent of total
0-19	59	1	12.3%	63	0	7.6%
20-29	157	109	54.7%	195	85	33.9%
30-39	16	104	24.7%	60	165	27.3%
40-49	1	29	6.2%	30	152	22.1%
50-59	0	6	1.2%	6	55	7.4%
60+	0	4	0.8%	1	13	1.7%
TOTALS	174	252		292	470	
AGE 20+						
(%)	40.8	59.2		38.3	61.7	

developments emerge that permit a tentative assessment of iron worker family and community bonds. Marital status, age, and the property holdings of unskilled workers provide one measure of the stability and achievement in these workers' lives.

The vast majority of the unskilled workers were single and property-less young men. However, the two groups of unskilled workers tended to be quite different. "Service" workers include, for instance, time-keep-ers and watchmen, men who held positions of some responsibility and who tended to be older, married men (77.8 percent in 1860 were mar-ried) with some property holdings (22 percent owned real estate). On the other hand, not surprisingly, the unskilled mill, furnace, and foundry hands, contained the lowest percentage of married men in the industry (47.4 percent in 1860) and had the lowest number of workers with real estate holdings relative to their number of any major group (7.7 per-cent).[52]

In 1880 the mills attracted younger men and a larger percentage of single men than in 1860. Although the 1880 census did not ask for real and personal estate, each person gave his relationship to the head of the household. By 1880, not only were married men still among the lowest percentage of unskilled workers, but the percentage actually dropped from 47.4 percent to 44.1 percent. This decline contrasts with marked increases in the skilled mill trades and seems tied to several develop-ments. Whereas no one under fifteen was listed as working in the iron industry in 1860, by 1880, 8.3 percent of the unskilled iron workers were fourteen and younger: one was only nine years old. However, the total percentage of adolescent unskilled iron workers and molders between the ages of fifteen and nineteen working in the mills had declined since 1860: the percentage of unskilled iron workers had fallen from 27.7 percent to 17.4 percent; and the percentage of molders had fallen from 12.3 percent to 7.6 percent.

There are several possible reasons that might explain this change. A decline in apprentices may account for part of the drop in the number of young skilled workers. In addition, teenage boys in 1880 may have chosen *not* to work in the iron industry, and younger boys were wel-comed into the mills to assume the burdensome unskilled tasks. The other skilled trades surveyed, however, all reflect a similar drop in the

---

[52] A word about these statistics: in tables 7 to 11 samples involving less than twenty are of dubious value. This is most true for statistics in the 1860 census for men of Scottish, Canadian, German, and "other" extraction.

number and/or percentage of employed boys between the ages of fifteen and nineteen.[53] Such decreases may simply have resulted from the delayed impact of the Civil War, rather than an increase in hardship that forced families to send even younger boys into the mills or a change in attitudes of young men toward these trades. The generation of young men fifteen to nineteen-years old in 1880 would have been born during the war, and it is distinctly possible that the employment figures of 1880 paralleled a low birth rate during the war and a population explosion immediately after the war, when the soldiers returned home. The high demand for workers in the iron industry and the relative low supply of young men may well have required the unskilled work force to be buttressed with the large crop of post-war babies. Similarly, vacancies created by war deaths, along with the labor demand of an expanding industrial marketplace, would have hastened the movement of young men into the skilled trades. A surprisingly large number of these skilled operatives, and especially the molders, were in their twenties; and they appear, by 1880, to have stayed and grown old and attached to their trade.

Data on property holdings among the skilled further reflects mobility and organizational patterns of ethnic culture that may have helped to unite these people during periods of stress. While the percentage of skilled workers owning property is considerably lower than that of the managerial class, in all cases, except that of the boiler makers (their small sample is the least reliable statistically), the percentage is above that of the unskilled mill hands.

The percentage of property holders rose from a meager 9.3 percent of the molders to a percentage in the high twenties for those trades conspicuous for the paucity of Irish workers (such as nailers and spikers, and pattern makers). However, when the Irish entered a trade, they seemed to have acquired property at a higher rate than other nationalities, even in those trades where their numbers were relatively few. This is seen in the distribution of real estate holdings by amount and nationality for the molders and unskilled workers (tables 8 and 9). The stronger showing of the Irish conforms to Thernstrom's findings in Newbury-

---

[53] This decline can be observed in and outside the iron industry. The number of workers below age twenty is in ratio to the total employed in the following two representative industries:

	1860	1880
Machinists	43/296	25/283
Puddler	6/165	1/211

TABLE 8

Marital Status of Iron Workers, 1860 and 1880, and Property Holdings of Iron Workers, 1860

Occupation	Percentage Married 1860	1880	Percentage Holding Property in 1860
Managerial	80.8	86.6	44.0
Unskilled:			
Laborers	47.4	44.1	7.7
Service	77.8	73.2	22.0
Skilled:			
Molders	52.1	57.0	9.3
Puddlers	58.2	79.5	10.3
Heaters	74.2	73.4	25.8
Rollers	52.9	61.3	18.3
Roughers	—	23.3	—
Boiler Makers	61.5	63.0	0.0
Nailers, Spikers	67.2	—	29.5
Stover Mounters	67.5	52.5	20.8
Pattern Makers	79.8	69.3	28.4
Engineers	61.4	82.7	14.0
Machinists	54.7	63.0	13.5
INDUSTRY TOTAL	58.6	54.4	14.6

TABLE 9

Property Holdings of Molders, 1860

Molders	Native American	Irish
Under $500	0	4
$500-$999	2	10
$1000-$1499	2	5
Over $1500	5	8
TOTAL	9	27
Percentage of the Ethnic Group in the Trade:	5.9%	10.2%
N =	152	266

port.[54] The percentage of Irish molders with real estate (10.2 percent) was almost double that of the native molders (5.9 percent). Thus in Troy, the molders' figures accurately reflected the city-wide pattern throughout the trades.

Almost all propertied individuals were married. And the higher propertied percentages correspond to higher percentages of married workers within a trade: while 74.2 percent of the heaters were married, 44 percent owned property; and, while 58.2 percent of the puddlers were married, 10.3 percent owned property (table 8). In addition, in contrast to the unskilled laborers, the percentage of married skilled men increased in the iron mills and furnaces from 55.3 percent in 1860 to 61.5 percent in 1880.

When men in the most militant Troy union, the molders, are compared by age, marital status, and ethnicity with the unskilled iron hands, several striking differences appear. As might be expected, while there was a large influx of unskilled boys under fifteen into the mills between 1860 and 1880, none of the molders was less than fifteen. More interesting, though, was the extraordinary percentage — no less than 54.7 percent — of molders in their twenties. This number is unequalled in any other trade, though it is approximated by the other more active iron unions, the puddlers (46.6 percent) and the rollers (47.1 percent).[55] The molders were not only a youthful group, but the figures for 1880 suggest that most molders remained in the trade. In 1860 there were only thirty molders in their forties (6.2 percent of all the molders), whereas in 1880 there were 182 (22.1 percent of all the molders). Meanwhile, the number of molders in their twenties remained fairly constant, increasing from 266 in 1860 to 280 in 1880 (table 7). The new young molders, however, may well have felt harder times than had their older relatives in these trades twenty years earlier. Consequently, like their counterparts among the unskilled workers, a smaller percentage of molders in their twenties and thirties were married in 1880.

One group of skilled iron workers merits special attention because it illustrates the significance of certain cultural or social patterns in differ-

---

[54] Thernstrom, *Poverty and Progress,* chapter five, theorizes that the Irish put their children to work in the factories earlier than other ethnic groups in order to save enough money to buy a house. To these transplanted peasants a home, food, and shelter, rather than education, provided stability, security, and status. More recently, Michael Katz, among others, has suggested that the Irish chose the factory rather than the school only because Catholic parochial education was not available. This does not negate the higher rate of Irish property holding, however.

[55] Compare this with the stove mounters (33 percent), pattern makers (31.1 percent), and nailers (22.5 percent).

ent occupational and ethnic groups. Heaters and roughers both belonged to the National Amalgamated Association of Iron, Steel, and Tin Workers of the United States. These trades worked closely together around the iron furnaces. But 23.3 percent of the roughers in 1880 were married, as compared to 73.4 percent of the heaters (table 8). In addition, every rougher was under forty years old, with 76.7 percent being in their twenties; the age span of the heaters stretched from the late teens to the sixties, with 38.3 percent forty and over. Consequently, although the two trades were closely allied, they evidently involved very different groups of men with distinct life patterns. In the next section, analysis of the household position and family structure of skilled and unskilled workers as well as the marital patterns for the different ethnic groups suggests something of the strength and character of different ethnic cultures. These distinctions permit a tentative assessment of the cohesiveness of the iron worker family and of certain cultural or ethnic ties. Again, Troy's post-Civil War social conflict focuses attention on the Irish, and especially the molders.

Marriage statistics suggest the particular and cohesive strength of Irish culture: the Irish married later than other groups and married within their own community.[56] Among both skilled molders and unskilled workers, marital statistics for the Irish and Americans diverged: between 1860 and 1880 the percentages of married American molders increased from 52.6 percent to 60.1 percent, and that of unskilled American laborers increased from 51.1 percent to 55.0 percent; by comparison, the percentages of married Irish molders also increased from 48.1 percent to 55.8 percent, but the percentage of unskilled Irish laborers declined from 45.1 percent to 40.5 percent. The marital statistics for the other ethnic groups are too scant to be of much value.[57]

Differences may be attributed to many as yet unknown factors. However, some possibilities come to mind: the average skilled worker was older than the average unskilled worker, and more of the former had arrived at the age for marriage; skilled workers were more affluent than unskilled workers and therefore could more easily afford marriage and at an earlier age; and marital customs made marriage at an early age

---

[56] This data confirms similar patterns seen in other working-class ethnic communities at this time, See, Daniel J. Walkowitz, "Working-Class Women . . . in Cohoes, New York."

[57] Men of German extraction married at rates comparable to those of the Irish for both the unskilled workers and the moulders, while Canadians had a percentage below average for unskilled workers.

more likely for one group than for another. The statistics on inter-marriage between national groups demonstrate the influence of ethnicity on marriage. The native American male, who had considerably more freedom of choice in this matter than his female counterpart, infrequently married outside his community; in two-thirds of the intermarriages involving a native American, a female married a male of immigrant extraction. (In contrast, in every immigrant group more males intermarried than did females.)

Men and women of Irish extraction were least likely to marry outside their ethnic community. Irish intermarried at a rate almost one half that of any other group. Only 13.7 percent of the Irish married someone outside their ethnic group, while the intermarriage percentage rose for those of American and English extraction to 23.2 percent and 32.4 percent respectively (table 10, column E). Irish families, however, were not just Irish; most were probably Irish Catholics. Since the Catholic Church threatened excommunication to any person who married outside the Church, the already low percentage of Irish intermarriages would most likely be even lower if the Scots-Irish and the Presbyterian Orange were not included.

Furthermore, certain ethnic groups clearly favored some ethnic national groups over others. When an Irish or Canadian male married outside his community, he usually chose an American female. An Englishman preferred an American or Irish woman. An American male most frequently married an Irish or English woman, and Scotsmen tended to woo English women. Women, of course, had their favorites as well. The Irish woman seems to have preferred the American or English male; the Canadian woman seems to have preferred the Irishman; and the American woman chose an Irish, English, or Canadian man. In all, the largely Protestant groups seemed to discriminate less, choosing freely from among any and all comers, while Irish Catholics evidenced the strongest, most cohesive cultural community.

Community organization easily translated into social and political power, which was especially significant in post-Civil War Troy during interchanges between politicians, policemen, molders, and manufacturers. In this social framework, did Irish family and household structure reflect the apparent cohesion of the Irish family? More needs to be known concerning the relationship between family life and social behavior, but some preliminary evidence indicates the importance of strong family ties in aiding members during times of crisis. During a bitter conflict among

TABLE 10

Intermarriage Between Ethnic Groups of Iron Workers in Ward 6 and 9, 1890

Females' Ethnicity	U.S.A.	Ire.	Can.	Engl.	Scot.	Other	(A) Total Mixed Females	(B) Mixed Females Males	(C) Total Mixed	(D) Total Married	(E) (C) as percent of (D)
U.S.A.	117	23	10	15	1	1	50	+26	74	318	23.2%
Ireland	14	202	2	10	3	0	29	— 6	64	468	13.7%
Canada	1	6	35	2	0	1	10	— 6	26	96	27.1%
English	6	5	2	49	3	2	18	—11	47	145	32.4%
Scotland	2	1	1	2	12	0	6	— 1	13	37	35.1%
Other	1	0	1	0	0	7	2	— 2	6	20	30.0%
Mixed Males:	24	35	16	29	7	4	115		230	1084	21.1%

neighboring Cohoes cotton workers in 1882, for example, wives and children of striking workers frequently intimidated non-union strike-breakers.[58]

It is necessary to understand further the impact that immigration, urbanization, and industrial capitalism had on the immigrant and his family. In *The Uprooted,* his classic narrative of the immigration experience, Oscar Handlin argued that the city intimidated and bewildered the immigrant, destroying much of his home and family life:

> The street in its strangeness is the evidence of the old home's disintegration. . . . Almost resignedly, the immigrants witnessed in themselves a deterioration. All relationships became less binding, all behavior more dependent on individual whim. . . . The inability to use force was the crowning irony of the immigrants' disorganization . . .[59]

The experience of Troy's immigrant iron workers challenges the accuracy of this view. Violence and social disorder characterized the city's history during these years, and Irish immigrant workers took an active part. Violence and conflict, however, can reflect a certain integrity and organization within a strong community. Household and family structure provide one index of the social base of organization and protest. Indeed, the household and family structure of skilled and unskilled iron workers of American, English and Irish extraction in ward six (a south ward) and ward ten (a north ward) in 1880 indicates little difference between the two immigrant groups and the native Americans (table 11). Many iron workers were boarders — an unskilled worker was twice as likely to be a boarder than was a skilled worker, and most boarders were Irish — and more needs to be understood about boarding-house life. The key fact, though, is that seventeen of every twenty iron workers who lived with a family lived in a two-parent family. Moreover, two-thirds lived in nuclear households. Thus, it is the apparent cohesion, and not the disintegration, of the iron worker family that seems evident.[60]

Equally important, the American and Irish household shared many more common characteristics with each other than either did with the English. Evidently the city did not mark the immigrant household with special scars. Among both skilled and unskilled men, the percentage of

---

[58] Daniel J. Walkowitz, "Working-Class Culture" (Ph.D. thesis), ch. 6. The importance of family ties can be seen in Edward P. Thompson and Eileen Yeo, eds., *The Unknown Mayhew* (New York, 1972); Michael Anderson, *Family Life in Nineteenth-Century Lancashire* (Cambridge, England, 1971); and, Judith R. Walkowitz and Daniel J. Walkowitz, " 'We Are Not Beasts of the Field:' Prostitution and the Poor."

[59] Oscar Handlin, *The Uprooted* (New York, 1951), 155, 163.

[60] Based solely on structural evidence, these conclusions are put forth most tentatively.

TABLE 11

Household and Family Structure of Iron Workers
in Wards 6 and 10, 1880
(number and percentage)

HOUSEHOLD STRUCTURE	UNSKILLED WORKERS				SKILLED WORKERS			
Ethnicity	U.S.A.	Engl.	Irish	TOTAL	U.S.A.	Engl.	Irish	TOTAL
Nuclear Family	62	54	215	331	46	26	165	237
	54.9	45.0	54.0	52.5	67.6	52.0	63.7	62.9
Extended Family	8	7	26	41	5	6	17	28
	7.1	5.8	6.5	6.5	7.4	12.0	6.6	7.4
Augmented Family	16	33	46	95	7	7	34	48
	14.2	27.5	11.6	15.1	10.3	14.0	13.1	12.7
Sub-family	6	3	7	16	1	3	8	12
	5.3	2.5	1.8	2.5	1.5	6.0	3.1	3.2
Mixed Adult Group	0	0	6	6	2	2	3	7
	0.0	0.0	1.5	1.0	2.0	4.0	1.1	1.9
Single	21	23	98	142	7	6	32	45
	17.7	19.2	24.6	22.5	10.3	12.0	12.4	11.0
N:	113	120	398	631	68	50	259	377
FAMILY STRUCTURE								
Two-parent	83	91	250	424	53	40	187	280
	90.2	93.8	85.0	87.8	89.8	95.2	83.5	86.2
One-parent	9	6	44	59	6	2	37	45
	9.8	6.2	15.0	12.2	10.2	4.8	16.5	13.8

English nuclear families is almost ten points below that of the other groups. But the English family did not leave other Englishmen "out in the cold." Among unskilled workers, the English household often included their friends and relatives: hence, their relatively high percentage of augmented families. And among skilled workers, the English family was also extended to include relatives as well as non-relatives: note, then, the relatively high percentage of extended and augmented English families.

While these figures demonstrate the basic similarity of *household* patterns among Irish, English and American iron workers, the Irish family was noticeably weaker. The incidence of skilled and unskilled iron workers that lived in households with "broken" families, families where children lived with only one parent, almost doubles in the Irish family. Of the sixty-two Irish iron workers who resided with a single parent, forty-seven (75.8 percent) lived with a widowed mother.

Not only was the percentage of Irish workers living in whole families significantly lower than the percentages for the other groups, but the percentage of Irish widowers and Irish sons living in a "broken" home easily outdistanced the figures for English and American families. Although many Irishmen probably first confronted the city as chiefly a peasant experience, it would be incorrect to ascribe this difference in the number of one-parent families simply to the general anomie of "urban life." And while the long hours of hot, heavy, and often dangerous labor in the mills surely took their toll, the relatively high percentage of Irish widows could also be attributed to Irish attitudes toward the family, to the Catholic Church's sanctions against divorce, remarriage, and non-legalized cohabitation, to distinct Irish immigration or migration habits, or to another feature of Irish culture.[61]

---

[61] This is a terribly complex matter. The strength of Irish culture, particularly the influence of the Catholic Church, has been seen in the low intermarriage rate among the Irish. Similarly, the Church provided strong sanctions against divorce. The small number of divorced individuals enumerated in the census, however, suggests that the expense of divorce and Church opposition made separation the practical alternative to workingclass divorce. In addition, during this period of rapid industrial growth, with frequent strikes and lockouts, men were continually forced to seek new employment. Lateral occupational mobility could only increase the considerable geographic mobility Thernstrom *(Poverty and Progress)* and others have found in urban America at this time. This, in turn, would increase the number of men likely to be out of town in search of work until either the Troy strike was settled or until a new situation was secure enough to send for the family. Lastly, Trojan "widows" may have lost their husbands to the workingman's perennial enemy — unemployment, underemployment, and poverty, and the resulting psychology of failure that turned men to drink, dissipation, and/or flight. Thus, Irish family structure may have been but the product of the trauma involved in the nineteenth-century industrial crunch.

Thus we have the Troy iron workers: largely immigrants and Irish between 1860 and 1880, they managed to secure positions throughout the iron industry, and to develop and maintain a cohesive community life. What was the typical iron worker like in 1860 and how had he progressed by 1880? In the earlier decade, he was, if unskilled, probably an unmarried Irishman between the ages of fifteen and thirty who owned no real estate and lived in one of the city's south wards. The representative skilled Troy iron worker was not much different. Also Irish, he was most likely a molder in his twenties who had recently married an Irish woman. They tended to live in a nuclear family in a rented house near the mill or foundry where he was employed. Not much had changed by 1880, except that the iron worker was even more likely to be of Irish extraction. The typical unskilled worker was now more likely to be single and younger. Similarly, the typical skilled worker in 1880 was now more likely to be a molder, married, with a strong family life, and twenty years older than his 1860 counterpart. James Turner and his family are representative of these iron workers.

Sixty-year old James Turner and his forty-year-old wife, Mary, had come from Ireland with their four sons around 1850.[62] In 1860 they lived on one floor of a two-story row house in south Troy, at 17 Brick Row, above the Troy Iron Works. They probably rented their flat, either from the iron company or from one of the local landlords, such as Thomas Hopkins, an Englishman with some $20,000 in real estate holdings, who lived a few blocks from the Turner family with his wife and three-year-old daughter. By 1860 the Turners had only been able to save about fifty-odd dollars. Now with Civil War imminent and the recurrent problems of rising prices and depressions plaguing them, if the family was ever to gain some security — money for the food and possibly land (real estate) that had been so precious in those last years in Ireland — then it was crucial that the sons find early employment in the mills. The youngest son, twelve-year-old Michael, and a daughter, now eight, who had been born in the new country, attended school, awaiting that time when they would enter the iron and collar mills respectively. Meanwhile, every morning before six A.M., Mr. Turner and his three older sons, aged fifteen, eighteen, and twenty, left Mary Turner home to keep house, and began another long day in the iron mills. Six days a week, Turner and the two younger sons worked as unskilled iron mill hands; the oldest

---

[62] The biography of the Turner family is reconstructed from the 8th Census, 1860, *Population;* 10th Census, 1880, *Population;* and *Troy City Directory* (annual), 1860-1880.

son was already a skilled roller in the mill. After eleven or twelve hours of hot and heavy work, which at times dragged on for as long as fourteen hours, they returned home for dinner. For this sixty-six to seventy-two-hour work week, the Turners received perhaps four dollars each, and the oldest son, as a skilled worker, perhaps as much as six dollars. These figures compared favorably with weekly wages of about four dollars paid to unskilled female shirt and collar factory workers.[63] On Sunday the family would travel to the nearest church (Presbyterian or Catholic)[64] in the center of Troy to receive spiritual instruction, see their countrymen, and consider their lot in this world and the next.

If this portrait seems restrictive, in large part it is because the long mill hours left little time for recreation. Aside from the union life of the skilled workers, what activities they did have were important to them. Masonic clubs, fire brigades, baseball clubs, and even ethnic politics were an essential part of the culture of the working class, much as they marked the life of the socially prominent. This aspect of their history is an important supplement to the portrait drawn from statistical data, but will have to be detailed elsewhere.[65] Basically, however, life revolved around the church and ethnic groups: Sunday school and church picnics, fraternal organizations, and nationalist groups such as the Fenians and Clan na Gael.

In 1880 only the eldest son, William, was listed as living in Troy. He had married an Irish girl, and moved to number 10 Brick Row, above the Troy Iron Works, a few doors from his parents. They had the first of many children that year, William, 2nd. Meanwhile, all three younger brothers followed William's lead, and by 1866 had become skilled iron rollers. By 1870 the family had reorganized. James Turner, the father, died in 1870, and his wife died a few years later. The two younger sons seemed to have moved out of Troy. And the two older sons, William and John, now both family men, became heaters in the iron mill. Their families still lived above the iron works: by 1880 John had died and his widow lived at 11 Brick Row; and William and his wife lived with their nine sons and one daughter a few blocks away in a four-family house at

---

[63] Eight Census, 1860, *Manufactures*.

[64] Without consulting and correlating local church records there is no way to tell if the Turner family was Orange (Scotch Presbyterian) or Green (Catholic).

[65] This material will be detailed in my book-length manuscript in process on class, culture, and ethnicity in mid-nineteenth century Troy and Cohoes. This manuscript supplements census data with the extensive use of local and national newspapers, union minutes, letters, labor reports, and other more traditional literary sources in order to discuss attitudes, traditions, values, and working-class behavior more fully.

the corner of De Freest Avenue and Campbell's Highway. William, 2nd, now twenty, had been a heater in the mill the past few years, but was now employed as a clerk in a saloon. His sixteen-year-old sister worked in a collar shop, his fifteen and fourteen-year old brothers labored in the iron mills, four brothers between the ages of five and twelve attended school, and their mother stayed at home with the two little boys. Between 1860 and 1880 iron workers like the Turners had made modest gains in the mills. Though the conditions and style of their life had not appeared to change dramatically, the family remained intact; food, clothing, and shelter had been provided, and their sons had gained training and skilled employment in the iron industry.

The Turner family's experience reflects that of the predominantly Irish immigrants and their children in the working class of Troy's iron industry. Through the 1870s and 1880s, with its violence and disorder, these workers built a strong union movement. The violence itself did not occur simply as a function of the unions' development. Troy's working-class did not struggle so much to gain more power as to preserve what advantages they had already won. Immigrant Irish workers dominated the iron factories in 1860, and during the next twenty years solidified their position in the industry. For an Irishman, skilled and even unskilled jobs in the iron mills provided greater security for food, clothing, and shelter than either peasant life and famine conditions in Ireland, or the meagre and uncertain day-laborer wages of their many Irish-American countrymen. One central fact cannot be overlooked: during this period, the position of the typical Irish iron worker did not decline, but seemed to improve. The Irishman had gained a firm foothold in the iron industry, and the industry fulfilled certain aspirations for the skilled laborer. Furthermore, the impact of a cohesive Irish culture was felt throughout the community: in industrial, political, civic, family, and cultural life. Why, then, did violence and disorder occur? One possible explanation is that Troy's iron worker community organized an effective labor movement in the 1860s. Their organization also included considerable ethnic, political and social power in the city. Moreover, the strength and cohesiveness of iron-worker ethnic culture was reflected in tightly knit ethnic residential patterns, and in nuclear families with low (notably among the Irish) intermarriage rates. But the workers saw the organization, coherence, stability, and success they had achieved menaced by employer organizations formed in the late 1860s and 1870s to assume control over them. Industrial capitalism demanded changes. So manufacturers attempted to control wages and production. Then they tried to control work conditions with time cards, apprenticeship regulations and, ultimately, the use of non-union labor. When these changes met resistance, they tried to impose order on the social conditions through police and political power. These controls threatened further to alienate the workers. Troy's iron workers resisted this assault on their culture, and violence ensued.

Once historians begin to understand the structure of certain social institutions such as the family, they will be in a position to learn about the relationship of such institutions to behavior. This essay has tried to suggest an organic model for such understanding and some of the ways in which statistics can contribute to the task. Much other data can be also useful — whether to focus on crime with police records or on property holdings with tax records, to cite but two examples. And of course they can also be used to help answer many different questions. William Sewell's fine study of Marseille workers, for example, makes splendid use of police records to provide a closer look at the participants in radical protest.[66] Thus, this article on Troy's iron workers only introduces limited statistical information for its hypothesis about the relationship between working-class culture and behavior. The combination of factors that could influence attitudes and with them behavior needs to be understood further as an interlocking complex of cultural patterns. Identifying and distinguishing between unskilled and skilled iron workers, between young men and old men, between the propertied and the unpropertied, between Irish and Scottish mill hands, between weak family units and strong family units, between Catholics and Protestants, etc., provide analytic and comparative keys to help unlock the meaning of the urban, industrial or even ethnic experience in America. Understanding working-class culture and social behavior, however, merely begins with identification and statistical analysis. To make the culture come alive one must write the history of the workers and their community in Troy and in other industrial towns and cities.

---

[66] William H. Sewell, "The Working Class of Marseille Under the Second Republic."

THE LABOR BOYCOTT IN NEW YORK CITY, 1880-1886

12

Michael A. Gordon

In late 1885, *Bradstreet's* devoted four pages to an examination of boycotts in 1884 and 1885. It reported 237 boycotts against newspapers and manufacturers of hats, cigars, carpets, clothing, footwear, and brooms. Boycotts also involved bakers, printers, brewery workers, starch factory laborers, a steamship company, a street railway, and even Chinese-made goods. In general, *Bradstreet's* remarked, since 1880 — when the Irish Land League adopted the weapon — the labor boycott had grown in a "marked" and "prodigious" fashion. In New York State, the labor boycott had become so common in 1885 that the State Bureau of Labor Statistics gave it considerable attention in its *Third Annual Report*. Statistics were lacking, but the Bureau considered the new tactic important enough to conduct hearings and publish some testimony. The following year, 165 boycotts were recorded in the State. And in 1887 the Bureau listed 242 boycotts, even though it noted that "the boycott, as a war measure, has not been resorted to quite as frequently in the past as in former years." The Bureau explained the popularity of the boycott: "The strike is negation. The boycott is action." It was a matter of "logical sequence." Strikes caused a loss of wages, and "the men have argued that they have a right to go further, and to compel a settlement of the issues. Hence the boycott." Evidence was not lacking to support the argument that boycotts were employed when strikes either failed or were lengthy. Of the 165 boycotts in 1886, 119 accompanied strikes.[1]

---

[1] *Bradstreet's,* December 19, 1885. New York State Bureau of Labor Statistics, *Third Annual Report* (for 1885), *Senate Documents,* III, no. 23 (1886). 133-144 (hereafter cited *Third Annual Report*), *Fourth Annual Report* (for 1886), *Assembly Documents,* V, no. 27 (1887) 420-457, 713, 738-743 (hereafter cited *Fourth Annual Report*). See also the Bureau's *Fifth Annual Report* (for 1887), *Assembly Documents,* V, no. 74 (1888), 521-522.

Source: From *Labor History* 16, no. 2 (Spring 1975): 184-229.

Historians have not overlooked labor's increasing use of the boycott in the 1880s. The 1886 trial of five New York City boycotters, in particular, is usually viewed as sparking Henry George's bid to become that city's mayor. A larger conceptual view sees the George campaign and widespread strikes and boycotts as part of the "Revival And Upheaval" that began in the late 1870s and culminated in the bitter labor conflict and political agitation of 1886-1887. But the problem of explaining the epidemic of 1885 and 1886 boycotts remains. Most labor historians have either uncritically supported the Bureau's argument that the boycotts supplemented strikes, dismissed the tactic as a mere adoption of the Irish practice, or have simply ignored it.[2]

Two older works, however, offered interesting (but untested) hypotheses concerning the boycott. In 1916, Leo Wolman called it a modern form of the social, religious, and political ostracism practiced centuries earlier by clergy and guilds against religious dissenters and transgressors of guild codes. Wolman cited the early experiences, however, just to point up a contrast: in early times, masters *and* journeymen established severe penalties to maintain guild standards, but trade unions used the boycott as a weapon against employers who had *no* voice in the formation of union rules. The boycott, in short, was far from "a spontaneous revulsion of feeling in the large masses of people against a certain individual, with the result that they determine to cease all intercourse with him, social as well as economic." Instead, Wolman went on, "it represents in most cases only the deliberate exercise by the officers

---

[2] On the effect of the trial see, for example, Selig Perlman, "Upheaval And Reorganization," in John R. Commons *et al., History of The Labour Movement in the United States* (New York, 1918), II, 446; Philip S. Foner, *History of The Labor Movement in the United States* (New York, 1955), II, 117-119; Joseph G. Rayback, *A History of American Labor* (New York, 1959), 169; Peter A. Speek, "The Single Tax And The Labor Movement," *Bulletin of The University of Wisconsin, Economics And Political Science Series,* VIII (October, 1917), 308; Thomas J. Condon, "Political Reform And The New York City Election of 1886," *New York Historical Society Quarterly,* XLIV (October 1960), 363-393. For the larger conceptual view see, for example, Foner, ch. 8; Rayback, chs. 11-12; Speek, chs. 4-6; Perlman, Part VI, Chs. 1-2, 6-9; Selig Perlman, *A History of Trade Unionism in The United States,* (New York, 1923), ch. 4; Anthony Bimba, *The History of The American Working Class* (New York, 1927), chs. 18-19; Foster Rhea Dulles, *Labor in America* (New York, 1949), chs. 7-8; and Norman Ware, *The Labor Movement in The United States, 1860-1895* (New York, 1929). Those generally agreeing with the Bureau are Perlman, *A History of Trade Unionism,* 85; Perlman, in Commons, 364; Bimba, 177; and Harry W. Laidler, *Boycotts And The Labor Struggle: Economic And Social Aspects* (New York, 1913), 91-92. Rayback simply says that "toward the end of 1884 labor took up the boycott." Dulles similarly offers no analysis. Foner examined some Knights of Labor correspondence and found that Knights used boycotts when strikes failed, as an organizing tool, and as a means to shut down anti-union firms in small communities. "In practically every case," he notes, "the boycott was used in retaliation only when the employers locked out members of the union and replaced them with scab labor."

and members of the union of a policy designed to blockade the establishments of hostile employers by interfering with their purchase of raw materials and their sale of finished products." The labor boycott in the 1880s rested less with historical antecedents than with labor's inability to control labor supply and productivity. In those industries where workers could not organize trades to conduct successful strikes, or where organization was impossible (as in prisons), unions attempted to prevent the *sale* of products, not their manufacture. The boycott was especially appealing to the thousands of largely unskilled immigrants, new to labor organizations, who found it a cheaper alternative to costly strikes. So Wolman's analysis, while offering important insights, ultimately conformed to the view that boycotts just supplemented strikes.[3]

Norman Ware alone attributed the use and success of the boycott to the appearance of "labor solidarity and class consciousness" — a new "social situation" created by the industrial revolution. "There were workingmen's commodities and there were middle- and upper-class commodities," Ware wrote more than forty years ago. The production of goods designed primarily for working-class consumption — beer, cheap clothing and furniture, inexpensive cigars — were sold chiefly in local working-class communities and not yet marketed nationally. So consumer consciousness, itself a function of class consciousness, could be most effective if a boycott involved products sold mainly in working-class areas. Adopted through the influence of the Irish, the labor boycott promised success only so long as the social structure and ideology remained intact.[4]

Such explanations readily relate the boycott to the inability of labor organizations to control the behavior of workers in strike situations, and to the growth of a particular working-class consciousness, but ignore much else. Any attempt to understand why the boycott was so widely used must begin by examining the identities of Gilded Age labor boycotters, the nature of their experiences, and how they themselves viewed the tactic. The boycott was conducted chiefly by immigrant workers in an industrializing society, and must be considered along side other as-

---

[3] Leo Wolman, "The Boycott in American Trade Unions," *Johns Hopkins University Studies in Historical And Political Science,* XXXIV (1916), 17-20, 25-26. Similar views tracing the boycott to ancient practices are expressed in Laidler, 27-28; William A. Hammond, "The Evolution of The Boycott," *The Forum,* I (June, 1886), 369-376; and John Burnett, "The Boycott As An Element in Trade Disputes," *The Economic Journal* (London), I (March, 1891), 163-173.

[4] Ware, 335, 336. By the time Ware's book was published, this working-class consumer consciousness had been replaced by "a large, consumer middle class." National markets catered to all segments of society. See 336, 337.

pects of immigrant culture and labor's behavior in those years. It was an *adaptation* — not an *adoption* — of the Irish practice. An isolated tactic, the boycott was inseparably related to other traditional forms of popular immigrant protest (such as mass demonstrations, parades, and rallies), and patterns of organizing for protection, which were common to the European rural and urban worlds so many New York workers had known.

Furthermore, the use of the boycott, and labor's activities in general, cannot be understood apart from Irish-American nationalist efforts in New York. The term "labor boycott" was indeed derived from Irish Land League boycotts against recalcitrant landlords which began in late 1880. But the practice was popularized in New York by Irish-American nationalist groups and city labor unions, themselves often industrial counterparts of Old World organizations. In the early 1880s, the symbiotic relationship between labor and nationalist activities blurred the distinctions separating some labor proposals from schemes for redressing Ireland's grievances. This blurring occurred principally because significant numbers of Irish immigrants believed that problems afflicting American workers and Irish peasants stemmed from the same sources. They viewed industrial and land monopoly as the aggrandizement of natural resources which God had intended to be shared by all. This belief strengthened communal and nationalist loyalties among Irish immigrant workers, and led them to demand land reform for Ireland *and* America. Within this context, the labor boycott and kindred acts of social ostracism were seen by such immigrants as customary and legitimate tactics against unscrupulous employers or against other workers who violated their rights to share God's bounty, just as they had been used in Ireland against landlords and others for similar reasons.

This study, then, focuses upon aspects of immigrant culture which help clarify the origin and meaning of the labor boycott. For reasons which will become evident, the Irish receive primary attention. From 1880, to the mass arrests and trials of labor boycotters in 1886, other immigrants, and native Americans, engaged in boycotts, and they will be examined as well.

I

The boycott in America was new only in name in the 1880s. Revolutionary mechanics and merchants, angered by the Stamp Act and by other British regulations, refused to import or purchase British goods.

Labor organizations also variously adopted the practice in the decades preceding the 1880s. And, too, William Lloyd Garrison and other abolitionists advocated boycotts against slave-made products. The labor boycotts of the 1880s, however, were rooted more in Old World experiences than in American soil (although these and earlier examples of "'non-intercourse" need to be thoroughly studied). They stemmed from the sporadic terrorism conducted by the Irish secret societies of Whiteboys and the like between the 1760s and 1870s, and from corresponding protective activities by workers in towns and cities.[5]

Whiteboyism was but one of several forms of agrarian societies. Religious associations like the Ribbonmen sought to protect Irish Catholic peasants from the depredations of Protestant landowners, tithe collectors, and Orangemen. Local factions, occasionally tied through kinship, took pride in whipping opponents at county fairs in tests of strength. Distinctions between these groups were not always clear. Organizations often shared a common grievance, object of attack, and membership. Moreover, all were firmly entrenched in a rural culture and a system of values which dictated behavior, and imposed sanctions against those who violated cultural norms.[6]

Whiteboy violence, in particular, was motivated by crunching poverty. Changing landholding arrangements, depressed economic conditions, and population increases form the stark outline of much Irish peasant history from the late eighteenth century to the Famine. Only the Na-

---

[5] On Revolutionary era boycotts see, for example, Bernard Knollenberg, *Origin of The American Revolution, 1759-1766* (rev. ed., New York, 1965), 178, 211; Richard B. Morris, *Government And Labor in Early America* (New York, 1946), 43, 525; and Lawrence H. Gipson, *The Coming of The American Revolution, 1763-1775* (New York, 1954), 219-222. On boycotts as practiced by labor organizations see, for example, Wolman, 23; Laidler, 69; George A. Stevens, *New York Typographical Union No. 6: Study of A Modern Trade Union And Its Predecessors,* New York State Assembly Documents, XII, no. 28, pt. 3 (1912), 2, 10-11; John B. Andrews, "Nationalisation (1860-1877)," in Commons, 22-23, 24-25; *The New York Times,* March 11, 1870. In *William Sylvis, Pioneer of American Labor* (New York, 1945), 179, Jonathan P. Grossman describes the January 1867 attempt by the Providence Barstow foundry to smash the Iron Molders' Union: "Boycott resolutions against the company, perhaps the first ever passed by a national trade union, were adopted at a molders' convention." They were printed in the *Iron Molders' Journal,* and distributed nationally. On abolitionist use of the practice see, for example, Walter H. Merrill, *Against The Wind: A Biography of William Lloyd Garrison* (Cambridge, Mass., 1963), 56, 80; Robin W. Winks, " 'A Sacred Animosity': Abolitionism in Canada," in Martin Duberman (ed.), *The Anti-Slavery Vanguard: New Essays on The Abolitionists* (Princeton, 1965), 334.

[6] Galen Broeker, *Rural Disorder And Police Reform in Ireland, 1812-36* (London, 1970), 8-16; Gale E. Christianson, "Secret Societies And Agrarian Violence in Ireland, 1790-1840," *Agricultural History,* XLVI (July, 1972), 369-384; Kevin B. Knowlan, "Agrarian Unrest in Ireland, 1800-1845," *University Review* (National University of Ireland), II, no. 6 (1958), 7-16. Hereward Senior's *Orangeism in Ireland And Britain, 1795-1836* (London, 1966), is an excellent study of that subject.

poleonic Wars provided a brief spark to Irish agriculture, and even then tenant farmers and cottiers who defaulted on contractural obligations were subject to eviction. The traditional peasant claim of using rented land in perpetuity was recognized only in Ulster. Elsewhere, rent prices and conditions of tenancy were generally the products of competition for land and landlord whims. Pressured by falling grain prices after 1815, many landowners sought to increase profits by returning portions of land to pasturage. In the process, the network of tenant farms and family subdivisions was splintered, and thousands were evicted. Even after the Famine, when the Irish rural population was reduced drastically and the cottier system all but disappeared, landowner influence in Parliament was too strong to permit a meaningful alteration of the landlord-tenant relationship based upon the peasants' customary rights.[7]

Since their Munster origins in the 1760s, the Whiteboys sought to defend by violence what the British Government and its courts would not protect by law. While grievances differed from county to county, the pattern of retaliation was similar. In Southern and Western Ireland (and parts of the Midlands), peasant raiders wearing white shirts destroyed fences and buildings belonging to landowners or their agents, and intimidated tithe collectors. Carders, Oakboys, Terry Alts, Rockites, Blackfeet, bound by secret oaths, conducted similar attacks. Whiteboy violence was also motivated by attempts to prevent landlords from employing outside farm labor, but reprisals were directed as much against agrarian "scabs" as their employers. One observer in 1836 aptly called the secret societies a "vast trades union for the protection of the Irish peasantry." Another writer put the societies' activities in a more appropriate perspective: "So miserable was the condition of the persons engaged in it," that Whiteboyism was "a struggle for mere existence." [8]

The analogy between combinations of rural and urban workers is even

---

[7] John E. Pomfret, *The Struggle for Land in Ireland, 1800-1923* (Princetown, 1930), chs. 1-4, *passim;* Kenneth H. Connell, *The Population of Ireland, 1750-1845* (Oxford, 1950). See also, Gale E. Christianson, "Population, The Potato, And Depression in Ireland: 1800-1830," *Eire-Ireland,* VII (Winter, 1972), 70-95.

[8] Broeker, 8-12; Christianson, "Secret Societies And Agrarian Violence in Ireland, 1790-1840;" Pomfret, 12-21; Thomas N. Brown, "Nationalism And The Irish Peasant, 1800-1848," *The Review of Politics,* XV (October, 1953), 426-429; Wayne G. Broehl, *The Molly Maguires* (Cambridge, Mass., 1964), 2-3, 12-15, 21-25; George O'Brien, *The Economic History of Ireland from The Union to The Famine* (New York, 1921), 369-398; R. B. McDowell, *Public Opinion And Government Policy in Ireland, 1801-1846* (London, 1952), ch. 1; and Nicholas Mansergh, *The Irish Question, 1840-1921* (London, [1940] 1965), ch. 1. George C. Lewis, *Local Disturbances in Ireland* (London, 1836), quoted in Broeker, 8. "Agrarian Outrages in Ireland," *North British Review,* II (August, 1847), 523.

more striking when evicted peasants are followed into Irish, Scottish, and English towns. Primarily manual laborers, Irish workers also encountered the new production techniques of the Industrial Revolution. In this new setting, they fought employers as they had their rural enemies. "We can cite no actual biographies," E. P. Thompson writes, "but there can be no doubt that some of these immigrants brought with them the traditions of these secret societies." Moreover, Thompson suggests that "from one aspect, Luddism may be seen as the nearest thing to a 'peasant's revolt' of industrial workers; instead of sacking the *chateaux,* the most immediate object which symbolised their oppression — the gig-mill or power-loom—was attacked."[9]

Trade unions, too, had much in common with Whiteboy associations. Unlike the Land League membership, which was mainly composed of substantial farmers and a significant number of townsmen, the Whiteboys included mostly small tenants and cottiers whose rent was paid from wages they earned as laborers. Whiteboys insisted on rent ceilings, limiting the annual number of working days, and hiring workers from their district only. Irish trade unionists sought minimum-wage guarantees, reduction in working hours, and regulations limiting the admission of apprentices.[10]

Beyond its attempt to defend peasant rights and culture, Whiteboyism aided the development of nineteenth-century Irish nationalism. By broadening their membership base, and cooperating with similar groups in contiguous districts, agrarian secret societies helped shatter the insularity of peasant life. Clandestine terror activities became a form of political behavior which championed peasant claims in ways the Repealers and Young Irelanders could never do. When such behavior became linked to proposals for fundamental land reform and the creation of an independent Ireland, as it was in the 1870s and 1880s, Parliament could no longer ignore the clear political message inherent in agrarian violence by merely seeking more expedient ways to suppress it.[11]

Throughout the 1870s, however, Irish farmers had little success in taking advantage of Parliament's complicated Land Act of 1870. By 1880,

[9] E. P. Thompson, *The Making of The English Working Class* (New York, 1963), 429-444, 600. See 596-599 for Irish influences on Luddism.

[10] Sam Clark, "The Social Composition of The Land League," *Irish Historical Studies,* XVII (September, 1971), 447-469; Christianson, 382-383; O'Brien, 397-398; Pomfret, 4-7. On trade-union activity in Ireland, see Rachel O'Higgins, "Irish Trade Unions And Politics, 1830-50," *The Historical Journal,* IV (1961), 208-217; and Jesse Dunsmore Clarkson, *Labor And Nationalism in Ireland* (New York, 1925), chs. 3, 4, 6.

[11] Brown, 429-445.

Ireland was on the brink of another famine. Agricultural prices had declined perilously, potato crops had been poor for two years, and farmers were heavily in debt. Hundreds of thousands in the western counties faced starvation and eviction. Tenants' Defense Associations, organized throughout Ireland in 1879, urged tenants to withhold rents from rack-renting landlords. When farmers did so, they, too, were evicted. Unable to find seasonal work in England because of poor crops there, agricultural laborers, whose budding National Union collapsed in 1879, were particularly hard hit. "Uncle Pat's Cabin" became a symbol of their wretched conditions in a manner not unlike an earlier uncle's cabin in America embodied for some the oppression of slaves. With no relief in sight, peasants responded with terror reminiscent of Whiteboyism. In 1880 alone, 2590 "agrarian outrages" were reported. Bands of vigilantes roamed the countryside maiming cattle, and threatening and assaulting farmers who paid unjust rents or took land of evicted tenants. Landlords were intimidated, and shots fired into "enemy" houses.[12]

The Irish National Land League grew out of this crisis, and closely followed the launching of the New Departure. Formed on October 21, 1879, at a Dublin conference of young Irish nationalists and land reformers, the Land League sought land reform legislation, reduced land rents, and supported those tenants refusing to pay all or part of their rents. While the league's unity became strained in succeeding years, few in Ireland or America disagreed that Charles Stewart Parnell and Michael Davitt were the principal spokesmen for Irish self-government and land reform. Parnell, the aristocratic M. P. and League leader, and Davitt, a former Fenian, well understood peasant culture. "The League's history," writes Thomas N. Brown, "reveals how closely the nationalist adapted himself to the peasant world, for the Land League's essential power lay in its legitimization of old Whiteboy techniques." By chan-

---

[12] For a discussion of the hard times and the evictions see Thomas N. Brown, *Irish-American Nationalism, 1870-1890* (Philadelphia, 1966), 86, 101; R. Barry O'Brien, *The Life of Charles Stewart Parnell, 1846-1891* (New York, 1898), 175-176. O'Brien notes (on 247) that 6,000 were evicted in 1879, and 10,457 in 1880. On the conditions and political activities of farmers and agricultural laborers, see John P. Huttman, 'Fenians And Farmers: The Merger of The Home-Rule And Owner-Occupancy Movement in Ireland, 1850-1915," *Albion,* III (Winter, 1971), 182-197; and Pamela Horn, "The National Agricultural Labourers' Union in Ireland, 1873-9," *Irish Historical Studies,* CVII (March, 1971), 340-352. See also, Charlotte G. O'Brien, "The Irish 'Poor Man'," *Nineteenth Century,* VIII (December, 1880), 876-887; Standish O'Grady, "The Irish Small Farmer," *The Fortnightly Review,* 2nd ser., XXVII (April 1, 1880), 568-579; "The Distress in Ireland," *The Dublin Review,* 3rd ser., III (April, 1880), 464-491; Philip H. Bagenal, " 'Uncle Pat's Cabin'," *Nineteenth Century,* XII (December, 1882), 925-938; and Justin McCarthy, "The Irish Peasantry," *Longman's Magazine,* I (February, 1883), 392-408.

nelling "'traditional village hostilities into nonviolent forms," the League devised a new and potent weapon — the boycott.[13]

The new tactic owed some of its technique to James Redpath. As an abolitionist, Redpath had urged slaves to revolt against the Southern regime, and later saw social ostracism practiced against carpetbaggers. While touring Ireland for the New York *Tribune* in 1880, he spoke to distraught peasants in Connemara, and made clear he now opposed violence. "How are you going to conquer?," he asked the people of Deenane on August 25. Violence would only result in bloody recriminations by the government. In suggesting a new strategy, he went straight to the core of peasant culture — social ostracism. Redpath explained:

> Call up the terrible power of social excommunication. If any man is evicted from his holding, let no man take it. If any man is mean enough to take it, don't shoot him but treat him as a leper. Encircle him with scorn and silence. Let no man nor woman talk to him or his wife or children.

Four days later, Parnell spoke at a mass meeting in Ennis and echoed Redpath's advice. "'Now, what would you do to a tenant who bids for a farm from which another has been evicted?,'" Parnell asked. Several voices cried out, "'Shoot him!'"

> I think I heard somebody say, 'Shoot him' (Cheers). I wish to point out to you a very much better way, a more Christian and charitable way, which will give the lost sinner an opportunity of repenting. (Laughter and 'Hear, hear.') When a man takes a farm from which another has been evicted, you must shun him on the roadside when you meet him, you must shun him in the streets of the town, you must shun him in the shop, you must shun him in the fair green and in the market-place, and even in the place of worship. By leaving him severely alone, by putting him into a moral convent, by isolating him from the rest of his fellow countrymen as if he were a leper of old, you must show him your detestation of the crime he has committed. If you do this you may depend on it that there will be no man so full of avarice, so lost to shame as to dare the public opinion of all right-thinking men in the country and transgress your unwritten code of laws. (Loud cheers.)[14]

---

[13] F. S. L. Lyons, *Ireland Since The Famine* (New York, 1971), 151-160; Robert Kee, *The Green Flag: A History of Irish Nationalism* (London, 1972), 371-373; Charles Stewart Parnell, "The Irish Land Question," *North American Review,* CXXX (April, 1880), 388-406. The belief that the New Departure and the Land League had common origins is convincingly challenged in T. W. Moody, "The New Departure in Irish Politics, 1878-9," in H. A. Cronne, T. W. Moody, and D. B. Quinn (eds.), *Essays in British And Irish History in Honour of James Eadie Todd* (London, 1949), 303-333; and in Brown, *Irish-American Nationalism,* ch. 5. On Irish problems and politics in the 1870s and 1880s, see Lawrence J. McCaffrey, *Irish Federalism in The 1870s: A Study in Conservative Nationalism* (Philadelphia, 1962); and L. P. Curtis, Jr., *Coercion And Conciliation in Ireland, 1880-1892: A Study in Conservative Unionism* (Princeton, 1963). Brown, *Irish-American Nationalism,* 195.

[14] Charles F. Horner, *The Life of James Redpath And The Development of The Modern*

Speeches by Parnell and other League officials carried the theme throughout Ireland.The new tactic was applied to anyone who broke the "unwritten code of laws." Father John O'Mally, the Kilomolara parish priest and League supporter, suggested the weapon's name. Shortly after the local Land League formally "ostracized" Captain Charles Boycott, the land agent at Lough Mask for Ulster's Lord Erne, and a substantial tenant himself, O'Mally told Redpath that Boycott's name might help popularize the practice. By the infamous Captain's own admission, area residents boycotted him with consummate skill.[15]

II

The Land League not only mustered Irish peasants in a campaign for land reform and home rule. In so doing, it also aroused nationalist sentiments among thousands of Irish-Americans who gave it substantial financial and political support. While many New York sympathizers were Irish immigrant workers, participants in Irish-American nationalist and labor activities represented a broad segment of that city's population. Quarrels between and among various nationalist factions often prevented common agreement on goals and methods. Groups in New York and elsewhere argued over the nature and timing of social reform and Irish self-government, how funds should be channelled to Ireland, the efficacy of violence, and even which body should tender official receptions to visiting Irish dignitaries. Many workers and liberal reformers in the Gilded Age disagreed in more fundamental ways.[16]

However much they may have differed over specific labor and nationalist proposals, Irish immigrant workers, in particular, had much in common. The oppression of rack-renting landlords, the British Government, and church officials; decades of poverty; ancient communal and tribal loyalties; a way of life revolving around the seasons, marriages, and fairs; a religion intimately bound in folklore; sporadic agrarian violence — these and other aspects of peasant culture did not merely

Lyceum (New York, 1926), 30. Redpath quoted in A. D. Vinton, "The History of Boycotting" *Magazine of Western History,* V (December, 1886), 212. *The Times* (London), September 30, 1880.

[15] The proscriptions against breaking Irish peasant codes is analogous to Mafia practices in peasant Sicily. See E. J. Hobsbawm, *Primitive Rebels* (Manchester, 1959), 30-56, T. H. Corfe, "The Troubles of Captain Boycott," *History Today* (November, 1964), 758-764, and *ibid.* (December, 1964), 854-862; Vinton, 213-215; *Notes And Queries,* 6th ser., III (January 8, 1881), 33; *The Irish World And American Industrial Liberator,* October 8, 1881 (hereafter cited *The Irish World*). Boycott's letter to *The Times* (London), October 18, 1880, describes his "ostracism." See also Norman D. Palmer, *The Irish Land League Crisis* (New Haven, Conn., 1940), 195-199.

[16] I discuss this and the article's thesis in greater detail in my Ph.D. dissertation, "Studies in

linger as memories among Irish immigrants in a new land. In a segmented, heterogeneous, industrializing city like New York, this shared experience provided the framework from which Irish immigrants confronted their new world. That experience had important consequences for the growth of New York's two leading federated labor organizations, the Central Labor Union (C. L. U.) and the Knights of Labor. From 1881 to 1886, these organizations furthered solidarity among New York City workers by their collective attempts to achieve better wages and working conditions, their political activities, and their support of Ireland's struggles with the English. By promoting parades, holidays, and mass demonstrations, they provided opportunities for immigrant workers to participate in familiar patterns of protest and recreation.[17]

The C. L. U., in fact, grew out of a mass meeting at Cooper Institute on January 30, 1882, called to send greetings to Ireland, and to demonstrate labor's support of the Land League's No Rent Manifesto. Numerous expressions of American sympathy for Ireland preceded the meeting. As early as 1879, American priests and others raised thousands of dollars for the relief of a well-publicized Irish food shortage. From January 2 to March 11, 1880, Parnell and John Dillon, son of the famous Young Irelander and himself a prominent nationalist, toured the United States explaining the Land League's programs and collecting money for its activities. On the morning of Parnell's departure for home (Dillon stayed on), a Fifth Avenue Hotel conference resulted in the formation of a temporary American Land League executive committee. While participants at the meeting included delegates from Irish-American benevolent and temperance societies, Irish workers also made known their concerns. A longshoremen's committee gave Parnell $1,000 and voiced its support of his efforts to abolish landlordism. A visit by Michael Davitt in May coincided with the adoption by the Irish National Land And Industrial League of America of its constitution. Meeting in New York on May 18 and 19, and with Davitt as its Central Secretary, the Industrial League avowed its support of Parnell and the Land League, but affirmed that Ireland's industrial — and not just its agricultural — problems must be solved before all grades of workers

Irish and Irish-American Thought and Behaviour in Gilded Age New York City'' (University of Rochester, 1977). Thomas N. Brown's previously cited *Irish-American Nationalism, 1870-1890* is an excellent study, and discusses the factional disputes and much more. See especially chs. 4, and 6 through 9.

[17] Thomas N. Brown, "Nationalism And The Irish Peasant, 1800-1848," 403-411, and *passim;* Owen Dudley Edwards, "The Burden of Irish History," in Owen Dudley

would have relief.[18]

The New York receptions for Parnell and Davitt were sponsored mainly by what *The New York Times* called "well-known gentlemen." Even an enthusiastic April 12, 1881, Cooper Institute rally, arranged by the Land League to express solidarity with Ireland and contempt for the Coercion Act, was presided over by judges and other prominent New Yorkers. Many New York workers, however, wanted a meeting of their own to voice sympathy with Ireland. In October, Robert Blissert, then a journeyman tailor and member of the Excelsior Labor Club (a socialist local assembly of the Knights), tirelessly visited union meetings seeking delegates to regular Science Hall sessions to help plan labor's show of support. By late November, Blissert had sufficient backing to issue a formal "Call to The Trade And Labor Unions of The United States." The time had come, Blissert said, for workers to unite in protest against the "tyrannous and dastardly action of the British Government" in suppressing Land League members. Labor's cause was everywhere the same, "in Ireland, in the refusal of the tillers of the soil to give the fruits of their labor as rent to the so-called owners of the soil," and in Europe and America where workingmen demanded fair wages, shorter hours, "and a full recognition of the dignity and usefulness of their calling."[19]

Throughout December and January, the Science Hall committee, representing some forty-five labor organizations, raised funds and made arrangements for the January 30 meeting. Calling itself the Central Organization of United Trade and Labor Unions of New York, Brooklyn, and Jersey City, the committee issued 20,000 printed invitations to the demonstration. On the day of the Cooper Hall meeting, *Truth* editor Louis F. Post praised the committee's work, and then explained why American workers approved of the Land League. Workingmen saw in "the underlying principle of the Irish struggle" the belief "that all the forces of nature belong of right to the people in common, and the products of labor to the producer." Post perceived a theme in the workers' mass meeting: "In the Irish cause they behold their own."[20]

Edwards (ed.), *Conor Cruise O'Brien Introduces Ireland* (New York, 1969), 21-32.
18 James J. Green, "American Catholics And The Irish Land League, 1879-1882," *Catholic Historical Review*, XXXV (April, 1949), 19-42; *The New York Times*, January 3, 5, 18, and March 12, 1880; *The Irish-American*, January 17, June 5, 12, 1880.
19 *The New York Times*, December 18, 1879, and April 13, 1881; *Truth*, October 29, November 2, 11, 18, 1881; *John Swinton's Paper*, February 28, 1886; *The Irish World*, February 11, 1882, and June 28, 1884; Speek, 270.
20 *Truth*, December 12, 19, and 25, 1881, January 9, 23, 30, 1882; *John Swinton's Paper*, February 28, 1886; *The Irish World*, December 24, 1881; *The Sun*, May 2, 1886.

Despite the bitter cold, an estimated 12,000 men and women attended the January 30 meeting. Many were forced to stand outside the hall. Banners and mottoes of the various trades and labor organizations decorated the walls. The Friendly Society of Operative Masons brought their band along, and almost everyone wore badges reading "Pay No Rent for Land." Speeches by prominent labor figures carried the evening's message. Blissert called attention to Ireland's fight against land monopoly, and to the parallel struggle in America. Ireland's cause was just and moral. Blissert said the Irish "have acted as the calmest and most reasoning people in the world. They have shown science in their conduct and peace in their proceedings, leaving force and violence to the representatives of their tyrants, and instead of resorting to the sword they have simply boycotted the false and traitorous neighbor." Other speeches came from Thompson H. Murch—Maine's stonecutter Congressman, George F. McNeill—editor of the *Paterson Daily Standard*, John Swinton—still an editor of the New York *Sun*, Sergey E. Schevitch (who spoke in German), Robert Bartholome of the Piano Makers' Union, Peter J. McGuire—organizer of the 1874 Tompkins Square demonstration and International Secretary of the Brotherhood of Carpenters and Joiners of America, and William Hanson—an Englishman who justified boycotts by explaining the "divine origin" of land, and by quoting Biblical proscriptions against its abuse. *Isaiah* provided Hanson's text: "Woe unto them that join house to house, that lay field to field, till there be no place, that they may be placed alone in the midst of the earth."[21]

Because of his loyalties to Ireland, and his belief that the Land League agitation had implications for American labor, Robert Blissert was undoubtedly encouraged by the turnout. Born in England to Irish parents in 1843, Blissert considered Ireland his native country, and took pride in telling at least one audience that his grandfather was among the

---

[21] *The Irish World*, February 11, 1882; *The Irish Nation*, February 4, 1880; *The New York Times*, January 31, 1882; *Truth*, January 31, 1882. On McNeill, see George E. McNeill (ed.), *The Labor Movement. The Problem of Today* (Boston, 1887), 611-612. On Peter J. McGuire, see Robert A. Christie, *Empire in Wood: A History of The Carpenters' Union* (Ithaca, N. Y., 1956), *passim;* and Herbert G. Gutman, "The Tompkins Square 'Riot' in New York City on January 13, 1874," *Labor History*, VI (Winter, 1965), 44-70, *passim*. I have not yet seen David N. Lyon's "The World of P. J. McGuire: A Study of The American Labor Movement, 1870-1890" (unpublished Ph.D. diss. University of Minnesota, 1972). For Swinton, see Marc Ross, "John Swinton, Journalist And Reformer: The Active Years, 1857-1887" (unpublished Ph.D. diss., New York University, 1969); and Frank T. Reuter, "John Swinton's Paper," *Labor History*, I (Fall, 1960), 298-307. A brief obituary on Thompson H. Murch is in *John Swinton's Paper*, January 9, 1887.

thousands of Irish patriots shot at the Battle of New Ross in 1798. Blissert praised Parnell as a leader, but turned to Michael Davitt and Henry George for solutions to land and industrial monopoly. The energetic tailor was active in the labor movement for many years. Blacklisted in England after the 1867 London tailors' strike, he came to America in 1868, took part in the American Section of the First International, and worked to strengthen New York's Amalgamated Trades and Labor Union (A. T. L. U.). While he opened a large shop at 852 Broadway in 1883, and moved his wife and nine children to Long Island, he remained active in Irish-American and labor affairs into the 1890s.[22]

Blissert was genuinely concerned about Ireland's plight, but it is clear that he also sought to use the January 30 meeting to launch a more progressive labor federation than the A. T. L. U. His plans began to materialize at that demonstration when Charles I. Miller called on delegates to arouse interest for a new united labor organization within their organizations. In the following weeks, representatives from numerous bodies debated issues, elected temporary officers (Blissert was chairman), decided not to join the A.T.L.U., and appointed a committee to formulate a constitution. The new association was also concerned about workers who had been fired for union activities. On April 9, it resolved: "That we shall use all our influence with our fellow workers not to trade with any business man who sells the wares of employers who ostracize their workmen for trying to preserve their rights as citizens and human beings."[23]

The constitution was ready by mid-April. The first plank of the "Declaration of Principles" stated that, as "Labor creates all wealth," workers were entitled to a "full share" of profits. Seeking to identify more firmly the interests of labor with universal land reform, Blissert suggested a substitute plank at the April 23, 1882 meeting. His proposal was appropriate. A year earlier, Dr. Thomas Nulty, the Bishop of Meath, issued a pastoral letter supporting attempts to abolish landlord-

---

22 Testimony of Robert Blissert, August 30, 1883, *Report of The Committee of the Senate upon The Relations between Labor And Capital* (Washington, 1885), I, 841; *Truth,* October 14, 17, and 24, 1881; *The Irish Nation,* April 29, 1882. On Blissert's work in the 1870s, see Samuel Bernstein, *The First International in America* (New York, 1962), 141; David Montgomery, *Beyond Equality: Labor And The Radical Republicans, 1862-1872* (New York, 1967), especially 189, 327; Samuel Gompers, *Seventy Years of Life and Labor* (New York, 1925), I, 141.

23 There had been some discussion on this point at a January 8 meeting of the Central Organization of The United Trade and Labor Unions (see *Truth,* January 9, 1882); *Ibid.,* February 27, March 13, 20, 27, 1882; *The New York Times,* March 20, 1882; See also the sketches in *John Swinton's Paper,* February 28, 1886; and *The Sun,* May 2, 1886. *Truth,* April 10, 1882.

ism. In the midst of heated debates over Gladstone's 1881 Land Act, which incorporated Isaac Butt's "Three F's" (fixity of tenure, fair rents, and free sale of improvements), Nulty added credence to claims by Davitt and *The Irish World* that Gladstone's bill would only perpetuate an evil system inconsonant with Divine intent. Nulty wrote that the land of every nation

> is the *common property* of the people of that country; because its real Owner — the Creator who made it — has transferred it as a voluntary gift to them. *Terram autem dedit filiis hominum.* ('The earth he hath given to the children of men.') Now, as every individual in every country is a creature and a child of God, and all His creatures are equal in His sight, any settlement of the Land of this or any other country that would exclude the humblest man in this or that country from his share of the common inheritance, would not only be an injustice and a wrong to that man, but would moreover be an impious resistance to the benevolent intentions of his Creator.

With only minor grammatical alterations, this statement was adopted at Blissert's suggestion by the fledgling labor organization.[24]

The constitution itself reflected this Irish-American radical influence, but also incorporated socialist, trade union, and Knights of Labor principles. The "Preamble" stated the need for "concentrating the working classes for their own natural protection, education, and social advancement." Language was added to the "Declaration of Principles" underscoring the necessity of working-class emancipation by positing the inevitable conflict between labor and capital. Yet C. L. U.'s "Object" was to help constituent groups achieve tangible results. Trade and labor organizations would be aided in increasing memberships, in arbitrating disputes with employers, and in establishing strike funds. By June, 1882, from fifty-to-sixty-thousand New York workers were represented in the C. L. U. Ten thousand more from that city, Brooklyn, and Jersey City were added the next year. The total included unskilled workers and those not affiliated with local unions.[25]

Just two months after adopting Nulty's statement, the C. L. U. spon-

---

[24] *Ibid.*, April 17, 1882; Nulty quoted in *The Irish World*, April 23, 1881; *Truth*, April 24, 1882. The constitution was formally adopted on May 7, and the name Central Labor Union taken shortly thereafter. See *ibid.*, May 8, 1882; *John Swinton's Paper*, February 28, 1886.

[25] *Ibid.*, October 14, 1883; *The Irish World*, June 17, 1882; Speek, 272. Writing in *John Swinton's Paper*, on February 28, 1886, J. T. McKechnie noted that while "The principles of the Central Labor Union have remained fixed during the four years of its existence. . . . The land question and the greenback question no longer offer themselves for discussion." Henry George's campaign the following fall revealed McKechnie's observation to be premature.

sored a mass demonstration on the eve of Michael Davitt's departure
for home. An estimated 35,000 people paraded in New York on July 5,
1882. Some fifty labor organizations (at least two of them German
unions) along with twelve bands were represented. Assembled from
Fourteenth to Twentieth Streets, and from Third to Fifth Avenues, the
procession moved out with banners and flags at 8:30 P.M., and surged
down Fourteenth Street to Union Square, where Cigar Makers' International Union No. 144 entertained onlookers by circling the area amidst
a blaze of firecrackers. Speakers were interrupted all evening as parade
contingents reached the platform. One banner on the platform read
"The No Rent Battle of Ireland is The Workingmen's Battle the World
Over." Delegates from over one hundred different labor organizations
who served on arrangement committees wore badges inscribed "Hurrah
for the Nationalization of the Land, for Davitt, and United Labor."

This slogan became the evening's theme. Robert Blissert proudly reminded the gathering that "one of the first planks" in C. L. U.'s platform "was the principles of Michael Davitt, 'The Land for The
People.'" The formal testimonial, prepared by Blissert but read by
secretary Matthew Maguire, thanked Davitt and Ireland for launching
a campaign that would free workers and peasants alike. "We are thoroughly persuaded," Maguire read, "that the emancipation of labor will
never be brought about until the land . . . ceases to be monopolized by
a few and is restored to the whole people, to whom it rightfully belongs." Davitt's speech significantly tied labor unity and land reform
to the theories of Henry George. "The land war in Ireland," he declared,
"can be called a general labor movement. (Great cheering.) It is the
uprising of the labor of Ireland against the robber-system of monopoly
that has confiscated the fruits of labor." The rent imposed by that system upon Irish labor (the peasantry) was an unjust and immoral tax
that could only be abolished by destroying landlordism. Davitt said
American workers faced similar problems, and reiterated the advice
Redpath and Parnell had given to Irish peasants by urging workers
everywhere to apply moral force and not violence. Other speeches by
John Swinton and P. J. McGuire continued the attack against land
monopoly, but Father Edward McGlynn summarized the moral appeal
of all the addresses in just four words. It was entirely appropriate for a
priest to speak for Davitt's principles, he stated. At issue was the Com-
mandment " 'Thou shalt not steal.' "[26]

[26] *The Irish Nation,* July 8, 1882; *The Irish World,* July 15, 1882; *Truth,* July 6, 1882.

On September 5, 1882, the C. L. U. sponsored still another mass demonstration. The monster parade and picnic, marking the first American Labor Day holiday, was similar in appearance to Old World labor festivals. Three divisions stepped off from Broadway at 10:30 A.M., and wound their way through the city to Union Square, where Mayors Terence V. Powderly and Daniel McLaughlin joined John Swinton, Robert Blissert, Henry Appleton, and representatives from eleven states and Washington, D. C., in reviewing the procession. *The Irish World* estimated that 250,000 watched as scores of labor organizations paraded (many in trade uniforms) with their bands and banners. Wagons carried bricklayers, furniture makers, and others who displayed examples of their trades. Some signs demanded an end to convict and child labor, tenement-house cigar manufacturing, and the anti-labor sections of the Penal Code. Others urged workers to vote for labor candidates. And among the many banners calling for land nationalization, one read "No Man can Make Land, hence no Man Should Own It."[27]

From Union Square, workers marched to a reservoir at Forty-Second Street and Fifth Avenue, where they dispersed. Many at once headed with their families to Elm Park for a day-long picnic. Some 50,000 people reportedly flocked to the park throughout the day. Trades nailed their banners and shields to trees on the edges of the park and set up camp. French, German, Irish, and American flags were prominently displayed. There was singing and dancing, and at one corner of the park speeches went on for four hours. Several papers commented on the affair. *The New York Times* noted that "nearly all were well clothed, and some wore attire of fashionable cut." *Truth* praised the workers' behavior by sarcastically expressing regret "that there were not at least a few cases of drunkenness and riotous conduct to afford our contemporaries an opportunity to deliver a good sound lecture." Another opinion saw broader implications in the event. "It was a cold day for the politicians if they had anticipated any aid and comfort from the occasion," *The Irish World* summarized. The demonstration pointed "to the good time coming when envy, jealousy, and bickerings shall cease forever, and all

---

[27] At a May 18, 1882, C. L. U. "No Rent" meeting, P. J. McGuire suggested that the first Monday in September " 'should be set aside as a festive day' " for labor. The 1882 holiday, however, was held on a Tuesday. In 1883, it took place on a Wednesday. See Foner, II, 96. The debate on the holiday's founder is discussed in Jonathan Grossman, "Who Is The Father of Labor Day?," *Labor History*, XIV (Fall, 1973), 612-623. This debate has masked the holiday's significance as representing surviving strains of preindustrial work habits and customs. See Herbert G. Gutman, "Work, Culture, and Society in Industrializing America, 1815-1919," *American Historical Review*, LXXVIII (June, 1973), 560.

our industrious people stand shoulder to shoulder in the struggle with the tripled-headed monster, interest, rent, and profit."[28]

The reference to politicians was not merely rhetorical. Independent political action was first considered by the C. L. U. on July 9, during a long and bitter freighthandlers' strike (discussed in section III). On July 19, a mass meeting of strikers in Union Square adopted resolutions accusing railroads of controlling governmental bodies and political parties, and called on workers "to form a political party opposed to monopoly in all its forms' . . . ." Land monopoly was a primary campaign target, but the forty-four C. L. U.-endorsed city, state, and congressional candidates (all of them union members) did poorly.[29]

A week before the elections, two receptions were tendered Henry George upon his return from a year's service as *The Irish World*'s correspondent in Ireland. A banquet at Delmonico's, attended chiefly by prominent New Yorkers, was held on Saturday evening, October 28. The previous evening, however, workers jammed into Cooper Union for labor's greeting. A committee from fifty-four different labor unions helped with arrangements. While Robert Blissert, Louis F. Post, and P. J. McGuire praised George and endorsed his principles, John W. Franklin provided the most eloquent address of the night. A bricklayer, and labor's mayoral candidate, Franklin was moved by his own participation among such prominent men. "Imagine my feelings as an humble mechanic to be called on to convey the gratitude and esteem that his moral work has caused to glow in the heart of labor for Mr. Henry George." Franklin believed "it was something above my ambition and expectation" to be asked to welcome George home. He defended *Progress and Poverty* by concluding that "to those who flaunt in our faces the sacred rights of property I would say, When the rights of property infringe on the rights of man and cause suffering to God's creatures, let the rights of man come first, and we will consider the rights of property afterwards." George stirred the audience with an interesting story. While in Ireland, an unnamed, but according to George "a dearly beloved prelate," questioned him thoroughly about his theories and convictions regarding land. When finished, the priest said he had merely wanted to insure that George knew his subject, and told him he had long been familiar with such tenets. As George told it, the priest explained "When

---

28 For the coverage and editorials, see *Truth,* September 6, 1882; *The New York Times,* September 6, 1882; *The Irish World,* September 16, 1882.
29 *The New York Times,* July 10, 1882; *Truth,* September 19, October 6, 22, 24, and November 24, 1882.

I was a little boy, sitting with my family round the peat fire, I heard the
same truths talked over by people who could not speak a word of English. [Great cheering.] It is the Old Irish System that made the land
belong to the people [George concluded to loud cheers], the tribe, sept,
or clan; and what we are struggling for is the revival of that old national
system."[30]

In his Labor Day speech at the picnic grounds, Robert Blissert had
suggested that, because the Knights of Labor opened its ranks to all
creeds and races, the Order might contribute more toward equality and
understanding than the Church. Neither Blissert nor *The Irish World*
would be gratified by the performance of Knights leaders in New York.
Within a few years, "envy, jealousy, and bickerings" in leadership
circles made it almost impossible for Knights there to function effectively. Like the C. L. U., however, the growth and temporary success
of the Knights in New York may have had much to do with Old World
experiences. Former members of European trade unions and rural protective societies likely found in both their member unions and federated
bodies organized, communal efforts similar to those they knew in Europe. This would have been particularly applicable when local assemblies and unions drew members from neighborhoods largely inhabited
by homogeneous immigrant groups. The insistence of New York's District Assembly No. 49 — a large, dissident, radical Knights assembly
— that secrecy within the Order be maintained has not been explained
by historians in terms of immigrant backgrounds. The feud between
D. A. No. 49 leaders and the Order over secrecy has instead been viewed
as a clash between fundamentalist and reformist principles.[31]

Secrecy was introduced into the Knights by Uriah Stephens, who
borrowed ceremonial practices from the Masons, Oddfellows, and
Knights of Pithias. The Molly Maguire riots, however, discredited secret
organizations, and Catholic clergy did not countenance secret oaths.
Faced with opposition, Knights leaders moved to eliminate some secret
portions in 1878. Their efforts were consummated at the September,
1881 General Assembly meeting in Detroit, where delegates voted to
abolish oaths and other secret aspects by January 1, 1882. Henry J.
Browne's *The Catholic Church And The Knights of Labor* clearly demonstrates that Terence V. Powderly's opposition to secrecy stemmed

---

[30] *The Irish World*, November 4, 1882. The arrangements committee list is in *Truth*, October 18, 1882.
[31] *Ibid.*, September 6, 1882.

from the Church's objections and, as Powderly readily explained to others, from his desire to increase the Order's membership by making public the Knights' name and objectives. Furthermore, James P. Rodechko writes: "Realizing the great numerical strength the Irish held within the Knights, Powderly carefully adapted the organization's program to the interests of its Irish Catholic membership."[32]

But what *were* the interests of Irish Catholic Knights? If the motives of Powderly and the Church seem clear, it remains uncertain how Irish workers viewed the secrecy issue. Irish Catholic peasants who banded together in clandestine, oath-bound activities, or who supported forms of social ostracism in the village or countryside, may have perceived the Knights's secret ceremonies as codifying a similar Old World "unwritten code of laws." And the Detroit meeting did not completely eradicate secrecy. The oath was replaced by a "pledge of honor," but Knights were prohibited, upon penalty of expulsion, from revealing the Order's business and ceremonials.[33]

Many New York Knights, in fact, bitterly opposed the changes. D. A. No. 49 was not formally organized until July 1, 1882, but its eventual leaders were active as Knights in New York and in Brooklyn. In the latter, they belonged to a secret clique within the District Assembly called the Home Club. Knights in these cities had sent Theodore Cuno (a Marxist), James Connolly, and Henry Taylor to the Detroit meeting. Cuno, who was named Grand Statistician there, had warned Powderly in October that New York and Brooklyn locals were upset at the changes. In November, George K. Lloyd, a New Yorker, wrote Powderly requesting a special dispensation permitting local Knights to disregard the Assembly's actions. Powderly claimed he lacked authority to grant the request. The Home Club successfully challenged Powderly and the new rules, and maintained strict secrecy until its own demise in 1887. Its insistence on secrecy, however, was not motivated solely

---

[32] Ware, 27-28, 34-35, 93; Henry J. Browne, *The Catholic Church And The Knights of Labor* (Washington, 1949), ch. 2, *passim,* but especially 58-64; Terence V. Powderly, *Thirty Years of Labor, 1859-1889* (Columbus, Ohio, 1890), 252-257, 559-561. James P. Rodechko, "Patrick Ford And His Search for America: A Case Study of Irish-American Journalism, 1870-1913" (unpublished Ph.D. diss., University of Connecticut, 1967), 21.

[33] Powderly, 559-61; Ware, 56n; Browne, 62-64; S. M. Jelley, *The Voice of Labor* (Philadelphia, 1887), 197, 204; Carroll D. Wright, "An Historical Sketch of The Knights of Labor," *The Quarterly Journal of Economics,* I (January, 1887), 137-168. For the ceremonial aspects, see Browne, 359-362; and John R. Commons *et al., A Documentary History of American Industrial Society* (Cleveland, 1911), X, 19-31. The importance of rituals for nineteenth-century social movements is discussed in Hobsbawm, ch. IX.

by a desire to preserve the fundamentalism of Stephens. Socialists within D. A. No. 49 sought to use the issue to gain control of the Order. A series of damaging internal feuds racked both D. A. No. 49 and the C. L. U. after 1886. They are important to our understanding of the fall of the Knights, the failure of the socialists' attempt to "bore from within," and the rise to dominance of "pure and simple trade unionism," but are developments beyond the scope of this study.[34]

The meaning of the secrecy issue for Irish immigrants will remain unclear until we determine how many of them were New York Knights, from what areas of Ireland they came, and their Old World occupations. Demographic data and the corroborative testimony of Irish immigrants is also an obvious requisite to understanding how Irish workers viewed the labor boycott. Two recently-published demographic studies are invaluable aids, but only further hard work can provide the kind of data suggested above.[35]

Irish immigrant workers furnished substantial *corroborative* testimony not only by participating in demonstrations and labor affairs, but also by their nationalist activities. In June 1881, *The New York Times* claimed it was useless to criticize Parnell and other Land League officials in hope of persuading Irish immigrants to abandon their support of the League. "Patrick and Bridget have their own guides in these things," the editorial sneered. "They will flock to hear the agitators . . . and will respond to their appeals with frantic applause and with money contributions far more liberal to the Land League than just to themselves. . . . The money that has kept the Land League together has come mostly from the day laborers and servant maids of America." The *Times* was not far off the mark. In issue after issue, *The Irish World, The Irish Nation,* and the *Irish-American* listed the names and amounts contributed to the Land League. There were, indeed, sizeable contributions from city officials and others, but most were one and two dollar dona-

---

[34] Ware, 94-95, 104, 108; Browne, 65-67; and Powderly, 560-561. In July 1886, for example, a C. L. U. reorganization established ten trade sections of 207 unions in New York and the immediate vicinity. The number fell to 142 by September, due in part to a rift with the Knights over the leadership of the Labor Day parade — itself the result of divisions between socialist, trade unionist, and Knights factions within the C. L. U. *John Swinton's Paper,* February 28 and August 22, 1886; Speek, 273; Ware, 278; and Howard Quint, *The Forging of American Socialism: Origins of The Modern Movement* (Indianapolis, [1953] 1964), 37-52. D. A. No. 49's squabbles are discussed in Ware, 93-96, 103-112. But see also *The New York Times's* regular coverage of leadership disputes beginning in June 1887.

[35] Robert E. Kennedy, Jr., *The Irish: Emigration, Marriage and Fertility* (Berkeley, 1973); and Ira Rosenwaike, *Population History of New York City* (Syracuse, N. Y., 1972), especially ch. 4.

tions from those whose names appeared in print only on such occasions.[36]

The Irish-American press and *Truth* also devoted attention to Land
League branch meetings. Established throughout many wards in New
York and adjacent cities following Parnell's visit in 1880, some branches
were named after League leaders or famous Irish patriots. There was
also a Boycotting Club in the West Side's Twentieth Ward, and a Boycotting League with offices at 552 Seventh Avenue. While some branch
names reflected members' differences over goals and tactics, all raised
funds for the Land League. Meetings were held in Catholic churches,
temperance society halls, school basements, and labor union headquarters. Press accounts usually gave few details, but occasionally featured
workers' participation, ward organizational efforts, and important
speeches. On April 25, 1880, for example, the Fourth Ward branch
met in the school room of St. James Catholic Church on New Bowery
Street. The parish priest told League members that priests belonged in
the vanguard of Ireland's struggle for freedom, and asserted that "The
Irish have the right to their own land—to the ownership thereof,"
and that land reform would lead to independence. At a New York
session of the Irish National Land and Industrial League on November
28, 1880, the League's president, Dr. William B. Wallace, told delegates that the Irish were justified in using the boycott, and gave succinct
instructions on how to use it against an enemy. "Let him live in your
midst," he directed, "but let him live as if he were accursed." In May
1881, Robert Blissert reminded workers at a Brooklyn Spread The Light
Club meeting that English and Irish workers had used boycotts for a
hundred years. He specifically cited two successful nonviolent boycotts
by English brickmakers and bakers in the 1850s and 1860s. On October 24, 1881, 500 Jersey City longshoremen, "headed by a band of
music," helped pack St. Michael's Institute to hear Parnell's mother
speak and, along with others, approved a resolution supporting the No
Rent Manifesto. And *The Irish Nation,* three months later, reported
on a membership campaign conducted by New York's First Ward
branch, of which the paper's editor, John Devoy, was president. A committee told branch members at St. Peter's Church on January 4, that it
had distributed 2500 circulars to residents of the First, Second, and
Third Wards, inviting all nationalities to participate in League efforts.
The handbills criticized those American newspapers supporting the Eng-

---

36 *The New York Times,* June 24, 1881.

lish "tyrants whose power George Washington struck down," and said the Irish "have arrayed against them all the power of a great and power-ful empire . . . which has created an aristocratic and land-owning class, at the expense of the down-trodden masses. . . ."[37]

The Irish World and many Land League branches shared these senti-ments, and urged boycotts of both British goods and the hostile New York Herald. "The young colonies of America," Patrick Ford's paper wrote, "when they could get no redress or justice from George III, 'Boy-cotted' all the English manufacturers. . . . And [Americans] did feel prouder, justly prouder, to wear their own homespun robes than the finest England sent them. . . . Try this plan my friends." Especially piqued at the Herald for its criticism of Irish boycotting, The Irish World reprinted 1770 accounts of boycotting from the Boston Gazette And Country Journal to remind Herald Readers that the Irish were "simply following in the footsteps of the inhabitants of Roxbury, Middleton, Acton, and other towns of Massachusetts." The citizens of Roxbury resolved not to buy from merchants importing British goods, and to read annually the names of offenders at the March town meeting. Little-ton residents agreed that such violators "shall suffer our high displeasure and contempt." And people in Acton declared "That from this time we will have NO COMMERCIAL OR SOCIAL CONNECTION with those who at this time do refuse to contribute to the relief of this abused country, . . . [and] that we will not afford them our custom but treat them with the utmost neglect, and all those who countenance them."[38]

At national conventions in Washington in 1882, and in Philadelphia in 1883, conservatives gained control of Irish-American activities in the United States. At Philadelphia, in fact, a new organization called the Irish National League of America was formed. Established in Ire-land by Parnell in October 1882, the League aimed at securing home rule first and not land reform. Consequently, "land" was significantly omitted from its name to reflect both Parnell's moderate politics after his release from Kilmainham Prison that year as well as the influence of strict Irish-American nationalists, and of conservatives who feared

[37] The Irish World, December 4, 25, 1880, January 1, 1881 On unsuccessful efforts to incorporate Parnell Land League branches under Irish National Land League jurisdic-tion, see The Irish Nation, January 28 and March 4, 1882. In May 1883 the Parnell branches agreed to unite with the new Irish National League. See ibid., May 12, 1883; The Irish American, May 8, 1880; The Irish World, December 4, 1880, May 21, 1881 (Spread The Light Clubs helped finance distribution of The Irish World in Ireland); Truth, October 25, 1881; The Irish Nation, January 7, 1882.
[38] The Irish World, December 25, 1880; January 22, 1881. On boycotting the Herald, see The Irish World, December 18, 1880, and January 15, 1881.

that the land reform schemes of Michael Davitt, Henry George, and *The Irish World* would bring fundamental changes to America, not just to Ireland. In New York, plans to merge with Parnell's new organization began in early 1883 and were completed by July. The city's Land League Executive Council and many ward branches adopted the League's platform, but Irish immigrant workers persisted in demanding radical changes for Ireland and America. While Parnellism dominated nationalist efforts in both countries, it by no means crushed the strain of Irish-American radicalism which Henry George's theories helped nourish, and from which George's 1886 mayoral campaign derived strength.[39]

III

Many of the labor boycotts considered here appear to strengthen aspects of Norman Ware's thesis that boycotts were most successful when directed at manufacturers of products oriented toward working-class consumers. A new dimension is added to Ware's interpretation when boycotts are considered within the historical framework sketched in the previous two sections. Moreover, if, as this study suggests, the labor boycott was a pre-industrial mode of protection familiar to immigrant workers, we should expect to find the tactic used in situations requiring defense, and not solely associated with organized labor boycotts.

One notable example occurred during the summer of 1882. On June 12 and 13, 600 freighthandlers went on strike against the New York Central and Hudson River Railroad for a three-cents-per-hour increase in wages (from seventeen to twenty cents). The strike at once spread to the freight depots and sheds of all major railroads along the Hudson River in New York and Jersey City, and even included the wharves of some steamship companies. Strikers received substantial support from newspapers, merchants, municipal councils in both cities, and others who bitterly opposed railroad monopolies. Some landlords delayed or cancelled rent payments, bakers donated free bread, and sympathetic citizens contributed to strike funds. Land League branches also aided strikers with money and resolutions of encouragement. (Not all help was accepted. The freighthandlers wanted no charity, and returned

---

[39] Brown, *Irish-American Nationalism,* 124-127, 155-158; Conor Cruise O'Brien, *Parnell And His Party, 1880-1890* (Oxford, 1957), 126-133; *The Irish Nation,* April 22, 1882, January 27, February 3, April 28, May 5, May 12, 26, June 2, 9, and July 6, 1883; *Truth,* May 22, 1883.

gifts they believed stemmed from that motive.) And New York's Board
of Trade, whose members suffered financially when goods rotted or
were delayed, even asked the Attorney General and the courts (without
success) to compel railroads to meet their obligations as common carriers by settling with strikers quickly and amicably. The strike lasted
until mid-August, and involved over 3,000 workers (most of them
Irish). Unable to prevent Castle Garden recruits from taking their
places, and disheartened by the long strike and its attendant privations,
the freighthandlers conceded defeat and returned to work or sought
other jobs.[40]

Throughout the strike, workers participated in numerous parades
and demonstrations. On one occasion, 1,000 New York workers,
dressed "in their Sunday clothes," reciprocated a gesture made the previous day by ferrying across the Hudson in order to join their Jersey
City counterparts at a Hamilton Park rally. They were accompanied by
some 200 Italian former "scabs." The next day, June 23, New York
strikers, wearing blue- and white-striped blouses, paraded along the
waterfront from the Bowery to Debrosses Street and back. Led by
five policemen and "a brass band and a man carrying a broom," the
men were joined by "hundreds" of other handlers and longshoremen
as they marched up West Street. A simple banner proclaimed in black
letters: "We are Free Men. We are Looking for Our Rights, and Will
Have Them." A police inspector as well as *The New York Times*
commended the 3,000 demonstrators for being orderly and sober. On
June 30, a rain-soaked crowd moved from Jersey City's Scottish-Amer-
ican Athletic Club grounds to St. Michael's Institute to hear John Swinton, Freight Handlers' Union Executive Committee president Jeremiah
Murphy, and others denounce railroad monopolies and urge workers
to persist in their struggle. Described by *The New York Times* as "the
most imposing labor demonstration ever known in that place," the
gathering adopted a resolution demanding government ownership of
railroads "as an absolute necessity for the preservation of the Republic." And at New York's St. Alphonsus Church, just a block from the
giant St. John's freight house, the Fifth Ward Land League branch
sponsored a farewell reception for Michael Davitt on July 11. Davitt
told strikers and others he would continue to advocate land reform, and
"that when landlordism is crushed" it would then be appropriate "to

---

[40] *The New York Times,* June 15, 18, 20-30, July 1, 7, 14, 15, 16, 18, 19, 20, 26, 29,
1882; "The Freight-Handlers' Strike," *Harper's Weekly,* XXVI (July 8, 1882), 427,
(July 22, 1882), 451; *Truth* June 21, 22, 24, July 14, 16, August 1-10, 1882.

discuss whether the nationalization of the land or peasant proprietary is the best for Ireland (applause)."[41]

At two other rallies, Robert Blissert continued the attack against railroad monopoly in ways particularly understandable to Irish laborers. At New York's Temperance Hall on July 3, freight-handlers and long-shoremen heard Blissert accuse politicians of selling out to English money. "English power," he said, "is as much felt in the City as in Ireland. English money owns the Erie, which has been grinding you down." Both political parties financed campaigns with "English gold," and workers were then "sold to the capitalist who controls the politician." On July 7, Blissert spoke to strikers from both cities at St. Michael's Institute, and followed Jeremiah Murphy and John Swinton, who congratulated workers on their peaceful conduct by comparing their behavior to the bloody 1877 strikes. *The Irish World* paraphrased Blissert's speech: "The cause of all your troubles is the private ownership of land . . . From the land comes everything. It is the great storehouse from which all things are drawn, while a few men are allowed to own it, they own you. . . . Until the Land Question is settled there is no hope. (Applause.)" Blissert went on to praise Henry George, to great approval, and closed by urging workers to "build up a true Republic where all men shall enjoy all the rights and benefits that a merciful God intended for us. (Cheers.)"[42]

Jersey City strike leaders were very familiar with the workers they led and with Irish customs. Jeremiah Murphy, who was elected president of the combined New York and Jersey City Union on June 28, was born near Cork in 1845. He worked in various factories in Ireland and Sourth Wales, was appointed a guard at Spike Island prison in Cork Harbor in 1869, and left for America in 1872 when his criticism of British policies led to troubles with government officials. A freight-handler and checker in Jersey City for ten years, Murphy was also active in nationalist affairs, and was given the honor of opening the July 5 Union Square reception for Davitt. Two other strike leaders were also natives of Cork. John R. McNamara was born in 1848, arrived in New York in 1864, and worked at several jobs before spending long years hauling freight on the docks. P. J. O'Sullivan, no newcomer to radical politics, was educated for the priesthood in France, and completed his English studies at Dundalk College. He returned to Cork to

41 *The New York Times*, June 22, 23, 24, July 1, 12, 1882; *The Irish Nation*, July 15, 1882.
42 *The New York Times*, July 4, 1882; *The Irish World*, July 15, 1882 (ellipses mine).

participate in the 1867 Fenian rising, drove a French Army ambulance in 1870, and was at the barricades in Paris a year later. He had been in America only two years when the strike erupted.[43]

Because the strike issue involved only transporters of goods, and not manufacturers, the freighthandlers had few reasons to organize economic sanctions against merchants. As previously noted, many businessmen openly supported the strike. The C. L. U. did ask member unions to boycott those merchants and manufacturers unwilling to contribute to strike funds, but it is unlikely that such action was necessary. Strikers were more concerned about other immigrants who took their jobs. On July 5, Murphy issued an "appeal to men of all nationalities" for support. "The raw immigrants from European cities are brought here by padrones and others," Murphy wrote, "and these poor creatures, unacquainted with our language or customs, are taken off the ships and put to work without being allowed to converse with anybody who would be likely to explain the real situation of affairs. We do not blame them. We pity them."[44]

While some fights between strikers and "scabs" occurred, the freighthandlers focused their efforts on preventing their own members from returning to work and breaking the strike. Just a day after his appeal was published, Murphy told a meeting of the union's Executive Council that "five or six" Jersey City tally men took back their old jobs,

> and we propose to boycott them. We shall have circulars containing their names printed and distributed over the city, and sent home to Ireland, too. We will march 1,000 men in front of their houses and let people know who the boycotted men are. We will not speak to them on the street, and you will see that this system of boycotting will go much further than using personal violence. We shall not harm them; they needn't fear that.

By July 8, a boycotting committee was organized, and the list of men to be ostracized expanded to eighty-three. The blacklist, printed in English and Italian, was to have been given to worshipers as they left church on Sunday, July 9, but Murphy ordered a delay. On July 15, he explained his action to strikers, and "to great applause," said the list would be distributed the next day. "They had waited patiently for these men to join them," *Truth* paraphrased Murphy's remarks, "but they preferred to be 'scabs,' and now they would treat them as such, and publish the list, and every man upon it should be shunned

[43] *Truth*, July 6, 9, 1882; *The New York Times*, June 29, July 6, 1882.
[44] *The New York Times*, July 3, 6, 1882.

like a leper." After yet another delay, the list was finally distributed in Catholic churches. While its effect is unknown, it is significant that the threat of social ostracism was made at all.[45]

The tactic may also have been used by others who worked on the docks. In March, 1881, a *Truth* reporter interviewed a New York longshoreman for its story, "How 'Longshoremen Live". Michael Ready said that for more than twenty years he had never passed "the limits of Old or Coenties Slips to look for a job." Longshoremen did not seek out work, he explained, but were hired by stevedores who walked along the waterfront. "There is an unwritten law of custom among the fraternity that was, with rare exceptions, adherred to," went Ready's account: "Should a 'longshoreman transgress, he would be tabooed and all possible obstacles thrown in his way in the future by the rest." [46]

Social ostracism was most successful in local neighborhoods or small communities. It frequently accompanied economic sanctions, and helped stimulate consumer consciousness. In April 1881, many Brooklyn unions boycotted baker John H. Schultz, who fired employees for joining a union. Twenty grocers refused to sell his bread, and 200 women visited his customers successfully demanding compliance with the boycott. In South Norwalk, Connecticut, from 1,200 to 1,500 hatters struck against four hat manufacturers for cutting wages and attempting to crush unions. A boycott was declared by L. A. No. 3356. "Our situation is becoming intolerable, and the whole community is influenced against us," a factory official reported in December, 1884. "We tried to board out [scabs] . . . and not a boarding house would recluse them. Even the restaurant keeper at the depot refused to supply them with food." And the watchman's wife, who fed the strike-breakers at the factory, was warned that she would be unable to buy anything in town. An appeal for wider support for the boycott came from John G. Caville, whose D. A. No. 49 had jurisdiction over L. A. No. 3356. "Now brothers, certainly we are not all hat makers," he wrote the Knights' *Journal of United Labor*, "but are not we the ones who wear hats?" At least three manufacturers agreed to union terms in May, and asked the C. L. U. to remove the boycott.[47]

---

45 *Ibid.*, June 29, July 7, 8, 12, 13, 27, 1882; *Truth,* July 9, 10, 12, 16, 17, 1882.
46 *Ibid.*, March 7, 1881.
47 *Journal of United Labor,* April 15, 1881, January 10, 1885; factory official quoted from the New York *World* in *John Swinton's Paper,* December 21, 1884; *The Irish World,* May 30, 1885.

In March 1885, hatters in Orange, New Jersey, boycotted the "foul" Berg hat factory. Curious about the effects, John Swinton journeyed to Orange, and later described the boycott as "the most striking exhibition of the power of the boycott yet seen in this country." Of the 2,000 workers employed in the town's twenty hat factories, nearly 100 worked for Berg. When some women hatters at Berg's decided to form a benevolent society, they were fired. Fifty-five journeymen struck in support. The Knights and trade unionists threatened a nation-wide boycott, but the most devastating blows came from secondary boycotts and social ostracism within the town itself. Swinton's account of a "foul" hatter's tale of woe demonstrates how well workers practiced social ostracism:

> He had gone into a barber's shop to get shaved, but the barber cried out 'foul' and refused to lather his face. He went to a saloon to get a glass of beer, but the beer-seller refused to draw it for him. His baker had refused him a loaf of bread, and his grocer a pound of sugar. His acquaintances refused to speak to him in the street, and when he went to Church, nobody else would sit in his pew.[48]

Meanwhile, some 3000 winders, setters, and weavers employed at Alexander Smith's Sons carpet mills in Yonkers carried their grievances to the community. A strike began on February 20 when employers refused to reinstate a ten per-cent wage reduction (imposed the previous December), to pay wages already due, and to rehire at least twenty women who were fired for joining a union. Most of the workers were young women, and seem to have been angrier at factory discipline than wage and hiring issues. In late March, the strikers' executive committee issued a statement including the principal demands, and a lengthy discussion of company fines for actions which the women thought harmless. The committee's complaints were specific:

> If a girl is caught looking out of a window her loom is stopped, and she is sent to the boss to explain, and very often she is docked for it. If a girl is discharged from any one department she cannot get employment in any other without first begging of her former boss permission to go to work, and they are not allowed to talk to one another during working hours, *or at noon time,* under penalty of being discharged. . . . They are not allowed to eat dinner together; even two sisters working in two different departments are not allowed to eat their meals together in the factory. . . .[49]

---

[48] *John Swinton's Paper,* April 5, 1885.
[49] *The New York Times,* February 22, 1885; *The Irish World,* March 7, April 4, 1885 (ellipses mine).

Unable to hire enough replacements, the company closed down for a few weeks in April and May. When the mills reopened, few strikers accepted the Smith's offer to rehire all but those who began the walkout on February 20. The company did find from 300 to 400 girls who would work but the women strikers, like the freight-handlers, concentrated on keeping old hands from returning. Swinton reported that they sometimes used "a father or mother, sister, brother or lover to help them. They never say that a man or store is *boycotted* —that is 'un-American' and they don't believe in it—but some tradesmen could tell a wonderful tale and the quiet 'ostracism' (that's an old word) will result in displacing 'capital' " in Yonkers.[50]

While Orange, South Norwalk, and Yonkers were relatively small communities, a boycott against luxuries and necessities intended strictly for working-class consumption could be effective even in a large city like New York. In March 1885, for example, the C. L. U. boycotted Peter Doegler's beer after he fired all union members. By September, over 300 saloons refused to carry it. Doegler came to terms in early October, and required all employees to join the Journeymen Brewers' Union. And on April 25, Williamsburgh shoe manufacturers Brennan and White discharged all women employees belonging to the shoemakers' union. When male workers walked out in disgust, "scabs" were hired, given loaded revolvers, and told they could expect violence. None occurred. Brennan and White had the women blacklisted in other Williamsburgh shoe factories, and sought female convicts from the Kings County Prison as replacements. The strikers issued a statement praising convicts who refused to work, and condemning Brennan, a former Crispin himself, for forgetting the importance and power of unions. "This power recognizes and guards the rights of capital as well as those of labor," the women reminded. "It has made known our sisters in Yonkers, in South Norwalk and in Philadelphia. We will live." A boycott, declared by the New York Protective Association (controlled by D. A. No. 49) and Brooklyn's Central Labor Union, was considerably successful. Shoe lasterer John Flynn told the State Bureau of Labor Statistics how it was conducted in local neighborhoods. He noted that the company "made a very cheap shoe."

---

50 *Ibid.*, May 23, 30, June 6, 1885; *John Swinton's Paper*, May 24, 1885. Three women, arrested for picketing the mills, became heroines. The C. L. U. and the Excelsior Labor Club honored Ellen Tracy, Lizzie Wilson, and Mary Carey at Irving Hall in late May. Each received a silver "Medal of Honor," inscribed "In Honor of Her Arrest As A Picket in The Yonkers Strike, May 18, 1885." *Ibid.*, June 7, 1885.

Committees "go right into our neighborhood, where we live and tell our mothers and sisters; we even do it ourselves; I have sent my sister to one, my brother to one, and my father to others."[51]

Boycotts against employers were often systematically organized by the C. L. U. and the Knights. At a January 14, 1883, C. L. U. meeting, in fact, secretary Matthew Maguire summarized the union's successes and failures during its first year, and urged that in the future workers wage boycotts instead of costly strikes. An important test of the effectiveness of organized boycotting arose the following December. Typographical Union No. 6—New York's English-speaking printers—voted to boycott Whitelaw Reid's *Tribune* when Reid's foreman broke a recent agreement without warning, called upon fifteen plainclothesmen to clear the paper's office of union printers and, with Reid's approval, refused to hire any more union typos. With C. L. U.'s aid, a printers' boycotting committee sent circulars to *Tribune* advertisers threatening to boycott the paper's customers, sought the support of other unions, and published a paper, *The Boycotter,* to state union grievances and publicize the boycott. From 1883 to 1892, the printers fought "outlaw" Reid on every front. Delegates were sent to state and national Republican conventions to urge the repudiation of the *Tribune* as the GOP's chief organ, but to little avail. Neither were the typos successful in substantially reducing *Tribune* advertising and subscriptions. Despite widespread labor support for the boycott, the *Tribune*'s national circulation hindered the union's chances for success. People unsympathetic to labor also read the "rat" sheet, and the paper held out until 1892, when the union finally won its demands. It won then only because Reid was a possible (and eventual) Republican nominee for Vice-President and had to rid himself and his party of the embarrassment that the printers had caused.[52]

Unlike the *Tribune,* the New York *Herold, Volkszeitung,* and *Sunday Review* were read almost solely by German workers. A boycott of these papers in December, 1885, by German Typographical Union No. 7 (with the C. L. U.'s help) lasted only a few weeks. Owners admitted that over 150 advertisements had been dropped, that they approached

---

[51] *Progress,* March 26, 1885; *John Swinton's Paper,* June 5, September 13, October 11, 1885; *Journal of United Labor,* June 10, 1885; testimony of John Flynn, in *Third Annual Report,* 140.

[52] *The Irish Nation,* January 20, 1883. The best published accounts are in George A. Stevens, 384-392; and Harry W. Baehr, Jr., *The New York Tribune Since The Civil War* (New York, 1936), 182-192.

bankruptcy, and hence conceded to demands for Union recognition.[53]

As the German printers' boycott suggests, the Irish were not the lone immigrant group conducting boycotts. German and Bohemian immigrants, in particular, faced problems similar to those confronting the Irish, and responded to them in similar ways. And there is much in their Old World histories which demonstrates that protective tactics like the boycott were integral to their cultures.[54]

In New York, thousands of German and Bohemian immigrants were employed as cigarmakers. A Cigar Makers' Progressive Union (C. M. P. U.) boycott of Straiton and Storm cigars arose from changes in manufacturing techniques, and ideological differences between the C. M. P. U. and Adolph Strasser's Cigar Makers' International Union (C. M. I. U.). However complicated its origin, the boycott was clearly protective in nature. Between 1867 and 1875, the introduction of the cigar mold splintered the traditional process of cigarmaking by enabling employers to hire unskilled workers as "filler breakers," or molders. An affront to the craft pride of older cigarmakers, the mold also forced German and Bohemian immigrants into large factories and tenement houses where they raced with the clock under a wage system based upon piecework.[55]

When Adolf Strasser became president of the C. M. I. U. in 1877, the Union lacked funds, its membership had declined to just 1,016, and the mold was being even more widely used in factories. By September 1881, the Union's membership had increased, and Strasser urged political action to achieve legislative reforms. Socialists within New York's C. M. I. U. Local No. 144, of which Samuel Gompers was president, accused Strasser of cooperating with *bourgeois* politicians. This split widened in that month's elections when Progressives defeated

---

53 *John Swinton's Paper*, December 20, 1885, January 3, 1886; *The Irish World*, January 9, 1886.
54 See, for example, Theodore S. Hamerow, *Restoration, Revolution, Reaction: Economics And Politics in Germany, 1815-1871* (Princeton, 1958), especially chs. 2, 3, 5, 6, 8 and 9; and the same author's *The Social Foundations of German Unification, 1858-1871: Struggles And Accomplishments* (Princeton, 1972), 205-211, 354-359; P. H. Noyes, *Organization And Revolution: Working-Class Associations in The German Revolutions of 1848-1849* (Princeton, 1966). For relevant Old World Bohemian background, see Jaroslav Purs, "The Situation of The Working Classes in The Czech Lands in The Phase of The Expansion And Completion of The Industrial Revolution (1849-1873)," *Historica*, VI (1963), 145-237; Stanley Pech, "Passive Resistance of The Czechs, 1863-1879," *The Slavonic And East European Review*, XXXVI (June, 1958), 434-452; and Pech's book, *The Czech Revolution of 1848* (Chapel Hill, N. C., 1969), especially 275-290.
55 Ware, 260; *John Swinton's Paper*, January 24, 1886; H. M. Gitelman, "Adolph Strasser And The Origins of Pure And Simple Unionism," *Labor History*, VI (Winter, 1965), 79.

Gompers' candidacy for re-election. Backed by Strasser, Gompers refused to abide by the election mandate, and the Progressives left the Internationals, gaining support from New York rollers, bunchers, packers, and some tenement-house workers.[56]

The C. M. P. U., composed chiefly of recently-arrived German and Bohemian immigrants, was formally organized on July 17, 1882, and held its first convention on May 13, 1883, in New York City. The Union's first constitution made clear Progressive loyalty to principles of the Socialist Labor Party, which had backed the Progressive bolt. Its organ, *Progress* (published in German, Bohemian, and English), incorporated those principles in attacking the capitalist wage system. "Piecework among other things," the journal wrote, "has a tendency to hasten the pauperization of the masses; cigarmakers before all others are threatened by this evil." A worker in a capitalist system "becomes apathetic, despondent and gradually lessens his claim upon a life of comfort and ease; step by step he renounces his rights upon the means of existence, he reduces his time of leisure and relaxation by working more to gain higher wages which have been reduced. . . ."[57]

From July to December 1883, Progressives fought against Strasser's efforts to crush its budding organization. By early 1884, tenement-house cigar manufacturers were pressing the courts to repeal a March 1883, State law prohibiting production of cigars in their establishments. Pending judicial review, the law was being widely evaded in New York City. As a precaution, however, over 1,200 cigarmakers and their families left tenement houses to form new settlements on Long Island, where they made cigars at lower rates than most factories in New York. These conditions, together with a recession, spurred some employers to cut wages on certain kinds of cigars. The C. M. P. U. had struck against three such companies for imposing reductions. On February 11, George Storm announced a "regulation" of wages on twenty-six kinds of work in his large factory on East Twenty-Seventh Street, resulting in reductions of up to twenty cents on rolling, and up to thirty cents on bunching. Storm claimed the "regulations" resulted from the

[56] Strasser was active for a time in the American Section of the First International. After the Tompkins Square riot, he and P. J. McGuire unsuccessfully tried to reunify their own Social Democratic Workingmen's Party with the American Section. (Gitelman, 74-79; McNeill, 590-591); Ware, 263-265; McNeill, 585-595; Gompers, 106-263, *passim.;* Bernard Mandell, *Samuel Gompers: A Biography* (Yellow Springs, Ohio, 1963), 20-42.

[57] The bolt from the C. M. I. U. almost crushed Union No. 144. Its membership fell from 5,000 in 1881, to from 500 to 600 in June, 1883. Progressives boasted nearly 6,000 members. *Progress,* February 20, May 1, 29, June 23, 1883, August, 1882.

revival of tenement-house work, and were to be accompanied by increases in rates from five to fifteen cents on five different kinds of jobs.[58]

Progressives charged Storm with bypassing an Arbitration Board established in the company following an 1877 strike. Concerned that they might not be able to control the board (composed of union and employer representatives), Straiton and Storm attempted to amend the 1877 agreement so as to enable them to dissolve the board at their discretion. When workers balked at this maneuver, the firm put its proposals to a vote, excluded dissidents from the polls, and fired the board president reputedly for not supporting the "regulations." Storm claimed acceptance of his scale "by an overwhelming majority"; Progressive shop members claimed overwhelming fraud, and some 500 union and 600 non-union men and women voted to strike. A boycott against the "Owl" firm was declared when "scabs" were hired, most of whom were supplied by Local No. 144. The C. L. U. sanctioned the boycott on March 9, when it learned that some old hands—non-Progressives—had asked to be rehired, and that Internationals had refused to call out its members in sympathy. D. A. No. 49 also declared a boycott, as did the Knights's General Executive Board, upon being told that Knights were being discharged by the company and replaced by "scabs." When that board, friendly to the C. M. I. U., learned the "scabs" were Internationals, it quickly rescinded the boycott order; D. A. No. 49 did not.[59]

Before March ended, Straiton and Storm claimed the strike had been settled. The firm now employed 1047 workers, and the only strike signs were pickets and policemen in front of the building. Progressives repeatedly charged, however, that police and non-strikers harassed pickets by assaulting and arresting them, that only twenty-seven men had returned to work, and that the boycott was effective. In May, the C. M. P. U. finally acknowledged defeat, blamed the Internationals for their failure, and removed the boycott from the official "Do Not Buy" list. The C. L. U. and D. A. No. 49 continued to boycott until January,

---

58 In July, Strasser and Union No. 144 cooperated with the United Cigarmanufacturers' Association in a lockout of 8,000 cigarmakers—almost all of them Progressives—by supplying strikebreakers and otherwise hindering Progressive efforts to organize factories. Strasser made other atttempts to destroy the Union in the fall (*ibid.*, August 1, 24, September 28, December 22, 1883; Ware, 266-267); Gompers, 194-197; *John Swinton's Paper*, February 3, 10, 1884. In 1884, the C. M. P. U. investigated cigarmakers' conditions in New York City. Its findings, *Die Lage der Cigarrenmacher* (New York, 1885), contain valuable sattistical information. *Progress*, February 22, 1884.

59 On the arbitration board, see *The New York Times*, December 9, 1878. *Progress*, February 22, 1884; testimony of George Storm, in *Third Annual Report*, 135; Ware, 269-270; *The Irish World*, March 15, 1884.

1886. Unable to prevent the Internationals from destroying their union, Progressives came to see reunification as the only means to mount a serious attack against capital. They were absorbed by D. A. No. 49 as Local Assembly No. 2814 in March, and rejoined the Internationals in September.[60]

IV

Throughout the strike and boycott, newspapers reported no acts of violence by Progressives. Immigrants soon learned, however, that boycotts were regarded by "respectable" citizens as violently intimidating and un-American. The first warnings came in early fall, 1885. A Jefferson City, Missouri, grand jury was investigating a recent railroad strike and boycott in the area. "Boycotting May Be Illegal," Swinton's headline read. The judge's charge to the jury indicated that more was involved than a question of the boycott's legality. "A system and name foreign to our institutions and language, known in Ireland as *boycotting*," the judge said, "is sought to be introduced among us as a means of compelling concessions in matters of conflicting interests." Combinations which tried to further the interests of their members were lawful. "But if the object of the combination is, or embraces the necessary effects of which is interfering with others' rights, the combination becomes a conspiracy, and may be dealt with as such."[61]

The exact meaning of "conspiracy" was defined in New York City courts in 1886, when roughly one hundred members of labor organizations were indicted on that and related charges in connection with strikes and boycotts. Only a few of these cases can be examined here. Understandably, bakers were among those waging the most numerous boycotts. "The baker's trade," the Bureau of Labor Statistics commented in 1886, "is one in which the unreasonably long hours, the poor pay and great privation have justified the men's attempts to better their condition." These conditions were the subjects of two letters written to *John Swinton's Paper* by New York baker Michael McGrath. The city's bakers, McGrath wrote in December 1883, worked up to

---

[60] *Ibid.,* March 15, 29, 1884; *John Swinton's Paper,* April 4, 27, May 11, 25, 1884; *Progress,* March 25, April 25, May 27, 1884. Straiton and Storm complained to Strasser that their cigars were still being boycotted in other Eastern states as late as November, 1885, and ordered 2,500 cigarmakers out of the factory until the boycott was completely removed (New York *Tribune,* November 15, 1885; *John Swinton's Paper,* November 22, 1885; *Progress,* November 28, 1885; *The Irish World,* January 2, 1886). For more complete details of the situation and its outcome, see *Progress,* November 18, and December 26, 1885; *The Irish World,* January 9, 1886; *Fourth Annual Report,* 527-539; Ware, 271-277.

[61] *John Swinton's Paper,* September 13, 1885.

sixteen hours a day. "Our trade is the worst trade in New York," he complained. Some journeymen bakers made as little as eight dollars a week under horrible conditions, while employers made heavy profits. McGrath described a tragic situation eight months later. Four German bakers had committed suicide, the causes of which McGrath attributed to degrading working and living conditions common to recently-arrived German immigrants. German employers could hire a baker from Castle Garden for a dollar a week. On such inadequate wages, he explained, the men were forced to live in the bakery, where leakage, poor sewerage, and gasses and steam from ovens made life unbearable. "These men have to work on an average of sixteen hours per day down in those poisonness [sic] cellars breathing that foul air, and it is nothing unusual to look around our beds and see the rats running about making fun as it were of our miserable surroundings." "Is it any wonder," he concluded, "they commit suicide?"[62]

The large number of neighborhood bakeries made union shops essential if bakers were to improve these conditions. The German Bakers' Union No. 1, an affiliate of the National Bakers' Union, adopted a policy limiting a day's work to twelve hours on weekdays, and fourteen on Saturdays. Walking delegates were instructed to investigate bakery working conditions and to determine if shops were unionized. When, on two occasions in early April 1886, a union committee failed to receive assurances from Mrs. Esther A. Gray that her four employees would be compelled to join the union and that she would maintain union conditions in her Hudson Street bakery, a boycott of her goods was declared. Mrs. Gray's bakery (the union claimed her husband, a plumber, owned it) was located in the city's West Side Ninth Ward. The Ward contained many Irish and German immigrants, and some native-born Americans. Picketing began on Monday, April 5. Throughout the week, *The New York Times* reported, "drunken and half-drunken men" distributed handbills, and insulted passersby. Union

---

[62] Between November 1, 1885, and October 31, 1886, 165 boycotts were reported in New York State. The most numerous were declared by cigarmakers (36), furniture workers (19), and bakers (15). The majority of boycotts were called to achieve a reduction in hours and an increase in wages (or against a decrease), and to protest employment of non-union men. It is impossible to determine from the Bureau's reports how many boycotts occurred in New York City, the ethnic distribution in various trades or, with some exceptions, the names of those against whom boycotts were issued. The Bureau asked such questions, but did not print results, *Ibid.,* 738-743. The original questionnaires are no longer extant (*Fourth Annual Report,* 738-744). See also the descriptions of wages and working conditions in the Bakers' Journeymen Union of New York, Brooklyn, and vicinity, *Die Sklaven der Backstube* New York, 1885). *John Swinton's Paper,* December 30, 1883; August 31, 1884.

members followed the bakery wagon on its rounds, made a list of her customers, and urged them to stop buying her goods. Neighborhood groceries refused to sell her bread. On Saturday, a policeman was stationed in front of her shop to prevent pickets from distributing handbills. Despite union efforts, Mrs. Gray maintained that her trade had increased, and that only "the very poorest class of trade" complied with the boycott. "I am doing fully as well, if not better than before these men came around here with their circulars," she reportedly told the *Tribune,* "and I do not need any other aid than the support and sympathy of people who believe that this is a free country."[63]

The "support and sympathy" came chiefly from the city's businessmen, and was due to the publicity given Mrs. Gray by the *Times, Tribune, Post,* and *Sun.* During the first two weeks of the boycott, money poured into the paper's offices, with instructions to buy her goods and donate them to charities. One contribution came from Charles Crocker, millionaire president of the Southern Pacific Railroad, who sent $50 and said he hoped she would "be sustained through this tyrannical attempt to dictate to you on the conduct of your business." And Mrs. Susan H. Wendell, of Hastings-on-Hudson, congratulated the new heroine for "especially upholding the rights of Americans, now sorely trampled upon and dragged through the mire" by hordes of "lawless and unprincipled men." Visitors to the city flocked to the famous Hudson Street bakery. Men and women from fashionable neighborhoods used the boycott as an excuse for a Saturday outing, and journeyed to Gray's shop where they bought pastries and gave them to workers' children in full view of the pickets. "The whole neighborhood, which is largely American," the *Times* chided, "backs her up against the ignorant Germans, who are unable to speak German intelligently." The paper did its best to arouse public indignation, but even *The Sun* had to agree with an on-duty policeman that the pickets were "sober," "orderly," and "decent."[64]

The unions next attempted to extend the boycott. On April 14, the executive committee of New York's seven bakers' unions agreed to

[63] *The Irish World,* February 6, 1886; *The Sun,* April 10, 11, 13, 1886. Conrad Stoeckler, a member of the boycotting committee, reported Mrs. Gray's men worked from seventeen to nineteen hours a day. (*Fourth Annual Report,* 749-749). *The New York Times,* April 9, 13, 19, 1886; *New York Tribune,* April 11, 14, 1886. For ward locations, see Kate Holladay Claghorn, "The Foreign Immigrant in New York City," *Reports of The Industrial Commission on Immigration* . . . ., 57 Cong., 1st sess., XV (1900), 470, and map 607A facing 470.
[64] *The New York Times,* April 11-18, 1886; *New York Tribune,* April 11, 13, 14, 1886; *John Swinton's Paper,* April 25, 1886; *The Sun,* April 11, 1886.

continue the boycott, discussed ways of cutting off Gray's flour supply, but took no action regarding a suggestion that her husband's plumbing shop be boycotted. The *Tribune* and the *Times* had had enough. The former saw the issue as one "not between capital and labor at all, but between four bakers who want to be free and other bakers who want to make them slaves." The latter organ called upon Americans to determine "whether this savage and un-American mode of warfare" was lawful. "The boycott is a foreign institution," the paper declared. "It is one of alien origin, and is set up here by persons who have not the faintest conception of what American citizenship is."[65]

The police could no longer withstand this sort of public pressure. On April 14, Jacob Raisel, Louis Schlontz, Charles Schuman, and Adam Flapnie were arrested on charges of disorderly conduct while picketing the bakery. Arraigned at the Jefferson Market police station before Justice Duffy, they were scolded, fined $12 each, and released. Later that Wednesday, four more were arrested and taken to the Charles Street station where they sang German songs for four hours while awaiting bail. Despite the arrests, Ernest Schmidt continued distributing handbills the next day. He and five others were quickly arrested. That same day, the Grays met with the District Attorney, Police Captain Copeland, and the Grand Jury to work out plans for indictments. Thirteen indictments were handed down on Friday; arrests were made early the next week. Based upon sections 168 and 553 of the Penal Code, the indictments were the first rendered against New York City boycotters. The bakers were charged with conspiring to interfere with Mrs. Gray's business, and with intimidating her and her customers. All were released on bail by Wednesday.[66]

While Mrs. Gray was being made a heroine by the city's respectable press, other important boycotts were also condemned. The boycott of George Theiss's Alhambra Saloon (more politely known as a "beer

65 Mrs. Gray's regular dealer complied with the boycott, and her new source of supply remained a mystery (*The New York Times*, April 15, 1886). *Ibid.*, April 13, 16, 1886; *New York Tribune*, April 14, 1886. For other similar views, many of which saw the boycott as ostracizing people from society, see "The Boycott," *Harper's Weekly*, XXX (April 24, 1886), 258; "The Lesson of The Day," *ibid.* (May 8, 1886), 290; "Two Kinds of Boycotting," *The Century*, n.s., X (June, 1886), 320-322; William Graham Sumner, "Industrial War," *The Forum*, II (September, 1886), 1-8; Sherman D. Thacher, "Boycotting," *New Englander And Yale Review*, n.s., IX (December, 1886), 1038-1042; and A. Lawrence Lowell, "Irish Agitation in America," *The Forum*, IV (September, 1887), 397-407.
66 One of the hand bills read, "Boycott the Cop in No. 12," a reference to John L. Van Wart, who lived at 12 Grove Street. On Wednesday, tyrant Van Wart had arrested some boys for playing baseball in the street (*The Sun*, April 15, 16, 1886). *The New York Times*, April 21, 1886; *The Irish World*, April 24, 1886.

garden" or "concert hall") grew out of a feud between Knights affiliates and a musicians' union. The Musical Mutual Protective Union (M. M. P. U.) was an open trade union of musicians. D. A. No. 49 had successfully tried to gain a foothold in the union, but was unable to persuade about 150 dissident musicians to join a new union, called the Carl Sahm Club. This more progressive, secret organization became a local assembly of D. A. No. 49, and was also a member of the C. L. U. It claimed that the M. M. P. U. blatantly disregarded the union scale. When two members of the Carl Sahm Club reported to their officers that Albert Eschert, a member of the M. M. P. U. and leader of Theiss's orchestra, violated the wage scale, a delegation was sent to Theiss on March 6 to demand that only Club members be employed, and that Theiss pay appropriate wages. Theiss maintained that he paid his men union wages, that they had never complained, and refused the demands. A boycott was then declared by the Carl Sahm Club, the bartenders' and waiters' union, and was sanctioned by the C. L. U.[67]

Between 75 and 150 pickets paraded in front of the saloon during the following two weeks. A few were arrested, but released. C. L. U. committees told Theiss's suppliers they would be boycotted unless they cut off his business. One dealer, George Ehret, had suffered the effects of a C. L. U. boycott in December 1884, for allegedly hiring strikebreakers during a strike. Faced witth another boycott, Ehret, who held a mortgage on Theiss's saloon, arranged a conference of C. L. U. officials and Theiss at his brewery on March 23. The C. L. U. committee consisted of waiters Max Dannhauser, Paul Wilzig, and Adolph Rosenberg; musician Hans Holdorf; bartender Michael Stroh; Archibald O'Leary of the Knights; and Charles Beadles of the C. L. U. The eight-hour meeting, which Ehret also attended, resulted in victory for the unions. Theiss signed an agreement promising to employ only union members and to pay union wages. But the conference also proved to be a blunder. Over Theiss's protests, the C. L. U. refused to lift the boycott until he paid $1,000 for boycotting expenses. Reluctantly, Theiss paid. He and Eschert next signed complaints against the first C. L. U. committee which visited Theiss on March 6. On April 23, Adam Schmidt, John Mollenhauer, Hans Holdorf, and Herman Wendler went before Justice Gorman in Essex Market Court, charged with conspiracy. Only Holdorf had been at the March 23 meeting, but it

[67] *Fourth Annual Report*, 745; *The New York Times*, April 24, 30, 1886.

was clear that Gorman considered anyone connected with the boycott guilty of extortion. "This is the most disgraceful case of blackmail," he told the defendants. "This boycotting and stopping another man's business ought to be put an end to." Each was released on $500 bail. Six days later, Eschert, Theiss, and a M. M. P. U. lawyer asked the District Attorney to lay the facts of the boycott before the Grand Jury. Early in May, indictments against the second C. L. U. committee were presented, charging extortion under sections 552, 553, and 554 of the Penal Code. Members of that delegation were summarily arrested, and released on $1,500 bail each.[68]

The boycotts against Mrs. Gray, Theiss and others had convinced substantial citizens that the "foreign institution" had to be destroyed. The boycott waged by the Bohemian Bakers' Union against widow Josephine Landgraf's bakery at 157 East Second Street further confirmed their fears. Bohemian journeymen bakers were subjected to the same conditions as journeymen bakers everywhere in the city. On Tuesday, April 13, the seventy-member Bohemian Union struck for $14 a week and the right to board where they chose. Forced to board with their employers, thus separated from their families, they had been receiving wages of from five to seven dollars a week. Mrs. Landgraf, a Bohemian, belonged to the Bohemian Boss Bakers' Union, and joined the German counterpart when her husband, a German, died. She employed three or four Germans and a like number of Bohemians in her little shop. When the strike was called by their union, the Bohemian bakers walked out.[69]

The strike issues at Landgraf's bakery were complicated by the Germans' decision to remain at work. Mrs. Landgraf was twice visited by Bohemian delegates on Wednesday, told that the Germans must stop baking Bohemian bread, and that she had to pay a $100 fine (later raised to $500). The Germans continued to bake the bread, and a boycott was declared on Wednesday night. Pickets immediately appeared in front of her shop. There was some violence. Fights broke out between German and Bohemian bakers on Wednesday, Thursday, and Saturday—and not for the obvious reason, that the Germans refused to strike in sympathy, but because they baked a bread almost solely made and consumed by Bohemians. German Bakers' Union No. 1 tried

---

68 *Fourth Annual Report,* 746-47, 752; *The New York Times,* April 24, 30, May 1, 2, 1886; *John Swinton's Paper,* December 21, 1884, January 25, 1885, June 27, 1886; 69 *The Sun,* April 18 and 19, 1886.

to resolve the problem on Sunday by offering the remaining bakers five dollars a week for the duration of the strike if they agreed to support the Bohemians. Three left; only the foreman stayed. Throughout the week, bakers picketed the shop and distributed circulars (printed in German and Bohemian) in the neighborhood, while two local Bohemian papers supplemented their efforts. On Saturday night, the Bohemian Union hired a band and paraded up Fourteenth Street, seeking more immigrant support. Mrs. Landgraf received contributions from the city's non-labor papers and their readers, but twenty-two grocers refused to resume trade with her. She was able to hire three German bakers, but her business declined, and the bakery wagon still only made trips to nearby charities.[70]

With the aid of a German-speaking ex-judge, Mrs. Landgraf testified before the Grand Jury on Tuesday, April 27. On Friday, the Jury filed into the Court of General Sessions for its last day of duty. All of the boycotting cases involving charges of conspiracy or extortion had been presented before this jury. It was a body which, to Swinton, represented a trend toward selecting Grand Juries "from a very superior class of citizens." Summarizing the long month's work, the foreman read a statement censuring the laxity of a judge and police captain who, in the Jury's opinion, had made the courts powerless to prevent boycotting. "A thorough examination" of the boycott had convinced the Grand Jury that it was

> an accursed exotic, and they urge every effort of our legislators, the Bench and the Bar, the press of the land, and every American citizen, to aid in exterminating this hydra-headed monster, dragging its loathsome length across this continent, sucking the very lifeblood from our trade and commerce, equally baneful to the employers and employed.[71]

On Monday, the new Grand Jury indicted seventeen members of the Bohemian Bakers' Union on charges of conspiracy and extortion. All were arrested in their homes near the Landgraf bakery early Wednesday morning. "The boycotters arrested yesterday for trying to starve out Mrs. Landgraf," *The New York Times* commented on Thursday, "turn out to be such recent importations into this country that they are unable even to speak the language, much less to understand American institutions." The paper charged that the Landgraf boycotters were of

---

[70] Differences between the bread is discussed in *The Sun,* April 19, 1886; *The New York Times,* April 18, 19, 21, 23, 24, 25, 28, 30, 1886.

[71] *John Swinton's Paper,* May 9, 1886; *The New York Times,* April 25, May 1, 1886.

the same stripe which rioted at the Williamsburgh sugar refineries, and which incited workers at mass meetings. "It is time to prevent the admission of this undesirable class of immigrant," the column concluded, "who are evidently as yet unfitted to appreciate or enjoy the blessings and privileges of a free government founded upon and maintained by law."[72]

The Theiss cases were the first to be tried. No argument could have swayed the court from its determination to convict the boycotters. Swept along by the panic and outrage following the Haymarket Square riot and the St. Louis violence, both judge and juries disposed of the litigation in short order. On June 25, Paul Wilzig was tried before the Irish-born Anglophile, George C. Barrett. Wilzig had been charged with extortion. (Section 552 of the Penal Code defined extortion as "the obtaining of property from another with his consent, induced by a wrongful use of force, or under color of official right." Section 553 described the threats which might constitute extortion, and Section 554 set punishment for anyone convicted of the crime at a maximum of five years in prison.) Theiss, Ehret, and Eschert each gave their accounts of the meetings and of the agreements. Wilzig was asked by his attorney to explain his understanding of the boycott. It was, Wilzig said through an interpreter, a peaceable attempt by labor to prevent others from dealing with someone with whom a union could not agree on union demands. He had committed no acts of violence, he especially emphasized, and had in fact counseled pickets to do the same, regardless of provocations. In one instance, Wilzig testified, Theiss told the boycotting committee that his "bouncer would club them out of his place" if they did not stay away. Further, the Central Labor Union had announced the boycott at the request of the musicians, bartenders, and waiters, and it was Charles Beadles of the C. L. U. who demanded $1,000 from Thiess, Wilzig claimed, not himself. Wilzig said he had only accepted Theiss's check on behalf of the C. L. U., and Theiss had only given it on the promise that the C. L. U. would drop its civil suit against his son for assaulting a striker. The prosecution's cross-examination, while having little to do with Wilzig's testimony, revealed the basis of the appeal being made to the jurors. Colonel John R. Fellows, asked Wilzig if he thought "Theiss had the right to employ whomever he pleased" for any wages that he could get them. "I do not," was the reply. "Are you a naturalized citizen of the United States?" "No,

---

[72] *Ibid.*, May 6, 1886.

Sir." "I thought not. That will do."[73]

In his charge to the jury, Barrett tried to clarify questions raised by each side during the trial concerning what actions were permissible under the law. He explained that workers could legally combine and peacefully bargain to obtain higher wages. They could also ask their friends to withdraw their patronage from persons whom they believed unjust to labor's cause. But a combination to prevent others from working at certain wages was a criminal conspiracy. Neither could workers "bring the power of combination to bear to injure the employers' business" by picketing, distributing handbills, or otherwise encouraging the public to boycott particular products or stores. "Not a hand need be raised—not an oath, not even a violent word be uttered—and yet in such a case I should leave it to a jury to say whether the attitude of [such] men was not under the pretense of moral suasion an attitude of real menace . . . and whether the whole object and purpose was not to intimidate the gentle patrons of the establishment and the general public." The jury retired at 5:30 P.M., and came back with a guilty verdict fifteen minutes later.[74]

Hans Holdorf came to trial on Monday, June 28, but most of the day was devoted to selecting a jury from a panel of over 150 prospective jurors. "The panel could not have been more representative of intelligent opinion," the *New York Times* assured. "It contained merchants, brokers, and manufacturers. Nearly every man owned a business or controlled one, and with hardly an exception they had heard of the case, and had opinions of their own about boycotts in general. . . ." The next day, Holdorf testified that he had committed no acts of violence, and that he had never considered doing so. The prosecution claimed that Holdorf made threats at the March 23 meeting and, therefore, was guilty of violent intimidation and of extortion. Barrett agreed. In his opinion, to boycott peacefully was to intimidate, and to intimidate was to do violence. "The essence of the overt act," he told the jury, "is intimidation." As for extortion, and the long meeting at which the agreement was reached, Barrett said "we cannot overlook the fact that

---

[73] The disposition of charges against the Gray boycotters is not known. On Barrett's background, see David McAdam, et. al. (eds.), *History of The Bench And The Bar of New York* (New York, 1897), II, 28-29; "Judge Barrett," *Harper's Weekly,* XXXIV (April 12, 1890), 273. Acts which could constitute extortion were those which: 1) did "unlawful injury" to a person or property of the threatened individual or to his family; 2) accused him or any of his family of a crime; 3) exposed the victim to "any deformity or disgrace"; or 4) exposed "any secret affecting him or any of them." (*Fourth Annual Report,* 752-753). *The New York Times,* June 24, 1886.
[74] *Ibid.; Fourth Annual Report,* 753-756.

that debate was necessarily colored by the existing boycott," with its implied acts of intimidation. The jury again returned a guilty verdict in fifteen minutes.[75]

When brought to trial on Wednesday, Stroh and Dannhauser immediately entered pleas of guilty. Rosenberg's trial lasted only two hours. O'Leary was remanded to the Court of General Sessions. The jury was exhausted, Barrett explained, and an air of conviction pervaded the court—O'Leary would get a fairer trial elsewhere. Two days later, July 2, the five men were sentenced to Sing Sing. "The moral guilt attaching to the crime of which you have been convicted," Barrett told them,

> is heightened by the fact that you are not American citizens. Such Socialistic crimes as these are breaches of national hospitality. What would you think of a man who, having sought asylum from oppression and poverty in a friend's house, then proceeded to violate his domestic rules, to disregard his customs, and to disturb the peace, order, and well-being of his household? Yet that is just what you and others of your union have been doing with a country that welcomed you and offered you equal privileges and opportunities with its native-born citizens.

Barrett sentenced Stroh and Rosenberg to thirteen months at hard labor. Wilzig and Holdorf received two years and ten months. Dannhauser faced prison for three years and eight months. Their fate, *The New York Times* wrote on July 3, "is a severe lesson to the unnaturalized foreigners who thus defied the law and violated the principles on which civilized society rests." Ostensibly tried and convicted for conspiracy and extortion, their real crimes against society, Swinton correctly noted, were boycotting and being immigrants.[76]

On the morning of July 7, Mrs. Landgraf sat in the rear of Barrett's courtroom and watched as lawyers selected a jury to hear the case against her eighteen boycotters. (Paul Kostka, president of the Bohe-

---

75 Holdorf's jury included a physician, a furnishing goods merchant, a manufacturer of packing boxes, a retired merchant, an organist, a liquor dealer, a "gentleman," a shirtmaker, a real estate broker, a coal dealer, and two watch dealers (*The New York Times,* June 29, 1886). *Fourth Annual Report,* 758.
76 *The New York Times,* July 1, 3, 1886; *Fourth Annual Report,* 752-760; *John Swinton's Paper,* July 11, 1886. On July 4, the C. L. U. ordered a boycott on Ehret's beer, charging that his testimony was instrumental in obtaining the convictions. Two weeks later, Ehret laid off one-fourth of his employees for lack of business. In saloons throughout the city, workers ordered beer and walked out without paying if they were served Ehret's. Neighborhood saloon-keepers either complied with the boycott, or armed themselves with clubs to insure payment. The boycott was not lifted until March 6, 1887 (*The New York Times,* July 5, 14, 15, 17, 20, 22, 23, 1886, and February 14, and March 7, 1887; *Fourth Annual Report,* 781-782).

mian Bakers' Union, had been added to the list.) The same panel from which the Theiss jurors were selected was used for the Landgraf cases. Of the twelve selected, four had served on Theiss juries. Charged with conspiracy and coercion under Sections 168 and 653 of the Penal Code, the defendants were tried as a group over the next four days. Conflicting testimonies did not, in Barrett's opinion, affect the question of whether the boycotters had conspired to prevent Mrs. Landgraf "from exercising her lawful calling or trade as a baker." "They may have done unmanly things," he told the jury, "things that seem unworthy of American citizenship and foreign to American methods, but they are not on trial for violations of good taste or the proprieties of civilized life." They were on trial, Barrett explained, for conspiracy and coercion, and the distribution of the boycotting circulars was relevant to each charge. "The mere fact that no violence was actually used in the street is not conclusive. It is for you to say whether the attitude of these men was not threatening. *Nor is it necessary that there should have been a direct threat.*" The distribution of the circulars was intimidation enough. The eighteen defendants were found guilty, and sentenced to short terms in the city prison on July 9.[77]

Ten days later, the C. L. U. Law Committee, headed by Louis F. Post, met with Governor David B. Hill to request a pardon for the Theiss boycotters. Hill asked the committee to submit answers to five broad legal questions bearing on the case. A special C. L. U. committee, chaired by James Redpath, immediately set to work, and submitted its report to the Governor on July 28. On October 9, Hill commuted the sentences of all five to 100 days (from July 3 to October 11). He explained that in addition to recommendations for clemency made by Redpath's committee, the New York Workingmen's State Assembly,

---

[77] At least two jurors complained that threats had been made against them, and asked to be dismissed (*The New York Times*, July 8, 1886). Section 168, no. 5, provided that "if two or more persons conspire . . . to prevent another from exercising a lawful trade or calling or doing any other lawful act by force, threats, intimidation," or by in any other way interfering with another's tools of employment, each is guilty of a misdemeanor. Section 653 defined as a misdemeanor any act to compel another person to do, or to refrain from doing something which the other person had a legal right to do, and to employ intimidation, threat, or violence on the person or any member of his family, or deprive him of his work tools in accompanying the act (*Fourth Annual Report*, 782, ellipses mine). Barrett told the Bohemians he would be lenient because they were ignorant of the law. The Theiss boycotters "were men of better education than you," and had committted blackmail. The men were sentenced to from ten to thirty days in prison (*Ibid.*, 786, 787). That same afternoon, Mrs. Landgraf's bakers quit, afraid for their safety if they remained. The woman announced she, too, was quitting, and would soon open a shop selling medicinal teas and herbs. For years her most popular product had been "M. Landgraf's Blood Purifying Tea." (*The New York Times*, July 10, 1886).

and the Knights of Labor he had received "petitions without number from all classes of people," and was convinced that the interests of justice would be best served by showing the men that the law was, in fact, their friend. It was no coincidence, however, that Hill issued the pardons at the same time that Tammany Hall announced Democrat Abram S. Hewitt as its candidate for mayor. The freed boycotters knew the meaning of Hill's action. Taken to Lincoln Hall upon their arrival in New York on October 12, the five men were greeted by a large welcoming committee. Wilzig expressed the sentiments of his fellow "criminals" by telling the audience: "I had rather stayed two months longer in prison than be looked upon as being the tool of Governor Hill to catch labor votes for his party. We have done our duty. You do yours at the election by voting for Henry George."[78]

George received almost 68,000 votes in that election. Hewitt got roughly 90,000, while Theodore Roosevelt polled some 60,000. Labor's campaign to elect Henry George still awaits serious study from the perspective of immigrant experiences and thought. The history of nineteenth-Century American workers, in general, deserves attention from a similar conceptual framework. This study has merely attempted to illuminate hitherto neglected aspects of that history.[79]

IMMIGRATION AND MODERNIZATION: THE CASE OF SLAVIC PEASANTS IN INDUSTRIAL AMERICA

13

John Bodnar

The study of the impact of modernization upon traditional, preindustrial cultures has usually been based upon a dichotomous model. Traditional and modern societies have been described as distinct categories. Passage from the former to the latter was assumed to involve the destruction of traditional culture and the eventual embracement of the new with its emphasis on materialism, individualism, and progress. If manifestations of a traditional culture were found in modern societies, they were thought to be minor residues of premodern society which were able briefly to withstand the disintegrating effects of modernization.[1]

Recent scholars have made a strong case for the persistence of preindustrial values. Especially impressive has been the work on modernization and women. Joan Scott and Louise Tilly, in a study of nineteenth century Europe, argued that preindustrial values "rather than a new individualistic idealogy" justified the work of working-class women. What they posited was a model of "continuity of traditional values and behavior in changing circumstances." They explained that behavior was less a product of new ideas than of the effects of old ideas operating in a new or changing concept. Since women's work was already justified in terms of family survival in peasant Europe, Scott and Tilly concluded that no change in values was needed to allow lower class women to work outside the home during the nineteenth century — "peasant values and family interests sent them to work."[2]

Descriptions of immigrant groups and peasants moving to industrial society have also noted the tenacity with which preindustrial cultural preferences and familial arrangements resisted disintegration and change. Italian families in Buffalo, New York, resisted the assumed destructive tendencies of industrialization by selecting only jobs which would minimize the separation of parent and child. Italian associational life, communal ties, and other cultural traits were found flourishing in twentieth century Chicago.[3] A study of boarding and lodging in American families revealed that families were malleable and not broken by the weight of industrialization. Indeed, they cushioned the "shock of urban life" for newcomers.[4]

A conclusion that the impact of modernization was minimal and less than destructive, however, would be premature. Studies from the Philadelphia Social History Project confirm that modernization took its toll and was not always resisted successfully. Industrial and technological change in nineteenth century Philadelphia frequently altered work in various skills, reduced the income and

Source: Copyright © 1975 by Peter N. Stearns. Reprinted from the *Journal of Social History,* vol. IX, pp. 44-71, reprinted by permission of the editor.

status of certain craftsmen, and enhanced opportunities for others.[5] The project's study of black families demonstrated clearly that urban conditions and economic status had an effect on the structure of families since black males suffered extremely high mortality rates in the city.[6] Additional studies have illustrated that the preindustrial legacy of slavery had much less impact upon the socioeconomic position of blacks in nineteenth century Philadelphia than did urban racism and structural inequality.[7]

What is needed is a model which allows for both persistence and change. Change, furthermore, cannot simply be equated with destruction or cultural breakdown. Often social change involved innovation and the creation of new behavioral strategies. Behavior in both peasant and proletarian worlds was often quite similar, since both groups operated under conditions of scarcity and restriction. Because of this basic similarity, modernization was frequently a dialectical process whereby the working class milieu reinforced many of the perceptions of the peasant. Certain customs were discarded to be sure, such as language, in the immigrant case, and others were obviously sustained. Both Scott and Tilly and McLaughlin hint at the need for a more dialectical model of modernization but both resort ultimately to a preindustrial framework as a determinant of working-class behavior.[8]

Explanations that preindustrial behavior persisted implicitly credit traditional culture with an independent endurance variable and assume that modern society is totally transformative. They leave little room for the possibility that urban-industrial society also positively nurtured behavioral patterns such as limited horizons, familial cooperation, fatalism, and anti-materialism which were as functional for proletarians as for peasants. They oversimplify, in other words, the modernization of values. Immigrant peasants usually lived in working-class environments. It was possible that in this arena preindustrial behavior neither disintegrated nor simply endured. It may have been reinforced. Working class immigrant behavior may have been more than simply a residue of the premodern past. Exigencies of the new socioeconomic order also necessitated a conservative, collectivist approach to life. Whether life was lived from harvest to harvest or paycheck to paycheck, workers still had to survive. Modernization may have involved a process of synthesis where traditional ways were integrated with working class pragmatism to produce distinct behavioral patterns.[9]

This paper will attempt to refine the interpretation of the impact of modernization on immigrant peasants. It will attempt to show that working-class behavior was not simply a residue from premodern worlds or on the other hand characterized by dissolution of traditional cultures. Urban, industrial society will be viewed as capable of eliciting behavioral patterns of its own which were similar to peasant culture. Here the dialectical process of modernization involves the interplay between tradition and working class necessity, producing a new working-class consciousness. This consciousness was a synthesis which was forged by immigrants themselves within the structural context of a new socioeconomic milieu. Slavic immigrants in industrial America will constitute the test sample. Perhaps the least studied of American immigrant groups, the adjustment process of Slavic newcomers from southern Poland, eastern Slovakia, the Ukraine, Croatia, Bosnia, Slovenia, and Serbia will be examined in hopes of refining our understanding of the impact modernization had upon immigrants from traditional societies.

It would admittedly be impossible to describe Slavic settlements in late nineteenth and early twentieth century America as devoid of old world traits. Familial relationships stand as prominent examples of elements resilient to the transformative nature of the urban-industrial milieu. Consider the roles assumed by various individuals in the Slavic family. An essentially hierarchical structure dominated by an authoritarian father characterized Slavic families in peasant Europe and America. An examination of Poles in Buffalo in the 1920's, for instance, found more than 90% of the Buffalo Poles believing that parents should exercise complete authority over their children.[10]

The expectation that children would contribute to the material support of the family was also characteristic of both European and American Slavs. In Pennsylvania mining districts Slavs not only exceeded all other ethnic groups in their use of child labor but routinely falsified their children's ages to obtain working permits. In Pittsburgh's South Side thousands of young Serbs spent their adolescent years working in glass factories until they could enter the steel mills. In Scranton 35% of Polish family income in 1911 was earned by children.[11]

Other characteristics of the Slavic peasant family were found long after settlement in America. The treatment of sexual attitudes continued without drastic change. Children were informed that erogenous zones were repulsive, bad, or nonexistent. An examination of Slovak-American Catholics revealed that sex was seldom discussed. For Slavic women sex continued to be primarily for the purpose of procreation.[12] As in Europe, moreover, greater control was exercised over older children than younger ones. A gradual progression existed from older children who were "tightly controlled" to the youngest who were much more uninhibited.[13]

A classic example of the perpetuation of peasant family alignments was demonstrated by the South Slavs. The prevalent family structure among premodern Croats and Serbs was the *zadruga*. Its main components were a communal, joint family which rested upon the supremacy of the older male member and the belief that other males should never leave their home. Sons and their wives and children would remain within the homes of their fathers. Daughters would leave upon marriage to become members of the *zadruga* of their husbands. Sons remained to contribute to the support of the communal family.[14]

In an examination of Yugoslav family structure in the immigrant steel town of Lackawanna, New York, the *zadruga* form of kinship arrangement was found persisting after two decades of settlement in America. The South Slav households had the highest rate of extended families among the town's ethnic groups, including Poles and Slovaks. Grandparents, married children, and other relatives abounded in the Yugoslav households. Thirty-four percent of Serbian and Croatian families were extended compared to only 20 percent of the Polish, Slovak, and Hungarian residents. Indeed, Yugoslavs lived in extended family households more than all other American immigrant groups according to studies conducted by the United States Immigration Commission. Moreover, over one out of every five Yugoslav households in Lackawanna had the families of married sons residing with the parents, an important feature of the *zadruga* pattern.[15]

If important aspects of family life continued in America, the religious practices of Slavic newcomers remained equally strong. The local parish continued to serve not only as a dominant center of religion but as a focus of community life.[16] Detroit Polish life, for instance, developed around St. Casimir's, St. Albertus, St. Josephats, and Sweetest Heart of Mary churches.[17] In Chicago early Poles identified their two largest communities by the names of their churches. "Stanislawowo," clustered around St. Stanislaus parish and "Wojciechowo" grew around the church of St. Adalbert. These communities were not only separated physically but seldom interacted. Jobs, schools, clubs, and churches were all located in these respective settlements and residents saw little need to extend their activities elsewhere.[18] "Stanislawowo" was an excellent example. It possessed a grade school, a high school, social clubs and religious societies. Organizations such as the "Macier z Polska" offered a variety of moral, cultural and "social training" activities for youth and adults. The parish continued its old world function as the cement of both religious and communal life.[19]

Slavs continued not only to practice their traditional religion and focus their social lives around their churches, but the spiritual orientation of peasant Europe with its emphasis upon non-secular rewards and religious values continued to influence Slavic attitudes. It was this residue of spiritual and religious values which explained the consistent anti-materialistic current which permeated Slavic-American thought. Throughout the first half-century of large scale Slavic settlement in America a consistent anti-materialism influenced the immigrant's mind. In the early 1890's, Polish newspapers were already mounting an assault upon the "Dollar God" of American culture. A Pole from Pennsylvania wrote *Dziennik Chicagoski* criticizing the tendency of American society to strain parental-child relationships by stressing "excess and wantoness." "The struggle for the dollar facilitated the losing of religion and patriotism so dear to us," the Polish newspaper feared. Numerous editorials and articles emphasized the evil effects of the pursuit of material wealth. In an 1894 editorial, *Zgoda* told Poles that a "reasonable honest drive" to improve your material being was good. The "idolistic pursuit of money at the expense of your soul," however, "would bring hatred and desperation." *Zgoda* continued, "good character and work are the greatest wealth."[20]

It was precisely because of this skepticism of the promise of American life that Poles emphasized Polish over American schools. One Polish journal called Polish schools the "watch-tower" of the Polish spirit. American schools were felt to be a "horrible example" where children learned little but disrespect for their parents.[21] American schools were not considered "adequate" for Polish children not only because they were "irreligious" but because they were thought to be permeated with secularism.[22]

Slovaks invariably echoed the Polish sentiments. In a series of essays in *Jednota* by a Slovak writer, Ivan Kramoris, the Slovak immigrant situation was analyzed. Kramoris posed the question, "But what are we to do in America." He explained that such a choice would be made in the framework of economic versus moral standards. Kramoris argued that an individual's morality actually influenced his economic life. Little doubt existed in Kramoris' mind that the eventual emphasis should be placed upon morality. Other writers concurred. "So many are cursed with the lust of acquiring things that they see no further ahead than their own selfish self," a Slovak editor exclaimed, "those who measure success by the material things acquired are lost in the fog of life."[23]

Characteristically, the anti-materialistic bias influenced Slovak views on education. *Osadne Hlasy* illustrated the drawbacks of the public schools in 1929. Children were taught but not "reared" in American schools, according to the Slovak journal, "they educate the mind but not the heart." J.T. Porincak, a Slovak, clarified the argument:

> With a public school education they [children] go forth into the world, lost completely to the Slovaks. Their idea of life is a breezy and snappy novel, a blood curdling movie and lots of money.
>
> But our duty to our people commands us to save our youth from the moral catastrophe that is confronting them.[24]

The Slavic-American skepticism toward public school was clearly manifested in various studies of school attendance and progress. In a 1911 study released by the United States Immigration Commission, Poles and Slovaks ranked lowest among ethnic groups in the largest urban centers. The percentage of Slavic children in school beyond the sixth grade was lower than the rate for the progeny of Irish and Jewish newcomers and Negroes. Beyond grade six, the group with the smallest percentage of children in the public schools of Chicago and Cleveland in 1911 were the Slovaks (4%). Poles ranked lowest in Buffalo, New Britain and Scranton and next to last in Cleveland and Milwaukee.[25]

Not surprisingly, computations of public high school attendance in 1910 found Slavic children noticeably absent. In Chicago, while 5% of black children and 6% of Polish Jewish children were attending the secondary schools, only 1% of the Poles and Slavaks were doing so. In Cleveland only one-half of one percent of Slovak children were in high school in 1910 as compared with 11% of Irish immigrant children, and 7% of Polish Jews who arrived in America at the same time.[26]

Where parochial school attendance figures were available, Slavic attendance invariably ranked behind native-born and second generation Irish children. In Milwaukee parochial schools in 1910, 15% of the children of native-born Catholics were in school and 10% of the second generation Irish. Only 2% of the Poles were attending, however, and no Slovaks. Polish and Slovak representation in Cleveland's parochial schools was better but considerably behind the native-born and Irish. New Britain had 19% of its Irish youth in Catholic schools after the sixth grade but none of its Polish youth.[27] In Scranton 99% of all Polish immigrant children in parochial school were in grades one to five only. In Shenandoah, Pennsylvania, 32% of the children of native-born Catholics were beyond the fourth grade. No Poles had advanced that far despite having been in Shenandoah for over thirty years by 1910.[28]

Clearly, then, the arguments detailing widespread cultural persistence in the transition process from premodern to modern societies apply to the Slavic immigrant in America. Slavs were not completely staggered by the tremors of urban-industrial society and their traditional culture proved resilient. But to characterize Slavic immigrant communities in urban America as simply extensions of peasant communalism would be erroneous. The entire framework of peasant behavior in eastern Europe was within a context of work and survival. The exigencies of working class status in the United States would not alter this fact. Immigrant life in industrial towns and cities would evolve a preoccupation with survival also. This process would not lead to a destruction of peasant culture, but it did not simply perpetuate it either. Rather, while fundamental elements of the premodern world view would be reinforced in modern society, behavioral changes occurred that could best be explained not in terms of destruction or persistence but in terms of innovation. Slavs created their own strategies for survival which both drew from the traditional and embraced the new. What remained the same was the framework in which this was done — a framework where survival was the preoccupation. This framework was as much an element of working-class status as of peasant traditionalism.

The strategies for survival developed in America were often subtle. The Slavic family, for instance, which maintained much of its peasant character was not completely unaltered. While it was traditional for the family to support itself collectively, innovations such as the use of carefully prepared budgets nearly always administered by the Slavic women became widespread.[29] The female assumed the position of fiscal manager in the Slavic immigrant family. A Slovak in McKeesport, Pennsylvania recalled that as long as his father worked he turned his pay over to his mother along with all of his brothers. Margaret Byington's famous survey of Homestead, Pennsylvania in 1910 found clear evidence of the extensive use of budgets by Slavs and their control by the immigrant woman. In the anthracite coal fields of Pennsylvania, Slavic mothers became the managers of smoothly functioning economic units where fathers and children automatically relinquished paychecks.[30]

Slavs in America also began to seek security in the peculiar context of working-class America. Denied opportunities for significant occupational mobility,[31] particularly since earlier arrivals such as the Irish and Germans already held skilled industrial jobs, Slavs turned intensely to home ownership as a means of solidifying their precarious economic status. In nearly every Slavic ethnic community in America immigrant savings and loan associations were established for the purpose of issuing home mortgages. Croatian immigrants organized the First Croatian Building and Loan Association in Chicago in 1910 in an immigrant's home. While it was difficult for some newcomers to relinquish their savings to an institution, deposits steadily increased. Loans were used predominantly to purchase homes and by 1935 the association had loaned over four million dollars for home mortgages.[32] Slovaks in Scranton, Pennsylvania, saved at the Bosak State Bank; Slovenes in southwestern Pennsylvania mining towns organized the Slovenian Savings and Loan Association in 1921 with branches in Strabane and Canonsburg. Croats in Gary, Indiana, initiated the America Savings and Loan Association for home mortgages. Before the Great Depression, Cleveland had five Polish savings and loan companies. Other representative institutions included the Croatian-American Building and Loan Association of Granite City, Illinois, the Pulaski Building and Loan Association and the Czecko-Slovak Building and Loan Association both of Chicago.[33] One Chicago real estate firm had eleven Poles to handle their "Polish business."[34] As one Croatian journal exclaimed, "a nation's basic wealth is its land and homes."[35]

Slavs exceeded nearly every ethnic group in urban America in purchasing homes. While the market value of their residences was consistently below native-born whites and other immigrant groups such as Germans, Irish, and Jews, seldom did anyone exceed their propensity to become homeowners.[36] In a nationwide survey conducted in 1930, the high rate of Slavic-American home ownership was dramatically revealed. In Akron, Bridgeport, Chicago and Cleveland, families originating from Czechoslovakia owned homes at a higher rate than all other immigrant groups. In Akron, Chicago, and Cleveland, Poles were second only to the Czechs and Slovaks. Polish families ranked highest in ownership rates in Buffalo, Toledo, Milwaukee, and Detroit. Slovaks were second in the later two cities. In all eight communities, Czechoslovak and Polish rates exceeded the ownership rates for families from England and Ireland with the exception of the Irish in Toledo. In Milwaukee, while 70% of the Poles, 63% of the Czechoslovaks, and 52% of the Yugoslavs owned homes, only about one-third of the English and Irish were home owners. In Akron, while 68% of all foreign-born families owned their own residences, 84% of the Czechoslovaks were home owners.[37] In Chicago, the rate of Czechoslovak home ownership was about 2.5 times higher than that of Russian Jews, although the property of the Jews was valued considerably higher.[38]

If Slavic home ownership is studied in smaller industrial centers where they were concentrated, the pattern further reveals their quest for economic security. In Pennsylvania mill towns Slavic ownership rates exceeded even the families of native-born whites. Serbs and Croats dominated the rates in Aliquippa, Farrell, and Steelton. Slovaks were the leading owners in Braddock, Duquesne, Homestead, and Munhall. In Homestead, Slovaks bought homes twice as much as native-white families. In the coal towns of Shenandoah, Wilkes-Barre, Mount Carmel, and Nanticoke, native-born whites were far behind Poles in acquiring housing. While 23% of the natives obtained their own home in Nanticoke, 57% of the Poles decided to become owners. Not surprisingly, in 1930 the foreign-born owned homes at a higher rates than the statewide average for all families in Pennsylvania, a state whose immigrant population was primarily southern and eastern European.[39]

In other areas as well, Slavs emerged as leading home owners. In Cicero, Illinois, while 22% of the native whites possessed their own residence, 67% of the Czechs and Poles were owners. Similar trends were evident in Lorain, Ohio, Lackawanna, New York, and New Britain, Connecticut.[40]

In addition to developing new strategies in America to obtain a modest degree of economic security, Slavs also manifested an intensified concern for ethnic communalism. They created elaborate ethnic community structures which surpassed the regionalism of their European experience. Upon arrival in America, Slavs seldom displayed powerful strains of ethnic identity. In Steelton, Pennsylvania, Croatians were deeply divided for a number of years by village (Bjelovar and Voyvodina) loyalties which they brought with them. One second generation Croat recalled that his parents, who emigrated from Bjelovar, attempted to discourage him from ever marrying a "Voyvodincia." Indeed, the two groups often argued over church affairs and the practice of certain Old World customs. These regional differences were overcome, however, when Croats faced a common problem in America. In Steelton their dispute with Slovenes which led to the ouster of the Slovenes from the Croatian-Slovenian Church brought about the end of European regionalism in favor of ethnic identity.[41]

The early attachment to village loyalties was certainly not unique to Steelton, neither was the triumph of ethnic nationalism over parochial interests. Slavs initially identified themselves by their place of birth, village, or region. Early immigrant fraternal lodges were usually begun along local lines. Slovak lodges in the coal fields of Pennsylvania were initially organized by counties of origin of Slovak newcomers, mostly from eastern Slovakia. Even in Steelton, Croats had five different fraternal lodges which reflected generally their European village origins.[42]

Local divisions, however, gave way to immigrant communities which, although frequently troubled by persistent factionalism, became culturally unified in the face of economic and social turmoil in America. Local fraternal lodges and societies in mining and manufacturing centers gradually joined groups from other localities to form national associations. The Polish National Alliance, the First Catholic Slovak Union, and the Croatian Fraternal Union all welded scattered ethnic communities into organizations which provided some economic benefit and much social exchange. While this movement had just emerged in the premigration societies in the late nineteenth century, it was expanded in industrial society due to the need for a more formal basis for community and the fragile economic security provided by industrial work.[42] Premodern tribalism was not destroyed or simply perpetuated in modern society but embellished.

While the national fraternal societies were a powerful force in bringing local immigrant settlements into the mainstream of the new American-ethnic communities, they suffered from frequent dissension and competition for support. In 1890, Peter V. Rovnianek helped found the National Slovak Society in Pittsburgh. All Slovaks were welcome whether they were Catholics, Protestants, or Freemasons. Rovnianek's organization was openly nationalistic. On the other hand, the Reverend Stefan Furdek established a strictly Catholic fraternal organization, the First Catholic Slovak Union in 1890. Furdek's stated objectives included a desire to preserve the Catholic faith.[32] Since the success of different immigrant societies often depended upon the degree to which they purported to uphold Old World culture and language, their very competitiveness served to strengthen a sense of immigrant identity in America. As a perceptive observer has noted, moreover, the leadership of the societies was drawn from immigrants of disparate social backgrounds as well as regions; immigrants who may have had little chance for association in the Old World now acted in concert to establish new institutions.[33]

Poles were particularly driven to heightened ethnic consciousness by their experience within the Roman Catholic Church. Significant was the Polish

National Catholic Church movement which began in Scranton in 1897. Polish workers in south Scranton began to argue for a greater voice in the management of church affairs. When the Irish bishop of Scranton termed them "disobedient," they established their own church and invited a young Polish priest, Francis Hodur, to guide them. By 1919 the Polish National Church movement, which substituted Polish for Latin in church services after Latin had been accepted for centuries in Poland, spread to over fifty congregations in America and eventually to scores of parishes in Poland itself. The schismatic Poles also founded their own fraternal union and publications.[34]

In Chicago, Poles that did not leave the Catholic church also began to assert their ethnic identity. Disturbed at the lack of Polish bishops and the suggestion of Chicago's Archbishop Mundelein that parishes would be based on territorial rather than nationality grounds, Chicago Polonia, manifesting a growing concern for their ethnic identity, issued its *I Polacci Negle Stati Uniti Dell' America Del Nord* statement in 1920. The document, a collaborative effort on the part of the General Union of Polish Clergy and the Polish Embassy to the Holy See, outlined the grievances of America's Polonia. It called for more Polish bishops, attacked the concept of territorial based churches — "churches of Poles were meant for the exclusive use of Poles" — and defended Polish schools as necessary for keeping family and language intact.[47]

Rising feelings of ethnicity seriously weakened and eventually divided the Uniate or Byzantine Church in America as well. The church was composed mostly of Rusins and Ukrainians. Resentment against the Ukrainian bishop, however, prompted Rusin clergy and laymen to organize the Greek Catholic Union in 1892.[48] The union, through its organ, *Amerikanskij Russki Viestnik,* and the Rusin Civilian Church Council eventually clarified its objectives. They included an attempt to halt the "Ukrainian policies" of the bishop. By 1918 the church was officially divided into Ukrainian and Rusin branches. As H.R. Niebuhr has pointed out, the immigrant church became more of a racial and cultural institution than a religious one.[49]

Economic exploitation also forced immigrants to coalesce around an emerging consciousness which was a blend of working-class status and heightened ethnic identity. Slavs were killed in a united labor protest at Lattimer, Pennsylvania, in 1897. The event evoked widespread criticism in the Slavic press against American officials who fired upon the striking miners. Croatians in Chicago contributed substantially to fellow Croats who struck mines in West Virginia, Colorado and Pennsylvania.[50] In 1891, to cite a case in point, a guard was slain at the Thompson Steel Works at Braddock, Pennsylvania, near Pittsburgh. Three Slovaks, Andrew Toth, Michael Sabol, and George Rusnak, were among sixty persons charged with the murder. Most received light sentences, but Toth, Sabol, and Rusnak were given the death penalty. Immediately Rovnianek's Slovak Union and Slovak organizations throughout the company rallied to the cause and sent petitions to the Pennsylvania Pardon Board requesting clemency be shown the three Slavs for "a crime which they did not commit." A standard petition form was printed in English and Slovak. Soon the forms, signed by hundreds of immigrants, were arriving at the pardon board. Each petition claimed that Slavic immigrants had been debarred from participation in public affairs and business in America:

> A great majority of us became servants, hewers of wood, drawers of water, workers in the mills, the mines, the fields, and the shops for a compensation which barely allowed us the necessaries of life . . . . We are buying lands, building houses, educating our children . . . . The hanging of these men will be a terrible blow to our people.[51]

While Slovaks were not successful in freeing Toth, Sabol, and Rusnak immediately, such incidents served to bring Slovaks together in the face of what seemed to be a threat to Slovak immigrants collectively.

Slavs were carefully establishing working-class worlds in America by integrating old world traditions with pragmatic innovations necessitated by the constrictions and realities of their socioeconomic status. This process was illustrated in the attitude they assumed toward an industrial society and the results they found in it. Rather than embracing the "American dream" of personal advancement through education and a career, Slavs sought mainly secure employment. Conditions in urban and industrial America only served to strengthen the peasant view of work as an instrument of survival, not success.

And here we can turn from generalizations to specific, personal reactions. The Slavic arrivals studied in this investigation were peasants from the most underdeveloped areas of southern and eastern Europe who eventually settled industrial mills, factories, and mines. Of those immigrants interviewed all arrived between 1902 and 1914 from Croatia, Bosnia, Galicia, and and the eastern counties of Slovakia. All but one had been agricultural workers or laborers in Europe. Indeed, 82% of all Serbians and 70% of all Slovaks emigrating from Austria -Hungary were agrarian-peasant workers.[52]

Since most Slavs shared a premodern background, they arrived with the traditional East European peasant's conception of work. Work was central to the Slavic peasant's existence. All of life, indeed survival, revolved around the yearly cycle of farm duties. Parents and children learned the routine tasks of the farm thoroughly, as performances of such tasks often made the difference between survival and a catastrophe.[53]

Even though many Slavs in Europe were transient before they came to America, they moved only as means of survival. Alternative jobs were sought only out of necessity. Southern Slavs frequently went to sea before 1918 and worked as sailors. When a necessary sum of money was accumulated, they returned to their villages and did not attempt to increase their wealth further. Gospodars, the elder heads of Yugoslav extended families, viewed factory work as temporary. One village elder proclaimed that if factory employment were lost, peasants would be unable to eat. Yet it was important to retain the land as a means of security. A gospodar stated:

> We work in the factory so that we can continue to hold onto the land and we hold onto the land because no one knows what is sure.[54]

The transient landless peasants who wondered throughout nineteenth-century Slovakia moved continuously in search of work as their only means of survival.[55]

Survival was always the preoccupation with the Slav and work was the instrument of survival. The East European peasant viewed the world as a source of "limited good." That is to say that no relationship existed between work and the acquisition of wealth. Wealth — as well as land, health, and security — were considered to exist in short supply and the peasant felt little could be done to alter this situation. In Slavic Europe children were continually taught to work hard; little else seemed available. Not surprisingly Russian peasants employed one criterion in determining the suitability of their daughter's prospective marriage partner: was the prospective son-in-law a "good worker."[57] Upward social success seemed unobtainable and irrelevant as they searched only for work. Zara Werlinich was a Serb who arrived in McKees Rocks, Pennsylvania in 1913. The seventh of thirteen children, he had little alternative but to leave his father's farm after it was inherited by his oldest brother. Upon his arrival he conceived a single goal: to get a job. "We all had to look for work," he recalled, "a job don't look for you." Werlinich was hired as a laborer in the Fort Pitt Foundry and remained a laborer for twenty years until the depression forced him out of work. He was gratified that the foundry provided a steady income.[57]

Werlinich's aims were shared by the majority of Slavic newcomers who sought steady work as a course of security. Consider the orientation of Sam Vignovic, a Serb who began working at a glass factory in Pittsburgh in 1914. "I was anxious to make money and support myself," Vignovic recalled, "I didn't care about a [particular] job even though it was hard." When Vignovic learned hourly wages were fifteen cents higher at the nearby Jones and Laughlin Steel plant, he changed positions. His reasoning was not based on a desire to raise his standard of living but to improve his savings in the event he lost his job.[58]

Other Slavs displayed similar modest and characteristically working-class intentions. A Serb (who requested anonymity) left the mountains of Bosnia in 1907 and arrived at the Carnegie Steel plant in Duquesne. He found his task of filling wheel-barrows with gravel and sand for brick-layers dreadful but reasoned that without work "they would put your plate upside down at the boarding house." George Hudock, a Bethlehem Slovak, wanted to operate a crane and rejected subsequent opportunities to earn more because those "opportunities" seemed less "steadier."[59]

Slavs logically viewed industrial work as quite desirable. One Pittsburgh Slav emphasized that many of his friends genuinely wanted to work in the steel mills because they disliked outdoor work which was irregular and "time passed quickly" in the steel plant. Another put the point more concisely, "the mill was considered a good place to work."[60] One Polish newcomer considered his ten hour day in America an improvement over the dawn to dusk routine he had followed in Europe.

If the initial aspirations of Slavic newcomers were modest, subsequent behaviorial evidence suggested they seldom displayed any attempt at risk-taking or attaining a higher position. If a steady job was the initial goal of Slavs, once obtained it was not easily abandoned. Valerian Duda came from Poland to McKeesport in 1906 at the age of seventeen. Along with other Poles he worked at the National Tube Plant of United States Steel. He retired forty-eight years later as a tester of galvanized pipe. Andrew Bodnar left Slovakia in 1913 and was taken by an uncle to a Homestead mill. He retired forty-seven years later as a "piler" of steel beams.[61]

The reluctance of Slavs to leave steady work was a pervasive theme. Walter Balawajder, a Pole, had learned the trade of cabinet-making in Europe. Upon his arrival in McKeesport, however, he worked in a steel mill. A decade later when he learned that the Westinghouse Company in Pittsburgh was planning on fabricating radio cabinets, he was excited by the possibility of returning to his original trade. When Westinghouse guaranteed him higher wages but not permanent work he decided to remain in the mill. "Once you build up that seniority," he reasoned, "there was no use to go somewhere else for something you weren't sure of." Similarly John Urczyk, a Ukrainian from Galicia, came to America in 1913 and obtained work at the Pressed Steel Car Company in McKees Rocks. He recalled fellow immigrants at Pressed Steel unwilling to leave even their particular department. Urczyk revealed that this reluctance to change occupations stemmed partially from a fear by Slavs that they would not know how to perform occupational tasks somewhere else.[62]

Most East European newcomers were forced to change occupations at one time or another but the moves were usually lateral rather than vertical, involuntary rather than voluntary. Economic dislocation influenced immigrant job changes more than a desire for social advancement.[63] Consider the experience of Valentine Bauer. Born in a Hungarian village, Bauer immigrated to Galitzin, Pennsylvania, at the age of nineteen where he worked for a decade in soft coal mines. When employment became sporadic at the mines Bauer contacted an uncle in Bethlehem and was hired as a blacksmith helper at the steel mill. Unable to sustain his family without an income during the 1919 steel strike, he began working at the Mack Truck Company in Allentown. He returned to the steel mill two years later. When employment became irregular during the 1930's, he was hired as a janitor for St. John's Hungarian Church and school. He occupied that position until his retirement in 1957. Bauer was emphatic in explaining his decision to remain as janitor, "The work was more steady." He elaborated:

> Well, we [immigrants] had to take what we got. I started in the mine. It used to be slack a lot so I would do farm work at Lorretto. I never wanted to leave Bethlehem. I was happy here and proud that I always lived in the fifth ward because my work is here and the church is here.[64]

Even more important than the modest character of the aspirations and achievements of the first generation was the fact that the majority of the immigrant children displayed little advancement over their parents. In a quantitative assessment of intergenerational occupational mobility among South Slavic immigrants in Steelton, Pennsylvania, less than one out of four sons was able to attain an occupational status above his father between 1920 and 1940. While a modest amount of occupation advancement occurred,[65] the children were quite similar in their aspirations and accomplishments to their parents.

Most immigrant sons began their working career early. Of 115 immigrant children interviewed, all but two were working by the age of fourteen.[66] George Porvasnik was representative. Porvasnik, the son of a Slovak immigrant, was born in Pittsburgh in 1911. He left school at the age of fourteen to work in a plant which manufactured chains. The constant odor of banana oil on chains caused him to bleed frequently from the nose and he left after six months. Porvasnik became a rivet heater at Pressed Steel and remained there for forty years. Other young Slavs began employment in the "glass houses" of south Pittsburgh and in the silk mills of south Bethlehem. These jobs usually served as a prelude to a lifetime of toil at nearby steel plants.[67]

While the occupational careers of second generation Slavs were unspectacular, they fulfilled many of their original occupational expectations. Robert Milanovich, a Serbian-American, worked at a Pittsburgh glass factory only until an opening occurred at the Jones and Laughlin steel mill. Milanovich reasoned that the mill was better than most jobs around. Sam Mervosh's sole aim was to get a job. He began working in a rolling mill where his father knew the superintendent. The position particularly appealed to Mervosh because it was removed from the heat of the blast furnaces. And, as Milanovich, he claimed that pay in the mill was better than most wages in south Pittsburgh. Charles Jablonski simply "aspired" to get away from school. Frank Horvath, a Bethlehem Hungarian, wanted only a steady job. Horvath insisted that he never thought of having anything more than he had. "I just wanted a job," he affirmed, "whether it be a garbage man or an iceman."[68]

Once the second generation became established in their careers, they demonstrated, like their fathers, a reluctance to change positions. Occupational alterations were viewed with caution. Lewis Buchek and Joseph Wiatrak both declined positions with the postal service because they did not wish to jeopardize their seniority at a mill. Prior to a strike which temporarily put him out of work, Lewis Kozo never considered leaving Bethlehem Steel. A strike forced him to work temporarily as a salesman. While he enjoyed sales, he quickly returned to the mill so as not to jeopardize his pension. Sam Mervosh never thought of leaving a Pittsburgh mill because he felt unqualified for any other position.[69]

In addition to limited horizons, the working-class attitudes of many Slavic- and Magyar-Americans to their work was reinforced by traditional family and neighborhood associations. One Hungarian eschewed the higher wages of Brooklyn Ship Yards so as not to sever his family ties in Bethlehem. Another Pole remained in Bethlehem for the same reason. Michael Komernitski stayed at a screw and bolt factory in McKees Rocks. He not only feared the loss of his pension but genuinely liked living among Slovaks, Poles, and Ukrainians in the McKees Rocks "bottoms."[70]

It should not be surprising that the aims of the second generation were modest and similar to those of their fathers. The influence of the immigrant parent was crucial in shaping the aspirations of the child. The concepts of work which Slavs developed in industrial America did not weaken quickly. Indeed, the absence of social mobility in the immigrant generation assured a continuation of Slavic working-class status and, therefore, limited horizons. Work was still conceived as an instrument of survival rather than a means to a career or social advancement.

Immigrant parents influenced their children in subtle ways. Many children viewed their immigrant fathers as, above all else, hard workers. If sons had any image of their father it included manual work as an inevitable aspect of life. Indeed, the fathers served as "models of immobility." A Polish-American described his parents as individuals who believed in "work, work, work, and work." A Bethlehem Slovak recalled that his father never talked of changing jobs but only of doing a good days work for the company.[71] A Serbian son in Pittsburgh remembered his father as a man esteemed by fellow Serbs for his application to his job. The Serbian son claimed his father's characteristics were representative of most Serbs. He clearly explained his father's motives as fear of the loss of his job. He argued:

> Those men were tireless. They did hard work. They stuck with their job; they didn't have to be driven. They were tireless and always feared the loss of their jobs since they had nothing to fall back on.[73]

Parents encouraged child labor as necessary for family survival. Sam Davich was required to work at age fourteen in a glass factory in Pittsburgh and turn over his earnings to his mother, as were most other immigrant children. Several Slovak girls went to work in Donora, Pennsylvania, when their father became ill and was able to work only part time in the mills. In Lyndora, Pennsylvania many Polish children were sent to Detroit in the late 1920's when news of jobs in the expanding automobile industry was received. One Ukrainian-American son explained that it was understood that a child helped his father because the parent "couldn't make out."[73]

Slavic children were not always sent to work randomly. In mining districts especially, but also in steel mills, fathers took their sons to work with them or at least secured for them their initial adult occupations.[74] More importantly, it was within these initial jobs that the second generation usually decided upon their career goals. Those who helped their fathers as coal loaders, for instance, usually viewed the position as "blaster," a less physically demanding task, as a job to work toward. Numerous young men were taught their first job skills by their fathers. Nick Kiak's first job was learning the operation of a crane from his father at the Bethlehem mill.[75] All but seven of over seventy second generation Slavs interviewed in southwestern Pennsylvania coal fields were taken into the mines by their fathers.[76] Premigration reliance on kinship helped to determine occupational patterns. But the industrial work situation itself was also influential in shaping career goals.

Slavic parents not only influenced their children by example and direct action but imparted definite views concerning education. A typical Slovak father stressed to his son that it was more important to learn a manual skill than attend school. Michael Zahorsky was assured by his father that if he learned a trade he would never go hungry. Zahorsky became a blacksmith. Frank Horvath quit school at age sixteen to work in a Bethlehem furniture factory. His brothers had already started peddling milk to help pay the family milk bill. Horvath's parents questioned whether school helped anyone survive. They argued that an opportunity to leave school and make money should never be avoided.[77]

When Slavic newcomers did insist on education, religious vocation and ethnic cultures were usually stressed. Michale Labeka's father taught him the role of cantor in the Ukrainian church. A cantor was paid to sing religious responses in many Slavic churches. Labeka later supplemented his income as a mill worker in Monessen with his earnings as a cantor. Bernard Gorczyca's parents sent him to a Polish seminary in Michigan at age fourteen. Other parents admonished their children to study their native tongue and religious instruction.[78]

Slavic-American newspapers reinforced the disdain of American education. Immigrant children were told that America stressed education excessively and that intelligence was inborn anyhow. A Slovak newspaper printed a letter from a student who argued that the aim of American-born Slovaks should be loyalty to home and parish "even though it doesn't help you make money." Another Slovak wrote to *Narodne Noviny* that Slovaks should strive only to be more religious and do their daily work. A Ukrainian periodical urged all Ukrainian-American mothers to see that 80% of their children's schooling was in Ukrainian subjects. The uneducated, according to *Svoboda,* were those who Americanized their names and forgot the immigrant culture. When *Amerikansko Slovenske Noviny* attacked American public schools in 1893 for "assimilating our children and turning them against their parents," it was only reflecting the pervasive distrust of most Slavs toward secular education. Not surprisingly a recent content analysis of Slovak-American newspapers concluded that Slovak editors praised education not as a source of social mobility but as a vehicle for cultivating morality and preserving the ethnic culture and language.[79] Clearly the anti-materialistic skepticism toward American schools cited earlier was reinforced by a socioeconomic status which valued steady work.

The plight of women in industrial society gave further evidence that different structural conditions were not necessarily effecting drastic change, which at the same time women's attitudes and work experience were not simply reflections of cultural persistence. The working-class world encountered by Slavic women was making demands quite similar to those of their European homeland. If work on peasant farms required extensive participation of women, the Slavic women in industrial America were just as taxed. Caring for boarders, packing countless lunches, raising children, managing finances were familiar to most Slavic wives. Work outside the home was frequently necessary and, despite the findings of McLaughlin on Buffalo's Italians, "head on collision" with industrial society could not always be minimized let alone avoided. Jobs were necessary for survival. Considerations such as selecting jobs which involved minimal family strain were secondary to family survival. In eastern Pennsylvania textile mills, Slavic women chose jobs which offered quicker placements on wage-earnings scales and could be learned rapidly. For this reason cigar factories were preferred to silk mills. Often women either took what was available, followed friends to a particular factory, or looked for employment where language was not a barrier.[80] The following characterization of a Polish housewife in Johnstown, Pennsylvania in 1915 by a social investigator revealed that the demands of survival in industrial society evoked behavior which included a synthesis of tradition (child bearing methods, use of farm animals) and working-class devices (continued earning of wages through selling milk and caring for lodgers).

Monday evening went to sister's to return wash board, having just finished day's washing. Baby born while there; sister too young to assist; women not accustomed to midwifery anyway, so she cut the cord herself. Got up and ironed the next day . . . . She milked cows and sold milk the day after baby's birth. This woman keeps cows, chickens, and lodgers; also earns money doing laundry and char work. The husband deserts her at times; he makes $1.70 a day . . . . Mother thin and wiry; looks tired and worn. Frequent fights in home.[81]

The fatalism and "limited horizons" of peasant women was often noted and attributed to the high incidence of child deaths. Rudolph Bell, in his study of a South Slavic village, noted that burying one's own child was an expected tragedy which contributed to the image of the world as a source of "limited good."[82] But infant mortality rates continued at a high level for Slavs in America. Positioned in squalid mill towns and coal mining districts, Slavs suffered from poor diets, unsanitary conditions, and subsequently, dying children. The infant mortality rate in the United States (children under one year of age) in 1917 was 94 per 100,000 population. Among Poles in Shenandoah, Pennsylvania it was 187 per 100,000. The average annual death rate from "diarrhea and enteritis" among children under two years of age in Shenandoah was 365.8 per 100,000 compared to 104.8 for all of Pennsylvania and 71.4 for the United States.[83]

In Johnstown, Pennsylvania, a center for Slavic steel workers and miners, Serbs and Croats had an infant mortality rate of 263.9 in 1912 compared to a rate of 124 for all persons in America. Indeed, the rate surpassed the 149 per 100,000 rate for Serbia itself between 1901 and 1905.[84] The fact that Serbian or Croatian women seldom had either a physician or a midwife was as much a result of their low economic resources as it was their ignorance of modern medical practices. In fact, midwives were not usually affordable to South Slavs in Johnstown.[85]

As a result of the squalor and conditions of working class life, child death remained an expected tragedy. The notes from the Johnstown study were graphic:

"Mother aged 31 years; 10 pregnancies in 10 years; 8 live born; 2 still born; 4 deaths in first year."

"Mother aged 30 years; 9 pregnancies in 11 years; 8 live births, 1 miscarriage reported; 3 deaths in first year due to pneumonia; malarial fever and rheumatism."

"Mother aged 35 years; 6 births in 12 years; 4 live births and 2 still births. All live born died in first year . . . . SAYS SHE HAD ALWAYS WORKED TOO HARD, KEEPING BOARDERS IN THIS COUNTRY AND CUTTING WOOD AND CARRYING IT AND WATER ON HER BACK IN THE OLD COUNTRY . . . . Father furious because all babies die; wore red necktie to funeral of last to show his disrespect for wife who can only produce children that die."[86]

The behavioral patterns exhibited by Slavic newcomers can best be described as neither innovations nor residues of a previous culture. They must be judged a synthesis. Modernization involved a clash of peasant culture and working-class pragmatism which resulted in a reinforcement of traditional behavior and perceptions. If a preoccupation with security and survival was necessary in eastern Europe, working-class conditions in America did little to alter that fact. The sources of immigrant behavioral patterns were found in both worlds. While the peculiar constellation of symbolic traits which derived from Europe, such as religion and ethnic identification, gave the appearance of vast ethnic differences among Slavs, on a structured level the behavior of all Slavic peasants in America was remarkably similar and revealed an ability to integrate their culture with an emerging working-class consciousness. Limited occupational mobility in America reinforced the limited horizons of peasant Slovakia, Croatia, and Poland. The economic need to cling to steady work reinforced the traditional familial ties which mitigated against seeking individual careers far from home and demanded contributions from children for family sustenance. The increased desire to retain ethnic culture and the anti-materialistic thrust of peasant life buttressed the working-class skepticism of public schooling. The high incidence of child death from industrial squalor insured the continuation of the relationship between infant death and fatalism from eastern Europe. Without extensive social mobility within modern society, the simple transfer from premodern to modern society would not in itself effect drastic change.

Modernization could also result in a different chemistry depending on the background of newcomers who were subjected to its impact and particular structural situations. In Britain the initial impact of industrialization on skilled artisans evoked elements of pride, political action, and "class combativity." It was not until the late nineteenth century that this aggressive working-class view gave way to a "conservative and defensive culture" which resembled that of Slavic peasants in America.[87] While Slavs in America were involved in several labor protests for increased wages, generally their conservative, defensive posture was evidenced soon after their arrival in the industrial milieu. Arriving with a strong, traditionalist cultural bent, the tiresome burden of working-class life, sustained by limited mobility through two generations, hastened the emergence of a "defensive posture." Looking at the process of modernization, a recent scholar has noted the reconstruction of tradition in modern societies. He points out that the process whereby the various dimensions of tradition became institutionalized "are in continuously close relation to the organizational aspects of the social division of labor in general"[88] The Slavic peasant who emigrated to the lower levels of the American social structure reconstructed his own world by fusing old and new behavioral strategies to meet the continuing demands of survival.

FOOTNOTES

Research for this essay was supported by grants from the American Council of Learned Societies, the Immigration History Research Center, University of Minnesota, and the Pennsylvania Historical and Museum Commission. The author would like to thank professor David Montgomery for his valuable criticisms.

1. William J. Goode, *The Family* (Englewood Cliffs, N.J., 1964) and Oscar Handlin, *The Uprooted* (New York, 1951).

2. Joan W. Scott and Louise A. Tilly, "Women's Work and the Family in Nineteenth Century Europe," *Comparative Studies in Society and History*, XVII (Jan., 1975), 41-43, 55. For an elaboration of this discussion see Peter Stearns, "Working Class Women in Britain, 1890-1914," in *Suffer and Be Still*, Ed. by Martha Vicinus (Bloomington, Ind.,

1972), p. 104. Teodor Shanin, "The Peasantry as a Political Factor" in *Peasants and Peasant Society: Selected Readings,* Ed. by T. Shanin (Baltimore, 1971), 241-44.

3. Virginia Yans McLaughlin, "Patterns of Work and Family Organizations: Buffalo's Italians," *Journal of Interdisciplinary History,* II (Autumn, 1971), 299-314; Rudolph Vecoli, "Contadini in Chicago: A Critique of the Uprooted," *Journal of American History* (Dec., 1964), 404-16.

4. John Modell and Tamara K. Hareven, "Urbanization and the Malleable Household: An Examination of Boarding and Lodging in American Families," *Journal of Marriage and the Family,* (Aug., 1973), 467-78.

5. Bruce Laurie, Theodore Hershberg and George Alter, "Immigrants and Industry: The Philadelphia Experience, 1850-1880," *Journal of Social History,* IX (Dec., 1975), 231-43.

6. Frank Furstenberg, Theodore Hershberg, and John Modell, "The Origins of the Female-Headed Black Family: The Impact of the Urban Experience," *Journal of Interdisciplinary History,* VI (Fall, 1975), 232.

7. Hershberg, "Free Blacks in Antebellum Philadelphia: A Study of Ex-Slaves, Freeborn, and Socioeconomic Decline," *Journal of Social History,* 5, (Winter, 1971-72), 194-204.

8. Scott and Tilly, "Women's Work and the Family in Nineteenth Century Europe," 436-37; Yans McLaughlin, "A Flexible Tradition," 441-42.

9. See Joel M. Halpern, "Peasant Culture and Urbanization in Yugoslavia," in *Contributions to Mediterranean Sociology,* Ed. by J.G. Peristiany (The Hague, 1968), 293.

10. Helen S. Zand, "Polish Family Folkways," *Polish-American Studies,* XIII (July-December, 1956). Niles Carpenter and Daniel Katz, "A Study of Acculturation in the Polish Group of Buffalo, 1926-1928," *University of Buffalo Studies,* VII (June, 1929), 128-29.

11. Interviews with Sam Davich, Pittsburgh, June 24, 1974, Pittsburgh Oral History Project (POHP), reel 35; Michael Komernitski, McKees Rocks, June 17, 1974, POHP, reel 16; Joe Rudiak, Pittsburgh, July 21, 1974, POHP, reel 19; John Wolota, Pittsburgh, June 14, 1974, POHP, reel 14. All tapes used in this study are on file at the Pennsylvania Historical and Museum Commission. *The Report on Conditions of Women and Child Wage Earners in the United States, IV: The Silk Industry,* 61 Cong., 2nd sess., sen. doc. 645 (19 vols.; Washington, 1911), presents data on over 800 immigrant family incomes in Pennsylvania and New Jersey.

12. Howard Stein, "An Ethno-Historic Study of Slovak-American Identity, McKeesport, Pennsylvania," (unpublished Ph.D. dissertation, Univ. of Pittsburgh, 1972), pp. 417-437. Peter Ostafin, "The Polish Peasant in Transition: A Study of Group Integration as a Function of Symbiosis and Common Definitions," (unpublished Ph.D. dissertation, University of Michigan, 1948), pp. 200-210.

13. Stein, "An Ethno-Historic Study of Slovak-American Identity," 430-37; Kazimierz Dobrowolski, "Peasant Traditional Culture," *Peasants and Peasant Societies,* ed. by Teodor Shanin (Baltimore, 1971), pp. 280-85.

14. Vera St. Erlich, *Family in Transition, A Study of 300 Yugoslav Villages* (Princeton, N.J., 1966), 32. On the evolution of the Zadruga see Emile Sicard, "La Zadruga Sud-Slave dans l'Evolution du Groupe Domestique," (published Ph.D. dissertation, University of Clermont-Ferrand, Paris), 373-76. See also v. Kriskovic, *Brvatsko Pravo Kucnih Zadruga; Listorijskodogmatski Nacrt* (Zagreb, 1925); *Definitivni Rezultati, Popisa Stonovnistva OK 31 Januara, 1921 God,* 254-55, 375-76. Fran Vrbanic, "One Hundred

Years of the Development of the Population of Croatia-Slavonia," Yugoslav Academy of Science and Art, *Rad,* CXL (Zagreb, 1899), 17-58. While some dispute exists over the existence of the classic zadruga in Slovenia, Slovene family structure was still essentially based on a "patriarchal, extended family" headed by a "gospodar." It is true that zadrugas never flourished in Moslem districts. These districts, however, did not supply any significant amount of immigrants to immigrant centers such as Lackawanna, Gary, Steelton, or Pittsburgh. See Irene Winner, *A Slovenian Village, Zerovnica* (Providence, 1971) pp. 58-78. Joel M. Halpern, *A Serbian Village* (New York, 1958), pp. 135-37.

15. See table I. U.S. Immigration Commission, *Immigrants in Industry,* Part 23: Summary Report on Immigrants in Manufacturing and Mining Canals.; (Wash., 1911), II, 502-12.

16. Joseph Parot, "The American Faith and the Persistence of Chicago Polonia," (unpublished Ph.D. dissertation, Northern Illinois University, 1971).

17. Thaddeus Radzialowski, "The View from a Polish Ghetto," *Ethnicity,* I (July, 1974), 125-32.

18. Edward R. Kantowicz, *Polish-American Politics in Chicago, 1888-1940* (Chicago, 1975), pp. 26-27; Joseph Parot, "Ethnic versus Black Metropolis: The Origins of Polish-Black Housing Tensions in Chicago," *Polish-American Studies,* 29 (Spring-Autumn, 1972), 8-12.

19. Parot, "The American Faith and the Persistence of Chicago Polonia, 1870-1920," pp. 107-112; John Bodnar, "Steelton's Immigrants: Social Relationships in a Pennsylvania Mill Town," (unpublished Ph.D. dissertation, University of Connecticut, 1975), Chapter II; Joze Zavertnik, *Ameriski Slovenci* (Chicago, 1925), 448-506; Imrich Mazar, *Dejiny Bingham Tonskych* Slovakov, 1879-1919 (Binghamton, N.Y., 1919). Timothy Smith, "Lay Initiative in the Religious Life of American Immigrants, 1880-1950," *Anonymous Americans,* ed. by Tamara Harven (Prentice-Hall, 1971), pp. 215-21.

20. F. Majer to *Dziennik Chicagoski,* Aug. 27, 1892, Chicago Foreign Language Press Survey (CFLPS), reel 49. July 22, 1892, p. 4; Aug. 27, 1892, CFLPS, reel 49. *Zgoda,* Nov. 14, 1894, p. 4; Jan. 19, 1899, p. 6.

21. *Dziennik Chicagoski,* June 6, 1896; Sep. 1, 1908, CFLPS, reel 49.

22. *Ibid.,* Jan. 3, 1928. The overtones of anti-semitism which prevaded the Polish ethnic community often focused on the alleged materialistic aims of the Jews, although Polish anti-semitism had deeper historical roots in Europe. See *Narod Polski,* Aug. 6, 1919, CFLPS, reel 49.

23. Ivan Kramoris, "The Slovak Immigrant Situation," *Jednota,* Apr. 19, 1934; p. 3. *Jednota,* June 10, 1936, p. 9. Jane Addams related the distress of a visiting Czech professor in Chicago over the "materialism" of America including a few Bohemians; see *Twenty Years at Hull House* (New York, 1910), p. 171. Slovaks expressed attitudes similar to Poles in sterotyping Jews as materialistic; see *Jednota,* Sep. 8, 1937, p. 3.

24. *Jednota,* Apr. 22, 1936, p. 9; May 8, 1936, pp. 8-9.

25. See table V.

26. See table VI.

27. See table VII.

28. 61 Cong., 3rd Sess., serial 5875, *The Children of Immigrants in Schools* (5 vols.; Washington, 1911), V, 95, 515, 909.

29. Scott and Tilly, "Women's Work and Family in Nineteenth Century Europe," 48-49. Scott and Tilly found evidence of fiscal management by women in some premodern families but reliance on budgets and their control by women was certainly innovative for east European peasants.

30. Stein, "An Ethno-Historic Study of Slovak-American Identity," p. 426; Margaret Byington, Homestead: The Households of a Mill Town (New York, 1910), pp. 152-57 contains valuable data on Slavic family budgets. Interviews from the Scranton Oral History Project (1973) on establish and financial role of the Slavic female. See also Peter Roberts, *Anthracite Coal Communities* (New York, 1904) and Bessie Pehotsky, *The Slavic Immigrant Woman* (Cincinnati, 1925).

31. The only two statistical studies of Slavic mobility are Barton, *Peasants and Strangers,* 107-112 and Bodnar, "Steelton's Immigrants: Social Relationships in a Pennsylvania Mill Town," (unpublished Ph.D. dissertation, University of Connecticut, 1975). The following table is based on material from Barton, p. 107-112 and Bodnar, p. 212 and shows occupational mobility in Steelton, Pennsylvania and Cleveland, Ohio between 1905 and 1925 for Slavic and Italian immigrants:

INTERCLASS MOBILITY	Cleveland 1910-1920	Steelton 1905-1915	Steelton 1915-1925
% of Manual Workers Climbing	9%	5%	5%
% of White Collar Skidding	22%	3%	10%
Number	300	127	261

Examinations of intergenerational mobility among Slavic-Americans are found in Bodnar, "Steelton's Immigrants," Chapter VII and Barton, *Peasants and Strangers*, pp. 107-112. The following table is drawn from the works cited above. The ratios for the intergenerational occupational mobility of Slavic and Italian sons in Steelton and Cleveland between 1920 and 1950 are:

	Cleveland (born 1901-10)	Cleveland (born 1911-20)	Steelton (born 1900-15)
% of Lower Class Origins Climbing	25%	30%	22%
% of Middle Class Origins Skidding	70%	50%	43%
Number	81	92	180

The National Opinion Research Center has found that the percentage of Slavs in American white collar jobs was lower than the percentage for all Protestant groups, Orientals, Jews, and Irish, German, and Italian Catholics; Greeley, *Ethnicity in the United States* (New York, 1974), pp. 42-43.

32. *Memorial Book, 25th Anniversary First Croatian Building and Loan Association, 1910-1935* (Chicago, 1935).

33. *Wiadomosci Codzienne,* Jan. 28, 1938, p. 6; Feb. 9, 1938, p. 2; Marie Prisland, *From Slovenia to America* (Chicago, 1968), pp. 78-87; *Zajednicar,* Apr. 26, 1939, p. 11; Jozep Pauco, *Slovenski Prieko/pnic v Americke* (Cleveland, 1972), pp. 38-40.

34. *Zogda,* July 19, 1893, p. 8.

35. *Majski Glas* (May Herald) (May, 1937), p. 17; see also *The New American*, III (May, 1936), p. 1.

36. For a comparison of real estate value see U.S. Census, *Fifteenth Census of the United States, 1930, Special Report on Foreign Born White Families by Country of Birth* (Washington, 1933), pp. 155-73.

37. See Table II.

38. U.S. Census, *Fifteenth Census of the United States, VI: Families*, pp. 658-712.

39. See Table III.

40. See Table IV.

41. Bodnar, "Steelton's Immigrants," Chapter VI.

42. Poles in Philadelphia always identified themselves by their villages of birth; see Caroline Golab, "The Polish Communities of Philadelphia, 1870-1920: Immigrant Distribution and Adaptation in Urban America," (unpublished Ph.D. dissertation, Univ. of Pennsylvania, 1971), pp. 233-34. See also Franciszek Bujak, *Zmiaca-Wies Powiatu Limanowskiego: Stosunki Gospodarcze i Spoleczne* (Krakow, 1903); Bodnar, "Steelton's Immigrants," Chapter VI.

43. Victor L. Greene, "For God and Country: The Origins of Slavic Catholic Self-Consciousness in America," *Church History*, XXXV (Dec., 1966), 446. Greene after a study of Chicago Poles, concluded that America made its immigrants ethnocentric. Similar conclusions are found in Timothy Smith, "Religious Denominations as Ethnic Communities: A Regional Case Study," *Church History*, XXXV (June, 1966), 226; Richard Kornblum, *Blue Collar Community* (Chicago, 1974), pp. 35, 187; Bodnar, "The Formation of Ethnic Consciousness, Slavic Immigrants in Steelton," *The Ethnic Experience in Pennsylvania* (Lewisburg, Pa., 1973), pp. 309-330.

44. Essential to studying the formation of the Slovak community is Konstantine Culen, *Dejiny Slovakov v. Amerike* (2 vols; Bratislava, 1942), I, 190-210; Jozef Pauco, *75 Rokov Prvej Katolicej Katolicej Slovensej Jednoty* (Middleton, Pa., 1970), pp. 5-15 and "Kratka Historia Pennsylvanskej Slov Jednoty," in *Pennsylvania Slovak Catholic Union Diamond Jubilee* (Pittson, Pa., 1968).

45. Barton, "Immigration and Social Mobility in an American City: Studies of Three Ethnic Groups in Cleveland, 1890-1950," (unpublished Ph.D. dissertation, Univ. of Michigan, 1971), pp. 146-47.

46. Theodore Andrews, *The Polish National Church in America and Poland* (London, 1953), pp. 29-44; Paul Fox, *The Polish National Catholic Church* (Scranton, n.d.), pp. 24-25, 119; Leo V. Zrzywkowski, "The Origin of the Polish National Catholic Church of St. Joseph County, Indiana," (unpublished Ph.D. dissertation, Ball State Univ., 1972).

47. Parot, "The American Faith and the Persistence of Chicago Polonia, 1870-1920," pp. 310-36.

48. Michael Roman, "Istorija Greko-Kaft Sojedenija," *Golden Jubilee, 1892-1942* (Munhall, Pa., 1942), pp. 39-74. Stephen Gulovich, "Rusin Exarchate in the United States," *Eastern Churches Quarterly*, VI (Oct.-Dec., 1946), 463-72; Walter C. Warzeski, *Byzantine Rite Rusins in Carpatho-Ruthenia and America* (Pittsburgh, 1971), pp. 113-17; Bohadan Procko, "The Ukrainian Catholic Church in America" (unpublished Ph.D. dissertation, Univ. of Ottawa, 1964).

49. H. R. Niebuhr, *The Social Sources of Denominationalism* (New York, 1929), pp. 223-24. Marshall Sklare, "The Ethnic Church and the Desire for Survival," in Peter I. Rose, *The Ghetto and Beyond* (New York, 1969), pp. 101-17.

50. *Novi Svijet,* Jan. 19, 1928, p. 3.

51. Dept. of Justice Papers, Board of Pardons, Clemency File, R.G. 56, Pennsylvania Historical and Museum Commussion. See Greene, *The Slavic Community on Strike* (Notre Dame, Ind., 1968), for an account of the Lattimer Massacre.

52. Johann Chemlai, "The Austrian Emigration, 1900-1914," in *Perspectives in American History,* VII (1973), 291-92, 341.

53. Joel M. Halpern, *A Serbian Village* (New York, 1958), p. 64. Eric Wolf, *Peasants* (Englewood Cliffs, N.J., 1966), pp. 65-70. Mary Matossian, "The Peasant Way of Life," in *The Peasant in Nineteenth-Century Russia,* ed. by Wayne S. Vucinich (Stanford, Cal., 1968), p. 39.

54. Irene Winner, *A Slovenian Village: Zerovnica* (Providence, 1971), pp. 108, 120-121.

55. Rudolph M. Bell, "The Transformation of a Rural Village: Istria, 1870-1972," *Journal of Social History,* 7 (Spring, 1974), 251-252. Mark Stolarik, "Immigration and Urbanization, The Slovak Experience, 1870-1918" (unpublished Ph.D. diss., Univ. of Minnesota, 1974), Chapter I. Stolarik deals with Slovak peasant transiency in Europe.

56. The concept of "limited good" was developed by George Foster, "Peasant Society and the Image of Limited Good," *American Anthropologist* 67 (April, 1965), 293-315. Foster's views are substantiated by Bell, "The Transformation of a Rural Village," 256-258. Both Bell and Foster emphasize the peasant's perception of "limited good." Sula Benet, trans. and ed., *The Village of Viratino,* (Garden City, N.Y., 1970), p. 107.

57. Interview with Zara Werlinich, Pittsburgh, Aug. 16, 1974, Pittsburgh Oral History Project (POHP), reel 3. This and all interviews used in this study were taped in Pennsylvania and are on file at the Pennsylvania Historical and Museum Commission. In addition to the author, interviews were conducted by Peter Gottlieb, Lynda Nyden, and Major Mason, all of the University of Pittsburgh, and Carl Romanek of The Pennsylvania State University at McKeesport.

58. Interview with Sam Vignovic, Pittsburgh, Aug. 6, 1974, POHP, reel 8.

59. Interviews with Anonymous, West Mifflin, Aug. 16, 1974, POHP, reel 2. George Hudock, Bethlehem, July 16, 1974, Bethlehem Oral History Project (BOHP), reels 3-4.

60. Interviews with Mike Palovich, Pittsburgh, Aug. 7, 1974, POHP, reel 20; Nick Winovich, Pittsburgh, Aug. 7, 1974, POHP, reel 8. A similar aspiration was made by an Illinois steel worker, Steve Dubi. He recalled: "When we were kids we we thought the steel mill was it. We'd see the men comin out, all dirty, black . . . . We thought they were strong men. We just couldn't wait to get in there." See Studs Terkel, *Working* (New York, 1974), p. 552.

61. Interviews with Valerian Duda, McKeesport, July 8, 1974, POHP, reel 36; Andrew Bodnar, Munhall, June 3, 1974, POHP, reel 25.

62. Interviews with Walter Balawajder, McKeesport, July 11, 1974, POHP, reel 16, similar experiences were encountered by Mike Backer, Glassport, June 24, 1974, POHP, reel 33; John Urczyk, McKees Rocks, June 27, 1974, POHP, reel 10.

63. In two-hundred interviews used in the preparation of this paper only ten immigrants ever indicated an attempt to leave their industrial pursuits to enter business for themselves. Mike Pavlovich, for instance, left the Jones and Laughlin Steel plant in 1912 and opened a small saloon in Pittsburgh. His venture failed after one year, however, and he returned to a mill job. Of those who did enter private business, several did so only upon retirement from industrial work. See interview with Mike Pavlovich, Pittsburgh, Aug. 7, 1974, POHP, reel 20.

64. Interview with Valentine Bauer, Bethlehem, July 24, 1974, BOHP, reel 13. Additional explanations of Slavic geographic mobility are detailed in all interviews but see especially the interview with Peter Hnat, McKees Rocks, June 26, 1974, POHP, reel 9.

65. See footnote 31.

66. All but two of the 115 immigrant sons interviewed in this study were born between 1902 and 1914.

67. Interviews with George Porvasnik, McKees Rocks, July 12, 1974, POHP, reel 21; Sam Davich, Pittsburgh, June 24, 1974, POHP, reel 17; Charles Jablonski, Bethlehem, July 11, 1974, BOHP, reel 5. Davich worked at Jones and Laughlin plant for forty years. Jablonski spent his last forty-six working years at Bethlehem Steel. A similar experience is related by Michael Zahorsky, Aliquippa, July 31, 1974, POHP, reel 7.

68. Interviews with Robert Milanovich, Pittsburgh, Aug. 5, 1974, POHP, reel 3; Sam Mervosh, Pittsburgh, Aug. 12, 1974, POHP, reel 18; Charles Jablonski, Bethlehem, July 11, 1974, BOHP, reel 5; Frank Horvath, Bethlehem, July 16, 1974, BOHP, reel 3. Another Bethlehem worker wanted only a "job he would like." See interview with Francis Vadaz, July 11, 1974, BOHP, reel 6.

69. Interviews with Jouis Buchek, McKees Rocks, July 17, 1974, POHP, reel 12; Joseph Wiatrak, McKees Rocks, July 1, 1974, POHP, reel 1; Lewis Kozo, Bethlehem, July 15, 1974, BOHP, reel 2; Sam Mervosh, Pittsburgh, Aug. 8, 1974, POHP, reel 18.

70. Interviews with Frank Horvath, Bethlehem, July 16, 1974, reel 3; Charles Jablonski, Bethlehem, July 11, 1974, BOHP, reel 5; Michael Komernitski, McKees Rocks, POHP, reel 16.

71. Interviews with Bernard Gorczyca, Pittsburgh, June 20, 1974, POHP, reel 4; Frank Horvath, Bethlehem, July 16, 1974, BOHP, reel 3.

72. Interviews with Anton Cindrich, Pittsburgh, June 25, 1974, POHP, reel 17. Similar statements were made by Walter Klis, Pittsburgh, July 2, 1974, POHP, reel 15.

73. Interview with J. Wolota, Pittsburgh, June 14, 1974, POHP, reel 14. See Geoffrey H. Steers, "Child-rearing Literature and Modernization Theory," *The Family in Historical Perspective, Newsletter*, (Winter, 1974), pp. 8-9. Benjamin Spock, *Baby and Child Care* (New York, 1968), p. 12; Philip Slater, *The Pursuit of Loneliness* (Boston, 1970), pp. 62-64.

74. Interviews with John Smitko, McKeesport, June 22, 1974, POHP, reel 34. Southwestern Pennsylvania Oral History Project, Pennsylvania Historical and Museum Commissions, reels 110-115.

75. Interviews with Joseph Slater, Dravosburg, July 2, 1974, POHP, reel 35. Nick Kiak, Bethlehem, July 11, 1974, BOHP, reel 9.

76. Interviews with Sam Davich, Pittsburgh, June 24, 1974, POHP, reel 17; Michael Komernitski, McKees Rocks, June 17, 1974, POHP, reel 16; Joe Rudiak, Pittsburgh, July 21, 1974, POHP, reel 19; John Wolota, Pittsburgh, June 14, 1974, POHP, reel 14. Southwestern Pennsylvania Oral History Project, reels 110, 112, 113, 129.

77. Interviews with Michael Zahorsky, Aliquippa, June 21, 1974, POHP, reel 7; Frank Horvath, Bethlehem, July 16, 1974, POHP, reel 3.

78. Interviews with Michael Labeka, McKees Rocks, June 18, 1974, POHP, reel 4; Bernard Gorczyca, Pittsburgh, June 20, 1974, POHP, reel 15; Joe Rudiak, Pittsburgh, July 21, 1974, POHP, reel 19.

79. *Svoboda,* Aug. 26, 1932, p. 3; *Narodne Noviny,* Apr. 16, 1930, p. 3; July 22, 1931, p. 5. Stolarik, "Immigration and Urbanization," pp. 161-173. This evidence contradicts T.L. Smith, "Immigrant Social Aspirations and American Education, 1880-1930," *American Quarterly,* 21 (Fall, 1969); p. 525, who claims that the immigration experience of southern and eastern Europeans intensified the concern for learning. A recent study of Greek-American immigrants found that hard work was stressed more than education. See Nicholas Tavushis, *Family and Mobility Among Greek Americans,* (Athens, 1972). Colin Greer argued that immigrant children attended school extensively only *after* economic stability was attained. "Public education was the rubber stamp of economic improvement," he claimed, "rarely has it been the boot strap;" see Greer, ed., *Divided Society: The Ethnic Experience in America,* p. 89.

80. Bessie Olga Pehotsky, *The Slavic Immigrant Women* (Cincinnati, 1925), pp. 10-37; Caroline Manning, *The Immigrant Woman and Her Job* (Washington, 1930), pp. 104-106.

81. U.S. Dept. of Labor, Children's Bureau, Publication 9 (Washington, 1915), p. 32.

82. Rudolph M. Bell, "The Transformation of a Rural Village: Istria, 1870-1920," *Journal of Social History,* 7 (Spring, 1974), 251-52; Irene Winner, *A Slovenian Village: Zerovnica* (Providence, 1971), pp. 230-39. Mary Matossian, "The Peasant Way of Life," in *The Peasant in Nineteenth-Century Russia,* ed. by Wayne Vucinich, (Stanford, Cal., 1968), p. 29.

83. U.S. Dept. of Labor, Children's Bureau, Publication 106 (Washington, 1922), p. 47.

84. U.S. Dept. of Labor, Children's Bureau, Publication 9 (Washington, 1915), pp. 11-12, 28.

85. *Ibid.,* pp. 13-16.

86. *Ibid.,* pp. 31-82. Similar findings can be found in studies of Gary, Indiana in Publication 12 (Washington, 1922), pp. 38-109. Emphasis is mine.

87. See E.P. Thompson, *The Making of the English Working Class* (New York, 1966), p. 832; Gareth Steadman Jones, "Working Class Culture and Working Class Politics in London, 1870-1900: Notes on the Remaking of a Working Class," *Journal of Social History,* 7 (Summer, 1974), 484.

88. S.N. Eisenstadt, "Post-Traditional Societies and the Continuity and Reconstruction of Tradition," *Daedalus,* 102 (Winter, 1973), 18.

Table 1. Family Structure in Selected Cities, 1880-1925[a]

	South Slavs, Lackawanna, 1925	North Slavs, Hungarians, Lackawanna, 1925	Southern Born Blacks, Boston, 1880	Italians New York City, 1905	Welsh, Scranton, 1880
Nuclear	30%	69%	56 %	59.9%	83%
Extended	34%	20%	10.6%	23.2%	3%
Augmented	60%	23%	33.3%	21.1%	14%
Number of Household	220	480		3,584	227

[a]Source: New York State Census for Lackawanna, 1925; Elizabeth Pleck, "The Two-Parent Household: Black Family Structure in Late-Nineteenth Century Boston," *Journal of Social History*, VI, (Fall, 1972), 21; Herbert Gutman, "Work, Culture, and Society in Industrializing America, 1815-1919," *American Historical Review*, LXXVIII (June, 1973), 588; John Bodnar, "Socialization and Adaptation: The Immigrant Families of Scranton," *Pennsylvania History*, XLIII (January, 1976).

Table 2[a]. Percentage of Foreign-Born Family Heads Owning Homes, Urban Areas, 1930

	F = B Families	F = B % Owners: City	England	Ireland	Italy	Czechoslovakia	Poland	Yugoslav
Akron	13,014	68%	64%	—	68%	84%	70%	—
Bridgeport	18,109	35%	24%	40%	37%	39%	34%	—
Chicago	357,519	42%	31%	—	40%	54%	49%	41%
Cleveland	99,395	50%	38%	52%	—	65%	54%	49%
Buffalo	49,606	51%	37%	56%	45%	54%	58%	—
Toledo	14,399	69%	59%	75%	—	69%	81%	—
Milwaukee	47,393	58%	36%	33%	—	63%	70%	52%
Detroit	145,593	51%	41%	50%	—	59%	69%	54%

[a]Source: Fifteenth Census of the United States, 1930, Special Report on Foreign-Born White Families By Country of Birth (Washington, 1933), 155-73.

Table 3. Slavic Homeownership in Pennsylvania, 1930[a]

	Penna.	Aliquippa	Braddock	Duquesne	Farrell	Homestead	Johnstown
Families	2,235,620	5,271	4,081	4,473	2,973	4,346	15,042
% Owners	54%	45%	24%	42%	49%	31%	40%
% Native Owners (White)	54%	39%	18%	33%	34%	23%	35%
% Foreign-born Owners	60%	54%	33%	54%	63%	46%	51%
Largest F = B Group[b]	Slavic	Serbo-Croat	Slovak	Slovak	Serbo-Croat	Slovak	Slovak

	Shenandoah	Steelton	Wilkes-Barre	Mount Carmel	Munhall	Nanticoke
Families	4,438	2,974	18,718	3,760	2,963	5,378
% Owners	35%	49%	45%	47%	65%	45%
% Native Owners (White)	27%	43%	33%	37%	55%	23%
% Foreign-born Owners	41%	69%	57%	72%	78%	57%
Largest F = B Group	Polish	Serbo-Croat	Polish	Polish	Slovak	Polish

[a]Computed from U.S. Census, *Fifteenth Census of the United States, VI: Families*, 658-712.

[b]Slavs formed about 50 percent of the foreign-born population of Pennsylvania in 1930. Poles and Slovaks accounted for the largest number of Slavs.

Table 4. Homeownership in Selected Towns, 1930[a]

	Cicero, Ill.	Lorain, Ohio	Lackawanna, N.Y.	New Britain, Conn.
Families	16,255	10,167	4,357	15,534
% Owners	55%	58%	43%	35%
% Native Owners (White)	22%	48%	40%	32%
% Foreign-born Owners	67%	69%	53%	40%
Largest F = B Group	Czech-Polish	Slovak-Polish	Polish-Serbo-Croat	Polish-Italian

aComputed from U.S. Census, *Fifteenth Census of the United States, VI: Families*, 233, 366-78, 939.

Table 5[a]. Public School Attendance of Native & Immigrant Children Beyond Grade 6, 1910

	NBW	Negro	Hebrew German	Hebrew Polish	Irish	South Italian	Polish	Slovak	
Buffalo	31%	18%	40%	39%	32%	10%	6%	—	
Chicago	24%	15%	26%	20%	19%	5%	6%	4%	
Cleveland	26%	17%	31%	23%	24%	7%	7%	5%	Croat 6% Slovene 8%
Milwaukee	23%	16%	—	—	25%	2%	10%	—	Slovene 7%
New Britain	40%	—	—	—	61%	—	6%	—	
Scranton	—	—	—	22%	—	11%	4%	5%	
Shenandoah	16%	—	—	—	28%	1%	1%	—	

aStatistics computed from 61 Cong., 3rd sess.; serial 5875, *The Children of Immigrants in Schools* (5 vols., Washington, 1911), II, 378, 648, 848, IV, 77, 477, V, 418, 508.

Table 6ᵃ. High School Attendance, Native & Immigrant Children, 1910.

	NBW	Negro	Hebrew German	Hebrew Polish	Hebrew Russian	Irish	South Italian	Polish	Slovak
Buffalo	12%	8%	19%	16%	——	13%	3%	2%	——
Chicago	9%	5%	10%	6%	——	6%	1%	1%	1 %
Cleveland	12%	8%	13%	7%	——	11%	1%	2%	.5%
Milwaukee	10%	9%	——	——	3%	12%	1%	2%	——
New Britain	19%	——	——	9%	——	43%	——	1%	——

ᵃStatistics computed from 61 Cong., 3rd sess.; serial 5875 (5 vols., Washington, 1911), II, 378, 648, 848; IV, 77, 477; V, 418, 508.

Table 7ᵃ. Parochial School Attendance by Ethnic Group Beyond Grade 6

	Native-born white	Irish	Polish	Slovak
Milwaukee	14.9%	10%	1.6%	0%
New Britain	22 %	26%	0 %	——
Cleveland	17 %	19%	5 %	10%

ᵃ61st Cong., 3rd sess., serial 5875, *The Children of Immigrants in Schools* (5 vols.; Washington, 1911), pp. 95, 515, 909.

VARIETIES OF WORKINGCLASS EXPERIENCE: THE WORKINGMEN OF SCRANTON, PENNSYLVANIA, 1855-1885

14

Samuel Walker

The response of American workingmen to industrialization in the nineteenth century was a complex and multidimensional phenomenon. The outlines of the emerging industrial-capitalist order were far from clear even to the most prescient observer. Like other Americans, workingmen were torn between a number of different interpretations of the changes that were engulfing society. Although the factory system was a common experience, it was one that affected different individuals and different groups in various ways.

Looking at the broad sweep of the industrialization process in America, historians have identified a number of different general factors that influenced the perceptions and actions of workingmen. The initial onset of industrialization, for example, was a very different experience from the changes that occurred later in the process. Geography was also important. The New England states industrialized early, and western and many southern areas industrialized relatively late. Different occupations were affected by industrialization at different times also. The social status of workingmen in small industrial communities was different from that of their counterparts in the large cities. Finally, the American workingclass experience was deeply affected by the continuing tensions among different ethnic and racial groups.[1]

This essay examines the varieties of workingclass experience in Scranton, Pennsylvania, from the mid-1850s through the mid-1880s. Although Scranton was hardly a typical industrial community, many aspects of its industrial history were common to other areas. The period covers the rapid transformation of Scranton from a small village into a major industrial center. The growth of the city and its industries attracted a volatile mixture of different ethnic groups. Finally instability in the anthracite coal industry —the foundation of the city's economy—together with a major depression in the mid-1870s brought on continued industrial conflict. Despite Scranton's uniqueness as an anthracite coal mining community, the experience of rapid industrialization and urbanization, ethnic group conflict, and industrial strife was common to all industrial communities in nineteenth-century America.[2]

As Scranton workingmen confronted the industrial revolution, they responded in a variety of ways. First, they expressed a "producer ideology" that rested on an identity of interests with their employers. In many respects, their employers shared the idea of a harmony of interests and reciprocated with a posture of paternalism. The second worker response was quite different. Sensing that they were losing their social and economic status, the workers developed an incipient class consciousness. Numerous expressions of collective action characterized workers' actions between the 1850s and 1880s. But the workers found it difficult to maintain a united front. The various occupations had different experiences with the advent of industrialization. The miners in particular regarded themselves as an aristocracy among Scranton workingmen. Thus the third type of response was a form of occupational identity that divided miners, laborers, and ironworkers among themselves. In the long run, however, ethnicity proved to be the most enduring source of identity for workingmen. Ethnic group consciousness formed the fourth major response.[3]

These four different responses were not mutually exclusive. Rather they competed with each other for influence over the thought and actions of Scranton workingmen. In some cases two of the factors merged and became indistinguishable. The solidarity of the Welsh coal miners, for example, was a potent combination of ethnic and occupational identity. Specific circumstances, meanwhile, could give added salience to a particular factor. Collective action and incipient class consciousness were most pronounced during the economic and political upheaval of 1876-1878. A full appreciation of the workers' experience in Scranton must take into account the complexity and fluidity of the situation. At one moment, groups of workers grasped at one solution to their problem; a few years later a different set of circumstances caused the same groups to define their situation in very different terms. Workingmen, after all, were capable of both wisdom and folly, like other human beings, and were quite ready to change their minds if circumstances changed.

The period from the mid-1850s through the mid-1880s forms a distinct chapter in the economic and social history of Scranton. It begins with the opening of the anthracite coal mining industry in the area, witnesses the rapid development of an oligopolistic corporate structure, and ends with the integration of the major local firms into the national economy. In the early 1850s the fate of the community was very much in the hands of resident Scrantonians. By the mid-1880s its fate was in the hands of impersonal market forces and nonresident finance capitalists.[4]

Local historians were correct in suggesting that the progress of their community could be attributed to the pioneering efforts of a handful of men. Although the city lay in the heart of incredibly rich anthracite coal deposits, the mountainous terrain prevented their full exploitation until the advent of the railroad in the 1850s. Colonel George W. Scranton rightly deserved the title of father of the community. He and a series of associates had begun producing iron in the 1840s. He survived a number of near disasters to form what eventually became the Lackawanna Iron and Coal Company. Using that firm as his base, Colonel Scranton began to push railroad development vigorously. Through construction, purchase, and rental, this resulted in the Delaware, Lackawanna and Western Railroad. The turning point in the history of the community came in 1856 with the opening of a direct rail connection with the port of New York City. Scranton then quickly became a major anthracite mining, iron manufacturing, and railroading center.[5]

The development of Scranton was rapid and spectacular. The population grew from 4,469 in 1850 to 17,093 in 1860 and then to an estimated 35,000 by 1870. Economic progress, however, exacted its price from the members of the Scranton family. The capital required for the expansion of family-owned firms came from New York financiers, and the Scrantons soon lost control of their companies. George and Joseph H. Scranton's iron manufacturing firm was rescued from disaster in 1846 by a contract to produce rails for the Erie Railroad. The railroad magnates provided the capital and gained control of the firm. In a similar fashion, outside capital was required to construct the various railroad lines that eventually formed the Delaware, Lackawanna and Western. Moreover "capitalists refused to subscribe to the railroad stocks unless they could have . . . an equal interest in the iron works." Thus although George Scranton was the driving force behind the economic development of the area, he and the other members of the family were reduced to the role of resident managers. New York interests controlled both the Lackawanna Iron and Coal Company and the Delaware, Lackawanna and Western Railroad, which they operated virtually as a single enterprise. The direct involvement of Scranton family members in the day-to-day activities of the firms remained high, and this role formed the basis for the impact of paternalism in industrial relations.[6]

By the 1860s the economic development of the northern anthracite region was reduced to a competition between two mining and transportation giants. On the one side stood the Scranton-based Lackawanna Iron and Coal Company and the DL&W Railroad. On the other stood the older firm, the Delaware and Hudson Canal Company, which also combined mining with railroading. The result of their competition was a furious expansion of the industry as each tried to gain market dominance over the other. By the late 1860s the two firms directly controlled over half the coal mined in the area and, through their near monopoly over transportation, effectively dominated the smaller anthracite producers. The northern operators as a group, meanwhile, competed vigorously with their counterparts in the southern anthracite region.[7]

The transformation of the Scranton economy from one of relatively small family-owned companies into one dominated by two giant industrial combinations forms the context in which two of the different workers' responses appeared. Incipient class consciousness arose from a sense that workers were becoming a class apart in the world of industrial capitalism. Yet the experience of the early years of industrialization continued to exert a strong influence. The first response, the belief in a harmony of interests and the producer ideology that underpinned it, was a product of this early experience. In his study of the American labor movement in the 1860s and early 1870s, David Montgomery argues that labor leaders subscribed to an "ideological syndrome of 'free agency,' self-improvement, and temperance," which "was capped by a commitment to a society in which all members were free to move upward on the basis of their own talents." The producer ideology, then, dictated that all men who worked had the potential to rise in society; no inherent conflicts divided workingmen from employers.[8]

The early industrial experience of Scranton lent credence to this view of society. In their own lives many workingmen had seen individuals rise from humble beginnings to positions of great wealth. Many Scranton workingmen, in fact, had worked side by side with the George Scrantons and Thomas Dicksons in the 1850s and 1860s. George Scranton, for example, wielded hammer and chisel in his initial attempts to manufacture iron. One workingman recalled the time when "Thomas Dickson, then General Superintendent . . . [of the Delaware and Hudson Coal Department] appeared with blue denim trousers and blouse on him. He took the hammer from one man and took his place for about fifteen minutes, then stepped over on the other side and spelled another man for fifteen minutes."[9]

Such instances of close fraternization on the job blurred distinctions of wealth and class. At the same time, the employers often took a personal interest in the welfare of their men. One account described George W. Scranton as "the poor man's friend," who had continued to operate his mines through the depression winter of 1857 because he allegedly said, "we *must* work [to] enable our men to work." Another employee recalled that Joseph Scranton had agreed to support his family when the father went to serve in the Union Army. Joe Scranton told the man, "Your pay goes right on, Fred, and I will take care of these [the children]." Others recalled that Joe Scranton had promised to match the wages of his competitors and had always taken pride in the sobriety of his men.[10]

These recollections, of course, should not be taken at face value. The number of strikes in the mid-1860s, for example, raises doubts about Joe Scranton's promise to match competitors' wages. Undoubtedly these accounts emphasized the best rather than the worst aspects of the past. Nostalgia had an important political function: romanticizing the past was a means of condemning present conditions. Workingmen frequently drew invidious comparisons between the first generation, George and Joe Scranton, and the latter's son, William, who was generally regarded as a local tyrant. Even with these qualifications in mind, however, the fond recollections of the past did represent a genuine sense of personal identification that transcended class lines.[11]

The physical structure of the city contributed to close relations between worker and employer. Even through the 1880s Scranton was primarily a walking city. Most people walked to and from their jobs. Coal miners, for example, settled into closely knit communities surrounding the largest mines. Frequently workingmen encountered their employers on the streets. The experience of Terence Powderly, who was an obscure journeyman machinist through the early 1870s, illustrates this phenomenon. In his diary, Powderly noted several occasions when he met and conversed with William W. Scranton. Once he was introduced to the industrialist's daughter and on another occasion shared the same chair in the barbershop with his employer. In short, the observation of the Pennsylvania Bureau of Industrial Statistics was accurate when it said that "in the early days the acquaintance among the people was far more general than it is at present; [people] were more nearly on the same plane socially, industrially, and morally, than they are today."[12]

Workingmen and industrialists even shared common social events. The annual typographers' union ball in 1872 was described as a major social event in the pages of the *Scranton Republican*. The fourth annual Brotherhood of Locomotive Engineers ball in 1873, meanwhile, was attended by George L. Dickinson and other "prominent railroad men." The seventh annual ball four years later again attracted a number of executives and was described as "one of the most successful social gatherings of the season." Among those in attendance was Walter Dawson, master mechanic for the DL&W and a man generally reviled by labor leaders in the community.[13]

The legacy of close relations between workingmen and employers made itself felt in industrial relations. Labor unions in the Scranton area continually stressed their belief in the mutual interests of employer and employee. Conciliation rather than conflict remained their major goal. The leaders of the 1876 machinists' strike in Scranton—a major strike that attracted national attention and, among other things, helped to destroy the Machinists and Blacksmiths Union—declared: "We seek no war with legitimate enterprise, but demand a just remuneration for our labor."[14] The term "legitimate enterprise" was crucial. Both workingmen and local businessmen made moral distinctions between various types of corporations.

The producer ideology enshrined small enterprise. The large corporation, however, was a different matter. During and after the 1871 coal miners' strike, local business leaders complained that the executives of the anthracite corporations—nonresidents of the community—cared nothing about the fate of the community. Vast and impersonal enterprises, responding to national market forces, the anthracite companies were "soulless" corporations."[15]

Throughout its history the Workingmen's Benevolent Association, the anthracite coal miners' union, stressed close cooperation between employers and employees. The union's major effort in the 1870s, in fact, was the development of a cooperative arrangement with the coal producers, one that would restrict production and thereby raise both prices and wages. The experiment failed because of the highly competitive nature of the anthracite industry, particularly the rivalry between producers in the northern and southern anthracite fields. But this did not prevent the leaders of the miners from continuing to believe that their fate rested with cooperation with the producers.[16] The Machinists and Blacksmiths Union adopted a similar perspective. The preamble to the union's constitution stated that "so far from encouraging a spirit of hostility to employers, all properly organized unions recognize an identity of interests between employer and employee."[17]

Scranton workingmen inherited a tradition of settling industrial disputes on a person-to-person basis. They had grown accustomed in the 1850s and at least through part of the 1860s to dealing with such problems on that basis. Thus even after control of the corporations had passed to New York financiers, workingmen sought to deal with the top officials directly. Repeatedly they sent delegations by train to meet with either the president or chairman of the board of directors. A committee of five workers went to New York to see Samuel Sloan, president of the DL&W, asking that a 10 percent pay cut be rescinded. And in September 1877, a delegation of coal miners again went to New York to see Sloan in hopes of ending the two and a half month old miners' strike. In June before the strike had begun, the miners had tried to arrange a meeting with the board of directors in order to air their grievances. The mayor of Scranton later testified that "this was one point the men tried to gain [in the 1871 miners' strike] . . . one they gained at this time. I never saw men seemingly more pleased with the result."[18]

These efforts by Scranton workingmen were increasingly futile, if not pathetic, gestures by the 1870s. In the developing system of industrial capitalism, the president and members of the board of directors were not involved directly in industrial disputes; such tasks were left to lower-level managers. Personal contact counted for little as decisions were calculated on the basis of impersonal market forces. It was this change that helped to give rise to attacks on the "soulless" corporation.

The producer ideology that flourished in the anthracite regions had an important impact on the Knights of Labor in the 1870s and 1880s. The program of the Knights continually stressed a harmony of interests between employers and employees. It is of no small significance that Terence Powderly, leader of the Knights, not only came of age during the era of the Workingmen's Benevolent Association but was a member and eventually an officer in the Machinists and Blacksmiths Union. Experiences and ideas that developed at the local level eventually influenced the ideological perspective of the first important national labor union.[19]

Significantly the actions of some industrialists in Scranton paralleled those of their workingmen. They too sought to cling to the old pattern of settling disputes directly. George Dickson, president of the Dickson Manufacturing Co., settled a June 1873 strike in twenty minutes by meeting with the strikers and promising to pay the men in four days (the strike involved a delay in the arrival of payday). And in June 1877, at the first sign of industrial unrest, William W. Scranton arrived on the scene immediately. He listened to the strikers' demands but said "he could not do anything, and he drove away." In the 1871 miners' strike, he personally stood guard at the opening of a mine to protect strikebreakers. And in the 1877 "riot," he led a group of about fifty armed men to protect the city from the rampaging mob of workingmen.[20]

The surviving remnants of paternalism were visible in the context of continuing and often bitter industrial strife. Because of the instability of the anthracite market, the Scranton area was torn by numerous strikes between the mid-1860s and the late 1870s. Workingmen perceived that their status in society was declining, and they were increasingly willing to see themselves as a separate class and to take collective action. Coal miners' strikes occurred in 1860, 1864, 1865, 1869, and 1871. Workers in the railroad shops went on strike for the eight-hour day in 1868. There were also numerous small disputes between the onset of the depression in the fall of 1873 and the final upheaval in the summer of 1877. The 1876 machinists' strike in Scranton, for example, was a struggle of national significance for the machinists' union.[21]

The two most important strikes of the period demonstrated the determination of the coal miners and their capacity for protracted strike activity. The 1871 strike lasted nearly six months, the 1877 nearly three. Both struggles were followed by the formation of insurgent workingmen's political parties. In 1872 the Labor Reform party narrowly missed capturing control of city government in Scranton. The 1877-1878 Greenback-Labor party was more successful. After sweeping the Luzerne County elections in the fall of 1877, the Greenbackers elected their candidate, Terence Powderly, mayor of Scranton in early 1878. The turn to independent political action and the choice of the word *labor* for the name of these parties testifies to the incipient growth of class consciousness on the part of Scranton workingmen in the 1870s.[22]

A close examination of the social sources of workingmen's activities in Scranton, however, suggests that class consciousness was extremely weak. The conflicting appeals of occupational identity and ethnic group consciousness divided the workingclass. The picture was ambiguous, for the very factors that divided workers also provided the mainspring for concerted action. That is to say, the miners were capable of effective action when acting together as miners. And in the case of the Scranton area coal miners, occupational and ethnic identities merged, for the bulk of the miners were proudly Welsh in background.

In the context of the Scranton community, the coal miners comprised a genuine aristocracy of labor. They brought with them skills and cultural traditions that they had developed in the anthracite fields of Wales. In 1880, Scranton had the third largest Welsh-American community in the United States, behind New York City and Pittsburgh. The Welsh miners settled into an aggressively middle-class community in Hyde Park, on the heights overlooking downtown Scranton. Although divided among several different Protestant denominations, the Welsh saw themselves as a united group vis-à-vis the Catholic Irish workers. Private homeowning was very high among the miners, and local businessmen cited them as an example for other workers to follow.[23]

In the coal mines a distinct hierarchy existed among the miners and the laborers. Miners were de facto bosses, supervising the laborers who worked under them and paying them out of their own earnings (based on a fixed rate per carload). The miners also enjoyed such indexes of status as the privilege of leaving work early while the laborers remained to load the last of the coal. The laboring jobs, meanwhile, were generally held by Irish-Americans and, to a lesser extent, German-Americans.[24]

Ethnic group consciousness underpinned the anthracite miners' union in the Scranton area. The Workingmen's Benevolent Association (WBA) was essentially an extension of the Welsh community. Like many other labor unions, the WBA evolved out of early fraternal organizations that engaged in self-help activities. One local historian observed that "in the sixties, Welsh and English miners . . . familiar with the workings of cooperative societies in their native land, organized a cooperative association. . . . The purpose of the venture was to reduce the cost of living." The first Miners' Benevolent Association in Hyde Park was organized in September 1862. It soon had eight branches and over one thousand members who paid twenty-five cents a month dues and were eligible for benefits of three dollars a week in case of injury. The stated purpose of the organization was "the amelioration of human suffering and the promotion of moral conduct, subordinant to which is the mutual protection and support of each other by the members as laborers." The miners also organized a host of building and loan societies to further their ambitions to become homeowners.[25]

The 1871 miners' strike clearly illustrated the effect of ethnic group consciousness among Scranton workingmen. The strike was organized in December 1870 by the predominantly Welsh WBA. After several weeks, the largely Irish and German laborers broke ranks and sought to return to work; they clearly hoped to displace the Welsh in the skilled mining jobs. The employers, of course, encouraged these efforts. The violence that flared on several occasions during the strike (at one point resulting in martial law) was the result of clashes between Welsh miners and the Irish and German laborers, not between workers and employers. Significantly, violent clashes involved entire ethnic communities, including women and children.[26]

The eventual failure of the 1871 strike led directly to the formation of the municipal Labor Reform party in early 1872. As the returns on election day indicated, the party drew virtually all of its support from the four predominantly Welsh GOP wards. The regular GOP virtually disappeared as a result of the miners' defection, while the Democratic party retained the loyalty of its constituents, the Irish laborers. The social base of the Labor Reform party, then, was almost entirely the Welsh miners. Ideologically it did not differ from either of the two mainstream parties; it advanced a cautious municipal reform program and did not advocate any proposals designed to benefit either coal miners or workingmen generally.[27]

A sense of craft exclusiveness characterized other occupations in the Scranton community. The Brotherhood of Locomotive Engineers and the typographers staged annual dances that were covered in the local press and attended by their employers. The perceived self-interest of different occupations hindered collective action even in the desperate days of the summer of 1877 when feelings of class consciousness were presumably at their height. The 1877 upheaval in Scranton began with a spontaneous walkout by workers in the iron mills. It occurred on July 24, one week after the initial outbreak of violence in Martinsburg, West Virginia. The next day brakemen and firemen went out on strike and "the City of Scranton was thus suddenly cut off from all communication with the outside world." The railroad strike then forced a suspension of coal mining. It was only then that the coal miners resolved not to return to work without a 25 percent pay increase. The different unions, however, were unable to maintain a solid front. Within a week the firemen and brakemen returned to their jobs without any gains. The miners felt betrayed but maintained their own strike for nearly three months. Weakened by the divisions among the workingclass, they too were forced to return to work eventually without any significant gains.[28]

The spread of the Knights of Labor into the Scranton area in 1876 and 1877 further illustrates the fact that craft and ethnic group identities provided the mainspring of workingmen's actions. Local assemblies were essentially fraternal associations, closely resembling other fraternal groups that were rooted in the different ethnic communities and often closely related to the church. The diaries of Terence Powderly provide an illuminaing glimpse into the wide variety of community organizations. Powderly himself was the quintessential joiner, moving freely from literary club, to debating club, to political club, and to labor union. The Irish-Catholic groups he joined were paralleled by similar groups in the Welsh-American and German-American communities.[29]

The surviving records of Local Assembly 222, Powderly's home local, and District Assembly 16 of the Knights of Labor further indicate the dominant mood of exclusivity. As other studies of the Knights of Labor have suggested, most assemblies were organized on the basis of specific crafts. Thus LA 222 was dominated by machinists. Other locals were eventually organized exclusively for German-American workingmen. The minutes of LA 222 indicate a primary concern with the mundane business of organizational life. There was little to distinguish it from the other fraternal groups in the community.[30]

Rivalries among the different ethnic groups also dominated the politics of District Assembly 16. Terence Powderly quickly emerged as the most prominent labor spokesperson among the Irish-Catholics of Scranton. He was challenged by Joshua R. Thomas, an iron molder and blacksmith who represented the Welsh community. Both men competed for leadership positions in the district assembly. Powderly, of course, eventually went on to become Grand Master Workman of the Knights. In the 1876-1877 expansion of the Knights in the Scranton area, conflict between Irish and Welsh workingmen was a constant source of difficulty.[31]

In the end, ethnic group identity provided the most enduring source of identity among Scranton workingmen. Several long-term processes bear out this view. One is the speed with which workingclass militancy dissipated. After its defeat in the 1872 municipal elections, the Labor Reform party vanished without a trace. Militancy also had a difficult time surviving the upheaval of 1877. After an initial upsurge of growth, the Knights of Labor quickly lost their organizational momentum. Even Terence Powderly's home local, LA 222, virtually collapsed and almost died in the spring of 1878. Only Powderly's personal intervention kept it alive over the next few years. His growing personal status, first as mayor of the city and then as Grand Master Workman of the Knights, helped him enormously in this regard. When prosperity returned to the area in late 1878 and early 1879, labor militancy practically vanished.[32]

The second index of the prominence of ethnic group consciousness, and the relative weakness of class consciousness, is the pattern of voting in local elections. Voting behavior, by ward, was remarkably consistent throughout the 1870s and 1880s. The Welsh miners were most heavily concentrated in wards 1, 2, 4, and 5 (the latter two representing the community of Hyde Park, which was virtually synonymous with the Welsh miners). In both local and national elections, these wards consistently gave at least 60 percent and often as high as 75 percent of their vote to Republican candidates. The Irish Catholics were most heavily concentrated in wards 3, 6, 7, 12, 18, 19, and 20. (Wards 6 and 7 were literally on the other side of the tracks from wards 4 and 5.) The Democratic vote in these wards often exceeded 90 percent in both local and municipal elections.[33]

Politics played a central role in the social structure of ethnic group communities in Scranton. It was the focal point for many vital institutions and, at the same time, provided an important source of ethnic group identity vis-à-vis other ethnic groups. Ethnicity, religion, and politics merged into a coherent whole. The Irish, for example, were defined both by their Catholicism and their near-total allegiance to the Democratic party. Similarly the Welsh defined themselves by their Protestantism (a common denominator that overrode denominational cleavages) and the fact that they were, according to one observer, "Republican to a man." The Germans exerted less political clout in Scranton, in part because they were divided between Protestants and Catholics.[34]

In each ethnic group community, organized religion provided the basis for a wide range of related social institutions. Terence Powderly, for example, rose to prominence as a political leader through his activity in a series of literary and debating clubs associated with the Catholic church. In the St. Columbkilles Young Men's Literary Society, the future labor leader practiced the arts of debating, public speaking, and mastering the details of running an organization (writing constitutions and bylaws and maintaining correspondence, for example).[35]

The web of community institutions included ethnic group newspapers. The editors of the various newspapers were almost always active political figures. Joseph Scranton led the middle-class, Anglo-Saxon, Republican element through his paper, the *Scranton Republican*. Frank Beamish, the reputed "Boss Tweed" of the city, ran his Democratic party machine through his editorship of the *Scranton Free Press*. Members of the Jones family spoke for the Welsh community through the Welsh-language weekly, the *Hyde Park Baner*. Nicholas Kiefer, also active in city politics, edited the weekly German-language *Herold*.[36]

Each newspaper carried extensive coverage of the activities of different groups in their respective ethnic group communities. Welsh religious and cultural events were reported in the *Banner* and the *Scranton Republican*; although not a Welsh newspaper, the latter had to be extremely solicitous of the most cohesive voting bloc in the GOP. Irish nationalism, meanwhile, received full treatment in the Democratic party papers, the machine-oriented *Free Press* and the reform-minded *Daily Times*. During election campaigns, ethnic group rivalry came to the fore. Republican papers reminded its readers that the opposition party was dominated by Irish-Catholics. In 1872, for example, the *Republican* denounced the Democratic mayoral candidate as "an unnaturalized Irish squire" and warned darkly of the threat of an all-Irish police force. Democratic newspapers, meanwhile, usually retaliated by reminding their readers that the Republicans were highly sympathetic to temperance and prohibition ideas. As community institutions, then, the newspapers served not simply as vehicles for their respective editors but more importantly as a means of mobilizing ethnic group solidarity. Party loyalty became the most visible expression of ethnic group identity.[37]

Voting patterns rooted in ethnicity survived labor insurgency with little disruption. The 1872 Labor Reform party, for example, drew over 80 percent of its total vote from wards 1, 2, 4, and 5 alone. It received virtually no support from the workingmen in the traditionally Democratic wards. The Labor Reform party, like the coal miners' strike that preceded it, was an extension of the Welsh mining community. This ethnic solidarity provided the great strength of both the strike and the insurgent political party but also set firm limits to their appeal to other workingmen.[38]

The political insurgency of 1877-1878 was a bit more complex. The Greenback-Labor party swept the county elections in the fall of 1876 and then elected Terence Powderly as mayor of Scranton in February 1878. Since Powderly was an Irish Catholic, the insurgent labor party appealed primarily to that ethnic group. Thus the election returns of February 1878 were virtually the mirror image of those in 1872; on this occasion the insurgent party was rooted in a traditionally Democratic constituency. Powderly carried all of the Democratic wards by the usual margins. In addition, he scored important gains among traditionally Republican workingmen. For example, he carried wards 1 and 2 and did extremely well in wards 4 and 5. The intensity of the industrial strife the previous year—the "riot" on August 1 and the eventual failure of a long miners' strike—was sufficient to drive many normally Republican workingmen into the arms of an essentially Democratic "labor" party.[39]

Labor insurgency cooled rapidly, however. There was a significant drop in support for the Greenback-Labor party among the Welsh miners even between November 1877 and February 1878. The Greenbackers' support in the Fourth Ward, for example, dropped from 67.3 percent to 41.1 percent. A similar decline occurred in the Fifth Ward. In short, traditional loyalties reasserted themselves within months after the upheaval of the summer of 1877. By the fall of 1878, voting patterns had returned completely to their normal condition. Although the Greenback-Labor party continued to exist in name, it was for all practical purposes little more than the local Democratic party under a different name.[40]

The return of normal voting patterns presented Mayor Terence Powderly with a difficult problem in his quest for reelection. He soon found it necessary to establish a reconciliation with the local Democratic party. In 1880 he was elected as a fusion Greenback-Democratic candidate and in 1882 was reelected to a third term as a regular Democrat. By then Greenbackism and labor insurgency had completely vanished. Moreover Powderly's reelection campaigns were marked by the prominence of the traditional ethnic rivalries as the major campaign issues (Republicans warning about an all-Irish police force and Democrats reminding their followers about the affinity of many Republicans for temperance).[41]

Although elected on an upsurge of workingmen's discontent, Powderly served six years as mayor in a fashion that was in no way different from that of any of his predecessors. The 1878 platform of the municipal Greenback-Labor party contained no planks that pertained specifically to the interests of workingmen. Nor did Powderly suggest that he would institute any labor-oriented program in his campaign. During his three terms he was, like other mayors of the period, essentially a figurehead. Powderly differed only to the extent that he used the office as a convenient base from which to pursue his outside interests, including his national role in the Knights of Labor. In short, neither Powderly himself nor his constituents expected the labor mayor of Scranton to be an aggressive and innovative advocate of workingclass interests. Soon after the upheaval of 1877, municipal politics returned to normal.[42]

In conclusion, a few caveats are in order. First, the dominant influences affecting the perception and behavior of workingmen in Scranton during its period of initial industrial growth were not mutually exclusive. No one factor was completely dominant at any given time, to the exclusion of others, and no group in the community subscribed to one rather than another. Rather these various influences were blended together in a complex and confusing mixture.

A second important caveat to this analysis is that it is restricted to a particular period in the history of Scranton. The period from the mid-1850s through the mid-1880s forms a distinct era in the history of the community. A number of important changes began to occur in the mid-1880s. First, industrialization continued apace, further altering the work experience in both mine and factory. The perceptions of workingmen by the turn of the century were undoubtedly far different from those of their predecessors in the initial phase of industrialization. Second, the advent of immigration from Eastern Europe profoundly altered the context of ethnic group relations. The new arrivals found themselves at the bottom of the social scale, while the established groups claimed a measure of higher status. The relationship of ethnicity and social class became even more complex.[43]

With these caveats in mind, we should consider briefly those aspects of the Scranton experience that merit safe generalization. Perhaps the most important of these is the fact that workingclass experience, even in a single community over a relatively short period of time, was very complex. Attitudes and behavior cannot be reduced to a simple formula. Moreover the ingredients in that mix—paternalism, class consciousness, occupational consciousness, ethnicity—were common to other industrial communities. A second issue concerns the impact of the local experience on the labor movement. The variety of perceptions and influences in the local community helps to explain the conflicting ideas to be found in the early labor movement. Within the Knights of Labor, for example, advocates of several different points of view tried to make themselves heard. This accounts in part for the continuing struggle within the order over such issues as strikes, temperance, the role of trade unions, and a host of other vital questions. Further examination of the workingclass experience at the local level—in the factories, the neighborhoods, the schools—will undoubtedly shed more light on the development of both workingclass culture and the labor movement at the national level.[44]

NOTES

1. Herbert G. Gutman, *Work, Culture, and Society in Industrializing America* (New York: Knopf, 1975); David Montgomery, "The 'New Unionism' and the Transformation of Workers' Consciousness in America, 1909-1922," *Journal of Social History* 7 (Summer 1974): 509-529; David Montgomery, "Workers' Control of Machine Production in the Nineteenth Century," *Labor History* 17 (Fall 1976): 485-509. Gutman and Montgomery are the two most prominent leaders of the new labor history, which emphasizes the complexities of workingclass experience.

2. This analysis is drawn from Samuel Walker, "Terence V. Powderly, 'Labor Mayor': Workingmen's Politics in Scranton, Pennsylvania, 1870-1885" (Ph.D. diss., Ohio State University, 1973).

3. Valuable insights are to be found in Rowland Berthoff, "The Social Order of the Anthracite Region, 1825-1902," *Pennsylvania Magazine of History and Biography* 89 (July 1965): 261-291, Wayne G. Broehl, *The Molly Maguires* (Cambridge: Harvard University Press, 1964), and Clifton K. Yearly, *Enterprise and Anthracite: Economics and Democracy in Schuylkill County, 1820-1875* (Baltimore: Johns Hopkins Press, 1961).

4. On the anthracite industry, see Eliot Jones, *Anthracite Coal Combination in the United States* (Cambridge: Harvard University Press, 1914); Peter Roberts, *The Anthracite Coal Industry* (New York: Macmillan, 1901); Yearly, *Enterprise and Anthracite.*

5. W. David Lewis, "The Early History of the Lackawanna Iron and Coal Company: A Study in Technological Adaptation," *Pennsylvania Magazine of History and Biography* 96 (October 1972): 424-468; B. H. Throop, *A Half Century in Scranton* (Scranton: The Republican, 1895), pp. 99-119.

6. F. L. Hitchcock, *A History of Scranton and Its People* (New York: Lewis Publishing, 1914), 1:36-37; David Craft, *A History of Scranton, Pennsylvania* (Dayton: United Brethren Publishing Co., 1891).

7. "A Revolution in the Coal Trade," *Pottsville* (Pa.) *Miner's Journal*, May 27, June 3, 1871; Yearly, *Enterprise and Anthracite*, pp. 154-162; Jules I. Bogen, *The Anthracite Railroads: A Study of American Railroad Enterprise* (New York: Ronald Press, 1927).

8. David Montgomery, *Beyond Equality: Labor and the Radical Republicans, 1862-1872* (New York: Vintage Books, 1967), pp. 204-205.

9. Repp memoirs, typescript manuscript, pp. 11-12, Lackawanna County Historical Society, Scranton, Pa.; Lewis, "Early History of the Lackawanna Iron and Coal Company," 456-468.

10. Repp memoirs, p. 13; J. A. Clark, *The Wyoming Valley* (Scranton: J. A. Clark, 1875), p. 117; "A Mill Hand This 22 Years," *Scranton Daily Times*, November 4, 1872.

11. William W. Scranton was compared to the "Autocrat of all the Russias" in letter to editor, *Scranton Daily Times*, October 18, 1877. See also *John Swinton's Paper* (New York), May 17, 1885; Hannah Powderly to Terence Powderly, August 3, 1877, Powderly Papers, Catholic University of America.

12. H. M. Alden, "The Pennsylvania Coal Region," *Harper's New Monthly Magazine* 27 (September 1863): 455-467; P. E. Gibbons, "The Miners of Scranton, Pennsylvania," *Harper's New Monthly Magazine* 55 (November 1877): 916-927; Pennsylvania, *Annual Report of the Secretary of Internal Affairs*, vol. 3, *Industrial Statistics* (1887), app. B, p. 2.

13. *Scranton Daily Times*, February 22, 1873; *Scranton Republican*, January 13, 1872, February 15, 1877. On Walter Dawson, see clippings in Powderly scrapbooks and comments in Terence Powderly, notebook (both circa 1877, unpaginated), Powderly Papers.

14. *Scranton Republican*, October 11, 1876.

15. *Scranton Daily Democrat*, February 16, 1871; *Scranton Republican*, February 8, October 31, 1872.

16. Marvin W. Schlegel, "The Workingmen's Benevolent Association: First Union of Anthracite Miners," *Pennsylvania History* 10 (October 1943): 243-267.

17. International Union of Machinists and Blacksmiths, *Constitution and Rules of Order*, 1874, copy in Powderly Papers.

18. *Scranton Republican*, June 17, 1873, March 10, 1874, September 7, 1877; Robert McKune, testimony in Pennsylvania, *Report of the Committee Appointed to Investigate the Railroad Riots in July, 1877* (Harrisburg, 1878), p. 705.

19. Samuel Walker, "Terence V. Powderly, Machinist, 1866-1877," *Labor History* 19 (Spring 1978): 165-184. A more detailed analysis of Powderly, his early career with the machinists and the Knights of Labor, and his ideological outlook, is found in Walker, "Terence V. Powderly, 'Labor Mayor.'" This interpretation differs greatly from the standard view of the Knights, expressed most fully in Gerald N. Grob, *Workers and Utopia: A Study of Ideological Conflict in the American Labor Movement, 1865-1900* (Chicago: Quadrangle Books, 1969).

20. *Scranton Republican*, June 17, 1873, July 25, 1877; *Scranton Daily Democrat*, May 26, 1871.

21. *Pottsville Miner's Journal*, July 29, 1865, June 26, 1869; *Scranton Republican*,

January–June, 1871; Thomas Murphy, *Jubilee History of Lackawanna County, Pennsylvania* (Topeka: Historical Publishing Co., 1928), 1:384-386.

22. Walker, "Terence V. Powderly," chap. 2.

23. Gibbons, "Miners of Scranton," 916-927; *Scranton Republican*, April 25, 1873; *New York Times*, May 15, 1869; see also a number of valuable letters in Alan E. Conway, ed., *The Welsh in America: Letters from Immigrants* (Minneapolis: University of Minnesota Press, 1961).

24. Gibbons, "Miners of Scranton," 916-927; G. O. Virtue, "The Anthracite Mine Laborer," United States Department of Labor, *Bulletin* 13 (1897): 728-774.

25. Murphy, *Jubilee History*, pp. 424-425; A. B. Galatian, comp., *History of the City of Scranton* (Scranton: Scranton Republican, 1867), pp. 80-81.

26. Hitchcock, *History of Scranton*, 1:488-492; *Scranton Republican*, April 21, 25, 1871; *Scranton Daily Democrat*, May 3, 10, 1871.

27. *Scranton Republican*, July 15, 24, 26, 1871, March 6, May 6, 1872.

28. Ibid., July 24, 1877–August 2, 1877.

29. Terence Powderly, diary, April 2, July 14, September 17, 1876, January 12, 26, 1877, Powderly Papers. See also Walker, "Terence W. Powderly."

30. Knights of Labor, Local Assembly 222, minutes, November 8, 16, 1876, May 17, 1877, March 14, December 15, 1878, Powderly Papers.

31. Knights of Labor, District Assembly 16 (originally DA 5, later redesignated DA 16), minutes, February 4, April 29, 1877, Powderly Papers.

32. Knights of Labor, LA 222, minutes, April 18, May 2, 30, December 15, 1878.

33. For a more detailed analysis, see Walker, "Terence V. Powderly, 'Labor Mayor,'" chap. 2.

34. The best account is Gibbons, "Miners of Scranton," 916-927.

35. These activities are detailed in Terence Powderly, diary, 1869-1876. See also Walker, "Terence V. Powderly, Machinist." Rowland Berthoff, "Social Order of the Anthracite Region," also provides an illuminating interpretation.

36. Hitchcock, *History of Scranton*, pp. 529-530; Craft, *History of Scranton*, pp. 365-366.

37. *Scranton Republican*, April 23, 1872, February 6, 20, 1882; *Scranton Daily Times*, February 22, 1882.

38. *Scranton Republican*, May 6, 1872; Walker, "Terence V. Powderly," chap. 2.

39. *Scranton Daily Times*, February 21, 1878; *Scranton Republican*, February 21, 1878.

40. Walker, "Terence V. Powderly, 'Labor Mayor,'" chap. 2.

41. *Scranton Republican*, January–February 1880, 1882, passim.

42. Walker, "Terence V. Powderly, 'Labor Mayor,'" chap. 5.

43. Milton Gordon, *Assimilation in America: The Role of Race, Religion and National Origins* (New York: Oxford University Press, 1964); Robert H. Wiebe, *The Segmented Society: An Introduction to the Meaning of America* (New York: Oxford University Press, 1975).

44. On the ideology of the Knights of Labor on one particular issue, see Samuel Walker, "Terence V. Powderly, the Knights of Labor and the Temperance Issue," *Societas—A Review of Social History* 5 (Autumn 1975): 279-293.

IMMIGRANTS IN THE NEW SOUTH: ITALIANS IN LOUISIANA'S SUGAR PARISHES, 1880-1910*

15

Jean Ann Scarpaci

Louisiana's sugar-cane fields comprise one of that state's leading industries. During the nineteenth century most of the sugar raised in the continental United States grew in the southeast and south central areas of Louisiana. The sugar parishes encircled New Orleans, lined the Mississippi River from its mouth northward to Baton Rouge, and extended westward into the region surrounding Bayou Lafourche and Bayou Teche.[1]

Sugarcane cultivation required a large labor force of skilled and unskilled workers. During the period of cultivation, from February through mid July, "hoe gangs" fought the advance of weeds into the rows of cane and kept the drainage ditches clear. During the harvesting or grinding months, from October through January, cane cutters and loaders sent a steady supply of cane to the sugar mill.[2]

Each fall, in the late nineteenth century, the harvest season or *zuccarata*, as they called it, attracted thousands of Italian laborers to Louisiana's sugarcane fields. These immigrants responded to the chronic scarcity of labor on the sugar plantations, but they were only a migratory or temporary element in the state's foreign-born population. The num-

* This essay benefitted from the incisive questions and comments offered by my colleagues Perra S. Bell and John G. Van Osdell. The original version was read before the American Historical Association convention in New Orleans, Louisiana, on December 30, 1972.

[1] J. Carlyle Sitterson, *Sugar Country: The Cane Sugar Industry in the South, 1753-1950* (Lexington, 1953), 267; Department of Commerce, Bureau of the Census, *Eleventh Census, 1890: Statistics of Agriculture*, 68, 394-395, 405; Thomas Lynn Smith, "Depopulation of Louisiana's Sugar Bowl," *Journal of Farm Economics*, XX (August 1938), 503-509.

[2] "Facts Concerning Domestic Cane Sugar Production: furnished in a letter to the New York Press by Walter Suthon, a planter of Houma, Louisiana," *Sugar Planters' Journal*, XXXII (April 19, 1902), 428-429, (Hereafter *SPJ*.)

Source: From *Labor History* 16, no. 2 (Spring 1975):165-183.

ber of Italians in the labor force of the plantation rose and fell in relation to the cultivating season as well as to the existence of higher paying jobs elsewhere in the United States.

Italians constituted the largest immigrant group in Louisiana around 1900. Census totals recorded an increase in Italian foreign-born from 2,527 in 1880 to 20,233 in 1910. Nor did these official figures reflect the seasonal influx of immigrant labor, which ranged from 30,000 to 80,000. After 1905, the totals sharply decreased. But Italian migration to the sugar parishes (illustrated in Census Chart I) only faintly suggests this pattern of increase in the foreign-born between 1880-1900 and decline in 1910.[3]

CENSUS CHART I

Italians and Native Whites of Italian Parentage In Louisiana's Sugar Parishes 1880-1910 (5 or more recorded)

Parishes	1880	1890*	1900*	1910**	1910***
Ascension	27	529	1,332	578	1,206
Assumption	9	270	770	460	926
Iberia	15	41	355	275	549
Iberville	13	645	886	865	1,701
Jefferson	139	380	1,012	1,209	2,455
Lafourche	6	149	830	343	626
Plaquemines	143	324	362	135	265
St. Bernard	2	15	123	238	524
St. Charles	4	323	626	254	615
St. James	8	317	1,218	699	1,225
St. John	3	249	450	144	293
St. Mary	17	207	1,639	1,246	2,363
Terrebonne	6	17	550	294	537
W. Baton Rouge	5	199	120	210	296

*Only foreign-born reported in 1880-1900 census
**Foreign-born   ***Native whites of Italian parentage

---

[3] *Tenth Census, 1880: Population,* 511-512 and *Thirteenth Census, 1910: Population,* 778-788. For estimates of floating population see Editorial, "Italian Immigration," *Daily Picayune,* August 12, 1904, 6, and Italy, Ministero Degli Affari Esteri, Commissariato Dell Emigrazione, *Bollettino Dell' Emigrazione, Anno 1904* (Roma, 1905), A. Ravaiolo, "La Colonizzazione Agricola Negli Stati Uniti," 32. Chart I was compiled from the following: *Tenth Census, 1880: Population,* 511-512; *Eleventh Census, 1890: Population,* I, 630-631; *Twelfth Census, 1900: Statistics of Population,* 757-58; *Thirteenth Census, 1910: Population,* 778-788.

Census Chart II illustrates the overall view of the distributions of the Italian population in the State.[4]

CENSUS CHART II

Italians Residing in the Sugar Parishes and in the State of Louisiana 1880-1910

	Sugar Parishes Foreign-Born	Total*	Entire State Foreign-Born	Total*
1880	397		2,527	
1890	3,665		7,767	11,076
1900	10,273		17,577	26,621
1910	6,940	13,681	20,223	42,911

*The total indicates the Italian foreign-born and the native whites, one or both of whose parents were born in Italy.

The immigrants, while on the plantation, shared the social status and wage scale of their black co-workers. They adapted to the new work experience, the new environment, and the plantation's work routine, yet they retained their Old World traditions. The continuous link with their native culture provided a group cohesiveness during their time on the plantation, a cohesiveness which remained after they moved from laborer to entrepreneur.

Throughout Reconstruction and well into the 1880s, both cotton and sugar planters complained about the "unreliability" and "inefficiency" of the blacks who comprised their labor force. They failed in their attempts to regiment these workers, who did not respond to their demands and who sought employment in the towns and cities. Furthermore, those agricultural workers remaining in the labor pool on the plantations produced less than the planters expected.[5]

According to many post-bellum plantation accounts, blacks quickly began to demonstrate their desire for economic independence. From 1865 through the 1880s, white planters considered them an unpredictable agricultural labor force. Seemingly dissatisfied with their unchanging existence as plantation labor, for which they received daily or monthly wages, blacks sometimes worked only for a short time and then left. Planters attributed such behavior to their refusal to grant wage advances,

---

[4] Census Chart II was compiled from statistics in Census Chart I, plus *Eleventh Census,* clxvii, 608, 685, 687, 689, *Twelveth Census,* 813-817, and *Thirteenth Census,* 773.

[5] Roger W. Shugg, *Origins of Class Struggle in Louisiana. A Social History of White Farmers and Laborers during Slavery and After, 1840-1875* (Baton Rouge, 1939), 258; Sitterson, *Sugar Country,* 243-245.

or to pay weekly instead of monthly or seasonally. Another cause of discontent involved the wage itself. Black laborers struck for higher wages during periods critical to the cultivation of the sugar crop. Occasionally, they left one plantation for another which offered higher wages. Their search for better work conditions extended over a wide regional and interstate area, with many blacks shuttling between Louisiana and Mississippi. After the Civil War, wages tended to move upward until the 1873 depression, when groups of planters agreed to reduce wages and their black workers refused to contract out on such a basis. These workers were also decidedly unsatisfied with the work schedule imposed upon them.[6]

Planters resented this "Ishmael" or travelling tendency of black workers. Those dependent upon blacks viewed their economic behavior as irresponsible and unreliable. Feeling trapped and fearful of labor trouble, some planters banded together to meet this black challenge. *Ad hoc* associations provided a united front when confronted by demands for higher wages. Their members agreed to pay a standard wage, in order to end the uncertain conditions of sugar cultivation. Some even used extreme measures to thwart migrating blacks, such as having them arrested as "debtors" or for violation of contracts; others effectively controlled the wharf areas and employed river patrols to prevent their field hands from leaving by boat.[7]

This "Negro Exodus" aroused serious concern among those planters who had counted on a permanent black labor force. Benjamin Singleton, a leader of the black movement, likened it to the exodus of Moses and the people of Israel. Many blacks moved to cities, both in the North and the South; others migrated North to work as farm laborers. They might, for instance, go to Kansas, where sugar beets were cultivated, being attracted by the better wage rates there. This veritable "Kansas fever" peaked in 1878. No accurate data is available about those who left the South. The largest migration, however, did occur in 1878-79; and it originated in Mississippi and Louisiana. Estimates ranged from 5,000 to 10,000. Whatever the precise number, it was potentially ruin-

---

[6] Sitterson, *Sugar Country,* 243-245. For more than a decade after the war blacks moved at the end of the year from one plantation to another, and during the first two weeks of each year the roads of the sugar region were lined with carts piled high with all their belongings. Although conditions at their new places were rarely better, many blacks continued to hope, and they also liked to exercise their rights as freedmen to change their employers.

[7] Morgan Dewey Peoples, "Negro Migration From the Lower Mississippi Valley to Kansas, 1879-1880" (unpublished Master's essay, Louisiana State University, 1950), 45.

ous to southern agriculture.[8]

The strikes of black agricultural workers in the early 1880s heightened planter pessimism regarding the possibility of keeping such labor on the plantation or controlling those who worked there. On April 19, 1881, strikes and riots broke out in St. Bernard Parish at cane planting time:

> . . . the strike assumed more serious proportions, verging into a riot. It is stated that about three or four hundred negroes banded together under the leadership of some of the Spaniards or "islang," and went from plantation to plantation, compelling the laborers to stop work until the planters consent to pay the wages demanded . . . . Finding it necessary to quell the turbulent disturbers a committee of planters called at the Governor's office and asked for the authorities of the State to assist them as the parish authorities are powerless.[9]

By April 21, Governor Louis Wiltz had instructed the sheriff in St. Bernard Parish to stop the "rioters" or call upon the militia to help. Instead of questioning their own harsh system, which failed to attract a sufficient and competent labor force, planters condemned the blacks for "deserting" the plantations, for demanding higher wages, and for failing to meet production quotas.[10]

A large supply of labor remained necessary for sugar cultivation, and labor shortages which had haunted the sugar industry in the post-Civil War years continued into the 1880s. Now convinced they could not control a black labor force, planters sought workers from other quarters. One enterprising planter succinctly summed up the situation: "The only draw back I fear is want of reliable labour. Old darkies good but dieing [sic] out. Young ones about good for nothing. Have sent to Portugal for 25 laborers and their families."[11]

Closer at hand was an established colony of Italians in New Orleans. Trade routes long had existed between Louisiana and Sicily, and a colony

---

[8] Walter L. Fleming, "Pap Singleton, The Moses of the Colored Exodus." *American Journal of Sociology*, XV, no. 1 (1909), 61-78; Peoples, "Negro Migration," 11; Roy Garvin, "Benjamin, or Pap Singleton and His Followers," *Journal of Negro History*, XXXIII (January 1948), 7, 11. Benjamin Singleton was responsible for founding eleven colonies in Kansas between 1873 and 1874, after an unsuccessful effort in 1870 with the Tennessee Real Estate and Homestead Association. By 1879 the movement had become a flood. Singleton wrote pamphlets on Sunny Kansas but "educated" blacks scorned his plans. By the end of 1879 he claimed to have brought 7432 blacks to Kansas.

[9] Riot in St. Bernard," *Daily Picayune*, April 19, 1881, 1.

[10] *Louisiana Capitolian* (Baton Rouge), April 21, 1881, 2. Strikes also occurred in St. John's parish during the spring of 1880 as reported in "Here and There," *Le Louisianais* (Convent, La,), April 17, 1880, 1.

[11] Sitterson, *Sugar Country*, 315. Sitterson cites a letter from Daniel Thompson to Cyrus Woodman, August 1, 1880 in C. L. Marquette (ed.), "Letters of a Yankee Sugar Planter," *Journal of Southern History*, VI (1940), 533.

of Italians, mainly merchants and in related occupations, had resided in New Orleans by mid-century. In 1850, 915 Italians lived in Louisiana; in 1870, the number had increased to 1,884. Approximately 97 percent of them were Sicilians — from north central, central, and western Sicily. Those emigrating directly had followed the citrus trade routes from Palermo and Messina to New Orleans.[12]

The connection between trade routes and emigration of people from the Mediterranean stirred the imagination of many white southerners after the Civil War. Expanded commercial ties had two advantages: first, it would increase both profits and economic activity; second, it might satisfy the need for laborers to develop Southern agricultural and industrial potential. In 1867, a conference on the problem of Southern commerce led to a request for government subsidies, through mail contracts, for a steamship line plying between Southern and Mediterranean ports. Delegates to this commercial convention suggested that there would be a "natural" balance of trade: ". . . considering that we grow cereals and they grow fruits — that we can export cotton, tobacco, rice and petroleum to them, and receive fruits, olive oil, wines, sardines and works of art in return. . . ."[13]

This trade route also might supply laborers directly to the South.

> We have to glance the eye over the map to see from whence these new supplies must come. The northern shores of the Mediterranean embracing Spain, Italy, Sicily and Sardinia, with Greece, are teeming with a population of fifty millions. The climate is the same as that of the Southern States. Their farmers, fruit growers and laborers would be at home in the sunny fields of the South. The climate which the Northern emigrant shuns they are accustomed to. While readily acquiring a knowledge of the course of agriculture now existing here, they would bring with them, and introduce, the modes of producing their various fruits and wines. The waste fields, now deserted, would, under their patient labor, become fruitful with the grape, the olive, the fig, the orange, the lemon and kindred products. . . .[14]

Other sources also acknowledged a connection between trade routes

---

12 *Seventh Census,* 1850, *Ninth Census,* 1870, 340-341; Cavalier Guido Rossati and R. Enotenico, "Gli Italiani nell Agricoltura degli Stati Uniti D'America," in *Gli Italiani Negli Stati D'America* (New York, 1906), 37; Italy, Ministero Degli Affari Esteri, Commissariato Generale Dell'Emigrazione, *Emigrazione E Colonie: Raccolta Di Rapporti Dell R. R. Agenti Diplomatici E Consolari,* III, *America* (Roma, 1909), 202-221; interview and letter from Gaetano Mistretta, Donaldsonville, Louisiana, February and November, 1966.

13 *Remarks on the Importance to the Nation in View of the Condition of the Southern States and the Prostration of Commerce, of Establishing Steamship Intercourse with the Nations of the Mediterranean Sea* (New York, 1867), 9.

14 *Ibid.,* 8.

and European immigration. James C. Kathman, Chief of the Bureau of Immigration for the State of Louisiana, compared Sicily's climate and fertility with Louisiana's. Both Kathman and General P. T. Beauregard spoke to this point in *De Bow's Review* in the 1860s. Beauregard also served as president of an Immigration and Homestead Association formed in 1873 to encourage foreigners to come to Louisiana.[15]

Mediterranean ports often appeared as destinations on Louisiana shipping lists. The location of New Orleans along with its position as a center of distribution for the midwest obviously was a factor in the development of such trade. Markets for specific commodities reflected the needs and resources of the trans-Mississippi West. Vessels laden with cotton and wheat sailed to European ports, returning with fresh fruit and other agricultural products for the American market.[16]

The citrus fruit trade was centered in Sicily; hence there was a long tradition of commercial transactions between that island and New Orleans. The ethnic make-up of New Orleans' business community began to reflect such contacts, as may be seen from names in business directories and in newspaper reports. The substantial Italian colony which developed in New Orleans before the Civil War revolved around the citrus fruit trade. Italians not only imported and distributed the fruit, but also unloaded the ships and peddled the fruit throughout New Orleans as well as in the suburbs.[17]

Immigration to Louisiana continued to follow the established citrus trade routes. During the late nineteenth century most of the ships bring-

---

[15] "Department of Immigration and Labor," *De Bow's Review*, IV n.s. (November, 1867), 474; *Address of the People in Behalf of the Louisiana Immigration and Homestead Company*, Louisiana State University Archives, Baton Rouge, P. T. Beauregard Papers.

[16] *Daily Picayune* (New Orleans), December 16, 1880, 1, notes the arrival of the British S. S. *Sciuda* from Palermo with 210 immigrants and a cargo of lemons. The *Daily Picayune*, December 8, 1887, 8, notes the arrival of the British S. S. *Elysia* with 613 Italians and a cargo of lemons and Mediterranean fruits to be shipped north and west by the Illinois Central Railroad. William Harris, State Commissioner of Agriculture and Immigration, in a pamphlet, *Louisiana Products, Resources and Attractions with a Sketch of the Parishes* (New Orleans, 1881), recorded exports of grain from New Orleans to the ports of Leghorn, Venice and Naples and exports of tobacco to Italy. This relationship between trade routes and immigrant traffic across the Atlantic receives attention in Marcus Lee Hansen, *Atlantic Migration*, Chapter VIII, "Commerce Bridges the Atlantic" (Cambridge, Mass., 1951), 172-198.

[17] Alice Fortier, *Louisiana, Comprising Sketches of Parishes, Towns, Events, Institutions and Persons Arranged in Cyclopedic Form* (4 vols. Madison, Wisconsin, 1914), III, 742-743, discusses one of New Orleans' leading Italian businessmen partnerships, the Vaccaro Brothers. Stefano Vaccaro, born in Contessa Entellina, Sicily, came to New Orleans in 1860 and from 1862 engaged in the fruit and produce business until 1893, when his sons, Felix, Luca, and Joseph took over. The Vaccaro Brothers first began at Decatur and North Peters Streets, and were wholesale dealers until 1898, when they began importing bananas and coconuts from Spanish Honduras to New Orleans whence they shipped these products across the country.

ing Italian immigrants and products to New Orleans left from Palermo. For example, in 1880 the British Steamship *Scuida* sailed from Palermo to New Orleans with 210 immigrants and a cargo of lemons from Messina and Palermo. The S. S. *Elysia* in 1887 sailed from Palermo to New Orleans with 613 Italian immigrants and a cargo of lemons as well as Mediterranean fruits. The S. S. *Utopia* with 796 Italians from Piana dei Greci, Sicily, sailed from Palermo to New Orleans in 1888. Sugar planters welcomed this convenient link between commerce, immigration, and a potential labor force for their plantations. In 1881 the Louisiana Sugar Planters' Association created a committee for Italian immigration which, from 1881 through 1908, in concert with the State Bureau of Agriculture and Immigration, supported efforts to recruit such immigrants.[18]

The majority of Italians still clustered around the city, but some individuals sought economic opportunities outside New Orleans itself. John Dymond of Plaquemines Parish, located south of New Orleans, was in 1870, the first sugar planter to hire an Italian laborer. During the next decade, Dymond and his neighbors offered jobs to other Italian immigrants. The census figures for Plaquemines Parish record the scattering of Italians in the sugar parishes as being 143 by 1880.[19]

This influx of Italian laborers was largely seasonal. They came directly from Italy to the cane fields at grinding time (October through December), and returned to their homeland immediately after the harvest, thereby following a nomadic pattern that had long been a way of life for Italian peasants. Augusto Miceli, a New Orleans attorney who arrived in America in the 1920s, reported that tramp steamers between New Orleans and Palermo would carry Italian "birds of passage" to Louisiana expressly for the grinding season. Charles Cangelosi of Baton Rouge noted that ships carrying immigrants for the plantations sometimes came directly up river to his community.[20]

[18] *Daily Picayune*, December 16, 1880, 1, December 8, 1887, 8 (this article notes that most of the passengers originated from Sicily and Southern Italy); *Weekly Times Democrat* (New Orleans), October 20, 1888, 3; "Cane and Corn," *Daily Picayune*, June 11, 1881, 1 and Minutes, May 12 and June 9, 1881, Louisiana State University Archives, Louisiana Sugar Planters' Association Papers. William Harris, State Commissioner of Agriculture and Immigration, in a pamphlet, *Louisiana: Products, Resources and Attractions with a Sketch of the Parishes* (New Orleans, 1881), recorded exports of grain from New Orleans to Leghorn, Venice, and Naples and exports of tobacco to Italy.

[19] "Italian Immigration." *Louisiana Planter and Sugar Manufacturer* (New Orleans), XXXVIII (September 22, 1906), 179-180 (hereafter LPSM); *Tenth Census, 1880: Population*, 511-512.

[20] Grazia Dore, "Some Social and Historical Aspects of Italian Emigration to America," trans., by Andrea Martonetty, *Journal of Social History*, II, no. 2 (1968), 110; Au-

Similarly, on a seasonal basis, during the 1890s and early 1900s, other Italian laborers began to migrate down into the sugar region from Chicago and New York, and Italians residing in New Orleans and in other Louisiana towns outside the sugar region often temporarily supplemented the labor force. This annual journey of Italian immigrants usually began in October and tapered off by March. For those from Chicago and New York there was the added attraction of being able to avoid the cold northern winters. One sugar planter observed:

> You see, our Dagoes have a way of going to Chicago for the summer months. They work in the sugar fields until May 1 or May 10, and then put out for Chicago where they work in shops, in mines and on railroads until winter sets in when they pack up and come to the sugar belt. Their fuel bills would be more than the railroad fares, and they make money on the deal.

It is clear, then, that much of the annual migration of Italians to Louisiana was internal as well as seasonal.[21]

Italian laborers on the plantation had to adjust to the firmly established work routine. Planters continued to welcome them as replacements for black labor, although the immigrant at best supplemented the native work force. Most Italians filled the unskilled, low-paying jobs that were essential to the cultivation and harvesting of sugar cane, for the planters did not change wages or work functions as the ethnic composition of the labor force changed.

Pay rolls and time books indicate that ordinary labor received 75 cents a day during the growing season. For grinding, teamsters and cane loaders received $1.40 per day, and cane cutters $1.25. Only the best workers held positions as teamsters and loaders. And only first-rate cane cutters received $1.25. The other workers—old men, women, and boys—were paid less, from 75 cents to $1.20 per day, depending upon the amount of work they could do. Their wages for cultivating the crops ranged from 25 to 60 cents. Whatever the labor, the work day lasted from sun up to sun down.[22]

In addition to his wages, the plantation laborer was given a house and a

gusto Miceli, interview in New Orleans, Louisiana, November 10, 1965; Mr. Luigi Scala, former Italian Consul at Independence, Louisiana, noted that steamship companies encouraged "birds of passage." (interview in Providence, Rhode Island, October 1966); letter from Mr. Charles Cangelosi, Baton Rouge, Louisiana, September 26, 1965.

21 "Importation of Porto [sic] Rican Sugar and Exportation of Italians: Interview with Hon. W. E. Howell of Lafourche Parish," *SPJ*, XXXI (August 31, 1901), 722-723.

22 Payroll for Dunboyne Plantation, January to December, 1897, Louisiana State University Archives, Edward J. Gay and Family Papers: Time Books 1898-1901 and 1905-1908; Facts Concerning Domestic Can Sugar," 428-429.

garden patch of about one-quarter acre; there he grew corn, peas, and sweet potatoes, aided by the plantation mules and plows furnished free of charge. He also received free fuel, which he hauled to his house by using the plantation team provided for this purpose.[23]

Vincent Brocato, who came from Cefalu, Sicily, to Raceland, Louisiana, in 1895 at age 22, described the housing for families as tenement-like buildings of one story divided into apartments. The single men lived in dormitories. All the houses were crudely built and, like most rural dwellings of that period, lacked indoor plumbing. Wood stoves and open fireplaces provided both heating and cooking facilities. Kerosene lamps provided the light.[24]

The plantation tasks requiring little skill, such as hoeing and ditching, were assigned to the Italians. When Donelson Caffery of St. Mary's Parish wrote to his son from Washington, D. C., in 1897, he noted: "Some few hundred Dagoes will be required to ditch the swamp land." This kind of work was necessary to keep the land dry. As hoe men and briarhook handlers, Italians were considered "superior" to other laborers; at least so the planters believed and they preferred them for this work in the cane fields.[25]

Some Italian immigrants believed that plantation work meant "plenty money" compared with economic rewards in Sicily, where poverty and misery had surrounded them. The habits of years of impoverishment at home helped ambitious and frugal laborers to survive in Louisiana and, in some cases, to get ahead. A. Piaggio, an Italian who visited Donaldsonville, Louisiana, in 1895, a time of depression in the sugar industry, explained how an immigrant family could achieve subsistence or better in the plantation setting:

> A family of five Italians, the father, the mother and three children, arriving on a cane plantation from Italy all set to work. Even in a depressed labor market, the father by working three watches of six hours each, at 50 cents a watch, could earn $1.50 a day. The mother could earn $1, and the children, even if only 5 years old manage as a rule to earn 10 cents a day. So that the aggregate of such an average family's work per day was about $3. . . .[26]

---

23 *Ibid.*

24 Interview with Mrs. Vincent Brocato, Raceland, Louisiana, November 14, 1965. Mrs. Brocato came to Raceland with her family in 1895. There they joined her father who had emigrated in 1894. Mrs. Brocato conveyed information from her own life and from her husband's experiences. Mr. Brocato was alive in 1965, but unable to provide an interview. See also interview with Mistretta.

25 Letter dated March 3, 1897, Letter Book 1866-1906, Louisiana State University Archives, Donelson Caffery and Family Papers; Hall Clipper, "Special Correspondent, *LPSM,* XXIV (June 9, 1900), 359.

26 Letter from John V. Baiamonti, Jr., Tickfaw, Louisiana, December 8, 1970. (Mr. Baia-

It is difficult to understand how these laborers could *save* money on wages ranging from 50 to 75 cents per day, even with the whole family working and even though, during the depression years, the wages did not compare unfavorably with those received by industrial workers. One old Sicilian said he saved money because he "ate nothing but *pane e cutadro* [bread and knife]." Ridley Le Blanc, who worked at Raceland Plantation in Louisiana, expanded on this account, describing Italian laborers as:

> very good workers in the fields. . . . They were good gardeners, raised goats, made and baked their own bread, made and formed their spaghetti, made cheese and made their clothes. They were self supporting and saved nearly all of their small earnings and quickly went into their own successful business.

Gaetano Mistretta, the son of an Italian merchant in Assumption Parish, supports these observations. His father's store accounts, Mistretta recalled, indicated that the immigrant laborers purchased very little. They either made or grew the necessities of life; they were accustomed to subsist on bread and cheese for an entire working day. The Italians, then, adjusted to the long-established work routine on the plantation and the kinds of work available, and so the wages and living conditions did not vary with the ethnic composition of the labor force.[27]

Although contemporaries predicted that Italians would soon replace black labor in the sugar region, blacks continued to dominate the work force between 1880 and 1910. For the Italian, direct contact with blacks as co-workers was a new experience. He faced a double adjustment, then; the first was to the work routine, the second to the indigenous socio-economic structure. Since Italians and black laborers shared the same positions in the plantation system, they also shared the low occupational status of agricultural labor.

The particular composition of the work force prompted comparisons between the two groups. Most of the studies, conducted by native whites, concluded that immigrant labor was more productive than black

---

monte interviewed Sicilian immigrants and their children in Tangipahoa Parish during the course of his research on the Italians in Tangipahoa Parish); "Italians Returning to their Fatherland," *Daily Picayune,* December 21, 1895, 9.

[27] Henry Marshall Booker notes in his study "Efforts of the South to Attract Immigrants, 1860-1900" (unpublished Ph.D. diss., University of Virginia, 1965), 54, that the Southern States paying the highest wages for farm labor with board for the period 1866-1899 were Texas, Florida, and Louisiana. Letter from Mr. George Piazza, a New Orleans attorney, September 29, 1965; letter from Mr. Ridley Le Blanc, December 1965, formerly connected with the Godchaux Company in Raceland, Louisiana; Mistretta letter and interview.

labor. In this competitive setting, hostility might conceivably have developed between black and Italian wage earners, but the immigrants seemed unperturbed. As one observer concluded, the Italians "have no rooted prejudice to competition with negro labor. Intermixture with negro labor can usually be obviated by the division of employment on plantations and any necessary association of the Italian whites with the blacks is not precluded by any race animosity." When blacks and Italians comprised the work force, Walter Fleming observed, as they did at Sunnyside Plantation in Arkansas, "there is no friction . . . between Italian and black; but there is no race mixture." One Louisiana planter affirmed that the forty families of Italian laborers on his plantation did not quarrel among themselves or with the other workers. The Italians, he stated, kept separate from the blacks in social relations and, in fact, the immigrants tended to keep their own counsel in all matters.[28]

Some individuals reported that all plantation workers, Italians, blacks, and those of French ancestry ate and lived together without any hostility. One informant claimed that it was not unusual to have a black family living next door to an Italian family. In the fields, work squads had both immigrant and black laborers, and when a black served as hoe gang boss, he did not encounter resentment from Italian crew members. Blacks, one might conjecture, served as on-the-job trainers for the newcomers.[29]

Although both conflict and violence did trouble some Italian-black relationships, newspapers did not report persistent hostility. Immediate events precipitated what instances there were of conflict rather than "racial" or national confrontation. Significantly, the press did not evaluate the fights, shootings, and thefts which occurred from 1880 to 1910 between Italians and Southern blacks as "racial" provocations. Certainly, Louisiana's Anglo-American society considered both these groups as violence prone, and Southerners were very sensitive to any evidence of "race" incompatibility. In fact, much of the crime committed by Italian and black workers occurred within their own ethnic communities. Southerners only became alarmed when they were personally affected.[30]

Consquently, Italians and blacks appear to have reacted with tolerance in their associations. Neutrality was the keynote. Immigrant acceptance of persons so unlike themselves in appearance, religion, language, and

---

28 Eliot Lord, *The Italian in America* (New York, 1905), 184; Walter Fleming, "Immigration to the Southern States," *Political Science Quarterly*, XX (June 1905), 297; Lee J. Langely, "To Build Up Louisiana: Needed Outside Capital and Labor will be Welcomed," *Manufacturers' Record* (Baltimore), XLV (April 14, 1904), 276-277.
29 Brocato interview and letter from Le Blanc.
30 *L'Italia* (Chicago), August 15-16, 1896.

specific customs may be largely explained by the Sicilians' general indifference to the world outside their town. *Campanilismo,* or provincialism, characterized the South Italians. They identified with their village existence, as Charlotte Chapman's study of Milocca, a Sicilian community indicates. Those who came from other Sicilian towns always retained their *furasteri,* or refugee, quality; and their offspring, though born in Milocca, were *furasteri* children. And such identities followed the Miloccese emigrants to Pittston, Pennsylvania, and Birmingham, Alabama. Chapman also observes that the individual's willingness to interact with groups or entities *within* the village varied according to his sense of identification. To the Sicilian, his family and town were his prime interests. All else for him was secondary. In Louisiana, the indifference with which the Sicilian regarded black labor reflected this scale of priorities and led to a minimum of interaction.[31]

When describing intergroup relations between immigrants and blacks, Mistretta and others claimed that Italian wage earners initially bore no ill-will toward their black co-workers. They had no reason to dislike the blacks and regarded them with curiosity, But once aware that they shared the same socio-economic position, at the lowest level of Southern society, they decided to avoid further association with blacks. Indeed, this decision was one factor in their resolve to leave the cane fields.[32]

An interview with Italians who had moved from sugar plantations to farming in Independence, Louisiana provided a detailed explanation:

> One Italian informant . . . said he and his family had been badly mistreated by a French plantation owner near New Roads. When asked how he had been mistreated, he stated that he and his family were made to live among the Negroes and were treated in the same manner. At first he did not mind because he did not know any difference, but when he learned the position that Negroes occupied in this country, he demanded that his family be moved to a different house and be given better treatment.

In fact, much of the criticism of plantation conditions derived from the observation that blacks occupied an inferior position in the South's social hierarchy. Representatives of the Italian government repeatedly stated their wish that Italians settle in the South on a par with the native Anglo-Saxon, and not compete with the native black for his title of agricultural proletariat.[33]

[31] Charlotte Gower Chapman, *Milocca: A Sicilian Village* (Cambridge, Mass., 1971), 151-157. Chapman collected her data on Milocca in 1928.
[32] Mistretta interview.
[33] Luther Williams, "The People of Tangipahoa Parish: A Sociological Comparison of

Thus, the exposure of the Italian immigrant to white prejudices ultimately influenced his attitude toward Southern blacks. He realized that treatment equal to that accorded the blacks was inferior treatment. And much of the conflict that developed between the groups reflected the upward mobility of Italians from laborer to tenant to farmer or businessman.

Economic competition had always threatened to create an environment of hostility between Italians and blacks on the plantation. The conclusions drawn from the studies of Alfred Holt Stone and others prompted some of the planters to continue to seek Italian workers. Stone, for example, emphasized that Italians worked harder, produced larger yields per acre, labored in all weather, and made greater sacrifices in order to accumulate savings, and implied that the blacks did not match these characteristics. Conceivably, the combination of an increasing number of Italian workers on the plantations and their reputation for high productivity would arouse hostility among the blacks. This increase, all evidence indicates, had been in direct response to an endemic labor scarcity and did not necessarily sharpen job competition. But blacks might well have regarded the immigrant as responsible for lowering wages because of his high rate of productivity.[34]

When depression hit the sugar industry, many Italians, rather than accepting lower wages, left the cane fields altogether. Repeal of the McKinley Tariff, which removed protection for domestic industry, also encouraged their departure. Perhaps the proximity of New Orleans and the relative ease of movement in and out of the sugar parishes and into industrial centers, acted as a "safety valve" for these Italian laborers. In any case, many of them viewed plantation work as merely temporary. It provided a means to accumulate savings in order to embark on a career as agricultural or business entrepreneur.[35]

Although the exodus of blacks from the South declined during the 1880s, planters also continued to record a decrease in their annual migration within the south, from a region where cotton was baled to the plantation which was grinding sugar. But this movement of blacks from staple farming to the lumber mill regions, and to southern towns and cities, did not remove them entirely from the plantation work force. Indeed, plant-

---

Two Ethnic Groups" (Unpublished Masters' essay, Louisiana State University, 1951), 85; Baron Des Planches and Italian Immigration," *LPSM*, XXXIV (April 21, 1906), 246.

34 Alfred Holt Stone, "Italian Cotton Growers in Arkansas," *American Monthly Review of Reviews*, XXXV (February 1907), 209-213.

35 "The Plantation Labor Problem," *LPSM*, XVII (December 5, 1896), 362.

ers still depended primarily upon black labor throughout the nineteenth century.[36]

Later, as the rate of immigration to Louisiana decreased, and as Italian sugar workers already there responded to better economic conditions elsewhere in the United States, planters again began to recruit blacks and whites from the cotton region. Obviously, the flow of Italians to Louisiana had not forced black laborers from the plantations as the literature of the period had predicted. A growing number of immigrants worked on the plantations until 1900 and planters always seemed anxious to employ more each year, but there apparently never was a sufficient number of Italians to meet the needs of the sugar industry. When blacks left the fields, Italians were recruited to fill their places; when Italian migration slackened, blacks were again courted. However the general pool of plantation labor remained insufficient.[37]

Louisiana's sugar plantations, as indicated, exposed the Italian immigrant to many new conditions and experiences, Nothing in his past had prepared him for the cycle of cane cultivation, the process of sugar refining, the English-speaking population, and the presence of black wage earners. He had to adapt these experiences to his own frame of reference, which was the strong cohesive group identity that had been brought over almost undiluted from Italy. Although gradually redefined in America, the basic pattern of values involving close ties with family, fellow villagers *(paesani)*, and co-nationals, remained. It provided a familiar setting which more than counterbalanced the unfamiliar aspects of American life.

Rather than these day-to-day patterns within the Italian-American community, the press mainly documented "sensational" or "colorful" events. It focused on incidents of conflict or violence, celebrations, and participation in local events. On the plantations much of the reported violence stemmed from disagreements over money or work assignments, where the conflicts were generally among family members and friends. In most cases of violence among Italians, the press assumed that the motives had been personal and that all the witnesses would remain

[36] Sitterson, *Sugar Country*, 315-317. David Hellwig's study of the blacks' response to immigration also considered their reaction to the South's attempt to recruit Italian labor. He noted that blacks displayed their displeasure against the recruiters, not their proteges. Hellwig found no massive conflict between the two groups. The blacks contrasted the virtues of a traditional labor source against the potential threat of "the Italian as corrupt, violent, anarchistic, prone to join unions and in general a threat to both the American and Southern way of life." Letter, September 30, 1973, St. Cloud, Minnesota.

[37] *Ibid.*

silent. (In such newspaper accounts, the stereotyping of Italians as violence prone was typical.) When an Italian fruit peddler, Luca Rizzo, shot his brother-in-law, Vito Corenno, on the Glenn Orange Plantation near Morgan City, the *Thibodaux Sentinel* noted ". . . these same parties had a cutting affair about two years ago and the usual dense ignorance of the shooting is shown by those who presumably know all about it, including the wounded man." This code of silence and determination to remain apart was also a direct legacy from the Old World, as Danilo Dolci has documented. Dolci, who has worked among the inhabitants of western and central Sicily, acknowledged these attitudes by referring to two proverbs: "The man who goes his own road can never go wrong," and " the man who plays alone never loses." As one Sicilian emigrant explained:

> If a man goes alone, he needn't get involved in any trouble. He goes his own way. He does whatever he pleases, he goes his own road. With other people as one says one thing, another says something else, and they can't agree.

This self-imposed isolation implies not the isolation of the individual but of his extended family group.[38]

Identification with the family group typical of life in Sicily and brought over intact to America, encouraged laborers to save money in order to send for their wives, Ship arrivals in New Orleans set the stage for family reunions. This tradition of close family ties included reprisals for family dishonor. An Italian laborer in Lafourche Parish carried out this private code when he shot and killed the prospective husband of his sixteen-year old sister. He had learned, observers hypothesized, that her fiance was already married to a woman in Italy. At any rate, it seems clear that the Old World code of honor which touched the family, making each member of a family responsible for the other's behavior, also functioned in Louisiana.[39]

The persistence of group cohesiveness impressed Count Gerolamo Moroni, Italian consul at New Orleans. In 1912, he observed that Italians preferred to work on the sugar plantations because these were situated near villages and cities in which Italian merchants resided. The merchant offered sociability as well as familiar commodities. Workers, further-

---

[38] "Italian Killed," *Thibodaux Sentinel*, May 29, 1909, 1; Danilo Dolci, *The Man who Plays Alone*, trans. by Antonia Cowan (Garden City, N. Y., 1970), 4.
[39] Chapman, *Milocca*, 73 "Southern States Items," *Daily Picayune*, August 30, 1894, 11; "Italian Murdered," Weekly *Thibodaux Sentinel*, October 13, 1900, 1.

more, lived in close proximity on plantations, and in effect formed small villages of their own. This retention of group cohesiveness, though thousands of miles from the Old World, probably played an important role in attracting Sicilians to Louisiana. Most of the newcomers had once lived in towns, more aptly termed "rural cities," with populations ranging from 2,000 upward to the tens of thousands. Life in America's isolated rural communities would not readily appeal to peasants who were accustomed to residential clusters. Certainly the proximity of a large Italian colony in New Orleans easily reached by train and boat helped the immigrant to feel that the environment was familiar.[40]

Mutual benefit or benevolent societies which were common in Sicily and had reinforced *campanilismo* in the Old World, served similarly in the United States. Including fraternal as well as welfare functions, they provided health benefits and burial costs, and they sponsored such social functions as anniversary celebrations, religious observances, and commemorations of American holidays, like Columbus Day. Many of these societies reflected the Old World emphasis upon town and regional loyalties. Six mutual benefit societies were listed for the sugar parishes in the Italian consul's report of 1910. Two other societies were recorded in the press. Indeed, the very names of some societies demonstrated their regional orientation. In addition to town and regional identities, Sicilian saints such as Santa Lucia and Santa Rosalia, as well as the Immaculate Conception, particularly revered by Sicilians, also provided names for societies. Whenever these societies staged a celebration, dignitaries representing the native American community participated. In 1907, when the Duca D'Aosta Association of Franklin sponsored a celebration, both Senator Murphy J. Foster and Lieutenant Governor J. Y. Sanders addressed the gathering. Such official attention to the Italian Americans who had become citizens encouraged them to support these politicians.[41]

We have seen that those Italians who remained in Louisiana as entrepreneurs continued to maintain that group cohesiveness which preserved

---

[40] *Bolletino Dell' Emigrazione, Anno 1913,* Gerolamo Moroni, "La Louisiana e L'immigrazione Italiana," 51-53; Rudolph Vecoli, "Contadini in Chicago: A Critique of *The Uprooted,*" *Journal of American History,* LIV (December 1964), 404-405.
[41] *Ibid.,* 413; Chapman, *Milocca,* 172-73; *Bollettino Dell' Emigrazione, Anno 1910,* Moroni, "Societa Italiane Nel Distretto Consolate di New Orleans," 1118-1193; "Over the State—Pattterson," *Kentwood Commercial,* June 18, 1895, 4; "Latest News in Louisiana," *Daily Picayune,* October 16, 1906, 16; "Latest News in Louisiana," *Ibid,* July 27, 1910, 14; *Bolletino Dell' Emigrazione, 1910;* Latest News in All Louisiana— Kenner," *Daily Picayune,* August 30, 1903, 14; "A Gala Day in Franklin," *St. Mary Banner* (Franklin), May 11, 1907, 3-4.

their ethnic identity. And as the immigrant moved out of the agricultural laborer class, he placed a wider distance between himself and his former black co-worker. He even acquired the race prejudice of Southerners — which was the price paid in exchange for social acceptance.

From available statistical data, it is difficult to determine precisely how many Italians actually worked on sugar plantations. Neither United States Census figures nor the yearly reports of the arrivals of immigrants in Louisiana reflect the volume and impact of this migration. Indeed, the temporary nature of work in the *zuccarata,* which caused a rapid turnover in the labor force, led to an internal migratory pattern. Workers from Chicago, Kansas City, St. Louis, New Orleans, and New York, as well as from Sicily, flooded the sugar regions each year seeking employment.

Even before 1910, a decreasing number of Italians came to work in the cane fields. Instead, some of them climbed out of the wage earner category and became economically self-sufficient. They achieved their goal through frugality and a singleminded concentration upon saving. Wages on the sugar plantations permitted ambitious immigrants to move into tenantry, share cropping, and eventually land ownership.

Yet, as we have seen, most of the temporary or seasonal migrants did not remain in Louisiana. They had originally followed the call of the annual *zuccarata* because wages and work conditions had seemed more favorable than elsewhere. Conditions soon changed, however, and by 1908 an Italian government official noted that an immigrant laborer could save one-fifth more over eight months of construction work than he could save in a year of farm labor.[42]

In addition, Louisiana's social climate caused some immigrants to leave. Italians shared with black workers the low status assigned to agricultural wage earners. Southerners considered such work dirty and undesirable, and placed the stamp of inferiority upon those who did it. The attitude was partly social in origin, a contempt for manual labor; and partly racial, the undesirable jobs were only for groups rated inferior by the native white community.

Italians might have been willing to tolerate these attitudes if good salaries were at stake, but not when they could obtain higher wages elsewhere. There were additional considerations: peonage, yellow fever,

---

42 Robert Foerster, *The Italian Emigration of Our Times* (New York, 1969. Originally published by Harvard University Press in 1919), 369. Foerster cites "Memorandum degl' instituti italiani di patronate per gli emigranti in sulle cause che ostacolano L'avviamento all' agricoltura degl' immigranti italiani negli Stati Uniti" in the *Bollettino Dell' Emigrazione, Anno 1909,* 9. The factors contributing to the decline of

the lynching of Italians, and Southern expressions of intolerance toward some immigrant customs, and these prompted many immigrants to leave Louisiana altogether. With the original attraction of high agricultural wages canceled by better economic opportunities elsewhere, Italian migrants no longer responded to the annual call of labor in the *zuccarata.*

immigration to Louisiana are discussed in Chapters V and VI of Jean Ann Scarpaci, "Italian Immigrants in Louisiana's Sugar Parishes: Recruitment, Conditions of Labor, and Community Relations, 1880-1910" (unpublished Ph.D. diss., Rutgers University, 1972).

16

COMMUNITY CHANGE AND CAUCASIAN ATTITUDES TOWARD THE CHINESE: THE CASE OF TWO CALIFORNIA MINING TOWNS, 1850-1870*

Ralph Mann

Of all the polyglot crowds of Forty-niners, the Chinese were perhaps the most alien to the American born, and probably no other group suffered so much violence at the hands of their fellow miners. Mistreatment of the Chinese and efforts by whites to drive them from the mines and from the United States have been explained by several different interpretations of the dynamics of Chinese-Anglo relations. Most historians accept the centrality of racial antipathy, adding reinforcing factors such as white fears of economic competition, political and union opportunism, unfavorable preconceptions of the Chinese and Chinese civilization, and the clash between Chinese and American goals and values in California.[1] In this paper, I hope to explain anti-Chinese outbreaks by investigating interactions between the Chinese and Caucasian communities of two neighboring California mining camps, Grass Valley and Nevada City, between 1850 and 1870. Although the camps' white inhabitants shared national anti-Chinese stereotypes and responded to statewide political and economic movements against the Chinese, the extent of this response depended on specific local issues. Sustained agitation occurred when a town's Anglo society found itself in crisis and saw its aspirations, or even its survival, as threatened by Chinese values or practices or by the growth of Chinatowns. There were two main periods of turmoil over the Chinese during the two decades: in the mid 1850s in Nevada City and in the late 1860s in Grass Valley. In each case Anglos stressed different aspects of the widely held negative image of the Chinese, corresponding to different problems within the white communities. The social history of the two camps and of the Chinese settlements in them provides a starting point for understanding when and why anti-Chinese rhetoric and violence crested.

Racial antipathy toward the Chinese was a constant; I have found no evidence suggesting either an increase or a decline in the belief that Chinese were basically inferior to whites. American miners carried west with them stereotypes of the Chinese and theories of Anglo-Saxon superiority and

*An earlier version of part of this paper was read at the meeting of the Organization of American Historians, Denver, Colorado, April 18, 1974. I wish to acknowledge financial support from the Penrose Fund of the American Philosophical Society and a grant-in-aid from the University of Colorado Council on Research and Creative Work.

did not change these ideas during the two decades I examined. Racism, then, created the mental preconditions for anti-Chinese brutality, though it explains neither its timing nor its extent. The whites of both Grass Valley and Nevada City took active parts on both sides of the political controversies concerning Chinese immigration and rights, but partisan movements had only transient influence in the camps unless they coincided with local social crises. Moreover, the issues behind racial clashes in Grass Valley and Nevada City often did not correspond with those of California's political Sinophobia. Finally, while statewide opponents of the Chinese presence often charged unfair labor competition and while these arguments were current from the first days of the camps, it was not until the late 1860s that economic fear of the Chinese became an important local concern, and then it arose because of growing occupational and ethnic divisions in the white communities. Although racism, California politics, and workingmen's fears all were vital factors, local social situations determined the response to state and national beliefs and movements and were the keys to Chinese-Anglo relations in the two towns.

Groups of Chinese miners began arriving in Grass Valley and Nevada City by late 1850. Although the Nevada County compilers of the state census of 1852 did not list Chinese as individuals, they enumerated 3,886 Chinese in the county, a figure not matched by the decennial federal censuses of 1860 and 1870.[2] The Chinese were met with a mixture of amused acceptance, paternalism, and violence. They were hired to work in the placers and then protected by their white employers from claim jumpers who insisted that they "should give way to white men."[3] Some whites praised them for honesty, industriousness, and minding their own business and confidently expected them to be both good customers for white merchants and carriers of Western civilization back to China. Others condemned them for lying, thieving, and clannishness and maintained that they were too obtuse to learn American customs. The newspapers in the camps displayed more interest than enmity, often demanding fair play for the Chinese, who were widely regarded simply as part of the color of the gold rush, as long as they did not compete directly with whites in the search for gold.[4]

The great increase in numbers of Chinese by 1852 helped produce, for the first time, talk of the Chinese undercutting white labor and physical resistance to Chinese migration into Nevada City and Grass Valley; however, both newspaper and diary references to the perils of the Chinese presence and to driving them from the diggings were concentrated in early and mid-May, immediately after and in some cases obviously in response to Governor Bigler's "special message" on the desirability of exclusion.[5] The hostility was not confined to the Chinese; Anglos accused other foreign-born miners and blacks of crimes against peace, property, and ad hoc mining law. The camps were participating in a statewide nativist crusade, which resulted in a tax on all foreign miners. After its passage, however, Chinese-white relations returned to where they had been before.[6] Whites still hired Chinese to work white-owned claims, and Chinese companies bought and worked their own mining ground. Completely contradictory views of the Chinese continued to coexist, but they were now more clearly political in origin; the Whig paper in Nevada City was more likely to praise the Chinese than was its Democratic rival. Both parties decried violence, and physical attacks on the Chinese subsided to their earlier level, becoming sporadic and usually associated with robbery. On occasion white posses searched for the white plunderers of Chinese camps, and when G. W. Hall was found guilty of murdering a Chinese miner, largely on Chinese evidence, the Nevada City public accepted the decision even after it was overturned by the California Supreme Court in 1854.[7] The anti-Chinese excitement of 1852 had only a passing impact in Grass Valley and Nevada City.

During the early 1850s definable Chinese districts began to develop in both camps. While white ethnic groups did not form neighborhoods of their own, spatial segregation based on race did occur; the Chinese and the tiny group of blacks lived apart. Wherever the Chinese migrated overseas in the nineteenth century, they established discrete communities for mutual support and for the preservation of their customs, but in the two towns this separation also reflected whites' racial antipathies, backed by force.[8] Chinatowns began to take shape by 1852 and 1853 in the downtown areas of the two camps. The Chinese leased buildings in the cheapest and roughest blocks, and there, surrounded by white saloons and brothels, they established their own stores, restaurants, and gambling dens.[9] Nevada City was more oriented toward placer mining than was Grass Valley, where the Chinese were excluded from the quartz gold mines, and therefore had a larger Chinese community. The Chinatown of Nevada City, already recognizable as a distinct enclave by late 1853, offered a wider range of services to Chinese miners; it had more merchants and more skilled and semiskilled craftsmen. Grass Valley's smaller Chinatown began on the town's outskirts and did not establish itself downtown until the late 1850s. The great majority of both Chinatowns' inhabitants were miners, but a slightly higher proportion in Grass Valley worked for the white community in such capacities as cook or washman, while more in Nevada City kept stores or followed trades that catered to the Chinese. In 1860 Nevada City's Chinatown was further developed; it was more nearly an autonomous community, with a population large enough to support a few Chinese businesses.[10] (See table 1.)

TABLE 1

Chinese Occupations, Male

	1860				1870			
	Grass Valley		Nevada City		Grass Valley		Nevada City	
Miners	275	90%	386	88%	171	50%	436	68%
Merchants	3	1%	17	4%	7	2%	10	2%
Physicians	0		1		6	2%	3	2%
Restaurant keepers	0		0		1		4	
Boardinghouse keepers	0		0		1			
Opium house keepers	0		0		0		3	
Druggists	0		1		0		1	
Washmen	13	4%	13	3%	10	3%	22	3%
Cooks	12	4%	11	3%	42	12%	58	9%
Quartz millhands	0		0		22	6%		
Saw millhands	0		0		0		1	
Brickmakers	0		0		1			
Carpenters	0		1		0		2	
Blacksmiths	0		0		0		2	
Cobblers	0		0		1		2	
Tailors	0		1		0		2	
Painters	0		0		1		2	
Barbers	0		5	1%	4	1%	4	1%
Gardeners	0		0		21	6%	13	2%
Clerks	0		0		1		1	
Fishermen	0		0		0		6	1%
Soap root diggers	0		0		0		25	4%
Wood choppers	0		0		10	3%	12	2%
Peddlers	0		0		1		3	
Gamblers	0		0		10	3%	9	1%
Common laborers	2	1%	0		23	7%	16	3%
Servants	0		0		6	2%	1	
Total adult males	305	100%	437	100%	339	99%	639	99+%
Total boys	0		2		4	1%	3	1 – %
Total Chinese males	305	100%	439	100%	343	100%	642	100%

SOURCE: The data for all tables was drawn from the following: *Population Schedules of the Seventh Census of the United States, 1850*, National Archives Microfilm Publications, microcopy 432, roll 36, California, Yuba City, pp. 547-610, 619-630; *Population Schedules of the Eighth Census of the United States, 1860*, National Archives Microfilm Publications, microcopy 653, roll 61, California, vol. 4, Napa and Nevada Counties, pp. 143-330; *Population Schedules of the Ninth Census of the United States, 1870*, National Archives Microfilm Publications, microcopy 593, roll 75, California, vol. 5., Napa and Nevada Counties, pp. 142-233, 271-322.

TABLE 2

Total Chinese Population

	1860			
	Grass Valley		Nevada City	
Adult males	305	95%	439	92%
Boys	0		2	
Adult females	15	5%	40	8%
Girls	0		1	
Total	320	100%	480	100%
	1870			
Adult males	339	89%	639	95%
Boys	4	1%	3	
Adult females	39	10%	27	4%
Girls	1		1	
Total	383	100%	670	100%

The census of 1860 shows that nearly all the inhabitants of both Chinatowns were young males. Very few, except for a handful of merchants and professionals, claimed to possess any personal or real estate. The census, admittedly unreliable where the Chinese were concerned, listed only five possible families and only three children. The few Chinese women were not listed by occupation; their living arrangements suggest, however, that almost all were prostitutes.[11] (See tables 2 and 4.)

This picture of the Chinese communities of Grass Valley and Nevada City agrees with both the standard description of the Chinese population in California as a whole and the realities of Chinese migration. Except for some merchants and professionals, the Chinese came to America as single men, dependent on regional companies organized by entrepreneurs from their home prefects for both their passage and their protection in the mines. Leaving their families behind them, they worked to improve their status in China, while their companies' merchants helped supply work and consumer goods.[12]

To say that a young Chinese arriving in the mines of Grass Valley or Nevada City in the early 1850s was attracted by the hope of quick wealth and a quick return home, that he left his wife, if he had one, behind, and that he had little identification with California as a possible home is not to say that he was different from his American-born counterpart. And to say that Chinatown served as a place where miners from the surrounding placers could find gamblers and women is not to say that Chinatowns differed greatly in the early 1850s from the Anglo camps that incorporated them.[13] By the mid-1850s, however, new forces were reshaping Anglo miners and camps, making them more unlike the Chinese and the China-towns, and creating the potential for clashes between the two groups.

The flush times of 1850 and 1851 in Grass Valley and Nevada City had produced all the familiar scenes of gold rush life: the packed saloons, the casual violence, and the miners always ready to follow the latest rumor of a strike. The towns were transient and temporary, both physically and in population. Vigilante groups organized against crime waves, and in many cases vigilantism came down to Anglo-Americans' trying to eject other ethnic groups from the camps. Crime, chaos, and the principal threats to orderly mining were believed to originate above all with the Sonorans and Sydney Ducks; the Chinese in comparison seemed model inhabitants.[14]

Townspeople recognized that even many American miners reveled in their escape from the social restraints that had characterized their eastern homes. As in all camps, Sunday was a day of business and of amusements, which for many centered around the gambling saloons, the brothels, or the bullfighting arena. The *Grass Valley Telegraph* bitterly complained that rowdyism was "countenanced by the leading citizens" in a way that would not have been tolerated back East. The *Nevada City Journal* agreed, finding the explanation in the fact that California was a "land of chance residences, not a home." Without local commitments, inhabitants ignored town laws and accepted gambling, Sabbath breaking, and all "the vices from Spanish life."[15] Journalists, ministers, and businessmen, led by Alonzo Delano, a banker and writer, and Aaron A. Sargent, an editor and politician, began to proclaim that acceptance of these immoral conditions was dangerous both to the individual and to the future prosperity of the towns themselves.[16]

The boom times in both camps passed very quickly, and mining became simply another job for wages. In 1851 the discovery of several leads of gold in quartz veins raised hopes that both camps could enjoy a permanent and secure existence by developing lode mining. Long before quartz mining actually supplanted the more individualistic placer mining in the towns' economies, the newspaper voices of the commercial interests began to celebrate the fireproof brick buildings that were going up to house large mercantile firms and the sound of industry, typified by the constant pounding of quartz mill stamps. The camps' leaders chose as their models New England mill towns, which they conceived of as places of prosperity and piety, and newspapers eagerly chronicled all local evidence of culture, refinement, and purity along with proofs of economic growth. Grass Valley stopped calling itself a camp and began referring to itself as a village. For some, by the end of 1851, the gold rush, with all its excesses, had become a "misty and almost forgotten era."[17]

Order was also essential to the salvation of the individual in the two camps; a virtuous boy could be led astray by the temptations of camp life. While Sargent, Delano, and others lauded the rough democracy of mining life, in which all men dressed alike and all had to work for survival, they also maintained that underneath the uncouth appearances, there might be men of culture, education, and talent, men really apart from the mass. Sargent exhorted his fellow New Englanders to remember and follow the traditions of the Puritans, while Delano seemed relieved to find "an innate sense of decency" in himself, under his beard and ragged clothes, and accordingly cleaned up.[18] Churches, schools, and middle-class deportment all could help bring the desperately desired stability, but hopes centered on the establishment of permanent homes, made possible by the arrival of women and children, the classic nineteenth-century civilizing agents. Delano's nostalgic miners plaintively called for a woman to "make us wear a shirt of a Sunday." The newspapers were overjoyed at evidence of wives and dependents coming "to form the basis of a lasting prosperity" by bringing the towns under the "healthy and softening influence of women and morality."[19]

Although the newspapers credited the new families with a great positive influence on the two camps, change could not occur overnight. In 1853, a recent bride wrote home from Nevada City, "This is a hard country as far as morals are concerned," and other women complained of hastily built, unfinished housing and garbage-strewn streets.[20] Some men expressed fears that the towns were not fit to receive ladies and, worse, might even contaminate them. William M. Stewart, a Nevada City attorney, claimed that women were borne along by the scramble for wealth to the point of abandoning and divorcing their husbands for men with better prospects. The mere existence of families would not be enough; before they could ameliorate society, there would have to be active attempts to tame the towns, led by the male solid citizens. All over American California, as in much of the United States, moral reform movements, most importantly temperance and Sabbatarianism, culminated in the early 1850s. Grass Valley's and Nevada City's ministers and editors enthusiastically enlisted in the fight.[21] Each town claimed California's largest chapter of the Sons of Temperance, and petitions suggested boycotting merchants who stayed open on Sunday. Lyceums debated local mores, and gambling and prostitution began to be attacked. Editorials and lyceum debaters demanded the enforcement of local moral ordinances, and hinted that, if officials failed, citizens should take the law into their own hands to close brothels and gambling halls. A real moral crusade took shape; between 1851 and 1855 meetings and resolutions against vice in all forms were both frequent and strident.[22]

In Grass Valley and Nevada City the foreign born had been preeminently identified with disorder; conversely the civilization that families were expected to promote was specifically Anglo-Saxon. There is fragmentary evidence that middle-class concern over loss of identity had racial overtones; respectable moral values were white.[23] By the mid-1850s most of the Australians and Mexicans had left the camps; but the Chinese were increasing in numbers and, since they were concentrated in the Chinatowns, in visibility. In the mid-1850s references to China Street and the "Celestial district" began to appear in Nevada City newspapers. While the Anglo community's leaders began to talk in terms of permanency, even though most whites remained transient, and while white gambling and prostitution at least temporarily became more circumspect, the Chinese gold seekers remained sojourners, and their leaders, the merchants, continued to maintain sojourners' institutions. It should come as no surprise that the Chinese, particularly in Nevada City, bore much of the brunt of the new white crusade for moral reform. A new emphasis appeared in the image of the Chinese; they were identified more and more with gambling, petty theft, and, especially, prostitution.[24] If American women represented everything conducive to order, Chinese women represented the opposite. A telling argument used against the Chinese stressed the cruelty with which men treated females; Chinese women were slaves, not saviors. Accounts of brawls and robberies in Chinese brothels, involving whites as well as the inhabitants of Chinatown, began to appear frequently in the newspapers, and white association with Chinese women was bitterly condemned.[25] It was also clear that the appearance of Chinese families would not end Sinophobia; a false rumor that the Chinese companies had decided to import the wives of men already in California brought cries for complete exclusion. Fears that the Chinese, ceasing to be "Celestial celibates," would become permanent residents were not, however, as frequently or as fervently expressed as concern over the moral danger presented by the bachelor colonies.[26]

The image of Chinese immorality and disorder was strong enough to allow the revival of a vigilante tradition that blamed the foreign born for community troubles. In 1854 and 1855, at the height of the moral campaigns in the camps, there were three citizens' raids into Nevada City's rapidly growing Chinatown, dispersing the denizens of the "Chinese houses of ill-fame." The *Nevada Journal* lamented the inefficacy of these attacks:

despite the "summary cleansing . . . the vermin have crawled back to their nests and hold out as aforetime." The newspapers pointed out that some disreputable whites, "natives of Port Sydney," were using moral indignation as a cover for looting the Chinese, but in general attacks on the Chinese district were condoned, even when the violence spread from brothels to Chinese miners' homes. The usual tone of response was humorous; "the boys" were having fun, and if the means were slightly reprehensible, the goals were widely accepted. With the future of the towns at stake, few whites would oppose anti-Chinese violence.[27]

The year 1855 was a peak one for anti-Chinese agitation all over the state. Alarmed at the growing numbers of Chinese immigrants in a time of depression, the legislature passed a foreign miners' tax aimed at the Chinese and designed to be exclusionary and coupled it with a prohibitive capitation tax to be paid by the ship's captain for every Chinese he brought to California.[28] In other mining areas, especially in Shasta County, the Chinese were driven out because of competition for jobs. On these issues, the Nevada county newspapers tried to assume a rational stance, opposing the higher tax on the grounds that the Chinese could not pay it, and condemning it and efforts to expel the Chinese because they would deprive mining counties of needed revenue and infringe upon the legal rights of the Chinese. The *Nevada Journal*, Sargent's paper and a leader in the moral crusade, accepted the raids on brothels but engaged the *Shasta Courier* in a controversy over Chinese rights. Whites could still adopt pragmatic, even paternalistic attitudes toward the Chinese in Nevada City if the emotional issue of the threat of Chinese vice to white stability could be avoided. Chinese labor was not a major issue in the towns in the mid-1850s as it was statewide; efforts to close the brothels were not accompanied by organized attempts to drive the Chinese out of the local mines.[29]

In the two decades after the gold rush, the mining economies of the two camps were never strong enough to eliminate all concern over their survival, but by the second half of the 1850s, it was clear that each town had, along with prosperous mines, well-established family neighborhoods and enough churches, schools, and ladies to ensure the prevalence of a traditional respectable morality. After 1855, newspaper references to the need to reform the camps declined, although brief outbursts caused by specific events, such as the opening of a hurdy-gurdy dance hall near a well-to-do neighborhood, continued. At intervals through the 1860s, off-duty volunteer fire companies "washed out" houses of ill fame, but the Chinese were no longer special targets.[30] The Chinese never lost their identification with an alien morality that could contaminate white society, and the arrest of Chinese gamblers and prostitutes remained a feature of crime news. But increased stability within the white community lessened the chance for holy war.[31]

In the 1860s the white and Chinese populations alike grew, although the numbers of both groups fluctuated in response to employment opportunities. The Chinese streamed out to work on the railroad and poured back into the Chinatowns when the work ended.[32] During the 1860s, whites became resigned to the permanency of Chinatown; parts of each town were recognized as Chinese territory. Both Chinatowns developed more complete societies, with a wider range of institutions to serve their inhabitants. Temples and a theater supplied traditional Chinese culture, and restaurants, physicians, and druggists multiplied to meet the physical needs of a growing population. There were more Chinese stores and also more opium dens, gamblers, and prostitutes. Buildings were still flimsy, although temples and merchant dwellings were often well furnished. Unlike the major white business districts, but like the white slums that continued to exist next door, the Chinatowns did not assume an air of solidity or prosperity.[33] (See tables 1 and 2.)

The Chinese continued to be almost without exception male, young, and single. The most common living unit in the Chinatowns was a tiny house or cabin occupied by four to six men. As quartz mines, which still largely barred Chinese employees, became more important in both towns' mining economies, the proportion of Chinese listing miner as their occupation declined, although the majority still dug for gold. Placer mining projects organized and manned by the Chinese grew in number, size, and importance until some of the largest placer operations in the two camps were Chinese. Chinese entrepreneurs developed other large-scale undertakings, the most spectacular being the digging and shipping of soap root fiber for use in mattress manufacture. The soap root concern employed over twenty-five laborers and expected thousands of dollars in profits. Chinese enterprises of this kind won grudging admiration from the white community.[34] For the rank and file, domestic work and common labor took on more importance; in both cases, work that was more town oriented than mining had been. The great majority of Chinese continued to work at jobs in which they did not directly compete with whites, but a handful worked beside whites as quartz mill hands or as skilled labor, and they could be seen as rivals to white labor. The emergence of these men, with the rise in numbers of domestics and common laborers, meant that more Chinese earned their livings at close quarters with whites than in the 1850s.[35] The census of 1870 listed most Chinese women as prostitutes —a description confirmed by their housing arrangements, in which three or more women often lived together or with one man. Few families and few children lived in the camps; a leading merchant might, however, maintain an establishment with more than one wife. (See tables 1, 3, and 4.)

While most Chinese continued to live in the Chinatowns or at all-Chinese mining sites on the outskirts of town, the Chinese population became somewhat more diffused throughout both Grass Valley and Nevada

City. Service workers such as cooks commonly lived in their places of employment, and other Chinese lived in laundries located in white neighborhoods. Outside the towns quartz mining companies, which employed both whites and Chinese, perforce created situations where the two groups lived in close proximity, as laborers lived near their work. In very rare cases Chinese and whites shared the same dwelling.[36]

Nevada City's Chinese population remained larger than Grass Valley's, and it was more mining oriented. Even with seven of ten Chinese in Nevada City listed by the census of 1870 as miners, the town supported a more varied occupational group than Grass Valley did because its larger Chinese community generated a greater range of supporting services. Not only gamblers and keepers of opium dens, as some whites believed, but also tailors, cobblers, peddlers, and restaurant keepers catered to the Chinese miners, supplementing the wares of the larger Chinese merchants. Only half of Grass Valley's Chinese mined, but a higher proportion of the nonminers performed specialized services for the white community. Although they both became larger and more complex, the relative positions of the two Chinatowns therefore remained the same between 1860 and 1870. (See tables 1 and 2.)

Both Chinatowns developed more traditional institutions during the 1860s; in particular the number of temples multiplied.[37] Chinese regional companies dominated both camps; whites believed that the Sze Yup and the Young Wo split control of the Chinese rank and file in both camps. When these rival companies staged a brief battle in the streets of Nevada City in 1869, together they mustered more than one hundred and fifty fighting men. Both towns also contained *tongs*, which feuded over women and mining rights, and occupational guilds, which set prices and attempted to regulate competition.[38]

During the 1860s, Anglo observers in each camp began to pattern their image of the Chinese after the Chinatowns. The Chinese districts were the abodes of alien powers, the *hui kuan.* More importantly, they were slum areas—noisome centers of crime and vice, but not dangerous if they were confined to one area of town. Citizens complained about noise emanating from the Chinese quarter, especially at the Chinese New Year when "the night was made hideous by the incessant rattle of firecrackers." Newspapers repeated continual accusations of odor pollution: "Their homes, if that sacred name can be degraded to mean the abode of a Chinaman, are surrounded with all the stenches that animal or vegetable decomposition can produce."[39] Whites came to identify the Chinatowns with the health hazards of dirt, refuse, and overcrowding, but fears of plague emanating from Chinatown were allayed by clean-up campaigns in which the Chinese cooperated with town authorities to dig and maintain sewers or to remove trash. Disease never became an important issue between the racial groups.[40]

TABLE 3

Chinese Occupations, Female, 1870

	Grass Valley		Nevada City	
Keeping house	5	13%	2	7%
Prostitute	34	85%	25	89%
Adults	39	98%	27	96%
Girls	1	2%	1	4%
Total female	40	100%	28	100%

Note: Females not listed by occupation in 1860.

TABLE 4

Men Living with Families by Origin

	Male Population	Living in Families	Percentage
Grass Valley, 1850			
Chinese	0	0	0
All others	408	13	3
Nevada City, 1850			
Chinese	0	0	0
All others	894	16	2
Grass Valley, 1860			
Chinese	305	2	1
All others	3,055	217	7
Nevada City, 1860			
Chinese	437	3	1
All others	2,286	321	14
Grass Valley, 1870			
Chinese	339	5	2
All others	2,786	971	35
Nevada City, 1870			
Chinese	639	2	1
All others	1,372	502	37

Anti-Chinese opinion in the early 1860s focused on crimes against property. Burglary replaced gambling or prostitution as the most common accusation; any unsolved theft was routinely blamed on the Chinese, who were considered innately larcenous. Whites, with or without the aid of town police, searched the Chinatowns for stolen articles, usually without success. White storekeepers claimed that Chinatown's merchants acted as receivers of stolen goods and hinted at large criminal conspiracies manipulated by the regional companies.[41] Racial contempt helped influence whites to treat Chinese crime differently from that of other ethnic groups; Chinese caught pilfering were commonly administered corporal punishment on the spot. In the late 1850s and early 1860s Nevada City placed convicted Chinese on chain gangs to repair the town streets. Finally, since a few white officials claimed that some Chinese preferred jail to trying to find work during the winter when mining was closed, alternative punishments—primarily the cutting of queues—were used, and the whipping post was advocated for Chinese only.[42]

In spite of suspected *tong* conspiracies, Chinese crime was seen as an annoyance, not a major disruption of the white community. Proven instances of Chinese crime were characteristically thefts of food or clothing, and the only serious crime against whites was stealing gold dust from mining operations. The Chinese of both Grass Valley and Nevada City fought among themselves, as individuals and as loyal members of the regional companies, but Anglos knew that the Chinese rarely offered violence to whites except in self-defense. While some whites scorned Chinese as too craven to fight back, others acknowledged that a legal system that would not allow a Chinese to testify against a person of another race made it hazardous for the Chinese to risk resistance. Although the Chinese commonly did repulse robberies and assaults, the belief of many whites that they were cowardly reduced the perceived danger of crime originating in Chinatown. Whites urged the Chinese to organize against bandits as a way of alleviating crime, arguing that Chinese passivity encouraged lawlessness. In one instance whites raised a purse to reward a party of Chinese who had killed a white bandit.[43] White officials never recognized, as they did with regard to other ethnic groups, that Chinese unemployment resulting from dependence on seasonal placer mining might cause the petty theft whites identified as characteristically Chinese. Anglos saw Chinatown as a place of disorder—vice ridden, dirty, an eyesore—but neither as desperately poor nor as overtly dangerous to whites unless they entered the district looking for trouble. No mobs attacked the Chinatowns to purify the camps, and few members of benevolent societies entered on charitable missions.

In the 1860s, then, most whites accepted or were resigned to the presence of the Chinatowns. When there was any attempt to expand them, to buy or to build in areas outside the downtown slums, however, whites resisted. In 1860 when the "Celestial population began to colonize" in a Nevada City district previously occupied solely by white merchants, a building the Chinese erected was torn down; when it was rebuilt, it was torn down again, with the implicit approval of the white population. At least one other attempt to expand was met in the same way, and newspaper accounts echoed the amused "boys will be boys" tone used for the raids on Chinese and white dives or brothels. Although Chinese were not physically assaulted in these incidents, it was made obvious that extralegal activity to keep the Chinatowns penned in one area was acceptable to whites; vigilante measures against alien presences in white areas, be they Chinese businesses or white brothels, were permissible.[44]

While tearing down houses that advanced the limits of Chinatown was a harmless amusement, the common practice of stoning or snowballing passing Chinese was interpreted in camp newspapers as evidence of a white social problem, the development of an idle and vicious youthful population. Chinese retaliation was applauded, even in one case in which it resulted in injury to an innocent Anglo bystander. Editors blamed parents for not teaching their children acceptable behavior; clearly some families were not helping to bring the expected order to the towns.[45] The newspapers did not identify youthful gang members by class, occupation, or ethnicity, although there was a tendency for Republican journals to place the blame for adult anti-Chinese actions on Irish laborers. To the advocates of social order, the raids of the 1850s had been acceptable because they were directed toward a specific goal: the removal of an immediate menace to the growth of the towns. Similarly, tearing down Chinese buildings in white areas was repelling a potential danger to white order and prosperity. Indiscriminate personal violence against Chinese, however, was never acceptable. Stoning Chinese was considered as reprehensible as robbing their camps. Appropriate responses suggested by editors when Chinese were harassed and injured included sending the children taking part to reform school and permitting Chinese to testify in court against their tormentors; the disruption of order was more dangerous than letting "dishonest" Chinese have access to the legal apparatus.[46]

The repudiation of anti-Chinese brutality accompanied a growing acceptance of the Chinese presence, based on increasing contact between the races and subsequent gains in white knowledgeability about Chinese. One important source of this familiarity was increased employment of Chinese domestic workers. Perhaps even more important was the beginning of social relations between the Chinese community leaders and their white counterparts. The Chinese elite initiated these meetings in order to defend their own interests by promoting peace. Several banquets were given by the Chinese to white business and political leaders during the 1860s; they were attended by males only and the whites did not reciprocate with invitations to their homes. In 1863 a Grass Valley minister described a banquet, given by the merchant Tin Ty for a carefully selected group of prominent whites, which obviously succeeded in raising the host's status in the estimation of his influential guests. The minister arrived with some nervousness, expecting to be served rats and rice, and received, to his relief, a typical Americal collation of the period. After the meal, Tin Ty attempted to explain Chinese beliefs and customs. On other occasions, Chinese merchants introduced their families to their guests, served and explained Chinese food, and presented Chinese music and dancing as entertainment.[47]

The guests, particularly newspaper editors, responded by publicizing previously unknown and favorable aspects of their hosts' culture. Whites tended to distinguish the cultured merchants from the rank and file in the Chinatowns. In one instance a merchant, Ah Sing, had been murdered while trying to stop a fight between a drunken Anglo and a Chinese prostitute. The Nevada City newspapers eulogized him as a "worthy and valuable citizen" who knew English and had a great and good influence on his countrymen, acquainting them with American laws and customs. But the account of his funeral also noted the presence of his wife, with other women considered his concubines, and condemned his marital arrangements. Although the few newspaper references to merchants' wives suggested that the Chinese could have "real" families, they were still usually contemptuous of Chinese women. Chinese merchants, as individuals, could win respect and clear up white misconceptions, but they could not raise the estimation of their poorer compatriots among whites or change the common image of Chinese women.[48]

Whites had often ventured into Chinatown, generally looking for illegal amusements, but during the 1860s they began to encounter and understand other aspects of Chinatown life. Whites visited the Chinese quarters during the Chinese New Year's celebration, were received as friends, and took their share of the food set out for guests. They attended the Chinese theater, although comprehending little that went on, and, more strikingly, they consulted Chinese doctors. Religious ceremonies, funerals, festivals, births, and marriages all attracted whites, and newspapers attempted—with a mixture of wonder, rejection, and condescending acknowledgment of Chinese sincerity—to explain the customs surrounding these occasions to white readers. Knowledge did not necessarily lead to acceptance; for example, the beginnings of Anglo understanding of the nature of the regional companies created disquiet concerning their power over the Chinese. There was, however, a growing sense among some whites at least that actions incomprehensible to them were not taken by the Chinese out of perversity but rather were the products of a complex total culture.[49]

The growing sophistication of white knowledge about the Chinese accompanied attempts to shape the Chinese into white patterns of behavior. Evidence that the Chinese were adopting even superficial American characteristics such as western clothes and weapons was offered by newspapers as proof that the Chinese could become "civilized." Sometimes the reports were simply mistaken, confusing traditional Chinese customs with American ones, as when the Chinese practice of leaving written greetings at the New Year was equated with American calling card customs. Other actions did suggest increasing Chinese understanding of Anglo practice, as when the beginning of a New Year's celebration was postponed to avoid the Sabbath.[50] More importantly, religious groups tried to further acculturation. Several denominations tried to teach English and Christianity to the Chinese throughout California during the 1850s and 1860s. The most important local attempt came in 1869 when the Methodist churches organized Sunday schools to teach English in both camps. Initially, especially in Nevada City, the response was favorable among both whites and Chinese. Attendance at the school grew from nine to forty-five, and the Chinese proved good students. However, as one teacher explained, racial stereotypes held by whites proved too powerful to overcome, and after hopeful starts, the schools failed as the Chinese became disgusted and quit at the failure of enough teachers to come forward to maintain instruction.[51] Some barriers between the races were falling, but the camps did not contain enough whites actively interested in the Chinese to support successfully an institution of acculturation such as the Methodist schools.

As in the early 1850s, whites recorded favorable characteristics of the Chinese, and some remained open-minded about them, regarding them as more than an exotic by-product of gold mining society. But racism continued to be a major determinant of white attitudes, and the old depictions of Chinese as immoral, dishonest, servile, and idolatrous continued to coexist with more positive portrayals of them as industrious and peaceful. The Chinese became less a threat and more an object of fun for the newspapers during the 1860s; Chinese immigration continued, one newspaper claimed, because of the inducements of "the numerous henroosts in the region and the good fare and comfortable quarters to be had in the county jail."[52] Most frequently references to the Chinese accused them of ignorance or cowardice. Chinese women remained objects of white disdain. When a Chinese male was arrested on the unlikely charge of grand larceny for abducting a Chinese woman, the *Grass Valley Union* passed it off by sneering that a "Chinawoman was too worthless a thing to form the basis of a crime of grand larceny." Editors depended on accounts of kidnappings, purchased brides, and feuds over prostitutes to liven the news. On the other hand, accounts of Chinese being married by American law were the most popular evidence of acculturation.[53] Chinese women and the Chinese lack of families, then, remained at the center of white concern, but in the mid-1860s, while the whites were largely at peace with themselves, fears of immoral influences or any other danger from the Chinese were not enough to arouse attempts to eject them.

This situation changed dramatically in the late 1860s. In 1867 and again in 1869 anti-Chinese political activity reached a frenzy all over California as the Democratic party attempted to reestablish itself after the disaster of the Civil War by allying with the depression-dogged workingmen's movement. The main theme of the resulting campaigns was that cheap Chinese labor allowed Republican capitalists to drive out unionizing whites; racist and antiaristocratic rhetoric provided powerful weapons against a party that could be identified as both the supporter of big business and the sponsor of the Fifteenth Amendment.[54] In the past, political movements against the Chinese had had little lasting effect on Grass Valley and Nevada City, but this time Grass Valley whites in particular responded, with important ramifications in race relations. The reason, once again, was a crisis within white society.

During the 1860s, gold mining in Grass Valley and to a lesser extent in Nevada City became more industrialized, more oriented toward large-scale, deep-shaft, hard-rock operations. Gold production, coupled with commerce with the mining towns of Nevada state, kept the two towns growing in both wealth and population. While most California mining camps declined, Nevada City and Grass Valley thrived.[55]

Prosperity brought increased social distances within the towns. Mining in particular was identified with certain ethnic groups. Experienced Cornish miners dominated the underground quartz work, since they enjoyed a near monopoly of the necessary skills; placer mining became more the province of the Chinese. As a result in Grass Valley, the quartz mining center, the Cornish became the largest ethnic group, and the American born declined until they made up only a quarter of the population. In Nevada City the American born continued to form a plurality, but the Chinese were a close second, and over 60 percent of the male inhabitants were foreign born. The Irish, the other large ethnic group, were heavily employed in various types of mining jobs, especially in surface labor at quartz mines.[56] While Americans left mining and frequently left town, those remaining concentrated in the professions and in merchandising. In both towns an American-born minority controlled the upper-class occupations, including most mine owning, while the foreign-born majority of the population held, in the main, less prestigious jobs. The Cornish, as a technological elite, ranked between the American born and most of the foreign born. The towns also developed neighborhoods clearly defined by the wealth and origin of the inhabitants. Crudely speaking, this meant that well-to-do Americans lived apart from poor Irish or middling Cornish, somewhat as they had always been separated from the Chinese.[57] (See tables 5 and 6.)

TABLE 5

Proportion of Occupations by Origin, 1860

	Professionals		Artisans		Miners		Unskilled		Male Population	
Grass Valley										
United States	79	44%	148	57%	1,005	39%	178	52%	1,409	44%
England	40	22%	40	16%	565	22%	40	12%	685	20%
Ireland	21	12%	31	12%	640	25%	57	17%	749	22%
Germany and Scandinavia	30	17%	32	12%	40	2%	10	3%	112	3%
France and Mediterranean	5	3%	5	2%	55	2%	26	8%	91	3%
area										
Canada	0		1		5		3	1%	9	
Latin America	0		1		0		0		1	
China	3	2%	0		275	11%	29	8%	305	9%
Total	178		258		2,585		341		3,361	
Nevada City										
United States	146	58%	222	61%	970	53%	154	55%	1,492	55%
England	15	6%	39	11%	235	13%	32	11%	321	12%
Ireland	4	2%	25	7%	130	7%	38	14%	197	7%
Germany and Scandinavia	52	21%	58	16%	70	4%	18	14%	198	7%
France and Mediterranean	16	6%	12	3%	25	1%	6	2%	59	2%
area										
Canada	1		5	1%	10	1%	2	1%	18	1%
Latin America	1		0		0		0		1	
China	18	7%	3	1%	386	21%	29	10%	439	16%
Total	253		364		1,826		279		2,722	

TABLE 6
Proportion of Occupations by Origin, 1870

	Professionals		Artisans		Miners		Unskilled		Male Population	
Grass Valley										
United States	101	47%	262	44%	195	12%	237	36%	795	25%
England	42	20%	136	23%	985	59%	50	8%	1,213	39%
Ireland	15	7%	84	14%	250	15%	87	13%	436	14%
Germany and Scandinavia	32	15%	60	10%	20	1%	38	6%	150	5%
France and Mediterranean area	4	2%	18	3%	30	2%	45	7%	97	3%
Canada	6	3%	26	4%	10		50	8%	92	3%
Latin America	0		1		0		2		3	
China	15	7%	4	1%	171	10%	144	22%	339	11%
Total	215		591		1,661		653		3,125	
Nevada City										
United States	107	56%	199	55%	300	28%	127	33%	733	36%
England	14	7%	39	11%	185	17%	11	3%	249	12%
Ireland	3	2%	17	5%	60	6%	21	5%	101	5%
Germany and Scandinavia	34	18%	51	15%	45	4%	31	9%	161	8%
France and Mediterranean area	8	4%	13	4%	15	1%	17	4%	53	3%
Canada	4	2%	13	4%	30	2%	22	5%	69	3%
Latin America	0		0		5		1		6	
China	21	11%	18	5%	436	41%	155	40%	639	32%
Total	191		350		1,076		385		2,011	

In 1869 in Grass Valley, where social distances were greater than in Nevada City, a mining strike placed these ethnic and occupational separations in clear relief. The Cornish-dominated Miners' Union had been formed primarily to protect Cornish jobs and traditional skills by opposing the introduction of dynamite and single-handed drilling into the mines to replace two-man teams using black powder. Wages were a secondary issue; however, in an attempt to create a common front with the Irish surface workers, the union demanded guaranteed wages for them. Resistance to the demands resulted in the closing of several mines.[58]

The mine owners, claiming that profitable operations required the new techniques, responded in a way that exacerbated ethnic and racial differences in the town. They attempted, by innuendo, to turn the Irish against the Cornish, aided by the usual antagonism between the two groups. More importantly, they threatened to reduce labor costs by replacing the Cornish with German, or even more provocatively, with Chinese miners. When violence flared against strikebreakers, it was rumored that Chinese habitations near the mines would be destroyed. Chinese strikebreakers were in fact not used and the Chinese houses were not attacked, but public opinion against union use of force helped bring the walkout to a close.[59]

The strike highlighted social tensions that enabled the Democratic party's anti-Chinese movement to attract support in the two camps, but particularly in Grass Valley in 1869 and at a level no previous political campaign had been able to match. Not only was this crusade on a larger scale, more organized, and more persistent than its California predecessors, but its anti-Chinese and anticapitalist rhetoric touched a sore point in the camps. In Nevada City and Grass Valley the battle became a vehicle, in part, for the resentments of the foreign born against the American-born elite, expressed through aggression against the Chinese, the American upper classes' potential weapon against the foreign born. In this context, contacts between Anglo and Chinese merchants and efforts by churches to teach English did not soothe animosity toward the Chinese; they inflamed it. The further fact that the same newspapers that extolled the gentility of Chinese leaders and the industriousness of Chinese workers supported, in theory, the use of cheap Chinese labor, did not promote racial peace. A pointed accusation against the Republican employers was that they preferred the Chinese to the Irish, both socially and as employees; Democrats accused the pro-Chinese of covert Know-Nothingism.[60] Editors, ministers, and businessmen might have developed a more favorable image of the Chinese during the 1860s, but the movement against the Chinese was heavily supported by Cornish and Irish miners and laborers who utilized all the old anti-Chinese stereotypes, especially that of slave labor, in an effort to drive them out of the camps. The defenders of Chinese cheap labor and the Chinese in general quickly recognized the potential political impact of partisan anti-Chinese activity and shifted as elections approached to argue that they, too, would like to see the Chinese go, but did not think there was a legal way to accomplish the goal. Pro-Chinese material became too dangerous politically and temporarily disappeared during the heat of the elections of 1867 and 1869. During these elections the Chinese were typically depicted as barbarians whose uncivilized standards of living enabled them to underbid and drive out white labor. Political agitators claimed that Chinese drained off American wealth to China and put no money in circulation within the American economy. This political campaign against the Republicans combined, uniquely, anti-Chinese and antiblack racism; as part of the struggle against the Fifteenth Amendment, Democrats claimed that it would grant suffrage to the Chinese, who would then overwhelm the California government. Democrats stigmatized the Republicans as the mongrel party, raising fears of miscegenation with both Chinese and Negroes.[61]

Election time brought anti-Chinese charges to their shrillest, but the effects were not as transient as they had been in the 1850s. The image of Chinese as unfair labor competitors persisted between elections and was not supplanted by either the old fixation with Chinese vice or any positive assessments. In 1867 a mob of miners briefly expelled Chinese from the neighboring camp of French Corral. When they were brought to trial for riot in Nevada City, only one was convicted. Long after the elections were over, advertisements appeared announcing that firms had fired their Chinese employees. A Grass Valley club, which aimed to protect ethnic workingmen by boycotting all who hired Chinese, survived the election of 1869 by several months.[62]

Anti-coolie clubs, boycotts, and the discharge of Chinese labor were certainly not unique to Grass Valley; local anti-Chinese activity drew on the state movement for techniques as well as political support. The usual explanations for the force of the California anti-Chinese agitation of the late 1860s are not, however, adequate for an understanding of the impact of the campaigns in the two camps. Simple economic arguments that may apply to much of the state do not explain the lasting local response to this agitation, since Grass Valley and Nevada City were prosperous, and Grass Valley was easily the leading gold producer in the state. Nor is a purely political explanation adequate; the Democratic party used the Chinese issue in the two towns in an effort to reestablish itself in county politics, as it did statewide, but the movement was most intense and persistent in Grass Valley, long a Democratic bastion. In Republican Nevada City, where the Democrats had to rebuild a shattered organization, a very bitter campaign against the Chinese did not sustain itself after the polls were closed.[63] The receptiveness of the camps to the agitation of 1867 and 1869 depended, then, in large part on local conditions. The Chinese were very visible in the late 1860s; their continued arrival in "shipments" under the aegis of the companies was frequently noted by the towns' newspapers. A few Chinese competed with whites for mine-related surface labor, especially in Grass Valley, and lived in separate camps at some major mining sites, including French Corral. The Chinese were conceivably a direct threat to European-born miners, especially during the Grass Valley strike. The overlapping leadership of the Miners' Union and the Anti-Coolie Association suggests that miners confirmed, from personal experience, the connection proclaimed by the Democratic party between capitalists and Chinese.[64]

When the disturbances of 1867 and 1869 are compared to those of 1855 and 1858, it becomes clear that public opinion had set limits on anti-Chinese activities. There were no attempts, despite rumors, to destroy the Chinatowns. There was no increase in the number of assaults on individual Chinese, and violence was not openly condoned by even the leaders of the Anti-Coolie Association, although they argued that failure to expel the Chinese would lead to bloodshed. The Chinese still had friends; social contacts between whites and Chinese did not cease, and favorable mention of the Chinese in the newspapers did not disappear. A few Chinese were fired, but the leading hotels kept their Chinese employees, and laundrymen and domestics living in white areas did not suffer unusual amounts of abuse. Even at the height of agitation in 1869, a minority defended the Chinese, a minority that considered itself the social and moral elite of the towns.[65] The anti-Chinese movement of 1867-1869 was more persistent than that of the crisis of 1854-1855, in part because the later statewide agitation was more organized, longer lasting, and more relevant to the felt needs of the white communities. The cardinal difference, however, was the fact that the social crisis of the mid-1850s could be and was resolved by the establishment of more families and more semblance of order, while the ethnic and occupational divisions of the late 1860s persisted and continued to generate emotional frustration and economic insecurity.

Racism, greed, and political manipulation cannot by themselves adequately explain Chinese-white relations, and racial attitudes and reactions were not static during the 1850s and 1860s. Despite preexisting stereotypes and constant racism, there was no doubt that the effectual image of the Chinese changed. In the 1850s, whites saw the Chinese as a totally alien group, whose lack of families and Anglo family values justified repression and even expulsion. In the 1860s, the Chinese were better known and had successfully developed interaction with influential whites who helped reduce mob violence against them. Anti-Chinese campaigns in the 1850s stressed vice; in the 1860s, servility—aspects of the anti-Chinese stereotype that corresponded to the strains of the times among whites. The basic difference between the two main periods of anti-Chinese tumult was that in the mid 1850s the entire white population, especially the articulate moral and commercial leaders, saw their own and the towns' future prosperity as endangered by the Chinese, while in the late 1860s only one segment of the white community felt threatened. Although a numerical majority and politically potent, these miners and laborers, often foreign born, could not unite the towns against the Chinese. The American-born leadership, who had countenanced violence before, now condemned it; the enemies of the Chinese were a greater threat to order, and possibly to the old elite, than the Chinese themselves.

In 1865 three Chinese brothels appeared on the edge of Chinatown, across from Nevada City's Methodist church. The newspapers fumed that they had "no business in such a locality" and that they shocked the decency of the neighborhood. Vigilante action was suggested: the "hose companies should wash them out or some other just though illegal procedure be . . . taken against them." In the end, however, a grand jury indicted these "sinks of hell," and they were closed by court order.[66]

NOTES

1. The standard works explaining American attitudes toward the Chinese are Elmer Sandmeyer, *The Anti-Chinese Movement in California* (Urbana, 1939); Alexander Saxton, *The Indispensable Enemy* (Berkeley and Los Angeles, 1971); Stuart Miller, *The Unwelcome Immigrant* (Berkeley and Los Angeles, 1969); Gunther Barth, *Bitter Strength* (Cambridge, Mass., 1964).

2. Patrick Tinloy, "Nevada County's Chinese," *Nevada County Historical Society Bulletin* 25 (Jan. 1971):1-4; Lorenzo Sawyer, *Way Sketches: Across the Plains in 1850* (New York, 1926), Dec. 2, 1850, 124-125; *California State Census of 1852*, Nevada County, DAR typescript, California State Historical Society, San Francisco.

3. *Nevada* (City) *Journal*, Oct. 9, 1851, 2:4, Oct. 16, 1851, 2:3, Sept. 13, 1851, 2:4.

4. Ibid., Aug. 19, 1853, 2:3, May 8, 1852, 1:2; *Grass Valley Telegraph*, Feb. 16, 1854, 2:4; *Nevada* (City) *Democrat*, March 22, 1854, 2:1-2; Sawyer, *Way Sketches*, 124-125.

5. *The Buckeye Rovers in the Gold Rush*, ed. H. Lee Scamehorn (Athens, Ohio, 1965), May 9, 1852, May 16, 1852, 161; *The Diary of a Forty-niner*, ed. Chauncey L. Canfield (New York, 1920), May 16, 1852, 232; *Nevada Journal*, May 1, 1852, 2:1-2, May 8, 1852, 2:5.

6. *Nevada Journal*, March 13, 1852, 2:3; for the California nativist movement, see Rodman Paul, "The Origin of the Chinese Issue in California," *Mississippi Valley Historical Review* 25 (Summer 1938):181-196; Leonard Pitt, "The Beginnings of Nativism in California," *Pacific Historical Review* 30 (Feb. 1961):23-38.

7. *Nevada Journal*, Aug. 19, 1853, 2:3, Feb. 25, 1853, 2:2, November 25, 1853, 1:1; *Nevada Democrat*, March 22, 1854, 2:1-2.

8. J. W. to Susan Winchester, Grass Valley, Nov. 19, 1853, Jonas Winchester Papers, California State Library, Sacramento. For Chinese overseas communities, see Stanford Lyman, "The Structure of Chinese Society in Nineteenth Century America" (Ph.D. diss.,

University of California, Berkeley), 1A, 41-45, 72A. For neighborhoods, see Ralph Mann, "The Decade After the Gold Rush," *Pacific Historical Review* 46 (Nov. 1972): 484-504.

9. Tinloy, "Nevada County's Chinese," passim; *Nevada Democrat*, Dec. 5, 1855, 2:1; *Grass Valley National*, Nov. 5, 1861, 3:2; *Nevada Journal*, Dec. 16, 1853, 2:2, July 7, 1854, 2:2.

10. Mann, "The Decade After the Gold Rush," 491, 494; *Nevada Journal*, Dec. 16, 1853, 2:2.

11. These inferences are drawn from the manuscript censuses, *Population Schedules of the Eighth Census of the United States, 1860*, National Archives Microfilm Publications, microcopy 653, roll 61, California, vol. 4, Napa and Nevada Counties, pp. 143-330.

12. Lyman, "The Structure of Chinese Society," 97, 277-80; Barth, *Bitter Strength*, 90, 111; Paul C. P. Siu, "The Sojourner," *American Journal of Sociology* 58 (July 1952): 34-36, 42.

13. Barth, *Bitter Strength*, 95. Cf. John Caughey, *Gold Is the Cornerstone* (Berkeley and Los Angeles, 1948), 177-190.

14. *Nevada Journal*, Nov. 20, 1851, 2:2, Nov. 15, 1851, 2:2, June 12, 1852, 2:1, June 26, 1852, 2:2; "The Story of a Gold Miner: Reminiscences of Edwin Franklin Morse," *California Historical Society Quarterly* 6 (Sept. 1927):226.

15. *The Letters of a Young Miner: Covering the Adventures of Jasper S. Hill During the Gold Rush, 1849-1852*, ed. Doyce B. Nunis, Jr. (San Francisco, 1964), July 5, 1851, 68-69; *Grass Valley Telegraph*, Oct. 31, 1854, 2:3, Oct. 15, 1853, 2:2; *Nevada Journal*, Oct. 9, 1851, 2:1, Oct. 23, 1851, 2:2, Dec. 6, 1851, 2:1; *Luzena Stanley Wilson: 49er*, ed. Correnah Wilson (Oakland, 1881, 1937), 28-29.

16. Alonzo Delano, *Pen-Knife Sketches or Chips off the Old Block* (San Francisco, 1853, 1934), passim; *Nevada Journal*, 1852, 1853, passim.

17. *Letters of a Young Miner*, June 12, 1851, 66; *Nevada Journal*, Sept. 13, 1851, 1:5; Oct. 2, 1851, 2:4; Delano, *Pen-Knife Sketches*, 67, 104; *Grass Valley Telegraph*, Oct. 31, 1854, 1:6, 2:1; Sept. 29, 1853, 2:1.

18. Alonzo Delano, *Old Block's Sketch Book* (1856; reprint ed., Santa Ana, Calif., 1947), 34-38; Delano, *A Live Woman in the Mines* (New York, n.d.), 22; *Nevada Journal*, Dec. 4, 1851, 2:4, Dec. 13, 1851, 2:2; Mollie Stafford, *The March of Empire Through Three Decades* (San Francisco, 1884), 81-82; Charles D. Ferguson, *The Experiences of a Forty-Niner* (Cleveland, 1888), 153.

19. Delano, *A Live Woman*, 22-23; Stafford, *March of Empire*, 77; *Nevada Journal*, Oct. 9, 1851, 2:1; April 19, 1851, 2:4; *Grass Valley Telegraph*, Oct. 9, 1855, 2:1, July 4, 1854, 2:2.

20. Mary Searls in Niles Searls, *The Diary of a Pioneer and Other Papers* (San Francisco, 1940), Dec. 9, 1853, 84; "Reminiscenses of Emily Lindsey Rolfe," *Nevada County Historical Society Bulletin* 20 (Dec. 1966):2.

21. Gilman Ostrander, *The Prohibition Movement in California, 1848-1933* (Berkeley and Los Angeles, 1957), 1-3, 11-12, 17-19; William Hanchett, "The Blue Law Gospel in Gold Rush California," *Pacific Historical Review* 24 (Nov. 1955): 362-363, 366-367; *Alonzo Delano's California Correspondence*, ed. Irving McKee (Sacramento, 1952), Aug. 30, 1851, 133; *Reminiscences of Senator William B. Stewart of Nevada* (New York, 1908), 65-66.

22. *Nevada Democrat*, March 1, 1854, 2:3, March 22, 1854, 3:1; *Grass Valley Telegraph*, March 30, 1854, 2:1, Dec. 22, 1853, 2:2, April 27, 1854, 1:4, Feb. 11, 1853, 2:4, Nov. 17, 1854, 2:3, Nov. 9, 1855, 2:2.

23. *Nevada Journal*, Oct. 23, 1851, 2:2, April 19, 1851, 2:4.

24. Ibid., Dec. 16, 1853, 2:2, Feb. 8, 1856, 1:6, March 22, 1854, 2:1-2, March 24, 1854, 2:6, Oct. 27, 1854, 2:3; *Grass Valley Telegraph*, Aug. 3, 1854, 2:1.

25. *Nevada Journal*, Aug. 8, 1856, 2:6, April 28, 1854, 2:5; *Grass Valley Telegraph*, Jan. 19, 1854, 2:3.

26. *Nevada Journal*, Oct. 27, 1854, 2:3; *Grass Valley Telegraph*, Aug. 3, 1854, 2:1; May 4, 1854, 2:1. Cf. Miller, *Unwelcome Immigrant*, 146-147, 150-151.

27. *Nevada Journal*, Aug. 25, 1854, 2:3, Jan. 12, 1855, 1:3, March 9, 1855, 1:4, March 23, 1855, 2:4; *Nevada Democrat*, Aug. 23, 1854, 2:1, Oct. 24, 1855, 2:4; *Nevada Journal*, Oct. 20, 1854, 2:3, Aug. 24, 1854, 2:4.

28. Mary R. Coolidge, *Chinese Immigration* (New York, 1909), 59; Sandmeyer, *The Anti-Chinese Movement*, 41-43.

29. *Nevada Journal*, Jan. 26, 1855, 2:3, Feb. 9, 1855, 2:3; Oct. 26, 1855, 2:4; *Nevada Democrat*, Dec. 19, 1855, 2:3.

30. *Nevada* (City) *Daily Transcript*, Oct. 16, 1866, 2:2; *Daily National Gazette* (Nevada City), Dec. 20, 1870, 3:1.

31. *Morning Transcript* (Nevada City), Nov. 26, 1860, 3:1; *Nevada Democrat*, Oct. 1, 1861, 3:1; *Nevada Journal*, May 22, 1857, 2:4, Aug. 29, 1857, 2:4.

32. *Nevada Daily Transcript*, Feb. 22, 1866, 3:1; *Grass Valley Daily Union*, March 22, 1866, 3:2; *Nevada* (City) *Daily Gazette*, Oct. 26, 1866, 3:1.

33. *Population Schedules of the Ninth Census of the United States, 1870*, National Archives Microfilm Publications, microcopy 593, roll 75, California, vol. 5, Napa and Nevada counties, 142-233, 271-322; *Nevada Daily Transcript*, Jan. 12, 1870, 3:1; *Nevada Daily Gazette*, July 25, 1854, 3:1, Nov. 17, 1870, 3:1.

34. *Daily National* (Grass Valley), Dec. 23, 1864, 3:1, Nov. 18, 1870, 3:1; *Nevada Daily Gazette*, April 14, 1869, 3:1; *Daily National Gazette*, Nov. 2, 1870, 3:1; *Nevada Daily Transcript*, July 9, 1869, 3:1, June 30, 1870, 3:1, Nov. 18, 1870, 3:1.

35. *Nevada Daily Gazette*, Nov. 28, 1867, 3:1; *Nevada Daily Transcript*, Aug. 22, 1869, 3:1.

36. *Population Schedules of the Ninth Census*, 144, 145, 206, 296, 311. Cf. David V. DuFault, "The Chinese in the Mining Camps of California: 1848-1870," *Historical Society of Southern California Quarterly* 41 (June 1959):167.

37. *Grass Valley National*, Aug. 25, 1863, 3:1; J. F. Putnam's Diary (1862), California State Historical Society, San Francisco, 195; *Nevada Journal*, Jan. 4, 1861, 3:1; *Nevada National* (Grass Valley), Jan. 7, 1860, 2:3.

38. *Daily National Gazette* (Nevada City), Aug. 6, 1870, 3:1; *Nevada Daily Gazette*, April 6, 1855, 3:1; *Nevada Daily Transcript*, Oct. 11, 1870, 3:1, Oct. 2, 1870, 3:1, Jan. 16, 1870, 3:1; *Nevada Daily Gazette*, Aug. 23, 1866, 3:1; *Grass Valley Daily Union*, July 22, 1865, 3:1; *Nevada Daily Gazette*, Aug. 19, 1865, 3:1; *Nevada Daily Transcript*, June 8, 1870, 3:1.

39. *Nevada Journal*, Jan. 4, 1861, 3:1, Aug. 24, 1860, 3:1, Jan. 18, 1861, 3:1, Feb. 11, 1859, 2:1; *Grass Valley Daily Union*, June 7, 1865, 3:1; *Daily National Gazette*, July 12, 1870, 3:1.

40. *Nevada Daily Transcript*, June 9, 1870, 3:1, Aug. 8, 1869, 3:1; *Daily National Gazette*, June 3, 1870, 3:1.

41. *Daily National* (Grass Valley), Sept. 15, 1864, 3:1; *Nevada Daily Transcript*, Jan. 11, 1870, 3:1; *Nevada Daily Gazette*, March 22, 1864, 3:1, March 24, 1864, 3:1; *Daily National*, Jan. 28, 1870, 3:1; *Daily National Gazette*, July 8, 1870, 3:1; *Nevada Daily Transcript*, March 25, 1865, 3:1; *Nevada Democrat*, Oct. 5, 1859, 3:2.

42. *Nevada Daily Transcript*, Feb. 4, 1864, 3:1; Mary Searls in Searls, *Diary of a Pioneer*, April 2, 1859, 89-90; *Nevada Democrat*, Jan. 18, 1860, 3:1; *Morning Transcript*, May 20, 1862, 3:1; *Nevada Journal*, Jan. 20, 1860, 3:1; *Daily National Gazette*, Oct. 11, 1870, 2:1.

43. *Nevada Daily Gazette*, June 21, 1869, 2:1, Nov. 22, 1866, 3:1, April 1, 1865, 3:1.

44. *Nevada Democrat*, Aug. 22, 1860, 3:1; *Nevada Journal*, Aug. 24, 1860, 3:1; *Nevada Daily Gazette*, Mar. 21, 1867, 3:1; *Daily National Gazette*, April 20, 1870, 2:1.

45. *Nevada Daily Gazette*, Feb. 1, 1866, 3:1; *Nevada Daily Transcript*, Aug. 7, 1870, 3:1, Feb. 1, 1866, 3:1; *Grass Valley Daily Union*, June 4, 1865, 3:1.

46. *Grass Valley Daily Union*, May 13, 1865, 3:1; *Nevada Daily Transcript*, July 24, 1868, 3:1; *Nevada Daily Gazette*, Jan. 25, 1868, 2:1.

47. *Nevada Daily Gazette*, Feb. 6, 1867, 3:1; *Grass Valley Daily Union*, Feb. 16, 1866, 3:1-2; *Daily National* (Grass Valley), Jan. 28, 1865, 3:1; *Nevada Daily Transcript*, Dec. 23, 1865, 3:1; R. F. Putnam's Diary (1862), 242-245.

48. *Nevada Journal*, Oct. 4, 1861, 3:2; *Grass Valley Daily Union*, Feb. 15, 1866, 3:1-2.

49. *Nevada National*, Jan. 7, 1860, 2:3; *Nevada Daily Gazette*, Jan. 25, 1868, 3:1, Nov. 2, 1869, 3:1, Sept. 15, 1868, 1:3, Feb. 24, 1869, 2:2, May 14, 1869, 3:2; *Grass Valley National*, Sept. 22, 1868, 3:1; *Daily National Gazette*, Sept. 19, 1870, 3:1, Oct. 14, 1870, 3:2; *Grass Valley Daily Union*, Oct. 14, 1865, 3:1, Feb. 15, 1866, 3:1-2.

50. *Nevada Daily Transcript*, Aug. 30, 1870, 3:1; *Nevada Daily Gazette*, Feb. 5, 1867, 3:1, Nov. 6, 1869, 3:1; *Nevada Democrat*, Jan. 25, 1860, 3:1; *Nevada Daily Transcript*, Feb. 6, 1862, 2:3.

51. Robert Seager II, "Some Denominational Reactions to Chinese Immigration to California, 1856-1892," *Pacific Historical Review* 28 (Feb. 1959): 51; *Nevada Daily Gazette*, Feb. 11, 1867, 3:1, March 16, 1869, 3:1, March 29, 1869, 3:1; *Nevada Daily Transcript*, Feb. 28, 1869, 3:1, April 9, 1869, 3:2, June 8, 1869, 2:2-3.

52. *Daily National Gazette*, July 8, 1870, 3:1.

53. *Nevada Daily Gazette*, April 1, 1865, 3:1, Nov. 6, 1869, 3:1, Dec. 25, 1867, 3:1; *Grass Valley Daily Union*, Oct. 17, 1865, 3:2; *Daily National* (Grass Valley), Feb. 2, 1869, 3:1.

54. Saxton, *Indispensable Enemy*, 88, 98.

55. Ralph Mann, "The Social and Political Structures of Two California Gold Mining Towns, Grass Valley and Nevada City, California, 1850-1870" (Ph.D. diss., Stanford University, 1970), 111-113.

56. Ibid., 121-127.

57. Ibid., 124-125, 130.

58. *Grass Valley Daily National*, April 22, 1869, 3:2, May 11, 1869, 3:3, April 28, 1869, 3:1; *Nevada Daily Transcript*, May 25, 1869, 2:1, 3:1, May 21, 1869, 2:2.

59. *Nevada Daily Gazette*, May 25, 1869, 2:1, May 17, 1869, 3:1; *Grass Valley Daily National*, Nov. 13, 1869, 3:1; *Nevada Daily Transcript*, June 26, 1869, 2:4; Rodman W. Paul, *California Gold* (Cambridge, Mass., 1947), 328.

60. *Nevada Daily Gazette*, Dec. 4, 1867, 2:1, Jan. 30, 1869, 2:2, July 17, 1869, 2:1, Aug. 4, 1869, 2:1, Aug. 13, 1869, 2:2-3.

61. *Daily National Gazette*, Oct. 20, 1870, 2:1, April 4, 1870, 2:2; *Daily National*, Aug. 28, 1869, 2:1-4, June 26, 1869, 2:1.

62. *Nevada Daily Gazette*, Dec. 12, 1867, 3:1, Dec. 14, 1867, 3:1, Feb. 7, 1868, 1:1, Nov. 12, 1869, 3:1; *Daily National*, Oct. 17, 1870, 3:1, Sept. 6, 1869, 3:1, Sept. 28, 1869, 3:1, Dec. 18, 1869, 3:1.

63. Victor G. Nee and Brett De Bary Nee, *Longtime Californ'* (New York, 1972), 44; Saxton, *Indispensable Enemy*, 80-81; Sandmeyer, *Anti-Chinese Movement*, 45.

64. *Daily National Gazette*, Sept. 16, 1870, 3:1, Sept. 6, 1869, 3:1.

65. *Nevada Daily Gazette*, Feb. 7, 1868, 1:1, Sept. 15, 1868, 1:3, Nov. 6, 1869, 3:1, Dec. 4, 1867, 3:1; *Daily National Gazette*, Nov. 18, 1870, 2:2.

66. *Nevada Daily Gazette*, Feb. 18, 1865, 2:2, May 2, 1865, 3:1; *Nevada Daily Transcript*, May 12, 1865, 3:1, May 13, 1865, 3:1.

BIBLIOGRAPHIC ESSAY

American labor historiography really begins with the massive, multivolume study of John R. Commons et al., *History of Labor in the United States*, 4 vols. (New York, 1918-1935). The interpretation of Commons and his University of Wisconsin associates has dominated the field of American labor history until recently and, it must be conceded, contributed much to our understanding of the subject. Unfortunately, however, the Commons study took a largely formal, institutional approach. Its primary emphasis was upon trade union developments and labor party programs— as these evolved from the idealistic anti-wage-system convictions of Jacksonian workingmen to the practical, bread-and-butter unionism of the AFL. The Commons tradition, at its best, has a spacious view of labor history about it. But it pictured trade unionism as a history of consensus and accommodation, found the major issues as being wages and union recognition, and generally assumed that the worker had no unique culture or community. It overlooked those cultural and social dynamics that profoundly shaped the experience of the workforce. It did not depict clashes in ideology, culture, or aspiration, perceiving things rather in terms of institutional struggle and material gain. Understandably it devolved into fact gathering and narrative, into a study of the material goals of organized labor—its pragmatic self-interest—and, as David Montgomery has observed, it projected an "economistic" model of workers' behavior.

Beginning with the 1960s, a generation of younger scholars, deeply influenced by Eric Hobsbawm and Edward P. Thompson, have responded to Montgomery's challenge to study "the cultural and intellectual life of the workingclasses." In 1968, Montgomery noted that American historians had yet to probe "the culture of the American mechanic" and the "impact of the spreading factory system on the cultural heritage of urban America's lower orders." This new generation, drawing on Hobsbawm's *Primitive Rebels* and *Labouring Men* as well as Thompson's landmark volume, *The Making of the English Workingclass* and several of his seminal essays has taken on this burden and gradually changed the face of American social and labor history. Like these two English scholars, they have inquired into the effect of community and social factors upon workingclass behavior and consciousness in order to understand both the wage earner and his conflicts. They recognized the wisdom of Perry Anderson's finding: "The actual movement of history is never a simple change—over from one pure mode of production to another; it is always composed of a complex series of social formations in which a number of modes of production are enmeshed together, under the dominance of one of them." And they endorsed Eugene Genovese's conclusion: "There is no excuse for identifying the economic origins of a social class with the developing nature of that class," since "every social class . . . [is] the product of a configuration of economic interests, a semi-autonomous culture, and a particular world outlook." Accepting such propositions, the new social historians have provided a fresh understanding of the connections between politics and economics, ideology and society. As a result of their work, we know something of social and geographic mobility patterns for selected groups of American workers—in Boston, Poughkeepsie, Philadelphia, as well as in small towns like Warren, Pennsylvania, and Cohoes, New York.

Most often, however, it was the preindustrial worker who was studied and rarely the informal or formal institutions that made up his community. Moreover, major aspects of workingclass thought and experience—consciousness, ideology, child rearing, sexual conduct, family life (extended or nuclear)—remain largely unexplored. What we know of the workingclass community and subcommunity, of its network of lodges, pubs, church social activities is limited to a very few industrial towns. Nor have the educational and welfare services of nineteenth-century unions been treated with authority by any social or labor historian. Even the highly visible impact of industrialization on society—the socioeconomic dislocations it produced for craftsman and trade alike, the effect upon social status and religious life, the ethnic conflict it triggered—is not fully understood. Needless to say, workforce consciousness and ideology, both origins and expressions, as well as the critical issue of embourgeoisement, have hardly received definitive treatment.

Herbert Gutman, in *Work, Culture and Society in Industrializing America* (New York, 1976), has made a start in helping us to understand the workings of the sunken two-thirds of that great iceberg of workingclass culture. In this highly suggestive small book, as well as in numerous articles on Pennsylvania and Ohio miners and nineteenth-century factory towns like Paterson, New Jersey, Gutman has provided a paradigm for the study of workingclass culture and belief, especially in small industrial communities. He has also given us a new appreciation of that workforce that did not join trade unions and of religious-ethnic factors in shaping consciousness and behavior. Alan Dawley's *Class and Community* (Cambridge, Mass.,

1976), a study of artisan shoemakers and the impact of modernization upon them, has also added to our knowledge of the symbiotic relationship of politics, economic change, and consciousness. Brian Greenberg, Daniel Walkowitz, Bruce Laurie, John Cumbler, and Thomas Dublin are among the new social historians who, in articles and forthcoming books, have studied workers, artisans, or immigrant factory operatives as carriers of preindustrial values. They have searched out the formal or informal institutions that shaped labor's values and ideology and showed how these institutions changed with the changing character of community and workforce.

While not ignoring labor's political expressions—and Dawley and Philip Silvia, among others, explore local, issue-oriented politics—the new social historians shift from Commons' emphasis on workingclass political organization and programs. As such, their scholarship differs from that of historians who have recently studied regional voting patterns, especially in the context of workingclass trends and issues: Paul Kleppner, *The Cross of Culture: A Social Analysis of Midwestern Politics, 1850-1900* (New York, 1970); Richard Jensen, *The Winning of the Midwest: Social and Political Conflict, 1888-1896* (Chicago, 1971); and Samuel McSeveney, *The Politics of Depression* (New York, 1972). This trio of historians, particularly Kleppner, has sought to understand the relation between voting behavior and ethno-cultural, especially religious, values.

The new scholarship is also distinct from, though greatly indebted to, Stephan Thernstrom's pioneering studies in social mobility: *Poverty and Progress* (Cambridge, Mass., 1964), *The Other Bostonians* (Cambridge, Mass., 1973), and such articles as "Immigrants and WASPS: Ethnic Differences in Occupational Mobility in Boston, 1890-1940" in S. Thernstrom and R. Sennett, eds., *Nineteenth-Century Cities* (New Haven, 1969), which includes highly suggestive observations on downward mobility. This new generation of social historians is not only familiar with Thernstrom's studies, it has been (at least some of its members have been) raised in the methodology of social mobility and the intricacies of residential and occupational coding. And some have remained loyal to their training, seeking to be rigorously scientific—to use statistics and computers toward the end of producing "a new social history." The results, more often than not, have been uninteresting, with scores of "anonymous Americans" being counted, categorized, indexed, traced, linked; yet somehow their history and experiences have eluded their counters. For all of the empirical knowledge that has surfaced, the cultural implications of this vast collection of demographic data have escaped researchers. Stuart Blumin's study of Kingston, New York, *The Urban Threshold: Growth and Change in a Nineteenth-Century American Community* (Chicago, 1976), typically relies upon quantitative analysis, but—like Thernstrom it should be emphasized

—never exclusively so. Indeed he uses traditional sources as well, toward the end of exploring shifting community patterns in an antebellum small town. So do Charles Buell, "The Workers of Worcester: Social Mobility and Ethnicity in a New England City, 1850-1880" (Ph.D. dissertation, New York University, 1974); Laurence Glasco, "Ethnicity and Social Structure: Irish, Germans, and Native-Born of Buffalo, New York, 1850-1860" (Ph.D. dissertation, State University of New York, Buffalo, 1973); and Douglas Shaw, "Making of an Immigrant City: Ethnic and Cultural Conflict in Jersey City, New Jersey" (Ph.D. dissertation, University of Rochester, 1973).

Committed to innovative scholarship, the new social historians have frequently explored topics neglected by conventional students. They have all looked to the social sciences for help but not always to mathematics or macroeconomics; some have relied instead upon the sociological tradition of Marx, Durkheim, and Jurgen Habermas, and others have been influenced by Raymond Williams and Antonio Gramsci in their effort to uncover the formative influences upon workingclass consciousness. To that end, they have begun to examine the relation of workers to leisure, child rearing, family structure, religious beliefs, and institutions and to develop pilot studies that explore the impact of industrialization and urbanism on workingclass culture and community life. Their research is far more sophisticated than comparable studies in the past, for they recognize the deficiencies of a historical analysis that examines nurture, the family, or religion as an "autonomous structure, independent of class confrontation [and] cultural interpenetration." Taking to heart this injunction of Talcott Parsons, they do not engage in any vulgar reductivism; indeed their work is frequently very complex and their conclusions tentative. Equally important, it addresses the relationship between society and consciousness, social existence, and ideology—what Keith Baker has termed "the cognitive aspects of social action." Recent investigations of immigrant wage earners are in this category and have precursors in Victor Greene's *Slavic Community on Strike: Immigrant Labor in Pennsylvania Anthracite* (Notre Dame, 1968); Clifton Yearley, *Enterprise and Anthracite: Economics and Democracy in Schuylkill County, 1820-1875* (Baltimore, 1961); Rowland Berthoff, *British Immigrants in Industrial America, 1790-1950* (Cambridge, Mass., 1953). They represent a distinct advance over the traditional approach to immigration history. Witness, for instance, Virginia Yans-McLaughlin's penetrating analysis of Italian workingclass family life in Buffalo, *Family and Community: Italian Immigrants in Buffalo, 1880-1930* (Ithaca, N.Y., 1977), and John Bodnar's *Immigration and Industrialization: Ethnicity in an American Mill Town, 1870-1940* (Pittsburgh, 1977), an investigation that uses census, marriage, and tax data, as well as the usual sources, to reconstruct community life.

Both works tell us something of how the newcomers entered the urban community as well as the factory system, how they joined the existing network of associations or established new ones, how complex community forces combined with Old World customs to affect behavior and consciousness.

David Montgomery's recent work has taken an equally promising direction. His essay, "The 'New Unionism' and the Transformation of Workers' Consciousness in America, 1909-1922," *Journal of Social History* 7 (1974), is a dress rehearsal for his forthcoming analysis of workers' control, which promises to be a quantum leap beyond Commons. Demands for worker control, he has concluded in this and other articles, challenged scientific management and the corporate ideology of unions and thus were a threat to both. Montgomery's *Beyond Equality: Labor and the Radical Republicans, 1862–1872* (New York, 1967), which was a subtle exploration of workingclass community and consciousness, demonstrated how mechanisms promoting consensus nationality often collapsed on the local level, how they might break on the "shoal of class conflict."

The work of younger social historians like Susan Hirsch, Charles Stephenson, and Paul Faler, possibly the most perceptive student of artisan ideology, has thus far appeared only in journals. These articles also suggest the continuing effort to follow Edward Thompson in analyzing social structure and patterns. The new scholarship generally has joined such an analysis to an investigation of the consciousness of the historical actors themselves, of their "images of power and authority, the popular mentalities" of deference as well as resistance. The result has been a conceptual approach that possesses spaciousness, subtlety, and analytical power.

INDEX

About the Contributors

John Bodnar, Chief, Division of History, Pennsylvania Historical and Museum Commission, has published *Immigration and Industrialization: Ethnicity in an American Mill Town, 1870-1940.*

Milton Cantor is Professor of History at the University of Massachusetts, Amherst.

John T. Cumbler, Assistant Professor of History at the University of Louisville, is the author of *Working-Class Community in Industrial America.*

Alan Dawley is a member of the History Department, Trenton State College.

Thomas Dublin teaches American social history at the University of California, San Diego. He is currently completing a monograph on women workers in the early Lowell mills.

Paul Faler is an Associate Professor of History at the University of Massachusetts, Boston.

Michael Feldberg, Research Associate, Department of Urban Affairs, Boston University, is the author of *The Philadelphia Riots of 1844: A Study of Ethnic Conflict.*

Michael Gordon has recently completed his doctoral dissertation at the University of Indiana.

Gary Kulik is a graduate student at Brown University and Curator of Slater Mill Historic Site, Pawtucket, Rhode Island.

Bruce Laurie is Assistant Professor of History at the University of Massachusetts, Amherst.

Ralph Mann teaches American social history at the University of Colorado, Boulder.

Jean Scarpaci is Associate Professor of History at Towson State University.

Philip Silvia, Jr., is an Associate Professor of History at Bridgewater State College.

Charles Stephenson is a member of the History Department, State University of New York, Brockport.

Samuel Walker is Assistant Professor of Criminal Justice at the University of Nebraska at Omaha. He is the author of the forthcoming *Popular Justice: A History of American Criminal Justice.*

Daniel Walkowitz teaches in the Department of History, University College, Rutgers University.

DATE DUE

GAYLORD   PRINTED IN U.S.A